FLORIDA

SCIENCE FUSION

fusion [FYOO • zhuhn] a combination of two or more things that releases energy

This **Interactive Student Edition** belongs to

Julea Kamga

Teacher/Room

Mr. Kos moski

HOLT McDOUGAL

HOUGHTON MIFFLIN HARCOURT

Consulting Authors

Michael A. DiSpezio

Global Educator
North Falmouth, Massachusetts

Michael DiSpezio is a renaissance educator who moved from the research laboratory of a Nobel Prize winner to the K–12 science classroom. He has authored or co-authored numerous textbooks and written more than 25 trade books. For nearly a decade he worked with the JASON Project, under the auspices of the National Geographic Society, where he designed curriculum, wrote lessons, and hosted dozens of studio and location broadcasts. Over the past two decades, he has developed supplementary material for organizations and shows that include PBS *Scientific American Frontiers, Discover* magazine, and the Discovery Channel. He has extended his reach outside the United States and into topics of crucial importance today. To all his projects, he brings his extensive background in science and his expertise in classroom teaching at the elementary, middle, and high school levels.

Marjorie Frank

Science Writer and
Content-Area Reading Specialist
Brooklyn, New York

An educator and linguist by training, a writer and poet by nature, Marjorie Frank has authored and designed a generation of instructional materials in all subject areas, including past HMH Science programs. Her other credits include authoring science issues of an award-winning children's magazine; writing game-based digital assessments in math, reading, and language arts; and serving as instructional designer and co-author of pioneering school-to-work software for Classroom Inc., a nonprofit organization dedicated to improving reading and math skills for middle and high school learners. She wrote lyrics and music for *SCIENCE SONGS*, which was an American Library Association nominee for notable recording. In addition, she has served on the adjunct faculty of Hunter, Manhattan, and Brooklyn Colleges, teaching courses in science methods, literacy, and writing.

Acknowledgments for Covers

Front cover: *satellite dishes* ©Robert Glusic/Photographer's Choice RF/Getty Images; *gecko* ©Pete Orelup/Flickr/Getty Images; *mountain biker* ©Jerome Prevost/TempSport/Corbis; *digital screen* ©Michael Melford/Stone/Getty Images; *Giant's Causeway* ©Rod McLean/Alamy.

Back cover: *fossils* ©Yoshishi Tanaka/amana images/Getty Images; *cells* ©Todd Davidson/Getty Images; *tarsier* ©Bruno Morandi/The Image Bank/Getty Images; *x-ray* ©Lester Lefkowitz/Taxi/Getty Images.

Printed in the U.S.A.

ISBN 978-0-547-36577-0

8 9 1421 14 13 12

4500395699 C D E F G

Michael R. Heithaus

Director, School of Environment and Society
Associate Professor, Department of Biological Sciences
Florida International University
North Miami, Florida

Mike Heithaus joined the Florida International University Biology Department in 2003. He has served as Director of the Marine Sciences Program and is now Director of the School of Environment and Society, which brings together the natural and social sciences and humanities to develop solutions to today's environmental challenges. While earning his doctorate, he began the research that grew into the Shark Bay Ecosystem Project in Western Australia, with which he still works. Back in the U.S., he served as a Research Fellow with National Geographic, using remote imaging in his research and hosting a 13-part *Crittercam* television series on the National Geographic Channel. His current research centers on predator-prey interactions among vertebrates, such as tiger sharks, dolphins, dugongs, sea turtles, and cormorants.

Donna M. Ogle

Professor of Reading and Language
National-Louis University
Chicago, Illinois

Creator of the well-known KWL strategy, Donna Ogle has directed many staff development projects translating theory and research into school practice in middle and secondary schools throughout the United States. She is a past president of the International Reading Association and has served as a consultant on literacy projects worldwide. Her extensive international experience includes coordinating the Reading and Writing for Critical Thinking Project in Eastern Europe, developing an integrated curriculum for a USAID Afghan Education Project, and speaking and consulting on projects in several Latin American countries and in Asia. Her books include *Coming Together as Readers; Reading Comprehension: Strategies for Independent Learners; All Children Read;* and *Literacy for a Democratic Society.*

Teacher Advisory Board

Lamica Caldwell
Tavares Middle School
Tavares, FL

Brad Carreker
Foundation Academy
Winter Garden, FL

Lisa J. Larson
Conway Middle School
Orlando, FL

Carolyn Levi
Kennedy Middle School
Rockledge, FL

Kerri McCullough
Windy Hill Middle School
Clermont, FL

Leyla Shaughnessy
Jones High School
Orlando, FL

Nancy Sneed Stitt
Meadowlawn Middle School
North St. Petersburg, FL

Sonia Watson
Tuskawilla Middle School
Oveido, FL

Antonio Young
Bay Point Middle School
St. Petersburg, FL

Program Advisors/Reviewers

Program Advisors

Rose Pringle, Ph.D.
Associate Professor
School of Teaching and Learning
College of Education
University of Florida
Gainesville, FL

Carolyn Staudt, M.Ed.
Curriculum Designer for Technology
KidSolve, Inc. / The Concord Consortium
Concord, MA

Content Reviewers

Paul D. Asimow, Ph.D.
Associate Professor of Geology and Geochemistry
Division of Geological and Planetary Sciences
California Institute of Technology
Pasadena, CA

Nigel S. Atkinson, Ph.D.
Professor of Neurobiology
Section of Neurobiology
The University of Texas at Austin
Austin, TX

Laura K. Baumgartner, Ph.D.
Postdoctoral Researcher
Pace Laboratory
Molecular, Cellular, and Developmental Biology
University of Colorado
Boulder, CO

Sonal Blumenthal, Ph.D.
Science Education Consultant
Austin, TX

Eileen Cashman, Ph.D.
Professor
Department of Environmental Resources Engineering
Humboldt State University
Arcata, CA

Wesley N. Colley, Ph.D.
Senior Research Scientist
Center for Modeling, Simulation, and Analysis
The University of Alabama in Huntsville
Huntsville, AL

Joe W. Crim, Ph.D.
Professor Emeritus
Department of Cellular Biology
The University of Georgia
Athens, GA

Elizabeth A. De Stasio, Ph.D.
Raymond H. Herzog Professor of Science
Professor of Biology
Department of Biology
Lawrence University
Appleton, WI

John E. Hoover, Ph.D.
Professor
Department of Biology
Millersville University
Millersville, PA

Charles W. Johnson, Ph.D.
Chairman, Division of Natural Sciences, Mathematics and Physical Education
Associate Professor of Physics
South Georgia College
Douglas, GA

Ping H. Johnson, Ph.D.
Associate Professor
Department of Health, Physical Education and Sport Science
Kennesaw State University
Kennesaw, GA

Tatiana A. Krivosheev, Ph.D.
Associate Professor of Physics
Department of Natural Sciences
Clayton State University
Morrow, GA

Louise McCullough, M.D., Ph.D.
Associate Professor of Neurology and Neuroscience
Director of Stroke Research and Education
University of Connecticut Health Center &
The Stroke Center at Hartford Hospital
Farmington, CT

Mark Moldwin, Ph.D.
Professor of Space Sciences
Atmospheric, Oceanic and Space Sciences
University of Michigan
Ann Arbor, MI

Hilary Clement Olson, Ph.D.
Research Scientist Associate V
Institute for Geophysics, Jackson School of Geosciences
The University of Texas at Austin
Austin, TX

Russell S. Patrick, Ph.D.
Professor of Physics
Department of Biology, Chemistry, and Physics
Southern Polytechnic State University
Marietta, GA

James L. Pazun, Ph.D.
Professor and Chairman
Chemistry and Physics
Pfeiffer University
Misenheimer, NC

L. Jeanne Perry, Ph.D.
Director (Retired)
Protein Expression Technology Center
Institute for Genomics and Proteomics
University of California, Los Angeles
Los Angeles, CA

Kenneth H. Rubin, Ph.D.
Professor
Department of Geology and Geophysics
University of Hawaii
Honolulu, HI

Michael J. Ryan, Ph.D.
Clark Hubbs Regents Professor in Zoology
Section of Integrative Biology
University of Texas
Austin, TX

Brandon E. Schwab, Ph.D.
Associate Professor
Department of Geology
Humboldt State University
Arcata, CA

Miles R. Silman, Ph.D.
Associate Professor
Department of Biology
Wake Forest University
Winston-Salem, NC

Marllin L. Simon, Ph.D.
Associate Professor
Department of Physics
Auburn University
Auburn, AL

Matt A. Wood, Ph.D.
Professor
Department of Physics & Space Sciences
Florida Institute of Technology
Melbourne, FL

Adam D. Woods, Ph.D.
Associate Professor
Department of Geological Sciences
California State University, Fullerton
Fullerton, CA

Teacher Reviewers

Lamica Caldwell
Tavares Middle School
Tavares, FL

Brad Carreker
Foundation Academy
Winter Garden, FL

Lynda L. Garrett, M.Ed.
Gamble Rogers Middle School
St. Augustine, FL

Barbara A. Humphreys
New River Middle School
Fort Lauderdale, FL

Lisa J. Larson
Conway Middle School
Orlando, FL

Sabine R. Laser
St. Cloud Middle School
St. Cloud, FL

Stacy Loeak
Rodgers Middle School
Riverview, FL

Susan McKinney
Nova Middle School
Davie, FL

Mindy N. Pearson, M.Ed. & NBCT
Van Buren Middle School
Tampa, FL

Kathleen M. Poe
Fletcher Middle School
Jacksonville Beach, FL

Barbara Riley
Science Education Consultant
Merritt Island, FL

Kimberly Scarola, M.Ed.
Pembroke Pines Charter Middle School
Pembroke Pines, FL

Leyla Shaughnessy, M.Ed.
Jones High School
Orlando, FL

Nancy Sneed Stitt, M.S.
Science Instructional Coach
Pinellas Park High School
Largo, FL

Contents in Brief

I can't see wind, but I can see how it moves a kite through the air!

It takes a change in temperature to pop popcorn!

Contents

Modern agriculture allows us to grow plants anywhere. Plants can even grow without soil!

Big Idea 6

Assignments:

I've seen lots of rust, but I never thought about it as a chemical reaction.

I wonder how hot air balloons rise in the atmosphere.

Unit test date: ______

Wildfires are often caused by lightning.

Assignments:

Contents *(continued)*

Big Ideas 11, 12 & 13 — *Assigned* — *Due*

Unit test date: ____

A roller coaster works by changing direction and speed to create a thrilling ride!

It's fascinating to see how cells work. We can watch a plant cell divide!

Unit test date:

Assignments:

Contents *(continued)*

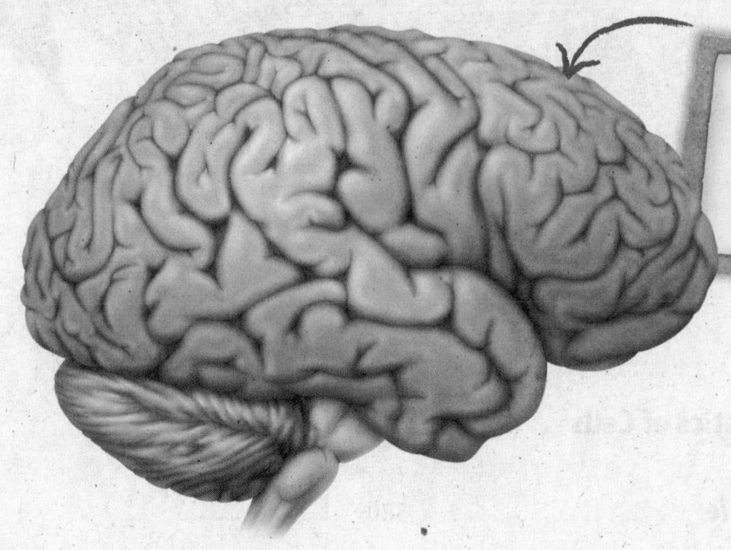

My brain controls everything my body does. It is my body's control center.

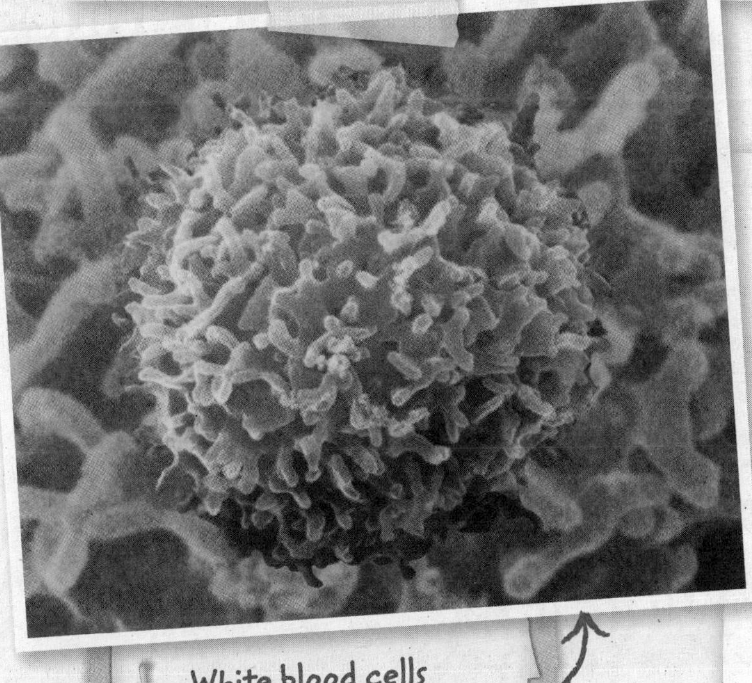

White blood cells patrol our bodies to keep out invaders.

Assignments:

Power up with Science Fusion!

Your program fuses . . .

Online Virtual Experiences

Inquiry-Based Labs and Activities

Active Reading and Writing

. . . to generate energy for today's science learner — you.

Be an active reader and make this book your own!

You can answer questions, ask questions, create graphs, make notes, write your own ideas, and highlight information right in your book.

By the end of the school year, your book will become a record of the knowledge and skills you learned in science.

Inquiry-Based Labs and Activities

ScienceFusion includes lots of exciting hands-on inquiry labs and activities, each one designed to bring science skills and concepts to life and get you involved.

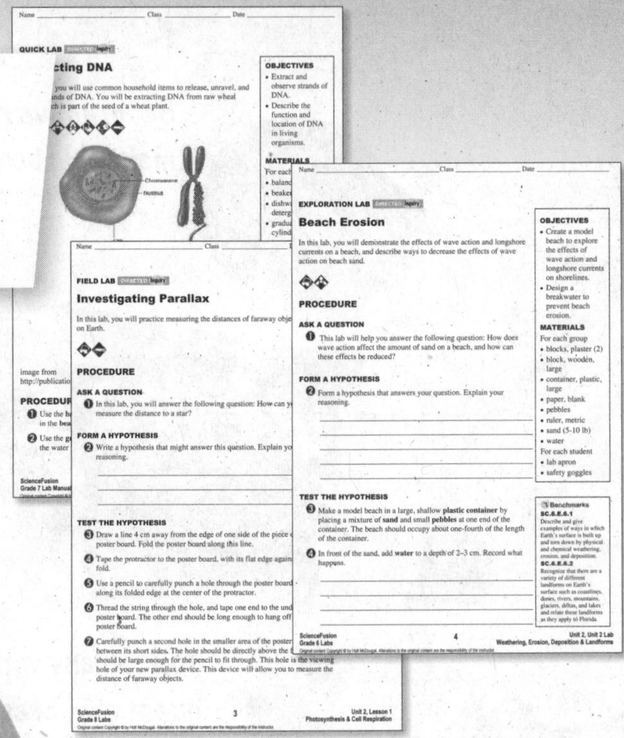

Name ______ Class ______ Date ______

QUICK LAB

cting DNA

you will use common household items to release, unravel, and
ands of DNA. You will be extracting DNA from raw wheat
ch is part of the seed of a wheat plant.

OBJECTIVES
- Extract and observe strands of DNA.
- Describe the function and location of DNA in living organisms.

MATERIALS
For each
- balanc
- beaker
- dishw deterg
- gradua cylind

image from
http://publicatio

PROCEDUR
1. Use the b in the bea
2. Use the g the water

ScienceFusion
Grade 7 Lab Manual

Name ______ Class ______

FIELD LAB

Investigating Parallax

In this lab, you will practice measuring the distances of faraway obje
on Earth.

PROCEDURE

ASK A QUESTION

1. In this lab, you will answer the following question: How can y measure the distance to a star?

FORM A HYPOTHESIS

2. Write a hypothesis that might answer this question. Explain yo reasoning.

TEST THE HYPOTHESIS

3. Draw a line 4 cm away from the edge of one side of the piece poster board. Fold the poster board along this line.
4. Tape the protractor to the poster board, with its flat edge again fold.
5. Use a pencil to carefully punch a hole through the poster board along its folded edge at the center of the protractor.
6. Thread the string through the hole, and tape one end to the und poster board. The other end should be long enough to hang off poster board.
7. Carefully punch a second hole in the smaller area of the poster between its short sides. The hole should be directly above the should be large enough for the pencil to fit through. This hole is the viewing hole of your new parallax device. This device will allow you to measure the distance of faraway objects.

ScienceFusion
Grade 8 Labs
3
Unit 2, Lesson 1
Photosynthesis & Cell Respiration
Original content Copyright © by Holt McDougal. Alterations to the original content are the responsibility of the instructor.

Name ______ Class ______ Date ______

EXPLORATION LAB

Beach Erosion

In this lab, you will demonstrate the effects of wave action and longshore currents on a beach, and describe ways to decrease the effects of wave action on beach sand.

PROCEDURE

ASK A QUESTION

1. This lab will help you answer the following question: How does wave action affect the amount of sand on a beach, and how can these effects be reduced?

FORM A HYPOTHESIS

2. Form a hypothesis that answers your question. Explain your reasoning.

TEST THE HYPOTHESIS

3. Make a model beach in a large, shallow **plastic container** by placing a mixture of **sand** and small **pebbles** at one end of the container. The beach should occupy about one-fourth of the length of the container.
4. In front of the sand, add **water** to a depth of 2–3 cm. Record what happens.

OBJECTIVES
- Create a model beach to explore the effects of wave action and longshore currents on shorelines.
- Design a breakwater to prevent beach erosion.

MATERIALS
For each group
- blocks, plaster (2)
- block, wooden, large
- container, plastic, large
- paper, blank
- pebbles
- ruler, metric
- sand (5-10 lb)
- water

For each student
- lab apron
- safety goggles

Benchmarks
SC.6.E.6.1
Describe and give examples of ways in which Earth's surface is built up and torn down by physical and chemical weathering, erosion, and deposition.
SC.6.E.6.2
Recognize that there are a variety of different landforms on Earth's surface such as coastlines, dunes, rivers, mountains, glaciers, deltas, and lakes and relate these landforms as they apply to Florida.

ScienceFusion
Grade 6 Labs
4
Unit 2, Unit 2 Lab
Weathering, Erosion, Deposition & Landforms
Original content Copyright © by Holt McDougal. Alterations to the original content are the responsibility of the instructor.

By asking questions, testing your ideas, organizing and analyzing data, drawing conclusions, and sharing what you learn...

You are the scientist!

Online Virtual Experiences

Explore cool labs, activities, interactive lessons, and videos in the virtual world—where science comes alive and you make it happen.

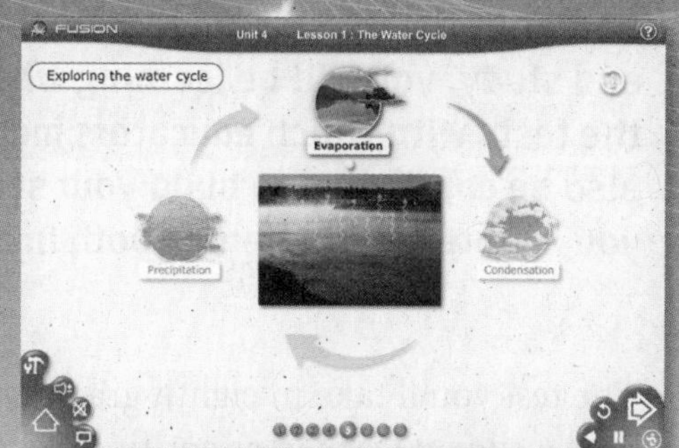

See your science lessons from a completely different point of view—a digital point of view.

Science Fusion! is a new source of energy... just for YOU!

Sunshine State Standards

An Overview and What It Means to You

This book and this class are structured around the Next Generation Sunshine State Standards. As you read, experiment, and study, you will be learning what you need to know to take the tests with which educators measure your progress. You will also be continuing to build your science literacy, which makes you a more skillful person both in and out of school.

The test you'll take in eighth grade is intended to measure how well you learned scientific facts and procedures, and how well you can apply them to situations you might find in the real world. What you remember long after that test, called enduring understandings, will help you see, measure, interpret, and evaluate many more situations you encounter in life.

The Next Generation Sunshine State Standards grew out of 18 Big Ideas that describe major themes and overarching concepts in science. The Big Ideas and Benchmarks appear throughout your book. Look for them on the opening pages of each Unit and Lesson.

The next few pages address several questions, including:

- What are the standards underlying the instruction?
- Where is each Benchmark found in this book?
- What makes the Benchmarks relevant to you now?
- What kinds of questions will you be asked in the tests?

Notice the **Essential Question** on the Lesson opener. This question is a hint to the enduring understanding you may take away from this lesson, long after you've studied it and passed a test and perhaps forgotten some of the details.

Find the name and number of the **Big Ideas** for the unit on the Unit opener.

Find the **Benchmarks** for each lesson on the Lesson opener.

Nature of Science

Big Idea 1 The Practice of Science

What It Means to You

You have done science without knowing it. If you've ever tried to understand something new to you by drawing on what you already knew, you have thought scientifically. Science is more than a collection of facts or the following of one method. It is an attempt to understand the natural world in way agreed upon by all.

Rift in ground at tectonic plate line

Benchmarks

SC.6.N.1.1 Define a problem from the curriculum, use appropriate reference materials to support scientific understanding, plan and carry out scientific investigation of various types, such as systematic observations or experiments, identify variables, collect and organize data, interpret data in charts, tables, and graphics, analyze information, make predictions, and defend conclusions.

Where to Check It Out Unit 1, Lessons 3, 4, & 5

SC.6.N.1.2 Explain why scientific investigations should be replicable.

Where to Check It Out Unit 1, Lesson 3

SC.6.N.1.3 Explain the difference between an experiment and other types of scientific investigation, and explain the relative benefits and limitations of each.

Where to Check It Out Unit 1, Lesson 3

SC.6.N.1.4 Discuss, compare, and negotiate methods used, results obtained, and explanations among groups of students conducting the same investigation.

Where to Check It Out Unit 1, Lesson 3

SC.6.N.1.5 Recognize that science involves creativity, not just in designing experiments, but also in creating explanations that fit evidence.

Where to Check It Out Unit 1, Lesson 1

Sample Question **Circle the correct answer.**

1 Lee reads of a scientific study claiming drinking lots of water improves memory. The study used a large number of subjects, controlled all variables carefully, and shared results openly with other scientists. Lee, who feels he knows a lot about how science works, still isn't convinced. What else might convince him?

A. If he knew the study took place in a large lab.

B. If he knew it was done at a university.

C. If he knew elaborate equipment was used.

D. If others were able to replicate the findings.

Nature of Science

Big Idea 2 The Characteristics of Scientific Knowledge

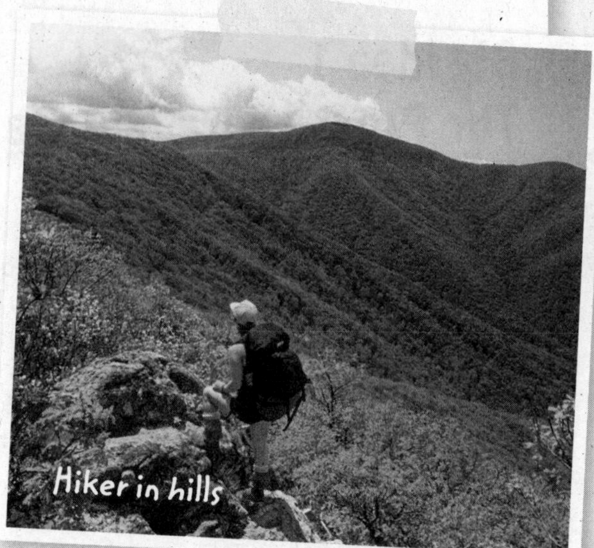
Hiker in hills

What It Means to You

Scientific knowledge is different from other forms of thought because it is based on empirical evidence, or evidence gained by the senses. Scientists gather a lot of empirical evidence before they try to form explanations from it. What this means is that scientific knowledge can be tested and measured. It can change when new evidence arises. Scientific knowledge is more than one person's opinion.

Benchmarks

SC.6.N.2.1 Distinguish science from other activities involving thought.

Where to Check It Out Unit 1, Lesson 1

SC.6.N.2.2 Explain that scientific knowledge is durable because it is open to change as new evidence or interpretations are encountered.

Where to Check It Out Unit 1, Lesson 2

SC.6.N.2.3 Recognize that scientists who make contributions to scientific knowledge come from all kinds of backgrounds and possess varied talents, interests, and goals.

Where to Check It Out Unit 1, Lessons 1& 5

Sample Question **Circle the correct answer.**

2 Miku made a list of activities she likes to do. Which activity would not be classified as scientific?

A. identifying rocks by color and texture

B. determining how fast her plant is growing by measuring the height of it every day

C. drawing pictures of superheroes she's created

D. making notes about how many hours the sun shines each day

Nature of Science

Big Idea 3 The Role of Theories, Laws, Hypotheses, and Models

What It Means to You

Learning science is like learning a language. Terms like *theory*, *model*, and *law*, while used losely in everyday language, have specific meanings in science.

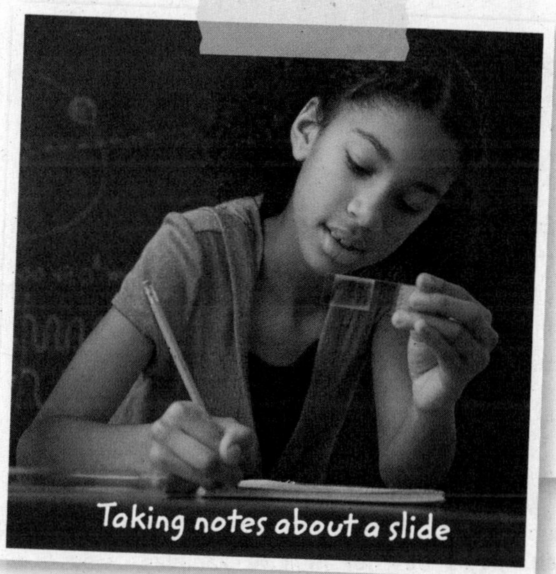

Taking notes about a slide

Benchmarks

SC.6.N.3.1 Recognize and explain that a scientific theory is a well-supported and widely accepted explanation of nature and is not simply a claim posed by an individual. Thus, the use of the term theory in science is very different than how it is used in everyday life.

Where to Check It Out Unit 1, Lesson 2

SC.6.N.3.2 Recognize and explain that a scientific law is a description of a specific relationship under given conditions in the natural world. Thus, scientific laws are different from societal laws.

Where to Check It Out Unit 1, Lesson 2

SC.6.N.3.3 Give several examples of scientific laws.

Where to Check It Out Unit 1, Lesson 2

SC.6.N.3.4 Identify the role of models in the context of the sixth grade science benchmarks.

Where to Check It Out Unit 1, Lesson 4

Sample Question **Circle the correct answer.**

3 Brianna observes that the air inside a balloon always seems to get smaller the colder the temperature gets. Which of the following is a scientific law that would describe this observation?

A. As temperature descreases, a gas's volume decreases.

B. Gases are made of tiny particles that move.

C. Balloons can only hold so much gas.

D. As temperature decreases, a gas's volume increases.

Earth Science

Big Idea 6 Earth's Structures

What It Means to You

Earth's surface is constantly being built up and torn down. As you look at the structures around you—the mountains, rivers, valleys, and lakes—you can see that Earth's surface is telling you a story. If you know about the internal and external forces that shape Earth's surface, its structures become a tale of the past.

Benchmarks

SC.6.E.6.1 Describe and give examples of ways in which Earth's surface is built up and torn down by physical and chemical weathering, erosion, and deposition.

Where to Check It Out Unit 2, Lessons 1, 2, & 3

SC.6.E.6.2 Recognize that there are a variety of different landforms on Earth's surface such as coastlines, dunes, rivers, mountains, glaciers, deltas, and lakes and relate these landforms as they apply to Florida.

Where to Check It Out Unit 2, Lessons 2, 3, & 4

Sample Question **Circle the correct answer.**

4 After a thunderstorm, Carlos noticed a small layer of sediment on the side of his driveway. Which of the following processes could have taken place during the storm to cause the sediment to be there?

A. combustion

B. deposition

C. disintegration

D. cyrstalization

Melting iceberg

Earth Science

Big Idea 7 Earth Systems and Patterns

What It Means to You

The sun does more than simply brighten the sky. It drives the flow of matter and energy through Earth's systems. Earth's air, land, water, weather, and almost all living things are influenced by the sun. Understanding conditions on Earth means understanding how all these different parts interact.

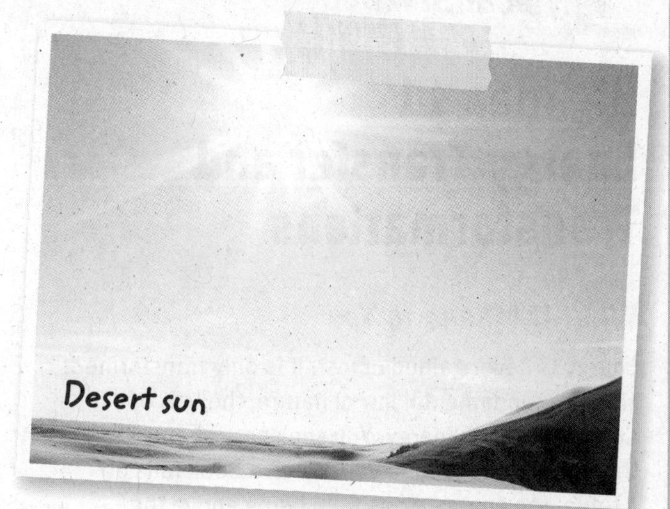

Desert sun

Benchmarks

SC.6.E.7.1 Differentiate among radiation, conduction, and convection, the three mechanisms by which heat is transferred through Earth's system.
Where to Check It Out Unit 3, Lesson 3

SC.6.E.7.2 Investigate and apply how the cycling of water between the atmosphere and hydrosphere has an effect on weather patterns and climate.
Where to Check It Out Unit 4, Lessons 1, 2, 3, & 6

SC.6.E.7.3 Describe how global patterns such as the jet stream and ocean currents influence local weather in measurable terms such as temperature, air pressure, wind direction and speed, and humidity and precipitation.
Where to Check It Out Unit 4, Lessons 2 & 3

SC.6.E.7.4 Differentiate and show interactions among the geosphere, hydrosphere, cryosphere, atmosphere, and biosphere.
Where to Check It Out Unit 3, Lessons 1 & 3

SC.6.E.7.5 Explain how energy provided by the sun influences global patterns of atmospheric movement and the temperature differences between air, water, and land.
Where to Check It Out Unit 3, Lessons 3 & 4

SC.6.E.7.6 Differentiate between weather and climate.
Where to Check It Out Unit 4, Lesson 6

SC.6.E.7.7 Investigate how natural disasters have affected human life in Florida.
Where to Check It Out Unit 4, Lesson 5

SC.6.E.7.8 Describe ways human beings protect themselves from hazardous weather and sun exposure.
Where to Check It Out Unit 4, Lesson 4

SC.6.E.7.9 Describe how the composition and structure of the atmosphere protects life and insulates the planet.
Where to Check It Out Unit 3, Lesson 2

Sample Question **Circle the correct answer.**

5 When energy from the sun hits the air above land, the air warms up and rises. Along a coastline, cooler air above the ocean flows toward the land and replaces this rising air. Which of the following best describes these processes?

A. conduction and convection

B. radiation and convection

C. conduction, convection, and radiation

D. radiation and conduction

Physical Science

Big Idea 11 Energy Transfer and Transformations

What It Means to You

Energy is never gained or lost. It is only transformed. This is a fundamental law of nature, the Law of Conservation of Energy. You see energy being transformed all around you. When a book falls off a table, the energy it has from being above the gound, potential energy, gets transformed into the energy of motion that carries it to the ground, kinetic energy. In a microwave oven, the radiant energy from microwaves gets turned into heat energy that raises the temperature of the food. When we speak of "saving energy," what we really means is trying to transform as much unusable energy as possible into usable forms.

Benchmark

SC.6.P.11.1 Explore the Law of Conservation of Energy by differentiating between potential and kinetic energy. Identify situations where kinetic energy is transformed into potential energy and vice versa.

Where to Check It Out Unit 5, Lesson 1

Sample Question **Circle the correct answer.**

6 Gordon throws a baseball into the air. It rises, stops when it reaches a certain height, and then falls back into his hand. When does the ball have its most potential energy?

A. When it is in Gordon's hands

B. As it travels up from Gordon's hands

C. At its highest point in the air

D. As it travels back to Gordon's hands

Physical Science

Big Idea 12 Motion of Objects

What It Means to You

Sometimes, the tiniest push or pull can start an object into motion. Objects in motion are all around us. They may move towards or away from us. They may circle around us or fly by us. The motions of all objects, however, can be described as the distance the object travels over a certain amount of time. We say the objects that move most quickly are the ones that travel the greatest distance in the least time.

Benchmark

SC.6.P.12.1 Measure and graph distance versus time for an object moving at a constant speed. Interpret this relationship.

Where to Check It Out Unit 5, Lesson 2

Sample Question **Circle the correct answer.**

7 A weather station records that the wind is moving at a velocity of 12 km/h northeast. Why is this a velocity and not a speed?

A. because it's given in SI units

B. because it's an average value for a given time

C. because it's a constant value

D. because both speed and direction are given

Physical Science

Big Idea 13 Forces and Changes in Motion

What It Means to You

Forces are what starts and stops all motion. Some forces, like friction between a bicycle and the pavement, act when objects are in contact. Other forces, like the gravitational pull of the sun on the Earth, act at a distance.

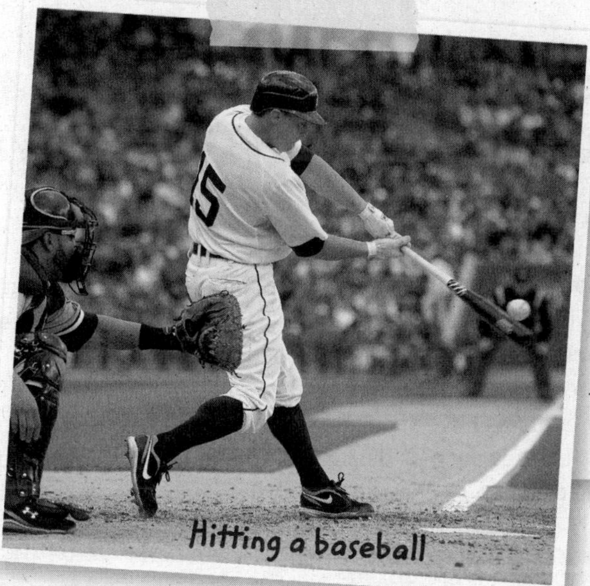
Hitting a baseball

Benchmarks

SC.6.P.13.1 Investigate and describe types of forces including contact forces and forces acting at a distance, such as electrical, magnetic, and gravitational.
Where to Check It Out Unit 5, Lessons 4 & 5

SC.6.P.13.2 Explore the Law of Gravity by recognizing that every object exerts gravitational force on every other object and that the force depends on how much mass the objects have and how far apart they are.
Where to Check It Out Unit 5, Lesson 5

SC.6.P.13.3 Investigate and describe that an unbalanced force acting on an object changes its speed, or direction of motion, or both.
Where to Check It Out Unit 5, Lesson 4

Sample Question **Circle the correct answer.**

8 Terance uses a hammer to hit a nail into a board on the wall. Later, he hits a nail into a board on the floor. How does gravity make it easier to hammer the nail in the second case?

A. Gravity pushes the board up to help the nail go in.

B. Gravity pulls the board and the nail toward each other.

C. Gravity pulls the hammer down so that it pushes on the nail.

D. Gravity pulls the nail down but does not pull on the hammer.

Life Science

Big Idea 14 Organization and Development of Living Organisms

What It Means to You

You're not as different from a plant as you might think. All living things share some characteristics. Like the tiniest bacteria, you also are composed of cells that perform the basic functions necessary for life. More complex organisms have specialized cells, which can form structures such as tissue and organs. Your body is made up of organ systems that work together to keep you alive.

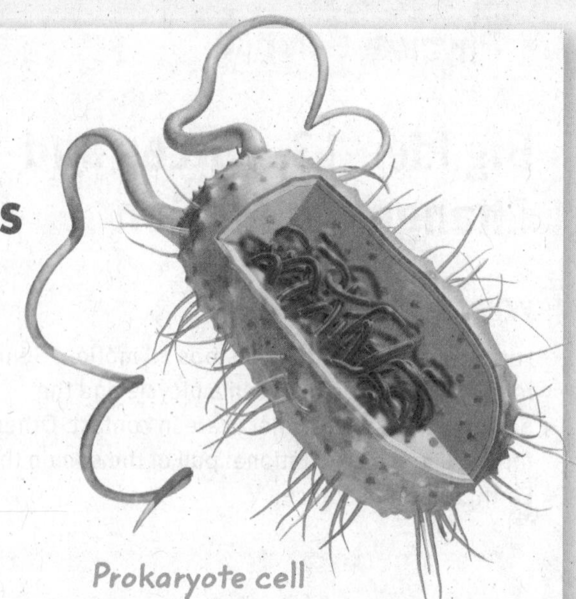

Prokaryote cell

Benchmarks

SC.6.L.14.1 Describe and identify patterns in the hierarchical organization of organisms from atoms to molecules and cells to tissues to organs to organ systems to organisms.
Where to Check It Out Unit 6, Lessons 2 & 4

SC.6.L.14.2 Investigate and explain the components of the scientific theory of cells (cell theory): all organisms are composed of cells (single-celled or multi-cellular), all cells come from pre-existing cells, and cells are the basic unit of life.
Where to Check It Out Unit 6, Lesson 1

SC.6.L.14.3 Recognize and explore how cells of all organisms undergo similar processes to maintain homeostasis, including extracting energy from food, getting rid of waste, and reproducing.
Where to Check It Out Unit 6, Lesson 5

SC.6.L.14.4 Compare and contrast the structure and function of major organelles of plant and animal cells, including cell wall, cell membrane, nucleus, cytoplasm, chloroplasts, mitochondria, and vacuoles.
Where to Check It Out Unit 6, Lesson 3

SC.6.L.14.5 Identify and investigate the general functions of the major systems of the human body (digestive, respiratory, circulatory, reproductive, excretory, immune, nervous, and musculoskeletal) and describe ways these systems interact with each other to maintain homeostasis.
Where to Check It Out Unit 7, Lessons 1, 2, 3, 4, 5, & 6

SC.6.L.14.6 Compare and contrast types of infectious agents that may infect the human body, including viruses, bacteria, fungi, and parasites.
Where to Check It Out Unit 8, Lesson 2

Sample Question **Circle the correct answer.**

9 Mariella is using a microscope to observe an organism from a sample of pond water. She observes that the cells of the organism have ribosomes, mitochondria, and lysosomes. She also observes that the cells do not have a cell wall. What type of organism is Mariella most likely to have found?

A. a plant

B. a fungus

C. an animal

D. a prokaryote

Additional Standards

The following standards from math, language arts, and health are part of this year's science curriculum. You will find them throughout the book, in the lessons where they best align.

Benchmarks

MA.6.S.6.2 Select and analyze the measures of central tendency or variability to represent, describe, analyze, and/or summarize a data set for the purposes of answering questions appropriately.

MA.6.A.3.6 Construct and analyze tables, graphs, and equations to describe linear functions and other simple relations using both common language and algebraic notation.

LA.6.4.2.2 The student will record information (e.g., observations, notes, lists, charts, legends) related to a topic, including visual aids to organize and record information and include a list of sources used.

LA.6.2.2.3 The student will organize information to show understanding (e.g., representing main ideas within text through charting, mapping, paraphrasing, summarizing, or comparing/contrasting).

HE.6.C.1.3 Identify environmental factors that affect personal health.

HE.6.C.1.8 Explain how body systems are impacted by hereditary factors and infectious agents.

UNIT 1

Nature of Science

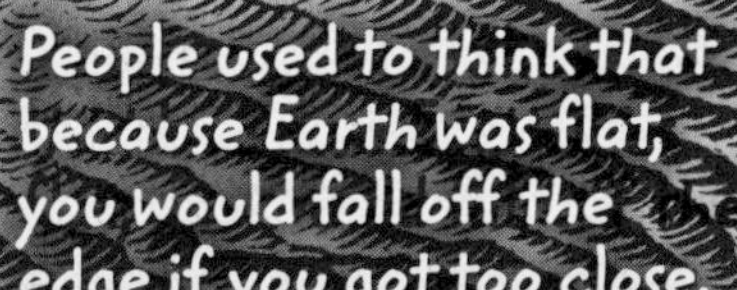

People used to think that because Earth was flat, you would fall off the edge if you got too close.

The Practice of Science

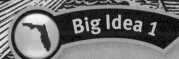

The Characteristics of Scientific Knowledge

Big Idea 3

The Role of Theories, Laws, Hypotheses, and Models

What do you think?

Careful observations and experiments provide us with new information that may change or confirm what we know about the world we live in. What is one way in which science has changed your view of the world?

Today, we know that Earth is a sphere.

Unit 1

Nature of Science

CITIZEN SCIENCE

Things Change

People used to have strange ideas about the world that they lived in. How science has changed some of those ideas is shown here.

1687

People used to think that the sun and planets revolved around Earth. In 1687, Newton described gravity and how it affects objects. His work explained why all of the planets, including Earth, must revolve around the much larger sun. Newton's work finally convinced people that the sun and not Earth was at the center of the solar system.

Sir Isaac Newton

1861

People used to think that living things could come from nonliving things, such as flies and beetles from rotting meat. This idea was called *spontaneous generation*. It was Pasteur's experiments that finally disproved this idea.

1950s

In 1915, people didn't believe Alfred Wegener when he proposed that the continents were moving slowly. It wasn't until the 1950s that advances in technology provided four different lines of evidence, which proved that continents do move. Wegener was right.

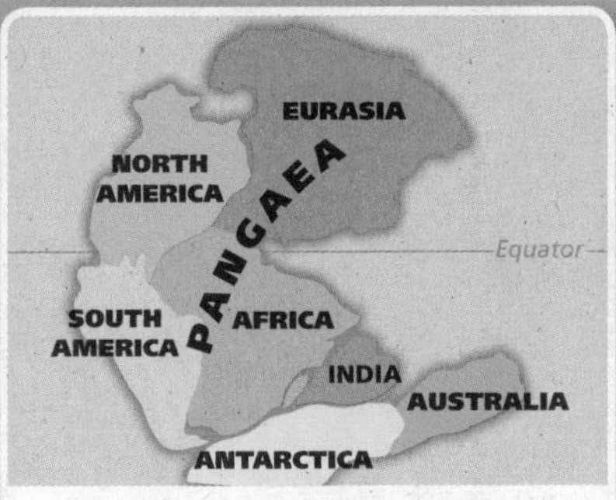

Modern continents used to be a part of Pangaea.

2008

People used to think that there were Martians on Mars. However, probes and landers have replaced ideas of little green men with real information about the planet. In 2008, we discovered water ice there.

Create Your Own Timeline

1 Think About It

Choose a favorite science topic and write it down below.

____

2 Conduct Research

Here are some questions to ask as you research your topic:

- What famous people contributed to the development of your topic and when?

____

____

____

- What images can you use to illustrate the changes that occurred to your topic over time?

____

____

____

3 Make A Plan

Sketch out how you would like to organize your information in the space below, including time, people involved, pictures, and brief passages showing the changes in your topic.

Take It Home

Describe what you have learned to adults at home. Then have them help you create a poster of how your topic has changed over time.

Lesson 1

What Is Science?

ESSENTIAL QUESTION

How is science different from other fields of study?

By the end of this lesson, you should be able to distinguish what characterizes science and scientific explanations from other forms of knowledge and recognize creativity in science.

A scientist studies the genetic code. To most people, this looks impossible to understand. To her eyes, it's a wealth of information.

Sunshine State Standards

SC.6.N.1.5 Recognize that science involves creativity, not just in designing experiments, but also in creating explanations that fit evidence.

SC.6.N.2.1 Distinguish science from other activities involving thought.

SC.6.N.2.3 Recognize that scientists who make contributions to scientific knowledge come from all kinds of backgrounds and possess varied talents, interests, and goals.

Engage Your Brain

1 Predict Check T or F to show which statement is true or false.

T	F	
☐	☐	Science can determine what book you will enjoy.
☐	☐	Scientists can often be creative when designing experiments.
☐	☐	Because they are well educated, scientists do not need to make many observations before coming to a conclusion.
☐	☐	Scientific results can be proven incorrect.

2 Contrast The pottery in the photo is known for its unique appearance. This is partly because of the glaze used on it. What is one question a scientist might ask about this pottery and one question a nonscientist might ask?

____

____

____

____

____

____

Active Reading

3 Apply Use context clues to write your own definition for the underlined word.

Example sentence

Having watched frogs in ponds her whole childhood, Reilley had a lot of empirical evidence about how they behaved.

empirical

____

____

____

____

Vocabulary Terms

- **science**
- **empirical evidence**

4 Identify As you read, place a question mark next to any words that you don't understand. When you finish reading the lesson, go back and review the text that you marked. If the information is still confusing, consult a classmate or teacher.

Science Is Everywhere

What does science study?

One way to define **science** is as the systematic study of natural events and conditions. It is a logical, structured way of thinking about the world. Scientists ask questions about nature. They try to give explanations to describe what they observe. Any explanation a scientist gives must rely on information available to everyone. It must be an explanation others can test.

You probably have done science yourself without knowing it. If you have looked around you and tried to explain what you saw in a way that could be tested, you have done science.

Active Reading

5 Apply As you read, underline examples of subjects that can be studied by science.

The Natural World

Science is subdivided into different branches. Each branch considers a different part of the world. Each branch, however, studies the world in the same logical and structured way.

Biology, or life science, is the study of all living things, from the smallest, one-celled organisms to mammals. Geology, or earth science, studies Earth, from the materials that make it up to the processes that shape it. Astronomy, the study of objects in outer space, often is included under Earth science. Physical science is the study of energy and all nonliving matter. Physical science includes both physics and chemistry.

These branches of science can and often do overlap. You might hear a scientist called a *biochemist* or *geophysicist*. Such terms refer to those whose work falls a little in each branch.

Think Outside the Book Inquiry

6 Infer List three questions you would like to have answered. Categorize them as scientific or nonscientific. For the nonscientific questions, can you rephrase them in a scientific way? Do you think you can answer every question scientifically?

Testable Ideas

What are types of questions scientists ask? Scientists ask questions that can be tested. They ask questions that have answers they can measure in some way. An explanation in science is usually agreed upon by many people and not just someone's opinion.

One way to understand how scientific thinking differs from other activities is to think of a sculptor making a piece of art. For example, consider the ice sculptor on the next page. Different people can have different ideas of the value of the art. Some may think it is beautiful. Others may find it ugly. Still another may think it's beautiful one day and ugly the next. These are all opinions. No one's opinion is more correct than another's. The types of books you like, the clothes you like to wear, or the foods you like to eat are not questions science normally addresses.

However, now think of other things the sculptor or onlooker might wonder about the piece. How long will an ice sculpture like this last before it melts? Might the sculpture stay frozen longer if something is used to treat the ice? Would using warmer tools make sculpting ice easier? Questions like these have testable answers. The results can be measured and compared. More important, they can be proved false. This is what distinguishes scientific questions from other kinds.

Visualize It!

7 Apply This sculptor wonders whether the piece may start to melt before it's finished. Is this a question he can investigate scientifically? Explain.

8 Explain This sculptor wonders if making the wings thinner would make the sculpture look more graceful. Is this a question that could be tested by science? Explain.

Tools like this thermometer help scientists make measurements.

9 Discriminate What other testable questions might one ask about the statue?

"Give me an explanation . . ."

What is a scientific explanation?

A scientific explanation describes a natural process. It relies heavily on evidence gained from direct observation and testing. It is an explanation that others can test and refute.

Evidence gained from observation is empirical evidence. **Empirical evidence** includes observations, measurements, and other types of data scientists gather. Scientists use these data to support scientific explanations. Personal feelings and opinions are not empirical evidence.

A scientist never should hide any evidence he or she claims supports a scientific explanation. Whatever that evidence might be, the scientist must disclose all of it, if he or she wants to be taken seriously. If one scientist does an experiment, other scientists must be able to do the same experiment and get the same results. This openness is what makes scientific explanations strong.

Scientific explanation can be complex and, perhaps, even unintelligible to nonscientists. This should not discourage you from at least trying to evaluate explanations you hear like a scientist would.

For example, what makes popcorn pop? You most likely have seen it pop. You probably even have some idea as to how it happens. Here is a scientific explanation for it you can evaluate.

The corn pops because of a change in temperature. All plants contain water. Maybe the rise in temperature causes that water in the shell to boil. When the water turns into a gas, it pushes the kernel apart. The popcorn "pops" when the hard outer shell explodes. This is an explanation you can evaluate.

Active Reading **10 List** Give two examples of things that are not empirical evidence.

EVIDENCE

LOGIC

TESTS

How is a scientific explanation evaluated?

Now that you have an explanation for what makes popcorn pop, you can try to evaluate it as a scientist might. Here is how you might proceed. For each step, some sample responses are provided. Try to think of others.

First, look at any empirical evidence. Think of all the evidence that might support the explanation. Think of the times you've seen popcorn pop. What have you noticed?

Second, consider if the explanation is logical. Does it contradict anything else you know? What about it don't you understand? What else might you also wish to know?

Third, think of other tests you could do to support your ideas. Could you think of a test that might contradict the explanation?

Last, evaluate the explanation. Do you think it has stood up to logic and testing? What about it might be improved?

The Scientific Explanation:
Popcorn pops because the rise in temperature causes the water in it to expand and "pop" the kernel outward.

The Evidence

For the first step, identify all the evidence you can think of for what causes popcorn to pop.

11 Identify What have you observed about how and when popcorn pops?

• Pops when placed in a microwave

• Pops on a stove top

The Logic

Second, consider if the explanation is consistent with other evidence you have seen.

12 Infer Describe how well your explanation agrees with all of the evidence you have and with all that you know.

• See that water does turn to a gas when heated

• Other things expand when heated

The Tests

Think of other tests you could do that would support the explanation.

13 Predict What other ways might you pop popcorn if this explanation is correct?

• Could pop it in a solar cooker

• Could pop it using hot air

The Conclusion

Last, evaluate the explanation. Describe its strong points. Describe how it might be improved.

14 Evaluate How strong do you think the explanation is? How might it be improved?

Creative Expression

How do scientists show creativity?

Active Reading

15 Apply Underline examples of creative solutions used by scientists to solve problems.

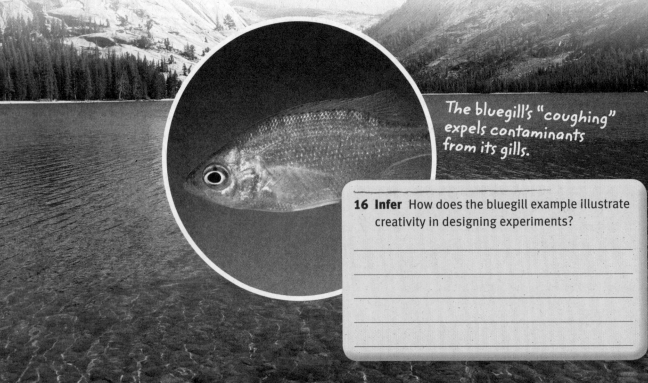

Scientists must rely only on what they can observe. They must always try to think logically. Indeed, this might seem dull. However, the best scientists are very creative. They can be creative both in the experiments they design and in the explanations they draw from them.

In Designing Experiments

How might creativity help in designing experiments? In one case, environmental scientists in the Washington, DC, area were looking for a method to detect harmful substances in drinking water. It would be too dangerous to have people drink the water directly, so they had to be creative.

Scientists knew bluegills are very sensitive to some contaminants. The fish "cough" to expel dirty water from their gills. Some scientists thought to use the fish coughing to identify contaminated water. They set bluegills in tanks in different locations. Sensors hooked up to the tanks detected the fishes' coughing and alerted monitors to potential harm. To ensure each fish's safety, a fish stayed in the tank only a short time.

The bluegill's "coughing" expels contaminants from its gills.

16 Infer How does the bluegill example illustrate creativity in designing experiments?

Newton claimed he got the idea for gravity when he saw an apple fall from a tree.

In Explaining Observations

Sometimes, a creative mind can put old evidence together in a new way. New explanations can often be as important as new observations.

Isaac Newton claimed the law of gravity came to him when he saw an apple fall. He reasoned that some force, gravity, pulled the apple to the ground. The question was why didn't gravity pull the moon to the ground as well?

Newton claimed it did. He explained the moon just didn't reach the Earth because it was moving too fast. To understand the idea, think of what would happen if you threw an apple as hard as you could. The harder you throw it, the farther it goes before gravity pulls it to the ground. What if you threw it so hard that it would travel once around the Earth before it reached the ground? This is what is happening to the moon. As it moves, Earth's gravity attracts it. It just moves too fast to fall to the ground.

Newton's explanation changed the understanding of motion forever. He had taken something many had seen, the fall of an apple, and explained it in a new way.

17 Devise Write a caption for this figure explaining how Newton related the moon to an apple falling to the ground.

____

____

____

____

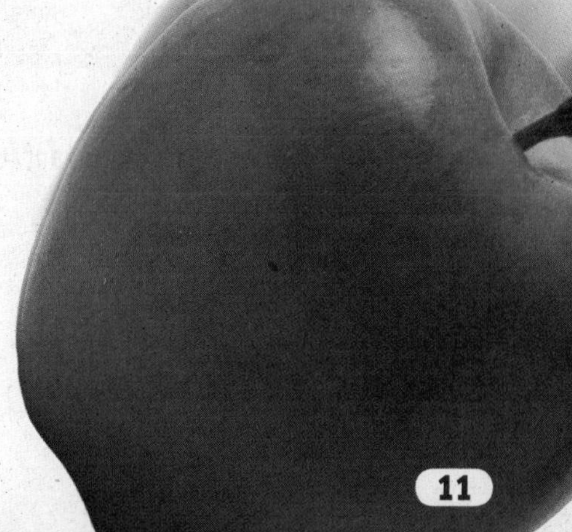

Visual Summary

To complete this summary, circle the correct word or phrase. Then use the key below to check your answers. You can use this page to review the main concepts of the lesson.

What Is Science?

Science is the systematic study of the natural world.

18 The natural sciences are normally divided into the life, earth, and physical / behavioral branches.

19 Science can / can't explain why you think a particular sculpture looks good.

Scientific explanations are supported by empirical evidence.

20 Empirical evidence includes observations / personal beliefs.

21 Scientific explanations are / are not able to be proved false.

Science can seem to be very dull work, but scientists are often very creative people.

22 Scientists are often creative in designing / comparing experiments.

23 Creative explanations must / need not rely on new observations.

Answers: 18 physical; 19 can't; 20 observations; 21 are; 22 designing; 23 need not

24 Hypothesize Why is it important that a scientist be both very logical and very creative?

Lesson Review

Vocabulary

Fill in the blanks with the term that best completes the following sentences.

1 The study of ____________________ involves the study of the natural world.

2 Science uses ____________________ to support its explanations.

Key Concepts

3 Distinguish You just bought a book titled *The Most Beautiful Artworks of the Century*. Is this likely to be a science book? Explain.

4 Determine A manufacturer claims its cleanser works twice as fast as any other. Could tests be performed to support the claim? Explain.

5 Contrast What is empirical evidence and what is it not?

6 Identify What are two ways in which scientists can show creativity?

Critical Thinking

Use this table to answer the following questions.

Color of flower	Number of butterfly visits	Number of moth visits
Red	11	0
Yellow	13	1
White	0	24

7 Distinguish For a science fair project, Ina wanted to investigate if flower color influenced the attraction of butterflies and moths. She made the table after observing the visits of butterflies and moths over a one-day period. Did she collect empirical evidence? Explain.

8 Infer Ina concludes that color does influence the attraction of butterflies and moths. Do you think this was a logical conclusion? Explain.

9 Judge Does being creative in doing science mean that a scientist should make things up? Why?

Lesson 2

Scientific Knowledge

ESSENTIAL QUESTION

How do we know about the world we live in?

By the end of this lesson, you should be able to identify examples of scientific knowledge and describe how they may change with new evidence.

Sunshine State Standards

SC.6.N.2.2 Explain that scientific knowledge is durable because it is open to change as new evidence or interpretations are encountered.

SC.6.N.3.1 Recognize and explain that a scientific theory is a well-supported and widely accepted explanation of nature and is not simply a claim posed by an individual. Thus, the use of the term theory in science is very different than how it is used in everyday life.

SC.6.N.3.2 Recongnize and explain that a scientific law is a description of a specific relationship under given conditions in the natural world. Thus, scientific laws are different from societal laws.

SC.6.N.3.3 Give several examples of scientific laws.

LA.6.4.2.2 The student will record information (e.g., observations, notes, lists, charts, legends) related to a topic, including visual aids to organize and record information and include a list of sources used.

This scientist is a paleontologist. She is very carefully removing small pieces of rock from fossilized bones. She is trying to uncover the fossil without damaging it.

Engage Your Brain

1 Conclude Fill in the blank with the word or phrase that you think correctly completes the following sentences.

A scientific ____________________ describes a basic principle of nature that always occurs under certain conditions.

A scientific model doesn't need to be something physical. It can also be a mathematical ____________________.

A good scientific theory is one that ____________________ the most evidence.

2 Predict Look at the two plants in the photo. What is different about the plant on the left? What do you think may have happened to it? How do you know this?

Active Reading

3 Apply Many scientific words, such as *model*, also have everyday meanings. Use context clues to write your own definition of the word *model*.

Example sentence

The **model** introduced by the automaker this year was a great improvement.

Example sentence

Rita was a **model** student.

Vocabulary Terms

- theory
- model
- law

4 Identify This list contains the vocabulary terms you'll learn in this lesson. As you read, circle the definition of each term.

Explain That!

What are some types of scientific explanations?

Active Reading **5 Identify** As you read, underline examples of scientific theories and models.

Science attempts to explain the world around us. Scientists make observations to collect information about the world. They then develop explanations for the things we see around us. Examples of scientific explanations are theories, models, and laws.

Theories

A scientific **theory** is a well-supported explanation about the natural world. Scientific theories have survived a great deal of testing. Theories explain the observations scientists have made. Scientists also use theories to make predictions about what they may not have seen yet. Theories are powerful things in science. They are much stronger than a hunch made by only one person.

Plate tectonics (playt tek•TAHN•ikz) is an example of a scientific theory. It states that Earth's outer layer is divided into individual plates. The plates move over Earth's surface and carry the landmasses with them.

The theory changed the study of Earth science greatly. Scientists found it could explain many things about the forces that shape Earth's surface. For example, they observed that most major earthquakes occur close to where plates meet and press against each other. In fact, scientists have yet to observe anything that opposes the theory. Plate tectonics helped scientists understand many natural events, such as mountain formation, volcanic eruption, and earthquake activity. It is a powerful scientific theory.

At this plate boundary in northeast Iceland, you can see the ground splitting.

Models

A scientific **model** is a representation of something in the natural world. Models allow scientists to study things that may be too large, too small, or in some way too difficult to study.

Again, be careful of how you think of a model. In science, models do not need to be physical things. A model can be a computer program or a mathematical equation. A model is anything familiar that helps scientists understand anything not familiar. Scientists use models to help them understand past, present, and even future events.

For example, if the land masses on Earth are moving, Earth's surface would not have looked the same millions of years ago. Scientists cannot know for sure what Earth's surface looked like. They can, however, attempt to make a model of it.

Maps are one example of a scientific model. Below are maps of what Earth's surface looks like today and what scientists think it looked like about 225 million years ago. The model shows that all land was once one big mega-continent. Scientists refer to this continent as *Pangaea* (pan•JEE•uh). The model shows how today's continents once formed Pangaea. Of course, the model of Pangaea does have its limitations. It does not allow scientists to study the "real thing," but it can give them a better sense of what Pangaea was like.

Active Reading

6 Infer What is the theory that can explain the model of Pangaea?

______

______

______

Visualize It!

7 Relate Write the names of today's continents where you think they were in Pangaea, using the spaces provided.

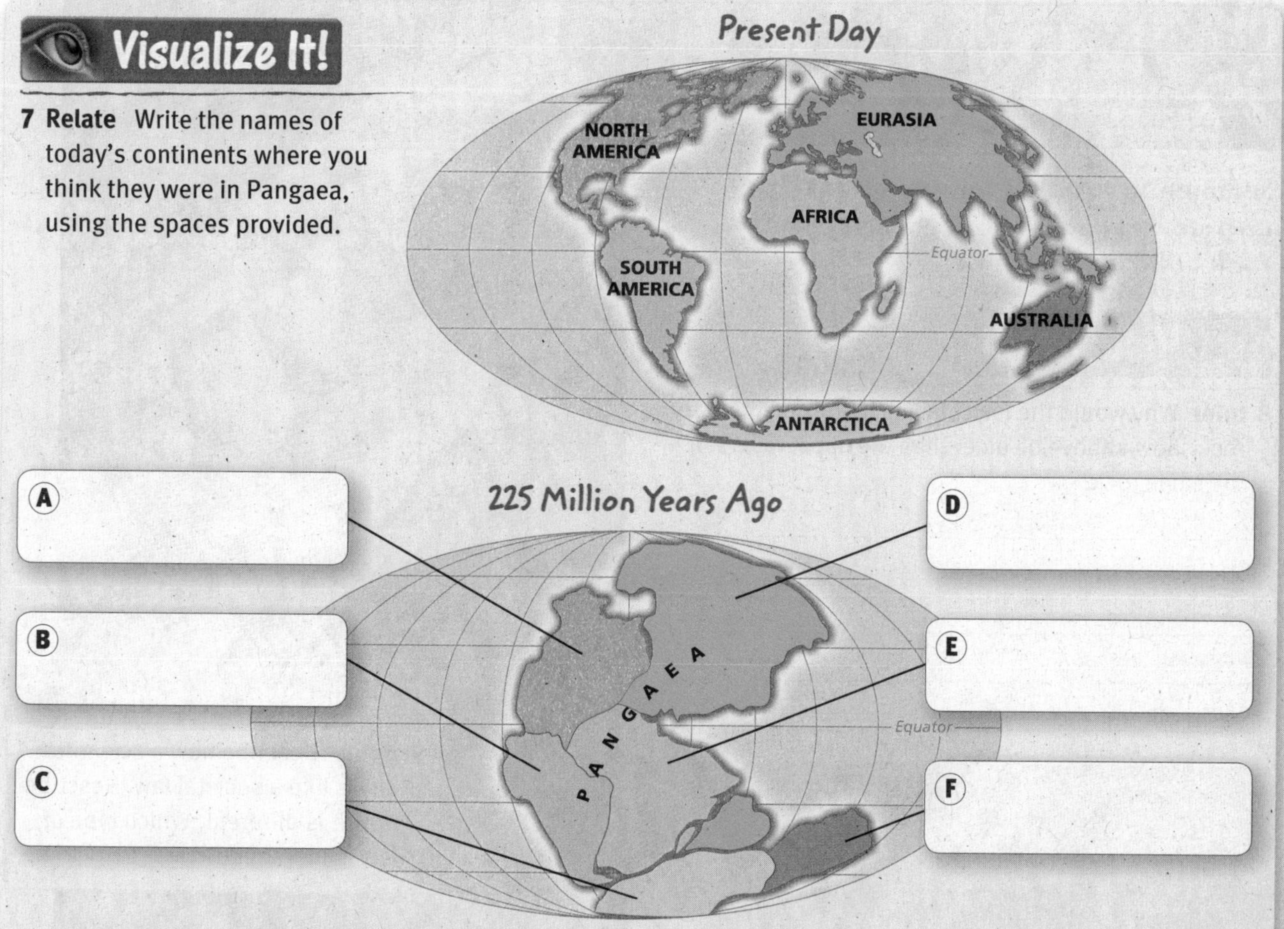

Laws

Theories and models often are modified as we learn more about the natural world. A scientific **law** describes a basic principle of nature that always occurs under certain conditions.

There are many scientific laws. The law of inertia states that an object in motion or at rest will stay in motion or at rest unless a force acts on it. Charles' law states that, at a constant pressure, as the temperature of a gas increases, its volume increases. Notice that laws simply tell you what to expect. For example, from the law of inertia, you can expect that an object at rest will stay at rest. Unlike a law in society, which is established, enforced, and sometimes changed, scientific laws are eternal and unchangeable.

Laws can be expressed in different ways. A law can be a statement or a mathematical equation. For example, Charles' law can be expressed mathematically as $V_1T_2 = V_2T_1$. This is just another way of showing the relationship between the volume and the temperature of a gas at a constant pressure.

Every branch of science has its scientific laws. In geology, the law of superposition states that any one layer of rock is always younger than the layer below it. Therefore, younger layers of rock will always overlie older layers. Again, the law is simply a description of what is seen.

Sedimentary rock is formed by particles carried by wind and water. Layers in the rock build up over time.

Visualize It!

8 Infer Why would the lower layers in the sedimentary rock shown above be older than the upper layers in the same rock?

Think Outside the Book Inquiry

9 Apply Describe how a scientific law is like a societal law. Describe how it is different. Which type of law is more restrictive?

Why It Matters

Bending the Law

WEIRD SCIENCE

Mutual Attraction

The law of gravity is a well-known scientific law. It states that the attraction of two masses to each other gets greater the larger the masses are and the closer they are. Isaac Newton first stated the law in the 1600s. He did not give a theory to explain gravity. He just described it.

Over 200 years later, Albert Einstein gave a theory that might explain how gravity works. He suggested that space curved around large masses. You can imagine the effect as similar to putting a heavy ball atop a tightly-stretched blanket. The more massive the ball, the more the blanket will curve. Large objects like stars curve space a great deal.

Bending Space

Scientists have proposed that vast amounts of unseen dark matter exist in outer space based on how its gravity affects the light from distant galaxies. The light appears to curve.

Throw a Curve!

Einstein proposed that large objects, like planets and stars, warped space. Gravity was the result of smaller objects "falling" down this warped space. The illustration shows how a large object, like the sun, warps space.

Extend

Inquiry

10 Identify How was Newton's description of gravity a law and not a theory?

11 Describe Describe a way you might try demonstrating Einstein's theory of gravity to a friend.

12 Infer Using Einstein's theory of gravity, explain why it's hard to notice the attraction of the small things on Earth to each other.

Consider the Source

What makes good scientific knowledge?

Active Reading

13 Identify As you read, underline two different theories for light.

What makes a good scientific theory or model? Good scientific knowledge does not always last forever. Theories and models often change with new evidence. The best scientific theories and models are those that are able to adapt to explain new observations.

The theory of light is an interesting example of how scientific knowledge can adapt and change. Scientists debated the theory of light for some time. At one time, scientists saw light as particles, and later as waves. The wave theory, however, seemed to explain more about light. For a long time, scientists accepted it. Light is still often depicted as waves.

Today, however, scientists view light as having both a particle nature and a wave nature. In a sense, the particle theory of light did not die. It was good scientific knowledge. It was just incomplete.

Most scientists today probably would agree that all scientific knowledge is incomplete. Even the best theories do not explain everything. Indeed, this is the reason science continues. The goal of science is best described as the attempt to explain as much as possible and to be open to change as new evidence arises. As you study science, perhaps the best advice to remember is that everything we know about the world is simply the best guesses we have made. The best scientists are those that are open to change.

Visualize It!

14 Apply The figures below model reflection in both the particle and wave theories of light. How might the particle theory have explained light passing through some objects and not others?

____

____

____

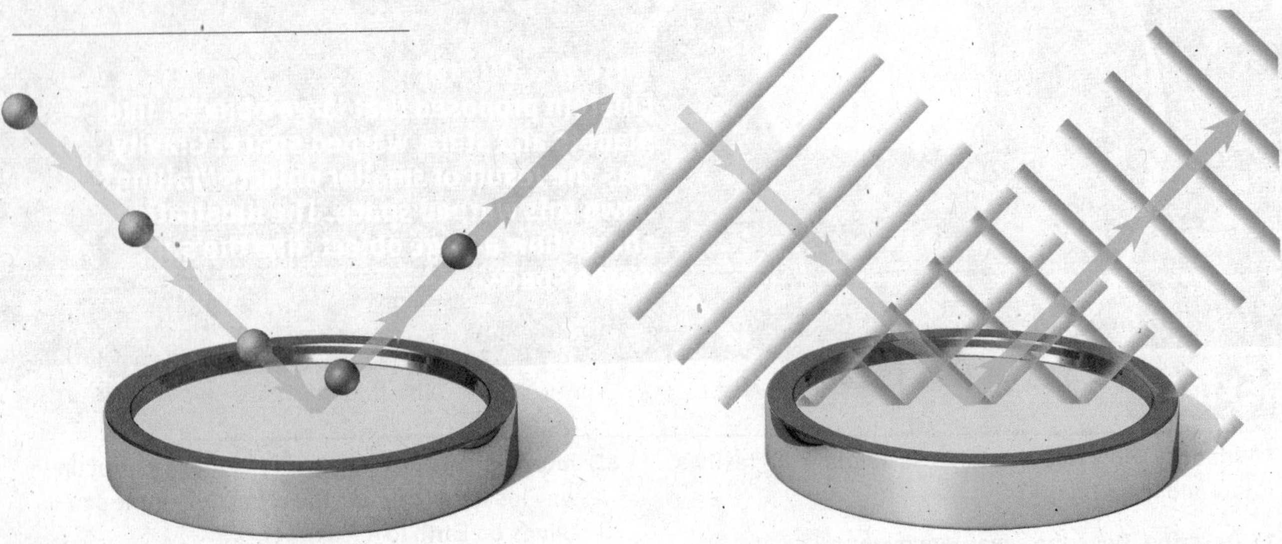

Reflection in the particle theory of light.

Reflection in the wave theory of light.

Information from places like NASA is reliable. Using our modern theory of light, NASA scientists can tell a lot about distant galaxies just by studying the light they see from them.

What makes a good source?

Where can you find good scientific knowledge? Because information can easily be sent across the world, you need to be able to separate reliable sources from the unreliable.

In general, you can trust information that comes from a government or university source. Nationally recognized research institutions, such as NASA, the Mayo Clinic, or Salk Institute, are also good sources. These institutions rely on their reputations. They would suffer if their information was found to be not accurate.

You should be cautious with publications more than a few years old. Remember, scientific knowledge changes. You should also be cautious of information made by those trying to sell a product. More often, their motivation is to use science to make money, not to instruct.

15 Evaluate In the table below, check the appropriate box indicating whether information from each source would be reliable, somewhat reliable, or not very reliable. Discuss your choices with others.

Government science agency (.gov site)	☐ reliable ☐ somewhat reliable ☐ not very reliable
Advertising agency	☐ reliable ☐ somewhat reliable ☐ not very reliable
Science textbook from 1985	☐ reliable ☐ somewhat reliable ☐ not very reliable
University (.edu site)	☐ reliable ☐ somewhat reliable ☐ not very reliable
Personal webpage	☐ reliable ☐ somewhat reliable ☐ not very reliable

Visual Summary

To complete this summary, check *true* or *false* below each statement. Then, use the key below to check your answers. You can use this page to review the main concepts of the lesson.

Scientific Knowledge

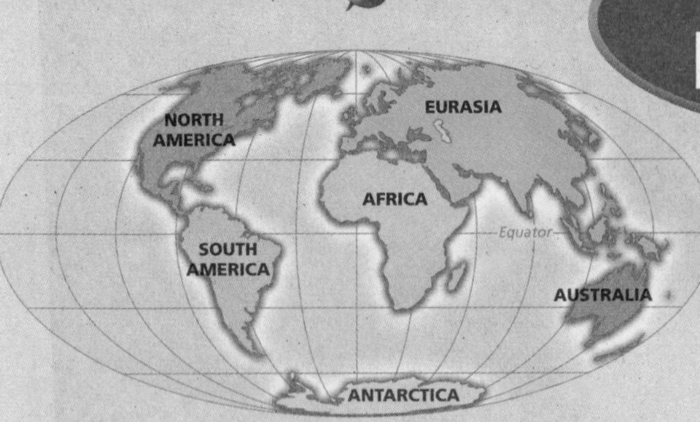

Models, Theories, and Laws
Models, theories, and laws are three types of scientific knowledge.

16 Any hunch you have is as good as a scientific theory.

☐ True ☐ False

17 Models can represent things that are too far away or too small to see.

☐ True ☐ False

18 Scientific laws can be thought of as general descriptions of what we see happening around us.

☐ True ☐ False

Adaptability of Scientific Knowledge
Scientific knowledge is durable, because it is open to change.

19 Scientific theories can change when new evidence is found.

☐ True ☐ False

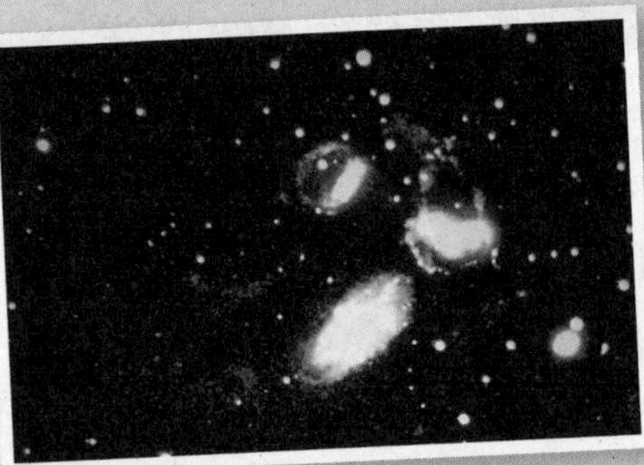

Reliable Sources
Sources for reliable scientific information include government agencies and research institutions, like NASA.

20 You can trust scientific information from advertisers, because they are selling a product.

☐ True ☐ False

Answers: 16 False; 17 True; 18 True; 19 True; 20 False

21 Relate Laws can be explained by theories. If a theory changes, does it mean the law must change? Explain.

Lesson Review

Vocabulary

Fill in the blank with the term or phrase that best completes the following sentences.

1 A(n) ______________________ is a representation of something in the natural world.

2 Unlike in society, a scientific ______________ is simply a description of what we see.

3 A scientific ______________________ has a lot of support and is more than just a "hunch."

Key Concepts

4 Differentiate How might a theory relate to a model?

5 Discriminate Where might you look on the Internet to find good scientific information about an illness?

6 Identify What two types of scientific knowledge can be expressed as mathematical equations?

7 Analyze Scientific theories can change over time as new information is discovered. If a scientific theory changes, does this mean that it was not a good theory to begin with?

Critical Thinking

The gravity of the sun and the moon affects tides on Earth. The model below shows the positions of the sun, the moon, and Earth during a spring tide. Use it to answer questions 8 and 9.

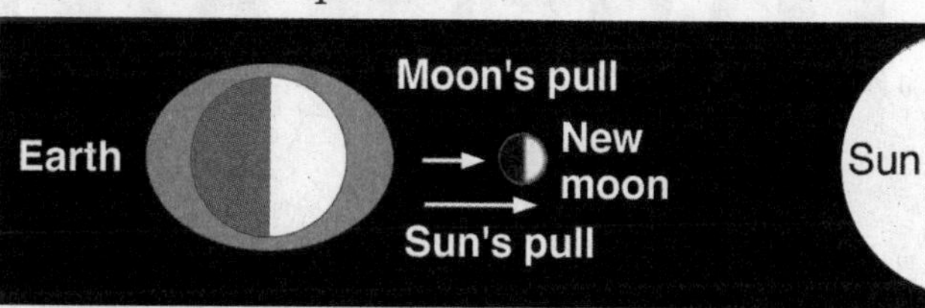

8 Analyze How does this model make it easier for someone to understand the sun's and the moon's influences on the tides?

9 Evaluate What do you think are the limitations of this model?

10 Evaluate Do you agree or disagree with the following statement? Explain your answer. Both theories and laws can be used to predict what will happen in a situation that has not already been tested.

Lesson 3

Scientific Investigations

ESSENTIAL QUESTION

How do scientists work?

By the end of this lesson, you should be able to summarize the processes and characteristics of different kinds of scientific investigations.

Sunshine State Standards

SC.6.N.1.1 Define a problem from the sixth grade curriculum, use appropriate reference materials to support scientific understanding, plan and carry out scientific investigation of various types, such as systematic observations or experiments, identify variables, collect and organize data, interpret data in charts, tables, and graphics, analyze information, make predictions, and defend conclusions.

SC.6.N.1.2 Explain why scientific investigations should be replicable.

SC.6.N.1.3 Explain the difference between an experiment and other types of scientific investigation, and explain the relative benefits and limitations of each.

SC.6.N.1.4 Discuss, compare, and negotiate methods used, results obtained, and explanations among groups of students conducting the same investigation.

LA.6.4.2.2 The student will record information (e.g., observations, notes, lists, charts, legends) related to a topic, including visual aids to organize and record information and include a list of sources used.

Particle accelerators such as the one shown here cause the particles that make up atoms to move at almost the speed of light. They allow scientists to investigate the nature of matter.

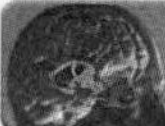

Engage Your Brain

1 Evaluate Check T or F to show whether you think each statement is true or false.

T	F	
☐	☐	Every scientific investigation is an experiment.
☐	☐	You could do an experiment to see if eating breakfast helps students raise their grades.
☐	☐	Scientists need fancy instruments to do experiments.
☐	☐	Scientists must repeat an experiment for it to be useful.

2 Infer What do you think the scientists who gathered the data for this graph were studying?

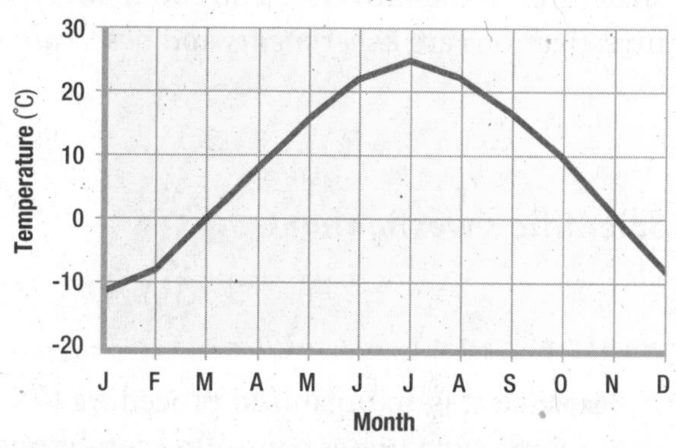

____

____

____

____

Active Reading

3 Synthesize The word *experiment* comes from the Latin word *experiri*, meaning "to try." What do you think the meaning of the word *experiment* is?

____

____

____

____

____

Vocabulary Terms

- **experiment**
- **observation**
- **hypothesis**
- **variable**
- **data**

4 Apply As you learn the meaning of each vocabulary term in this lesson, write a sentence of your own using the term.

Scientists at Work!

What are some types of scientific investigations?

Scientists carry out investigations to learn about the natural world—everything from the smallest particles to the largest structures in the universe. The two main types of scientific investigations are *experiments* and *observations.*

Scientific Investigations

Experiments

An **experiment** is an organized procedure to study something under controlled conditions. Experiments are often done in a laboratory. This makes it easier to control factors that can influence a result. For example, a scientist notices that a particular kind of fish is becoming less common in a lake near his home. He knows that some fish need more oxygen than others. To find out if this local fish species is being harmed by decreased oxygen levels, he might do the following experiment. First, he measures oxygen levels in the lake. Then, he sets up three tanks of water in a laboratory. The water in each tank has a different level of oxygen. Other factors that might affect fish, such as temperature, are the same in all three tanks. The scientist places the same number of fish in each tank. Then he collects information on the health of the fish.

Active Reading **5 Infer** Why would the scientist in the example want the temperature to be the same in all three tanks?

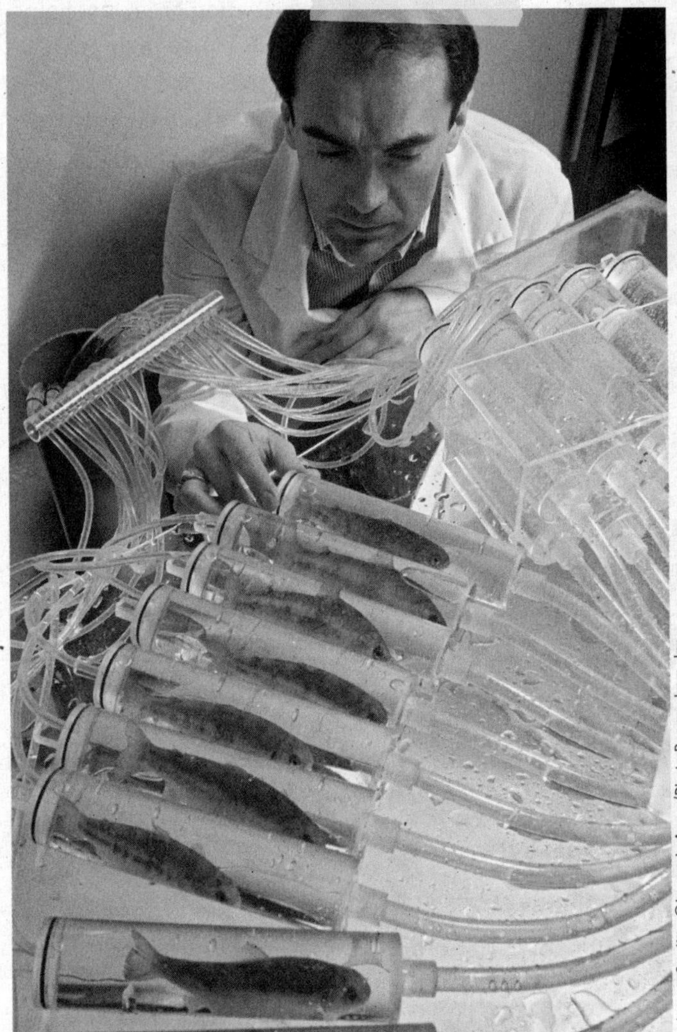

This scientist is studying salmon in a controlled laboratory experiment.

6 **Analyze** List the factors that the scientists cannot control in the field investigation shown in this picture.

This scientist is observing salmon in their natural environment in Mongolia.

Active Reading

7 **Identify** As you read, underline reasons why a scientist might choose to do observations that do not involve experiments.

Other Types of Investigations

Observation is the process of obtaining information by using the senses. The word can also refer to the information obtained by using the senses. Although scientists make observations while conducting experiments, many things cannot be studied under controlled conditions. For example, it is impossible to create or manipulate a star. But astronomers can observe stars through telescopes.

Observations of the natural world are generally less precise than experiments because they involve factors that are not controlled by scientists. However, they may give a better description of what is actually happening in nature.

Important scientific observations can be made anywhere. The scientist who experiments with fish and oxygen levels in the example you read on the opposite page might observe a lake to find out which animals and plants live in it. His observations may or may not support the findings of the laboratory experiment.

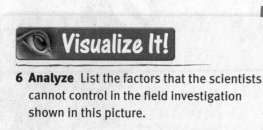

Another type of investigation is the creation of models, which are representations of an object or system. Models are useful for studying things that are very small, large, or complex. For example, computer models of Earth's atmosphere can help scientists forecast the weather.

Why Ask Why?

What are some parts that make up scientific investigations?

The work that scientists do can vary greatly. Some scientists spend much of their time outdoors. Others mostly work in laboratories. Yet scientific investigations have some basic things in common.

Hypothesis

A **hypothesis** (hy•PAHTH•ih•sis) is a testable idea or explanation that leads to scientific investigation. A scientist may think of a hypothesis after making observations or after reading findings from other scientists' investigations. The hypothesis can be tested by experiment or observation.

For example, imagine that while outside after a snowstorm, you notice that plant leaves seem to be healthy. You wonder how the leaves stayed alive because the temperature was below freezing during the storm. You also know that heat does not pass as easily through snow as it does through air. With this information, you could make the following hypothesis: "The leaves on the plants stayed healthy because the snow cover slowed their loss of heat." This is a hypothesis that could be tested by an experiment.

These scientists are removing a mummy discovered in Peru. Because Peru's climate is so dry, some DNA is preserved.

Mummies such as this one have been preserved by the cold, dry climate of the Andes Mountains in Peru.

Think Outside the Book

8 Apply Think of something you have observed or read about that interests you. Then, write a hypothesis about it.

Elements of Investigations

This scientist is analyzing DNA found in a mummy from Peru.

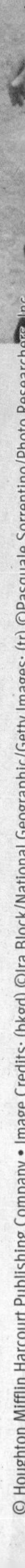

Variables

A **variable** is any factor that can change in an experiment, observation, or model. When scientists plan experiments, they try to change only one variable and keep the other variables constant, or unchanged. However, it may not be possible to control all the variables that can affect the results.

Suppose you decide to test the hypothesis that snow protects leaves from below-freezing temperatures. If you did the experiment in the field, you would not be able to control many variables. But you could set up a laboratory experiment to test your hypothesis. First, you would put similar plants in two chambers. Both chambers would be cooled to the same temperature. You would cover the plants in one chamber with snow and leave the plants in the other chamber without a snow cover. The snow cover is the variable you want to test. You would try to keep all the other variables the same in both chambers. For example, when you open one chamber to pour snow on the plants, you would keep the other chamber open for the same amount of time.

Observations and Data

Data are information gathered by observation or experimentation that can be used in calculating or reasoning. Everything a scientist observes in an investigation must be recorded. The setup and procedure of an experiment also need to be recorded. By carefully recording this information, scientists make sure that they will not forget important details.

The biologist shown in the photo above would record the results of her analysis of mummy DNA. In addition, she would identify the type of tissue that was examined—whether it came from a tooth or bone, for example. She would also record the type of instrument used to examine the tissue and the procedures that she followed. All of these details may be important when she reports her findings. The information will also help other scientists evaluate her work.

9 Identify What kind of data would you record for an experiment testing whether snow protects leaves from cold temperatures?

Many Methods

What are some scientific methods?

Scientific methods are the ways in which scientists answer questions and solve problems. There is no single formula for an investigation. Scientists do not all use the same steps in every investigation or use steps in the same order. They may even repeat some of the steps. The following graphic shows one path a scientist might follow when conducting an experiment.

10 Diagram Using a different color, draw arrows showing another path a scientist might follow if he or she were observing animals in the wild.

Defining a Problem

After making observations or reading scientific reports, a scientist might be curious about some unexplained aspect of a topic. A scientific problem is a specific question that a scientist wants to answer. The problem must be well-defined, or precisely stated, so that it can be investigated.

Forming a Hypothesis and Making Predictions

When scientists form a hypothesis, they are making an educated guess about a problem. A hypothesis must be tested to see if it is true. Before testing a hypothesis, scientists often make predictions about what will happen in an investigation.

Planning an Investigation

A scientific investigation must be carefully planned so that it tests a hypothesis in a meaningful way. Scientists need to decide whether an investigation should be done in the field or in a laboratory. They must also determine what equipment and technology are required and how materials for the investigation will be obtained.

Identifying Variables

Before conducting a controlled experiment, scientists identify all the variables that can affect the results. Then they decide which variable should change and which ones should stay constant. Some variables may be impossible to control.

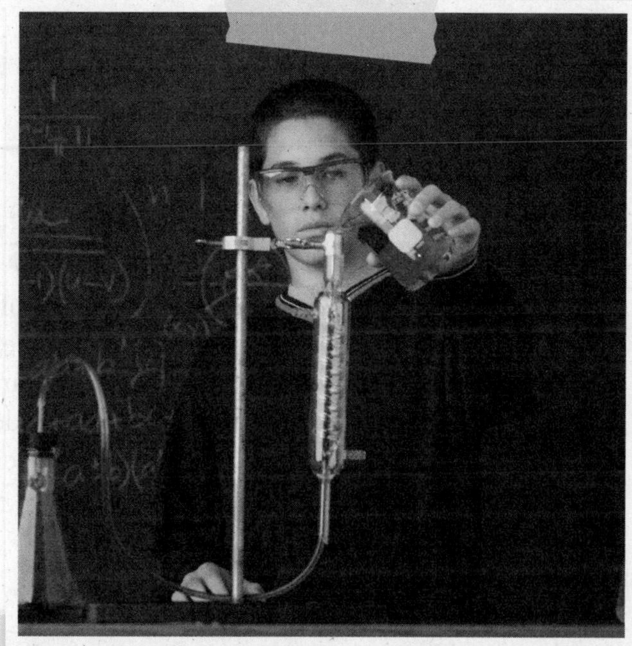

Collecting and Organizing Data

The data collected in an investigation must be recorded and properly organized so that they can be analyzed. Data such as measurements and numbers are often organized into tables, spreadsheets, or graphs.

Interpreting Data and Analyzing Information

After they finish collecting data, scientists must analyze this information. Their analysis will help them draw conclusions about the results. Scientists may have different interpretations of the same data because they analyze it using different methods.

Defending Conclusions

Scientists conclude whether the results of their investigation support the hypothesis. If the hypothesis is not supported, scientists may think about the problem some more and try to come up with a new hypothesis to test. When they publish the results of their investigation, scientists must be prepared to defend their conclusions if they are challenged by other scientists.

Use It or Lose It

How are scientific methods used?

Scientific methods are used to study any aspect of the natural world. They can also be used in the social sciences, which focus on human society. It is often harder to control variables in the social sciences. Nevertheless, these fields are made stronger by the methods developed for physical, life, and earth science.

Think Outside the Book **Inquiry**

11 Plan Suppose that you want to investigate something using scientific methods. First, define a problem. Then, plan a scientific investigation using the methods discussed in the previous pages.

Use of Scientific Methods

Different Situations Require Different Methods

After forming a hypothesis, scientists decide how they will test it. Some hypotheses can be tested only through observation. Others must be tested in laboratory experiments. However, observation and experiments are often used together to build scientific knowledge. For example, if you want to test the strength of a metal used in airplane construction, you may study it in a laboratory experiment. But after conducting the experiment, you may want to inspect airplanes that have flown for a period of time to see how the metal holds up under actual flight conditions.

If an investigation does not support a hypothesis, it is still useful. The data from the investigation can help scientists form a better hypothesis. Scientists may go through many cycles of testing and data analysis before they arrive at a hypothesis that is supported.

12 Apply Give another example of a scientific investigation that would require both observation and experiments.

____

____

____

____

Scientific Methods Are Used in Physical Science

Physical science includes the study of physics and chemistry. Scientists have used physics to figure out how gecko lizards stick to walls and ceilings.

Various explanations of the gecko's unique ability have been developed. Some scientists thought that static electricity helps geckos stick to walls. Others thought that the gecko produces a kind of glue from its feet. But experiments and observations did not support these hypotheses.

When a team of researchers studied the gecko's feet with a microscope, they found that each foot was covered with hundreds of thousands of tiny hairs. After measuring the force exerted by each hair against a surface, they came up with two possible hypotheses. One hypothesis was that geckos stick to walls because the hairs interact with a thin film of water. The other hypothesis was that the weak forces between the hairs and a surface combine to produce a force great enough to hold the gecko to the surface.

The team designed an experiment to test both hypotheses. The experiment showed that the force of a gecko's hair against a surface was the same whether or not the surface had any water on it. The scientists concluded that the gecko sticks to walls because of the combined forces of the hairs on its feet.

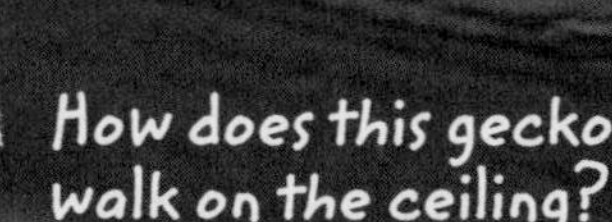
How does this gecko
walk on the ceiling?

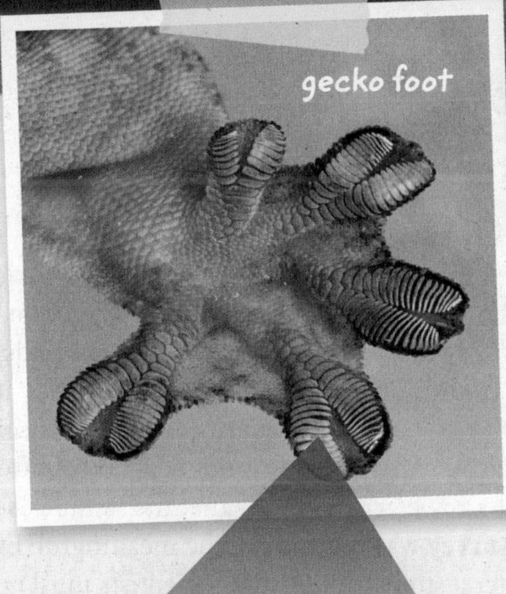
gecko foot

This is a close-up picture of the tiny hairs on a gecko's foot.

13 Relate Fill in the flow chart below with examples of the scientific methods used in the gecko investigation.

Defining a Problem

↓

Forming a Hypothesis

↓

Collecting Data

Getting It Right

What are some ways to confirm that an investigation is valid?

Scientific investigations should be carried out with great care. But scientists are only human. Sometimes they fail to plan properly. They may make mistakes in collecting or analyzing data because they are in a hurry. On rare occasions, irresponsible scientists produce false results on purpose. Fortunately, there are procedures that help expose flawed investigations.

Evaluating Investigations

Peer Review

Before a study is published, it is read by scientists who were not involved in the investigation. These peer reviewers evaluate the methods used in a study and the conclusions reached by its authors. For example, a reviewer could decide that an experiment was not properly controlled. Or a reviewer might say that the sample used in a survey was too small to be meaningful. Even after a study is published, scientists must answer questions raised by other scientists.

Replication

An important way to confirm an investigation is for other scientists to replicate it, or repeat the investigation and obtain the same findings. To make this possible, scientists must disclose the methods and materials used in the original study when they publish their findings. Not every investigation needs to be replicated exactly. But if a study cannot be supported by the results of similar investigations, it will not be accepted by the scientific community.

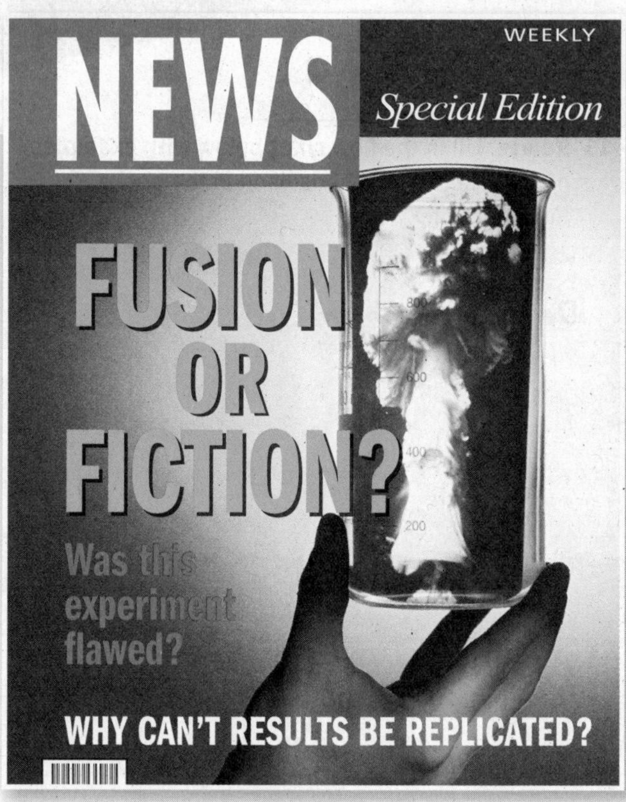

WEEKLY
NEWS
Special Edition
FUSION OR FICTION?
Was this experiment flawed?
WHY CAN'T RESULTS BE REPLICATED?

In 1989 a pair of scientists reported that they had accomplished cold nuclear fusion. The possibility of a cheap source of energy excited the public. However, other scientists considered the claim impossible. Attempts to replicate the findings failed.

Think Outside the Book

14 Evaluate Research the cold fusion news reported in 1989. Write a few paragraphs about the study. Did the study exhibit the characteristics of a good scientific investigation? Explain.

How can you evaluate the quality of scientific information?

Scientific information can be found on the Internet, in magazines, and in newspapers. It can be difficult to decide which information should be trusted. The most reliable scientific information is published in scientific journals.

The most reliable information on the Internet is on government or academic webpages. Other sites should be examined closely for errors, especially if they are selling things.

Although the lab reports that you prepare for school might not be published, you should try to meet the same standards of published studies. For example, you should provide enough information so that other students can replicate your results.

Visualize It!

15 Apply List two examples of poor scientific methodology found in this student's lab report.

Problem: How does the amount of sunlight affect the growth of plants?

Hypothesis: Plants that spend more time in the sunlight will grow taller because plants grow taller in warm conditions.

Changed variables: amount of time in the sunlight and type of plant

Constant variables: amount of water

Materials: plants, water, sunlamp, ruler

Procedure: Take the plants and put them under the sunlamp. Leave some of them under the lamp for longer amounts of time than others.

Data Table:

Plant number	Length of time in sunlight per day	Height after 2 weeks
1	5 hours	8 inches
2	8 hours	12 inches

16 Assess Would you believe this result or would you be skeptical of it? Explain your answer.

Visual Summary

To complete this summary, circle the correct word from each set of words. Then, use the key below to check your answers. You can use this page to review the main concepts of the lesson.

Types of Scientific Investigations

Scientists carry out investigations through experiments and observation.

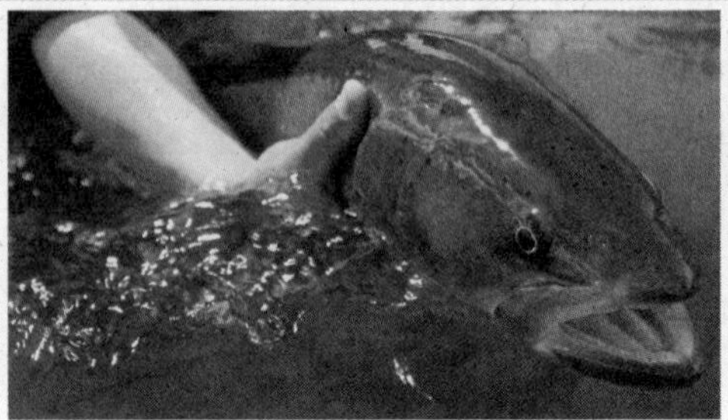

17 Scientific investigations that involve testing a single variable are called models / experiments / theories.

18 Hypotheses / Models / Observations are often made before other types of investigations are done.

Scientific Methods

Scientists use scientific methods to answer questions and solve problems.

19 A problem / hypothesis / variable must be tested to see if it is supported.

20 Scientists must decide which data / hypotheses / variables will stay constant in an experiment.

Scientific Investigations

Characteristics of Good Scientific Investigations

There are procedures that separate good scientific investigations from flawed ones.

21 The findings of experiments are generally not accepted until they are published / proven / replicated.

22 The most reliable scientific information comes from reporters / scientists / companies working in a particular field.

Answers: 17. experiments, 18. observations, 19. hypothesis, 20. variables, 21. replicated, 22. scientists

23 Relate What is the relationship between a scientific problem and a hypothesis?

Lesson Review

Vocabulary

Fill in the blank with the term that best completes the following sentences.

1 A(n) ______________ determines what will be tested in a scientific experiment.

2 All of the ______________ gathered in an investigation must be recorded.

3 A good scientific ______________ can be repeated by someone else and the same results will be found.

Key Concepts

Example	Scientific Method
4 Identify Scientists use instruments to record the strength of earthquakes in an area.	
5 Identify Scientists decide that in an experiment on fish, all the fish will be fed the same amount of food.	

6 Identify What are two key characteristics of a good scientific investigation?

7 Explain Why is it important for scientists to share information from their investigations?

Critical Thinking

Use this drawing to answer the following questions.

8 Analyze Which variable changes in the investigation depicted in the drawing?

9 Conclude Identify one variable that is kept constant for both groups in this experiment.

10 Infer What kind of data might be collected for this experiment?

11 Evaluate Which is less likely to be a reliable source of information, the webpage of a university or the webpage of a scientist who is trying to sell a new invention? Explain.

Lesson 4

Representing Data

ESSENTIAL QUESTION

In what ways can you organize data to fully understand them?

By the end of this lesson, you should be able to use tables, graphs, and models to display and analyze scientific data.

Scientists depend on tools called seismographs to record the motion of earthquakes. The graph produced by a seismograph is called a seismogram. This seismogram shows the ground motion of an earthquake that hit the United Kingdom in 2007.

Sunshine State Standards

SC.6.N.3.4 Identify the role of models in the context of the sixth grade science benchmarks.

MA.6.S.6.2 Select and analyze the measures of central tendency or variability to represent, describe, analyze, and/or summarize a data set for the purposes of answering questions appropriately.

MA.6.A.3.6 Construct and analyze tables, graphs, and equations to describe linear functions and other simple relations using both common language and algebraic notation.

LA.6.4.2.2 The student will record information (e.g., observations, notes, lists, charts, legends) related to a topic, including visual aids to organize and record information and include a list of sources used.

Engage Your Brain

1 Predict Check T or F to show whether you think each statement is true or false.

T	F	
☐	☐	Scientific models have been used to show results of scientific experiments.
☐	☐	Certain types of graphs are better than others for displaying specific types of data.
☐	☐	Most graphs are confusing and unnecessary.
☐	☐	If something can be shown in a table, then it should not be shown in a graph.

2 Evaluate Name two things about the model shown that are similar to the object that the model represents. Then name two things about the model that are different.

Active Reading

3 Apply Many words, such as *model*, have multiple meanings. Use context clues to write your own definition for each meaning of the word *model.*

Example sentence
After getting an *A* on another test, Julio's teacher told him he was a model student.

model:

Example sentence
For her science project, Samantha created a model of the solar system.

model:

Vocabulary Term

- **model**

4 Identify As you read this lesson, underline examples of models.

Crunching Data!

How do scientists make sense of data?

Before scientists begin an experiment, they often create a data table for recording their data. *Data* are the facts, figures, and other evidence gathered through observations and experimentation. The more data a scientist collects, the greater is the need for the data to be organized in some way. Data tables are one easy way to organize a lot of scientific data.

Scientists Organize the Data

A data table provides an organized way for scientists to record the data that they collect. Information that might be recorded in data tables are times, amounts, and *frequencies,* or the number of times something happens.

When creating a data table, scientists must decide how to organize the table into columns and rows. Any units of measurement, such as seconds or degrees, should be included in the column headings and not in the individual cells. Finally, a title must always be added to describe the data in the table.

The data table below shows the number of movie tickets sold each month at a small theater.

Movie Tickets Sold Monthly

Month	Number of tickets
January	15,487
February	12,654
March	15,721
April	10,597
May	10,916
June	11,797
July	18,687
August	18,302
September	16,978
October	10,460
November	11,807
December	17,497

Do the Math You Try It

5 Extend Circle the row in the table that shows the month when the greatest number of tickets were sold. Then circle the row that shows the month when the least number of tickets were sold. Finally, subtract the least number from the greatest number to find the range of the number of tickets sold.

________ – ________ = ________

greatest number of tickets — least number of tickets — range

Scientists Graph and Analyze the Data

In order to analyze their collected data for patterns, it is often helpful for scientists to construct a graph of their data. The type of graph they use depends upon the data they collect and what they want to show.

A *bar graph* is used to display and compare data in a number of separate categories. The length, or height, of each bar represents the number in each category. For example, in the movie theater data, the months are the categories. The lengths of the bars represent the number of tickets sold each month.

Other types of graphs include line graphs and circle graphs. A *line graph* is often used to show continuous change over time. A *circle graph,* or pie chart, is used when you are showing how each group of data relates to all of the data. For example, you could use a circle graph to depict the number of boys and girls in your class.

Active Reading

5 Interpret What kind of data would you display in a bar graph?

____

____

____

____

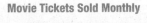

Visualize It!

7 Analyze The data in the graph below are the same as the data in the table at the left. During what three months are the most movie theater tickets sold?

____

____

____

Movie Tickets Sold Monthly

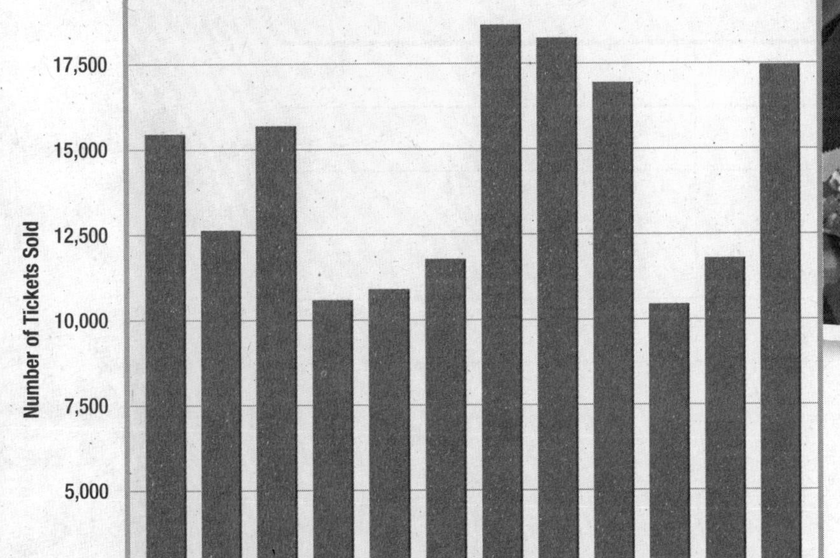

8 Extend What other kind of data could you collect at home that might show differences over the course of a year?

____

____

____

____

Graph It!

What do graphs show?

Graphs are visual representations of data. They show information in a way that is often easier to understand than data shown in tables. All graphs should have a title explaining the graph.

In certain types of graphs, the data displayed on the horizontal axis are the values of the *independent variable*. This is the variable that is deliberately manipulated in an investigation. For example, if you collect rainfall data over four weeks, the week number is the independent variable because you have chosen to collect data once a week. You have manipulated the time interval between data collections.

The data displayed on the vertical axis are the values of the *dependent variable*. This is the variable that changes as a result of the manipulation of one or more independent variables. For example, the inches of rainfall per week is the dependent variable.

Visualize It!

9 Complete The data at the right show the amount of rain, in inches, that fell in each of four weeks at a school. Use the empty table below to organize the data. Include a title for the table, the column headings, and all of the data.

Week 1: 0.62 in.
Week 2: 0.40 in.
Week 3: 1.12 in.
Week 4: 0.23 in.

Title ______________________

Headings	
Data	

Do the Math You Try It

10 Extend The average, or mean, of the rainfall data is the sum of the data values divided by the number of data values. Calculate the mean of the rainfall data. Round your answer to the nearest hundredth.

____ + ____ + ____ + ____ = ____
Weeks 1 through 4 — Sum

____ ÷ ____ ≈ ____
Sum — Number of data values — Mean

How are graphs constructed?

To make a bar graph of the rainfall data at the left, first draw a horizontal axis and a vertical axis. Next, write the names of the categories to be graphed along the horizontal axis. Include an overall label for the axis as well. Next, label the vertical axis with the name of the dependent variable. Be sure to include the units of measurement. Then create a scale along the axis by marking off equally spaced numbers that cover the range of the data collected. For each category, draw a solid bar using the scale on the vertical axis to determine the height. Make all the bars the same width. Finally, add a title that describes the graph.

Active Reading

11 Identify As you read, number the steps used to construct a graph. You may want to rely on signal words that indicate a new step, such as *then* or *next*.

12 Graph Construct a bar graph of the rainfall data at the left. On the lines provided, include a title for the graph and axis labels. Use a scale of 0.20 in. for the horizontal axis, and label the bars on the vertical axis.

Title: ______________________

Amount of Rainfall (in.)

0.0

Week 1 ______ ______ ______

____

Visualize It!

13 Analyze During which week was the rainfall amount approximately twice what it was during week 4? Use your graph to explain.

____

____

____

____

This rain gauge is used to gather and measure liquid precipitation.

Model It!

What types of models can be used to represent data?

A crash-test dummy, a mathematical equation, and a road map are all models that represent real things. A **model** is a representation of an object or a process that allows scientists to study something in greater detail. A model uses something familiar to help you understand something that is not familiar.

Models can represent things that are too small to see, such as atoms. They can also represent things that are too large to see fully, such as Earth. Models can be used to explain the past and the present. They can even be used to predict future events. Two common kinds of scientific models are physical models and mathematical models.

14 Apply As you read, underline different ways that scientists use models.

Physical Models

Physical models are models that you can touch. Toy cars, models of buildings, maps, and globes are all physical models. Physical models often look like the things they represent. For example, this model of Earth shows that Earth is divided into three layers—the crust, the mantle, and the core. The table below shows the estimated densities of each of Earth's layers.

Density of Earth's Layers

Layer	Density (g/cm^3)
crust	2.7–3.3
mantle	3.3–5.7
core	9.9–13.1

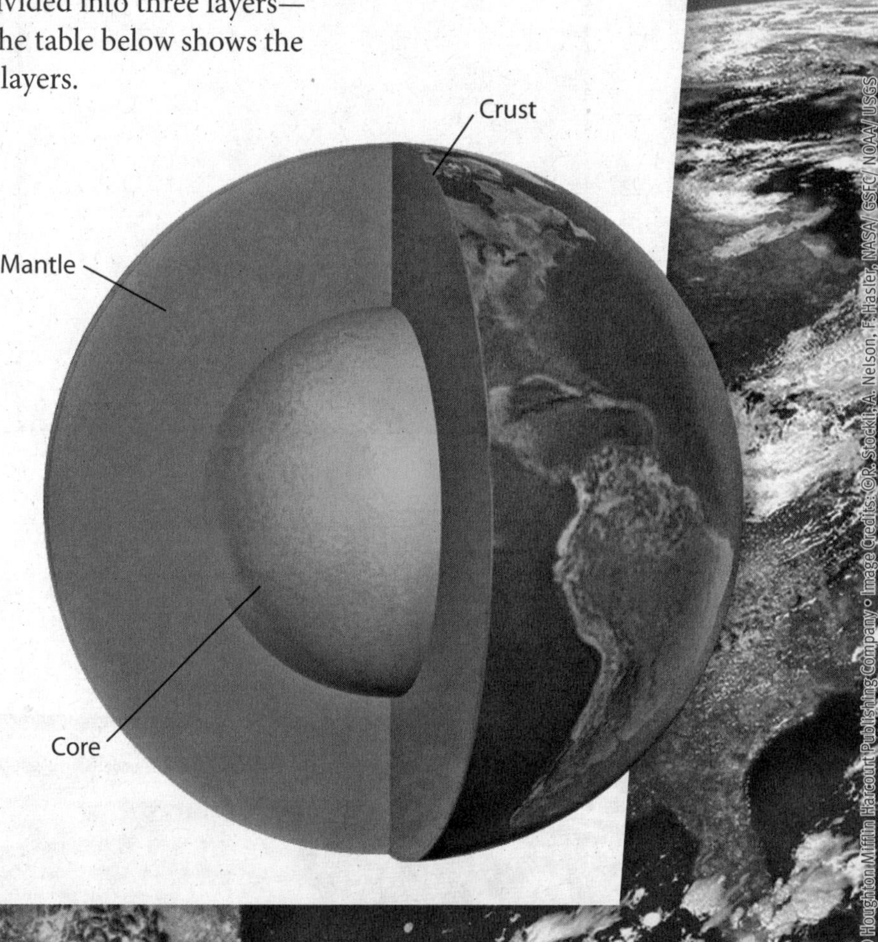

15 Analyze The table shows the estimated densities of Earth's layers. Write the layers of Earth in order of most dense to least dense.

____

____

Mathematical Models

Every day, people try to predict the weather. One way to predict the weather is to use mathematical models. A *mathematical model* is made up of mathematical equations and data. Some mathematical models are simple. These models allow you to calculate things such as how far a car will travel in an hour or how much you would weigh on the moon.

Other mathematical models are so complex that computers are needed to process them. Some of these very complex models, such as population growth, have many variables. Sometimes, certain variables that no one thought of exist in the model. A change in any variable could cause the model to fail.

Do the Math **You Try It**

16 Calculate The air we breathe is made up of 78% nitrogen, 21% oxygen, and 1% other gases. Use three different colored pencils to color the appropriate number of squares in the grid for each of these percentages.

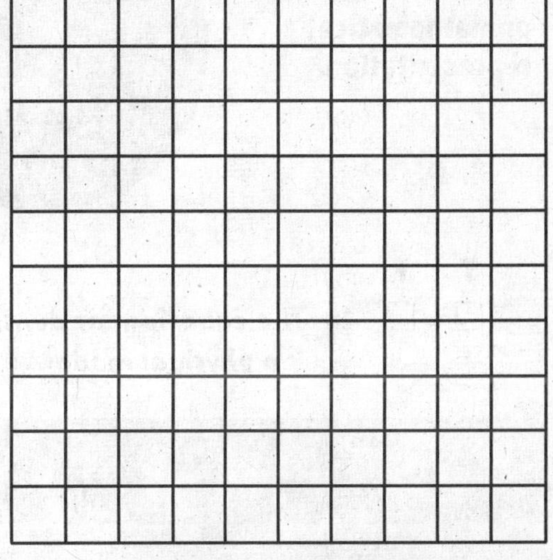

What are some benefits and limitations of models?

Just as models can represent things that are too small or too large to see, models benefit scientists in other ways. They allow scientists to change variables without affecting or harming the subject that they are studying. For example, scientists use crash-test dummies to study the effects of car accidents on people.

All models are limited because they are simplified versions of the systems that they try to explain. Simplification makes a model easy to understand and use. However, information is left out when a model is made.

Additionally, all models can change. Models can change if a scientist finds new data or thinks about concepts in a new way. Sometimes, new technology challenges existing models. Or, technology may help create new models that allow us to understand the world differently.

Think Outside the Book **Inquiry**

17 Apply With a classmate, discuss the benefits and limitations of globes and maps as physical models.

Visual Summary

To complete this summary, check the box that indicates true or false. Then, use the key below to check your answers. You can use this page to review the main concepts of the lesson.

Representing Data

A scientific model can be a visual or mathematical representation.

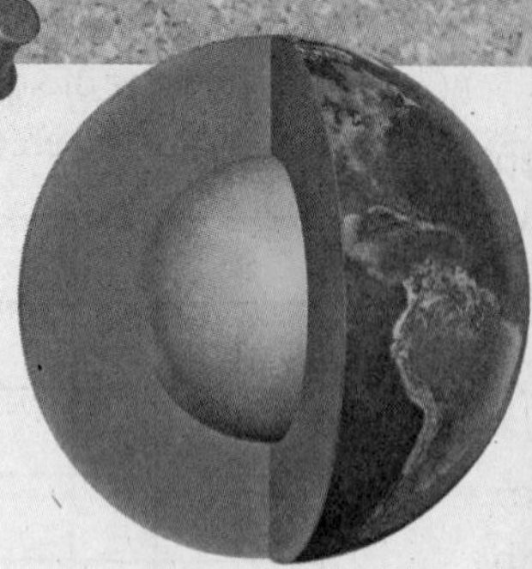

T F

☐ ☐ **18** The equation for density is a physical model.

A table can be used to record and organize data as it is being collected.

Density of Earth's Layers	
Layer	Density (g/cm^3)
crust	2.7–3.3
mantle	3.3–5.7
core	9.9–13.1

T F

☐ ☐ **19** Units of measurement should be placed with the column or row headings in tables.

A graph is a visual display of data that shows relationships between the data.

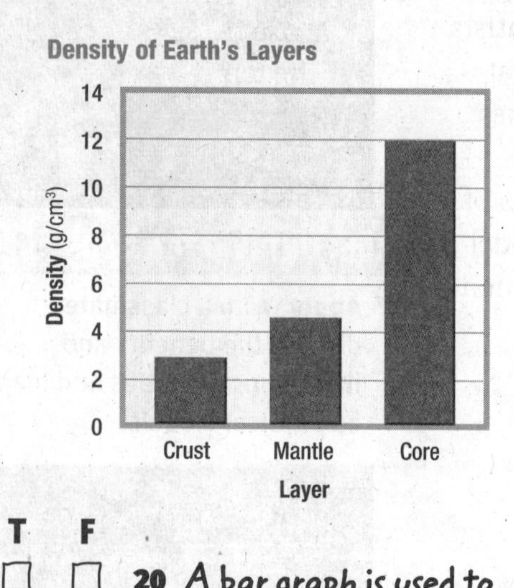

T F

☐ ☐ **20** A bar graph is used to show continuous data.

Answers: 18 F; 19 T; 20 F

21 Synthesize Provide an example of something in the natural world that could be depicted in each of the following ways: a table, a graph, and a model. (Use examples not given in this lesson.)

Lesson Review

Vocabulary

Fill in the blank with the term that best completes the following sentences.

1 A(n) ______________________ can be a visual or mathematical representation of an object or a process.

2 After data are collected, they are often arranged in a(n) ______________________.

3 Data can be arranged in visual displays called ______________________ to make identifying trends easier.

Key Concepts

4 Differentiate How is a physical model different from a mathematical model?

5 Identify A data table shows the height of a person on his birthday each year for ten years. What is the dependent variable?

6 Judge Which kind of graph would be best for depicting data collected on the weight of a baby every month for six months?

7 Apply What kind of model would you use to represent the human heart?

Critical Thinking

Use this graph to answer the following questions.

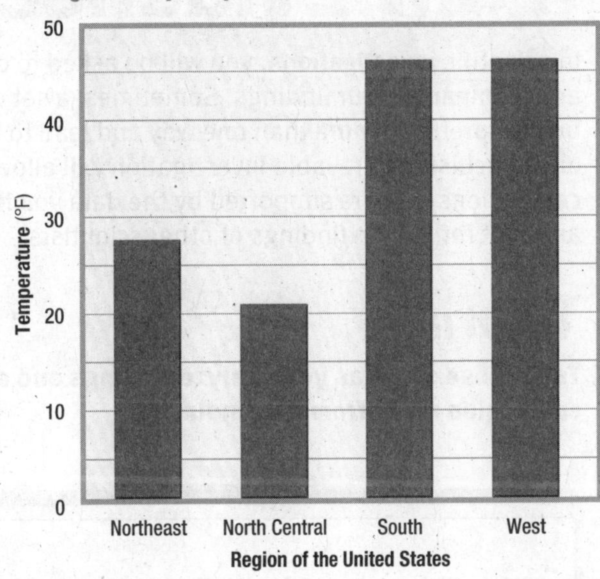

8 Identify Which region of the country has the coldest January temperatures?

9 Estimate How can you use the graph to determine the range of the temperature data? Write the range to the nearest degree.

10 Apply Give an example of a physical model and explain one limitation of the model. Then give an example of a mathematical model and explain one limitation.

Think Science

Making Conclusions from Evidence

In scientific investigations, you will be asked to collect data and summarize your findings. Sometimes, a set of data can be interpreted in more than one way and lead to more than one conclusion. A reliable investigation will allow you to make conclusions that are supported by the data you have collected, and that reflect the findings of other scientists.

Sunshine State Standards

SC.6.N.1.1 Define a problem from the sixth grade curriculum, use appropriate reference materials to support scientific understanding, plan and carry out scientific investigation of various types, such as systematic observations or experiments, identify variables, collect and organize data, interpret data in charts, tables, and graphics, analyze information, make predictions, and defend conclusions.

LA.6.4.2.2 The student will record information (e.g., observations, notes, lists, charts, legends) related to a topic, including visual aids to organize and record information and include a list of sources used.

Tutorial

Take these steps as you analyze findings and evaluate a conclusion made from the findings.

Flu Prevention Breakthrough

A medical study has shown that a new drug, Compound Z, protected children from the flu. The results of the study that was conducted last year showed that only 5% of students who were taking Compound Z were affected by the flu. During the same period of time, 20% of the general population was affected by the flu.

Researchers do not know exactly how Compound Z protects children from the flu.

1 What conclusion is made by the study? Identify the conclusion or interpretation of the data that is being made in the study.

2 What evidence or data is given and does the data support the conclusion? Identify all the observations and findings that are presented to support the conclusion. Decide whether the findings support the conclusion. Look for information and data in other studies that replicate the experiments and verify the conclusion.

3 Should other data be considered before accepting the conclusion as true? There may be more than one way to interpret findings of scientific work, and important questions left unanswered. When this happens, plan to make observations, look for more information, or do further experiments that could eliminate one explanation as a possibility.

Other data should be considered before the conclusion above can be supported. For example, data should be gathered to determine the percentage of children who were not taking Compound Z and got the flu. And, within the 20% of the general population who got the flu, what percentage were children?

You Try It!

Climate change is one of the most debated issues in modern science.

In the past 100 years, Earth's average global temperature has risen more than 0.74 °C. In 2008, the cold La Niña current in the Pacific caused the average global temperature to drop, but the global average was still warmer than any year from 1880 to 1996. The concentration of the greenhouse gas carbon dioxide (CO_2), rose from by about 76 parts per million from 1958 to 2008. Many people interpret this to mean that human activity is causing global climate change. However, evidence from the geologic record shows that Earth's climate has experienced even larger climate changes in the past.

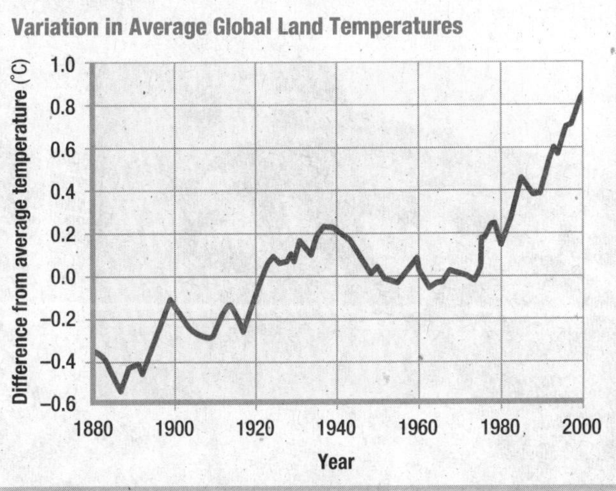

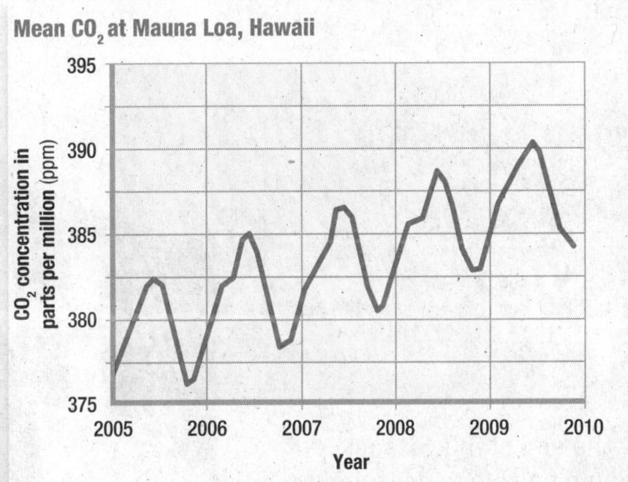

1 Gathering Data The graphs shown above are taken from a study on climate change. Identify trends or patterns that you observe in the graphs.

2 Making a Conclusion Draw a conclusion that is supported by the data you describe. Summarize your conclusion in a single paragraph.

3 Analyzing Data Which conclusions are supported by the data in the graphs? Which conclusions are not supported by the data?

4 Making Predictions What other data do you need to further support your conclusion?

Take It Home

Find an article that makes a conclusion based on a scientific study. Evaluate the conclusion and determine whether the evidence given supports the conclusion. Bring the article to class and be prepared to discuss.

Lesson 5

Science and Society

ESSENTIAL QUESTION

How does science affect our lives?

By the end of this lesson, you should be able to describe the impact that science has had on society and the role of scientists throughout history and today.

Science deepens our understanding of the world and improves the quality of our lives. Science also influences the ways we interact with one another.

Sunshine State Standards

SC.6.N.2.3 Recognize that scientists who make contributions to scientific knowledge come from all kinds of backgrounds and possess varied talents, interests, and goals.

Engage Your Brain

1 Predict Check T or F to show whether you think each statement is true or false.

T	F	
☐	☐	Science has very few career opportunities and does not impact our lives.
☐	☐	Good scientists are creative, logical thinkers and keen observers.
☐	☐	Only scientists are capable of scientific thinking.

2 Identify List the first five things you did this morning after you woke up. Put a checkmark next to any of these things that were made possible by the work of scientists.

Active Reading

3 Derive Many English words have their roots in other languages. Use the Latin word below to make an educated guess about the meaning of the word *scientific*.

Latin word	Meaning
scientia	knowledge

Example sentence

After years of scientific experimentation and observation, the researcher reported a major discovery.

scientific:

Vocabulary

4 Identify As you read, place a question mark next to any words you don't understand. When you finish reading the lesson, go back and review the text that you marked. If the information is still confusing, consult a classmate or a teacher.

A Mighty Impact!

What does science affect?

Active Reading

5 Apply As you read, underline examples of advances in science that have impacted you today.

For centuries, people have been asking questions and seeking answers. Even before there were people known as scientists, people engaged in scientific exploration. Science has had a great impact on all of us. Most likely, you can think of ways science affects your life already. You may be surprised to discover how large the influence of science really is.

The Way We Think

How do you see yourself? People used to think that Earth was the center of the universe. They thought the objects in the sky moved around them. They thought the sky existed only for them to look at. These beliefs made people feel very special.

We now know Earth is just one planet in one solar system. Earth orbits the sun and rotates once each day. When people realized this, they had to rethink their place in the universe. They had to rethink just how special they believed themselves to be. Scientific findings affect how we see ourselves.

Space science, 100 BCE

Space science, Today

Visualize It!

6 Explain Why might learning of the vastness of outer space affect how people see themselves?

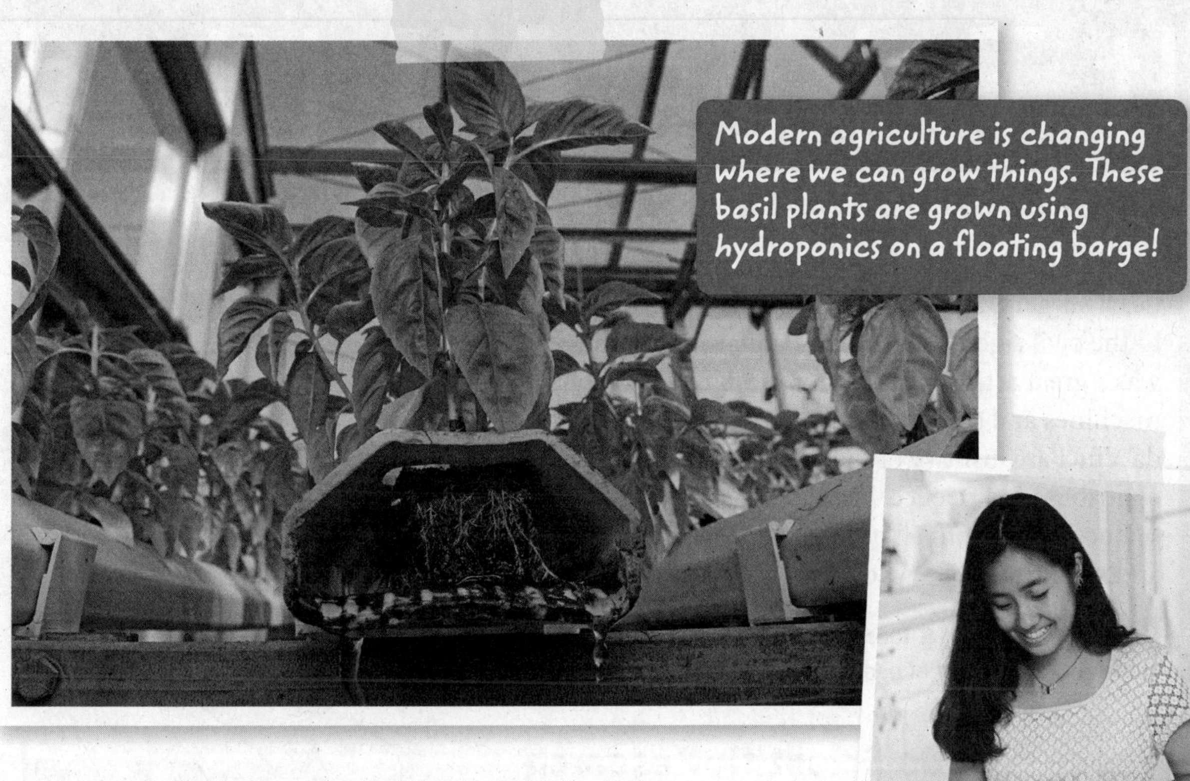

Modern agriculture is changing where we can grow things. These basil plants are grown using hydroponics on a floating barge!

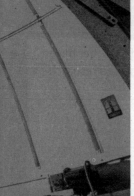

The Way We Live Our Lives

Our daily activities have been affected by advances in science, too. In industrialized countries, many people enjoy clean water and sanitary living conditions. Scientists frequently find new ways for us to conserve and protect resources. Medicines have eliminated many health concerns. Cars, trains, and airplanes take us where we want to go. Weather forecasts tell us what to expect, and then we can dress appropriately. Satellites and cables allow us to communicate with others from all over the world. Most of these things were not even imaginable just 100 years ago.

Society became more complex with the beginning of farming. People joined together to grow crops for the benefit of all. World population has been able to grow so large today because of advances in farming. We can now grow crops in soil once thought to be infertile. Thanks to science, we can even grow plants with no soil at all! Hydroponics (HY•druh•pahn•iks), or growing plants without soil, may one day allow us to live in outer space.

7 Compare When your grandparents were growing up, they ate mostly foods grown or produced near them. Describe how the food you eat is different from the food your grandparents ate as a result of science's impact on agriculture and transportation.

It Takes **All** Kinds

Who contributes to science?

Myra Logan was the first female to perform open-heart surgery. She also played piano and contributed to the civil rights movement. Leonardo da Vinci was a great artist. He also drew designs for flying machines and studied human anatomy. Logan and da Vinci are just two of the many people who have contributed to science. People who contribute to science come from all backgrounds, fields of interest, and skill groups. So who contributes to science?

Active Reading **8 Identify** As you read, underline some characteristics of people who do scientific research.

Those Who Do Scientific Research

Scientists are curious, creative, and enjoy solving problems. Scientists do research to answer questions and to investigate and challenge prevailing ideas. Some scientists work in life science, like immunologist Cesar Milstein, who researches viruses like AIDS. Physicist Chien Shiung Wu, a physical scientist, spent time in laboratories with radioactive elements. Mary Leakey, an archaeologist and Earth scientist, unearthed ape fossils in the field.

Leonardo da Vinci and his design for a flying machine

Klaus Radermacher uses robots and computers to make custom prosthetics. Prosthetics are artificial body parts that can replace missing, damaged, or diseased parts.

Visualize It!

9 Predict What problem might Radermacher have been trying to solve when he began his research?

People in Many Fields

The number of men and women who get paid to do scientific research is not very high. However, the opportunities open to those who are willing to learn and think like a scientist in other fields are almost limitless.

Many occupations use science. Medical and dental technicians help doctors and dentists keep people in good health. Architects use the laws of physics to design stable homes and offices. People who dye and style hair use chemistry when mixing hair dye and relaxing solutions. In the growing field of forensics, police officers use science to help them solve crimes. Auto engineers use physics to design aerodynamic cars.

Forensic technician

Auto engineers design vehicles.

10 Infer What might motivate someone to study forensics?

11 Describe Fill in the second column with a description of how a person might use science in each of the careers. Fill in the last row of the table with a career you might like to have.

Career	Science applications
Firefighter	
Pharmacist	
Chef	

Anyone Who Asks Scientific Questions and Seeks Answers

Active Reading

12 Identify As you read, underline questions that science can help you answer.

An important point to remember is that anyone can think and act like a scientist and do science. Have you wondered why certain plants always flower at about the same time of year? Have you wondered what the center of Earth is like? Have you wondered why sugar dissolves faster in hot liquids than in cold ones? If you have asked questions and thought about finding the answers, you have acted like a scientist.

Do not be embarrassed to ask impossible questions. A lot of what we take for granted today was once thought impossible. You may even discover that you are asking the same questions many scientists still ask.

13 Relate Questions about the world can pop into your mind at any time. Write down something you've thought about recently as you've gone about your usual activities. Then write how you might investigate it.

Is time travel possible?

Can a computer be built that can sense people's feelings?

Can plants be used to "clean up" the increased levels of carbon dioxide in our atmosphere?

Think Outside the Book

14 State What is your daring dream? Write a scientific question you would like to answer, regardless of how impossible it might seem to do.

Why It Matters

Let the Games Begin

Robotics tournaments, model car races, and science fairs offer opportunities for you to explore and share your interest in science with others. You may even win a prize doing it!

Robot Challenge

This robot was built and operated by students at a San Diego robotics competition. Robots aren't just for competitions, though. Robots can be built for search and rescue missions, manufacturing, and other roles.

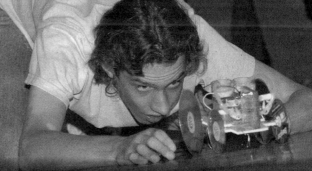

Fast and Friendly

This student is racing a model car he built. The car is powered by hydrogen fuel cells. Hydrogen fuel cells may be an environmentally friendly power source for cars of the future!

Extend

Inquiry

15 Select Which would you be most interested in entering: a science fair, a robotics competition, or a model car race? Why?

16 Identify Use the Internet to find a science competition in your area. Consider visiting it!

17 Plan Make a poster, draw a model, or write a paragraph explaining an idea you have for a science competition.

Visual Summary

To complete this summary, check the box that indicates true or false. Then use the key below to check your answers. You can use this page to review the main concepts of the lesson.

Science and Society

Impact of Science

The work of scientists has changed the way we live and think about the world.

	T	F	
18	☐	☐	As science has advanced, technology has advanced.
19	☐	☐	Agriculture and medicine are affected by science.

Who Does Science

Scientists are curious about the world and enjoy exploring it. They may work in laboratories, in the field, or in other locations.

	T	F	
20	☐	☐	Only people who work in science use scientific thinking skills.
21	☐	☐	People from all backgrounds, interests, and cultures can contribute to science.

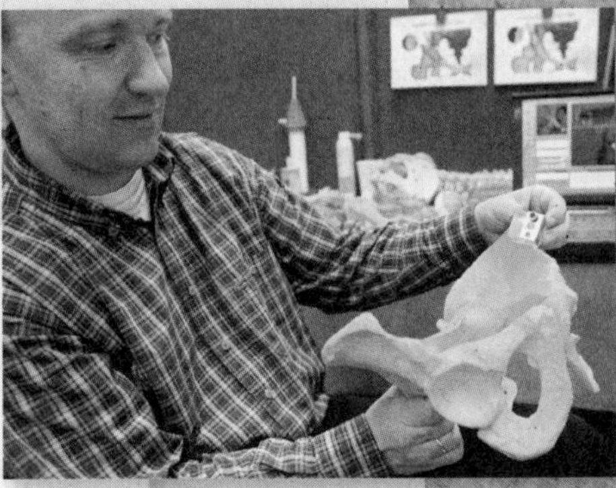

Answers: 18. T; 19. T; 20. F; 21. T

22 **Predict** Identify two changes in your world that might occur if funding for scientific research were cut drastically.

Lesson Review

Vocabulary

Fill in the blanks with the term or phrase that best completes the following sentences.

1 A(n) __________ may work in a lab or in the field and conducts research to discover new things.

2 The impact of science on __________ includes improvements in medicine, new technology, and more diverse food sources.

Key Concepts

3 Apply Identify two areas of science or technology that make your life easier, safer, or otherwise better than your grandparents' lives were.

4 List Name three characteristics of scientists that are important to their work but are also found in nonscientists.

Critical Thinking

5 Devise Imagine that one tree outside your school looks unhealthy, although all the other trees seem healthy and strong. Describe how you could apply scientific thinking to the situation.

Use this table to answer the following questions.

Scientists and Their Contributions

When	Who	What
1660s	Robert Hooke	Identified and coined the word *cells* using early microscopes
Late 1700s	Antoine Lavoisier	Identified oxygen and oxygen's role in respiration and combustion
Early 1900s	Marie Curie	Experimented with radioactivity and identified new chemical elements
Early 1980s	Luis Alvarez	Used geological evidence to show that a meteor struck Earth and proposed that this led to the extinction of dinosaurs

6 Categorize The main branches of science are life science, physical science, and Earth and space science. Identify a branch of science that was affected by each of these scientists.

7 Justify Why do you think the work of scientists cannot be pinned down to a single year?

8 Debate Do you think the contributions of these scientists are still valuable, even though some were made hundreds of years ago? Explain your answer.

My Notes

Unit 1 Summary

is an important step in

Representing Data → Scientific Investigations

What Is Science?

impacts the relationship between

Scientific Knowledge → Science and Society

1 **Interpret** The Graphic Organizer above shows that scientific knowledge can impact society. Explain why this is so.

2 **Distinguish** Explain the difference between scientific investigations and scientific knowledge.

3 **Judge** "Representing data is not an important part of scientific investigations." Describe why this statement is incorrect.

4 **Support** Explain why there is not one "scientific method."

Benchmark Review

Name ______________________

Multiple Choice

Identify the choice that best completes the statement or answers the question.

1 Scientists do many types of work. Their work often includes making field observations, conducting surveys, creating models, and carrying out experiments. Which description characterizes an experiment?

A. observation of plants or animals in their natural environment

B. physical or mathematical representation of an object or process

C. an organized procedure to study something under controlled conditions

D. collection of data from the unregulated world for comparative purposes

2 Raul wants to investigate how the angle of a ramp affects the speed of an object rolling down the ramp. He can conduct his investigation in a number of different ways. Which investigation should he perform?

F. observe different bicyclists riding down hills of varying steepness

G. record the time it takes one bicyclist to ride down hills of varying steepness

H. perform an experiment in a lab in which the angle of the ramp is controlled and the speed of a rolling cart is measured

I. observe video of various objects rolling down hills and estimate the angle of the hill and the speed of the object

3 Lida fills two balloons with the same amount of air. Balloon 1 remains at room temperature. Lida places balloon 2 in a freezer. The following diagram shows that the volume of the balloon in the freezer shrinks.

Balloon 1

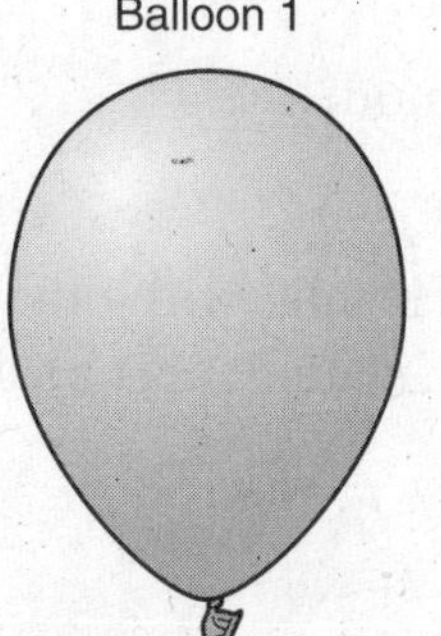

Balloon 2

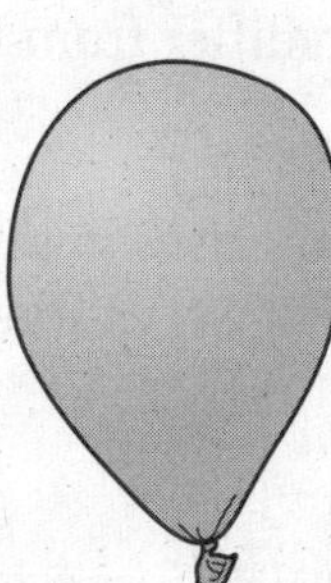

Which statement is a law that describes the results of Lida's balloon experiment?

A. Decreasing the amount of a gas decreases its temperature.

B. The volume of a gas increases when the temperature decreases.

C. The volume of a gas decreases when the temperature decreases.

D. Decreasing temperature decreases the volume of a gas because the molecules slow down.

Benchmark Review

4 Ryan made a list of activities that are scientific and activities that are not scientific. Which activity should Ryan classify as **not** scientific?

F. sorting rocks by color and size

G. measuring the height of a plant every day

H. climbing to the top of a very tall mountain

I. making notes about how many hours the sun shines each day

5 The diagram shows Niels Bohr's theory about how electrons are arranged in atoms. He thought electrons traveled on specific paths around a nucleus. The current theory is that electrons exist in certain cloudlike regions around a nucleus.

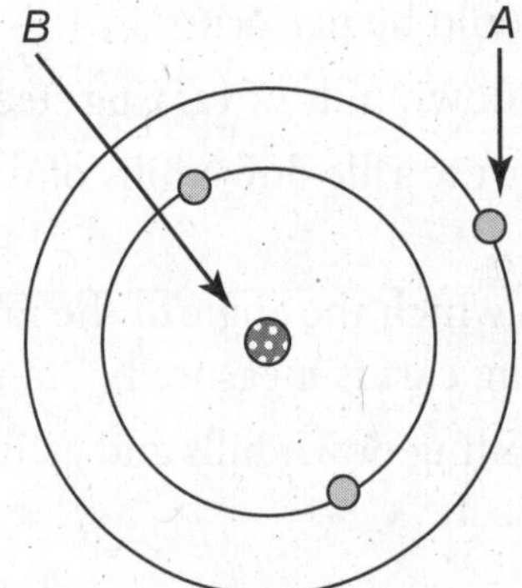

How would a model of the current theory **differ** from Bohr's model?

A. It would be the same as Bohr's model.

B. Object A would differ from Bohr's model.

C. Object B would differ from Bohr's model.

D. Both objects A and B would differ from Bohr's model.

6 Bryce observes that the sun always rises in the east. He talks with others and finds that everyone has the same observation. Which statement is a scientific law?

F. The sun rises in the east.

G. Why does the sun rise in the east?

H. The sun appears in the east because of Earth's rotation pattern.

I. If the sun appears in the east, then I am in the Western Hemisphere.

Name ____________________

7 Scientists use different types of tools to investigate how and why things happen. Here are some examples of these tools:

- a diagram of a food chain in the Everglades
- a plastic replica of the human digestive system
- a mathematical equation for finding the speed of an object

Which word describes **all** of these examples?

A. experiment
B. hypothesis
C. model
D. observation

8 Three different lab groups perform experiments to determine the density of the samples of iron. They have all rounded the density to the nearest whole number.

Group	Mass of iron (g)	Volume of iron (cm^3)	Density of iron (g/cm^3)
1	32	4	8
2	48	6	8
3	?	5	8

What is the mass of iron for group 3?

F. 5 g
G. 8 g
H. 40 g
I. 64 g

9 Lee wants to make sure she understands the components of a good scientific investigation. She knows that it should be controlled and have a large sample size. Also, she thinks that the results should be communicated to other scientists. Which is another component that is necessary for a good investigation?

A. It must be conducted in a big lab.
B. It must be run by a university scientist.
C. It must be done with expensive equipment.
D. It must be able to be replicated by other scientists.

Benchmark Review

10 A friend who knows a lot about science reads in a book that a piece of black paper will get warmer in sunlight than a piece of white paper. Which of these is a scientific reaction to this information?

F. Accept the statement as true because your friend knows about science.

G. Design an experiment to show whether the statement is correct or incorrect.

H. Believe the statement because it was written in a book, so you can trust it to be true.

I. Tell your friend that the statement makes no sense because color does not affect temperature.

11 University of Florida scientists developed a new type of wound dressing that keeps bacteria out of the wound. What is a conclusion that you can make from this information?

A. Scientific discoveries always lead to new technologies.

B. Scientists often respond to the needs in our society.

C. Scientific advances are always made in the field of medicine.

D. Scientists may make discoveries that have no impact on society.

12 Joe tells Mai his theory about why sea turtles nest on the beach instead of in the ocean. He says, "The turtle eggs would sink to the bottom of the ocean, and the baby turtles would drown." Joe says his uncle, a fisherman, told Joe this information. Mai tells Joe that his theory is not scientific. Why does Joe's idea not meet the requirements to be a scientific theory?

F. Joe's idea is already a scientific law.

G. Joe's idea is not supported by scientific evidence.

H. Joe's idea is a good guess that can be tested by experiments.

I. Joe and his uncle are not scientists.

UNIT 2

Weathering, Erosion, Deposition, and Landforms

Most of Florida's underground caves are also under water, which makes them ideal for diving.

What do you think?

Florida has many caves underground. If a cave is close to Earth's surface and its roof is weak, the roof may fall in, forming a sinkhole. How might these caves have formed?

Sinkholes often form suddenly.

Unit 2

Weathering, Erosion, Deposition, and Landforms

CITIZEN SCIENCE

Save a Beach

Like many other features on land, beaches can also change over time. But what could be powerful enough to wash away a beach? Waves and currents.

1 Define the Problem

People love to visit the beach. Many businesses along the beach survive because of the tourists that visit the area. But in many places, the beach is being washed away by ocean waves and currents.

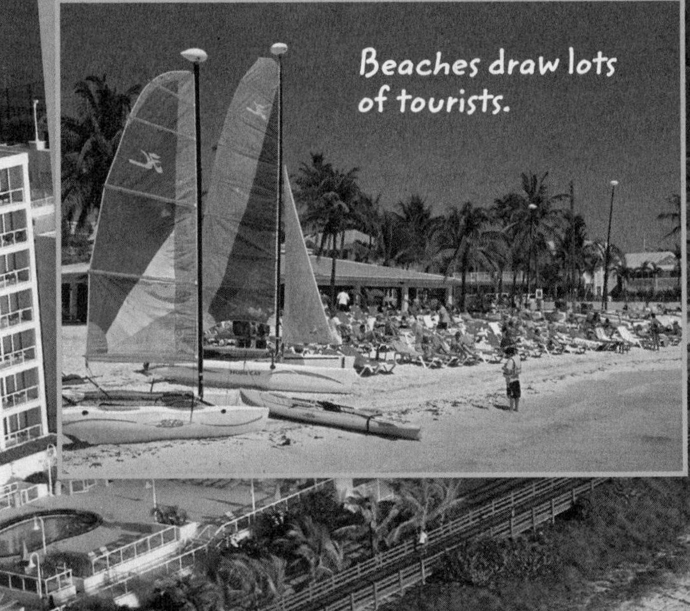

Beaches draw lots of tourists.

(2) Think About It

When waves from the ocean hit the beach at an angle, the waves will often pull some of the sand back into the ocean with them. These sands may then be carried away by the current. In this way, a beach can be washed away. What could you do to prevent a sandy beach from washing away? Looking at the photo below, design a way to prevent the beach from washing away. Then conduct an experiment to test your design.

Check off the questions below as you use them to design your experiment.

- ☐ How will you create waves?
- ☐ At what angle should the waves hit the beach?
- ☐ Will people still be able to use the beach if your method were used?

Waves carry the sands back into the ocean with them.

(3) Make a Plan

A Make a list of the materials you will need for your experiment in the space below.

____

____

____

B Draw a sketch of the set up in the space below.

C Conduct your experiment. Briefly state your findings.

____

____

____

Take It Home

Find an area that may be eroding in your neighborhood, such as the banks of a pond or road. Study the area. Then, prepare a short presentation for your class on how to prevent erosion in this area.

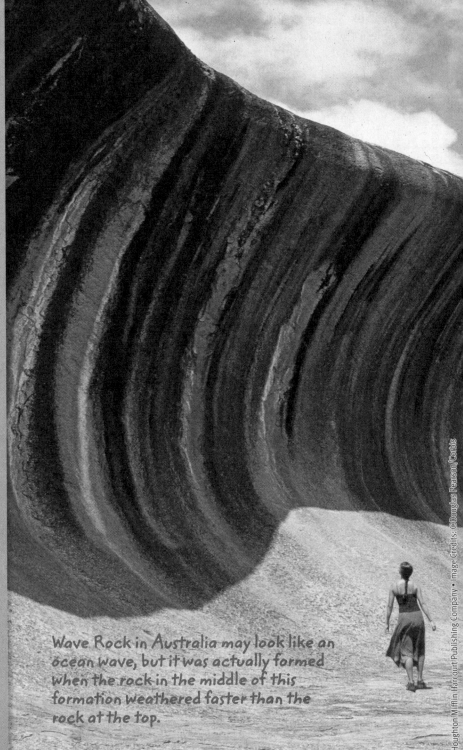

Lesson 1

Weathering

ESSENTIAL QUESTION

How does weathering change Earth's surface?

By the end of this lesson, you should be able to analyze the effects of physical and chemical weathering on Earth's surface, including examples of each kind of weathering.

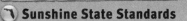

Sunshine State Standards

SC.6.E.6.1 Describe and give examples of ways in which Earth's surface is built up and torn down by physical and chemical weathering, erosion, and deposition.

LA.6.2.2.3 The student will organize information to show understanding (e.g., representing main ideas within text through charting, mapping, paraphrasing, summarizing, or comparing/contrasting).

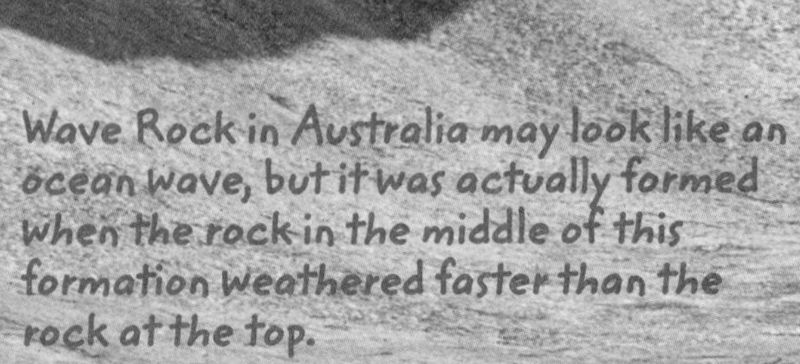

Wave Rock in Australia may look like an ocean wave, but it was actually formed when the rock in the middle of this formation weathered faster than the rock at the top.

Engage Your Brain

1 Predict Check T or F to show whether you think each statement is true or false.

T	F	
☐	☐	Rocks can change shape and composition over time.
☐	☐	Rocks cannot be weathered by wind and chemicals in the air.
☐	☐	A rusty car is an example of weathering.
☐	☐	Plants and animals can cause weathering of rocks.

2 Describe Your class has taken a field trip to a local stream. You notice that the rocks in the water are rounded and smooth. Write a brief description of how you think the rocks changed over time.

Active Reading

3 Synthesize You can often find clues to the meaning of a word by examining the use of that word in a sentence. Read the following sentences and write your own definition for the word *abrasion*.

Example sentences

Bobby fell on the sidewalk and scraped his knee. The abrasion on his knee was painful because of the loss of several layers of skin.

abrasion:

Vocabulary Terms

- **weathering**
- **physical weathering**
- **abrasion**
- **chemical weathering**
- **oxidation**
- **acid precipitation**

4 Apply As you learn the definition of each vocabulary term in this lesson, create your own definition or sketch to help you remember the meaning of the term.

BreakIt Down

What is weathering?

Did you know that sand on a beach may have once been a part of a large boulder? Over millions of years, a boulder can break down into many smaller pieces. The breakdown of rock material by physical and chemical processes is called **weathering**. Two kinds of weathering are *physical weathering* and *chemical weathering.*

What causes physical weathering?

Active Reading

5 Identify As you read, place the names of some common agents of physical weathering in the graphic organizer below.

Rocks can get smaller and smaller without a change in the composition of the rock. This is an example of a physical change. The process by which rock is broken down into smaller pieces by physical changes is **physical weathering**. Temperature changes, pressure changes, plant and animal actions, water, wind, and gravity are all agents of physical weathering.

As materials break apart, they can become even more exposed to physical changes. For instance, a large boulder can be broken apart by ice and water over time. Eventually, the boulder can split in two. Now there are two rocks exposed to the agents of physical weathering. In other words, the amount of surface area exposed to the agents of physical weathering increases. The large boulder can become thousands of tiny rocks over time as each new rock increases the amount of surface area able to be weathered.

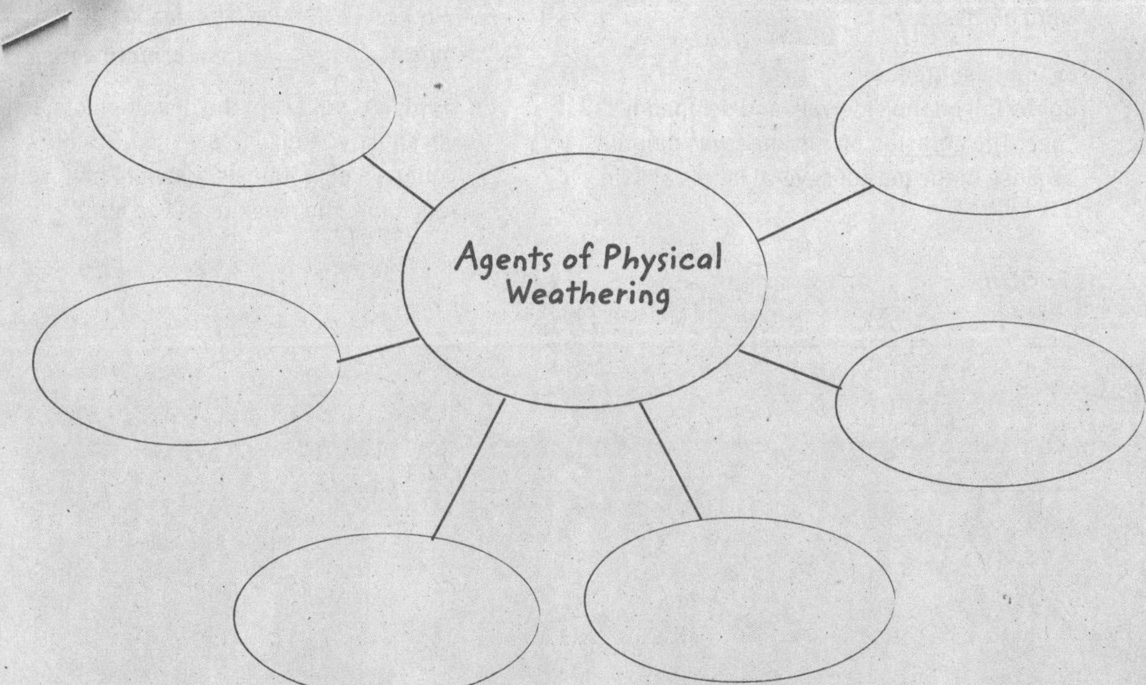

Visualize It!

6 Describe Write a caption for each of the images to describe the process of ice wedging

Ice Wedging

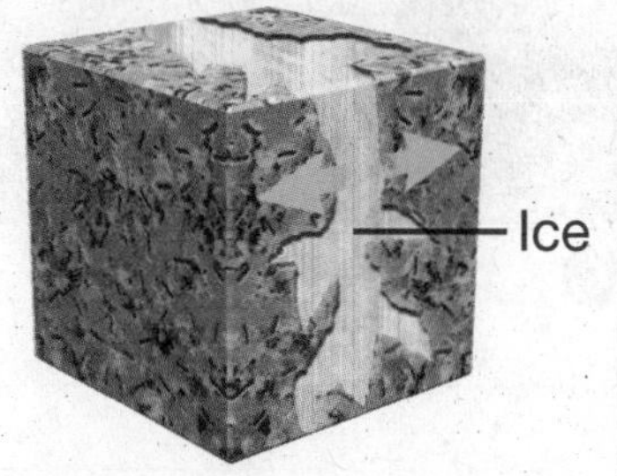

Temperature Change

Changes in temperatures can cause a rock to break apart. A rise in temperature will cause a rock to expand. A decrease in temperature will cause a rock to contract. Repeated temperature changes can weaken the structure of a rock, causing the rock to crumble. Even changes in temperature between day and night can cause rocks to expand and contract. In desert regions differences in day and night temperatures can be significant. Rocks can weaken and crumble from the stress caused by these temperature changes.

Ice wedging, sometimes known as *frost wedging*, can also cause rocks to physically break apart, as shown in the image below. Ice wedging causes cracks in rocks to expand as water seeps in and freezes. When water collects in cracks in rock and the temperature drops, the water may freeze. Water expands as it freezes to become ice. As the ice expands, the crack will widen. As more water enters the crack, it can expand to an even larger size. Eventually, a small crack in a rock can cause even the largest of rocks to split apart.

7 Hypothesize Where on Earth would physical weathering from temperature changes be most common? Least common? Explain.

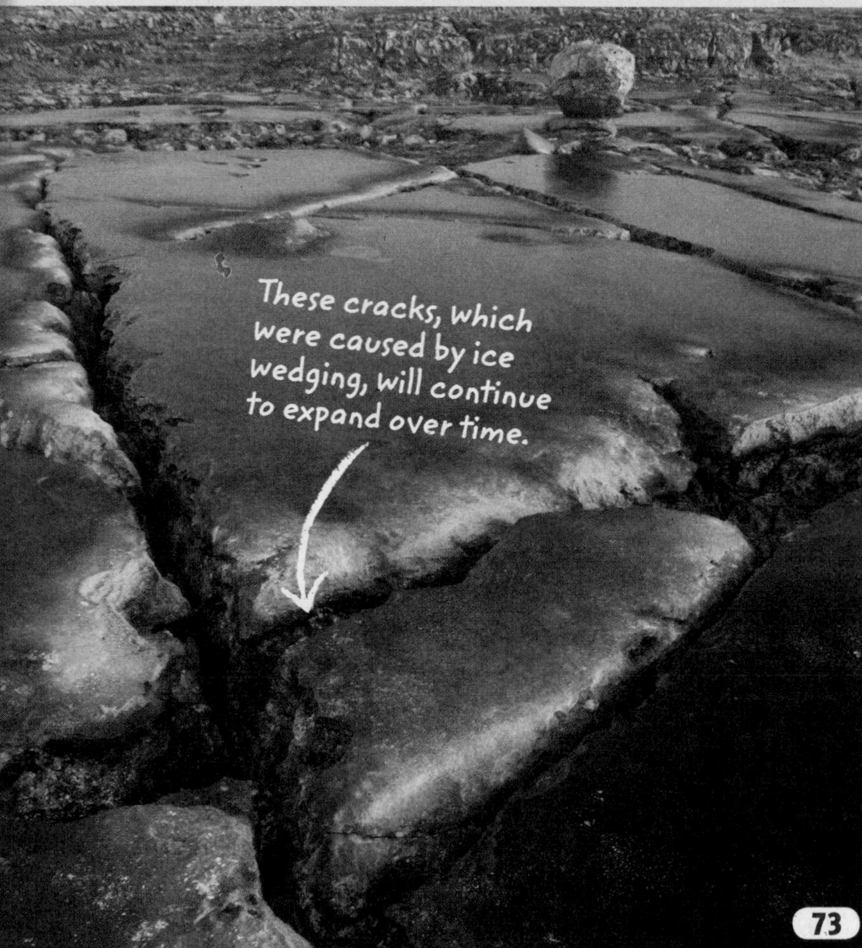

These cracks, which were caused by ice wedging, will continue to expand over time.

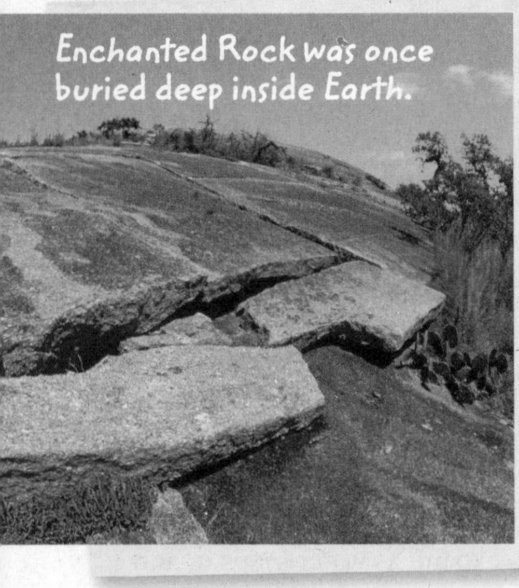
Enchanted Rock was once buried deep inside Earth.

Pressure Change

Physical weathering can be caused by pressure changes. Rocks formed under pressure deep within Earth can become exposed at the surface. As overlying materials are removed above the rock, the pressure decreases. As a result, the rock expands, causing the outermost layers of rock to separate from the underlying layers, as shown to the left. *Exfoliation* (ex•foh•lee•AY•shun) is the process by which the outer layers of rock slowly peel away due to pressure changes. Enchanted Rock in Texas is a 130 m–high dome of granite that is slowly losing the outermost layers of rock due to exfoliation and other processes.

Animal Action

Animals can cause physical weathering. Many animals dig burrows into the ground, allowing more rock to be exposed. Common burrowing animals include ground squirrels, prairie dogs, ants, and earthworms. These animals move soils and allow new rocks, soils, and other materials to be exposed at the surface, as shown below. Materials can undergo weathering below the surface, but are more likely to be weathered once exposed at the surface.

Prairie dog

Visualize It!

8 Describe Write a caption for each animal describing how it might cause physical weathering.

A ________________

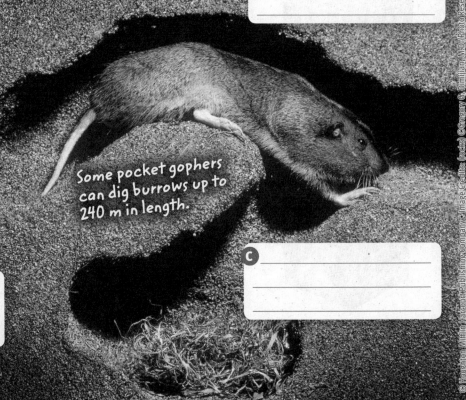

Earthworm

B ________________

Some pocket gophers can dig burrows up to 240 m in length.

C ________________

Wind, Water, and Gravity

Rock can be broken down by the action of other rocks over time. **Abrasion** (uh•BRAY•zhuhn) is the breaking down and wearing away of rock material by the mechanical action of other rock. Three agents of physical weathering that can cause abrasion are moving water, wind, and gravity. Also, rocks suspended in the ice of a glacier can cause abrasion of other rocks on Earth's surface.

In moving water, rock can become rounded and smooth. Abrasion occurs as rocks are tumbled in water, hitting other rocks. Wind abrasion occurs when wind lifts and carries small particles in the air. The small particles can blast away at surfaces and slowly wear them away. During a landslide, large rocks can fall from higher up a slope and break more rocks below, causing abrasion.

9 Identify As you read, underline the agents of weathering that cause abrasion.

Rocks are tumbled in water, causing abrasion.

Wind-blown sand can blast small particles away.

Rocks can be broken down in a landslide.

Plant Growth

You have probably noticed that just one crack in a sidewalk can be the opening for a tiny bit of grass to grow. Over time, a neglected sidewalk can become crumbly from a combination of several agents of physical weathering, including plant growth. Why?

Roots of plants do not start out large. Roots start as tiny strands of plant matter that can grow inside small cracks in rocks. As the plant gets bigger, so do the roots. The larger a root grows, the more pressure it puts on rock. More pressure causes the rock to expand, as seen to the right. Eventually, the rock can break apart.

Think Outside the Book Inquiry

10 Summarize Imagine you are a rock. Write a short biography of your life as a rock, describing the changes you have gone through over time.

This tree started as a tiny seedling and eventually grew to split the rock in half.

Reaction

What causes chemical weathering?

Chemical weathering changes both the composition and appearance of rocks. **Chemical weathering** is the breakdown of rocks by chemical reactions. Agents of chemical weathering include oxygen in the air and acids.

Reactions with Oxygen

Oxygen in the air or in water can cause chemical weathering. Oxygen reacts with the compounds that make up rock, causing chemical reactions. The process by which other chemicals combine with oxygen is called **oxidation** (ahk•si•DAY•shun).

Rock surfaces sometimes change color. A color change can mean that a chemical reaction has taken place. Rocks containing iron can easily undergo chemical weathering. Iron in rocks and soils combines quickly with oxygen that is dissolved in water. The result is a rock that turns reddish orange. This is rust! The red color of much of the soil in the southeastern United States and of rock formations in the southwestern United States is due to the presence of rust, as seen in the image below.

Active Reading

11 Identify As you read, underline examples of chemical weathering.

Reactions with Acid Precipitation

Acids break down most minerals faster than water alone. Increased amounts of acid from various sources can cause chemical weathering of rock. Acids in the atmosphere are created when chemicals combine with water in the air. Rain is normally slightly acidic. When fossil fuels are burned, other chemicals combine with water in the atmosphere to produce even stronger acids. When these stronger acids fall to Earth, they are called **acid precipitation** (AS•id prih•sip•ih•TAY•shun). Acid precipitation is recognized as a problem all around the world and causes rocks to break down and change composition.

Active Reading **12 Describe** How does acid precipitation cause rocks to weather faster?

____

____

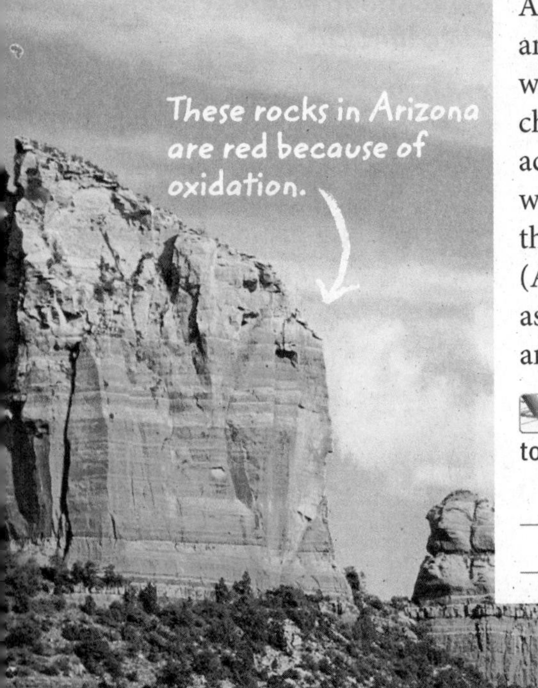

These rocks in Arizona are red because of oxidation.

Reactions with Acids in Groundwater

Water in the ground, or groundwater, can cause chemical weathering. As groundwater moves through spaces or cracks in rock, acids in the water can cause rocks to dissolve. A small crack in a rock can result in the formation of extensive cave systems that are carved out over time under Earth's surface, as shown to the right. The dissolved rock material is carried in water until it is later deposited. Stalactites (stuh•LAHK•tyt) and stalagmites (stuh•LAHG•myt) are common features in cave systems as dissolved chemicals are deposited by dripping water underground.

The dissolved rock from acidic groundwater can later be deposited in different locations.

Reactions with Acids in Living Things

Acids are produced naturally by certain living organisms. For instance, lichens (LY•kuhns) and mosses often grow on rocks and trees. As they grow on rocks, they produce weak acids that can weather the rock's surface. As the acids move through tiny spaces in the rocks, chemical reactions can occur. The acids will eventually break down the rocks. As the acids seep deeper into the rocks, cracks can form. The rock can eventually break apart when the cracks get too large.

This gear is rusted, which indicates that a chemical reaction has taken place.

Think Outside the Book

13 Apply Think of an item made by humans that could be broken down by the agents of physical and chemical weathering. Describe to your classmates all of the ways the item could change over time.

Visual Summary

To complete this summary, fill in the blanks with the correct word or phrase. Then use the answer key to check your answers. You can use this page to review the main concepts of the lesson.

Weathering

Physical weathering breaks rock into smaller pieces by physical means.

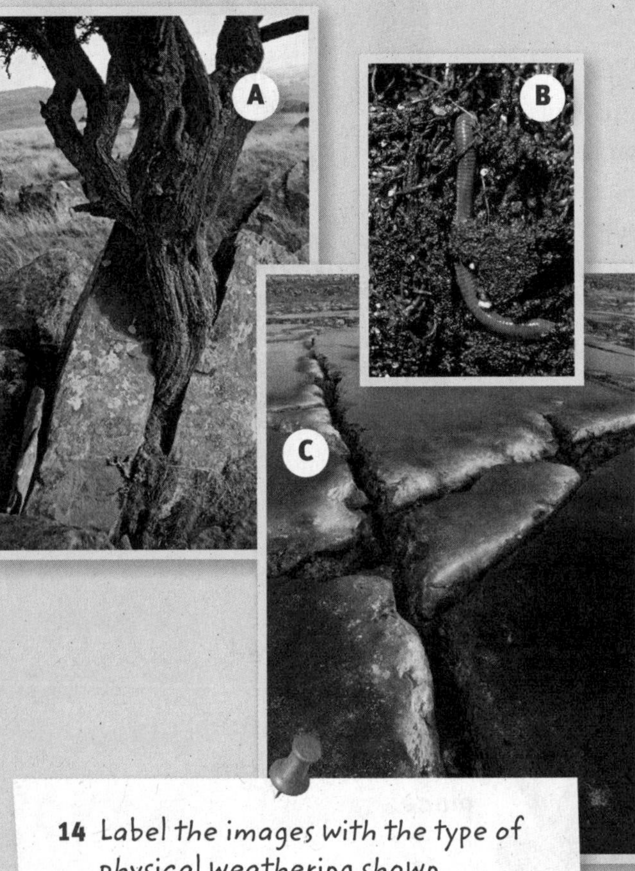

14 Label the images with the type of physical weathering shown.

A ______________________

B ______________________

C ______________________

Chemical weathering breaks down rock by chemical reactions.

15 Label the images with the type of chemical weathering shown.

A ______________________

B ______________________

Answers: 14. A, plant growth; B, animal action; C, ice wedging; 15. A, oxidation; B, reactions with acids

16 Relate Why are some rocks more easily weathered than other rocks?

Lesson Review

Vocabulary

Fill in the blank with the term that best completes the following sentences.

1 Acid precipitation is an agent of _______________ weathering.

2 The gradual wearing away or breaking down of rocks by abrasion is a type of _______________ weathering.

3 The process of _______________ causes rocks to change composition when reacting with oxygen.

4 The mechanical breakdown of rocks by the action of other rocks and sand particles is called _______________

Key Concepts

5 Compare What are some similarities and differences between physical and chemical weathering?

6 List Provide examples of physical weathering and chemical weathering in the chart below.

Physical Weathering	Chemical Weathering

7 Compare What are some similarities between ice wedging and plant root growth in a rock?

Critical Thinking

Use the graph to answer the following questions.

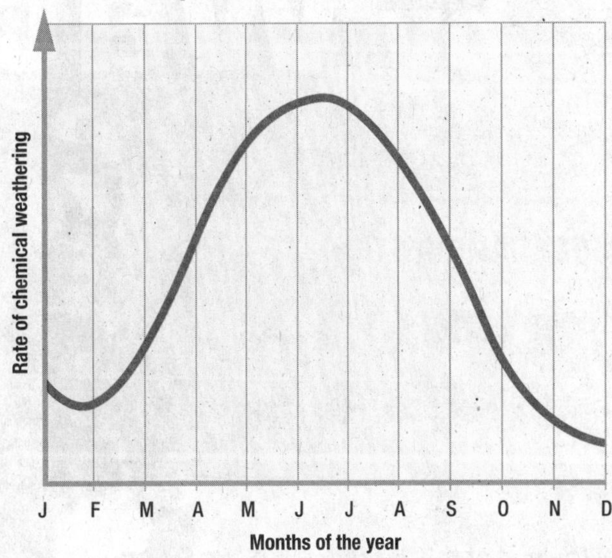

8 Analyze Which two months had the highest rates of chemical weathering?

9 Apply Why do you think those two months had the highest rates of chemical weathering?

10 Infer Coastal regions are often affected by abrasion. What processes would cause increased abrasion along a coastal region? Explain.

Lesson 2

Erosion and Deposition by Water

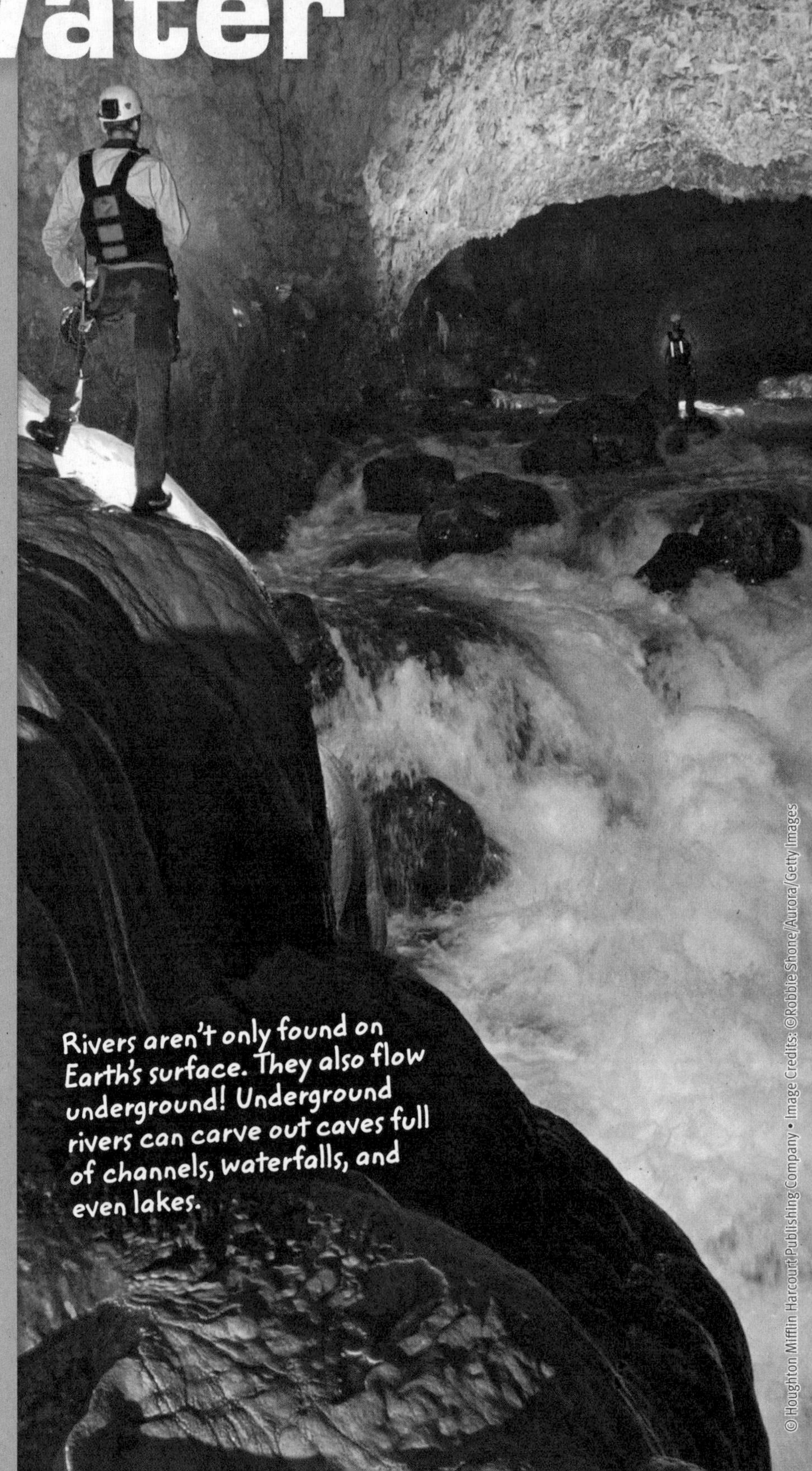

Rivers aren't only found on Earth's surface. They also flow underground! Underground rivers can carve out caves full of channels, waterfalls, and even lakes.

ESSENTIAL QUESTION

How does water change Earth's surface?

By the end of this lesson, you should be able to relate the processes of erosion and deposition by water to the landforms that result from these processes.

Sunshine State Standards

SC.6.E.6.1 Describe and give examples of ways in which Earth's surface is built up and torn down by physical and chemical weathering, erosion, and deposition.

SC.6.E.6.2 Recognize that there are a variety of different landforms on Earth's surface such as coastlines, dunes, rivers, mountains, glaciers, deltas, and lakes and relate these landforms as they apply to Florida.

MA.6.A.3.6 Construct and analyze tables, graphs, and equations to describe linear functions and other simple relations using both common language and algebraic notation.

LA.6.2.2.3 The student will organize information to show understanding (e.g., representing main ideas within text through charting, mapping, paraphrasing, summarizing, or comparing/contrasting).

Engage Your Brain

1 Predict Check T or F to show whether you think each statement is true or false.

T	F	
☐	☐	Water is able to move rocks as big as boulders.
☐	☐	Rivers can help to break down mountains.
☐	☐	Water cannot change rock underneath Earth's surface.
☐	☐	Waves and currents help to form beaches.

2 Explain Write a caption that explains how you think this canyon formed.

Active Reading

3 Synthesize Several of the vocabulary terms in this lesson are compound words, or two separate words combined to form a new word that has a new meaning. Use the meanings of the two separate words to make an educated guess about the meaning of the compound terms shown below.

flood + plain = floodplain

ground + water = groundwater

shore + line = shoreline

sand + bar = sandbar

Vocabulary Terms

- **erosion**
- **deposition**
- **floodplain**
- **delta**
- **alluvial fan**
- **groundwater**
- **shoreline**
- **beach**
- **sandbar**
- **barrier island**

4 Apply As you learn the definition of each vocabulary term in this lesson, create your own definition or sketch to help you remember the meaning of the term.

Go with the Flow

How does flowing water change Earth's surface?

If your job was to carry millions of tons of rock and soil across the United States, how would you do it? You might use a bulldozer or a dump truck, but your job would still take a long time. Did you know that rivers and other bodies of flowing water do this job every day? Flowing water, as well as wind and ice, can move large amounts of material, such as soil and rock. Gravity also has a role to play. Gravity causes water to flow and rocks to fall downhill.

By Erosion

Acting as liquid conveyor belts, rivers and streams erode soil, rock, and sediment. *Sediment* is tiny grains of broken-down rock. **Erosion** is the process by which sediment and other materials are moved from one place to another. Eroded materials in streams may come from the stream's own bed and banks or from materials carried to the stream by rainwater runoff. Over time, erosion causes streams to widen and deepen.

By Deposition

After streams erode rock and soil, they eventually drop, or deposit, their load downstream. **Deposition** is the process by which eroded material is dropped. Deposition occurs when gravity's downward pull on sediment is greater than the push of flowing water or wind. This usually happens when the water or wind slows down. A stream deposits materials along its bed, banks, and mouth, which can form different landforms.

5 Compare Fill in the Venn diagram to compare and contrast erosion and deposition.

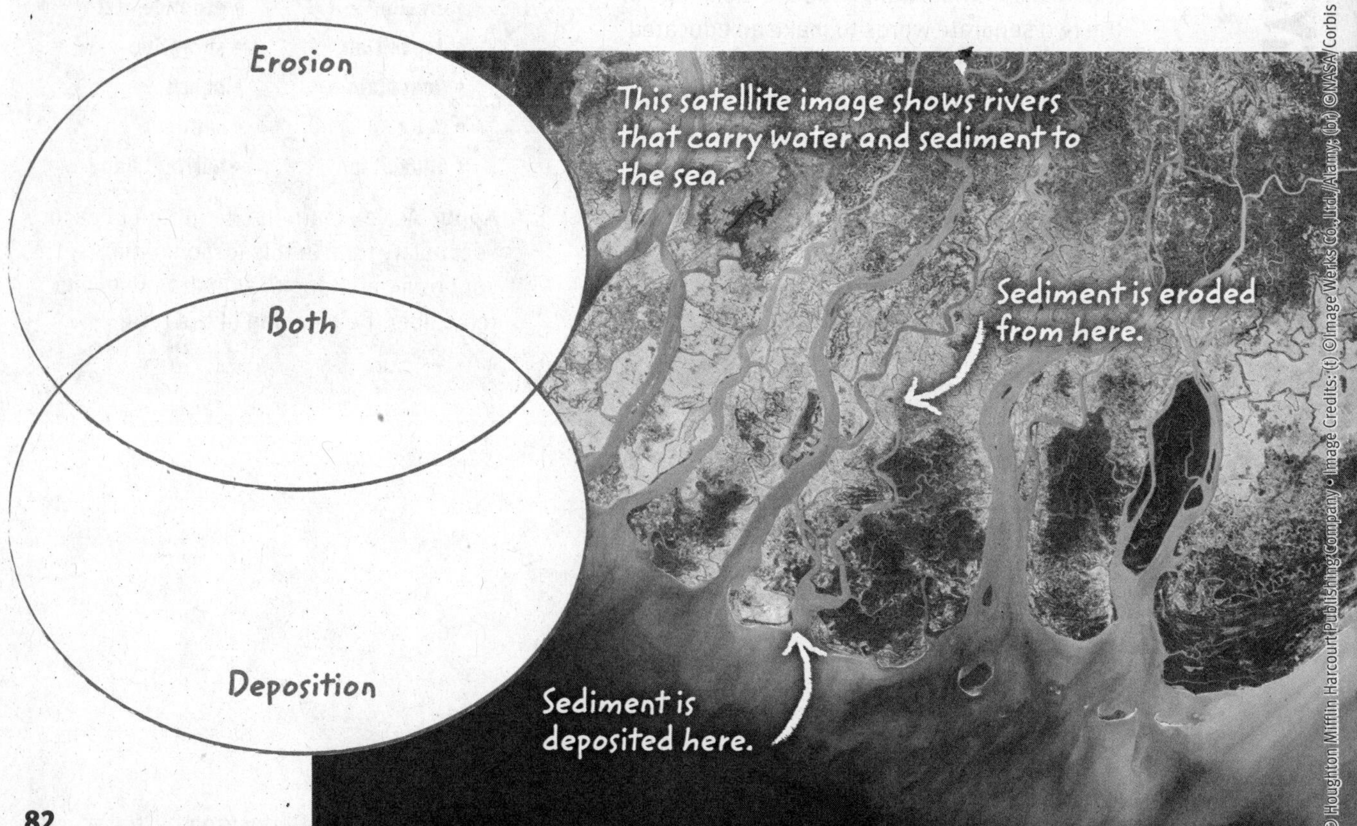
Erosion
Both
Deposition
This satellite image shows rivers that carry water and sediment to the sea.
Sediment is eroded from here.
Sediment is deposited here.

What factors relate to a stream's ability to erode material?

Some streams are able to erode large rocks, while others can erode only very fine sediment. Some streams move many tons of material each day, while others move very little sediment. So what determines how much material a stream can erode? A stream's gradient, discharge, and load are the three main factors that control what sediment a stream can carry.

Gradient

Gradient is the measure of the change in elevation over a certain distance. You can think of gradient as the steepness of a slope. The water in a stream that has a high gradient—or steep slope—moves very rapidly because of the downward pull of gravity. This rapid water flow gives the stream a lot of energy to erode rock and soil. A river or stream that has a low gradient has less energy for erosion, or erosive energy.

Load

Materials carried by a stream are called the stream's *load*. The size of the particles in a stream's load is affected by the stream's speed. Fast-moving streams can carry large particles. The large particles bounce and scrape along the bottom and sides of the streambed. Thus, a stream that has a load of large particles has a high erosion rate. Slow-moving streams carry smaller particles and have less erosive energy.

Discharge

The amount of water that a stream carries in a given amount of time is called *discharge*. The discharge of a stream increases when a major storm occurs or when warm weather rapidly melts snow. As the stream's discharge increases, its erosive energy, speed, and load increase.

Active Reading

6 Explain Why do some streams and rivers cause more erosion and deposition than others?

______

______

______

Do the Math

River Gradient Plot

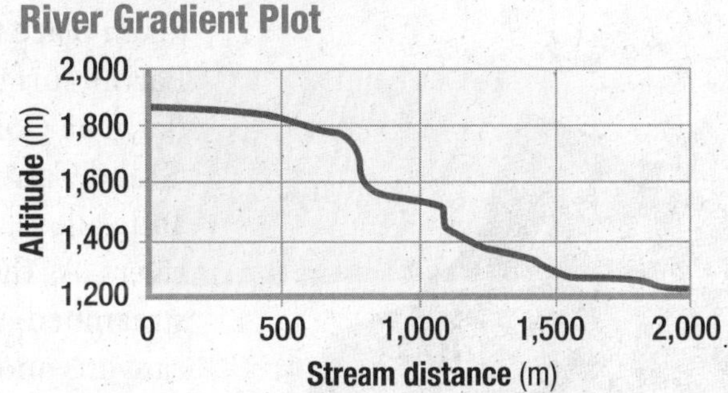

A river gradient plot shows how quickly the elevation of a river falls along its course. The slope of the line is the river's gradient. The line has a steep slope at points along the river where the gradient is steep. The line has a nearly level slope where the river gradient is shallow.

Identify

7 Along this river, at which two approximate altitude ranges are the gradients the steepest?

______

______

______

8 At which altitude ranges would you expect the highest streambed erosion rate?

______

______

______

9 At which altitude ranges would you expect the slowest streambed erosion rate?

______

______

______

Run of a River

What landforms can streams create?

A stream forms as water erodes soil and rock to make a channel. A *channel* is the path that a stream follows. As the stream continues to erode rock and soil, the channel gets wider and deeper. Over time, canyons and valleys can form.

Think Outside the Book

10 Apply Discuss with your classmates some landforms near your town that were likely made by flowing water.

Canyons and Valleys by Erosion

The processes that changed Earth's surface in the past continue to be at work today. For example, erosion and deposition have taken place throughout Earth's history. Six million years ago, Earth's surface in the area now known as the Grand Canyon was flat. The Colorado River cut down into the rock and formed the Grand Canyon over millions of years. Landforms, such as canyons and valleys, are created by the flow of water through streams and rivers. As the water moves, it erodes rock and sediment from the streambed. The flowing water can cut through rock, forming steep canyons and valleys.

Visualize It!

11 Apply On the lines below, label where erosion and deposition are occurring.

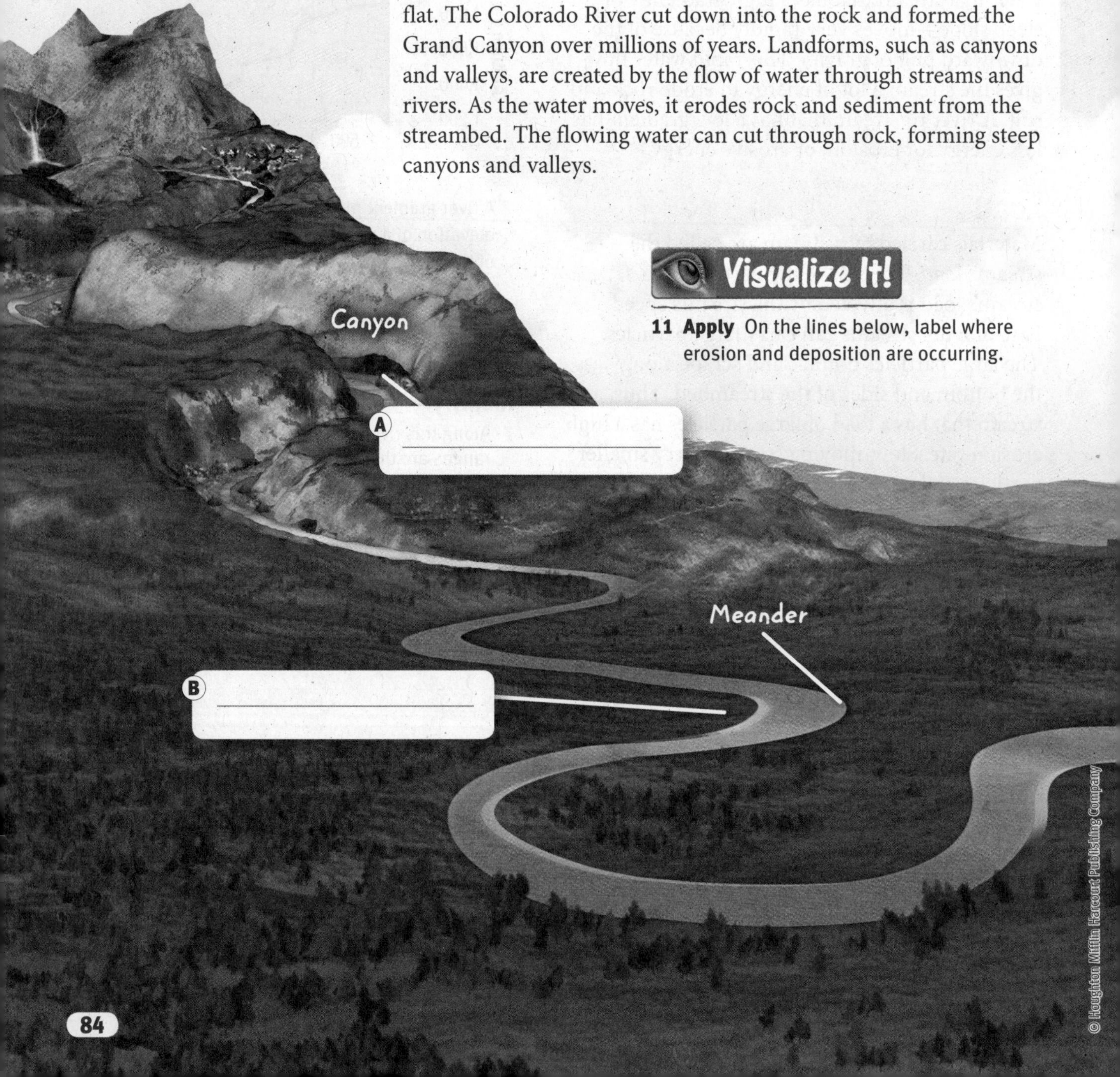

Canyon

A ______________________

Meander

B ______________________

Floodplains by Deposition

When a stream floods, a layer of sediment is deposited over the flooded land. Many layers of deposited sediment can form a flat area called a **floodplain**. Sediment often contains nutrients needed for plant growth. Because of this, floodplains are often very fertile.

As a stream flows through an area, its channel may run straight in some parts and curve in other parts. Curves and bends that form a twisting, looping pattern in a stream channel are called *meanders*. The moving water erodes the outside banks and deposits sediment along the inside banks. Over many years, meanders shift position. During a flood, a stream may cut a new channel that bypasses a meander. The cut-off meander forms a crescent-shaped lake, which is called an *oxbow lake*.

Deltas and Alluvial Fans by Deposition

When a stream empties into a body of water, such as a lake or an ocean, its current slows and it deposits its load. Streams often deposit their loads in a fan-shaped pattern called a **delta**. Over time, sediment builds up in a delta, forming new land. Sometimes the new land can extend far into the lake or ocean. A similar process occurs when a stream flows onto a flat land surface from mountains or hills. On land, the sediment forms an alluvial fan. An **alluvial fan** is a fan-shaped deposit that forms on dry land.

12 Identify As you read, underline the definitions of *delta* and *alluvial fan*.

13 Compare Compare and contrast alluvial fans and deltas.

____

____

____

____

____

Floodplain

C _______________

Oxbow lake

Delta

More Waterworks

What landforms are made by groundwater erosion?

As you have learned, rivers cause erosion when water picks up and moves rock and soil. The movement of water underground can also cause erosion. **Groundwater** is the water located within the rocks below Earth's surface. Slightly acidic groundwater can cause erosion by dissolving rock. When underground erosion happens, caves can form. Most of the world's caves formed over thousands of years as groundwater dissolved limestone underground. Although caves are formed by erosion, they also show signs of deposition. Water that drips from cracks in a cave's ceiling leaves behind icicle-shaped deposits known as *stalactites* and *stalagmites*. When the groundwater level is lower than the level of a cave, the cave roof may no longer be supported by the water underneath. If the roof of a cave collapses, it may leave a circular depression called a *sinkhole*.

Active Reading **14 Explain** How does groundwater cause caves to form?

____

____

Stalactites are caused by deposition.

Groundwater can erode rock, causing caves to form.

Visualize It!

15 Apply Describe what may have happened underground to cause this sinkhole to form.

____

____

____

____

What forces shape a shoreline?

A **shoreline** is the place where land and a body of water meet. Ocean water along a shoreline moves differently than river water moves. Ocean waves crashing against the shoreline have a great deal of energy. Strong waves may erode material. Gentle waves may deposit materials. In addition to waves, ocean water has *currents,* or streamlike movements of water. Like waves, currents can also erode and deposit materials.

Waves

Waves play a major part in building up and breaking down a shoreline. Waves slow down as they approach a shoreline. The first parts of the shoreline that waves meet are the *headlands,* or pieces of land that project into the water. The slowing waves bend toward the headlands, which concentrates the waves' energy. A huge amount of energy is released when waves crash into headlands, causing the land to erode. The waves striking the areas between headlands have less energy. Therefore, these waves are more likely to deposit materials rather than erode materials.

Currents

When water travels almost parallel to the shoreline very near shore, the current is called a *longshore current*. Longshore currents are caused by waves hitting the shore at an angle. Waves that break at angles move sediment along the coast. The waves push the sand in the same angled direction in which they break. But the return water flow moves sand directly away from the beach. The end result is a zigzag movement of the sand. As sand moves down a beach, the upcurrent end of the beach is eroded away while the downcurrent end of the beach is built up.

As waves approach a shoreline, they bend toward the headlands and crash against them. The energy in the waves between the headlands is spread out, so they have less erosive power.

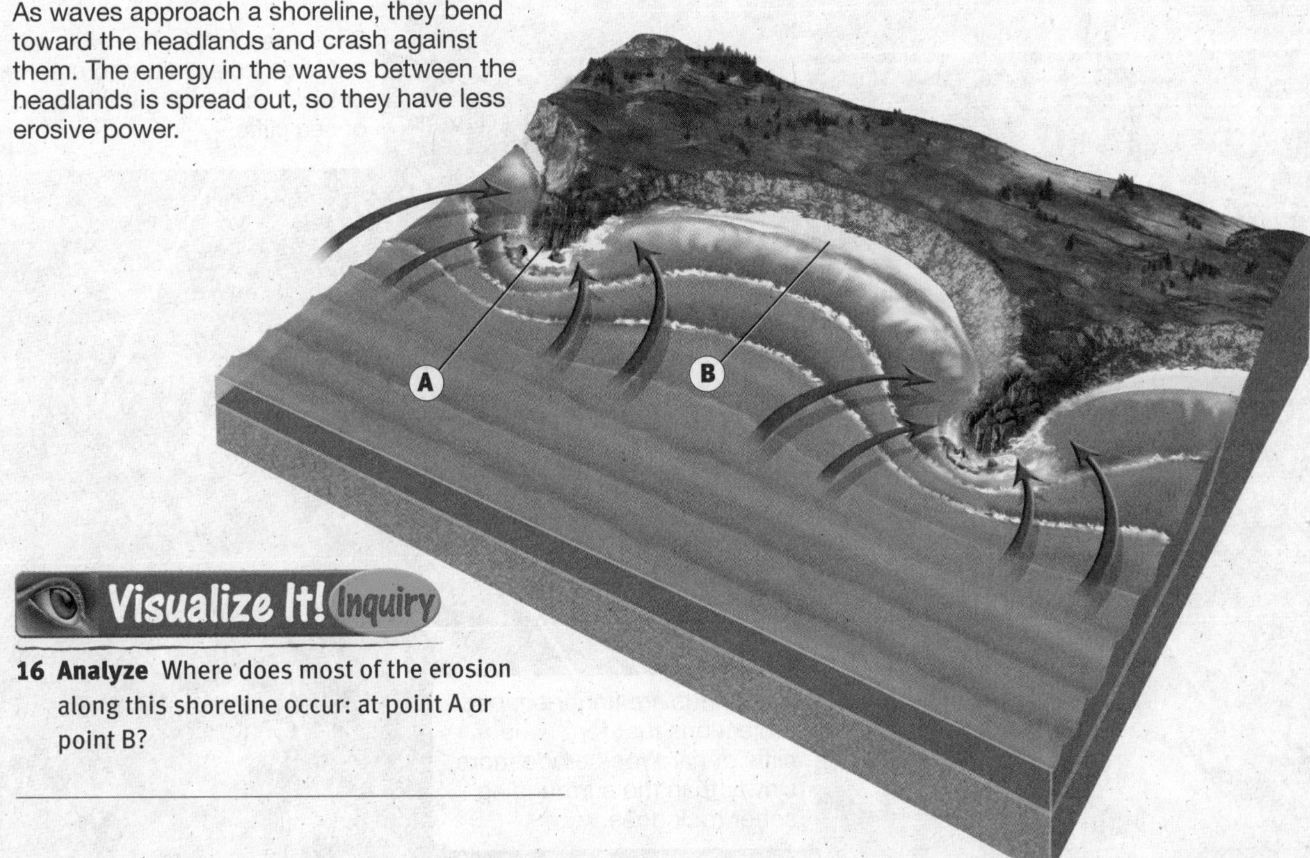

Visualize It! Inquiry

16 Analyze Where does most of the erosion along this shoreline occur: at point A or point B?

____

What coastal landforms are made by erosion?

Active Reading

17 Identify As you read, underline the sentence that summarizes the factors that determine how fast a shoreline erodes.

Wave erosion produces a variety of features along a shoreline. The rate at which rock erodes depends on the hardness of the rock and the energy of the waves. Gentle waves cause very little erosion. Strong waves from heavy storms can increase the rate of erosion. During storms, huge blocks of rock can be broken off and eroded away. In fact, a severe storm can noticeably change the appearance of a shoreline in a single day.

In addition to wave energy, the hardness of the rock making up the coastline affects how quickly the coastline is eroded. Very hard rock can slow the rate of erosion because it takes a great deal of wave energy to break up hard rock. Soft rock erodes more rapidly. Many shoreline features are caused by differences in rock hardness. Over time, a large area of softer rock can be eroded by strong waves. As a result, part of the shoreline is carved out and forms a bay.

Sea caves form when waves cut large holes into fractured or weak rock along the base of sea cliffs.
Wave-cut platforms form when a sea cliff is worn back from shore, producing a nearly level platform beneath the water at the base of the cliff.
Headlands are finger-shaped projections that form when cliffs of hard rock erode more slowly than the surrounding softer rock does.

Sea Cliffs and Wave-cut Platforms

A *sea cliff* forms when waves erode and undercut rock to make steep slopes. Waves strike the cliff's base, wearing away the rock. This process makes the cliff steeper. As a sea cliff erodes above the waterline, a bench of rock usually remains beneath the water at the cliff's base. This bench is called a *wave-cut platform*. Wave-cut platforms are almost flat because the rocks eroded from the cliff often scrape away at the platform.

Sea Caves, Arches, and Stacks

Sea cliffs seldom erode evenly. Often, headlands form as some parts of a cliff are cut back faster than other parts. As the rock making up sea cliffs and headlands erodes, it breaks and cracks. Waves can cut deeply into the cracks and form large holes. As the holes continue to erode, they become *sea caves*. A sea cave may erode even further and eventually become a *sea arch*. When the top of a sea arch collapses, its sides become *sea stacks*.

18 Summarize Complete the chart by filling in descriptions of each coastal landform.

Coastal Landform	Description
Headland	
Sea cave	
Sea arch	
Sea stack	
Wave-cut platform	

Sea arches form when wave action erodes sea caves until a hole cuts through a headland.

Sea stacks form when the tops of sea arches collapse and leave behind isolated columns of rock.

19 Analyze Which of these features do you think took longer to form: the sea stack, sea arch, or sea cave? Explain.

Shifting Sands

What coastal landforms are made by deposition?

Waves and currents carry a variety of materials, including sand, rock, dead coral, and shells. Often, these materials are deposited on a shoreline, where they form a beach. A **beach** is an area of shoreline that is made up of material deposited by waves and currents. A great deal of beach material is also deposited by rivers and then is moved down the shoreline by currents.

Beaches

You may think of beaches as sandy places. However, not all beaches are made of sand. The size and shape of beach material depend on how far the material has traveled from its source. Size and shape also depend on the type of material and how it is eroded. For example, in areas with stormy seas, beaches may be made of pebbles and boulders deposited by powerful waves. These waves erode smaller particles such as sand.

Visualize It!

20 Infer Would it take more wave energy to deposit sand or the rocks shown on this beach? Explain.

____

____

____

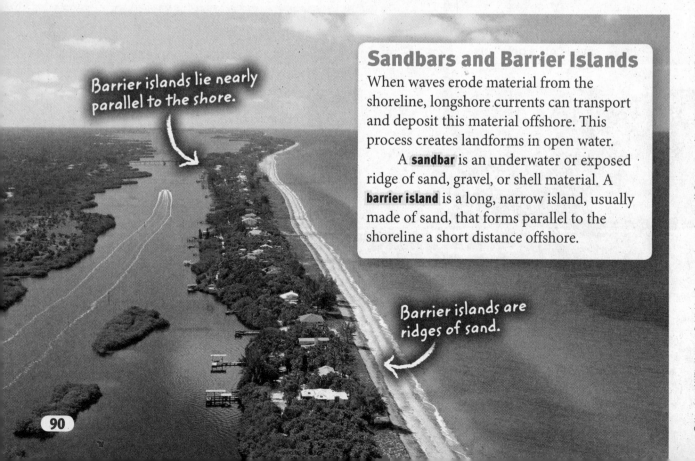

Barrier islands lie nearly parallel to the shore.

Barrier islands are ridges of sand.

Sandbars and Barrier Islands

When waves erode material from the shoreline, longshore currents can transport and deposit this material offshore. This process creates landforms in open water.

A **sandbar** is an underwater or exposed ridge of sand, gravel, or shell material. A **barrier island** is a long, narrow island, usually made of sand, that forms parallel to the shoreline a short distance offshore.

Why It Matters

EYE ON THE ENVIRONMENT

Living on the Edge

Barrier islands are dynamic landforms that are constantly changing shape. What's here today may be gone tomorrow!

Barrier islands

Landform in Limbo

Barrier islands are found all over the world, including the United States. They can be eroded away by tides and large storms. The barrier island at the left was eroded by a hurricane. Because of erosion, the shape of a barrier island is always changing.

Building on Barriers

Barrier islands are popular spots to build vacation homes and hotels. Residents of barrier islands often use anti-erosion strategies to protect their property from erosion by tides and storms. Short-term solutions include using sand bags, like those shown on the right, to slow down erosion.

Extend

Inquiry

21 **Explain** Give a step-by-step description of how a barrier island could form.

22 **Identify** Research different technologies and strategies people can use to slow the erosion of a barrier island.

23 **Model** Choose one of the anti-erosion methods identified in your research and design an experiment to test how well the technology or strategy slows down the process of erosion.

Visual Summary

To complete this summary, fill in the blanks. Then use the key below to check your answers. You can use this page to review the main concepts of the lesson.

Erosion and Deposition by Water

Streams alter the shape of Earth's surface.

24 Caused by erosion: canyons, valleys

Caused by deposition: floodplains, deltas, ________________

Groundwater erodes and deposits materials.

25 Caused by erosion: caves, ________________

Caused by deposition: stalactites, stalagmites

Waves and currents change the shape of the shoreline.

26 Caused by erosion: bays, inlets, headlands, wave-cut platforms, sea cliffs, sea caves, sea stacks, ________________

Caused by deposition: beaches, sandbars, barrier islands

Answers: 24. alluvial fans; 25. sinkholes; 26. sea arches

27 Explain How do erosion and deposition work together to form a delta?

Lesson Review

Vocabulary

Circle the term that best completes the following sentences.

1 *Erosion/Deposition* occurs when materials drop out of wind or water.

2 When a river flows into an ocean, it slows down and deposits materials in its *alluvial fan/delta.*

3 When a river periodically floods and deposits its sediments, a flat area known as a *floodplain/shoreline* forms over time.

Key Concepts

Complete the table below.

Landform	How It Forms
Canyon	**4 Explain**
Sinkhole	**5 Explain**
Sea cave	**6 Explain**

7 Synthesize How does gravity relate to a stream's ability to erode and deposit materials?

8 Identify What are the two main factors that affect how quickly a coastline erodes?

9 Describe How does a longshore current change a beach?

Critical Thinking

Use this graph, which shows erosion and deposition on a beach, to answer questions 10–11.

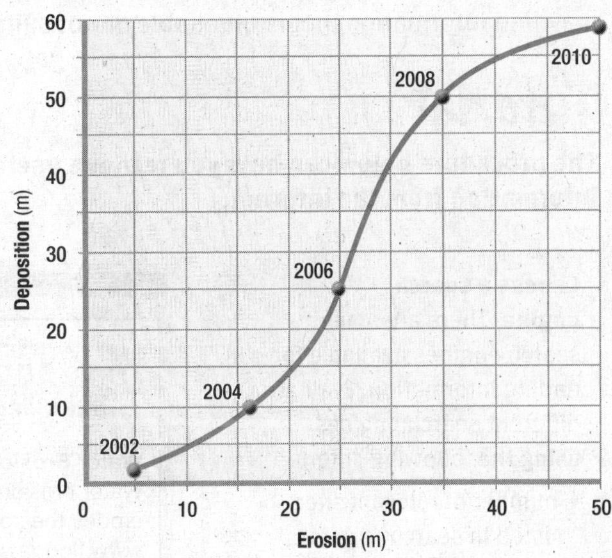

10 Analyze In 2004, was there more erosion or deposition taking place?

11 Evaluate Explain how waves and currents are affecting this beach over time.

12 Hypothesize Many communities pump groundwater to irrigate crops and supply homes with water. How do you think overpumping groundwater is related to the formation of sinkholes?

Think Science

Searching the Internet

The Internet can be a great tool for finding scientific information and reference material. But, because the Internet contains so much information, finding useful information on it may be difficult. Or, you may find information that is unreliable or not suitable.

Sunshine State Standards

LA.6.4.2.2 The student will record information (e.g., observations, notes, lists, charts, legends) related to a topic, including visual aids to organize and record information and include a list of sources used.

Tutorial

The procedure below can help you retrieve useful, reliable information from the Internet.

Choose a search engine There are many search engines available for finding information. Evaluate different search engines using the following criteria:

- number of relevant sites listed in search results;
- how easy the search engine is to use;
- how fast the search is; and
- how easy the documents on the site are to access, and what type of documents they are.

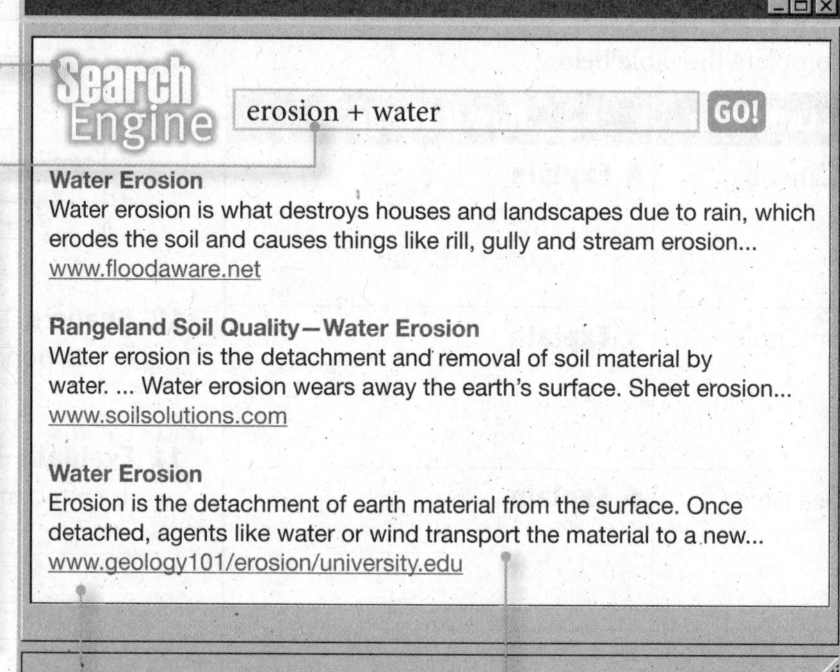

Search Engine
erosion + water
GO!
Water Erosion
Water erosion is what destroys houses and landscapes due to rain, which erodes the soil and causes things like rill, gully and stream erosion...
www.floodaware.net
Rangeland Soil Quality—Water Erosion
Water erosion is the detachment and removal of soil material by water. ... Water erosion wears away the earth's surface. Sheet erosion...
www.soilsolutions.com
Water Erosion
Erosion is the detachment of earth material from the surface. Once detached, agents like water or wind transport the material to a new...
www.geology101/erosion/university.edu

Choose and enter keywords Identify specific keywords for the topic of interest. You can make lists or draw concept maps to help you think of keywords or key phrases. Enter your keyword(s) into the search engine. You can enter one keyword at a time, or you can enter multiple keywords. You can put the word *and* or + between two keywords to find both words on the site. Use the word *or* between two keywords to find at least one of the keywords on the site. Use quotations ("like this") around keywords to find exact matches.

Look at the URL Examine the address in the search results list. Ask yourself if a reliable organization is behind the webpage such as government agencies (.gov or .mil), educational institutions (.edu), and non-profit organizations (.org). Avoid personal sites and biased sources, which may tell only one side of a story. These types of sources may lead to inaccurate information or a false impression.

Look at the content of the webpage Decide whether the webpage contains useful information. Read the page's title and headings. Read the first sentences of several paragraphs. Look at tables and diagrams. Ask yourself: How current is the webpage?; Are the sources documented?; and Are there links to more information? Decide whether the webpage contains the kind of information that you need.

You Try It!

Weathering is the physical and chemical alteration of rock.

Weathering processes have led to the formations you see here in Bryce Canyon. Study the photo and then do some research on the Internet to find out more about weathering processes.

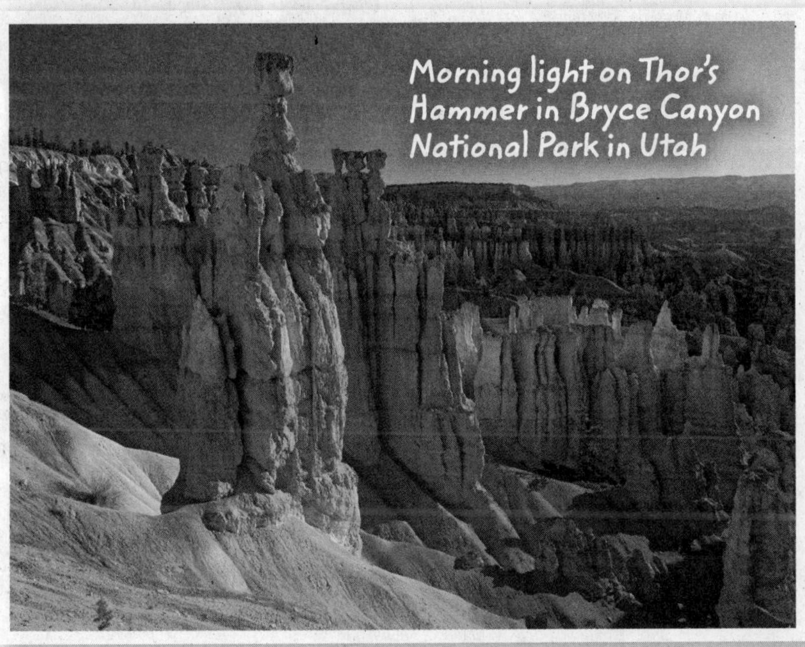

Morning light on Thor's Hammer in Bryce Canyon National Park in Utah

1 Choosing Keywords Think about what you want to learn about mechanical weathering. You may want to focus on one topic, such as frost wedging, exfoliation, or thermal expansion. Choose relevant keyword(s) or phrases for the topic that you are researching.

2 Searching the Internet Enter the keywords in a search engine. Which keywords or phrases prompted the most relevant and reliable sites?

3 Evaluating Websites Use the table below to evaluate websites on how useful they are and on the quality of the information. As you visit different websites for your research, make notes about each site's relevance and suitability.

Website	Comments

Lesson 3

Erosion and Deposition by Wind, Ice, and Gravity

ESSENTIAL QUESTION

How do wind, ice, and gravity change Earth's surface?

By the end of this lesson, you should be able to describe erosion and deposition by wind, ice, and gravity as well as identify the landforms that result from these processes.

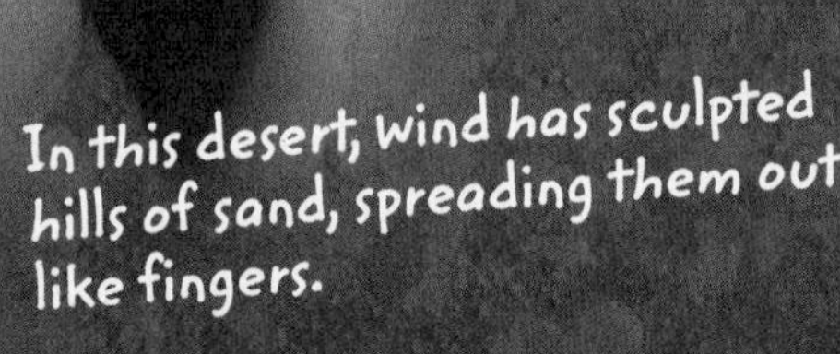

In this desert, wind has sculpted hills of sand, spreading them out like fingers.

Sunshine State Standards

SC.6.N.3.4 Identify the role of models in the context of the sixth grade science benchmarks.

SC.6.E.6.1 Describe and give examples of ways in which Earth's surface is built up and torn down by physical and chemical weathering, erosion, and deposition.

SC.6.E.6.2 Recognize that there are a variety of different landforms on Earth's surface such as coastlines, dunes, rivers, mountains, glaciers, deltas, and lakes and relate these landforms as they apply to Florida.

Engage Your Brain

1 Predict How do you think wind can erode materials?

2 Infer The dark bands you see in the photo on the right are dirt and rocks frozen in the ice. What do you think will happen to the dirt and rocks when the ice melts?

Active Reading

3 Define In this lesson, you will be learning about how different agents of erosion can abrade rock. Use a dictionary to look up the meaning of the word *abrade*. Record the definition:

Now use the word *abrade* in your own sentence:

As you read this lesson, circle the word *abrade* whenever you come across it. Compare the sentences that include this word with the sentence you wrote above.

Vocabulary Terms

- dune
- loess
- glacier
- glacial drift
- creep
- rockfall
- landslide
- mudflow

4 Apply As you learn the definition of each vocabulary term in this lesson, create your own definition or sketch to help you remember the meaning of the term.

Gone with the

How can wind shape Earth?

Have you ever been outside and had a gust of wind blow a stack of papers all over the place? If so, you have seen how wind erosion works. In the same way that wind moved your papers, wind moves soil, sand, and rock particles. When wind moves soil, sand, and rock particles, it acts as an agent of erosion.

Abraded Rock

When wind blows sand and other particles against a surface, it can wear down the surface over time. The grinding and wearing down of rock surfaces by other rock or by sand particles is called *abrasion.* Abrasion happens in areas where there are strong winds, loose sand, and soft rocks. The blowing of millions of grains of sand causes a sandblasting effect. The sandblasting effect slowly erodes the rock by stripping away its surface. Over time, the rock can become smooth and polished.

Desert Pavement

The removal of fine sediment by wind is called *deflation.* This process is shown in the diagram below. During deflation, wind removes the top layer of fine sediment or soil. Deflation leaves behind rock fragments that are too heavy to be lifted by the wind. After a while, these rocks may be the only materials left on the surface. The resulting landscape is known as desert pavement. As you can see in the photo below, desert pavement is a surface made up mostly of pebbles and small, broken rocks.

Visualize It!

5 Describe How did the desert pavement in this photo most likely form?

____

____

____

Wind

Dunes

Wind carries sediment in much the same way that rivers do. Just as rivers deposit their loads, winds eventually drop the materials that they are carrying. For example, when wind hits an obstacle, it slows and drops materials on top of the obstacle. As the material builds up, the obstacle gets larger. This obstacle causes the wind to slow more and deposit more material, which forms a mound. Eventually, the original obstacle is buried. Mounds of wind-deposited sand are called **dunes**. Dunes are common in deserts and along the shores of lakes and oceans.

Generally, dunes move in the same direction the wind is blowing. Usually, a dune's gently sloped side faces the wind. Wind constantly moves material up this side of the dune. As sand moves over the crest of the dune, the sand slides down the slip face and makes a steep slope.

Loess

Wind can carry extremely fine material long distances. Thick deposits of this windblown, fine-grained sediment are known as **loess** (LOH•uhs). Loess can feel like the talcum powder a person may use after a shower. Because wind carries fine-grained material much higher and farther than it carries sand, loess deposits are sometimes found far away from their source. Loess deposits can build up over thousands and even millions of years. Loess is a valuable resource because it forms good soil for growing crops.

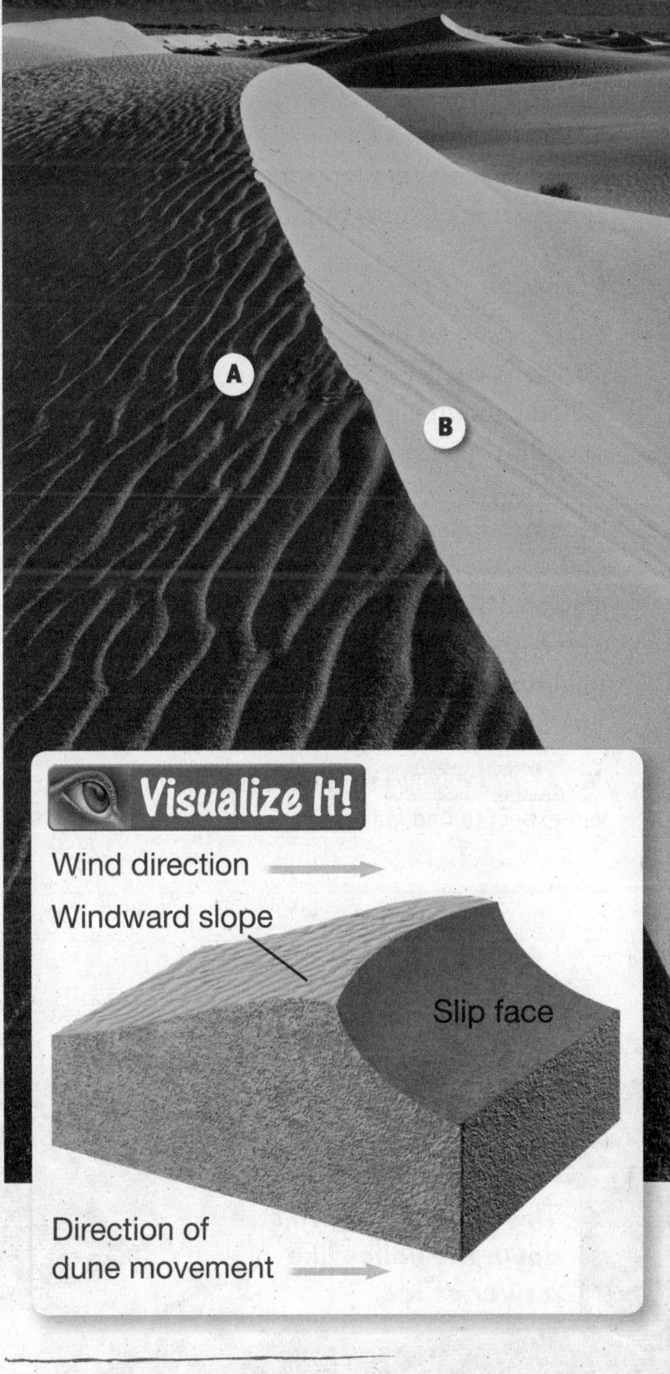

6 Infer Why do you think loess can be carried further than sand?

7 Determine Look at the photo above the illustration. Which direction does the wind blow across the photographed dune: from left to right or right to left?

8 Identify Which side of the dune in the photograph is the slip face: A or B?

Groovy Glaciers

What kinds of ice shape Earth?

Have you ever made a snowball from a scoop of fluffy snow? If so, you know that when the snow is pressed against itself, it becomes harder and more compact. The same idea explains how a glacier forms. A **glacier** is a large mass of moving ice that forms by the compacting of snow by natural forces.

Think Outside the Book

9 Apply Find out whether glaciers have ever covered your state. If so, what landforms did they leave behind?

Flowing Ice

Glaciers can be found anywhere on land where it is cold enough for ice to stay frozen year round. Gravity causes glaciers to move. When enough ice builds up on a slope, the ice begins to move downhill. The steeper the slope is, the faster the glacier moves.

As glaciers move, they pick up materials. These materials become embedded in the ice. As the glacier moves forward, the materials scratch and abrade the rock and soil underneath the glacier. This abrasion causes more erosion. Glaciers are also agents of deposition. As a glacier melts, it drops the materials that it carried. **Glacial drift** is the general term for all of the materials carried and deposited by a glacier.

Active Reading **10 Infer** Where in North America would you expect to find glaciers?

____

____

____

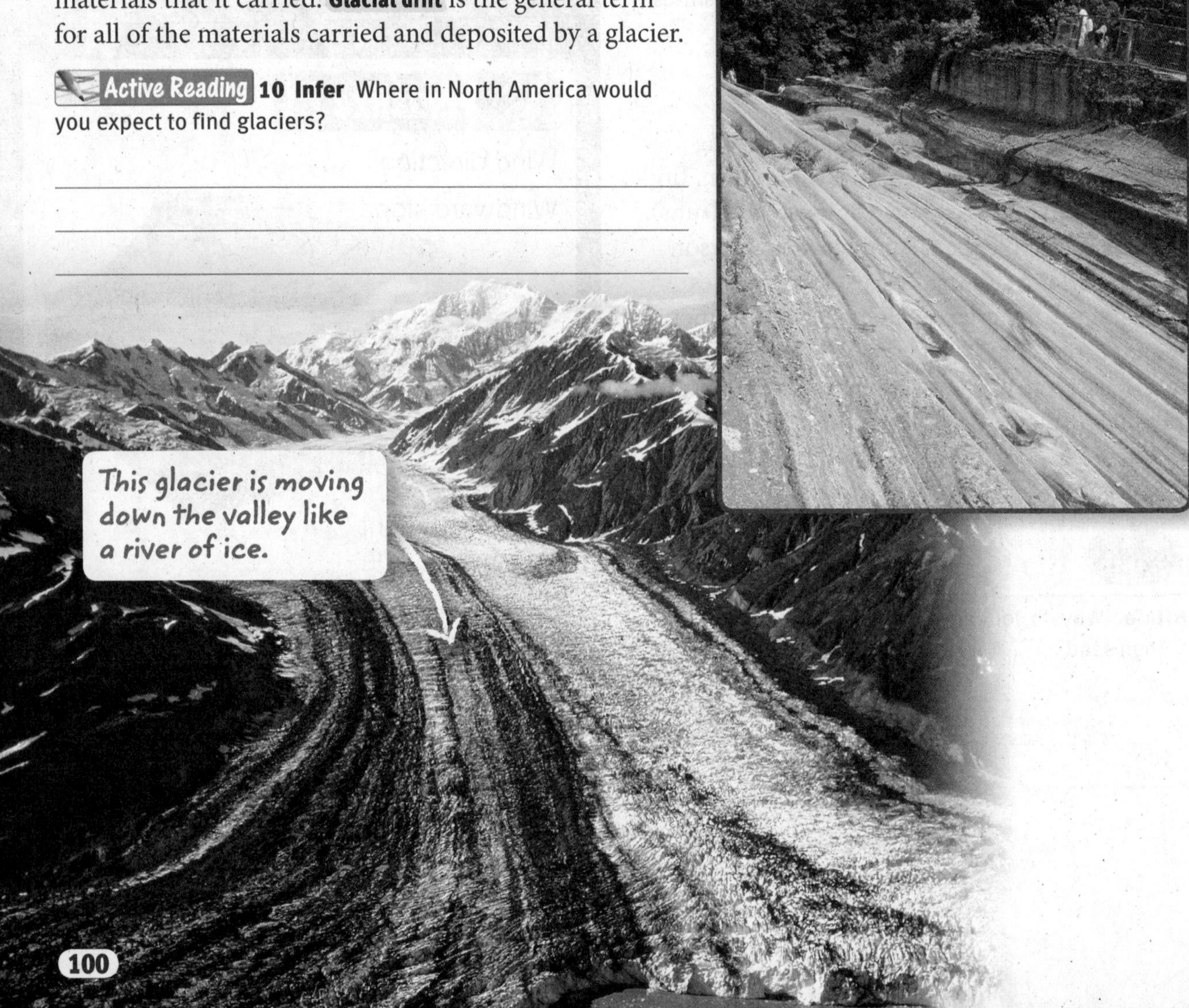

As a glacier flowed over this rock, it scratched out these grooves.

This glacier is moving down the valley like a river of ice.

Alpine Glaciers

An alpine glacier is a glacier that forms in a mountainous area. Alpine glaciers flow down the sides of mountains and create rugged landscapes. Glaciers may form in valleys originally created by stream erosion. The flow of water in a stream forms a V-shaped valley. As a glacier slowly flows through a V-shaped valley, it scrapes away the valley floor and walls. The glacier widens and straightens the valley into a broad U-shape. An alpine glacier can also carve out bowl-shaped depressions, called *cirques* (surks), at the head of a valley. A sharp ridge called an *arête* (uh•RAYT) forms between two cirques that are next to each other. When three or more arêtes join, they form a sharp peak called a *horn*.

Visualize It!

11 Summarize Use the illustration below to write a description for each of the following landforms.

Landforms made by alpine glaciers	Description
Arête	
Cirque	
Horn	
U-shaped valley	

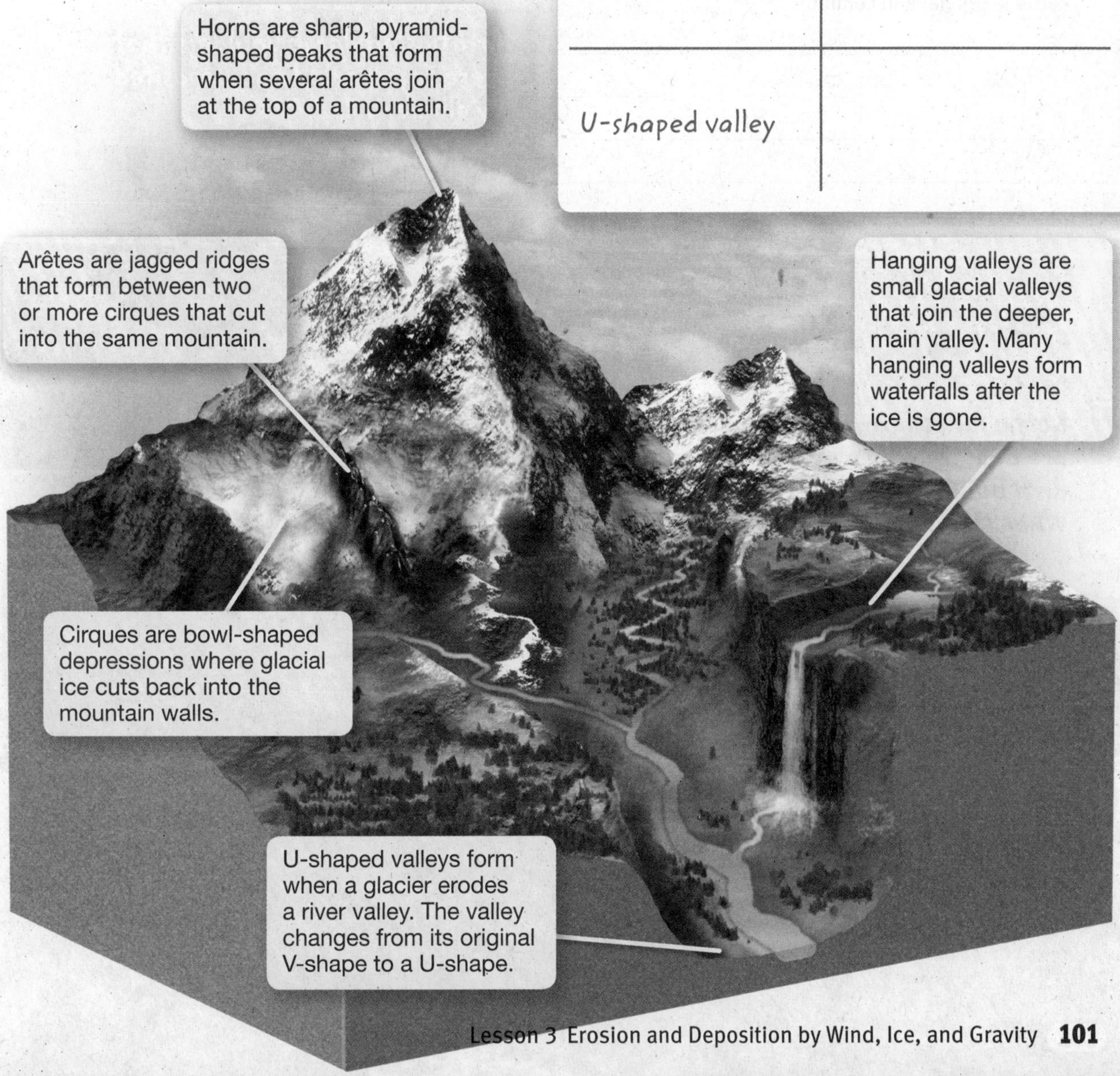

Horns are sharp, pyramid-shaped peaks that form when several arêtes join at the top of a mountain.

Arêtes are jagged ridges that form between two or more cirques that cut into the same mountain.

Hanging valleys are small glacial valleys that join the deeper, main valley. Many hanging valleys form waterfalls after the ice is gone.

Cirques are bowl-shaped depressions where glacial ice cuts back into the mountain walls.

U-shaped valleys form when a glacier erodes a river valley. The valley changes from its original V-shape to a U-shape.

Continental Glaciers

Continental glaciers are thick sheets of ice that may spread over large areas, including across entire continents. These glaciers are huge, continuous masses of ice. Continental glaciers create very different landforms than alpine glaciers do. Alpine glaciers form sharp and rugged features, whereas continental glaciers flatten and smooth the landscape. Continental glaciers erode and remove features that existed before the ice appeared. These glaciers smooth and round exposed rock surfaces in a way similar to the way that bulldozers can flatten landscapes.

Erosion and deposition by continental glaciers result in specific, recognizable landforms. Some of the landforms are shown below. Similar landforms can be found in the northern United States, which was once covered by continental glaciers.

12 Compare What does the formation of erratics and kettle lakes have in common?

Erratics are large boulders that were transported and deposited by glaciers.

Kettle lakes form when chunks of ice are deposited by a glacier and glacial drift builds up around the ice blocks. When the ice melts, a lake forms.

Why It Matters

Melting the Ice

What would you do if an Ice Age glacial dam broke and let loose millions of gallons of water? Get out of the way and get ready for some erosion!

A Crack in the Ice

During the last Ice Age, a huge ice dam held back Glacial Lake Missoula, a 320-km-long body of water. Then one day, the dam burst. Water roared out, emptying the lake in less than 48 hours!

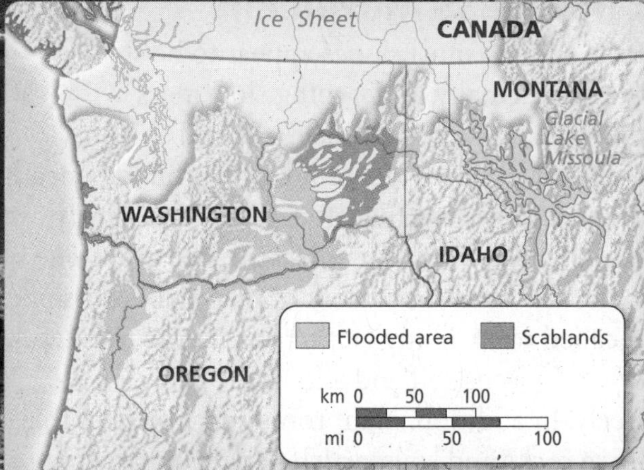

Giant ripple marks from the Missoula floods

Large-Scale Landforms

The erosion caused by the roaring water carved out a landscape of huge waterfalls, deep canyons, and three-story-high ripple marks. Many of these features are in an area called the Scablands.

History Repeats Itself

Lake Missoula eventually reformed behind another ice dam. The breaking of the dam and the floods repeated about 40 more times, ripping away topsoil and exposing and cracking the bedrock.

Extend

Inquiry

13 Relate Where have you seen ripple marks before and how do they compare to the ripple marks shown in the photo on this page?

14 Explain How do you think the three-story-high ripple marks shown here were formed?

15 Model Use sand, pebbles, and other materials to model how a severe flood can alter the landscape. Photograph or illustrate the results of your investigation. Present your results in the form of an animation, slide show, or illustrated report.

Slippery Slopes

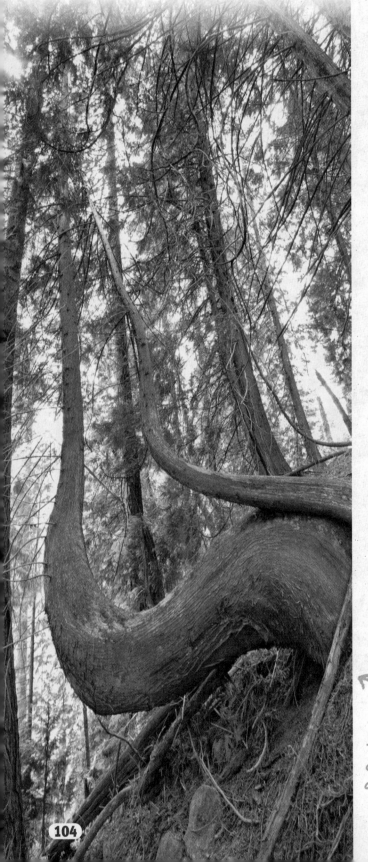

How can gravity shape Earth?

Although you can't see it, the force of gravity, like water, wind, and ice, is an agent of erosion and deposition. Gravity not only influences the movement of water and ice, but it also causes rocks and soil to move downslope. This shifting of materials is called *mass movement*. Mass movement plays a major role in shaping Earth's surface.

Slow Mass Movement

Even though most slopes appear to be stable, they are actually undergoing slow mass movement. In fact, all the rocks and soil on a slope travel slowly downhill. The ground beneath the tree shown on the left is moving so slowly that the tree trunk curved as the tree grew. The extremely slow movement of material downslope is called **creep**. Many factors contribute to creep. Water loosens soil and allows the soil to move freely. In addition, plant roots act as wedges that force rocks and soil particles apart. Burrowing animals, such as gophers and groundhogs, also loosen rock and soil particles, making it easier for the particles to be pulled downward.

16 Analyze As the soil on this hill shifts, how is the tree changing so that it continues to grow upright?

____

____

____

The shape of this tree trunk indicates that creep has occurred along the slope.

Rapid Mass Movement

The most destructive mass movements happen suddenly and rapidly. Rapid mass movement can be very dangerous and can destroy everything in its path. Rapid mass movement tends to happen on steep slopes because materials are more likely to fall down a steep slope than a shallow slope.

While traveling along a mountain road, you may have noticed signs along the road that warn of falling rocks. A **rockfall** happens when loose rocks fall down a steep slope. Steep slopes are common in mountainous areas. Gravity causes loosened and exposed rocks to fall down steep slopes. The rocks in a rockfall can range in size from small fragments to large boulders.

Another kind of rapid mass movement is a landslide. A **landslide** is the sudden and rapid movement of a large amount of material downslope. As you can see in the photo on the right, landslides can carry away plants. They can also carry away animals, vehicles, and buildings. Heavy rains, deforestation, construction on unstable slopes, and earthquakes increase the chances of a landslide.

A rapid movement of a large mass of mud is a **mudflow**. Mudflows happen when a large amount of water mixes with soil and rock. The water causes the slippery mud to flow rapidly downslope. Mudflows happen in mountainous regions after deforestation has occurred or when a long dry season is followed by heavy rains. Volcanic eruptions or heavy rains on volcanic ash can produce some of the most dangerous mudflows. Mudflows of volcanic origin are called lahars. Lahars can travel at speeds greater than 80 km/h and can be as thick as wet cement.

17 Identify List five events that can trigger a mass movement.

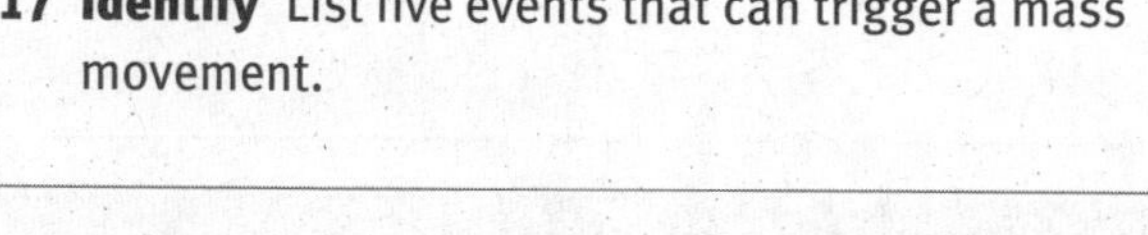

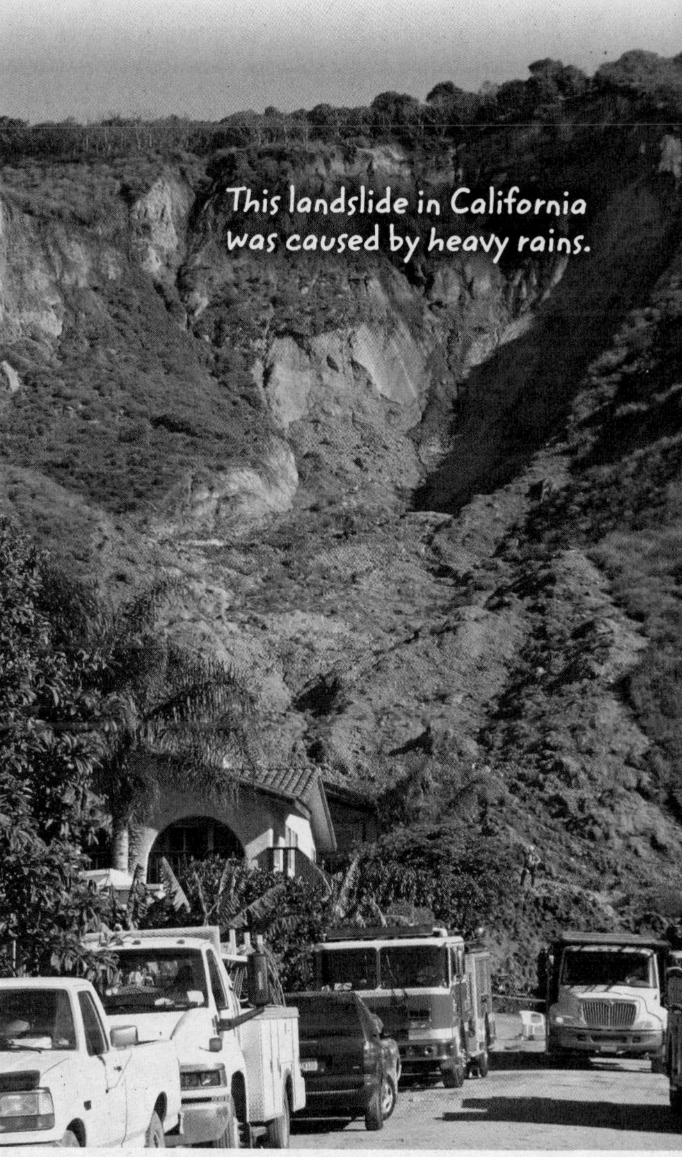

This landslide in California was caused by heavy rains.

18 Infer On which slope, A or B, would a landslide be more likely to occur? Explain.

Visual Summary

To complete this summary, fill in the blanks with the correct word or phrase. Then, use the key below to check your answers. You can use this page to review the main concepts of the lesson.

Erosion and Deposition by Wind, Ice, and Gravity

Wind forms dunes and desert pavement.

19 Wind forms dunes through: ________________

20 Wind forms desert pavement through: ________________

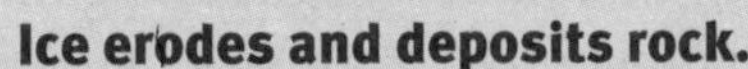

Ice erodes and deposits rock.

21 Alpine glaciers make landforms such as:

____

____

____

____

____

22 Continental glaciers make landforms such as:

____

____

____

Gravity pulls materials downward.

23 Type of slow mass movement: ________________

24 Three major types of rapid mass movement:

________________ ________________ ________________

Answers: 19 deposition; 20 erosion, deflation; 21 arêtes, cirques, horns, hanging and U-shaped valleys; 22 kettle lakes, erratics; 23 creep; 24 rock fall, landslide, mudflow

25 Summarize Describe the role that gravity plays in almost all examples of erosion and deposition.

Lesson Review

Vocabulary

Use a term from the section to complete each sentence below.

1 When an obstacle causes wind to slow down and deposit materials, the materials pile up and eventually form a ________________

2 Large masses of flowing ice called ________________ are typically found near Earth's poles and in other cold regions.

3 Very fine sediments called ________________ can be carried by wind over long distances.

4 As glaciers retreat, they leave behind deposits of ________________

Key Concepts

5 Explain How can glaciers cause deposition?

6 Compare Compare and contrast how wind and glaciers abrade rock.

7 Distinguish What is the difference between creep and a landslide?

Critical Thinking

Use the diagram to answer the question below.

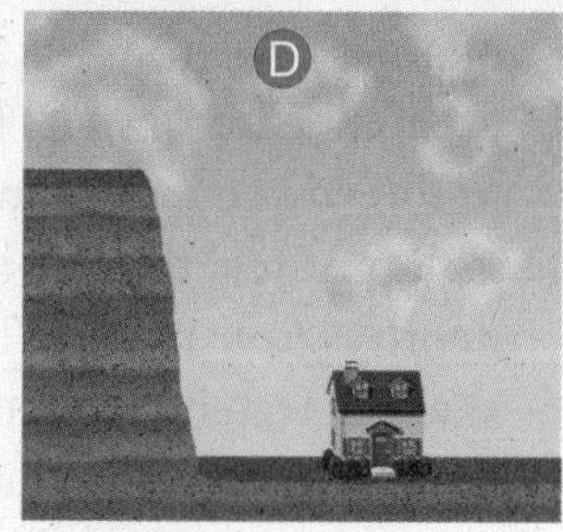

8 Synthesize Which of the four locations would be the best and worst places to build a house? Rank the four locations and explain your reasoning.

9 Integrate Wind erosion occurs at a faster rate in deserts than in places with a thick layer of vegetation covering the ground. Why do you think this is the case?

Focus on FLORIDA

Tampa Bay Estuary

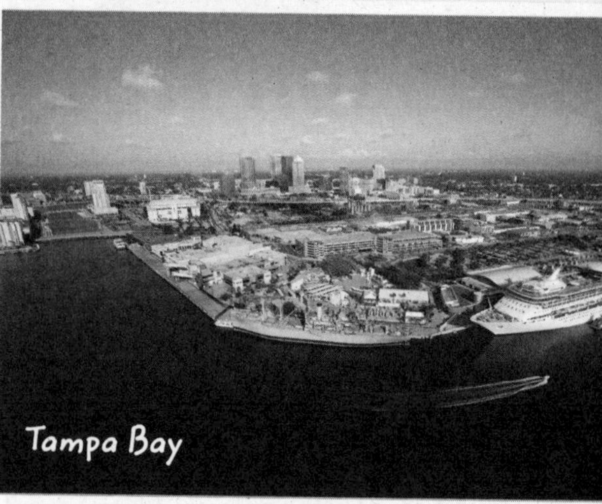
Tampa Bay

Protecting a Rich Ecosystem

Tampa Bay is home to an enormous number of animals—from microscopic plankton to the great blue heron. The largest open-water estuary in Florida covers almost 250 kilometers. Despite its large area, the Bay is very shallow. The average depth is four meters. This wide expanse of warm, shallow water supports important habitats like mangrove forests, marshes, and underwater seagrass beds. It provides a home to more than 200 species of fish. However, the Bay's ecosystem is threatened by pollution. Nitrogen runoff from residential areas is the chief pollutant. It changes the chemistry of the water, and kills the phytoplankton. In 1991, the government created the Tampa Bay Estuary Program (TBEP) as part of a program to restore bays in the United States. The TBEP conducts ongoing research on how to protect the bay and its diversity. In order to work with people who know the area well, the TBEP often asks for advice from the community.

Manatee

Protecting Manatees

Florida has become a year-long home to manatees. These gentle marine mammals grow to an average length of three meters and can weigh up to 1,500 kilograms. Manatees are an important part of their ecosystem. They maintain seagrass beds with their grazing. However, while they are feeding on seagrass, near the surface of the water, manatees can be injured or even killed in collisions with boats. Almost all manatees in Florida have scars from collisions.

You can help protect the manatee population by:

- Watching out for them in shallow, coastal waters, near seagrass beds;
- Following the speed limit signs for boats; and
- Keeping trash out of the water.

Take It Home

Create a poster that informs people of 10 ways they can protect the wildlife and different habitats in Tampa Bay. Include photos or illustrations in your poster.

Brown pelican

Birds of the Bay

The different habitats in Tampa Bay attract about twenty-five species of birds. Key habitats for these birds include islands, mudflats, seagrass meadows, and open waters. Islands provide protection for nests from predators and other disturbances. Mudflats and seagrass meadows offer fishing grounds for shorebirds like the brown pelican. Open waters are ideal habitats for birds like loons and ducks.

The birds in Tampa Bay make their homes on some of the area's most desirable waterfront real estate. As a result, many bird habitats are under threat from development and increased human presence. We can help protect bird populations by being respectful of nesting sites by keeping their habitats free of litter.

Math Connection

Complete the table. Round each percent to the nearest tenth. Check that your percents add up to 100%.

Type of Debris	Total Number of Pieces Reported	Percent of Total Debris
Cigarette butts	93,985	
Plastic pieces	34,766	
Foam plastic pieces	32,770	
Glass bottles	31,078	
Plastic caps/lids	30,787	
Plastic food bags	30,635	
Plastic straws	26,684	
Metal drink cans	24,992	
Glass drink bottles	19,356	
Paper pieces	16,645	
Other	30,366	
TOTAL	372,064	

Spoonbills feed on a mangrove island in the Tampa Bay estuary

Lesson 4

Landforms and Florida

ESSENTIAL QUESTION

How are Earth's landforms related to Florida?

By the end of this lesson, you should be able to describe some of the landforms found on Earth's surface and give examples of landforms found in Florida.

Forests, swamps, lakes, islands, and rivers provide shelter for many endangered plants and animals in and near the Florida Everglades.

 **Sunshine State Standards**

SC.6.E.6.2 Recognize that there are a variety of different landforms on Earth's surface such as coastlines, dunes, rivers, mountains, glaciers, deltas, and lakes and relate these landforms as they apply to Florida.

Engage Your Brain

1 Predict Check T or F to show whether you think each statement is true or false.

T	F	
☐	☐	Florida has been covered by glaciers in the past.
☐	☐	Florida has several mountains.
☐	☐	Florida is one of the flattest of the 50 states.
☐	☐	Rivers can erode land and deposit sediment.

2 Explain Imagine you are assigned to make a brochure welcoming visitors to the state of Florida. What kinds of landforms and sites would you recommend and why?

Active Reading

3 Synthesize The term *delta* was first used to describe a landform by an ancient Greek historian named Herodotus. He coined the term after the Greek letter Δ. Use the Greek letter and the example sentence to write your own definition of a *delta*.

Term	Greek letter
delta	Δ

Example sentence

The Mississippi River forms a large delta as the river flows into the Gulf of Mexico.

delta:

Vocabulary Terms

- mountain
- glacier
- lake
- river
- delta
- coastline
- dune

4 Apply As you learn the definition of each vocabulary term in this lesson, create your own definition or sketch to help you remember the meaning of the term.

What is a mountain?

Active Reading

5 Identify As you read, underline the characteristics of mountains.

A **mountain** is a region of increased elevation on Earth's surface that rises to a peak. One way a mountain can form is when the collision of tectonic plates causes the Earth's crust to uplift, or rise. Another way mountains form is through the eruption of volcanoes.

The highest point in Florida is Britton Hill near the Alabama border, which is 105 m in elevation. Mountains typically have an elevation of at least 300 m, meaning Florida does not have mountains! In fact, Florida and Louisiana tie for second place on a list of states with the lowest average elevation.

Mountains are important sources of *sediment*. Sediment refers to any pieces of rock that have been broken down from existing rock over time. Sediments can be transported to new locations by the actions of wind, ice, and water. For example, a portion of the Appalachian Mountains have become rounded and worn down, as shown below. Sediment from the Appalachian Mountains is continually being transported to areas including Florida. In fact, millions of years ago these sediments formed layers of sedimentary rock, which helped build up the land that is Florida today.

Visualize It!

6 Analyze What other states might have sediments from the Appalachian Mountains? Explain.

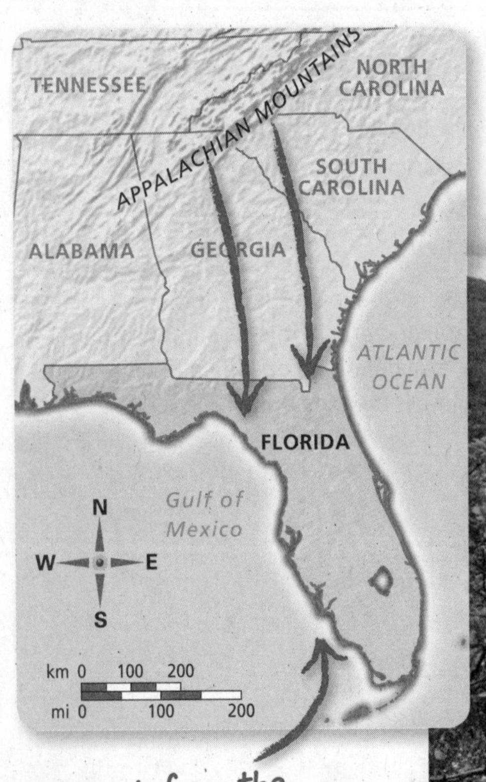

Sediments from the Appalachian Mountains were transported to Florida.

The rounded hills of the Appalachian Mountains in Shenandoah National Park, Virginia.

What is a glacier?

How can mountains get broken down into sediments? One method is through the action of glaciers. A **glacier** (GLAY•sher) is a mass of gradually moving or flowing ice. As snow and ice build on a mountain, the glacier can begin to move down the mountain. Glaciers scrape and relocate rocks as they move, forming sediments. In the photo below, a glacier is moving down through mountains in Alaska, creating sediments. Glaciers can be found at high elevations and near Earth's poles.

An *ice sheet* is a very large glacier that covers a large area. Approximately 18,000 years ago, much of Canada and the northern portion of the United States were covered by an ice sheet. During this glacial period, the sea level on Earth was reduced as the water was stored in the ice. As a result, the land area of Florida was much larger than it is today. Once the ice sheet began to melt, sediments were deposited throughout the United States. In addition, the sea level rose again, altering Florida's shape and size.

Think Outside the Book Inquiry

8 Apply The sand on most beaches was originally produced by the erosion of rock. Imagine you are a piece of sand on a beach in Florida. Describe your life, beginning as a rock at the top of a mountain and ending as a grain of sand on the beach.

Visualize It!

7 Analyze What might happen to the sea level if all the water in Earth's glaciers were suddenly released?

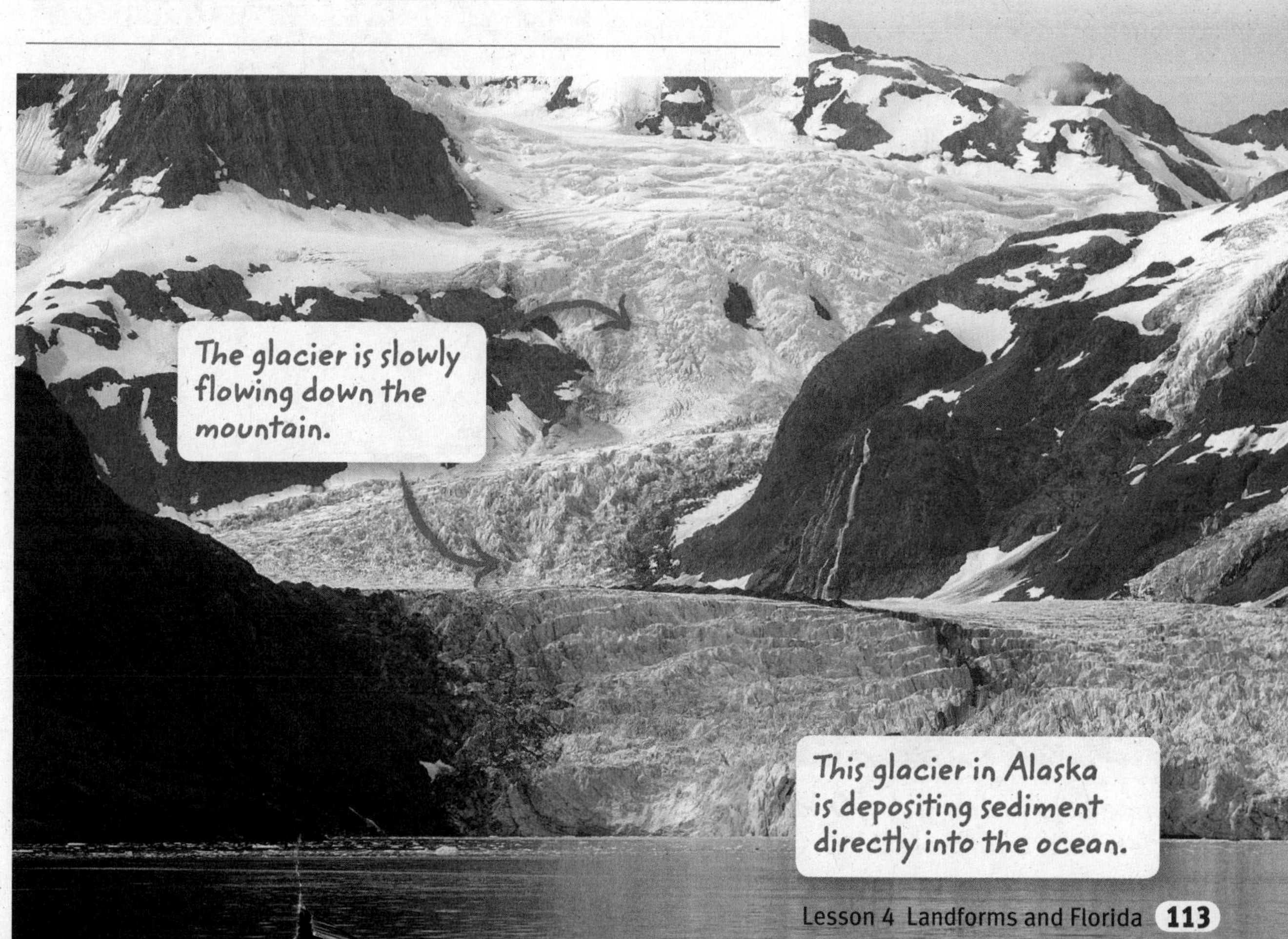

The glacier is slowly flowing down the mountain.
This glacier in Alaska is depositing sediment directly into the ocean.

Let's hit the water!

What is a lake?

Florida has approximately 30,000 lakes of varying size. A **lake** is a body of fresh or salt water that is surrounded by land. Lakes are fed by streams and rivers that carry water and sediment. The largest lake in Florida is Lake Okeechobee (oh•kih•CHOH•bee). This lake is part of a larger water system, called a watershed, that includes the Everglades wetlands area in South Florida.

Many of the lakes in Florida are sinkhole lakes. A sinkhole is a hole in the ground caused by the collapse of an underground cavern. Often, sinkholes become plugged by sediments and later get filled by water, forming sinkhole lakes. Lake Eola in the photo below is a sinkhole lake. If the plugs in a sinkhole are opened, it is like draining the water from a bathtub. In 1999, Lake Jackson near Tallahassee, Florida, drained as the sediment plug opened and the water flowed out, almost draining the entire lake.

Active Reading **9 Identify** How does a sinkhole lake form?

____

____

____

____

Lake Eola in downtown Orlando, Florida, is a sinkhole lake.

What is a river?

Rivers are one method of transporting sediment. A **river** is a large, natural stream of water that flows into an ocean or other large body of water, such as a lake. Rivers start as smaller flowing bodies of water, called streams, at higher elevations. The streams can combine to eventually form rivers that flow along a channel. In Florida, most of the rivers are relatively short and do not flow quickly because of the flat elevation of the state.

Rivers change course over time as they break down the river banks, or sides of the river, and deposit sediment. During times of excessive flow, rivers can flood, leading to significant damage to human structures and farm areas. Examples of Florida rivers include the St. Johns, the Apalachicola (ap•uh•lach•ih•KOH•luh), the Suwannee (suh•WAH•nee), and the Peace.

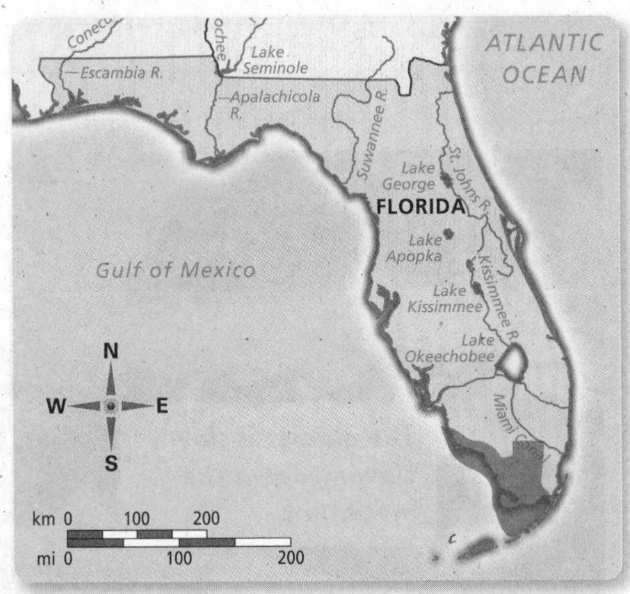

Visualize It!

10 Identify The shaded area at the tip of Florida represents the approximate location of Everglades National Park. How can lakes and rivers in Florida supply water to the Everglades?

____

____

____

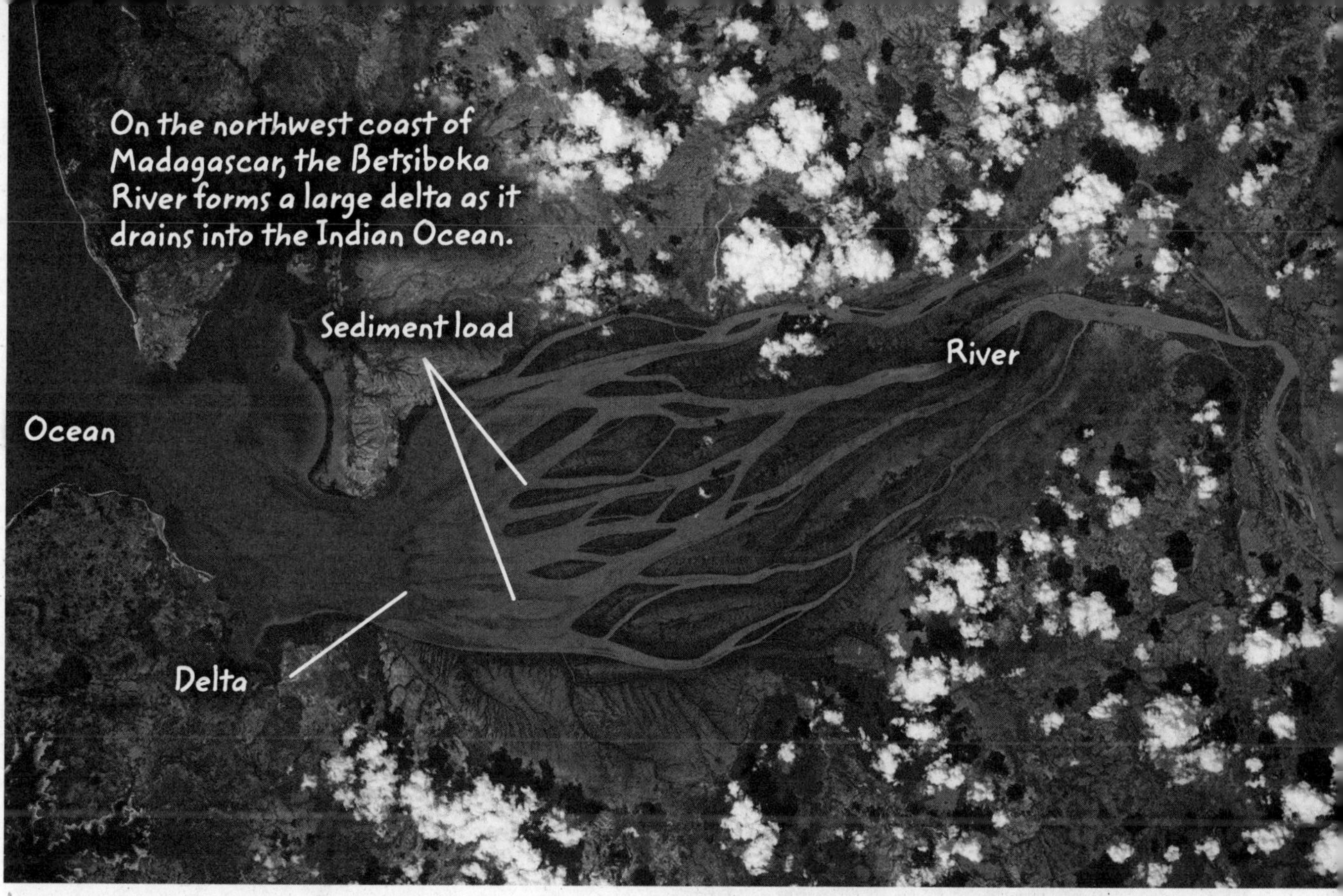

On the northwest coast of Madagascar, the Betsiboka River forms a large delta as it drains into the Indian Ocean.
Sediment load
River
Ocean
Delta

What is a delta?

When a river reaches a lake, ocean, or other body of water, the sediments carried in a river can form a delta. A **delta** (DEL•tuh) is a deposit, formed by sediment, that accumulates at the mouth of a river. These landforms are often, but not always, triangular in shape.

Deltas form as rivers slow down when they reach other bodies of water. When a river is no longer confined within a river channel, the velocity, or speed, of the water is reduced. Once velocity is reduced, the river deposits the sediments previously suspended in the water. The sediment then builds up and extends out from the shore to form a delta.

Most of Florida's rivers carry a limited amount of sediment and do not flow very fast. Therefore, Florida rivers do not form large or significant deltas. An exception to this is the Apalachicola River in the Florida Panhandle. The river is part of a larger river system that begins in the Appalachian Mountains and ends in the Florida Panhandle. Sediments are carried in the river and deposited into the Gulf of Mexico, forming deltas.

Active Reading

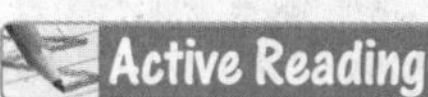

11 Identify As you read, fill in the form below to summarize what you learn about deltas.

Delta

Definition

Formation

Example

Surf's Up

Active Reading

12 Identify As you read, underline the factors that can change the characteristics of a coastline.

What is a coastline?

Florida has a long coastline. A **coastline** is a dynamic boundary between land and the ocean. Coastlines can vary from rocky coasts with high, sharp cliffs, to gently-sloping sandy beaches. A number of factors control the characteristics of coastlines including waves, wind, sediment supply, tides, and the geology of the region.

Coastlines are *dynamic*, or constantly changing. One way a coastline can change is by the action of ocean waves. Ocean waves can slowly break down rock forming sediments along a coastline. Tides can then carry these sediments towards the coast, or away from it. In addition, sea level can change over time, changing the shape and size of coastlines.

The coastline of Florida offers many recreational areas and important shipping ports. On the western coast of Florida, the coastline forms where the land meets the Gulf of Mexico. Beaches there include Pensacola Beach and Clearwater Beach. On the eastern coast, Florida meets the Atlantic Ocean. Beaches include Flagler Beach, Daytona Beach, and Cocoa Beach.

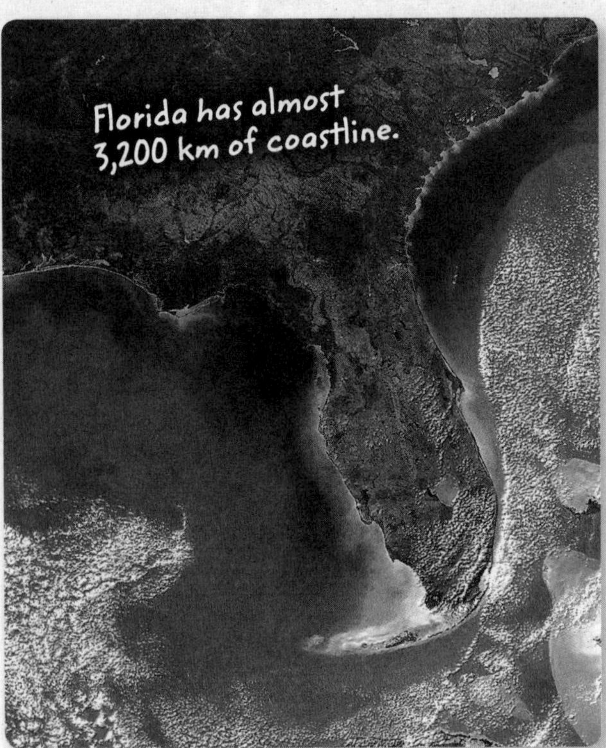
Florida has almost 3,200 km of coastline.

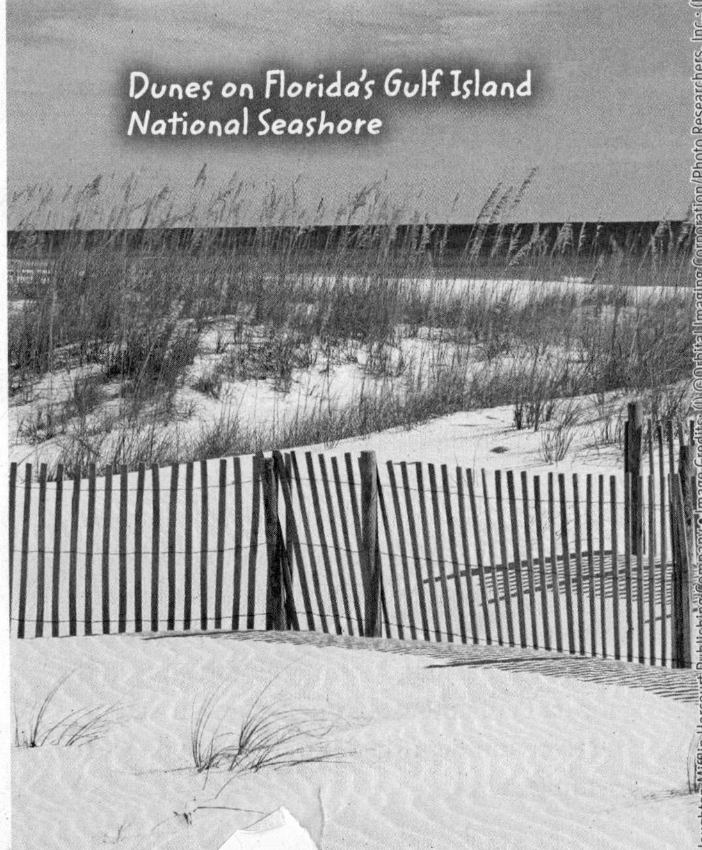
Dunes on Florida's Gulf Island National Seashore

13 Infer Why are coastlines important? List 3 ways you think coastlines might be important to the environment or to humans.

What is a dune?

Sand does not easily stay in one location because of the small size of sand grains. Mounds of sand, as seen in the photo below, often form as wind carries and then deposits sand particles. A **dune** is a mound of wind-deposited sand. Dunes are found in both desert and coastal regions. In the desert, winds can be very strong. Sand gets carried and deposited into varying sizes of dunes, from small hills to mountain-sized dunes.

Coastal dunes form along coastlines. The shape of a beach, the sand supply, the wind direction, and the type of sand can determine the types of dunes formed. Dunes can have a variety of shapes including star-shaped, crescent, and straight dunes. In Florida, coastal dunes are fairly small and are found behind sandy beaches. The dunes offer important protection for many species of plants and animals. Unfortunately, dunes can be destroyed as a result of human activities and natural processes.

Many conservation efforts are used to protect dunes. For example, various types of vegetation, such as sea oats, can be planted on a dune surface. The root systems of these plants help to hold the sand in place, as shown in the photo below. Fences are also installed to help maintain dunes by slowing the wind. Many locations have sand ladders, or wooden walkways, that prevent human trampling of the dunes.

Human activities can affect the location and amount of sand on a beach.

Visualize It!

14 Explain How can a fence protect dunes in Florida?

Visual Summary

To complete this summary, check the box that indicates true or false. Then, use the key below to check your answers. You can use this page to review the main concepts of the lesson.

Landforms

Mountains and glaciers produce sediment.

T F

☐ ☐ **15** Sediment from the Appalachian Mountains helped form Florida.

Lakes and rivers are part of Florida watersheds.

T F

☐ ☐ **16** A river carrying sediment can flow into a lake.

Coastlines have dunes formed by the wind.

T F

☐ ☐ **17** Dunes can occur on coastlines or in the desert.

Deltas form as rivers slow down.

T F

☐ ☐ **18** Deltas commonly form where rivers meet land surfaces.

Answers: 15 True; 16 True; 17 True; 18 False

19 Relate How can processes in other states, and even other countries, affect landforms in Florida?

Lesson Review

Vocabulary

Fill in the blank with the term that best completes the following sentences.

1 A ______________________________ may form where a river enters a large body of water, such as a lake or an ocean.

2 __________________________ is a large body of water surrounded by land.

3 Changes in sea level can result from water being locked inside a __________________________

4 An elevated surface formed by volcanoes or when tectonic plates move together is a ______________________________

Key Concepts

5 Identify List 4 specific examples of different landforms in Florida by completing the table below.

Type of landform	Example

6 Explain How are sediments created and how do those sediments make new landforms?

____

____

____

7 Explain Although there are no glaciers in Florida, how have glaciers affected Florida?

____

____

____

____

____

Critical Thinking

Use this map to answer the following questions.

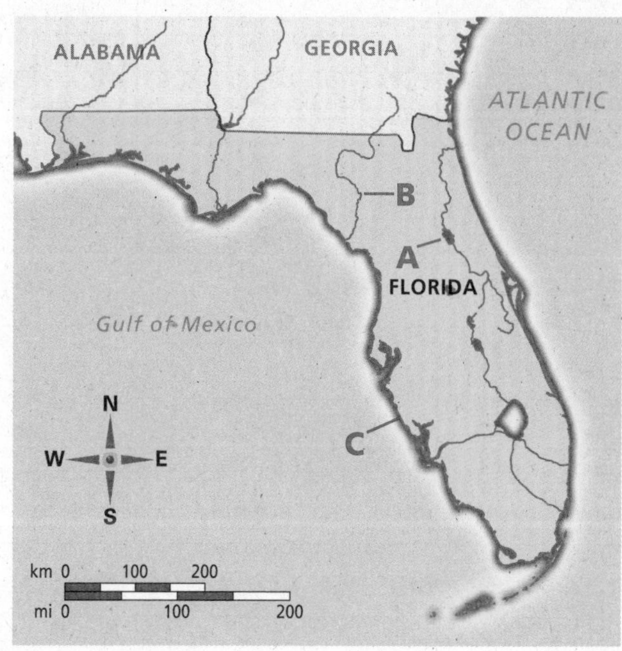

8 Identify Which location is most likely to have a dune? Explain.

____

____

____

9 Apply In location B, what can you conclude about the sediments carried in the river?

____

____

____

10 Analyze If many of the lakes in Florida are sinkhole lakes, what can you conclude about the geology beneath Florida's surface? Explain.

____

____

____

____

____

My Notes

Unit 2 **Summary**

Landforms and Florida

are affected by

Weathering

Erosion and Deposition by Water, Wind, Ice, and Gravity

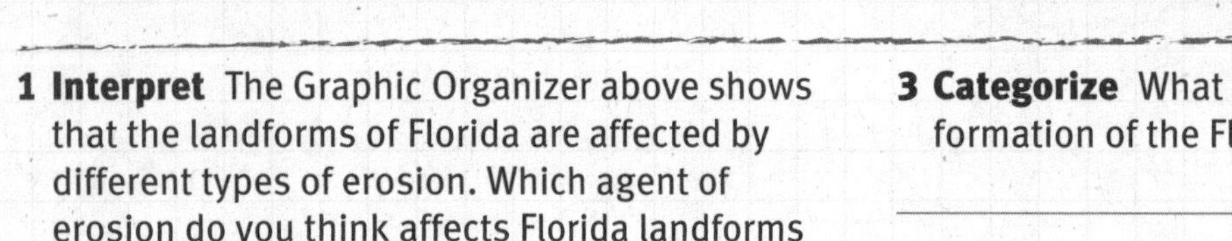

1 Interpret The Graphic Organizer above shows that the landforms of Florida are affected by different types of erosion. Which agent of erosion do you think affects Florida landforms the most?

2 Contrast Distinguish between physical weathering and chemical weathering.

3 Categorize What agent is responsible for the formation of the Florida landforms called dunes?

4 Analyze How do living things contribute to the physical and chemical weathering of rocks?

Benchmark Review

Name ______________________________

Multiple Choice

Identify the choice that best completes the statement or answers the question.

1 Emily used a tray filled with dirt as a model of a stream. Emily poured water into the top of the tray and observed how much erosion happened. Emily then increased the slope of the tray and repeated the experiment.

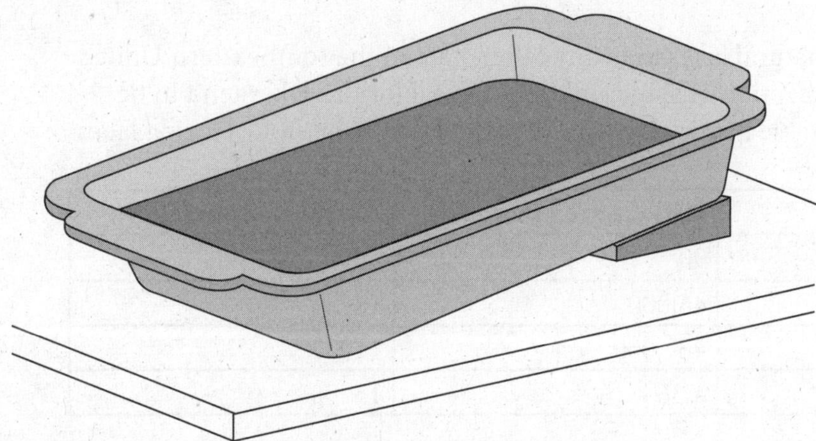

What would happen when the slope of the tray increased?

A. The speed of the water and the amount of erosion would increase.

B. The speed of the water and the amount of erosion would decrease.

C. The speed of the water would increase, while the amount of erosion would decrease.

D. The speed of the water would decrease, while the amount of erosion would increase.

2 All types of glaciers erode the land as they move slowly across it. How would you describe the landscape made by alpine glaciers compared to the landscape made by continental glaciers?

F. Alpine glaciers create U-shaped valleys, and continental glaciers create V-shaped valleys.

G. Alpine glaciers produce rugged landscapes, and continental glaciers produce flat landscapes.

H. Alpine glaciers form smooth landscapes, and continental glaciers form hilly landscapes.

I. Alpine glaciers make flattened landscapes, and continental glaciers make uneven landscapes.

Benchmark Review

3 Crops are often grown on floodplains because floodplains are usually very fertile. What is the **main** reason that floodplains are fertile?

A. Floodplains receive high amounts of rainfall.

B. Their flat surfaces result in little erosion of the soil.

C. Sediment is deposited on the plain each time it floods.

D. The soil takes in and holds the water from each flood.

4 Florida has more natural lakes than any other state in the southeastern United States. With the exception of some sinkhole lakes, Florida's lakes tend to be very shallow. The table below gives some information about four Florida lakes.

Lake	Surface area (acres)	Average depth (ft)
Annie	90	68
George	46,000	10
Okeechobee	467,000	11
Washington	4,364	13

Based on the information, which lake is **most likely** to be a sinkhole lake?

F. Lake Annie

G. George

H. Okeechobee

I. Lake Washington

5 Wind can affect a landscape in many ways. In the desert, wind can remove sediment near the surface, leaving gravel behind. The gravel becomes packed and smooth. What is the term for what is formed by this process?

A. desert gravel

B. desert asphalt

C. desert concrete

D. desert pavement

6 Marley has a vegetable garden in her yard. During a storm, heavy rain falls. The rain runs over the garden, and some of the soil is washed away. Which term **best** describes this movement of soil from one place to another?

F. deposition

G. discharge

H. erosion

I. weathering

7 While on a trip, Veronica saw the landforms shown in the following pictures.

Which of the following processes formed the landforms shown?

A. the transport and deposition of sediment by ice
B. the transport and deposition of sediment by water
C. the transport and deposition of sediment by wind
D. the transport and deposition of sediment by gravity

8 Sediments from mountains many miles away are now in the area known as Florida. Which is the **best** explanation as to how most of these sediments moved so far away from where the mountains are now?

F. The wind blew the sediments there.
G. The sediments were transported and deposited by streams and rivers.
H. This range of mountains used to be much farther south than it is now.
I. Rocks form more small, easily transported sediment on the southern side of mountains.

9 Riley rubs two rocks together. She notices that some of the surface of one of the rocks was worn away to form small particles. What has happened to that rock?

A. It was eroded.
B. It was dissolved.
C. It was exfoliated.
D. It was weathered.

Benchmark Review

10 Rainwater fills in a crack in a rock. The water freezes in a cold climate. After the water thaws, it evaporates. The crack left behind is larger than it was originally.

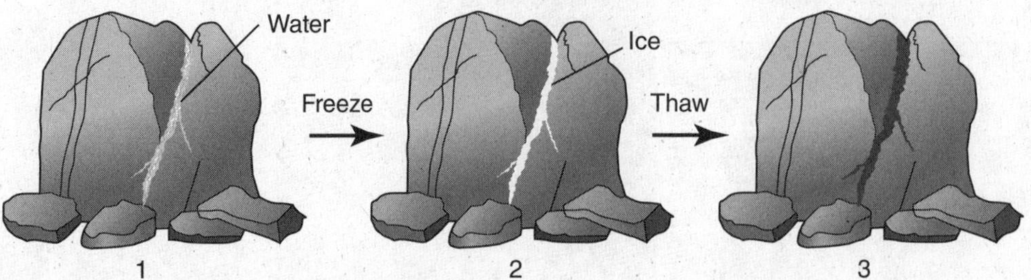

What is the physical weathering factor?

F. air

G. ice

H. rock

I. water

11 For millions of years, large amounts of glacial ice formed on Earth, covering huge areas of land. It then melted, or receded. When large amounts of glacial ice formed, large amounts of water froze. When the glacial ice melted, it released water into the oceans. Based on this information, what effect did glaciers have on the formation of Florida?

A. Florida's coastlines were eroded only during cold periods.

B. Florida's coastlines were eroded only during warm periods.

C. Different parts of Florida's coastlines were eroded during warm and cold periods.

D. Florida's mountains were eroded only during warm periods.

12 Sandy beaches make up most of the Florida coastline. Beach sand is the product of abrasion. Which is an example of abrasion of a rock?

F. a color change due to exposure to air

G. a shape change due to exposure to wind

H. a hole forming due to a reaction with water

I. a layer falling off due to a lessening of pressure

UNIT 3

Energy in the Earth System

Big Idea 7

Earth Systems and Patterns

Waves break on the reef crest, which protects the lagoon and shoreline behind it from the energy of the waves.

Organisms of the reef crest can stand high-energy waves.

What do you think?

Large amounts of energy can be transferred from one place to another through winds and waves. Sometimes, winds and waves can be destructive. How do we protect ourselves from powerful winds and waves?

Unit 3

Energy in the Earth System

CITIZEN SCIENCE

Clearing the Air

In some areas, there are many vehicles on the roads every day. Some of the gases from vehicle exhausts react with sunlight to form ozone. There are days when the concentration of ozone is so high that it becomes a health hazard. Those days are especially difficult for people who have problems breathing. What can you do to reduce gas emissions?

1 Think About It

A How do you get to school every day?

____

____

____

B How many of the students in your class come to school by car?

____

Gas emissions are high during rush-hour traffic.

2 Ask a Question

How can you reduce the number of vehicles students use to get to school one day each month?

With your teacher and classmates, brainstorm different ways in which you can reduce the number of vehicles students use to get to school.

Ride a bicycle to school.

Check off the points below as you use them to design your plan.

- ☐ how far a student lives from school
- ☐ the kinds of transportation students may have available to them

3 Make a Plan

A Write down different ways that you can reduce the number of vehicles that bring students to school.

B Create a short presentation for your principal that outlines how the whole school could become involved in your vehicle-reduction plan. Write down the points of your presentation in the space below.

C In the space below, design a sign-up sheet that your classmates will use to choose how they will come to school on the designated day.

Take It Home

Give your presentation to an adult. Then have them brainstorm ways in which they can reduce gas emissions every day.

Lesson 1

Earth's Spheres

ESSENTIAL QUESTION

What are the parts of the Earth system?

By the end of this lesson, you should be able to describe Earth's spheres and provide examples of interactions between the spheres.

Emperor penguins spend time on land, and need to breathe in oxygen from the air.

These penguins also swim and hold their breath for about 18 min as they hunt for fish. What do you have in common with these penguins?

Sunshine State Standards

SC.6.E.7.4 Differentiate and show interactions among the geosphere, hydrosphere, cryosphere, atmosphere, and biosphere.

MA.6.A.3.6 Construct and analyze tables, graphs, and equations to describe linear functions and other simple relations using both common language and algebraic notation.

Engage Your Brain

1 Predict Check T or F to show whether you think each statement is true or false.

T	F	
☐	☐	Earth is made up completely of solid rocks.
☐	☐	Animals live only on land.
☐	☐	Water in rivers often flows into the ocean.
☐	☐	Air in the atmosphere can move all over the world.

2 Analyze Think about your daily activities and list some of the ways in which you interact with Earth.

Active Reading

3 Synthesize You can often define an unknown word if you know the meaning of its word parts. Use the word parts and sentence below to make an educated guess about the meaning of the word *geosphere*.

Word part	Meaning
geo-	earth
-sphere	ball

Example sentence:
Water flows across the surface of the geosphere.

geosphere:

Vocabulary Terms

- **Earth system**
- **geosphere**
- **hydrosphere**
- **cryosphere**
- **atmosphere**
- **biosphere**

4 Apply As you learn the definition of each vocabulary term in this lesson, create your own notecards to help you remember the meaning of the term.

What on Earth?

What is the Earth system?

A system is a group of related objects or parts that work together to form a whole. From the center of the planet to the outer edge of the atmosphere, Earth is a system. The **Earth system** is all of the matter, energy, and processes within Earth's boundary. Earth is a complex system made up of many smaller systems. The Earth system is made of nonliving things, such as rocks, air, and water. It also contains living things, such as trees, animals, and people. Matter and energy continuously cycle through the smaller systems that make up the Earth system. The Earth system can be divided into five main parts—the geosphere (JEE•oh•sfir), the hydrosphere (HY•druh•sfir), the cryosphere (KRY•uh•sfir), the atmosphere, and the biosphere.

Visualize It!

5 Identify Fill in the boxes under each of the three labels that have lines. List an example of that sphere. Write whether that example is a living thing or a nonliving thing.

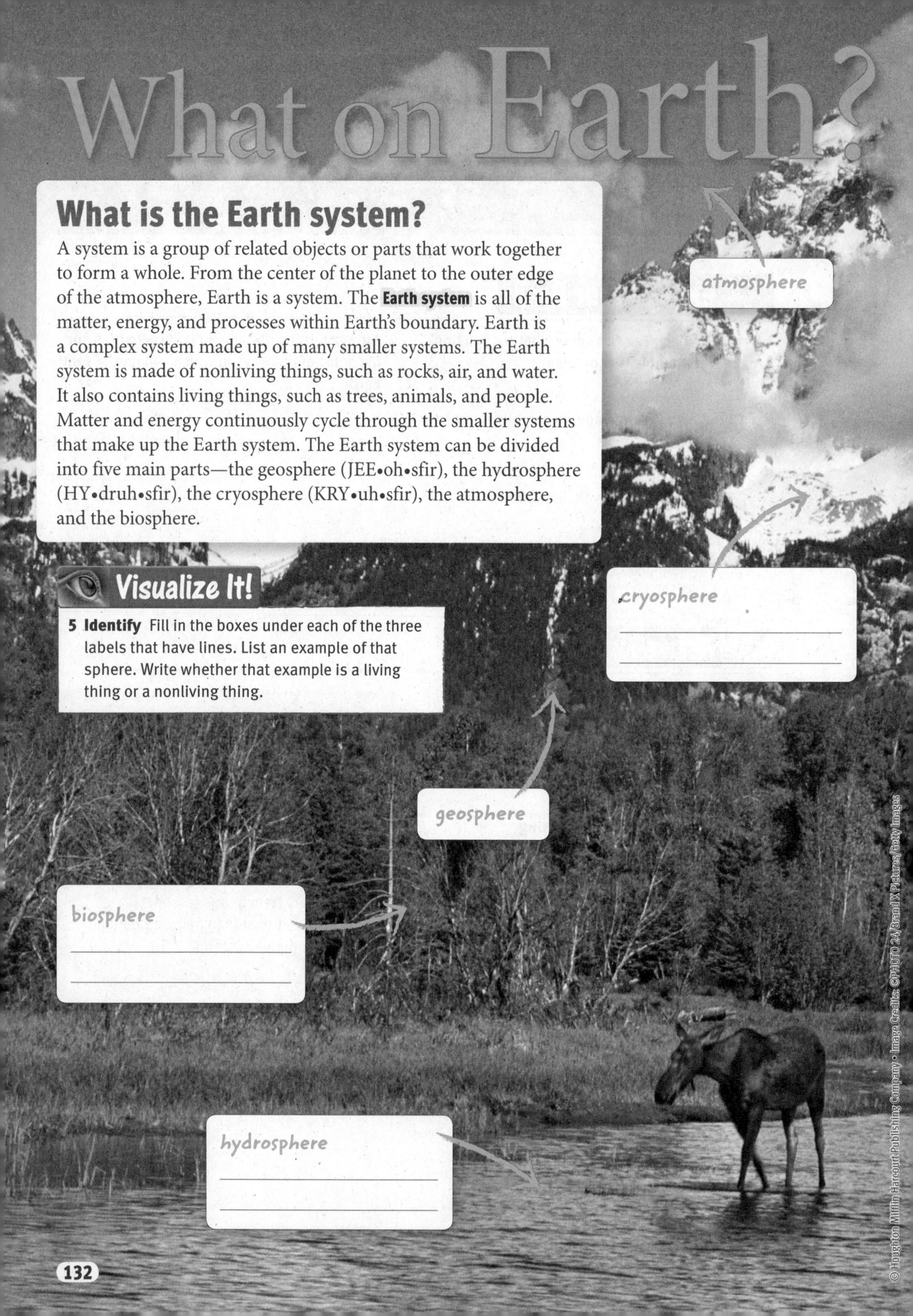

atmosphere

cryosphere

___

___

geosphere

biosphere

___

___

hydrosphere

___

___

What is the geosphere?

Active Reading **6 Identify** As you read, underline what each of the three different compositional layers of the geosphere is made up of.

The **geosphere** is the mostly solid, rocky part of Earth. It extends from the center of Earth to the surface of Earth. The geosphere is divided into three layers based on chemical composition: the crust, the mantle, and the core.

The crust is the thin, outermost layer of the geosphere. The crust is divided into plates that move slowly over Earth's surface. The crust beneath the oceans is called oceanic crust, and is only 5 to 10 km thick. The continents are made of continental crust, and ranges in thickness from about 15 to 70 km. Continental crust is thickest beneath mountain ranges. The crust is made mostly of silicate minerals.

The mantle lies just below the crust. A small layer of the solid mantle, right below the crust, is just soft enough to flow. Movements in this layer move the plates of the crust. The mantle is about 2,900 km thick. It is made of silicate minerals that are more dense than those in the crust are.

The central part of Earth is the core, which has a radius of 3,400 km. It is made of iron and nickel and is very dense.

Crust
The crust is the thin, solid outermost layer of Earth. It is made mostly of silicates.

Mantle
The mantle is the hot layer of rock between Earth's crust and core. The mantle is more dense than Earth's crust is.

Core
The core is Earth's center. The core is about twice as dense as the mantle is.

7 Summarize Fill in the table below, with the characteristics of each of the geosphere's compositional layers.

Compositional layer	Thickness	Relative density

Got Water?

What is the hydrosphere?

The **hydrosphere** is the part of Earth that is liquid water. Ninety-seven percent of all of the water on Earth is the saltwater found in the oceans. Oceans cover 71% of Earth's surface. The hydrosphere also includes the water in lakes, rivers, and marshes. Clouds and rain are also parts of the hydrosphere. Even water that is underground is part of the hydrosphere.

The water on Earth is constantly moving. It moves through the ocean in currents, because of wind and differences in the density of ocean waters. Water also moves from Earth's surface to the air by evaporation. It falls back to Earth as rain. It flows in rivers and through rocks under the ground. It even moves into and out of living things.

Active Reading

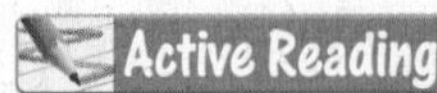

8 Identify What are two things through which water moves?

____

____

Visualize It!

9 Identify Write whether the example of water in each photo is part of the hydrosphere or the cryosphere.

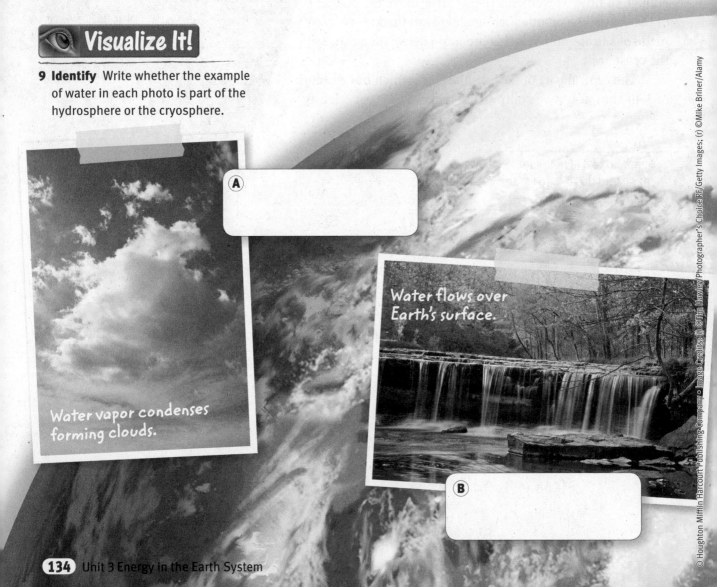

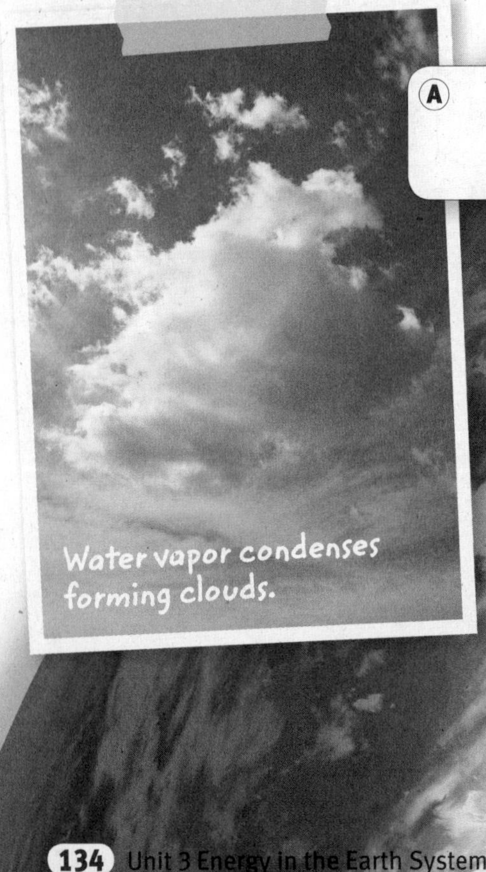

Water vapor condenses forming clouds.

A ______________________

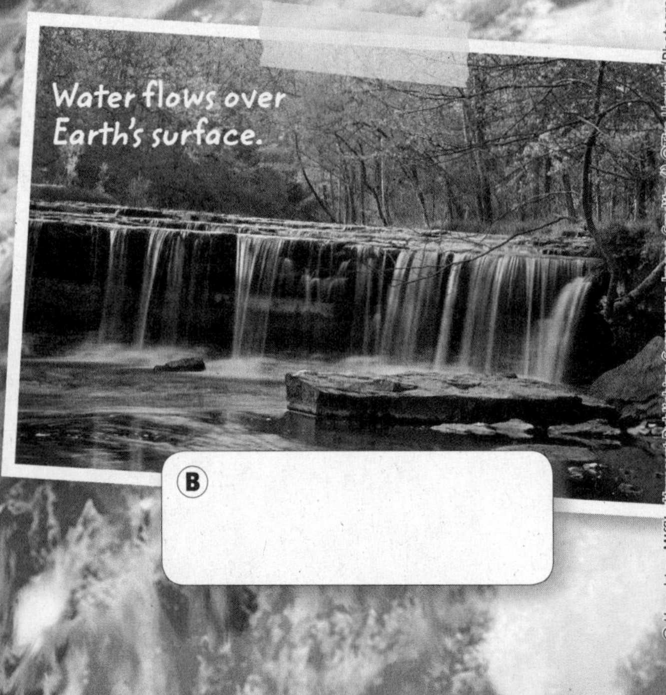

Water flows over Earth's surface.

B ______________________

What is the cryosphere?

Earth's **cryosphere** is made up of all of the frozen water on Earth. Therefore, all of the snow, ice, sea ice, glaciers, ice shelves, icebergs, and frozen ground are a part of the cryosphere. Most of the frozen water on Earth is found in the ice caps in Antarctica and in the Arctic. However, snow and glaciers are found in the mountains and at high latitudes all over the world. The amount of frozen water in most of these areas often changes with the seasons. These changes, in turn, play an important role in Earth's climate and in the survival of many species.

10 Compare Fill in the Venn diagram to compare and contrast the hydrosphere and the cryosphere.

Hydrosphere	Both	Cryosphere

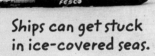

Ships can get stuck in ice-covered seas.

Ⓒ

Ⓓ

Water moves in ocean currents across huge distances.

What a Gas!

What is the atmosphere?

The **atmosphere** is a mixture of mostly invisible gases that surrounds Earth. The atmosphere extends outward about 500 to 600 km from the surface of Earth. But most of the gases lie within 8 to 50 km of Earth's surface. The main gases that make up the atmosphere are nitrogen and oxygen. About 78% of the atmosphere is nitrogen. Oxygen makes up 21% of the atmosphere. The remaining 1% is made of many other gases, including argon, carbon dioxide, and water vapor.

The atmosphere contains the air we breathe. The atmosphere also traps some of the energy from the sun's rays. This energy helps keep Earth warm enough for living things to survive, and multiply. Uneven warming by the sun gives rise to winds and air currents that move large amounts of air around the world.

Parts of the atmosphere absorb and reflect harmful ultraviolet (UV) rays from the sun, protecting Earth and its living things. Other parts of the atmosphere cause space debris to burn up before reaching Earth's surface and causing harm. Have you ever seen the tail of a meteor across the sky? Then you have seen a meteoroid burning up as it moves through the atmosphere!

Do the Math **You Try It**

11 Identify Fill in the blank in the key with the percentage of oxygen in the atmosphere.

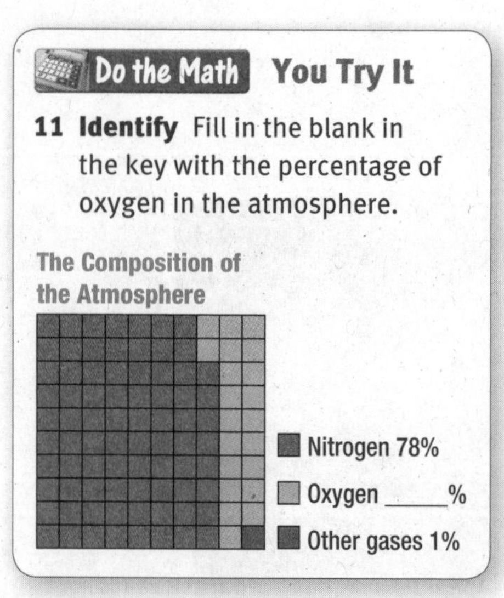

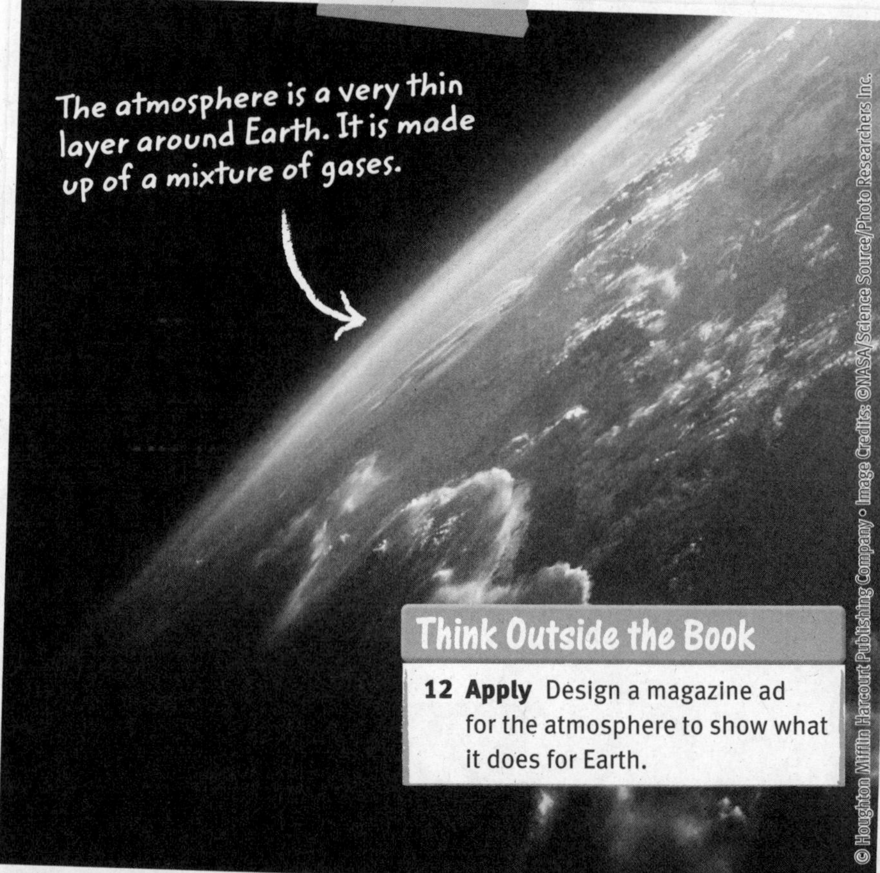

The atmosphere is a very thin layer around Earth. It is made up of a mixture of gases.

Think Outside the Book

12 Apply Design a magazine ad for the atmosphere to show what it does for Earth.

What is the biosphere?

The **biosphere** is made up of living things and the areas of Earth where they are found. The rocks, soil, oceans, lakes, rivers, and lower atmosphere all support life. Organisms have even been found deep in Earth's crust and high in clouds. But no matter where they live, all organisms need certain factors to survive.

Many organisms need oxygen or carbon dioxide to carry out life processes. Liquid water is also important for most living things. Many organisms also need moderate temperatures. You will not find a polar bear living in a desert because it is too hot for the polar bear. However, some organisms do live in extreme environments, such as in ice at the poles and at volcanic vents on the sea floor.

A stable source of energy is also important for life. For example, plants and algae use the energy from sunlight to make their food. Other organisms get their energy by eating these plants or algae.

Active Reading

13 Identify What factors are needed for life?

____

____

Visualize It! Inquiry

14 Predict What would happen if the biosphere in this picture stopped interacting with the atmosphere?

____

____

____

____

____

____

These crabs and clams live on the deep ocean floor where it is pitch dark. They rely on special bacteria for their food. Why are these bacteria special? They eat crude oil.

The hair on the sloth looks green because it has algae in it. The green color helps the sloth hide from predators. This is very useful because the sloth moves very, very slowly.

What's the Matter?

How do Earth's spheres interact?

Earth's spheres interact as matter and energy change and cycle between the five different spheres. A result of these interactions is that they make life on Earth possible. Remember that the Earth system includes all of the matter, energy, and processes within Earth's boundary.

If matter or energy never changed from one form to another, life on Earth would not be possible. Imagine what would happen if there were no more rain and all of the freshwater drained into the oceans. Most of the life on land would quickly die. But how do these different spheres interact? An example of an interaction is when water cycles between land, ocean, air, and living things. To move between these different spheres, water absorbs, releases, and transports energy all over the world in its different forms.

Visualize It!

15 Analyze Fill in the boxes below each photo with the names of at least two spheres that are interacting in that photo.

Rain provides water for living things.
A
The deer carcass is being decomposed by many kinds of organisms.
B

Matter Can Be Exchanged Between Spheres

Earth's spheres interact as matter moves between spheres. For example, the atmosphere interacts with the hydrosphere or cryosphere when rain or snow falls from the air. The opposite also happens as water from the hydrosphere and cryosphere moves into the atmosphere.

Sometimes, matter moves through different spheres. For example, some bacteria in the biosphere remove nitrogen gas from the atmosphere. These bacteria then release a different form of nitrogen into the soil, or geosphere. Plants in the biosphere use this nitrogen to grow. When the plant dies and decays, the nitrogen is released in different forms. One of these forms returns to the atmosphere.

Active Reading **16 Identify** What is the relationship between Earth's spheres and matter?

____

Energy Can Be Exchanged Between Spheres

Earth's spheres also interact as energy moves between them. For example, plants use solar energy to make their food. Some of this energy is passed on to animals that eat plants. Some of the energy is released into the atmosphere as heat as the animals move around. Some of the energy is released into the geosphere when organisms die and decay. In this case, energy entered the biosphere and moved into the atmosphere and geosphere.

Energy also moves back and forth between spheres. For example, solar energy reflected by Earth's surface warms up the atmosphere, creating winds. Winds create waves and surface ocean currents that travel across the world's oceans. When warm winds and ocean currents reach colder areas, thermal energy moves into the colder air, warming it up. In this case, the energy has cycled between the atmosphere and the hydrosphere.

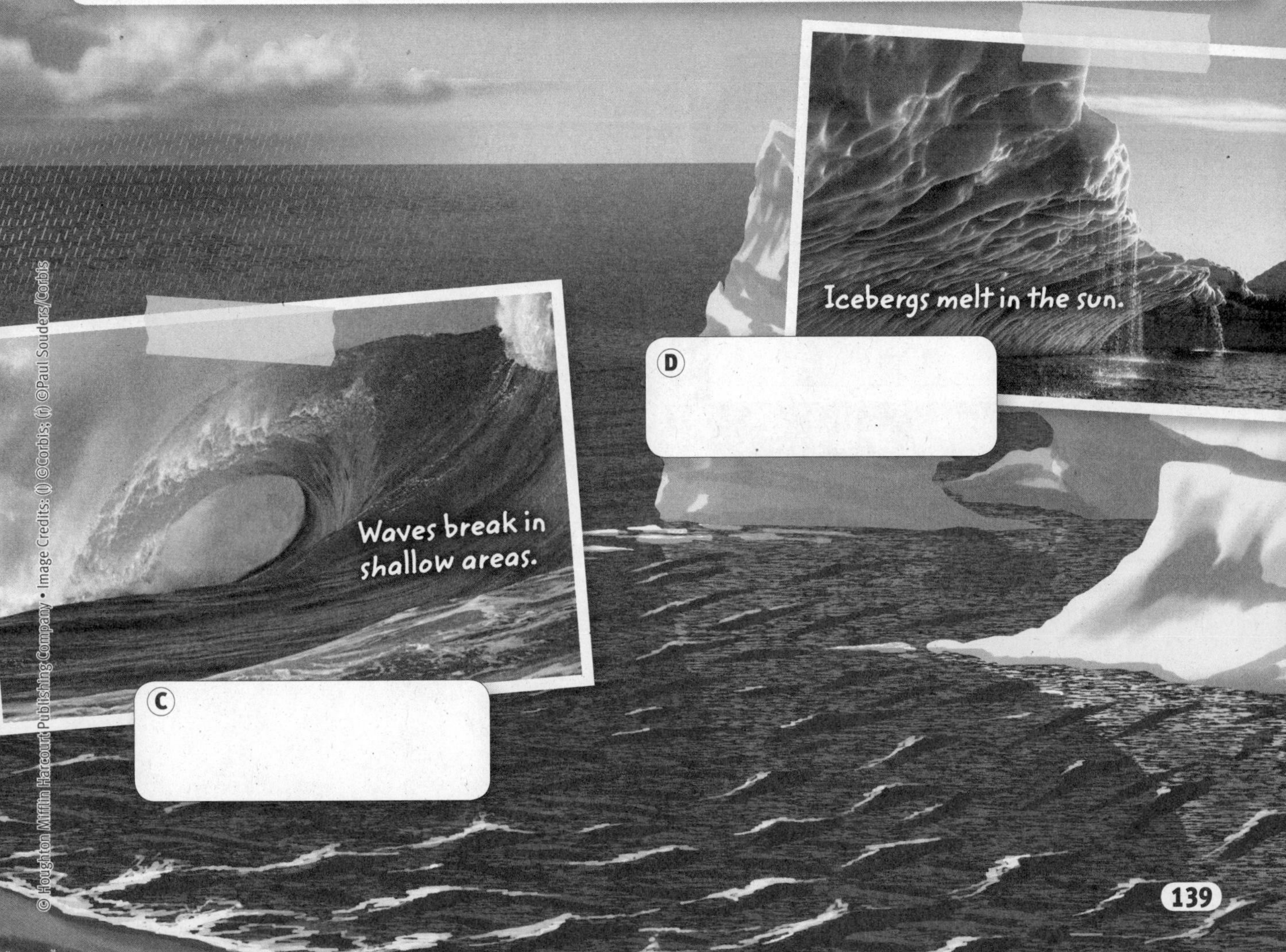
Icebergs melt in the sun.
D
Waves break in shallow areas.
C

Visual Summary

To complete this summary, fill in the box below each photo with the name of the sphere being shown in the photo. Then use the key below to check your answers. You can use this page to review the main concepts of the lesson.

Earth's Spheres

17 ______________________

18 ______________________

21 ______________________

20 ______________________

19 ______________________

Answers: 17 geosphere; 18 biosphere; 19 cryosphere; 20 hydrosphere; 21 atmosphere

22 Synthesize Diagram an interaction between any two of Earth's spheres.

Lesson Review

Vocabulary

Circle the term that best completes each of the following sentences.

1 The ice caps in the Antarctic and the Arctic are a part of the *geosphere/cryosphere/biosphere.*

2 Most of the water on Earth can be found in the *biosphere/hydrosphere/geosphere.*

3 The *hydrosphere/geosphere/atmosphere* protects organisms that live on Earth by blocking out harmful UV rays from the sun.

Key Concepts

Location	Sphere
4 Identify Forms a thin layer of gases around Earth	
5 Identify Extends from Earth's core to Earth's crust	
6 Identify Extends from inside Earth's crust to the lower atmosphere	

7 Describe What does the Earth system include?

8 Analyze Which spheres are interacting when a volcano erupts and releases gases into the air?

9 Identify What are the two most common gases in the atmosphere?

10 Describe How do Earth's spheres interact?

Critical Thinking

Use this graph to answer the following question.

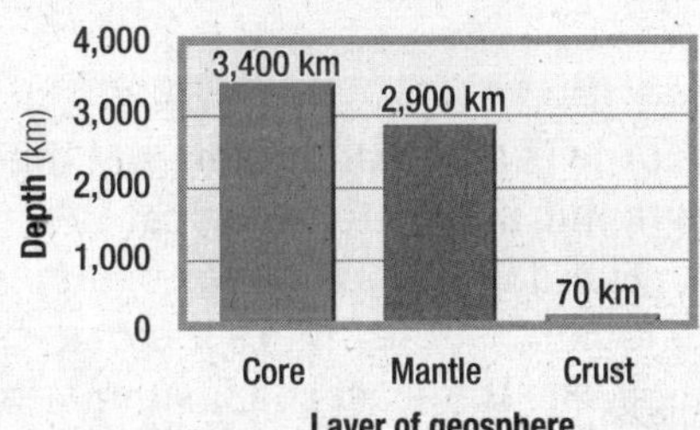

11 Analyze What is the diameter of the geosphere?

12 Identify Name two ways in which the Earth system relies on energy from the sun?

13 Analyze How does the biosphere rely on the other spheres for survival?

14 Infer Where is most of the liquid water on Earth, and what would have to be done so that humans could drink it?

People in Science

Evan B. Forde

OCEANOGRAPHER

Pillow lava on the ocean floor, seen from ***Alvin***

Evan B. Forde is an oceanographer at the Atlantic Oceanographic and Meteorological Laboratory in Miami, Florida. His main areas of study have included looking at the different processes occurring in the U.S. east coast submarine canyons. To study these canyons, Evan became the first African American to participate in research dives in underwater submersibles—machines that can take a human being under water safely—such as *Alvin*. He is currently studying how conditions in the atmosphere relate to the formation of hurricanes.

Evan graduated with degrees in Geology and Marine Geology and Geophysics from Columbia University in New York City. Along with his scientific research, he is committed to science education. He has developed and taught courses on Tropical Meteorology at the University of Miami. Keeping younger students in mind, he created an oceanography course for middle-school students through the Miami-Dade Public Libraries. Evan speaks often to students about oceanography and the sciences, and is involved with many community youth projects.

Social Studies Connection

Mendocino Canyons
Monterey Canyon
Sur Canyon
Hueneme Canyon
Santa Monica Canyon
Redondo Canyon
Scripps Canyon
La Jolla Canyon
San Francisco
CALIFORNIA
Los Angeles
San Diego
BAJA CALIFORNIA
MEXICO
PACIFIC OCEAN
N
W
E
S
San Lucas Canyon

Research the Monterey Submarine Canyon shown on the map. Find out its size and if it is still considered one of the largest canyons off the Pacific Coast. Research the kind of organisms that can live there.

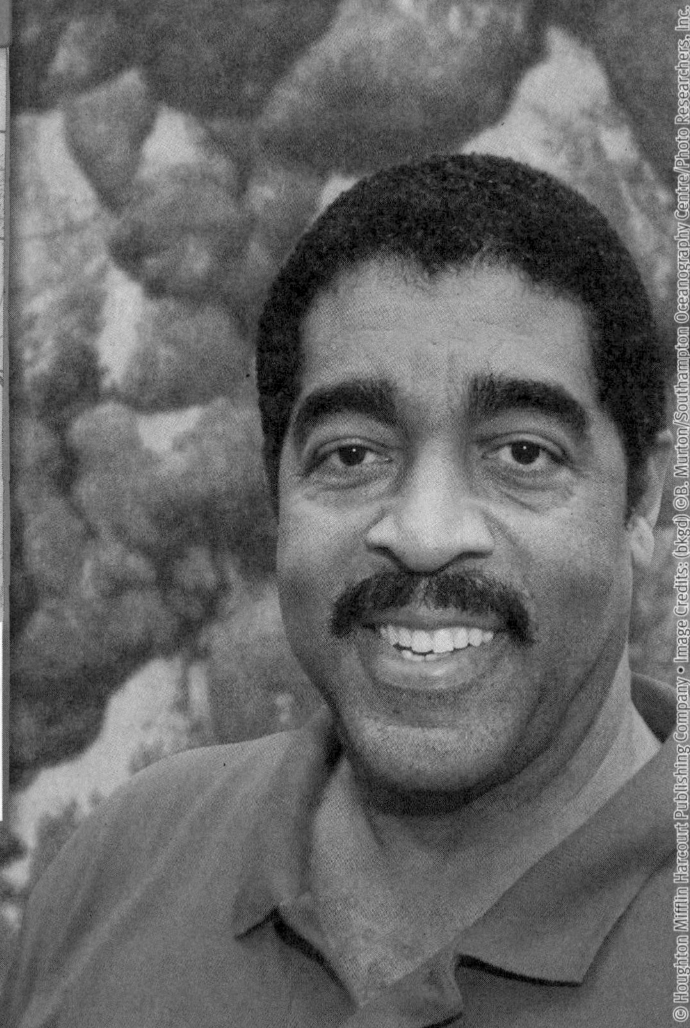

Evan B. Forde

JOB BOARD

Wind Turbine Technician

What You'll Do: Operate and maintain wind turbine units, including doing repairs and preventative maintenance.

Where You Might Work: You will need to travel often to the different wind farms that have wind turbines. Some technicians may have the chance to travel to wind farms in different countries to complete repairs on wind turbines.

Education: Typically, technicians will graduate from a wind energy program. Technicians should have a solid understanding of math, meteorology, computer, and problem solving skills.

Other Job Requirements: To do these tasks, you will need to climb wind towers as high as 125 meters, so it is helpful if you do not have a fear of heights.

Environmental Engineering Technician

What You'll Do: Help environmental engineers and scientists prevent, control, and get rid of environmental hazards. Inspect, test, decontaminate, and operate equipment used to control and help fix environmental pollution.

Where You Might Work: Offices, laboratories, or industrial plants. Most technicians have to complete field work, so they do spend time working outdoors in all types of weather.

Education: You will need an associate's degree in environmental engineering technology, environmental technology, or hazardous materials information systems technology.

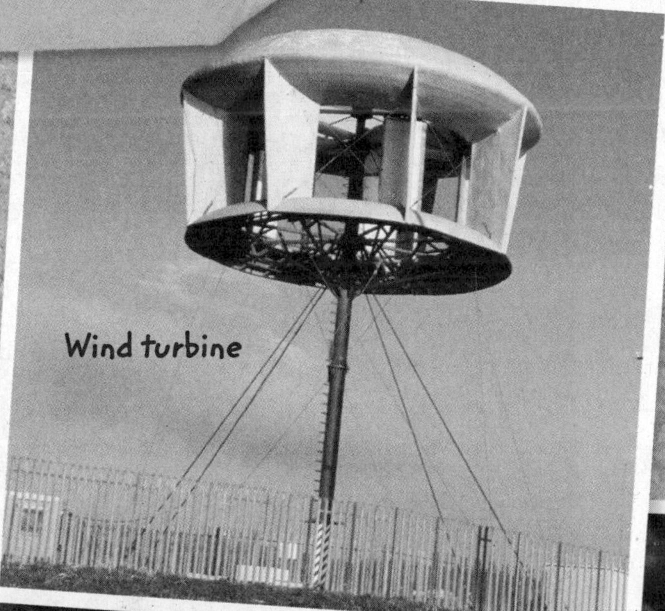
Wind turbine

Lesson 2

The Atmosphere

ESSENTIAL QUESTION

What is the atmosphere?

By the end of this lesson, you should be able to describe the composition and structure of the atmosphere and explain how the atmosphere protects life and insulates Earth.

The atmosphere is a very thin layer compared to the whole Earth. However, it is essential for life on our planet.

Sunshine State Standards

SC.6.E.7.9 Describe how the composition and structure of the atmosphere protects life and insulates the planet.

Engage Your Brain

1 Predict Check T or F to show whether you think each statement is true or false.

T	F	
☐	☐	Oxygen is in the air we breathe.
☐	☐	Pressure is not a property of air.
☐	☐	The air around you is part of the atmosphere.
☐	☐	As you climb up a mountain, the temperature usually gets warmer.

2 Explain Does the air in this balloon have mass? Why or why not?

Active Reading

3 Synthesize Many English words have their roots in other languages. Use the ancient Greek words below to make an educated guess about the meanings of the words *atmosphere* and *mesosphere*.

Greek word	Meaning
atmos	vapor
mesos	middle
sphaira	ball

atmosphere:

mesosphere:

Vocabulary Terms

- **atmosphere**
- **air pressure**
- **thermosphere**
- **mesosphere**
- **stratosphere**
- **troposphere**
- **ozone layer**
- **greenhouse effect**

4 Apply As you learn the definition of each vocabulary term in this lesson, create your own definition or sketch to help you remember the meaning of the term.

Up and Away!

What is Earth's atmosphere?

The mixture of gases that surrounds Earth is the **atmosphere**. This mixture is most often referred to as air. The atmosphere has many important functions. It protects you from the sun's damaging rays and also helps to maintain the right temperature range for life on Earth. For example, the temperature range on Earth allows us to have an abundant amount of liquid water. Many of the components of the atmosphere are essential for life, such as the oxygen you breathe.

A Mixture of Gases and Small Particles

As shown below, the atmosphere is made mostly of nitrogen gas (78%) and oxygen gas (21%). The other 1% is other gases. The atmosphere also contains small particles such as dust, volcanic ash, sea salt, and smoke. There are even small pieces of skin, bacteria, and pollen floating in the atmosphere!

Water is also found in the atmosphere. Liquid water, as water droplets, and solid water, as snow and ice crystals, are found in clouds. But most water in the atmosphere exists as an invisible gas called water vapor. Under certain conditions, water vapor can change into solid or liquid water. Then, snow or rain might fall from the sky.

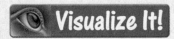

Visualize It!

5 Identify Fill in the missing percentage for oxygen.

Nitrogen is the most abundant gas in the atmosphere.

Oxygen is the second most abundant gas in the atmosphere.

The remaining 1% of the atmosphere is made up of argon, carbon dioxide, water vapor, and other gases.

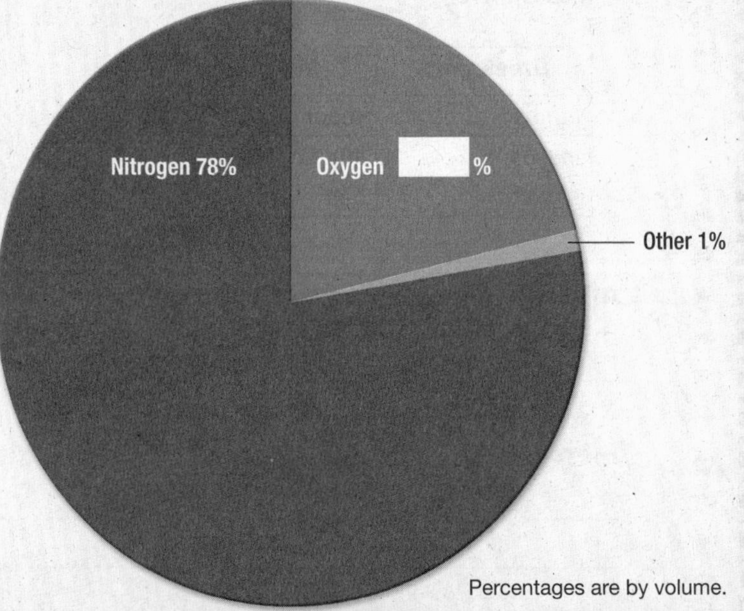

How do pressure and temperature change in the atmosphere?

The atmosphere is held around Earth by gravity. Gravity pulls gas molecules in the atmosphere toward Earth's surface, causing air pressure. **Air pressure** is the measure of the force with which air molecules push on an area of a surface. At sea level, air pressure is over 1 lb for every square centimeter of your body. That is like carrying a 1-liter bottle of water on the tip of your finger!

However, air pressure is not the same throughout the atmosphere. Although there are many gas molecules that surround you on Earth, there are fewer and fewer gas molecules in the air as you move away from Earth's surface. So, as altitude increases, air pressure decreases.

As altitude increases, air temperature also changes. These changes are mainly due to the way solar energy is absorbed in the atmosphere. Some parts of the atmosphere are warmer because they contain a high percentage of gases that absorb solar energy. Other parts of the atmosphere contain less of these gases and are cooler.

Active Reading

6 Identify As you read, underline what happens to temperature and to pressure as altitude increases.

Inquiry

7 Explain Why does a mountain climber need an oxygen supply at very high altitudes, even though the air still contains 21% oxygen?

____

____

____

At high altitudes such as the top of Mount Everest, air pressure and temperature are lower than they are at sea level.

Look Way Up

What are the layers of the atmosphere?

Earth's atmosphere is divided into four layers, based on temperature and other properties. As shown at the right, these layers are the troposphere (TROH•puh•sfir), stratosphere (STRAT•uh•sfir), mesosphere (MEZ•uh•sfir), and thermosphere (THER•muh•sfir). Although these names sound complicated, they give you clues about the layers' features. *Tropo-* means "turning" or "change," and the troposphere is the layer where gases turn and mix. *Strato-* means "layer," and the stratosphere is where gases are layered and do not mix very much. *Meso-* means "middle," and the mesosphere is the middle layer. Finally, *thermo-* means "heat," and the thermosphere is the layer where temperatures are highest.

Think Outside the Book

8 Describe Research the part of the thermosphere called the ionosphere. Describe what the aurora borealis is.

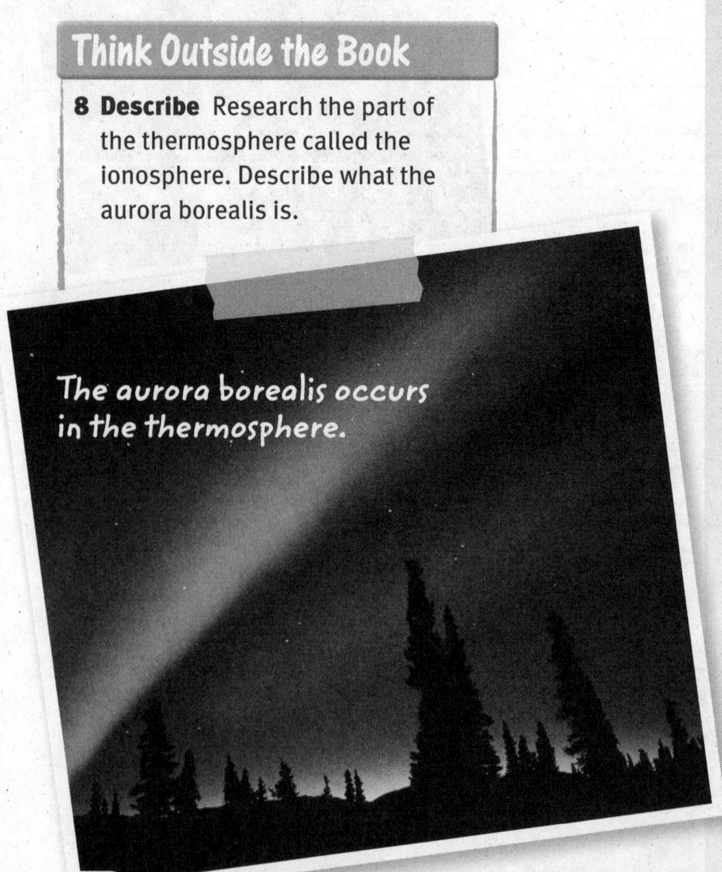

The aurora borealis occurs in the thermosphere.

Thermosphere

The **thermosphere** is the uppermost layer of the atmosphere. The temperature increases as altitude increases because gases in the thermosphere absorb high-energy solar radiation. Temperatures in the thermosphere can be 1,500 °C or higher. However, the thermosphere feels cold. The density of particles in the thermosphere is very low. Too few gas particles collide with your body to transfer heat energy to your skin.

Mesosphere

The **mesosphere** is between the thermosphere and stratosphere. In this layer, the temperature decreases as altitude increases. Temperatures can be as low as –120 °C at the top of the mesosphere. Meteoroids begin to burn up in the mesosphere.

Stratosphere

The **stratosphere** is between the mesosphere and troposphere. In this layer, temperatures generally increase as altitude increases. Ozone in the stratosphere absorbs ultraviolet radiation from the sun, which warms the air. An ozone molecule is made of three atoms of oxygen. Gases in the stratosphere are layered and do not mix very much.

Troposphere

The **troposphere** is the lowest layer of the atmosphere. Although temperatures near Earth's surface vary greatly, generally, temperature decreases as altitude increases. This layer contains almost 80% of the atmosphere's total mass, making it the densest layer. Almost all of Earth's carbon dioxide, water vapor, clouds, air pollution, weather, and life forms are in the troposphere.

Visualize It!

In the graph, the green line shows pressure change with altitude. The red line shows temperature change with altitude.

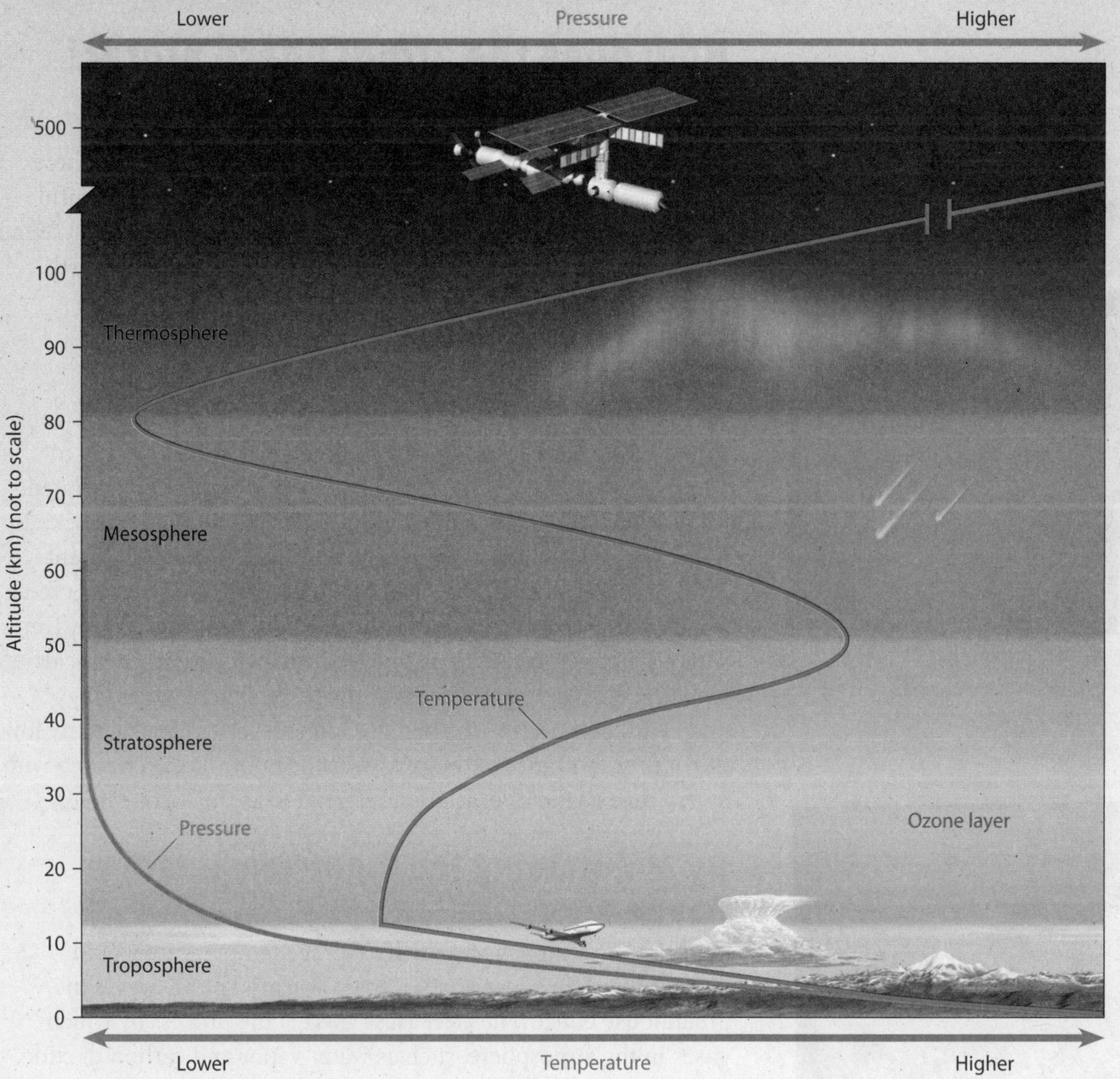

The layers of the atmosphere are defined by changes in temperature.

9 Analyze Using the graph and descriptions provided, indicate if air pressure and temperature increase or decrease with increased altitude in each layer of the atmosphere. One answer has been provided for you.

Layer	Air pressure	Temperature
Thermosphere	decreases	
Mesosphere		
Stratosphere		
Troposphere		

Here Comes

How does the atmosphere protect life on Earth?

The atmosphere surrounds and protects Earth. The atmosphere provides the air we breathe. It also protects Earth from harmful solar radiation and from space debris that enters the Earth system. In addition, the atmosphere controls the temperature on Earth.

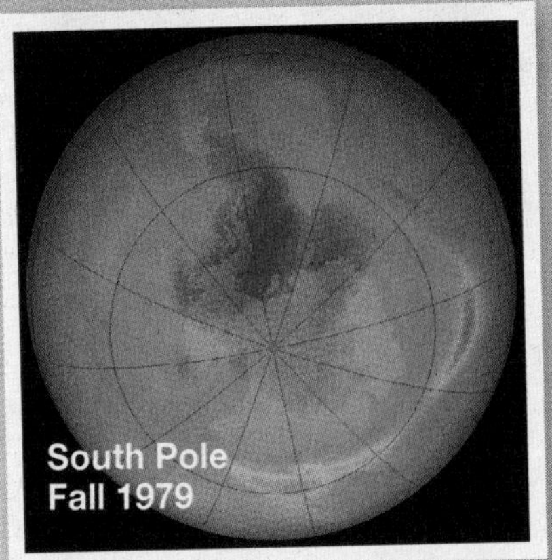

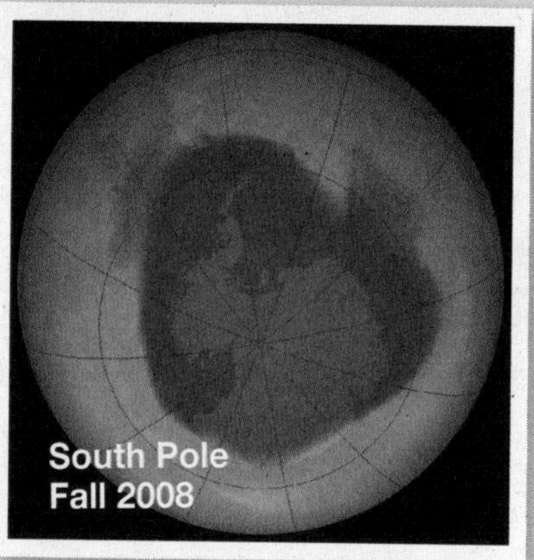

10 Compare How did the ozone layer over the South Pole change between 1979 and 2008?

___

___

___

By Absorbing or Reflecting Harmful Radiation

Earth's atmosphere reflects or absorbs most of the radiation from the sun. The **ozone layer** is an area in the stratosphere, 15 km to 40 km above Earth's surface, where ozone is highly concentrated. The ozone layer absorbs most of the solar radiation. The thickness of the ozone layer can change between seasons and at different locations. However, as shown at the left, scientists have observed a steady decrease in the overall volume of the ozone layer over time. This change is thought to be due to the use of certain chemicals by people. These chemicals enter the stratosphere, where they react with and destroy the ozone. Ozone levels are particularly low during certain times of the year over the South Pole. The area with a very thin ozone layer is often referred to as the "ozone hole."

By Maintaining the Right Temperature Range

Without the atmosphere, Earth's average temperature would be very low. How does Earth remain warm? The answer is the greenhouse effect. The **greenhouse effect** is the process by which gases in the atmosphere, such as water vapor and carbon dioxide, absorb and give off infrared radiation. Radiation from the sun warms Earth's surface, and Earth's surface gives off infrared radiation. Greenhouse gases in the atmosphere absorb some of this infrared radiation and then reradiate it. Some of this energy is absorbed again by Earth's surface, while some energy goes out into space. Because greenhouse gases keep energy in the Earth system longer, Earth's average surface temperature is kept at around 15°C (59°F). In time, all the energy ends up back in outer space.

Active Reading **11 List** Name two examples of greenhouse gases.

___

___

the Sun . . .

The Greenhouse Effect

Greenhouse gas molecules absorb and emit infrared radiation.

Without greenhouse gases in Earth's atmosphere, radiation from Earth's surface is lost directly to space.

Average Temperature: -18°C

With greenhouse gases in Earth's atmosphere, radiation from Earth's surface is lost to space more slowly, which makes Earth's surface warmer.

Average Temperature: 15°C

sunlight infrared radiation

The atmosphere is much thinner than shown here.

12 Illustrate Draw your own version of how greenhouse gases keep Earth warm.

Visual Summary

To complete this summary, fill in the blanks with the correct word or phrase. Then, use the key below to check your answers. You can use this page to review the main concepts of the lesson.

Both air pressure and temperature change within the atmosphere.

13 *As altitude increases, air pressure*

____

The atmosphere protects Earth from harmful radiation and helps to maintain a temperature range that supports life.

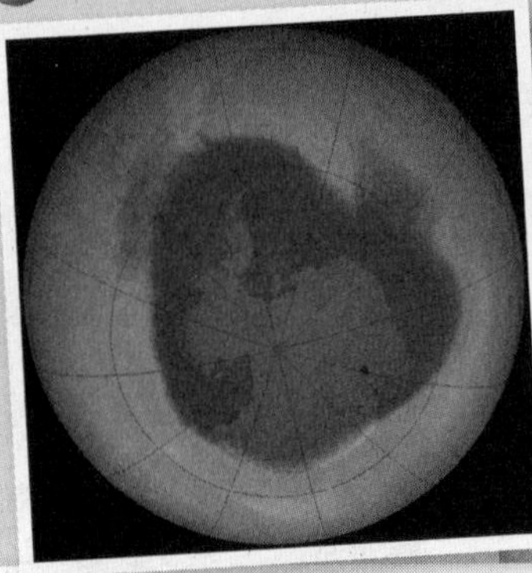

14 *Earth is protected from harmful solar radiation by the*

____

The Atmosphere

The atmosphere is divided into four layers, according to temperature and other properties.

15 *The four layers of the atmosphere are the*

____

____

____

____

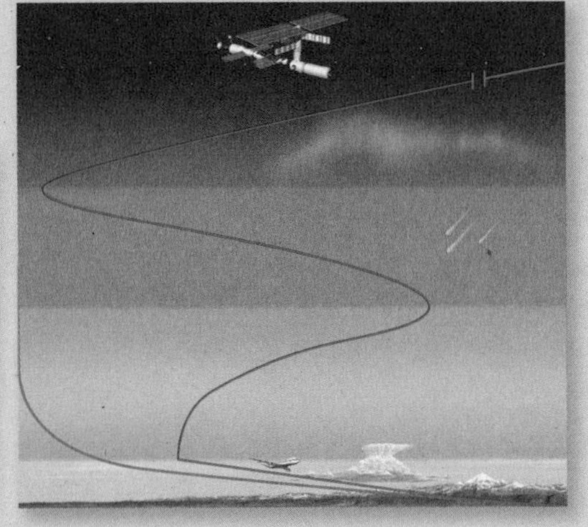

Answers: 13 decreases; 14 ozone layer; 15 troposphere, stratosphere, mesosphere, thermosphere

16 Hypothesize What do you think Earth's surface would be like if Earth did not have an atmosphere?

Lesson Review

Vocabulary

Fill in the blanks with the terms that best complete the following sentences.

1 The ____________________ is a mixture of gases that surrounds Earth.

2 The measure of the force with which air molecules push on a surface is called ____________________.

3 The ____________________ is the process by which gases in the atmosphere absorb and reradiate heat.

Key Concepts

4 List Name three gases in the atmosphere.

5 Identify What layer of the atmosphere contains the ozone layer?

6 Identify What layer of the atmosphere contains almost 80% of the atmosphere's total mass?

7 Describe How and why does air pressure change with altitude in the atmosphere?

8 Explain What is the name of the uppermost layer of the atmosphere? Why does it feel cold there, even though the temperature can be very high?

Critical Thinking

9 Hypothesize What would happen to life on Earth if the ozone layer was not present?

10 Criticize A friend says that temperature increases as altitude increases because you're moving closer to the sun. Is this true? Explain.

11 Predict Why would increased levels of greenhouse gases contribute to higher temperatures on Earth?

Use this graph to answer the following questions.

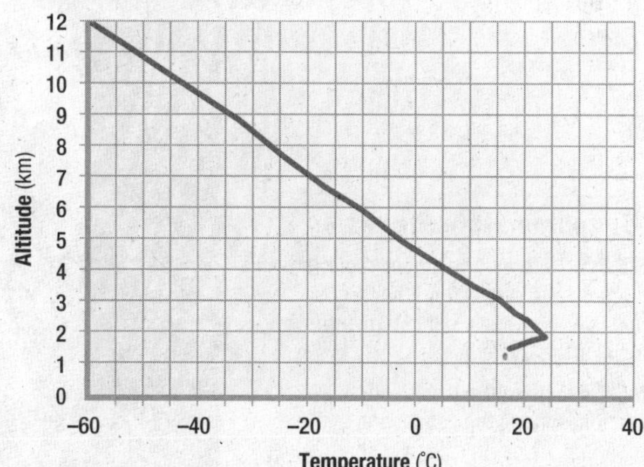

12 Analyze The top of Mount Everest is at about 8,850 m. What would the approximate air temperature be at that altitude? ____________

13 Analyze What is the total temperature change between 3 km and 7 km above Earth's surface? ____________

Lesson 3

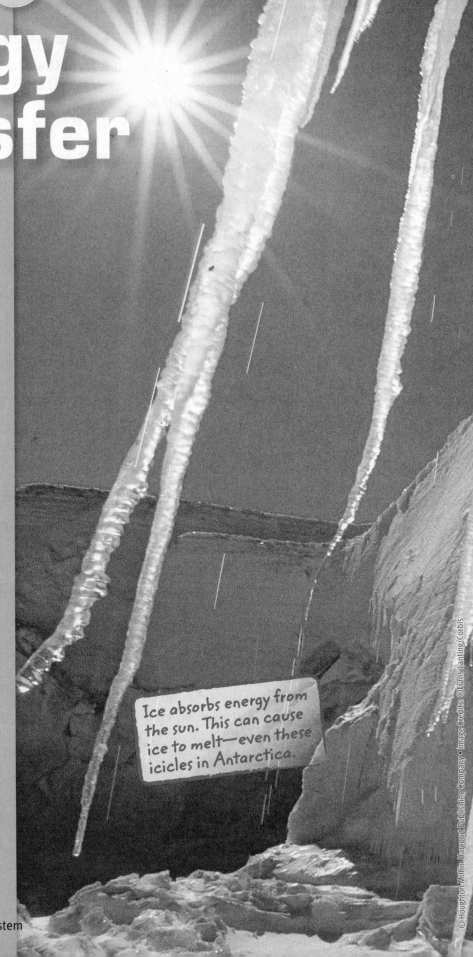

Energy Transfer

ESSENTIAL QUESTION

How does energy move through Earth's system?

By the end of this lesson, you should be able to summarize the three mechanisms by which energy is transferred through Earth's system.

Ice absorbs energy from the sun. This can cause ice to melt—even these icicles in Antarctica.

Sunshine State Standards

SC.6.E.7.1 Differentiate among radiation, conduction, and convection, the three mechanisms by which heat is transferred through Earth's system.

SC.6.E.7.4 Differentiate and show interactions among the geosphere, hydrosphere, cryosphere, atmosphere, and biosphere.

SC.6.E.7.5 Explain how energy provided by the sun influences global patterns of atmospheric movement and the temperature differences between air, water, and land.

LA.6.2.2.3 The student will organize information to show understanding (e.g., representing main ideas within text through charting, mapping, paraphrasing, summarizing, or comparing/contrasting).

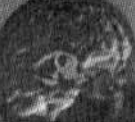

Engage Your Brain

1 Describe Fill in the blank with the word or phrase that you think correctly completes the following sentences.

An example of something hot is

____

An example of something cold is

____

The sun provides us with

____

A thermometer is used to measure

____

2 Explain If you placed your hands around this mug of hot chocolate, what would happen to the temperature of your hands? Why do you think this would happen?

____

Active Reading

3 Apply Many scientific words, such as *heat*, are used to convey different meanings. Use context clues to write your own definition for each meaning of the word *heat*.

The student won the first heat of the race.

heat:

____

The man wondered if his rent included heat.

heat:

____

Energy in the form of heat was transferred from the hot pan to the cold counter.

heat:

____

Vocabulary Terms

- temperature
- thermal energy
- thermal expansion
- heat
- radiation
- convection
- conduction

4 Identify This list contains the vocabulary terms you'll learn in this lesson. As you read, circle the definition of each term.

Hot and Cold

How are energy and temperature related?

All matter is made up of moving particles, such as atoms or molecules. When particles are in motion, they have kinetic energy. Because particles move at different speeds, each has a different amount of kinetic energy.

Temperature (TEMM•per•uh•choor) is a measure of the average kinetic energy of particles. The faster a particle moves, the more kinetic energy it has. As shown below, the more kinetic energy the particles of an object have, the higher the temperature of the object. Temperature does not depend on the number of particles. A teapot holds more tea than a cup. If the particles of tea in both containers have the same average kinetic energy, the tea in both containers is at the same temperature.

Thermal energy is the total kinetic energy of particles. A teapot full of tea at a high temperature has more thermal energy than a teapot full of tea at a lower temperature. Thermal energy also depends on the number of particles. The more particles there are in an object, the greater the object's thermal energy. The tea in a teapot and a cup may be at the same temperature, but the tea in the pot has more thermal energy because there is more of it.

5 Analyze Which container holds particles with the higher average kinetic energy?

____

____

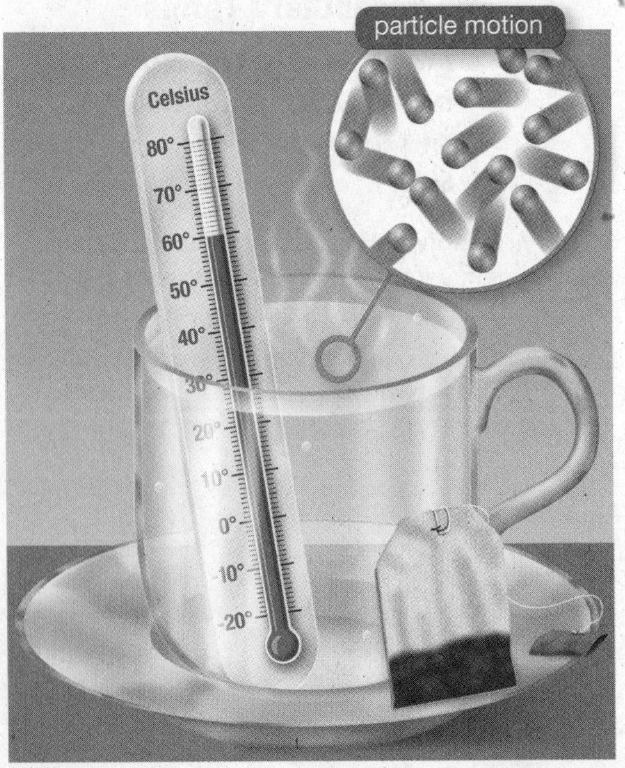

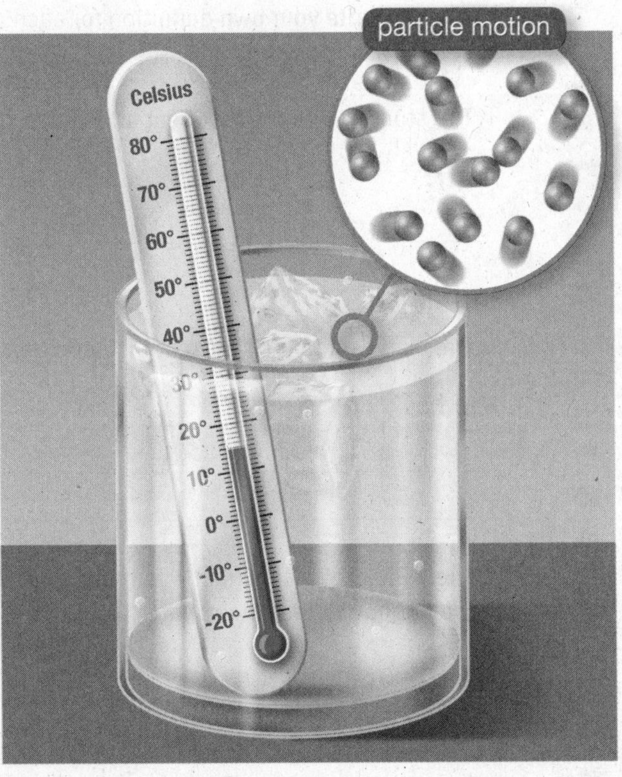

What is thermal expansion?

When the temperature of a substance increases, the substance's particles have more kinetic energy. Therefore, the particles move faster and move apart. As the space between the particles increases, the substance expands. The increase in volume that results from an increase in temperature is called **thermal expansion**. Most substances on Earth expand when they become warmer and contract when they become cooler. Water is an exception. Cold water expands as it gets colder and then freezes to form ice.

Thermal expansion causes a change in the density of a substance. *Density* is the mass per unit volume of a substance. When a substance expands, its mass stays the same but its volume increases. As a result, density decreases. Differences in density that are caused by thermal expansion can cause movement of matter. For example, air inside a hot-air balloon is warmed, as shown below. The air expands as its particles move faster and farther apart. As the air expands, it becomes less dense than the air outside the balloon. The less-dense air inside the balloon is forced upward by the colder, denser air outside the balloon. This same principle affects air movement in the atmosphere, water movement in the oceans, and rock movement in the geosphere.

6 Predict What might happen to the hot-air balloon if the air inside it cooled down?

7 Apply Why would an increase in the temperature of the oceans contribute to a rise in sea level?

When the air in this balloon becomes hotter, it becomes less dense than the surrounding air. So, the balloon goes up, up, and away!

Getting Warm

What is heat?

8 Identify As you read, underline the direction of energy transfer between objects that are at different temperatures.

You might think of the word *heat* when you imagine something that feels hot. But heat also has to do with things that feel cold. In fact, heat is what causes objects to feel hot or cold. You may often use the word *heat* to mean different things. However, in this lesson, the word *heat* has only one meaning. **Heat** is the energy that is transferred between objects that are at different temperatures.

Energy Transferred Between Objects

When objects that have different temperatures come into contact, energy will be transferred between them until both objects reach the same temperature. The direction of this energy transfer is always from the object with the higher temperature to the object with the lower temperature. When you touch something cold, energy is transferred from your body to that object. When you touch something hot, like the pan shown below, energy is transferred from that object to your body.

Visualize It!

9 Predict Draw an arrow to show the direction in which energy is transferred between the pan and the oven mitts.

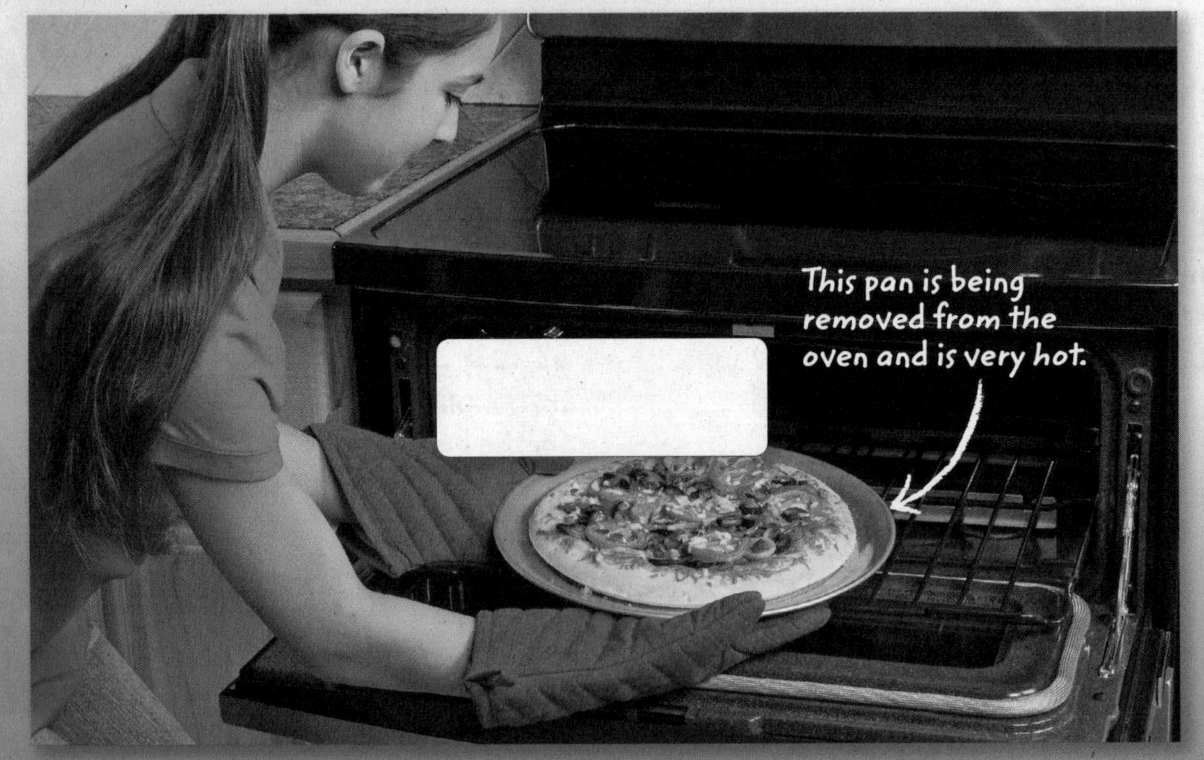

This pan is being removed from the oven and is very hot.

Why can the temperatures of land, air, and water differ?

When the same amount of energy is being transferred, some materials will get warmer or cooler at a faster rate than other materials. Suppose you are walking along a beach on a sunny day. You may notice that the land feels warmer than the air and the water, even though they are all exposed to the same amount of energy from the sun. This is because the land warms up at a faster rate than the water and air do.

Specific Heat

The different rates at which materials become warmer or cooler are due to a property called *specific heat*. A substance that has a high specific heat requires a lot of energy to show an increase in temperature. A substance with a lower specific heat requires less energy to show the same increase in temperature. Water has a higher specific heat than land. So, water warms up more slowly than land does. Water also cools down more slowly than land does.

10 Predict Air has a lower specific heat than water. Once the sun goes down, will the air or the water cool off faster? Why?

The temperatures of land, water, and air may differ—even when they are exposed to the same amount of energy from the sun.

Heat

How is energy transferred by radiation?

On a summer day, you can feel warmth from the sun on your skin. But how did that energy reach you from the sun? The sun transfers energy to Earth by radiation. **Radiation** is the transfer of energy as electromagnetic (ee•LEK•troh•mag•NEH•tik) waves. Radiation can transfer energy between objects that are not in direct contact with each other. Many objects other than the sun also radiate energy as light and heat. These include a hot burner on a stove and a campfire, shown below.

Electromagnetic Waves

Energy from the sun is called *electromagnetic radiation*. This energy travels in waves. You are probably familiar with one form of radiation called *visible light*. You can see the visible light that comes from the sun. Electromagnetic radiation includes other forms of energy, which you cannot see. Most of the warmth that you feel from the sun is infrared radiation. This energy has a longer wavelength and lower energy than visible light. Higher-energy radiation includes x-rays and ultraviolet light.

Visualize It!

11 Analyze Write a caption for the campfire photo on the right. Make sure the caption relates the image to radiation.

Energy from this hot burner is being transferred by radiation.

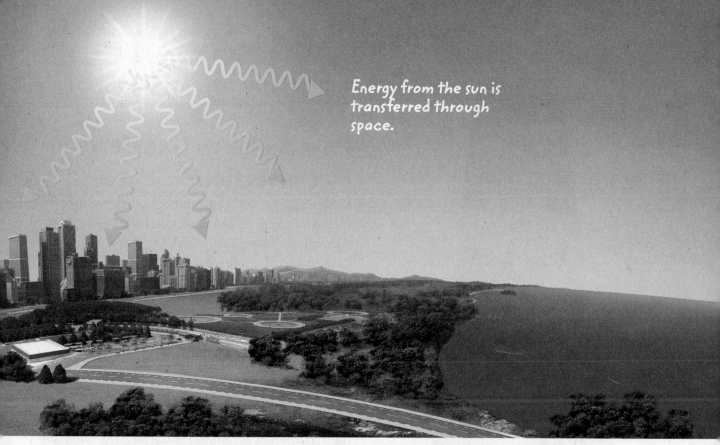

Energy from the sun is transferred through space.

Where does radiation occur on Earth?

We live almost 150 million km from the sun. Yet almost all of the energy on Earth is transmitted from the sun by radiation. The sun is the major source of energy for processes at Earth's surface. Receiving that energy is absolutely vital for life on Earth. The electromagnetic waves from the sun also provide energy that drives the water cycle.

When solar radiation reaches Earth, some of the energy is reflected and scattered by Earth's atmosphere. But much of the energy passes through Earth's atmosphere and reaches Earth's surface. Some of the energy that Earth receives from the sun is absorbed by the atmosphere, geosphere, and hydrosphere. Then, the energy is changed into thermal energy. This thermal energy may be reradiated into the Earth system or into space. Much of the energy is transferred through Earth's systems by the two other ways—convection and conduction.

12 Summarize Give two examples of what happens when energy from the sun reaches Earth.

Think Outside the Book

13 Apply Research ultraviolet radiation from the sun and its role in causing sunburns.

Heating Up

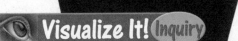

How is energy transferred by convection?

Have you ever watched a pot of boiling water, such as the one below? If so, you have seen convection. **Convection** (kun•VECK•shuhn) is the transfer of energy due to the movement of matter. As water warms up at the bottom of the pot, some of the hot water rises. At the same time, cooler water from other parts of the pot sink and replace the rising water. This water is then warmed and the cycle continues.

Convection Currents

Convection involves the movement of matter due to differences in density. Convection occurs because most matter becomes less dense when it gets warmer. When most matter becomes warmer, it undergoes thermal expansion and a decrease in density. This less-dense matter is forced upward by the surrounding colder, denser matter that is sinking. As the hot matter rises, it cools and becomes more dense. This causes it to sink back down. This cycling of matter is called a *convection current*. Convection most often occurs in fluids, such as water and air. But convection can also happen in solids.

wax

energy sources

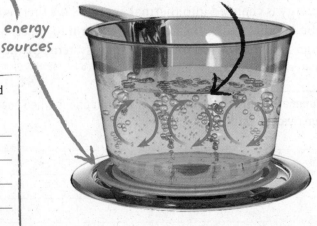

14 Apply How is convection related to the rise and fall of wax in lava lamps?

Where does convection occur on Earth?

If Earth's surface is warmer than the air, energy will be transferred from the ground to the air. As the air becomes warmer, it becomes less dense. This air is pushed upward and out of the way by cooler, denser air that is sinking. As the warm air rises, it cools and becomes denser and begins to sink back toward Earth's surface. This cycle moves energy through the atmosphere.

Convection currents also occur in the ocean because of differences in the density of ocean water. More dense water sinks to the ocean floor, and less dense water moves toward the surface. The density of ocean water is influenced by temperature and the amount of salt in the water. Cold water is denser than warmer water. Water that contains a lot of salt is more dense than less-salty water.

Energy produced deep inside Earth heats rock in the mantle. The heated rock becomes less dense and is pushed up toward Earth's surface by the cooler, denser surrounding rock. Once cooled near the surface, the rock sinks. These convection currents transfer energy from Earth's core toward Earth's surface. These currents also cause the movement of tectonic plates.

Active Reading **15 Name** What are three of Earth's spheres in which energy is transferred by convection?

____

Visualize It!

16 Apply Draw the convection current that could occur in the body of water in this image.

Convection currents occur throughout the Earth system.

Ouch!

How is energy transferred by conduction?

Have you ever touched an ice cube and wondered why it feels cold? An ice cube has only a small amount of energy, compared to your hand. Energy is transferred to the ice cube from your hand through the process of conduction. **Conduction** (kun•DUHK•shuhn) is the transfer of energy from one object to another object through direct contact.

Direct Contact

Remember that the atoms or molecules in a substance are constantly moving. Even a solid block of ice has particles in constant motion. When objects at different temperatures touch, their particles interact. Conduction involves the faster-moving particles of the warmer object transferring energy to the slower-moving particles in the cooler object. The greater the difference in energy of the particles, the faster the transfer of energy by conduction occurs.

Active Reading **17 Apply** Name two examples of conduction that you experience every day.

____

____

____

____

These desert sands would feel hot because of conduction.

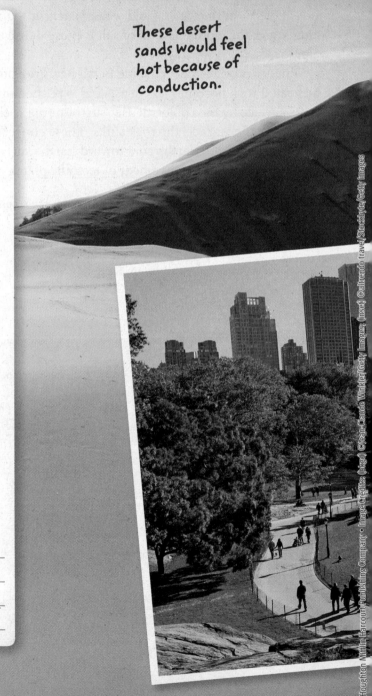

Where does conduction occur on Earth?

Energy can be transferred between the geosphere and the atmosphere by conduction. When cooler air molecules come into direct contact with the warm ground, energy is passed to the air by conduction. Conduction between the ground and the air happens only within a few centimeters of Earth's surface.

Conduction also happens between particles of air and particles of water. For example, if air transfers enough energy to liquid water, the water may evaporate. If water vapor transfers energy to the air, the kinetic energy of the water decreases. As a result, the water vapor may condense to form liquid water droplets.

Inside Earth, energy transfers between rock particles by conduction. However, rock is a poor conductor of heat, so this process happens very slowly.

Visualize It!

18 Compare Does conduction also occur in a city like the one shown below? Explain.

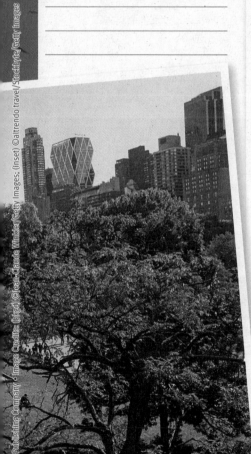

19 Summarize Complete the following spider map by describing the three types of energy transfer. One answer has been started for you.

Types of Energy Transfer

Radiation

Transfer of energy as

Visual Summary

To complete this summary, fill in the blanks with the correct word or phrase. Then, use the key below to check your answers. You can use this page to review the main concepts of the lesson.

Heat is the energy that is transferred between objects that are at different temperatures.

20 The particles in a hot pan have ____________ kinetic energy than the particles in a cool oven mitt.

Energy Transfer

Energy can be transferred in different ways.

21 The three ways that energy can be transferred are labeled in the image as

A: ____________________

B: ____________________

C: ____________________

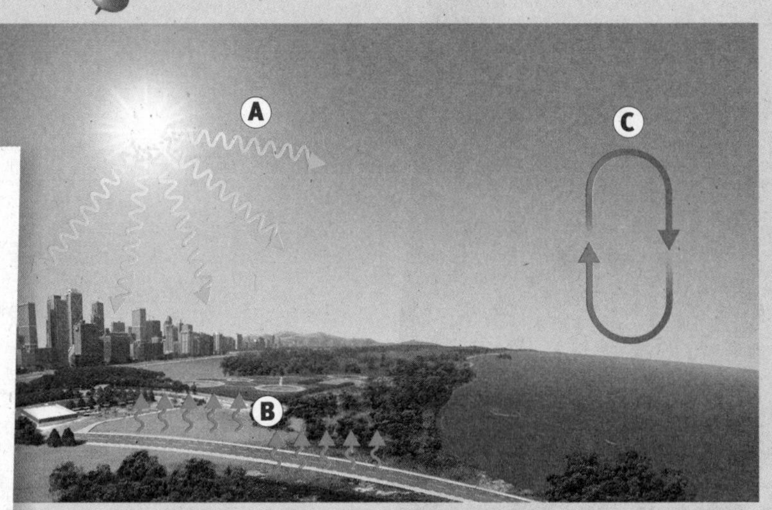

Answers: 20 more; 21 A: radiation, B: conduction, C: convection

22 Apply What type of energy transfer is responsible for making you feel cold when you are swimming in cool water? Explain your answer.

Lesson Review

Vocabulary

In your own words, define the following terms.

1 radiation

2 convection

3 conduction

Key Concepts

4 Compare What is the difference between temperature, thermal energy, and heat?

5 Describe What is happening to a substance undergoing thermal expansion?

6 Explain What is the main source of energy for most processes at Earth's surface?

7 Summarize What happens when two objects at different temperatures touch? Name one place where it occurs in Earth's system.

8 Identify What is an example of convection in Earth's system?

Critical Thinking

9 Apply Why can metal utensils get too hot to touch when you are cooking with them?

10 Predict You are doing an experiment outside on a sunny day. You find the temperature of some sand is 28°C. You also find the temperature of some water is 25°C. Explain the difference in temperatures.

Use this image to answer the following questions.

11 Analyze Name one example of where energy transfer by radiation is occurring.

12 Analyze Name one example of where energy transfer by conduction is occurring.

13 Analyze Name one example of where energy transfer by convection is occurring.

Lesson 4

Wind in the Atmosphere

ESSENTIAL QUESTION

What is wind?

By the end of this lesson, you should be able to explain how energy provided by the sun causes atmospheric movement, called wind.

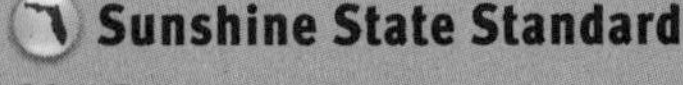
Sunshine State Standards

SC.6.E.7.3 Describe how global patterns such as the jet stream and ocean currents influence local weather in measurable terms such as temperature, air pressure, wind direction and speed, and humidity and precipitation.

SC.6.E.7.5 Explain how energy provided by the sun influences global patterns of atmospheric movement and the temperature differences between air, water, and land.

Although you cannot see wind, you can see how it affects things like these kites.

Engage Your Brain

1 Predict Check T or F to show whether you think each statement is true or false.

T	F	
☐	☐	The atmosphere is often referred to as air.
☐	☐	Wind does not have direction.
☐	☐	During the day, there is often a wind blowing toward shore from the ocean or a large lake.
☐	☐	Cold air rises and warm air sinks.

2 Explain if you opened the valve on this bicycle tire, what would happen to the air inside of the tire? Why do you think that would happen?

Active Reading

3 Synthesize You can often define an unknown phrase if you know the meaning of its word parts. Use the word parts below to make an educated guess about the meanings of the phrases *local wind* and *global wind*.

Word part	Meaning
wind	movement of air due to differences in air pressure
local	involving a particular area
global	involving the entire Earth

local wind:

global wind:

Vocabulary Terms

- **wind**
- **jet stream**
- **Coriolis effect**
- **local wind**
- **global wind**

4 Identify This list contains the vocabulary terms you'll learn in this lesson. As you read, circle the definition of each term.

Blow It Out!

What causes wind?

The next time you feel the wind blowing, you can thank the sun! The sun does not warm the whole surface of the Earth in a uniform manner. This uneven heating causes the air above Earth's surface to be at different temperatures. Cold air is more dense than warmer air is. Colder, denser air sinks. When denser air sinks, it places greater pressure on the surface of Earth than warmer, less-dense air does. This results in areas of higher air pressure. Air moves from areas of higher pressure toward areas of lower pressure. The movement of air caused by differences in air pressure is called **wind**. The greater the differences in air pressure, the faster the air moves.

Areas of High and Low Pressure

Cold, dense air at the poles creates areas of high pressure at the poles. Warm, less-dense air at the equator forms an area of lower pressure. This pressure gradient results in global movement of air. However, instead of moving in one circle between the equator and the poles, air moves in smaller circular patterns called *convection cells,* shown below. As air moves from the equator, it cools and becomes more dense. At about 30°N and 30°S latitudes, a high-pressure belt results from the sinking of air. Near the poles, cold air warms as it moves away from the poles. At around 60°N and 60°S latitudes, a low-pressure belt forms as the warmed air is pushed upward.

Visualize It!

5 Identify In the white oval area on the map, draw the convection cell that was left out. Use a pencil to indicate warm air and a pen to indicate cool air.

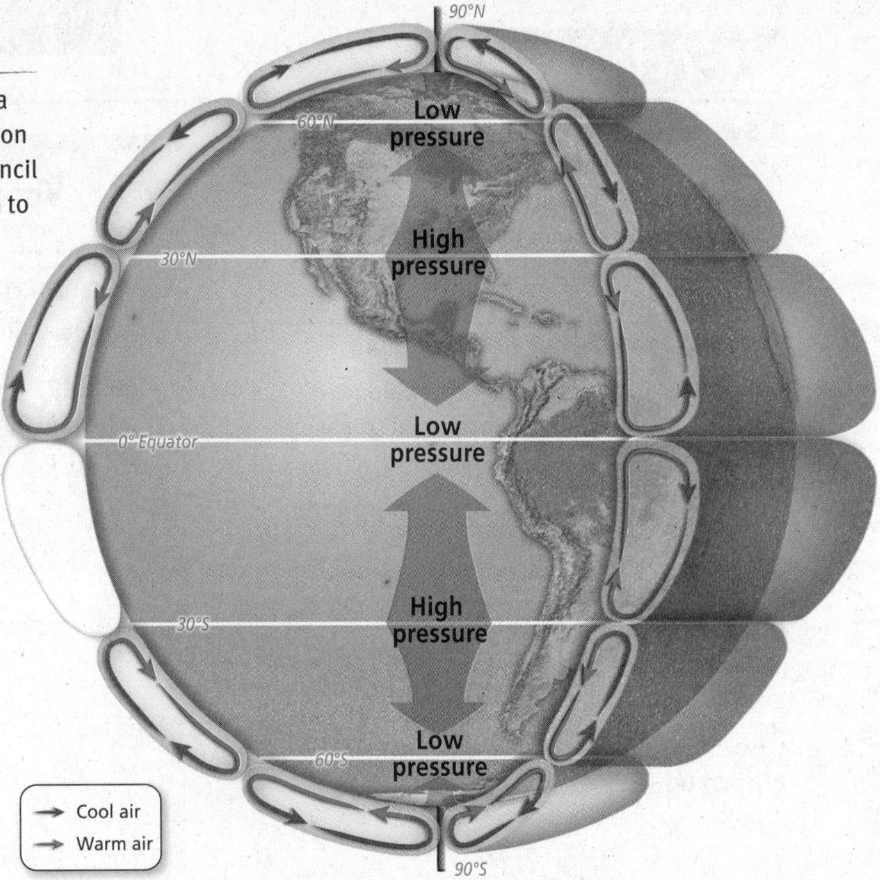

90°N
60°N
Low pressure
High pressure
30°N
Low pressure
0° Equator
High pressure
30°S
60°S
Low pressure
90°S
Cool air
Warm air

The warming and cooling of air produces pressure belts every 30° of latitude.

How does Earth's rotation affect wind?

Pressure differences cause air to move between the equator and the poles. If Earth was not rotating, winds would blow in a straight line. However, winds are deflected, or curved, due to Earth's rotation, as shown below. The apparent curving of the path of a moving object from an otherwise straight path due to Earth's rotation is called the **Coriolis effect** (kawr•ee•OH•lis ih•FEKT). This effect is most noticeable over long distances.

Because each point on Earth makes one complete rotation every day, points closer to the equator must travel farther and, therefore, faster than points closer to the poles do. When air moves from the equator toward the North Pole, it maintains its initial speed and direction. If the air travels far enough north, it will have traveled farther east than a point on the ground beneath it. As a result, the air appears to follow a curved path toward the east. Air moving from the North Pole to the equator appears to curve to the west because the air moves east more slowly than a point on the ground beneath it does. Therefore, in the Northern Hemisphere, air moving to the north curves to the east and air moving to the south curves to the west.

6 Identify As you read, underline how air movement in the Northern Hemisphere is influenced by the Coriolis effect.

Visualize It!

7 Label In the white ovals on the map, draw the direction and path of the winds that would occur at those locations on Earth.

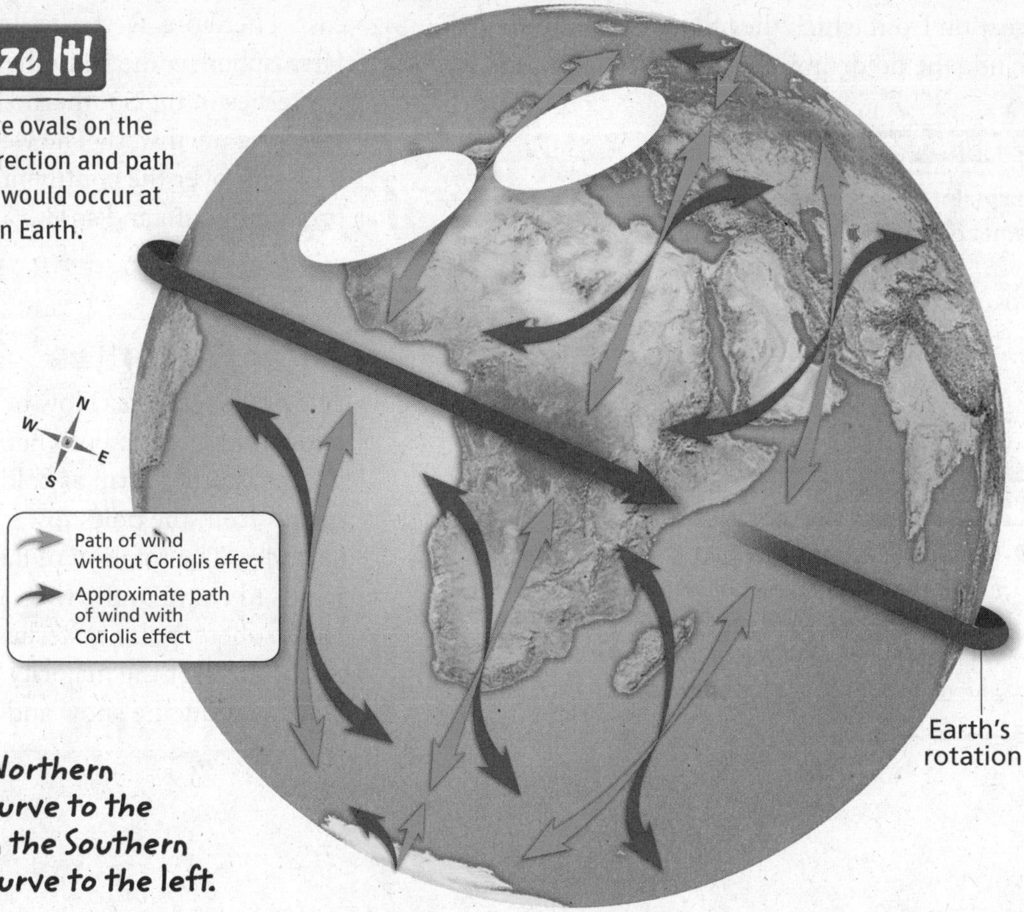

N
W
E
S

Path of wind without Coriolis effect

Approximate path of wind with Coriolis effect

Earth's rotation

Winds in the Northern Hemisphere curve to the right. Winds in the Southern Hemisphere curve to the left.

Blowin' Around

What are examples of global winds?

Recall that air travels in circular patterns called convection cells that cover approximately 30° of latitude. Pressure belts at every 30° of latitude and the Coriolis effect produce patterns of calm areas and wind systems. These wind systems occur at or near Earth's surface and are called **global winds**. As shown at the right, the major global wind systems are the *polar easterlies* (EE•ster•leez), the *westerlies* (WES•ter•leez), and the *trade winds*. Winds such as polar easterlies and westerlies are named for the direction from which they blow. Calm areas include the doldrums and the horse latitudes.

Active Reading

8 Explain If something is being carried by westerlies, what direction is it moving toward?

Think Outside the Book Inquiry

9 Model Winds are described according to their direction and speed. Research wind vanes and what they are used for. Design and build your own wind vane.

Trade Winds

The trade winds blow between 30° latitude and the equator in both hemispheres. The rotation of Earth causes the trade winds to curve to the west. Therefore, trade winds in the Northern Hemisphere come from the northeast, and trade winds in the Southern Hemisphere come from the southeast. These winds became known as the trade winds because sailors relied on them to sail from Europe to the Americas.

Westerlies

The westerlies blow between 30° and 60° latitudes in both hemispheres. The rotation of Earth causes these winds to curve to the east. Therefore, westerlies in the Northern Hemisphere come from the southwest, and westerlies in the Southern Hemisphere come from the northwest. The westerlies can carry moist air over the continental United States, producing rain and snow.

Polar Easterlies

The polar easterlies blow between the poles and 60° latitude in both hemispheres. The polar easterlies form as cold, sinking air moves from the poles toward 60°N and 60°S latitudes. The rotation of Earth causes these winds to curve to the west. In the Northern Hemisphere, polar easterlies can carry cold Arctic air over the majority of the United States, producing snow and freezing weather.

Visualize It!

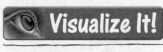

10 Identify Label the polar easterlies, the westerlies, and the trade winds in the white boxes on the map.

The major global wind systems

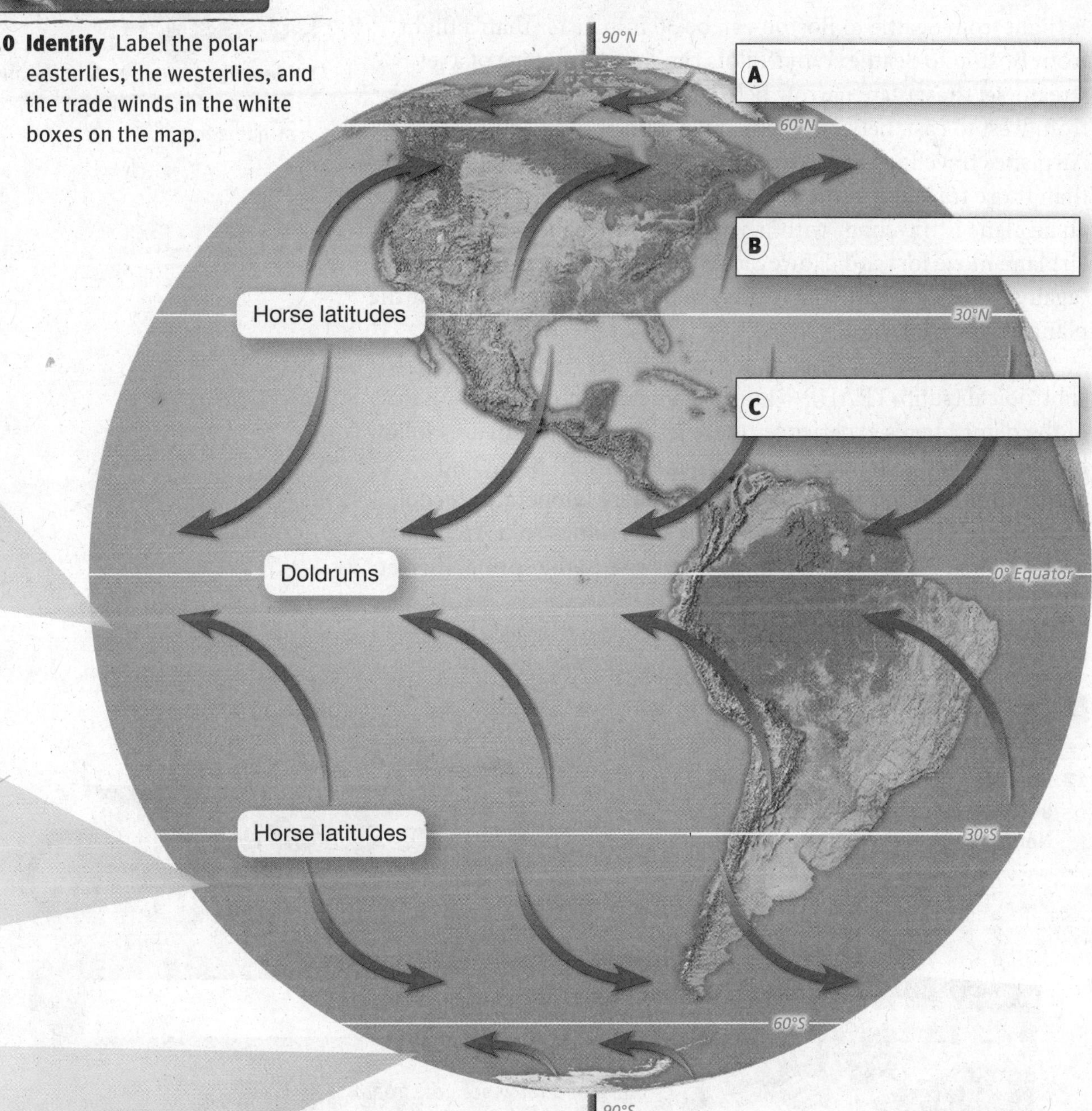

The Doldrums and Horse Latitudes

The trade winds of both hemispheres meet in a calm area around the equator called the *doldrums* (DOHL•druhmz). Very little wind blows in the doldrums because the warm, less-dense air results in an area of low pressure. The name doldrums means "dull" or "sluggish." At about 30° latitude in both hemispheres, air stops moving and sinks. This forms calm areas called the *horse latitudes*. This name was given to these areas when sailing ships carried horses from Europe to the Americas. When ships were stalled in these areas, horses were sometimes thrown overboard to save water.

The Jet Streams

A flight from Seattle to Boston can be 30 min faster than a flight from Boston to Seattle. Why? Pilots can take advantage of a jet stream. **Jet streams** are narrow belts of high-speed winds that blow from west to east, between 7 km and 16 km above Earth's surface. Airplanes traveling in the same direction as a jet stream go faster than those traveling in the opposite direction of a jet stream. When an airplane is traveling "with" a jet stream, the wind is helping the airplane move forward. However, when an airplane is traveling "against" the jet stream, the wind is making it more difficult for the plane to move forward.

The two main jet streams are the polar jet stream and the subtropical (suhb•TRAHP•i•kuhl) jet stream, shown below. Each of the hemispheres experiences these jet streams. Jet streams follow boundaries between hot and cold air and can shift north and south. In the winter, as Northern Hemisphere temperatures cool, the polar jet stream moves south. This shift brings cold Arctic air to the United States. When temperatures rise in the spring, this jet stream shifts to the north.

11 Identify As you read, underline the direction that the jet streams travel.

Visualize It!

12 Identify Label the polar jet stream and the subtropical jet stream in the Northern Hemisphere.

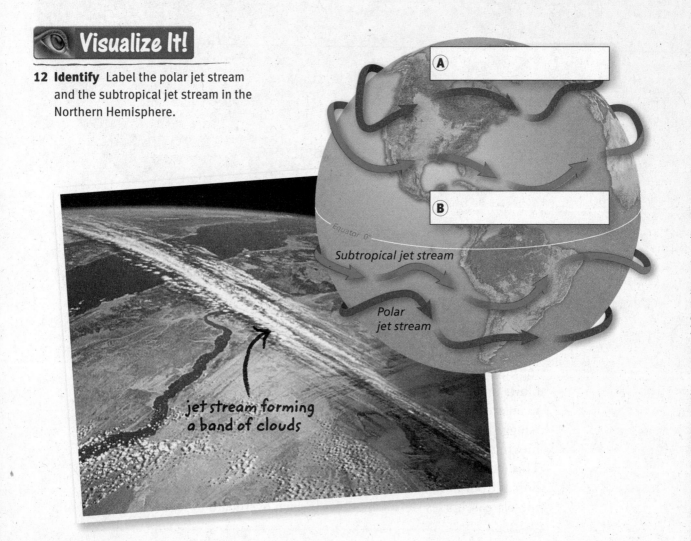

A

B

Equator 0°

Subtropical jet stream

Polar jet stream

jet stream forming a band of clouds

Why It Matters

EYE ON THE ENVIRONMENT

Desert Trades

How does some of the Sahara end up in the Americas? Global winds carry it.

Trade Wind Carriers
Trade winds can carry Saharan dust across the Atlantic Ocean to Florida and the Caribbean.

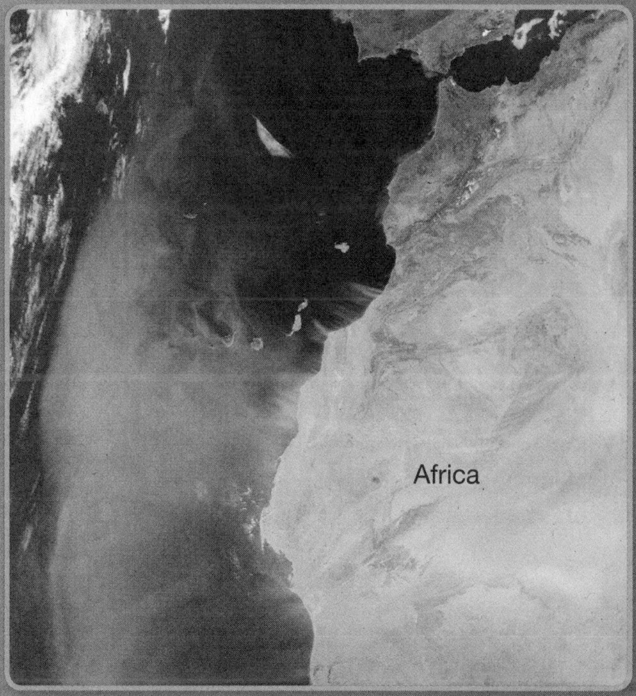

Florida Meets the Sahara
This hazy skyline in Miami is the result of a dust storm. Where did the dust come from? It all started in the Sahara.

The Sahara
The Sahara is the world's largest hot desert. Sand and dust storms that produce skies like this are very common in this desert.

Extend

Inquiry

13 Explain Look at a map and explain how trade winds carry dust from the Sahara to the Caribbean.

14 Relate Investigate the winds that blow in your community. Where do they usually come from? Identify the wind system that could be involved.

15 Apply Investigate how winds played a role in distributing radioactive waste that was released after an explosion at the Chernobyl Nuclear Power Plant in Ukraine. Present your findings as a map illustration or in a poster.

Feelin' Breezy

What are examples of local winds?

Active Reading

16 Identify As you read, underline two examples of geographic features that contribute to the formation of local winds.

Local geographic features, such as a body of water or a mountain, can produce temperature and pressure differences that cause local winds. Unlike global winds, **local winds** are the movement of air over short distances. They can blow from any direction, depending on the features of the area.

Sea and Land Breezes

Have you ever felt a cool breeze coming off the ocean or a lake? If so, you were experiencing a sea breeze. Large bodies of water take longer to warm up than land does. During the day, air above land becomes warmer than air above water. The colder, denser air over water flows toward the land and pushes the warm air on the land upward. While water takes longer to warm than land does, land cools faster than water does. At night, cooler air on land causes a higher-pressure zone over the land. So, a wind blows from the land toward the water. This type of local wind is called a land breeze.

17 Analyze Label the areas of high pressure and low pressure.

sea breeze

Ⓑ ____________ pressure

Ⓐ ____________ pressure

land breeze

Ⓓ ____________ pressure

Ⓒ ____________ pressure

Valley and Mountain Breezes

Areas that have mountains and valleys experience local winds called mountain and valley breezes. During the day, the sun warms the air along the mountain slopes faster than the air in the valleys. This uneven heating results in areas of lower pressure near the mountain tops. This pressure difference causes a valley breeze, which flows from the valley up the slopes of the mountains. Many birds float on valley breezes to conserve energy. At nightfall, the air along the mountain slopes cools and moves down into the valley. This local wind is called a mountain breeze.

Visualize It!

18 Analyze Label the areas of high pressure and low pressure.

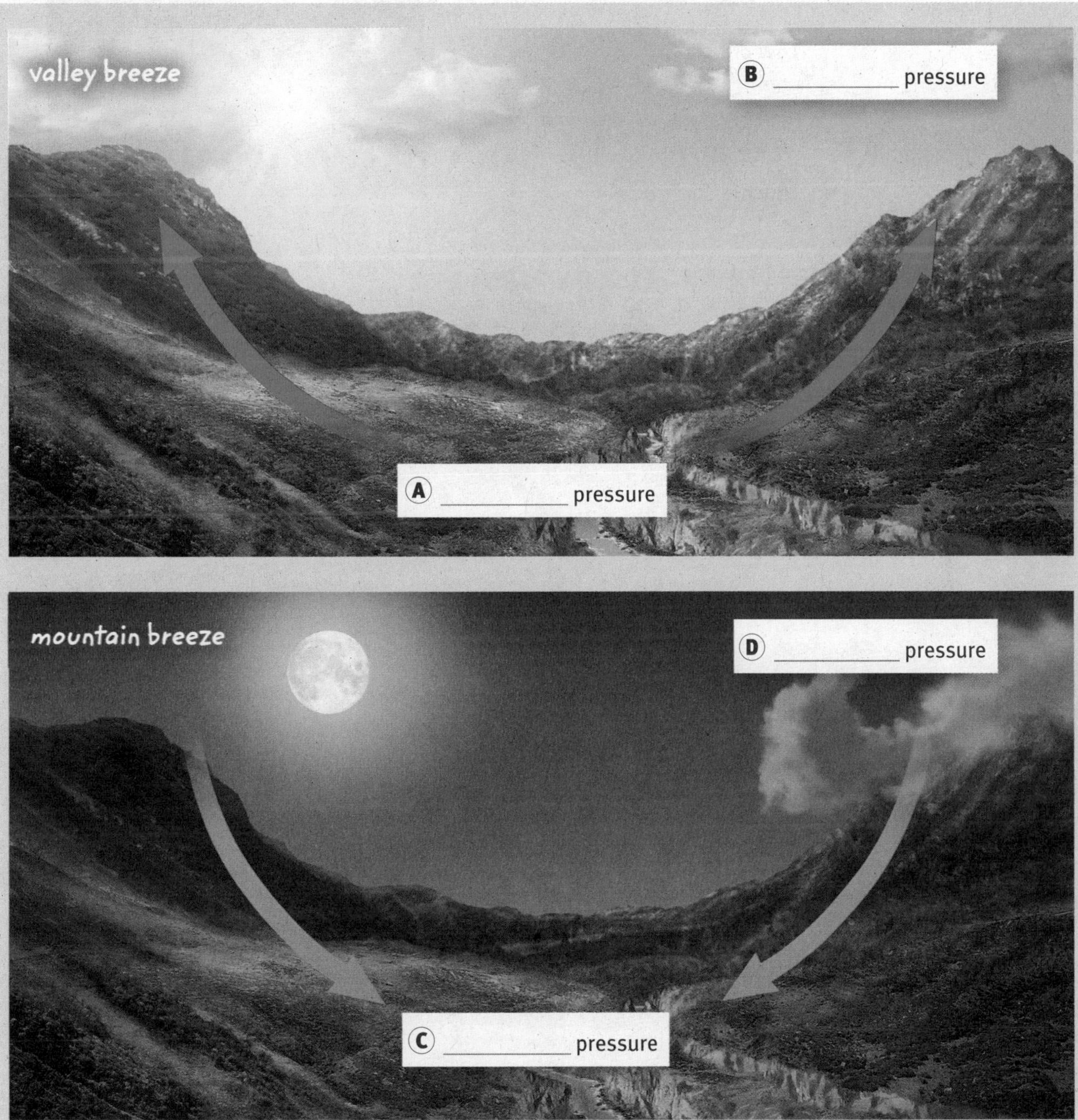

Visual Summary

To complete this summary, circle the correct word or phrases. Then use the key below to check your answers. You can use this page to review the main concepts of the lesson.

Wind is the movement of air from areas of higher pressure to areas of lower pressure.

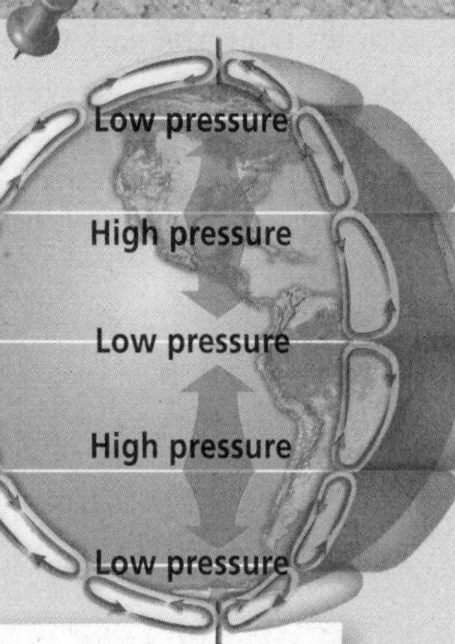

19 Cool air sinks, causing an area of high / low air pressure.

Global wind systems occur on Earth.

20 High-speed wind between 7 km and 16 km above Earth's surface is a jet stream / mountain breeze.

Wind in the Atmosphere

Geographic features can produce local winds.

21 During the day, an area of high / low air pressure forms over water and a sea / land breeze occurs.

Answers: 19 high; 20 jet stream; 21 high, sea

22 Explain Would there be winds if the air above Earth's surface was the same temperature everywhere? Explain your answer.

Lesson Review

Vocabulary

Fill in the blanks with the term that best completes the following sentences.

1 Another term for air movement caused by differences in air pressure is

____

2 Pilots often take advantage of the ______________________, which are high-speed winds between 7 km and 16 km above Earth's surface.

3 The apparent curving of winds due to Earth's rotation is the ______________________

Key Concepts

4 Explain How does the sun cause wind?

5 Predict If Earth did not rotate, what would happen to the global winds? Why?

6 Explain How do convection cells in Earth's atmosphere cause high- and low-pressure belts?

7 Describe What factors contribute to global winds? Identify areas where winds are weak.

8 Identify Name a latitude where each of the following occurs: polar easterlies, westerlies, and trade winds.

Critical Thinking

9 Predict How would local winds be affected if water and land absorbed and released heat at the same rate? Explain your answer.

10 Compare How is a land breeze similar to a sea breeze? How do they differ?

Use this image to answer the following questions.

11 Analyze What type of local wind would you experience if you were standing in the valley? Explain your answer.

12 Infer Would the local wind change if it was nighttime? Explain.

Think Science

Evaluating Claims

Scientific methods teach us how to evaluate ideas or claims to find out if they are credible, and if our explanations are reliable and logical. We can apply critical thinking to all matters in life—even to things like deciding what detergent to buy or what to eat.

Ever since the 1930s, the legend of the Loch Ness monster living in their deep lake had become part of everyday life for the people of Inverness, Scotland. But there has been much controversy over whether or not the Loch Ness monster really exists. Who do we believe? In this case, using scientific thinking to evaluate the credibility of the claim can help.

Sunshine State Standards

SC.6.N.3.1 Recognize and explain that a scientific theory is a well-supported and widely accepted explanation of nature and is not simply a claim posed by an individual. Thus, the use of the term theory in science is very different than how it is used in everyday life.

LA.6.2.2.3 The student will organize information to show understanding (e.g., representing main ideas within text through charting, mapping, paraphrasing, summarizing, or comparing/contrasting).

Tutorial

Consider the evidence surrounding the Loch Ness monster claim—does the creature exist or not? How will you evaluate the evidence to come to a conclusion? Follow the steps below to shape your argument.

1 What were the methods used to collect the data? Think critically and find out why an explanation or claim has been accepted by looking at the experiments, data, and methods used to support the idea.

2 Has the data presented been tested with further observations? Think about whether the evidence supports the explanation or claim. Sometimes, facts are used to support a claim even though they cannot be retested or reproduced.

3 Is there any evidence that contradicts the explanation or claim? Is there a reasonable alternative explanation? It is important to know whether any evidence casts doubt on the explanation or claim.

Huge monster found in Scotland! Could it be a surviving dinosaur?

This is a famous photograph from 1934, showing the Loch Ness Monster. In 1994, the actual fraudster reported the "monster" as being only 14 inches tall and created by fastening an artificial head to a toy submarine.

You Try It!

Evaluating whether or not scientific evidence supports a claim can be useful in science and in everyday life. Read the brochure below, and assess the validity of the claims as you answer the questions that follow.

Geo-Vento Energy

Let Us Install Wind Turbines at Your School

The use of wind turbines to generate electrical energy at your school will:

Save nonrenewable resources!

Save money!

Say "goodbye" to electric bills!

Geo-Vento offers the following proof:

- A school in Cape Cod, MA, generates all of its electrical energy from wind turbines. This school no longer pays any electric bills.
- It is a well-established theory that wind is an excellent energy source throughout the United States. No more electric bills for anyone!

1 Evaluating Methods Evaluate the claims made in the brochure. What evidence in the brochure supports these claims?

2 Determining Factual Accuracy Is the evidence in the brochure related to the claims that are made? Explain your answer.

3 Communicating Results Can you think of evidence that might disprove the claims that are made? Share your answer with your classmates and record their ideas.

4 Evaluating Theories Do you think the theory offered as proof is scientific? Why might this statement not be widely accepted?

5 Forming Alternative Hypotheses Write a claim that is a reasonable alternative to one of the claims made in the brochure. Consider and list the evidence you need to back it up.

Take It Home

With an adult, find a newspaper or magazine that appears to make scientific claims about a product. Carefully evaluate the claims and determine whether you think they are valid. Bring the ad to class and be prepared to share your evaluation.

Lesson 5

Ocean Currents

ESSENTIAL QUESTION

How does water move in the ocean?

By the end of this lesson, you should be able to describe the movement of ocean water, explain what factors influence this movement, and explain why ocean circulation is important in the Earth system.

This iceberg off the coast of Newfoundland broke off an Arctic ice sheet and drifted south on ocean surface currents.

Sunshine State Standards

SC.6.E.7.3 Describe how global patterns such as the jet stream and ocean currents influence local weather in measurable terms such as temperature, air pressure, wind direction and speed, and humidity and precipitation.

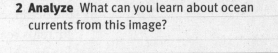

Engage Your Brain

1 Predict Check T or F to show whether you think each statement is true or false.

T	F	
☐	☐	Ocean currents are always cold.
☐	☐	Continents affect the directions of currents.
☐	☐	Currents only flow near the surface of the ocean.
☐	☐	Wind affects currents.
☐	☐	The sun affects currents near the surface of the ocean.

2 Analyze What can you learn about ocean currents from this image?

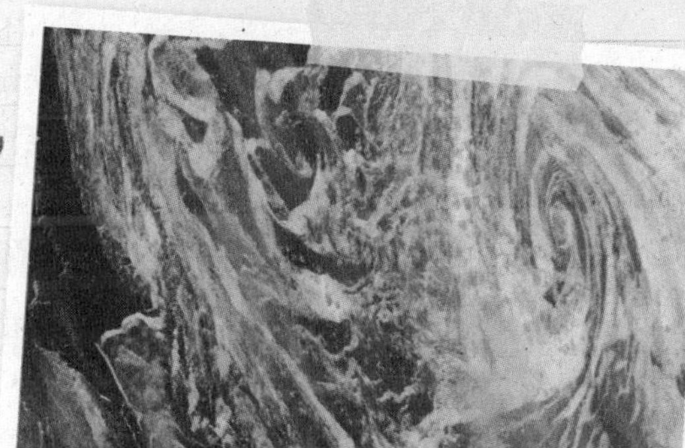

This image shows sea ice caught in ocean currents.

Active Reading

3 Synthesize You can often define an unknown word if you know the meaning of its word parts. Use the word parts and sentence below to make an educated guess about the meaning of the word *upwelling*.

Word part	Meaning
up-	from beneath the ground or water
well	to rise

Example Sentence

In areas where upwelling occurs, plankton feed on nutrients from deep in the ocean.

upwelling:

Vocabulary Terms

- **ocean current**
- **surface current**
- **Coriolis effect**
- **deep current**
- **convection current**
- **upwelling**

4 Apply As you learn the definition of each vocabulary term in this lesson, create your own definition or sketch to help you remember the meaning of the term.

Going with the Flow

What are ocean currents?

The oceans contain streamlike movements of water called **ocean currents**. Ocean currents that occur at or near the surface of the ocean, caused by wind, are called **surface currents**. Most surface currents reach depths of about 100 m, but some go deeper. Surface currents also reach lengths of several thousand kilometers and can stretch across oceans. An example of a surface current is the Gulf Stream. The Gulf Stream is one of the strongest surface currents on Earth. The Gulf Stream transports, or moves, more water each year than is transported by all the rivers in the world combined.

Infrared cameras on satellites provide images that show differences in temperature. Scientists add color to the images afterward to highlight the different temperatures, as shown below.

Active Reading

5 Identify As you read, underline three factors that affect surface currents.

What affects surface currents?

Surface currents are affected by three factors: continental deflections, the Coriolis effect, and global winds. These factors keep surface currents flowing in distinct patterns around Earth.

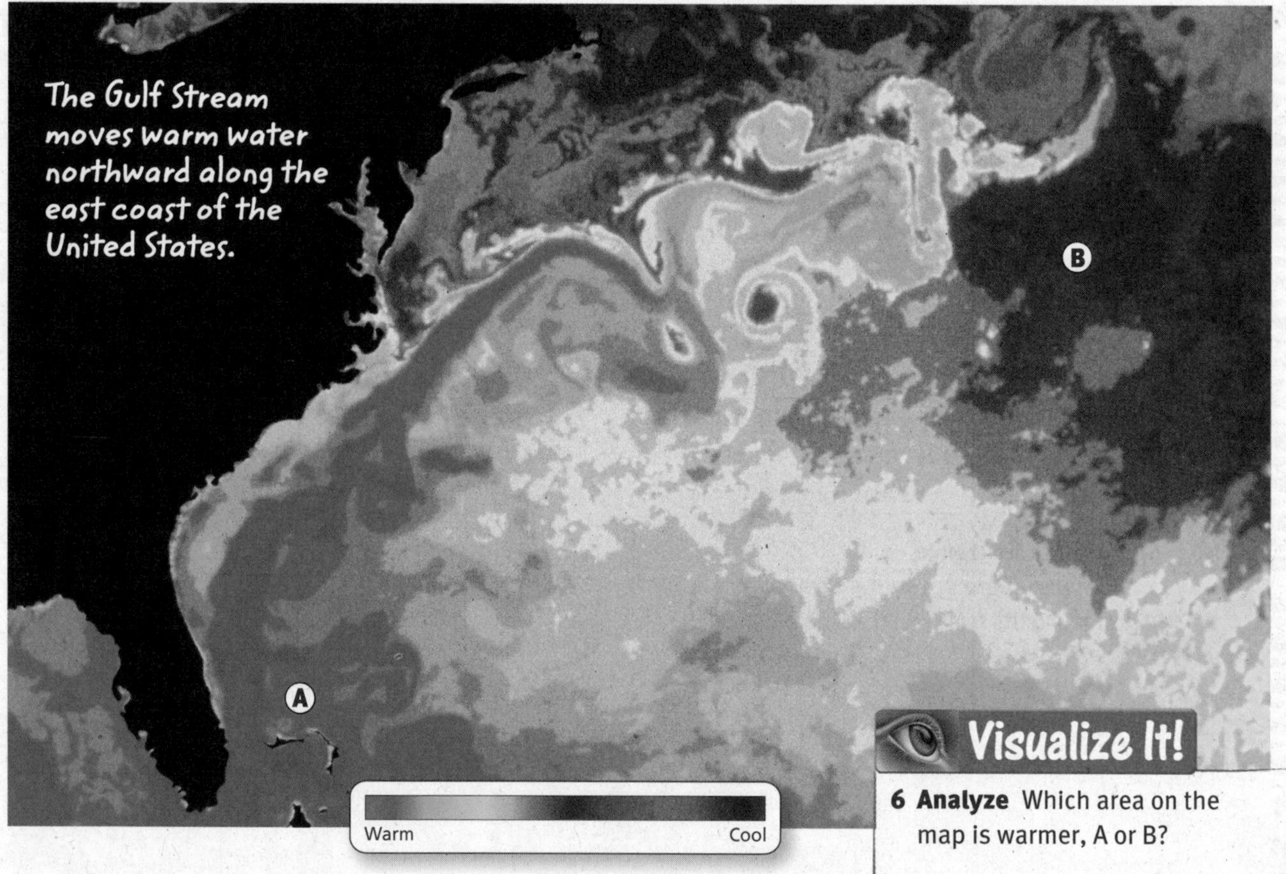

The Gulf Stream moves warm water northward along the east coast of the United States.
B
A
Warm
Cool

Visualize It!

6 Analyze Which area on the map is warmer, A or B?

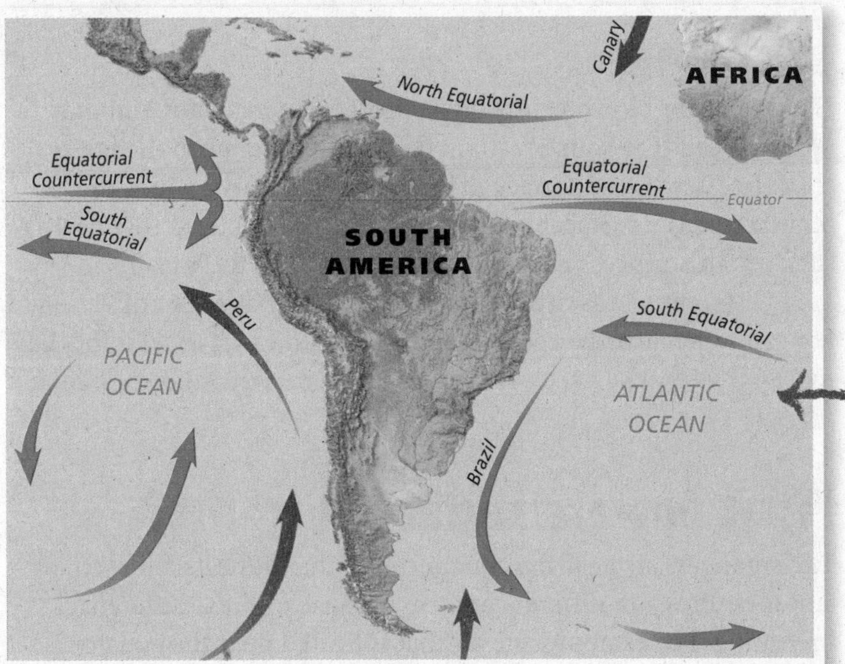

7 Identify Circle areas on the map where ocean currents have been deflected by a land mass.

Currents change direction when they meet continents.

Continental Deflections

If Earth's surface were covered only with water, surface currents would simply travel continually in one direction. However, water does not cover the entire surface of Earth. Continents rise above sea level over about one-third of Earth's surface. When surface currents meet continents, the currents are deflected and change direction. For example, the South Equatorial Current turns southward as it meets the coast of South America.

The Coriolis Effect

Earth's rotation causes all wind and ocean currents, except on the equator, to be deflected from the paths they would take if Earth did not rotate. The deflection of moving objects from a straight path due to Earth's rotation is called the **Coriolis effect** (kawr•ee•OH•lis ih•FEKT). Earth is spherical, so Earth's circumference at latitudes above and below the equator is shorter than the circumference at the equator. But the period of rotation is always 24 hours. Therefore, points on Earth near the equator travel faster than points closer to the poles.

The difference in speed of rotation causes the Coriolis effect. For example, wind and water traveling south from the North Pole actually go toward the southwest instead of straight south. Wind and water deflect to the right because the wind and water move east more slowly than Earth rotates beneath them. In the Northern Hemisphere, currents are deflected to the right. In the Southern Hemisphere, currents are deflected to the left.

The Coriolis effect is most noticeable for objects that travel over long distances, without any interruptions. Over short distances, the difference in Earth's rotational speed from one point to another point is not great enough to cause noticeable deflection.

In the Northern Hemisphere, currents are deflected to the right.

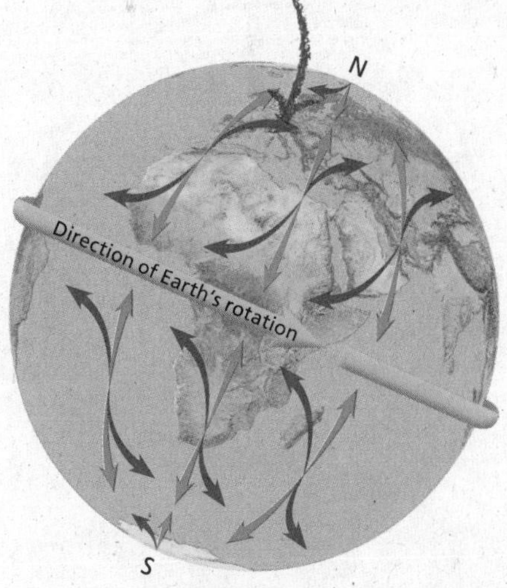

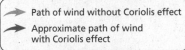

Path of wind without Coriolis effect
Approximate path of wind with Coriolis effect

Global Winds

Have you ever blown gently on a cup of hot chocolate? You may have noticed that your breath makes ripples that push the hot chocolate across the surface of the liquid. Similarly, winds that blow across the surface of Earth's oceans push water across Earth's surface. This process causes surface currents in the ocean.

Different winds cause currents to flow in different directions. For example, near the equator, the winds blow east to west for the most part. Most surface currents in the same area follow a similar pattern.

What powers surface currents?

The sun heats air near the equator more than it heats air at other latitudes. Pressure differences form because of these differences in heating. For example, the air that is heated near the equator is warmer and less dense than air at other latitudes. The rising of warm air creates an area of low pressure near the equator. Pressure differences in the atmosphere cause the wind to form. So, the sun causes winds to form, and winds cause surface currents to form. Therefore, the major source of the energy that powers surface currents is the sun.

8 Analyze Fill in the cause-and-effect chart to show how the sun's energy powers surface ocean currents.

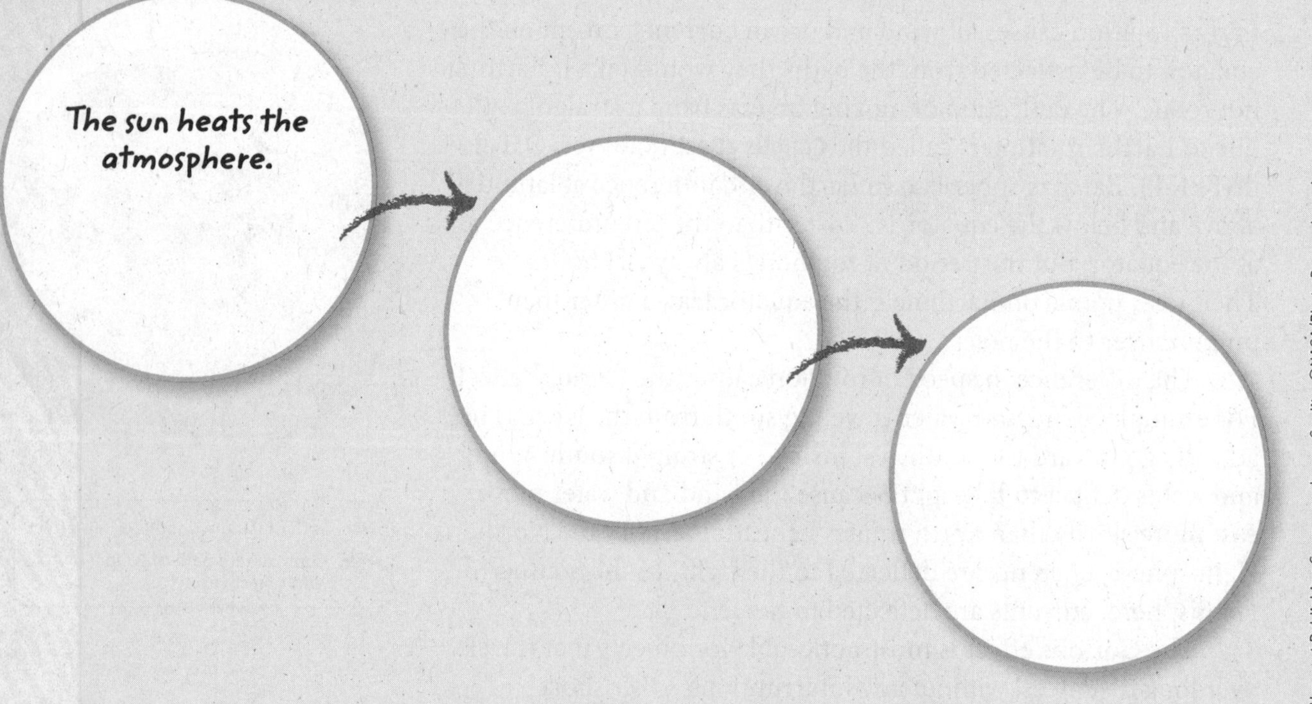
The sun heats the atmosphere.

Global Surface Winds

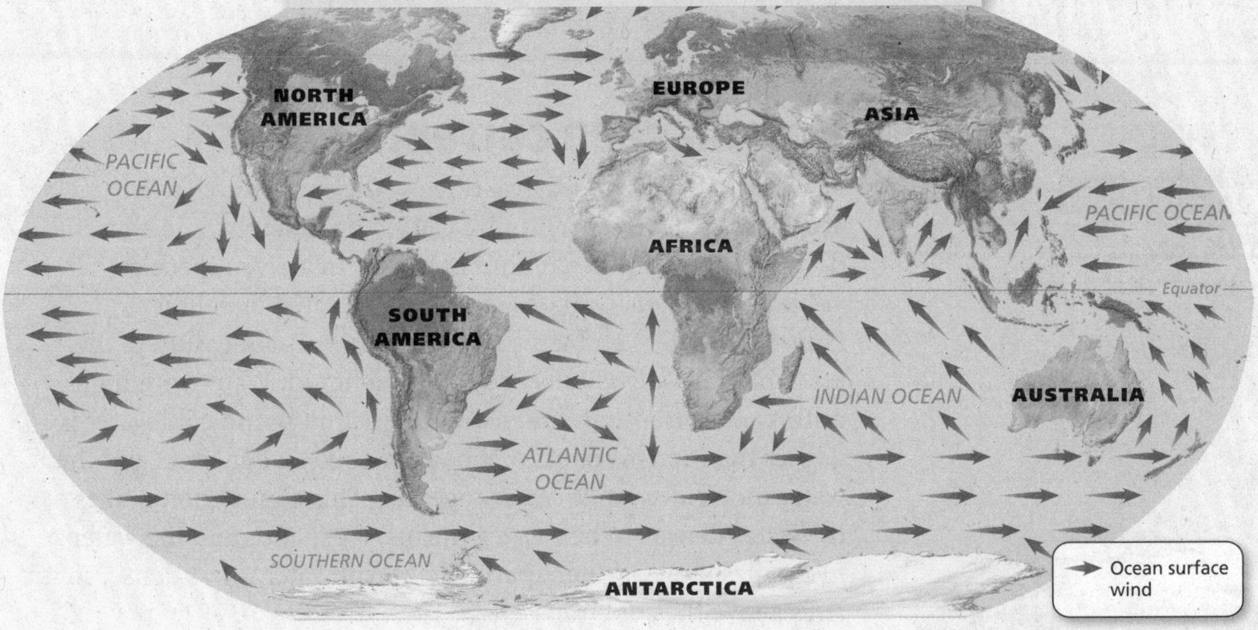

Global Surface Currents

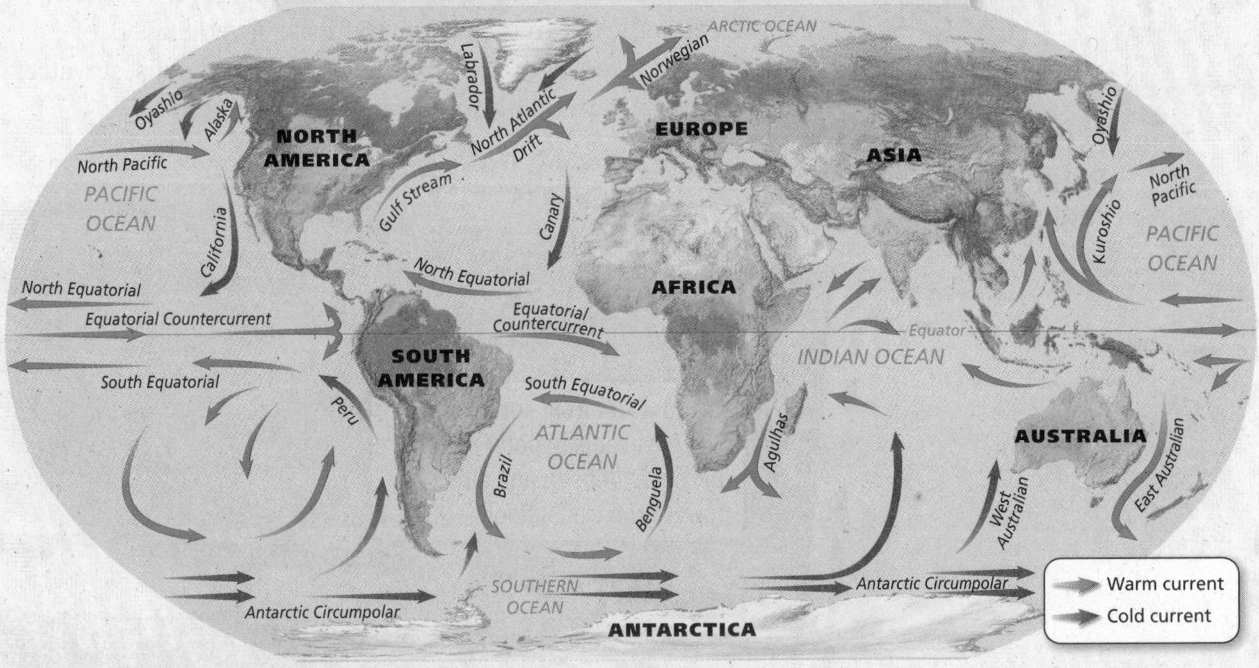

Visualize It!

9 Analyze Circle the same area on each map. Describe what you observe about these two areas.

Current Events

How do deep currents form?

Active Reading

10 Identify As you read, underline the cause of deep currents.

Movements of ocean water far below the surface are called **deep currents**. Deep currents are caused by differences in water density. *Density* is the amount of matter in a given space or volume. The density of ocean water is affected by salinity (suh•LIN•ih•tee) and temperature. *Salinity* is a measure of the amount of dissolved salts or solids in a liquid. Water with high salinity is denser than water with low salinity. And cold water is denser than warm water. When water cools, it contracts and the water molecules move closer together. This contraction makes the water denser. When water warms, it expands and the water molecules move farther apart. The warm water is less dense, so it rises above the cold water.

When ocean water at the surface becomes denser than water below it, the denser water sinks. The water moves from the surface to the deep ocean, forming deep currents. Deep currents flow along the ocean floor or along the top of another layer of denser water. Because the ocean is so deep, there are several layers of water at any location in the ocean. The deepest and densest water in the ocean is Antarctic Bottom Water, near Antarctica.

Polar region

Convection current

B — Warm water from surface currents cools in polar regions, becomes denser, and sinks toward the ocean floor.

C — Deep currents carry colder, denser water in the deep ocean from polar regions to other parts of Earth.

Visualize It!

11 Illustrate Complete the drawing at part B on the diagram.

What are convection currents?

As you read about convection currents, refer to the illustration below. Surface currents and deep currents are linked in the ocean. Together they form convection currents. In the ocean, a **convection current** is a movement of water that results from density differences. Convection currents can be vertical, circular, or cyclical. Think of convection currents in the ocean as a conveyor belt. Surface currents make up the top part of the belt. Deep currents make up the bottom part of the belt. Water from a surface current may become a deep current in areas where water density increases. Deep current water then rises up to the surface in areas where the surface current is carrying low-density water away.

Think Outside the Book Inquiry

12 Apply Write an interview with a water molecule following a convection current. Be sure to include questions and answers. Can you imagine the temperature changes the molecule would experience?

How do convection currents transfer energy?

Convection currents transfer energy. Water at the ocean's surface absorbs energy from the sun. Surface currents carry this energy to colder regions. The warm water loses energy to its surroundings and cools. As the water cools, it becomes denser and it sinks. The cold water travels along the ocean bottom. Then, the cold water rises to the surface as warm surface water moves away. The cold water absorbs energy from the sun, and the cycle continues.

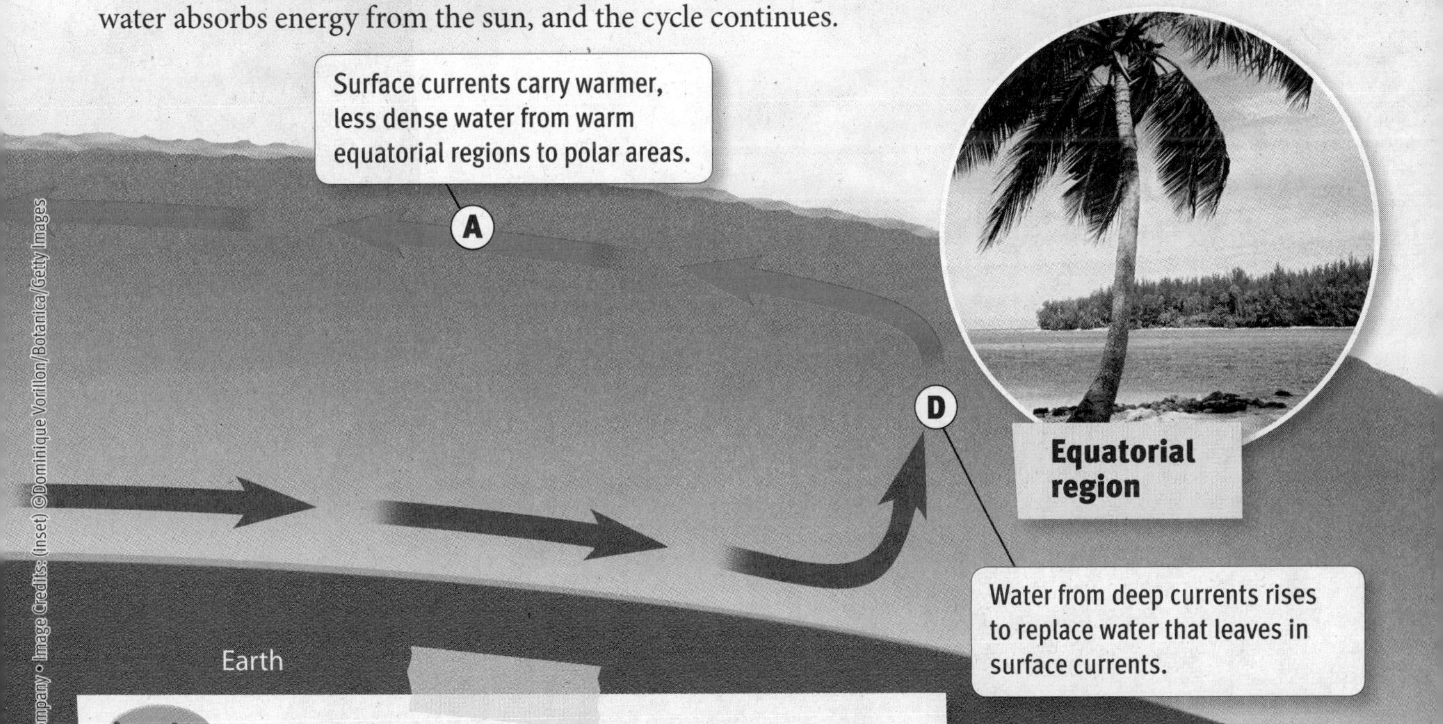

Inquiry

13 Inquire How are convection currents important in the Earth system?

Note: Drawing is not to scale.

That's Swell!

What is upwelling?

Active Reading

14 Identify As you read, underline the steps that occur in upwelling.

At times, winds blow toward the equator along the northwest coast of South America and the west coast of North America. These winds cause surface currents to move away from the shore. The warm surface water is then replaced by cold, nutrient-rich water from the deep ocean in a process called **upwelling**. The deep water contains nutrients, such as iron and nitrate.

Upwelling is extremely important to ocean life. The nutrients that are brought to the surface of the ocean support the growth of phytoplankton (fy•toh•PLANGK•tuhn) and zooplankton. These tiny plants and animals are food for other organisms, such as fish and seabirds. Many fisheries are located in areas of upwelling because ocean animals thrive there. Some weather conditions can interrupt the process of upwelling. When upwelling is reduced, the richness of the ocean life at the surface is also reduced.

The livelihood of these Peruvian fishermen depends on upwelling.

15 Predict What might happen to the fisheries if upwelling stopped?

____

____

____

____

____

____

On the coast of California, upwelling sustains large kelp forests.

During upwelling, cold, nutrient-rich water from the deep ocean rises to the surface.

Why It Matters

Hitching a Ride!

What do coconuts, plankton, and sea turtles have in common? They get free rides on ocean currents.

World Travel

When baby sea turtles are hatched on a beach, they head for the ocean. They can then pick up ocean currents to travel. Some travel from Australia to South America on currents.

Sprouting Coconuts!

This sprouting coconut may be transported by ocean currents to a beach. This transport explains why coconut trees can grow in several areas.

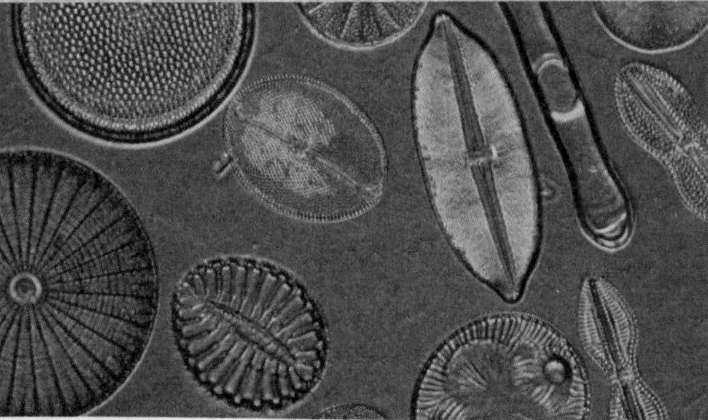

Fast Food

Diatoms are a kind of phytoplankton. They are tiny, one-celled plants that form the basis of the food chain. Diatoms ride surface currents throughout the world.

Extend

Inquiry

16 Identify List three organisms transported by ocean currents.

17 Research Investigate the Sargasso Sea. State why a lot of plastic collects in this sea. Find out whether any plastic collects on the shoreline nearest you.

18 Explain Describe how plastic and other debris can collect in the ocean by doing one of the following:

- make a poster
- write a poem
- write a song
- write a short story

Traveling the World

What do ocean currents transport?

Active Reading

19 Identify As you read, underline the description of how energy reaches the poles.

Ocean water circulates through all of Earth's ocean basins. The paths are like the main highway on which ocean water flows. If you could follow a water molecule on this path, you would find that the molecule takes more than 1,000 years to return to its starting point! Along with water, ocean currents also transport dissolved solids, dissolved gases, and energy around Earth.

20 Describe Choose a location on the map. Using your finger, follow the route you would take if you could ride a current. Describe your route. Include the direction you go and the landmasses you pass.

Antarctica is not shown on this map, but the currents at the bottom of the map circulate around Antarctica.

Ocean Currents Transport Energy

Global ocean circulation is very important in the transport of energy in the form of heat. Remember that ocean currents flow in huge convection currents that can be thousands of kilometers long. These convection currents carry about 40% of the energy that is transported around Earth's surface.

Near the equator, the ocean absorbs a large amount of solar energy. The ocean also absorbs energy from the atmosphere. Ocean currents carry this energy from the equator toward the poles. When the warm water travels to cooler areas, the energy is released back into the atmosphere. Therefore, ocean circulation has an important influence on Earth's climate.

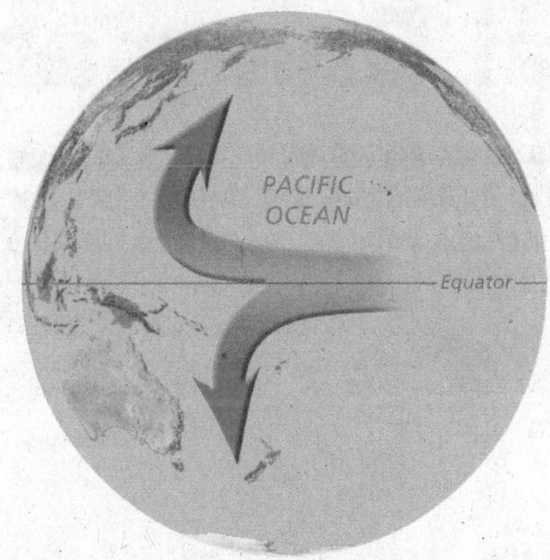

In the Pacific Ocean, surface currents transport energy from the tropics to latitudes above and below the equator.

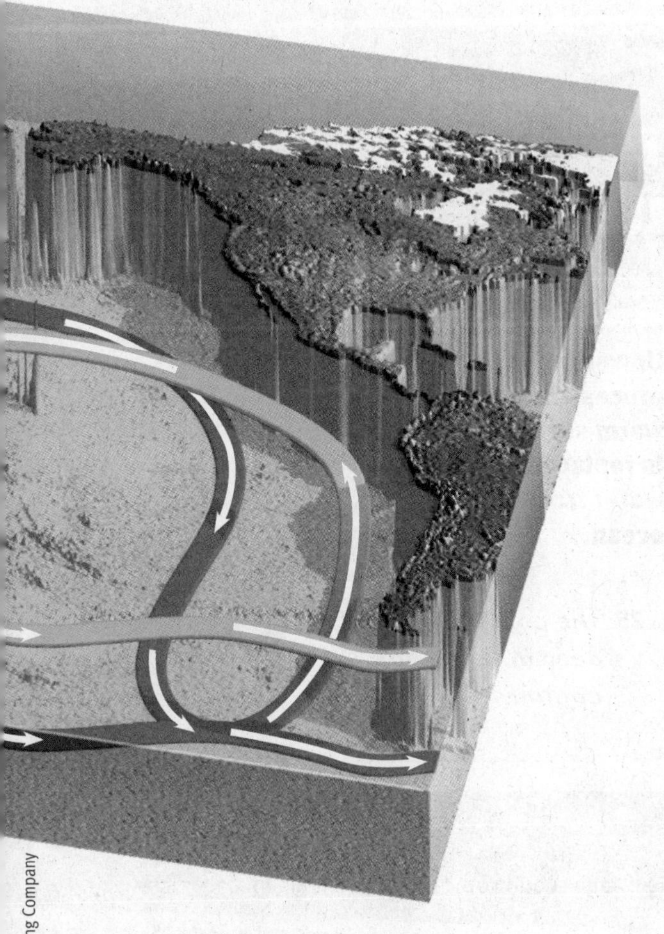

Ocean Currents Transport Matter

Besides water, ocean currents transport whatever is in the water. The most familiar dissolved solid in ocean water is sodium chloride, or table salt. Other dissolved solids are important to marine life. Ocean water contains many nutrients—such as nitrogen and phosphorus—that are important for plant and animal growth.

Ocean water also transports gases. Gases in the atmosphere are absorbed by ocean water at the ocean surface. As a result, the most abundant gases in the atmosphere—nitrogen, oxygen, argon, and carbon dioxide—are also abundant in the ocean. Dissolved oxygen and carbon dioxide are necessary for the survival of many marine organisms.

21 List Write three examples of matter besides water that are transported by ocean currents.

Visual Summary

To complete this summary, draw an arrow to show each type of ocean current. Fill in the blanks with the correct word. Then use the key below to check your answers. You can use this page to review the main concepts of the lesson.

Ocean Currents

Surface currents are streamlike movements of water at or near the surface of the ocean.

22 The direction of a surface current is affected by

_______________,

_______________,

and _______________

Deep currents are streamlike movements of ocean water located far below the surface.

23 Deep currents form where the

____

of ocean water increases.

A convection current in the ocean is any movement of matter that results from differences in density.

24 A convection current in the ocean transports matter and

____

Upwelling is the process in which warm surface water is replaced by cold water from the deep ocean.

25 The cold water from deep in the ocean contains

____

Answers: 22 continental deflections, the Coriolis effect, global winds; 23 density; 24 energy; 25 nutrients

26 Describe State the two general patterns of global ocean circulation.

Lesson Review

Vocabulary

Fill in the blanks with the terms that best complete the following sentences.

1 ______________________ are streamlike movements of water in the ocean.

2 The ______________________ causes currents in open water to move in a curved path rather than a straight path.

3 ______________________ causes cold, nutrient-rich waters to move up to the ocean's surface.

Key Concepts

4 Explain List the steps that show how the sun provides the energy for surface ocean currents.

5 Explain State how a deep current forms.

6 Describe Explain how a convection current transports energy around the globe.

7 List Write the three factors that affect surface ocean currents.

Critical Thinking

Use this diagram to answer the following questions.

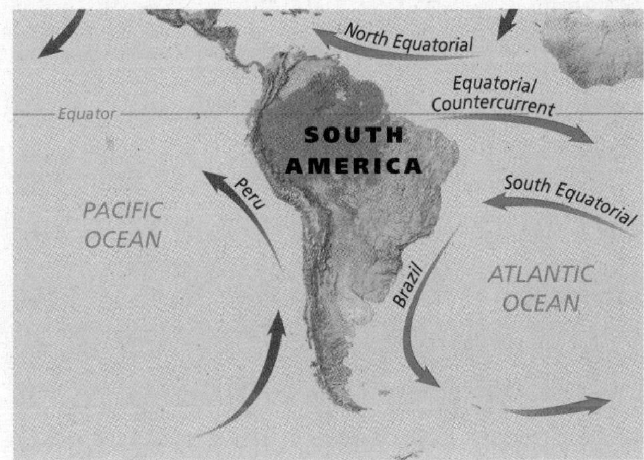

8 Apply Explain why the direction of the South Equatorial current changes.

9 Apply If South America were not there, explain how the direction of the South Equatorial current would be different.

10 Apply Describe how surface currents would be affected if Earth did not rotate.

My Notes

Unit 3 Summary

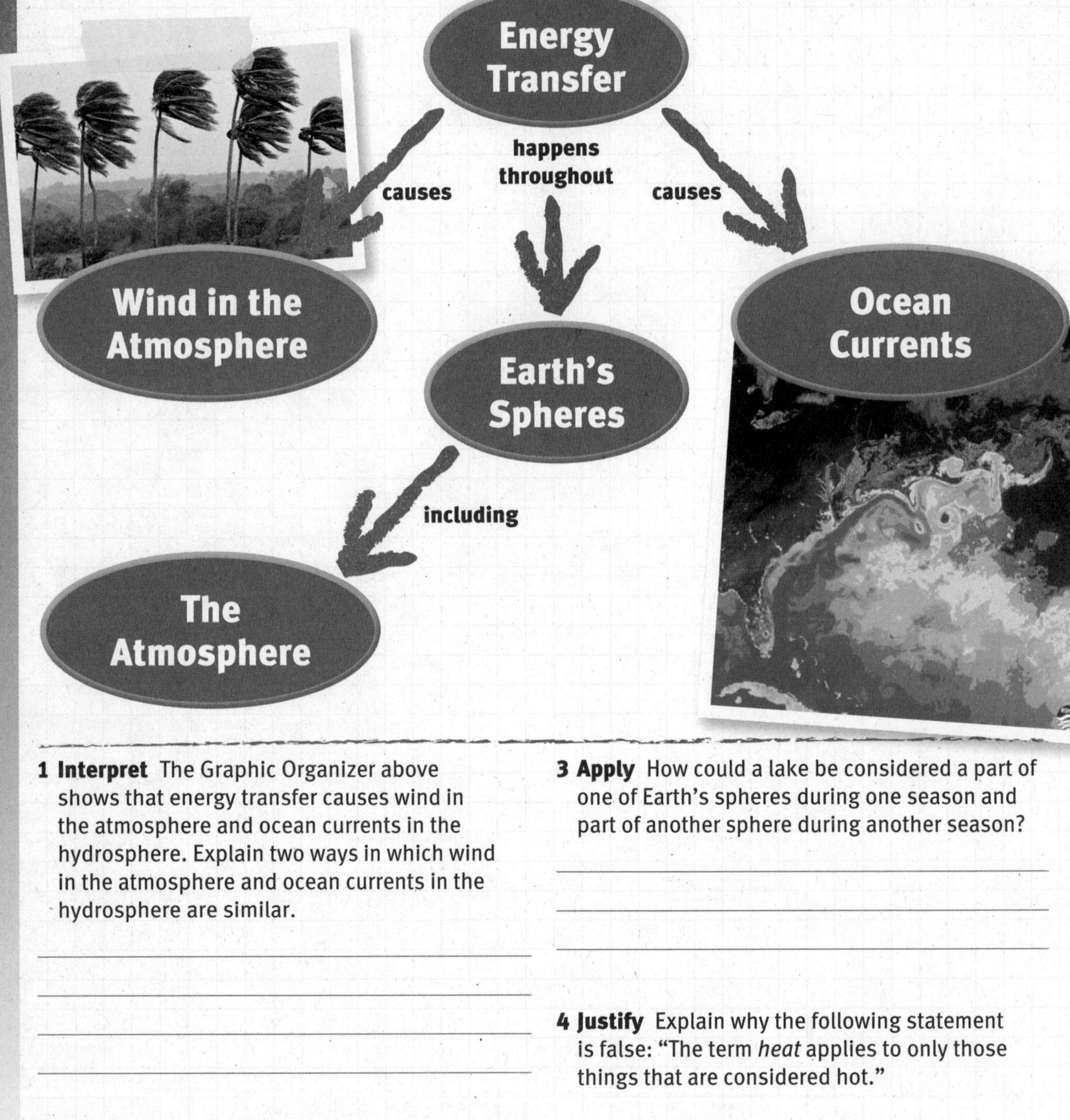

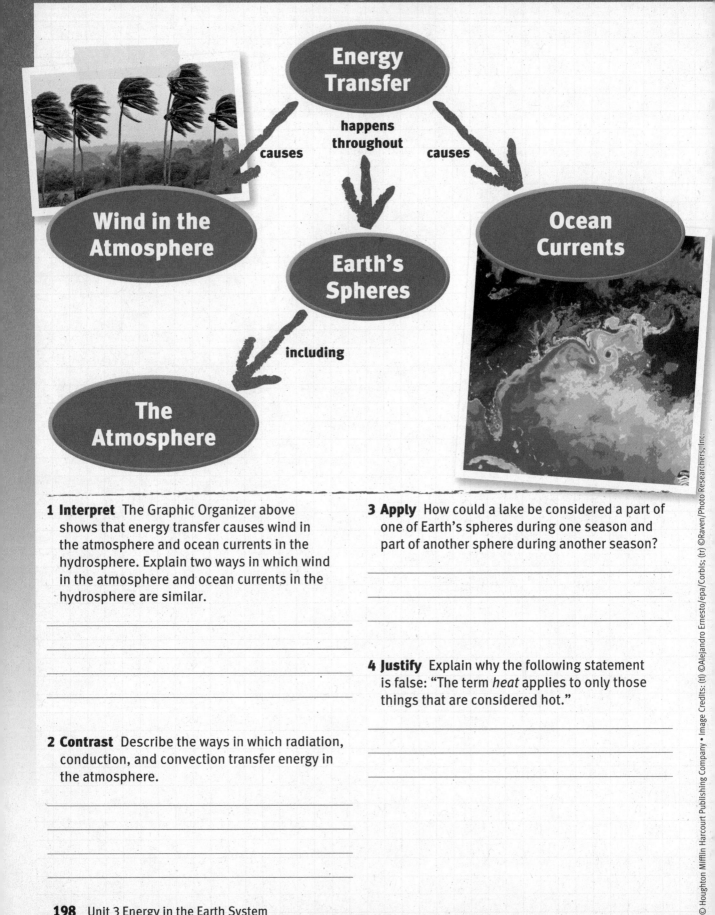

1 **Interpret** The Graphic Organizer above shows that energy transfer causes wind in the atmosphere and ocean currents in the hydrosphere. Explain two ways in which wind in the atmosphere and ocean currents in the hydrosphere are similar.

2 **Contrast** Describe the ways in which radiation, conduction, and convection transfer energy in the atmosphere.

3 **Apply** How could a lake be considered a part of one of Earth's spheres during one season and part of another sphere during another season?

4 **Justify** Explain why the following statement is false: "The term *heat* applies to only those things that are considered hot."

UNIT 4

Weather and Climate

Strong winds create huge waves that crash on shore.

Big Idea 7

Earth Systems and Patterns

What do you think?

The weather can change very quickly. In severe weather, people and pets can get hurt, and property can be damaged. Can you think of ways to keep people, pets, and property safe?

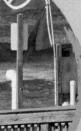

Warning flags are used to show how safe this beach is.

Unit 4

Weather and Climate

CITIZEN SCIENCE

Exit Strategy

When there is an emergency, knowing what to do helps keep people as safe as possible. So what's the plan?

1 Think About It

A Do you know what to do if there were a weather emergency while you were in school?

____

B What kinds of information might you need to stay safe? List them below.

____

____

____

____

____

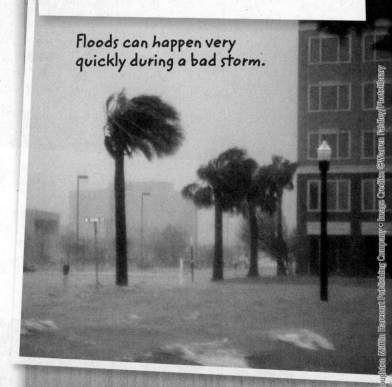

Floods can happen very quickly during a bad storm.

② Ask a Question

How well do you know your school's emergency evacuation plan? Obtain a copy of the school's emergency evacuation plan. Read through the plan and answer the following questions as a class.

A Is the emergency evacuation plan/map easy for students to understand?

____

B How would you know which way to go?

____

____

C How often do you have practice drills?

____

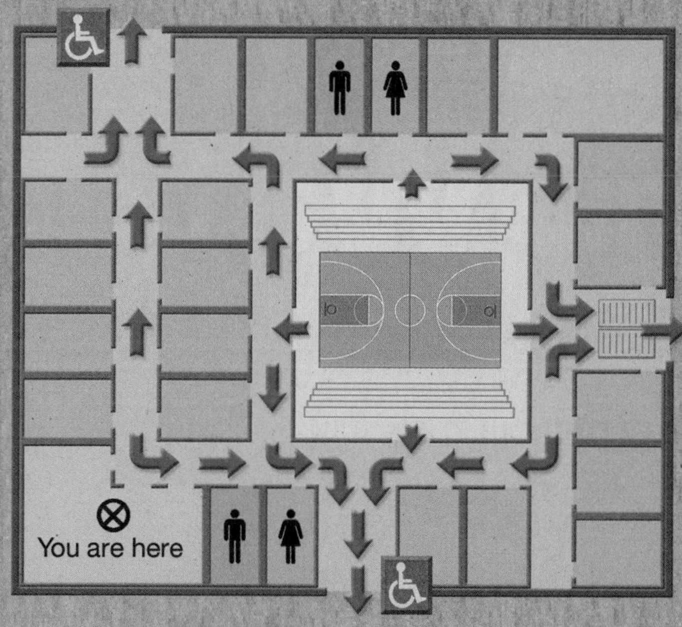

EMERGENCY EVACUATION ROUTE

③ Propose and Apply Improvements

A Using what you have learned about your school's emergency evacuation plan, list your ideas for improvements below.

____

____

____

____

____

____

B Develop and give a short oral presentation to your principal about your proposal on ways to improve the school's emergency evacuation plan. Write the main points of your presentation below.

____

____

____

____

____

C As a class, practice the newly improved emergency evacuation plan. Describe how well the improved emergency evacuation plan worked.

____

____

____

____

____

____

____

____

Take It Home

With an adult, create an emergency evacuation plan for your family or evaluate your family's emergency evacuation plan and propose improvements.

Lesson 1

The Water Cycle

ESSENTIAL QUESTION

How does water change state and move around on Earth?

By the end of this lesson, you should be able to describe the water cycle and the different processes that are part of the water cycle on Earth.

When do clouds touch the sea? When it rains. This is one way in which water from the air returns to Earth's surface. Can you think of other ways in which water returns to Earth?

Sunshine State Standards

SC.6.E.7.2 Investigate and apply how the cycling of water between the atmosphere and hydrosphere has an effect on weather patterns and climate.

SC.6.E.7.4 Differentiate and show interactions among the geosphere, hydrosphere, cryosphere, atmosphere, and biosphere.

Engage Your Brain

1 **Predict** Circle the word or phrase that best completes the following sentences.

The air inside a glass of ice would feel *warm/cold/room temperature*.

Ice would *melt/evaporate/remain frozen* if it were left outside on a hot day.

Water vapor will *condense on/evaporate from/melt into* the glass of ice from the air.

The ice *absorbs energy from/maintains its energy/releases energy into* the surroundings when it melts.

2 **Analyze** Using the photo above, solve the word scramble to answer the question: What happens to ice as it warms up?

T I G A C N S E H E A S T T

Active Reading

3 **Synthesize** You can often define an unknown word if you know the meaning of the word's origin. Use the meaning of the words' origins and the sentence below to make an educated guess about the meaning of *precipitation* and *evaporation*.

Latin word	Meaning
praecipitare	fall
evaporare	spread out in vapor or steam

Example sentence

Precipitation, in the form of rain, helps replace the water lost by evaporation from the lake.

precipitation:

evaporation:

Vocabulary Terms

- **water cycle**
- **evaporation**
- **transpiration**
- **sublimation**
- **condensation**
- **precipitation**

4 **Apply** As you learn the definition of each vocabulary term in this lesson, write out a sentence using that term to help you remember the meaning of the term.

What goes up...

What is the water cycle?

Movement of water between the atmosphere, land, oceans, and even living things makes up the **water cycle**. Rain, snow, and hail fall on the oceans and land because of gravity. On land, ice and water flow downhill. Water flows in streams, rivers, and waterfalls such as the one in the photo, because of gravity. If the land is flat, water will collect in certain areas forming ponds, lakes, and marshland. Some water will soak through the ground and collect underground as groundwater. Even groundwater flows downhill.

Water and snow can move upward if they turn into water vapor and rise into the air. Plants and animals also release water vapor into the air. In the air, water vapor can travel great distances with the wind. Winds can also move the water in the surface layer of the ocean by creating ocean currents. When ocean currents reach the shore or colder climates, the water will sink if it is cold enough or salty enough. The sinking water creates currents at different depths in the ocean. These are some of the ways in which water travels all over Earth.

Visualize It!

5 Analyze What is the relationship between gravity and water in this image?

How does water change state?

Water is found in three states on Earth: as liquid water, as solid water ice, and as gaseous water vapor. Water is visible as a liquid or a solid, but it is invisible as a gas in the air. Water can change from one state to another as energy is absorbed or released.

Water absorbs energy from its surroundings as it *melts* from solid to liquid. Water also absorbs energy when it *evaporates* from liquid to gas, or when it *sublimates* from solid to gas. Water releases energy into its surroundings when it *condenses* from gas to liquid. Water also releases energy when it *freezes* from liquid to solid, or *deposits* from gas to solid. No water is lost during these changes.

6 Identify As you read, underline each process in which energy is absorbed or released.

Visualize It!

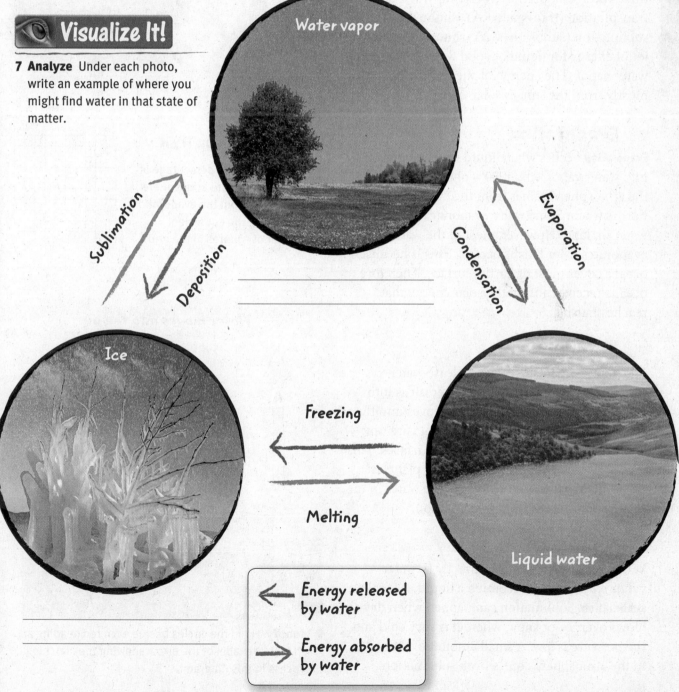

7 Analyze Under each photo, write an example of where you might find water in that state of matter.

Water vapor

Sublimation

Deposition

Evaporation

Condensation

Ice

Freezing

Melting

Liquid water

Energy released by water

Energy absorbed by water

The evaporating water leaves behind a dry, cracked lake bed.

How does water reach the atmosphere?

Water reaches the atmosphere as water vapor in three ways: evaporation (i•VAP•uh•ray•shuhn), transpiration (tran•spuh•RAY•shuhn), and sublimation (suhb•luh•MAY•shuhn). It takes a lot of energy for liquid or solid water to turn into water vapor. The energy for these changes comes mostly from the sun, as solar energy.

◯ Evaporation

Evaporation occurs when liquid water changes into water vapor. About 90% of the water in the atmosphere comes from the evaporation of Earth's water. Some water evaporates from the water on land. However, most of the water vapor evaporates from Earth's oceans. This is because oceans cover most of Earth's surface. Therefore, oceans receive most of the solar energy that reaches Earth.

◯ Transpiration

Like many organisms, plants release water into the environment. Liquid water turns into water vapor inside the plant and moves into the atmosphere through stomata. Stomata are tiny holes that are found on some plant surfaces. This release of water vapor into the air by plants is called **transpiration**. About 10% of the water in the atmosphere comes from transpiration.

◯ Sublimation

When solid water changes directly to water vapor without first becoming a liquid, it is called **sublimation**. Sublimation can happen when dry air blows over ice or snow, where it is very cold and the pressure is low. A small amount of the water in the atmosphere comes from sublimation.

Do the Math **You Try It**

8 Graph Show the percentage of water vapor in the atmosphere that comes from the evaporation by coloring the equivalent number of squares in the grid.

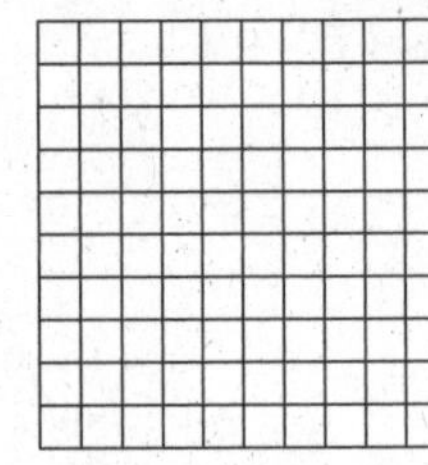

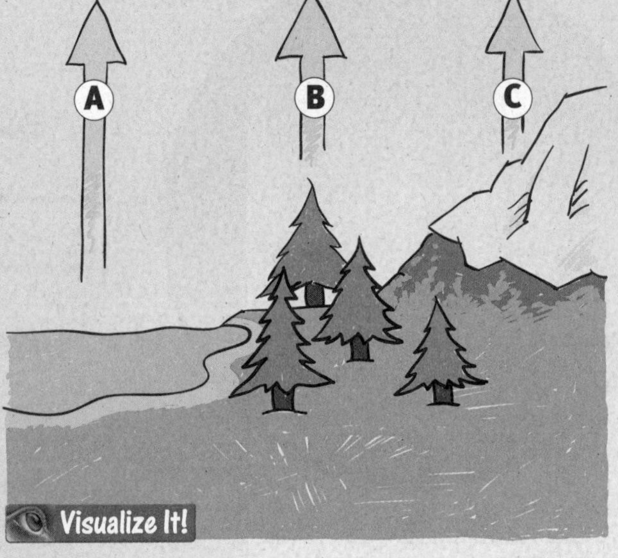
Water moves into the air.
A
B
C

Visualize It!

9 Identify Fill in the circles beside each red heading at left with the label of the arrow showing the matching process in this diagram.

What happens to water in the atmosphere?

Water reaches the atmosphere as water vapor. In the atmosphere, water vapor mixes with other gases. To leave the atmosphere, water vapor must change into liquid or solid water. Then the liquid or solid water can fall to Earth's surface.

◯ Condensation

Remember, **condensation** (kahn•den•SAY•shuhn) is the change of state from a gas to a liquid. If air that contains water vapor is cooled enough, condensation occurs. Some of the water vapor condenses on small particles, such as dust, forming little balls or tiny droplets of water. These water droplets float in the air as clouds, fog, or mist. At the ground level, water vapor may condense on cool surfaces as dew.

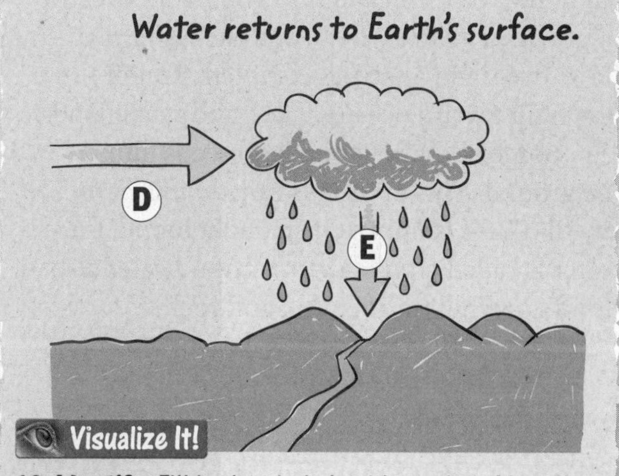

10 Identify Fill in the circle beside each red heading at left with the label of the arrow showing the matching process in this diagram.

◯ Precipitation

In clouds, water droplets may collide and "stick" together to become larger. If a droplet becomes large enough, it falls to Earth's surface as precipitation (pri•sip•i•TAY•shuhn). **Precipitation** is any form of water that falls to Earth from clouds. Three common kinds of precipitation shown in the photos are rain, snow, and hail. Snow and hail form if the water droplets freeze. Most rain falls into the oceans because most water evaporates from ocean surfaces and oceans cover most of Earth's surface. But winds carry clouds from the ocean over land, increasing the amount of precipitation that falls on land.

11 Summarize Fill in the boxes to describe how precipitation forms.

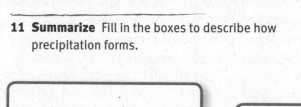

________________	→ Small droplet
________________	→ Large droplet falls to Earth.

How does water move on land and in the oceans?

After water falls to Earth, it flows and circulates all over Earth. On land, water flows downhill, both on the surface and underground. However, most of Earth's precipitation falls into the oceans. Ocean currents move water around the oceans.

Runoff and Infiltration

All of the water on land flows downhill because of gravity. Streams, rivers, and the water that flows over land are types of *runoff*. Runoff flows downhill toward oceans, lakes, and marshlands.

Some of the water on land seeps into the ground. This process is called *infiltration* (in•fil•TRAY•shuhn). Once undergound, the water is called *groundwater*. Groundwater also flows downhill through soil and rock.

12 Compare How do runoff and groundwater differ?

Visualize It!

13 Summarize Write a caption describing how water is moving in the diagram above.

Icebergs can be carried over long distances by ocean currents.

Ice Flow

Much of Earth's ice is stored in large ice caps in Antarctica and Greenland. Some ice is stored in glaciers at high altitudes all over Earth. Glaciers cover about 10% of Earth's surface. Glaciers can be called "rivers of ice" because gravity also causes glaciers to flow slowly downhill. Many glaciers never leave land. However, some glaciers flow to the ocean, where pieces may break off, as seen in the photo, and float far out to sea as icebergs.

Ocean Circulation

Winds move ocean water on the surface in great currents, sometimes for thousands of miles. At some shores, or if the water is very cold or salty, it will sink deep into the ocean. This movement helps create deep ocean currents. Both surface currents and deep ocean currents transport large amounts of water from ocean to ocean.

Water Works

What does the water cycle transport?

In the water cycle, each state of water has some energy in it. This energy is released into or absorbed from its surroundings as water changes state. The energy in each state of water is then transported as the water moves from place to place. Matter is also transported as water and the materials in the water move all over Earth. Therefore, the water cycle moves energy and matter through Earth's atmosphere, land, oceans, and living things.

Think Outside the Book

14 Apply With a classmate, discuss how the water cycle transfers energy.

Energy

Energy is transported in the water cycle through changes of state and by the movement of water from place to place. For example, water that evaporates from the ocean carries energy into the atmosphere. This movement of energy can generate hurricanes. Also, cold ocean currents can cool the air along a coastline by absorbing the energy from the air and leaving the air cooler. This energy is carried away quickly as the current continues on its path. Such processes affect the weather and climate of an area.

Matter

Earth's ocean currents move vast amounts of water all over the world. These currents also transport the solids in the water and the dissolved salts and gases. Rivers transfer water from land into the ocean. Rivers also carry large amounts of sand, mud, and gravel as shown below. Rivers form deltas and floodplains, where some of the materials from upstream collect in areas downstream. Rivers also carve valleys and canyons, and carry the excess materials downstream. Glaciers also grind away rock and carry the ground rock with them as they flow.

Visualize It!

15 Identify What do rivers, such as the ones in the photo, transport?

____

____

Visualize It! The Water Cycle

Water is continuously changing state and moving from place to place in the water cycle. This diagram shows these processes and movements.

16 Identify Label each arrow to show which process the arrow represents.

17 Identify Shade in the arrows that indicate where water is changing state.

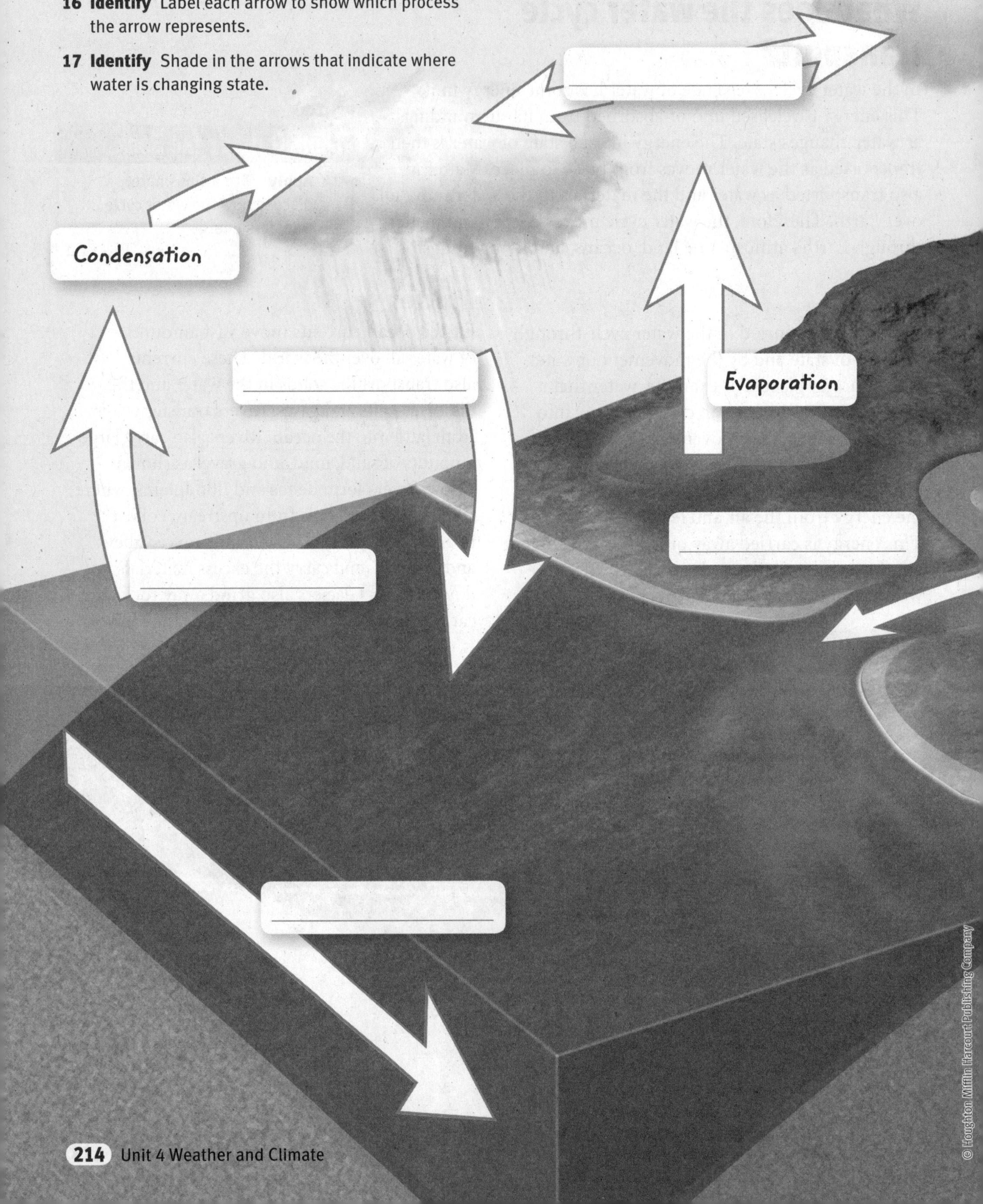

Condensation

Evaporation

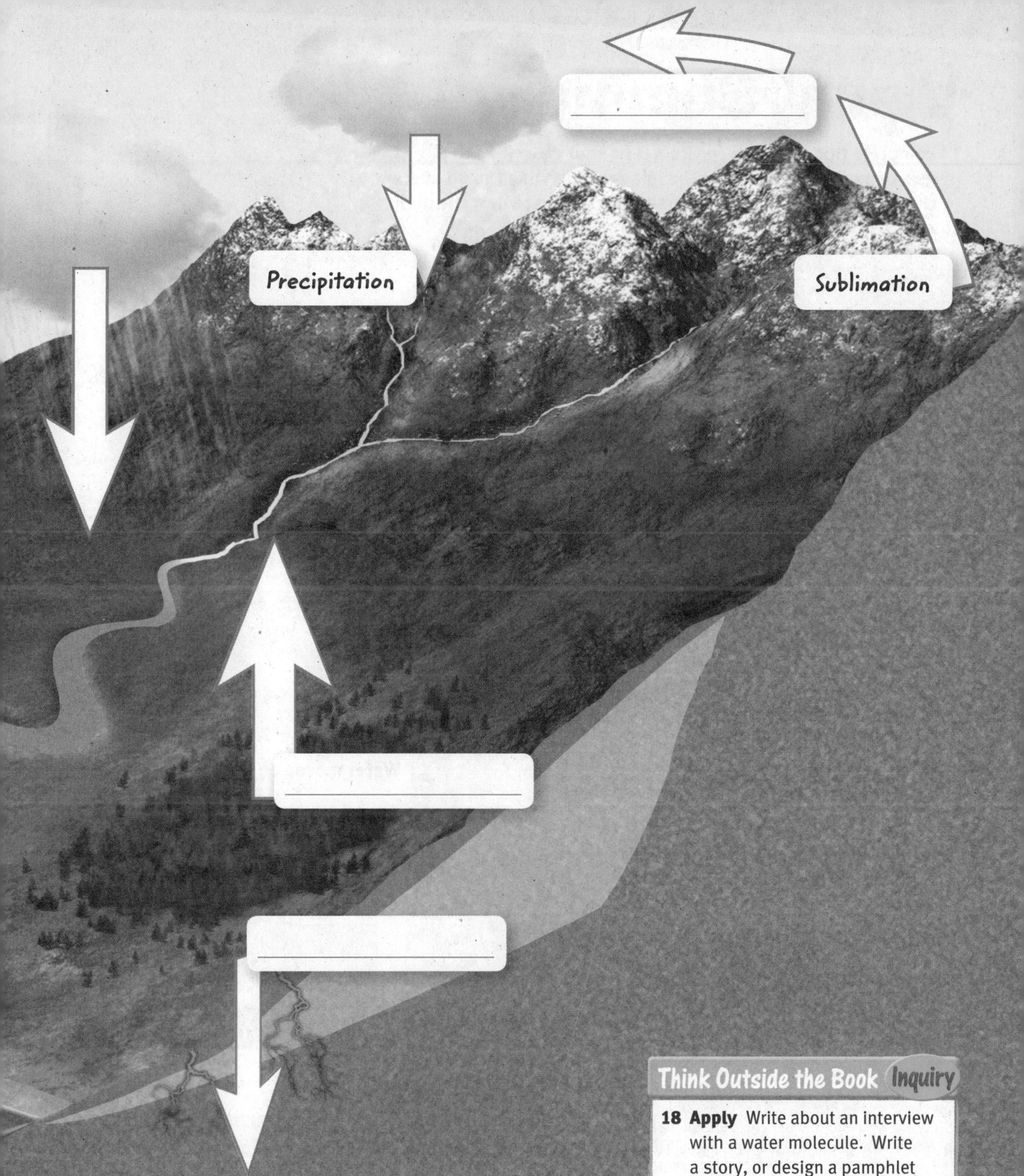

Precipitation

Sublimation

Think Outside the Book Inquiry

18 Apply Write about an interview with a water molecule. Write a story, or design a pamphlet describing one possible trip that a water molecule could take through the water cycle. Share your project with classmates.

Visual Summary

To complete this summary, write a term that describes the process happening in each of the images. Then use the key below to check your answers. You can use this page to review the main concepts of the lesson.

Water moves in the atmosphere.

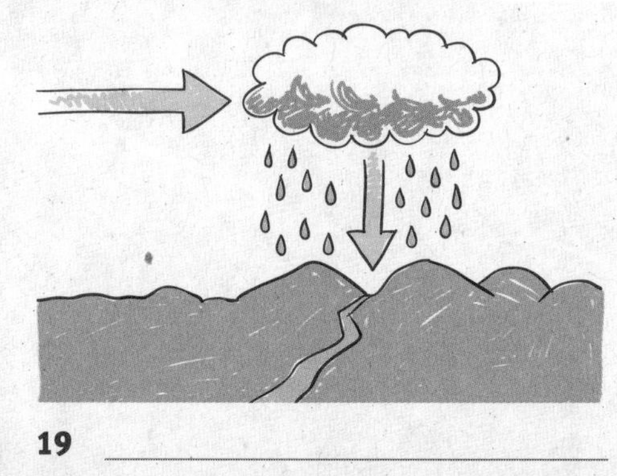

19 ______________________

The Water Cycle

Water moves on land and in oceans.

20 ______________________

Water moves into the atmosphere.

21 ______________________

Answers: 19 condensation or precipitation; 20 iceflow, runoff, infiltration, or ocean current; 21 evaporation, transpiration, or sublimation

22 Predict Describe what might happen to the water cycle if less solar energy reached Earth and how Earth's climate would be affected.

Lesson Review

Vocabulary

Write the correct label A, B, C, or D under each term to indicate the definition of that term.

1 water cycle

2 evaporation

3 precipitation

4 condensation

A The change of state from a liquid to a gas

B The change of state from a gas to a liquid

C The movement of water between the atmosphere, land, oceans, and living things

D Any form of water that falls to Earth's surface from the clouds

Key Concepts

5 Identify List the three ways in which water reaches the atmosphere and tell which way accounts for most of the water in the atmosphere.

6 Classify Which of the processes of the water cycle occur by releasing energy?

7 Identify What happens to water once it reaches Earth's surface?

8 Summarize Describe how three common types of precipitation form.

Critical Thinking

Use the image below to answer the following question.

9 Apply Describe the energy changes occurring in the process shown above.

10 Infer Why does the amount of water that flows in a river change during the year?

11 Predict During a storm, a tree fell over into a river. What might happen to this tree?

12 Evaluate Warm ocean currents cool as they flow along a coastline, away from the equator. Explain what is transported and how.

Lesson 2

Elements of Weather

ESSENTIAL QUESTION

What is weather and how can we describe different types of weather conditions?

By the end of this lesson, you should be able to describe elements of weather and explain how they are measured.

Weather stations placed all around the world allow scientists to measure the elements, or separate parts, of weather.

A researcher checks an automatic weather station on Alexander Island, Antarctica.

Sunshine State Standards

SC.6.E.7.2 Investigate and apply how the cycling of water between the atmosphere and hydrosphere has an effect on weather patterns and climate.

SC.6.E.7.3 Describe how global patterns such as the jet stream and ocean currents influence local weather in measurable terms such as temperature, air pressure, wind direction and speed, and humidity and precipitation.

Engage Your Brain

1 Predict Check T or F to show whether you think each statement is true or false.

T	F	
☐	☐	Weather can change every day.
☐	☐	Temperature is measured by using a barometer.
☐	☐	Air pressure increases as you move higher in the atmosphere.
☐	☐	Visibility is a measurement of how far we can see.

2 Describe Use at least three words that might describe the weather on a day when the sky looks like the picture above.

____

____

____

____

Active Reading

3 Distinguish The words *weather, whether,* and *wether* all sound alike but are spelled differently and mean entirely different things. You may have never heard of a wether—it is a neutered male sheep or ram.

Circle the correct use of the three words in the sentence below.

The farmer wondered *weather / whether / wether* the cold *weather / whether / wether* had affected his *weather / whether / wether.*

Vocabulary Terms

- weather
- humidity
- relative humidity
- dew point
- precipitation
- air pressure
- wind
- visibility

4 Apply As you learn the definition of each vocabulary term in this lesson, create your own definition or sketch to help you remember the meaning of the term.

Wonder about Weather?

What is weather?

Weather is the condition of Earth's atmosphere at a certain time and place. Different observations give you clues to the weather. If you see plants moving from side to side, you might infer that it is windy. If you see a gray sky and wet, shiny streets, you might decide to wear a raincoat. People talk about weather by describing factors such as temperature, humidity, precipitation, air pressure, wind, and *visibility* (viz•uh•BIL•i•tee).

What is temperature and how is it measured?

Temperature is a measure of how hot or cold something is. An instrument that measures and displays temperature is called a *thermometer*. A common type of thermometer uses a liquid such as alcohol or mercury to display the temperature. The liquid is sealed in a glass tube. When the air gets warmer, the liquid expands and rises in the tube. Cooler air causes the liquid to contract and fill less of the tube. A scale, often in Celsius (°C) or Fahrenheit (°F), is marked on the glass tube.

Another type of thermometer is an electrical thermometer. As the temperature becomes higher, electric current flow increases through the thermometer. The strength of the current is then translated into temperature readings.

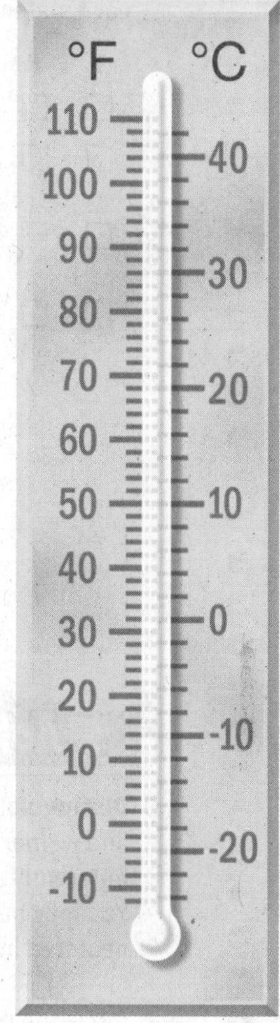

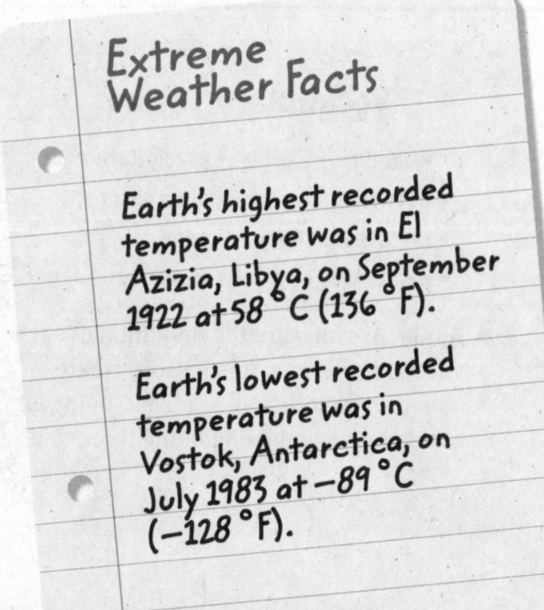

Extreme Weather Facts
Earth's highest recorded temperature was in El Azizia, Libya, on September 1922 at 58 °C (136 °F).
Earth's lowest recorded temperature was in Vostok, Antarctica, on July 1983 at −89 °C (−128 °F).

5 Identify Color in the liquid in the thermometer above to show Earth's average temperature in 2009 (58 °F). Write the Celsius temperature that equals 58 °F on the line below.

___

What is humidity and how is it measured?

As water evaporates from oceans, lakes, and ponds, it becomes water vapor, or a gas that is in the air. The amount of water vapor in the air is called **humidity**. As more water evaporates and becomes water vapor, the humidity of the air increases.

Humidity is often described through relative humidity. **Relative humidity** is the amount of water vapor in the air compared to the amount of water vapor needed to reach saturation. As shown below, when air is saturated, the rates of evaporation and condensation are equal. Saturated air has a relative humidity of 100%. A psychrometer (sy•KRAHM•i•ter) is an instrument that is used to measure relative humidity.

Air can become saturated when evaporation adds water vapor to the air. Air can also become saturated when it cools to its dew point. The **dew point** is the temperature at which more condensation than evaporation occurs. When air temperature drops below the dew point, condensation forms. This can cause dew on surfaces cooler than the dew point. It also can form fog and clouds.

Active Reading

6 Identify Underline the name of the instrument used to measure relative humidity.

7 Sketch In the space provided, draw what happens in air that is below the dew point.

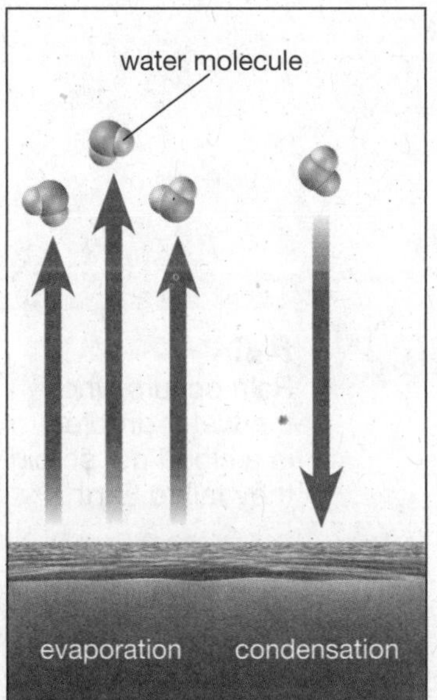

In unsaturated air, more water evaporates into the air than condenses back into the water.

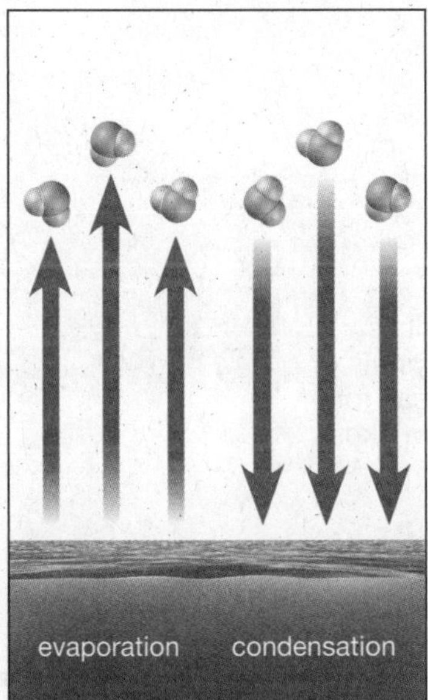

In saturated air, the amount of water that evaporates equals the amount that condenses.

When air cools below its dew point, more water vapor condenses into water than evaporates.

8 Explain Why does dew form on grass overnight?

What is precipitation and how is it measured?

Water vapor in the air condenses not only on Earth's surfaces, but also on tiny particles in the air to form clouds. When this water from the air returns to Earth's surface, it falls as precipitation. **Precipitation** is any form of water that falls to Earth's surface from the clouds. The four main forms of precipitation are rain, snow, hail, and sleet.

Rain is the most common form of precipitation. Inside a cloud, the droplets formed by condensation collide and form larger droplets. They finally become heavy enough to fall as raindrops. Rain is measured with a rain gauge, as shown in the picture below. A funnel or wide opening at the top of the gauge allows rain to flow into a cylinder that is marked in centimeters.

Snow forms when air temperatures are so low that water vapor turns into a solid. When a lot of snow has fallen, it is measured with a ruler or meterstick. When balls or lumps of ice fall from clouds during thunderstorms it is called *hail*. Sleet forms when rain falls through a layer of freezing air, producing falling ice.

9 Synthesize What are two ways in which all types of precipitation are alike?

____

____

____

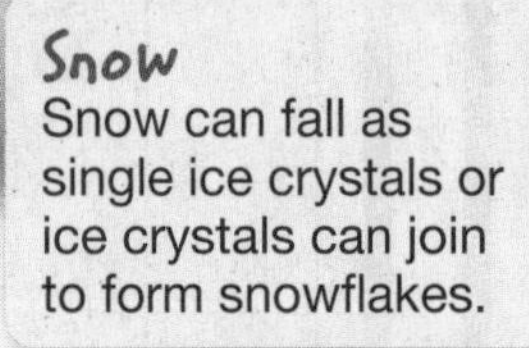

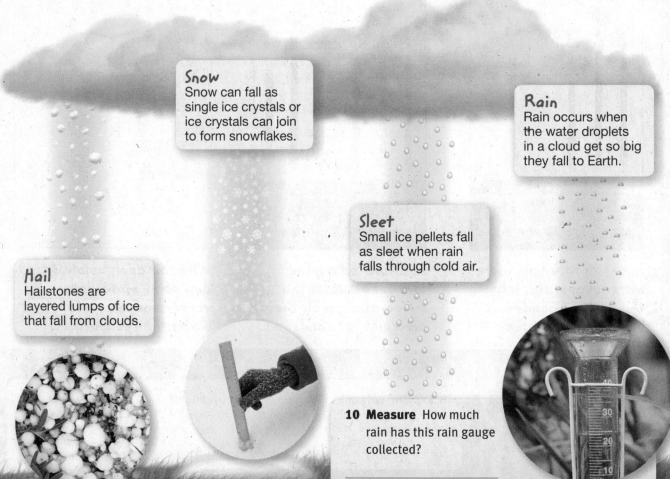

Snow
Snow can fall as single ice crystals or ice crystals can join to form snowflakes.

Rain
Rain occurs when the water droplets in a cloud get so big they fall to Earth.

Sleet
Small ice pellets fall as sleet when rain falls through cold air.

Hail
Hailstones are layered lumps of ice that fall from clouds.

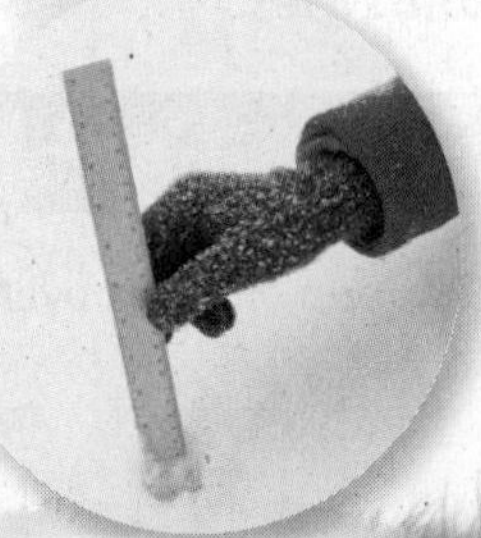

10 Measure How much rain has this rain gauge collected?

____

Why It Matters

Watching Clouds

EYE ON THE ENVIRONMENT

Cirrus Clouds

Cumulus Clouds

Stratus Clouds

As you can see above, cirrus (SIR•uhs) clouds appear feathery or wispy. Their name means "curl of hair." They are made of ice crystals. They form when the wind is strong.

Cumulus (KYOOM•yuh•luhs) means "heap" or "pile." Usually these clouds form in fair weather but if they keep growing taller, they can produce thunderstorms.

Stratus (STRAY•tuhs) means "spread out." Stratus clouds form in flat layers. Low, dark stratus clouds can block out the sun and produce steady drizzle or rain.

If you watch the sky over a period of time, you will probably observe different kinds of clouds. Clouds have different characteristics because they form under different conditions. The shapes and sizes of clouds are mainly determined by air movement. For example, puffy clouds form in air that rises sharply or moves straight up and down. Flat, smooth clouds covering large areas form in air that rises gradually.

Extend

Inquiry

11 Reflect Think about the last time you noticed the clouds. When are you most likely to notice what type of cloud is in the sky?

12 Research Word parts are used to tell more about clouds. Look up the word parts *-nimbus* and *alto-*. What are cumulonimbus and altostratus clouds?

The Air Out There

What is air pressure and how is it measured?

Scientists use an instrument called a barometer (buh•RAHM•i•ter) to measure air pressure. **Air pressure** is the force of air molecules pushing on an area. The air pressure at any area on Earth depends on the weight of the air above that area. Although air is pressing down on us, we don't feel the weight because air pushes in all directions. So, the pressure of air pushing down is balanced by the pressure of air pushing up.

Air pressure and density are related; they both decrease with altitude. Notice in the picture that the molecules at sea level are closer together than the molecules at the mountain peak. Because the molecules are closer together, the pressure is greater. The air at sea level is denser than air at high altitude.

Air pressure and density are lower at a high altitude.

Air pressure and density are higher at sea level.

Visualize It!

13 Identify Look at the photos below and write whether wind direction or wind speed is being measured.

An anemometer measures:

____

A wind vane measures:

____

What is wind and how is it measured?

Wind is air that moves horizontally, or parallel to the ground. Uneven heating of Earth's surface causes pressure differences from place to place. These pressure differences set air in motion. Over a short distance, wind moves directly from higher pressure toward lower pressure.

An anemometer (an•uh•MAHM•i•ter) is used to measure wind speed. It has three or four cups attached to a pole. The wind causes the cups to rotate, sending an electric current to a meter that displays the wind speed.

Wind direction is measured by using a wind vane or a windsock. A wind vane has an arrow with a large tail that is attached to a pole. The wind pushes harder on the arrow tail due to its larger surface area. This causes the wind vane to spin so that the arrow points into the wind. A windsock is a cone-shaped cloth bag open at both ends. The wind enters the wide end and the narrow end points in the opposite direction, showing the direction the wind is blowing.

What is visibility and how is it measured?

Visibility is a measure of the transparency of the atmospheree. Visibility is the way we describe how far we can see, and it is measured by using three or four known landmarks at different distances. Sometimes not all of the landmarks will be visible. Poor visibility can be the result of air pollution or fog.

Poor visibility can be dangerous for all types of travel, whether by air, water, or land. When visibility is very low, roads may be closed to traffic. In areas where low visibility is common, signs are often posted to warn travelers.

14 Explain What are two factors that can affect visibility?

____

____

Fog forms as land cools overnight, causing water vapor in the air above the land to condense.

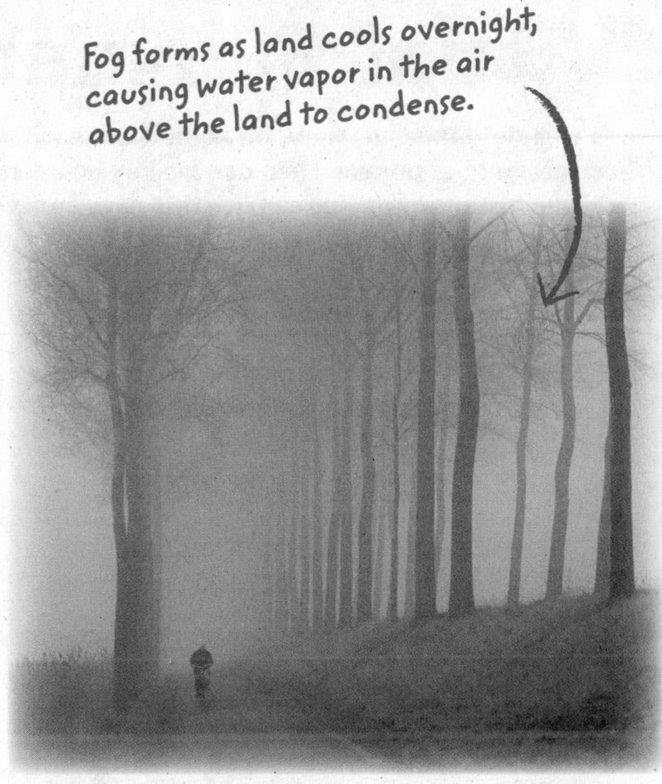

What are some ways to collect weather data?

Many forms of technology are used to gather weather data. The illustration below shows some ways weather information can be collected. Instruments within the atmosphere can make measurements of local weather conditions. Satellites can collect data from above the atmosphere.

15 Infer What are the benefits of stationary weather collection? Moving weather collection?

____

____

____

____

Airplane

Ground station

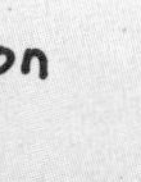

Stationary
Some forms of technology provide measurements from set locations.

Moving
Some forms of technology report changing measurements along their paths.

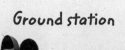

Weather buoy

Ship

Visual Summary

To complete this summary, fill in the blanks with the correct word or phrase. Then use the key below to check your answers. You can use this page to review the main concepts of the lesson.

Elements of Weather

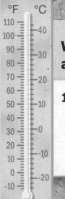

Weather is a condition of the atmosphere at a certain time and place.

16 Weather is often expressed by describing ________________, humidity, precipitation, air pressure, wind, and visibility.

Humidity describes the amount of water vapor in the air.

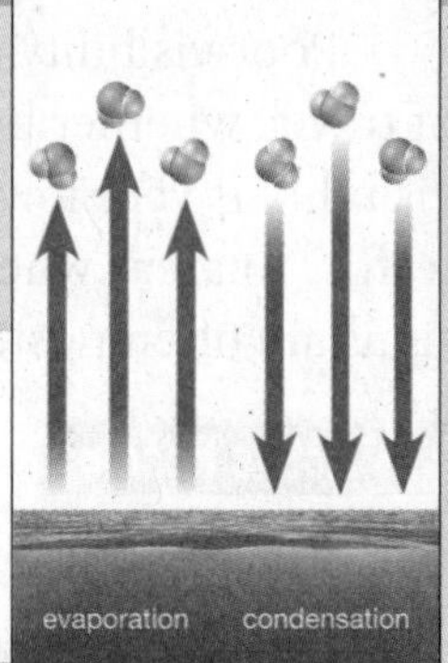

17 The amount of moisture in the air is commonly expressed as ____________ humidity.

Uneven heating of Earth's surface causes air pressure differences and wind.

18 Wind moves from areas of ____________ pressure to areas of ____________ pressure.

Visibility describes how far into the distance objects can be seen.

19 Visibility can be affected by air pollution and ______

Precipitation occurs when the water that condenses as clouds falls back to Earth in solid or liquid form.

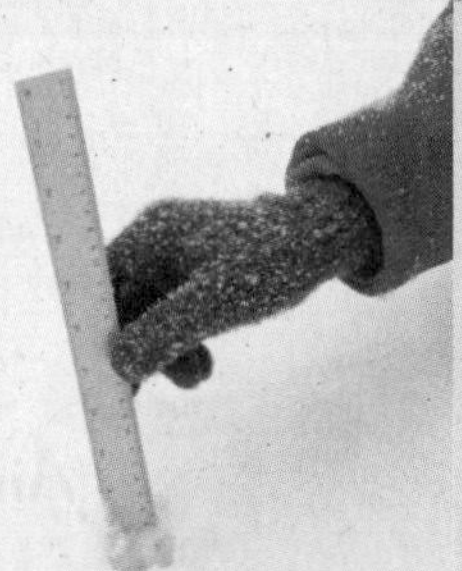

20 The main types of precipitation are hail, snow, ________________, and rain.

Answers: 16 temperature; 17 relative; 18 higher, lower; 19 fog; 20 sleet

21 Synthesize What instruments would you take along if you were going on a 3-month field study to measure how the weather on a mountaintop changes over the course of a season?

Lesson Review

Vocabulary

In your own words, define the following terms.

1 weather ______

2 humidity ______

3 air pressure ______

4 visibility ______

Key Concepts

Weather element	Instrument
5 Identify Measures temperature	
	6 Identify Is measured by using a barometer
7 Identify Measures relative humidity	
	8 Identify Is measured by using a rain gauge or meterstick
9 Identify Measures wind speed	

10 List What are four types of precipitation?

Critical Thinking

11 Apply Explain how wind is related to the uneven heating of Earth's surfaces by the sun.

12 Explain Why does air pressure decrease as altitude increases?

13 Synthesize What is the relative humidity when the air temperature is at its dew point?

The weather data below was recorded from 1989–2009 by an Antarctic weather station similar to the station in the photo at the beginning of this lesson. Use these data to answer the questions that follow.

	Jan.	Apr.	July	Oct.
Mean max. temp. (°C)	2.1	−7.4	−9.9	−8.1
Mean min. temp. (°C)	−2.6	−14.6	−18.1	−15.1
Mean precip. (mm)	9.0	18.04	28.5	16.5

14 Identify Which month had the lowest mean minimum and maximum temperatures?

15 Infer The precipitation that fell at this location was most likely in what form?

Lesson 3

What Influences Weather?

ESSENTIAL QUESTION

How do the water cycle and other global patterns affect local weather?

By the end of this lesson, you should be able to explain how global patterns in Earth's system influence weather.

The weather doesn't always turn out the way you want. But learning about the factors that affect weather can help you plan your next outing.

Sunshine State Standards

SC.6.E.7.2 Investigate and apply how the cycling of water between the atmosphere and hydrosphere has an effect on weather patterns and climate.

SC.6.E.7.3 Describe how global patterns such as the jet stream and ocean currents influence local weather in measurable terms such as temperature, air pressure, wind direction and speed, and humidity and precipitation.

Engage Your Brain

1 Predict Check T or F to show whether you think each statement is true or false.

T	F	
☐	☐	The water cycle affects weather.
☐	☐	Air can be warmed or cooled by the surface below it.
☐	☐	Warm air sinks, cool air rises.
☐	☐	Winds can bring different weather to a region.

2 Explain How can air temperatures along this coastline be affected by the large body of water that is nearby?

Active Reading

3 Infer A military front is a contested armed frontier between opposing forces. A *weather front* occurs between two air masses, or bodies of air. What kind of weather do you think usually happens at a weather front?

Vocabulary Terms

- **air mass**
- **front**
- **jet stream**

4 Apply As you learn the definition of each vocabulary term in this lesson, create your own definition or sketch to help you remember the meaning of the term.

Water, Water

How does the water cycle affect weather?

Weather is the short-term state of the atmosphere, including temperature, humidity, precipitation, air pressure, wind, and visibility. These elements are affected by the energy received from the sun and the amount of water in the air. To understand what influences weather, then, you need to understand the water cycle.

In the water cycle, shown to the right, water is constantly being recycled between liquid, solid, and gaseous states. The water cycle is the continuous movement of water between the atmosphere, the land, the oceans, and living things. The water cycle involves the processes of evaporation, condensation, and precipitation.

Evaporation occurs when liquid water changes into water vapor, which is a gas. Condensation occurs when water vapor cools and changes from a gas to a liquid. A change in the amount of water vapor in the air affects humidity. Clouds and fog form through condensation of water vapor, so condensation also affects visibility. Precipitation occurs when rain, snow, sleet, or hail falls from the clouds onto Earth's surface.

Active Reading

5 List Name at least 5 elements of weather.

____

____

____

Visualize It!

6 Summarize Describe how the water cycle influences weather by completing the sentences on the picture.

(A) Evaporation affects weather by ______________________________

____

____

Everywhere . . .

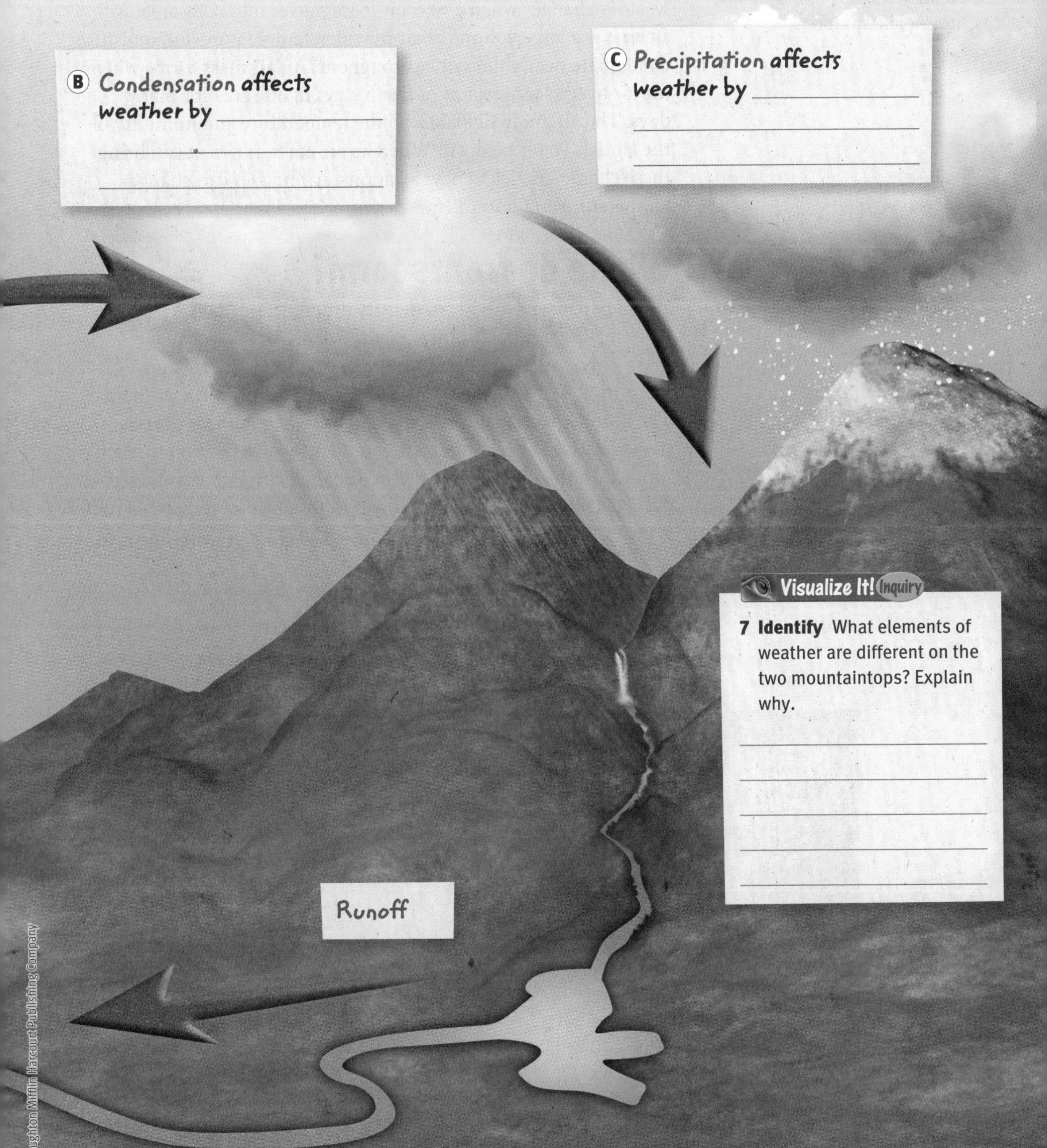

Ⓑ Condensation affects weather by ______________________

Ⓒ Precipitation affects weather by ______________________

Runoff

Visualize It! Inquiry

7 Identify What elements of weather are different on the two mountaintops? Explain why.

Putting Up a Front

How do air masses affect weather?

Active Reading

8 Identify As you read, underline how air masses form.

You have probably experienced the effects of air masses—one day is hot and humid, and the next day is cool and pleasant. The weather changes when a new air mass moves into your area. An **air mass** is a large volume of air in which temperature and moisture content are nearly the same throughout. An air mass forms when the air over a large region of Earth stays in one area for many days. The air gradually takes on the temperature and humidity of the land or water below it. When an air mass moves, it can bring these characteristics to new locations. Air masses can change temperature and humidity as they move to a new area.

Where do fronts form?

When two air masses meet, density differences usually keep them from mixing. A cool air mass is more dense than a warm air mass. A boundary, called a **front**, forms between the air masses. For a front to form, one air mass must run into another air mass. The kind of front that forms depends on how these air masses move relative to each other, and on their relative temperature and moisture content. Fronts result in a change in weather as they pass. They usually affect weather in the middle latitudes of Earth. Fronts do not often occur near the equator because air masses there do not have big temperature differences.

The boundary between air masses, or front, cannot be seen, but is shown here to illustrate how air masses can take on the characteristics of the surface below them.

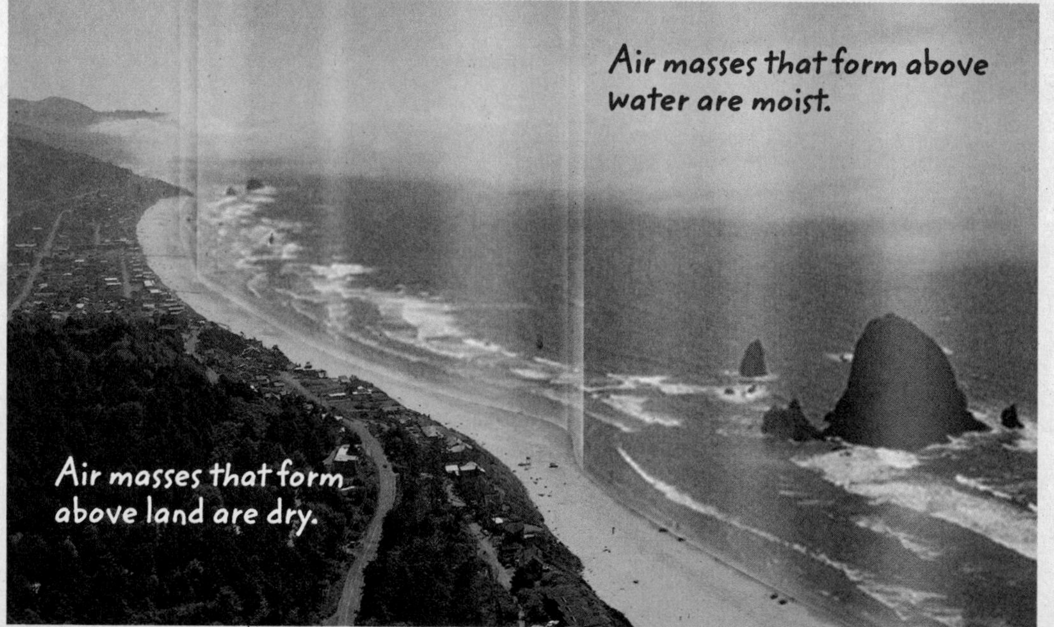

Air masses that form above water are moist.
Air masses that form above land are dry.

Cold Fronts Form Where Cold Air Moves under Warm Air

Warm air is less dense than cold air is. So, a cold air mass that is moving can quickly push up a warm air mass. If the warm air is moist, clouds will form. Storms that form along a cold front are usually short-lived but can move quickly and bring heavy rain or snow. Cooler weather follows a cold front.

9 Apply If you hear that a cold front is headed for your area, what type of weather might you expect?

____

____

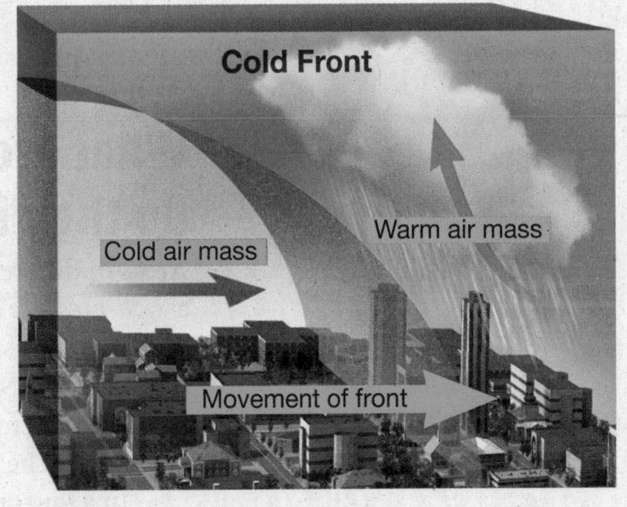

Warm Fronts Form Where Warm Air Moves over Cold Air

A warm front forms when a warm air mass follows a retreating cold air mass. The warm air rises over the cold air, and its moisture condenses into clouds. Warm fronts often bring drizzly rain and are followed by warm, clear weather.

10 Identify The rainy weather at the edge of a warm front is a result of

- ☐ the cold air mass that is leaving.
- ☐ the warm air rising over the cold air.
- ☐ the warm air mass following the front.

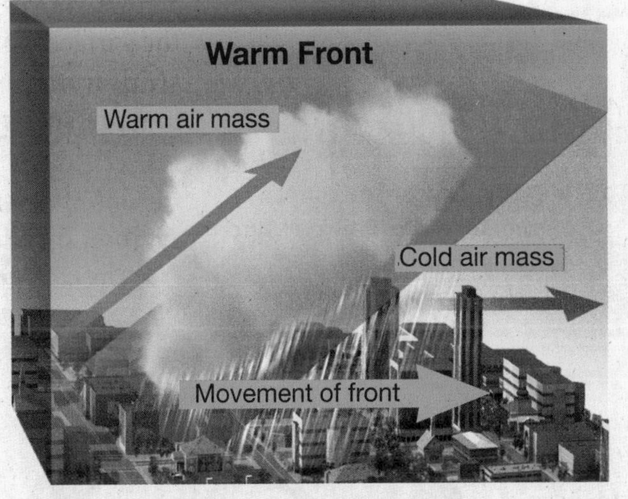

Stationary Fronts Form Where Cold and Warm Air Stop Moving

In a stationary front, there is not enough wind for either the cold air mass or the warm air mass to keep moving. So, the two air masses remain in one place. A stationary front can cause many days of unchanging weather, usually clear.

11 Infer When could a stationary front become a warm or cold front?

____

____

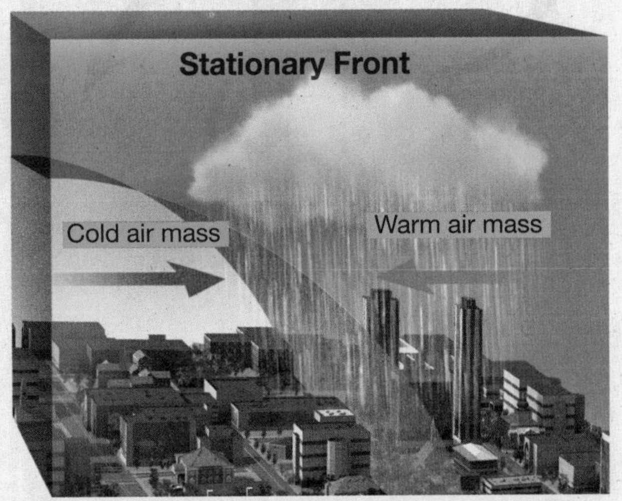

Feeling the **Pressure!**

What are pressure systems, and how do they interact?

Areas of different air pressure cause changes in the weather. In a *high-pressure system*, air sinks slowly down. As the air nears the ground, it spreads out toward areas of lower pressure. Most high-pressure systems are large and change slowly. When a high-pressure system stays in one location for a long time, an air mass may form. The air mass can be warm or cold, humid or dry.

In a *low-pressure system*, air rises and so has a lower air pressure than the areas around it. As the air in the center of a low-pressure system rises, the air cools.

The diagram below shows how a high-pressure system can form a low-pressure system. Surface air, shown by the black arrows, moves out and away from high-pressure centers. Air above the surface sinks and warms. The green arrows show how air swirls from a high-pressure system into a low-pressure system. In a low-pressure system, the air rises and cools.

12 Identify Choose the correct answer for each of the pressure systems shown below.

A high-pressure system can spiral into a low-pressure system, as illustrated by the green arrows below. In the Northern Hemisphere, air circles in the directions shown.

A In a high-pressure system, air

- ☐ rises and cools.
- ☐ sinks and warms.

B in a low-pressure system, air

- ☐ rises and cools.
- ☐ sinks and warms.

How do different pressure systems affect us?

When air pressure differences are small, air doesn't move very much. If the air remains in one place or moves slowly, the air takes on the temperature and humidity of the land or water beneath it. Each type of pressure system has it own unique weather pattern. By keeping track of high- and low-pressure systems, scientists can predict the weather.

High-Pressure Systems Produce Clear Weather

High-pressure systems are areas where air sinks and moves outward. The sinking air is denser than the surrounding air, and the pressure is higher. Cooler, denser air moves out of the center of these high-pressure areas toward areas of lower pressure. As the air sinks, it gets warmer and absorbs moisture. Water droplets evaporate, relative humidity decreases, and clouds often disappear. A high-pressure system generally brings clear skies and calm air or gentle breezes.

Low-Pressure Systems Produce Rainy Weather

Low-pressure systems have lower pressure than the surrounding areas. Air in a low-pressure system comes together, or converges, and rises. As the air in the center of a low-pressure system rises, it cools and forms clouds and rain. The rising air in a low-pressure system causes stormy weather.

A low-pressure system can develop wherever there is a center of low pressure. One place this often happens is along a boundary between a warm air mass and a cold air mass. Rain often occurs at these boundaries, or fronts.

13 Match Label each picture as a result of a high- or low-pressure system. Then, draw a line from each photo to its matching air-pressure diagram.

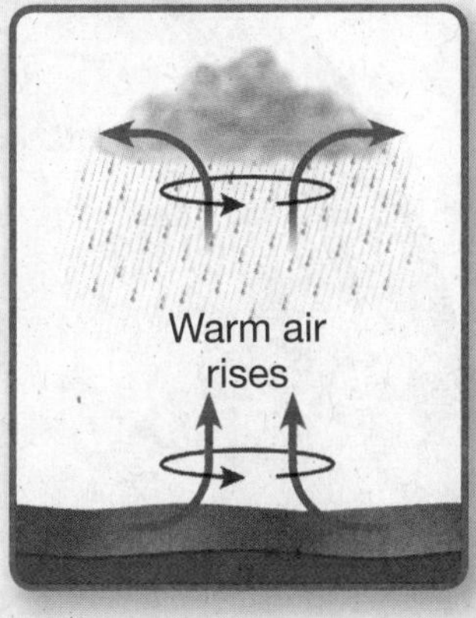

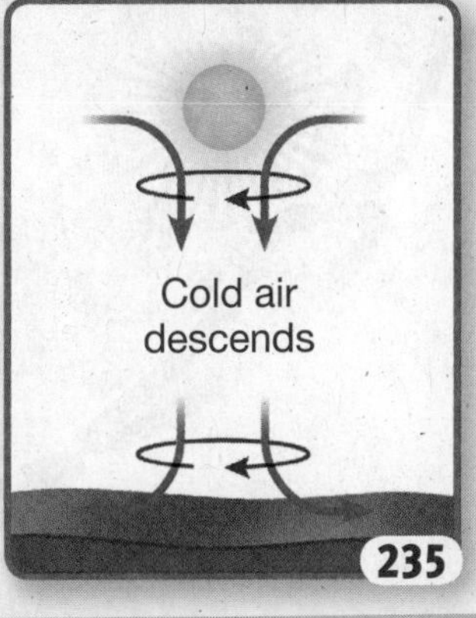

Windy Weather

How do global wind patterns affect local weather?

Winds are caused by unequal heating of Earth's surface—which causes air pressure differences—and can occur on a global or on a local scale. On a local scale, air-pressure differences affect both wind speed and wind direction at a location. On a global level, there is an overall movement of surface air from the poles toward the equator. The heated air at the equator rises and forms a low-pressure belt. Cold air near the poles sinks and creates high-pressure centers. Because air moves from areas of high pressure to areas of low pressure, it moves from the poles to the equator. At high altitudes, the warmed air circles back toward the poles.

Temperature and pressure differences on Earth's surface also create regional wind belts. Winds in these belts curve to the east or the west as they blow, due to Earth's rotation. This curving of winds is called the *Coriolis effect* (kawr•ee•OH•lis eff•EKT). Winds would flow in straight lines if Earth did not rotate. Winds bring air masses of different temperatures and moisture content to a region.

Visualize It!

14 Apply Trade winds bring

- ☐ cool air to the warmer equatorial regions.
- ☐ warm air to the cooler, higher latitudes.

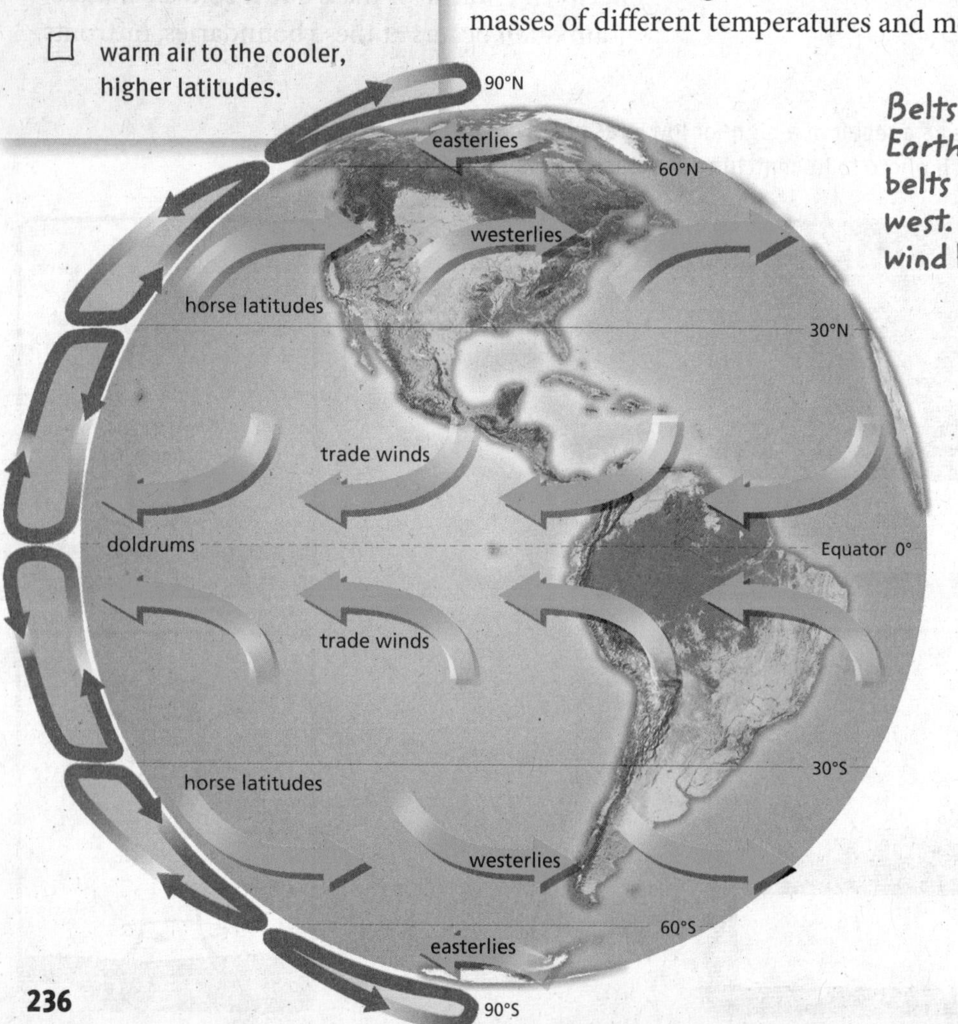

Belts of global winds circle Earth. The winds in these belts curve to the east or west. Between the global wind belts are calm areas.

How do jet streams affect weather?

Long-distance winds that travel above global winds for thousands of kilometers are called **jet streams**. Air moves in jet streams with speeds that are at least 92 kilometers per hour and are often greater than 180 kilometers per hour. Like global and local winds, jet streams form because Earth's surface is heated unevenly. They flow in a wavy pattern from west to east.

Each hemisphere usually has two main jet streams, a polar jet stream and a subtropical jet stream. The polar jet streams flow closer to the poles in summer than in winter. Jet streams can affect temperatures. For example, a polar jet stream can pull cold air down from Canada into the United States and pull warm air up toward Canada. Jet streams also affect precipitation patterns. Strong storms tend to form along jet streams. Scientists must know where a jet stream is flowing to make accurate weather predictions.

Active Reading **15 Identify** What are two ways jet streams affect weather?

In winter months, the polar jet stream flows across much of the United States.

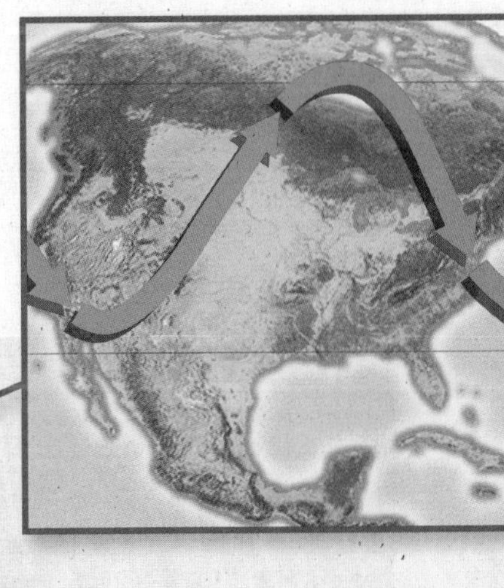

Polar jet stream

Subtropical jet streams

Polar jet stream

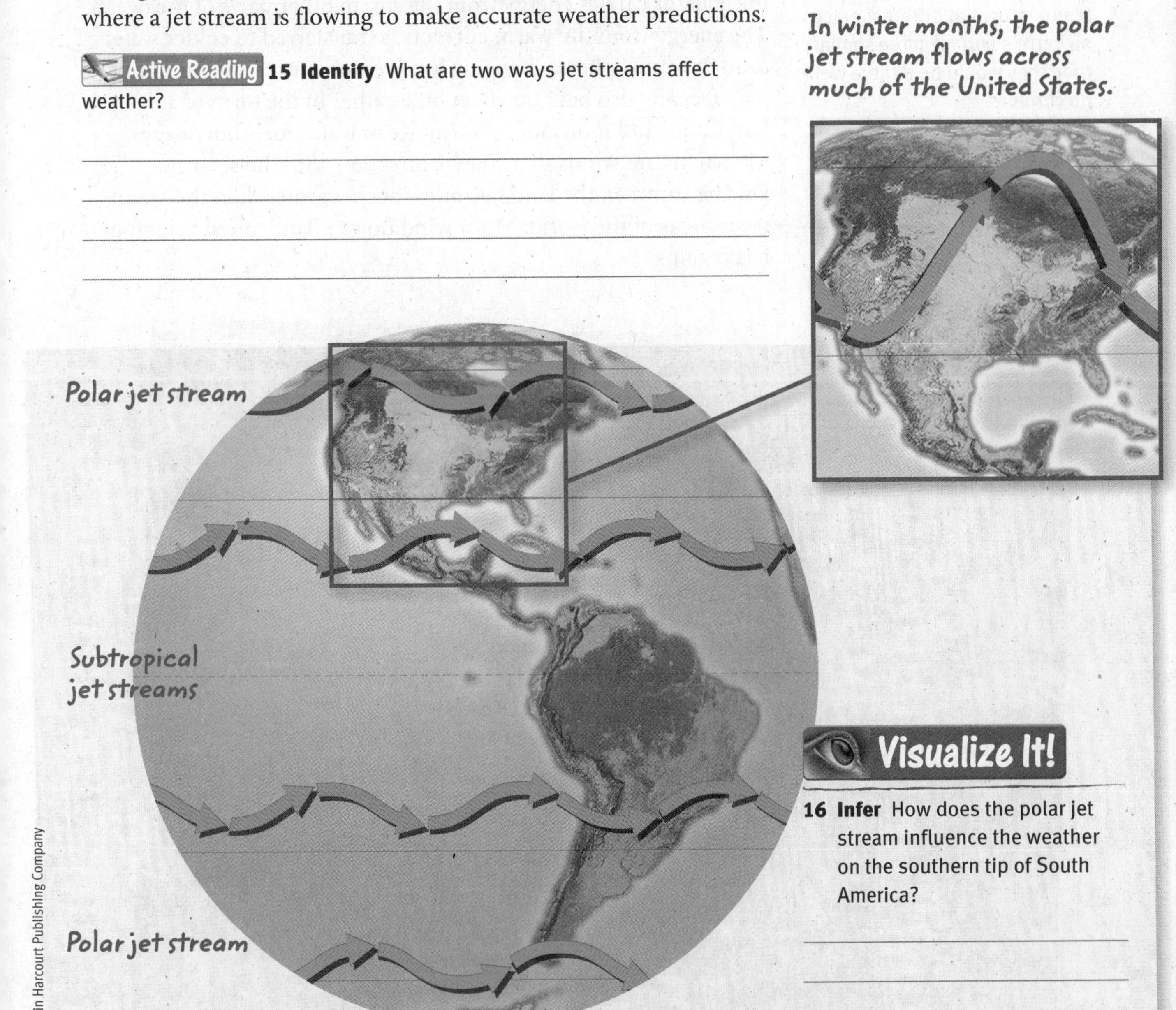

Visualize It!

16 Infer How does the polar jet stream influence the weather on the southern tip of South America?

Ocean Effects

How do ocean currents influence weather?

The same global winds that blow across the surface of Earth also push water across Earth's oceans, causing surface currents. Different winds cause currents to flow in different directions. The flow of surface currents moves energy as heat from one part of Earth to another. As the map below shows, both warm-water and cold-water currents flow from one ocean to another. Water near the equator carries energy from the sun to other parts of the ocean. The energy from the warm currents is transferred to colder water or to the atmosphere, changing local temperatures and humidity.

Oceans also have an effect on weather in the form of hurricanes and monsoons. Warm ocean water fuels hurricanes. Monsoons are winds that change direction with the seasons. During summer, the land becomes much warmer than the sea in some areas of the world. Moist wind flows inland, often bringing heavy rains.

Visualize It!

17 Summarize Describe how ocean currents help make temperatures at different places on Earth's surface more similar than they would be if there were no currents.

Warm current
Cold current
Surface currents are caused by winds. They distribute energy across Earth's surface, changing local temperature and humidity.

Cool Ocean Currents Lower Coastal Air Temperatures

As currents flow, they warm or cool the atmosphere above, affecting local temperatures. The California current is a cold-water current that keeps the average summer high temperatures of coastal cities such as San Diego around 26 °C (78 °F). Cities that lie inland at the same latitude have warmer averages. The graph below shows average monthly temperatures for San Diego and El Centro, California.

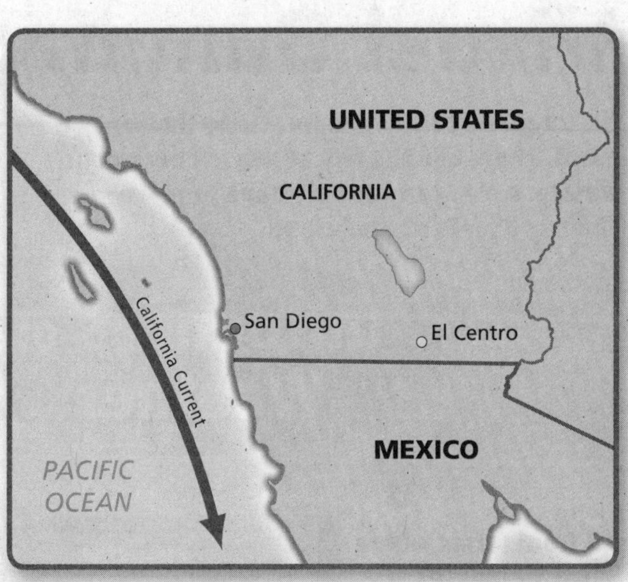

Visualize It!

18 Explain Why are temperatures in San Diego, California, usually cooler than they are in El Centro, California?

____

____

____

Average Monthly Temperatures

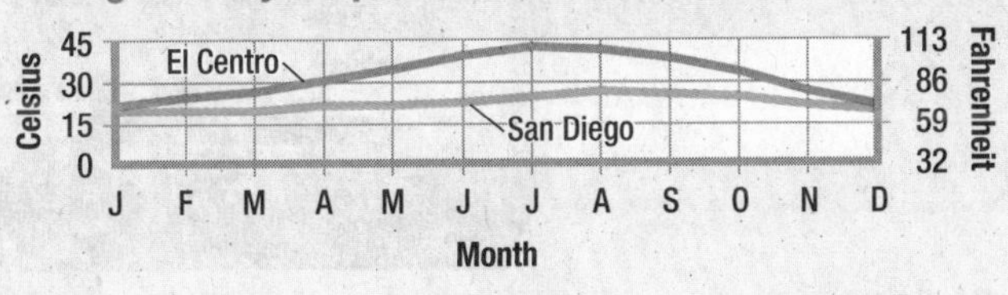

Source: weather.com

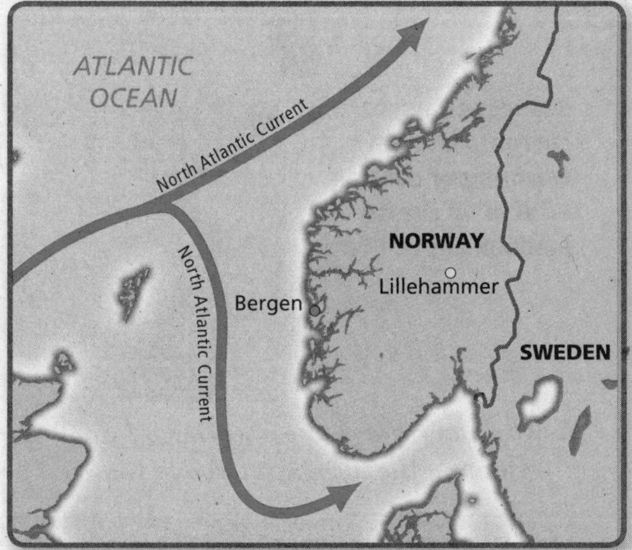

Average Monthly High Temperatures

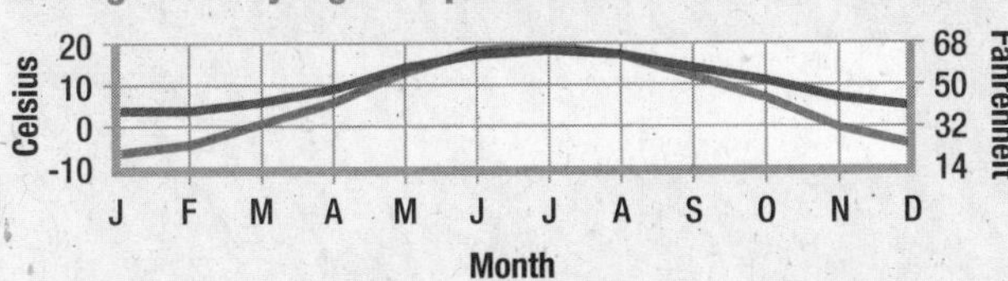

Source: worldweather.org

Warm Ocean Currents Raise Coastal Air Temperatures

In areas where warm ocean currents flow, coastal cities have warmer winter temperatures than inland cities at similar latitudes. For example, temperatures vary considerably from the coastal regions to the inland areas of Norway due to the warmth of the North Atlantic Current. Coastal cities such as Bergen have relatively mild winters. Inland cities such as Lillehammer have colder winters but temperatures similar to the coastal cities in summer.

Visualize It!

19 Identify Circle the city that is represented by each color in the graph.

- ■ Lillehammer/Bergen
- ■ Lillehammer/Bergen

Visual Summary

To complete this summary, circle the correct word. Then, use the key below to check your answers. You can use this page to review the main concepts of the lesson.

Influences of Weather

Understanding the water cycle is key to understanding weather.

20 Weather is affected by the amount of oxygen / water in the air.

A front forms where two air masses meet.

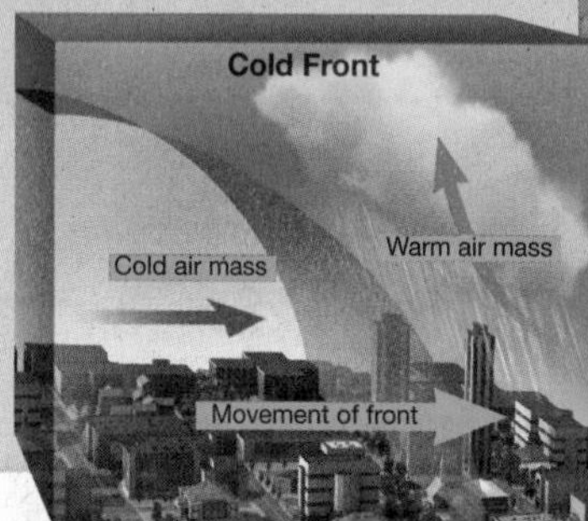

21 When a warm air mass and a cool air mass meet, the warm / cool air mass usually moves upward.

Low-pressure systems bring stormy weather, and high-pressure systems bring dry, clear weather.

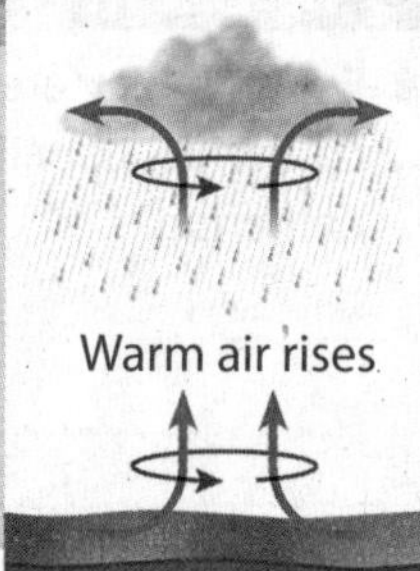

22 In a low-pressure system, air moves upward / downward.

Pressure differences from the uneven heating of Earth's surface cause predictable patterns of wind.

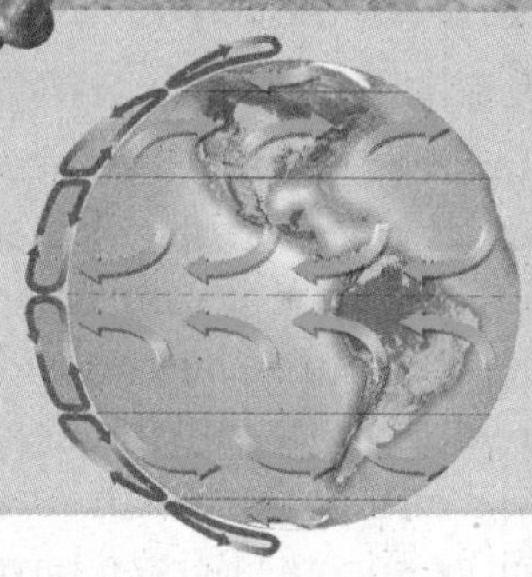

23 Global wind patterns occur as, due to temperature differences, air rises / sinks at the poles and rises / sinks at the equator.

Global ocean surface currents can have warming or cooling effects on the air masses above them.

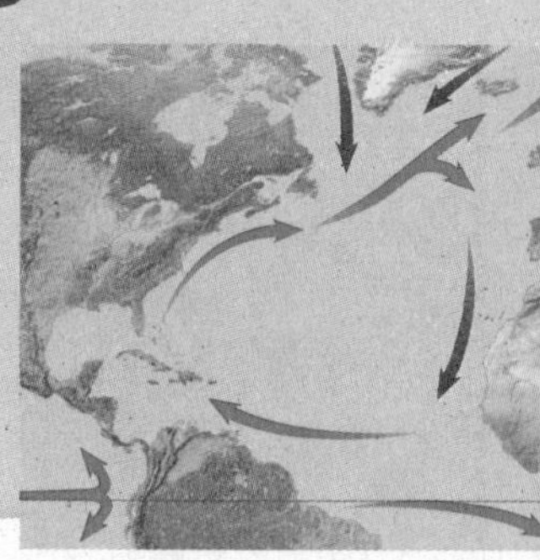

24 Warm currents have a warming / cooling effect on the air masses above them.

Answers: 20 water; 21 warm; 22 upward; 23 sinks; rises; 24 warming

25 Synthesize How do air masses cause weather changes?

Lesson Review

Vocabulary

For each pair of terms, explain how the meanings of the terms differ.

1 *front* and *air mass*

2 *high-pressure system* and *low-pressure system*

3 *jet streams* and *global wind belts*

Key Concepts

4 **Apply** If the weather becomes stormy for a short time and then becomes colder, which type of front has most likely passed?

5 **Describe** Explain how an ocean current can affect the temperature and the amount of moisture of the air mass above the current and above nearby coastlines.

6 **Synthesize** How does the water cycle affect weather?

Critical Thinking

Use the diagram below to answer the following question:

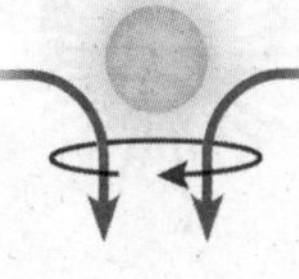

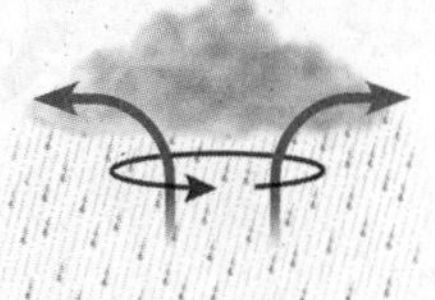

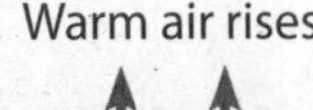

7 **Interpret** How does the movement of air affect the type of weather that forms from high-pressure and low-pressure systems?

8 **Explain** How does the polar jet stream affect temperature and precipitation in North America?

9 **Describe** Explain how changes in weather are caused by the interaction of air masses.

Focus on FLORIDA

Florida's Weather Community

Storm Chasers

Storm chasing in the armored Tornado Intercept Vehicle 2

During a storm, most people try to escape it, take shelter, and hide. But there are a few people that run *after* storms! These people are known as storm chasers. They chase storms to gather information for scientific research. Storm chasers often have a training in meteorology and work for government agencies like the National Oceanic and Atmospheric Administration.

In southern states like Florida, storm chasing occurs during the summer months. Using special equipment, storm chasers track weather data to find a storm. Sometimes they drive for hours without finding a single storm. But on other days, they'll get lucky.

Keeping Pets Safe

In 2004, Florida was hit by the devastating Hurricane Charley. Along with many of the displaced human citizens, countless numbers of pets, livestock, and wildlife were victims. The Humane Society of the United States coordinated efforts with animal organizations in Florida to create a spot for emergency animal care. Volunteers worked together with a mobile veterinary team to treat and shelter animals.

The Florida Association of Kennel Clubs (FAKC) was one of the organizations that helped the animal rescue effort during Hurricane Charley. The FAKC organized the transfer of more than 100 abandoned dogs to shelters in Colorado. The organization also provided supplies like hay, water, and medications for homeless livestock, and reunited lost animals with their owners.

To prepare for Hurricane Floyd, flamingos at the Miami Zoo were rounded up and kept indoors.

Math Connection

Pick three cities or towns in Florida. Research annual rainfall for those places. Compare the results in a bar graph. Which place has the greatest amount of precipitation? Which place has the least? Find out where in the state each place is located. How does the location affect the annual precipitation?

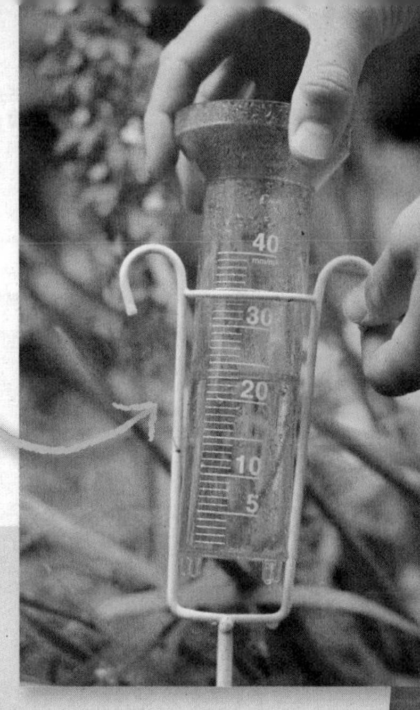

A rain gauge can measure the amount of rainfall an area receives.

The Community Collaborative Rain, Hail & Snow Network (or CoCoRaHS)

You may not be able to control the weather, but you could help track it! The Community Collaborative Rain, Hail & Snow Network (CoCoRaHS) is a unique volunteer network whose main goal is to track and measure precipitation. People of all ages can participate—you just need an interest in reporting weather conditions. As a volunteer, every time rain, hail, or snow arrives in your area, you will measure the precipitation from as many places as possible. Measurements have to take place around the same time every day, usually around 6:00 a.m. to 8:00 a.m. The equipment volunteers use includes a high capacity plastic rain gauge, a foil-covered Styrofoam hail pad, a set of metal hail pad mounting clips, and a package of information and forms for recording data. The information sent in by CoCoRaHS volunteers is used by government agencies, scientists, and many other people in your community.

During Florida's storm season, hurricanes can damage or destroy property.

Take It Home

Look up the weather forecast for your area. Record the predicted amounts of precipitation for the next five days. On each day, measure the amount of precipitation or look up the actual data. How do the predicted data compare with the actual data?

Lesson 4

Severe Weather and Weather Safety

ESSENTIAL QUESTION

How can humans protect themselves from hazardous weather?

By the end of this lesson, you should be able to describe the major types of hazardous weather and the ways human beings can protect themselves from hazardous weather and from sun exposure.

Lightning is often the most dangerous part of a thunderstorm. Thunderstorms are one type of severe weather that can cause a lot of damage.

Sunshine State Standards

SC.6.E.7.8 Describe ways human beings protect themselves from hazardous weather and sun exposure.

HE.6.C.1.3 Identify environmental factors that affect personal health.

Engage Your Brain

1 Describe Fill in the blanks with the word or phrase that you think correctly completes the following sentences.

A ________________ forms a funnel cloud and has high winds.

A flash or bolt of light across the sky during a storm is called ________________

________________ is the sound that follows lightning during a storm.

One way to protect yourself from the sun's rays is to wear ________________

2 Identify Name the weather event that is occurring in the photo. What conditions can occur when this event happens in an area?

____

____

____

____

Active Reading

3 Synthesize Use the sentence below to help you make an educated guess about what the term *storm surge* means. Write the meaning below.

Example sentence
Flooding causes tremendous damage to property and lives when a storm surge moves onto shore.

storm surge:

____

____

____

____

Vocabulary Terms

- thunderstorm
- lightning
- thunder
- hurricane
- storm surge
- tornado

4 Apply As you learn the definition of each vocabulary term in this lesson, create your own definition or sketch to help you remember the meaning of the term.

Take Cover!

What do we know about thunderstorms?

SPLAAAAAT! BOOOOM! The loud, sharp noise of thunder might surprise you, and maybe even make you jump. The thunder may have been joined by lightning, wind, and rain. A **thunderstorm** is an intense local storm that forms strong winds, heavy rain, lightning, thunder, and sometimes hail. A thunderstorm is an example of severe weather. Severe weather is weather that can cause property damage and sometimes death.

Thunderstorms Form from Rising Air

Thunderstorms get their energy from humid air. When warm, humid air near the ground mixes with cooler air above, the warm air creates an updraft that can build a thunderstorm quickly. Cold downdrafts bring precipitation and eventually end the storm by preventing more warm air from rising.

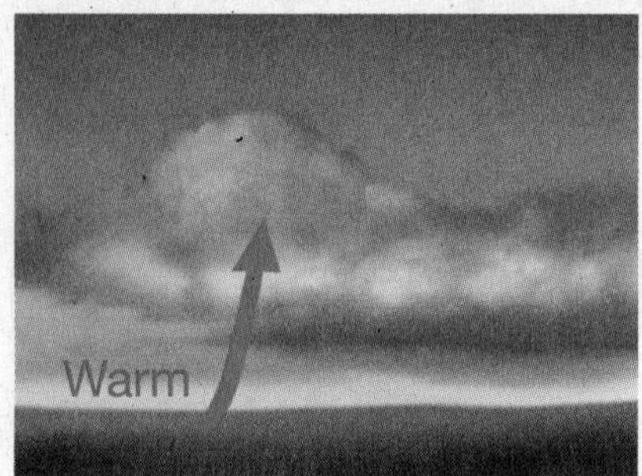

Step 1
In the first stage, warm air rises and forms a cumulus cloud. The water vapor releases energy when it condenses into cloud droplets. This energy increases the air motion. The cloud continues building up.

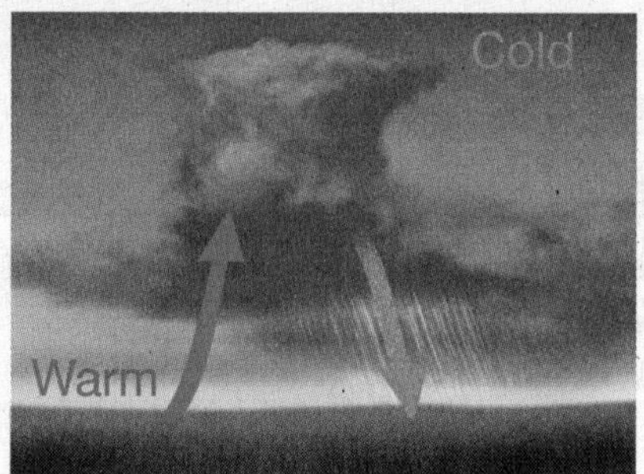

Step 2
Ice particles may form in the low temperatures near the top of the cloud. As the ice particles grow large, they begin to fall and pull cold air down with them. This strong downdraft brings heavy rain or hail.

Step 3
During the final stage, the downdraft can spread out and block more warm air from moving upward into the cloud. The storm slows down and ends.

5 Describe What role does warm air play in the formation of a thunderstorm?

Lightning is a Discharge of Electrical Energy

If you have ever shuffled your feet on a carpet, you may have felt a small shock when you touched a doorknob. If so, you have experienced how lightning forms. **Lightning** is an electric discharge that happens between a positively charged area and a negatively charged area. While you walk around, electrical charges can collect on your body. When you touch someone or something else, the charges jump to that person or object in a spark of electricity. In a similar way, electrical charges build up near the tops and bottoms of clouds as pellets of ice move up and down through the clouds. Suddenly, a flash of lightning will spark from one place to another.

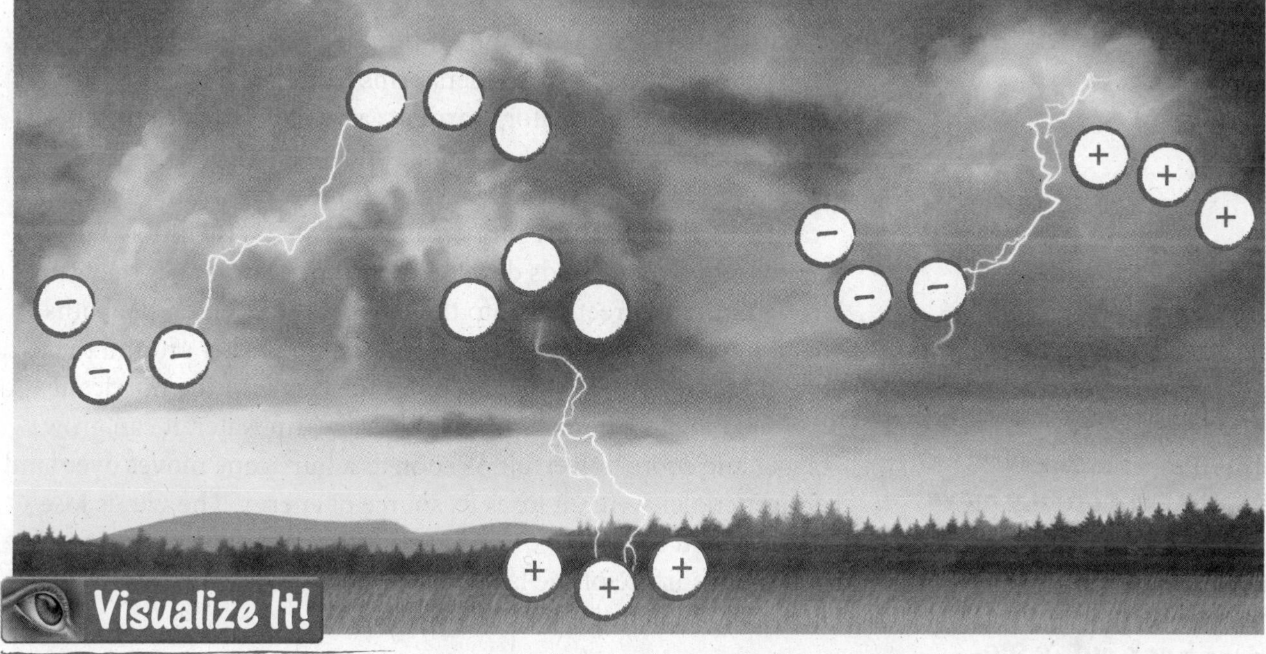

6 Label Fill in the positive and negative charges in the appropriate spaces provided.

Lightning forms between positive and negative charges. The upper part of a cloud usually carries a positive electric charge. The lower part of the cloud carries mainly negative charges. Lightning is a big spark that jumps between parts of clouds, or between a cloud and Earth's surface.

Thunder Is a Result of Rapidly Expanding Air

7 Identify As you read, underline the explanation of what causes thunder during a storm.

When lightning strikes, the air along its path is heated to a high temperature. The superheated air quickly expands. The rapidly moving air causes the air to vibrate and release sound waves. The result is **thunder**, the sound created by the rapid expansion of air along a lightning strike.

You usually hear thunder a few seconds after you see a lightning strike, because light travels faster than sound. You can count the seconds between a lightning flash and the sound of thunder to figure out about how far away the lightning is. For every 3 seconds between lightning and its thunder, add about 1 km to the lightning strike's distance from you.

Plan Ahead!

What do we know about hurricanes?

Active Reading

8 Identify As you read, underline the definition of *hurricane*.

A **hurricane** is a tropical low-pressure system with winds blowing at speeds of 119 km/h (74 mi/h) or more—strong enough to uproot trees. Hurricanes are called typhoons when they form over the western Pacific Ocean and cyclones when they form over the Indian Ocean.

Hurricanes Need Water to Form and Grow

A hurricane begins as a group of thunderstorms moving over tropical ocean waters. Thunderstorms form in areas of low pressure. Near the equator, warm ocean water provides the energy that can turn a low-pressure center into a violent storm. As water evaporates from the ocean, energy is transferred from the ocean water into the air. This energy makes warm air rise faster. Tall clouds and strong winds develop. As winds blow across the water from different directions into the low-pressure center, the paths bend into a spiral. The winds blow faster and faster around the low-pressure center, which becomes the center of the hurricane.

As long as a hurricane stays above warm water, it can grow bigger and more powerful. As soon as a hurricane moves over land or over cooler water, it loses its source of energy. The winds lose strength and the storm dies out. If a hurricane moves over land, the rough surface of the land reduces the winds even more.

Hurricanes in the Northern Hemisphere usually move westward with the trade winds. Near land, however, they will often move north or even back out to sea.

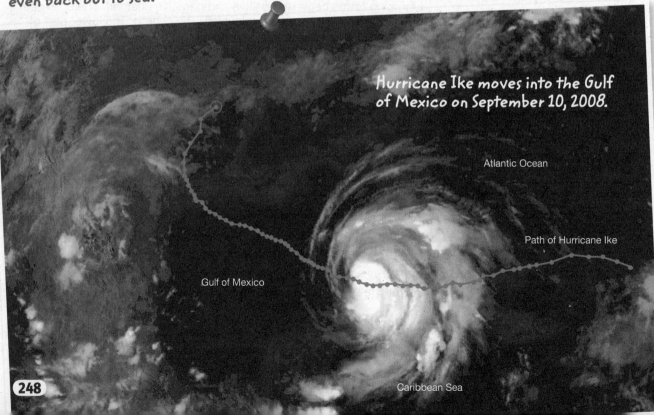

Hurricane Ike moves into the Gulf of Mexico on September 10, 2008.

Hurricanes Can Cause Extensive Damage

A hurricane can pound a coast with huge waves and sweep the land with strong winds and heavy rains. The storms cause damage and dangerous conditions in several ways. Hurricane winds can lift cars, uproot trees, and tear the roofs off buildings. Hurricanes may also produce tornadoes that can cause even more damage. Heavy rains from hurricanes may make rivers overflow their banks and flood nearby areas. When a hurricane moves into a coastal area, it also pushes a huge mass of ocean water known as a **storm surge**. In a storm surge, the sea level rises several meters, backing up rivers and flooding the shore. A storm surge can be the most destructive and deadliest part of a hurricane. Large waves add to the damage. A hurricane may affect an area for a few hours or a few days, but the damage may take weeks or even months to clean up.

Active Reading

9 Describe What are three of the dangers associated with hurricanes?

____

____

The storm surge and debris from Hurricane Ike cover a street on September 12, 2008, in Seabrook, Texas.

Think Outside the Book Inquiry

10 Apply With a classmate, discuss why hurricanes are more likely to make landfall in Florida than they are to hit California. You may need to refer to a map of ocean currents to find the answer.

☑ Secure Loose Objects!

What do we know about tornadoes?

A **tornado** is a destructive, rotating column of air that has very high wind speeds and that is sometimes visible as a funnel-shaped cloud. A tornado forms when a thunderstorm meets horizontal winds at a high altitude. These winds cause the warm air rising in the thunderstorm to spin. A storm cloud may form a thin funnel shape that has a very low pressure center. As the funnel reaches the ground, the higher-pressure air rushes into the low-pressure area. The result is high-speed winds, which cause the damage associated with tornadoes.

Clouds begin to rotate, signaling that a tornado may form.

The funnel cloud becomes visible as the tornado picks up dust from the ground or particles from the air.

The tornado moves along the ground before it dies out.

Think Outside the Book

11 Illustrate Read the description of the weather conditions that cause tornadoes and draw a sketch of what those conditions might look like.

Most Tornadoes Happen in the Midwest

Tornadoes happen in many places, but they are most common in the United States in *Tornado Alley*. Tornado Alley reaches from Texas up through the midwestern United States, including Iowa, Kansas, Nebraska, and Ohio. Many tornadoes form in the spring and early summer, typically along a front between cool, dry air and warm, humid air.

Tornadoes Can Cause Extensive Damage

The danger of a tornado is mainly due to the high speed of its winds. Winds in a tornado's funnel may have speeds of more than 400 km/h. Most injuries and deaths caused by tornadoes happen when people are struck by objects blown by the winds or when they are trapped in buildings that collapse.

12 Identify As you read, underline what makes a tornado so destructive.

13 Summarize In the overlapping sections of the Venn diagram, list the characteristics that are shared by the different types of storms. In the outer sections, list the characteristics that are specific to each type of storm.

Thunderstorms

Hurricanes

Tornadoes

14 Conclude Write a summary that describes the information in the Venn diagram.

Be Prepared!

What can people do to prepare for severe weather?

Severe weather is weather that can cause property damage, injury, and sometimes death. Hail, lightning, high winds, tornadoes, hurricanes, and floods are all part of severe weather. Hailstorms can damage crops and cars and can break windows. Lightning starts many forest fires and kills or injures hundreds of people and animals each year. Winds and tornadoes can uproot trees and destroy homes. Flooding is also a leading cause of weather-related deaths. Most destruction from hurricanes results from flooding due to storm surges.

Think Outside the Book Inquiry

15 Apply Research severe weather in your area and come up with a plan for safety.

Plan Ahead

Have a storm supply kit that contains a battery-operated radio, batteries, flashlights, candles, rain jackets, tarps, blankets, bottled water, canned food, and medicines. Listen to weather announcements. Plan and practice a safety route. A safety route is a planned path to a safe place.

Listen for Storm Updates

During severe weather, it is important to listen to local radio or TV stations. Severe weather updates will let you know the location of a storm. They will also let you know if the storm is getting worse. A *watch* is given when the conditions are ideal for severe weather. A *warning* is given when severe weather has been spotted or is expected within 24 h. During most kinds of severe weather, it is best to stay indoors and away from windows. However, in some situations, you may need to evacuate.

Follow Flood Safety Rules

Sometimes, a place can get so much rain that it floods, especially if it is a low-lying area. So, like storms, floods have watches and warnings. However, little advance notice can usually be given that a flood is coming. A flash flood is a flood that rises and falls very quickly. The best thing to do during a flood is to find a high place to stay until it is over. You should always stay out of floodwaters. Even shallow water can be dangerous because it can move fast.

What can people do to stay safe during thunderstorms?

Stay alert when thunderstorms are predicted or when dark, tall clouds are visible. If you are outside and hear thunder, seek shelter immediately and stay there for 30 min after the thunder ends. Heavy rains can cause sudden, or flash, flooding, and hailstones can damage property and harm living things.

Lightning is one of the most dangerous parts of a thunderstorm. Because lightning is attracted to tall objects, it is important to stay away from trees if you are outside. If you are in an open area, stay close to the ground so that you are not the tallest object in the area. If you can, get into a car. Stay away from ponds, lakes, or other bodies of water. If lightning hits water while you are swimming or wading in it, you could be hurt or killed. If you are indoors during a thunderstorm, avoid using electrical appliances, running water, and phone lines.

How can people stay safe during a tornado?

Tornadoes are too fast and unpredictable for you to attempt to outrun, even if you are in a car. If you see or hear a tornado, go to a place without windows, such as basement, a storm cellar, or a closet or hallway. Stay away from areas that are likely to have flying objects or other dangers. If you are outside, lie in a ditch or low-lying area. Protect your head and neck by covering them with your arms and hands.

How can people stay safe during a hurricane?

If your family lives where hurricanes may strike, have a plan to leave the area, and gather emergency supplies. If a hurricane is in your area, listen to weather reports for storm updates. Secure loose objects outside, and cover windows with storm shutters or boards. During a storm, stay indoors and away from windows. If ordered to evacuate the area, do so immediately. After a storm, be aware of downed power lines, hanging branches, and flooded areas.

16 Apply What would you do in each of these scenarios?

Scenario	What would you do?
You are swimming at an outdoor pool when you hear thunder in the distance.	
You and your family are watching TV when you hear a tornado warning that says a tornado has been spotted in the area.	
You are listening to the radio when the announcer says that a hurricane is headed your way and may make landfall in 3 days.	

Use Sun Sense!

How can people protect their skin from the sun?

Active Reading

17 Identify As you read, underline when the sun's ray's are strongest during the day.

Human skin contains melanin, which is the body's natural protection against ultraviolet (UV) radiation from the sun. The skin produces more melanin when it is exposed to the sun, but UV rays will still cause sunburn when you spend too much time outside. It is particularly important to protect your skin when the sun's rays are strongest, usually between 10 A.M and 4 P.M.

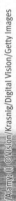

Know the Sun's Hazards

It's easy to notice the effects of a sunburn. Sunburn usually appears within a few hours after sun exposure. It causes red, painful skin that feels hot to the touch. Prolonged exposure to the sun will lead to sunburn in even the darkest-skinned people. Sunburn can lead to skin cancer and premature aging of the skin. The best way to prevent sunburn is to protect your skin from the sun, even on cloudy days. UV rays pass right through clouds and can give you a false feeling of protection from the sun.

Wear Sunscreen and Protective Clothing

Even if you tan easily, you should still use sunscreen. For most people, a sun protection factor (SPF) of 30 or more will prevent burning for about 1.5 h. Babies and people who have pale skin should use an SPF of 45 or more. In addition, you can protect your skin and eyes in different ways. Seek the shade, and wear hats, sunglasses, and perhaps even UV light-protective clothing.

Have fun in the sun! Just be sure to protect your skin from harmful rays.

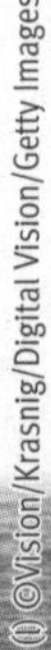

How can people protect themselves from summer heat?

Heat exhaustion is a condition in which the body has been exposed to high temperatures for an extended period of time. Symptoms include cold, moist skin, normal or near-normal body temperature, headache, nausea, and extreme fatigue. *Heat stroke* is a condition in which the body loses its ability to cool itself by sweating because the victim has become dehydrated.

Limit Outdoor Activities

When outdoor temperatures are high, be cautious about exercising outdoors for long periods of time. Pay attention to how your body is feeling, and go inside or to a shady spot if you are starting to feel light-headed or too warm.

Drink Water

Heat exhaustion and heat stroke can best be prevented by drinking 6 to 8 oz of water at least 10 times a day when you are active in warm weather. If you are feeling overheated, dizzy, nauseous, or are sweating heavily, drink something cool (not cold). Drink about half a glass of cool water every 15 min until you feel like your normal self.

Visualize It!

18 Describe List all the ways the people in the photo of the beach may have protected themselves from overexposure to the sun.

Drinking water is one of the best things you can do to keep yourself healthy in hot weather.

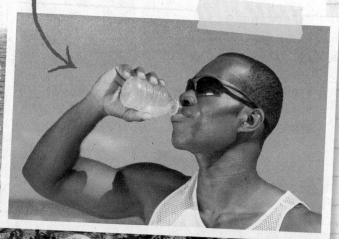

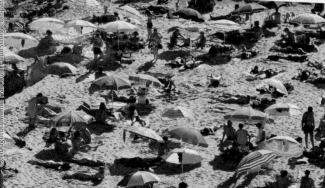

Know the Signs of Heat Stroke

Active Reading **19 Identify** Underline signs of heat stroke in the paragraph below.

Heat stroke is life threatening, so it is important to know the signs and treatment for it. Symptoms of heat stroke include hot, dry skin; higher than normal body temperature; rapid pulse; rapid, shallow breathing; disorientation; and possible loss of consciousness.

What to Do In Case of Heat Stroke

- ☐ Seek emergency help immediately.
- ☐ If there are no emergency facilities nearby, move the person to a cool place.
- ☐ Cool the person's body by immersing it in a cool (not cold) bath or using wet towels.
- ☐ Do not give the person food or water if he or she is vomiting.
- ☐ Place ice packs under the person's armpits.

Visual Summary

To complete this summary, circle the correct word or phrase. Then use the key below to check your answers. You can use this page to review the main concepts of the lesson.

Severe Weather

Thunderstorms are intense weather systems that produce strong winds, heavy rain, lightning, and thunder.

20 One of the most dangerous parts of a thunderstorm is lightning / thunder.

A hurricane is a large, rotating tropical weather system with strong winds that can cause severe property damage.

21 An important step to plan for a hurricane is to buy raingear / stock a supply kit.

Tornadoes are rotating columns of air that touch the ground and can cause severe damage.

22 The damage from a tornado is mostly caused by associated thunderstorms / high-speed winds.

It is important to plan ahead and listen for weather updates in the event of severe weather.

23 One of the biggest dangers of storms that produce heavy rains or storm surges is flooding / low temperatures.

Prolonged exposure to the sun can cause sunburn, skin cancer, and heat-related health effects.

24 One of the best ways to avoid heat-related illnesses while in the sun is to stay active / drink water.

Answers: 20 lightning; 21 stock a supply kit; 22 high-speed winds; 23 flooding; 24 drink water

25 Synthesize What are three ways in which severe weather can be dangerous?

Lesson Review

Vocabulary

Draw a line that matches the term with the correct definition.

1 hurricane

2 tornado

3 severe weather

4 thunderstorm

5 storm surge

A a huge mass of ocean water that floods the shore

B a storm with lightning and thunder

C a violently rotating column of air stretching to the ground

D weather that can potentially destroy property or cause loss of life

E a tropical low-pressure system with winds of 119 km/h or more

Key Concepts

6 Thunder is caused by ______________________

7 An electrical discharge between parts of clouds or a cloud and the ground is called ______________________

8 The sun's ultraviolet rays can cause skin damage including sunburn and even skin ______________________

9 Explain How can a person prepare for hazardous weather well in advance?

10 Describe What can people do to stay safe before and during a storm with high winds and heavy rains?

Critical Thinking

Use the map below to answer the following question.

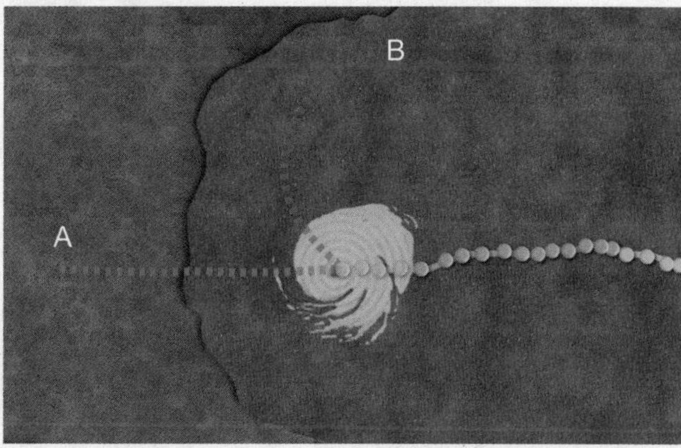

11 Interpret Would a hurricane be more likely to remain a hurricane if it reached point A or point B? Explain your answer.

12 Explain Why do hurricanes form in tropical latitudes?

13 Describe What two weather conditions are needed for tornadoes to form?

14 Explain Why is hail sometimes dangerous?

15 Summarize What can you do to avoid overexposure to the sun's rays?

Lesson 5

Natural Disasters in Florida

Tornadoes can touch down anywhere in Florida—including downtown Miami. This 1997 tornado injured five people and caused a massive power outage.

ESSENTIAL QUESTION

How do natural disasters affect Florida?

By the end of this lesson, you should be able to describe the natural disasters that affect Florida, including their economic impact and their effects on people.

Sunshine State Standards

SC.6.E.7.7 Investigate how natural disasters have affected human life in Florida.

HE.6.C.1.3 Identify environmental factors that affect personal health.

Engage Your Brain

1 **Predict** Check T or F to show whether you think each statement is true or false.

T	F	
☐	☐	It is safe to explore sinkholes.
☐	☐	Thunderstorms can cause flash floods.
☐	☐	Florida experiences more hurricanes than any other state.
☐	☐	Tornadoes are rare in Florida.

2 **Assess** What natural disasters do you think could affect the house shown below?

Active Reading

3 **Synthesize** You can often determine the meaning of a word when you look at context clues, or how the word is used in a sentence. Use the sentence below to guess the definition of *muck fire*.

Example sentence:

Muck fires start when lightning strikes the ground and the dead matter making up the soil starts to burn.

muck fire:

Vocabulary Terms

- **sinkhole**
- **wildfire**
- **muck fire**

4 **Apply** As you learn the definition of each vocabulary term in this lesson, create your own definition or sketch to help you remember the meaning of the term.

When It Rains, It Pours

Which parts of a thunderstorm can be dangerous?

Florida has lots of thunderstorms. Thunderstorms often happen in the summer when the air over the land is warm and moist. Cooler air over the Gulf of Mexico or the Atlantic Ocean blows toward the land. The cool air pushes the warm, moist air upward. As the moist air rises, it begins to cool. The moisture in the cooling air condenses into large, dark clouds. Thunderstorms result from these large clouds. Thunderstorms can be very dangerous and may cause lots of damage in Florida. Heavy rains, hail, lightning, and high winds are all dangers associated with thunderstorms.

Heavy Rain and Flash Floods

Thunderstorms can produce very heavy rains in a short period of time. When this occurs, the soil may not be able to absorb all of the rain. Instead, the water may rush into streambeds, drainage ditches, and valleys. The water can quickly accummulate and cause a flash flood. A *flash flood* is a sudden, local flood of great volume and short duration. Flash floods can be extremely powerful and dangerous. These floods can occur in a few minutes and can wash away people, cars, and even houses! Because of the speed and power of a flash flood, stay away from streams if thunderstorms are in the area. If a stream rises high enough to cover a road, do not cross the road even if you are in a large vehicle.

Hail

Severe thunderstorms sometimes produce hail. Hailstones are chunks of ice that fall as precipitation. Hail first starts as small ice crystals near the top of a thunderstorm cloud where the air is very cold. As the ice falls downward into a warmer part of the cloud, it is covered in a thin layer of water. Strong winds may then drive the forming hail upward again. The thin layer of water freezes and the hail grows larger. Hailstones may be lifted and dropped many times in this way until they become as large as grapefruit! These hailstones can smash car windows and damage roofs and other property. They can even kill livestock. Smaller hail can also cause damage. For example, small hail can bruise plants, damaging crops.

hailstones

Active Reading **5 Identify** What are some of the effects of hail?

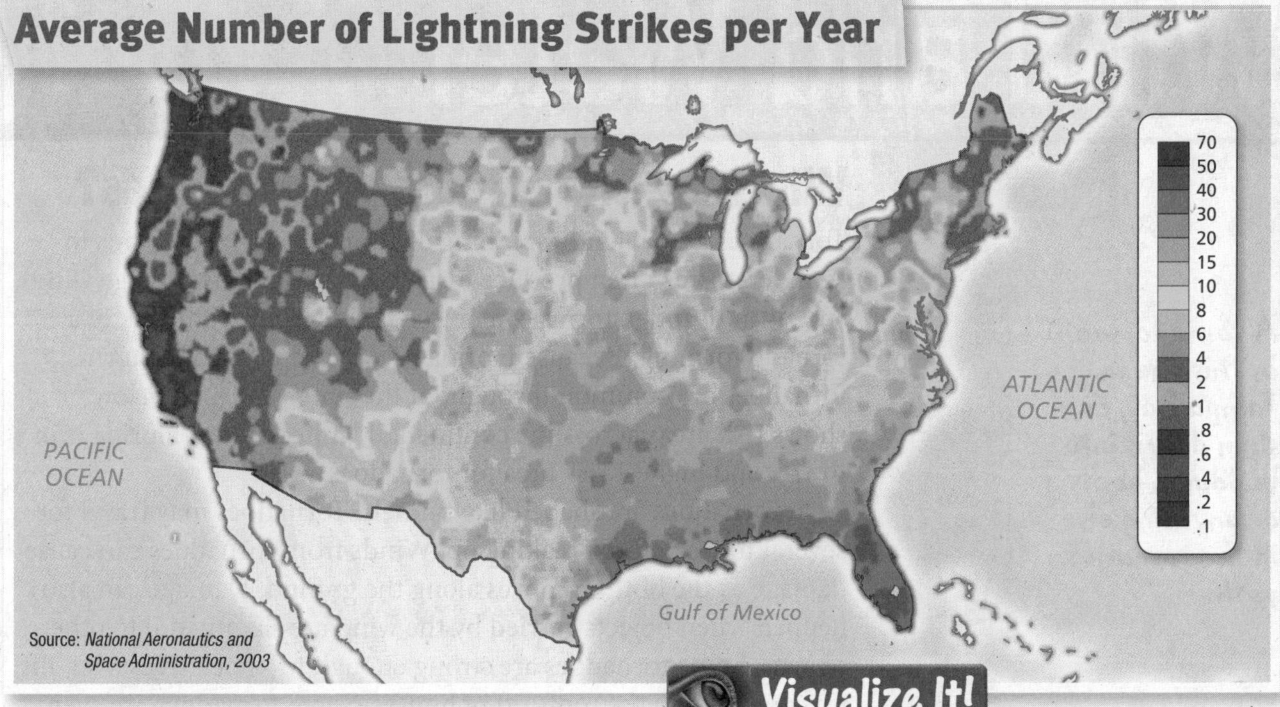

Lightning

Look at the map above. The map shows that Florida is often struck by lightning. In fact, Florida has more injuries and deaths caused by lightning than any other state. So, what is lightning, exactly? Lightning is an electric discharge that takes place in clouds or between a cloud and the ground. There are several types of lightning, but cloud-to-ground lightning is the most dangerous to people. If it strikes a person, it can seriously injure or kill them. Lightning may also damage power lines and property. In addition, lightning can start fires. Some of these fires help maintain Florida's ecosystems, while other fires are dangerous to people and property.

High Wind

Thunderstorms can produce intense winds that blow 50–160 km/h. These winds can be strong enough to blow trees down. They can also knock down power lines. Thunderstorms can produce sudden, dangerous bursts of air that move toward the ground and then spread out. These downburst winds are so strong that they are sometimes mistaken for tornadoes. They can destroy crops, knock down buildings or airplanes, and even move cars!

Visualize It!

6 Identify Which part of the country experiences the most lightning strikes?

____

____

lightning

Think Outside the Book

7 Apply In your journal, write about some experiences you've had with thunderstorms.

Wind and Water

A tornado, such as this one in Tampa Bay, can slam debris into buildings, boats, or anything else in the tornado's path.

What are the effects of tornadoes?

Tornadoes are violently spinning columns of air. High winds in thunderstorms often produce tornadoes. In fact, the average wind speeds in thunderstorms can be used to determine the risk of a tornado forming. Because Florida gets so many thunderstorms, tornadoes are common throughout the state. The map below shows risk areas across the continental United States. Florida is in the second highest risk area for tornadoes.

Tornadoes are shaped like funnels. Tornadoes may travel for several miles before breaking up. Winds from tornadoes can cause damage as the bottom moves along the ground. Damage can also happen when objects carried by the wind are slammed into other objects. Some tornadoes are strong enough to knock trees over, lift up cars, and rip the roofs off of houses. Some tornadoes are even strong enough to completely flatten a well-built building.

Active Reading **8 Identify** What are some of the effects of tornadoes?

Risk of Tornadoes

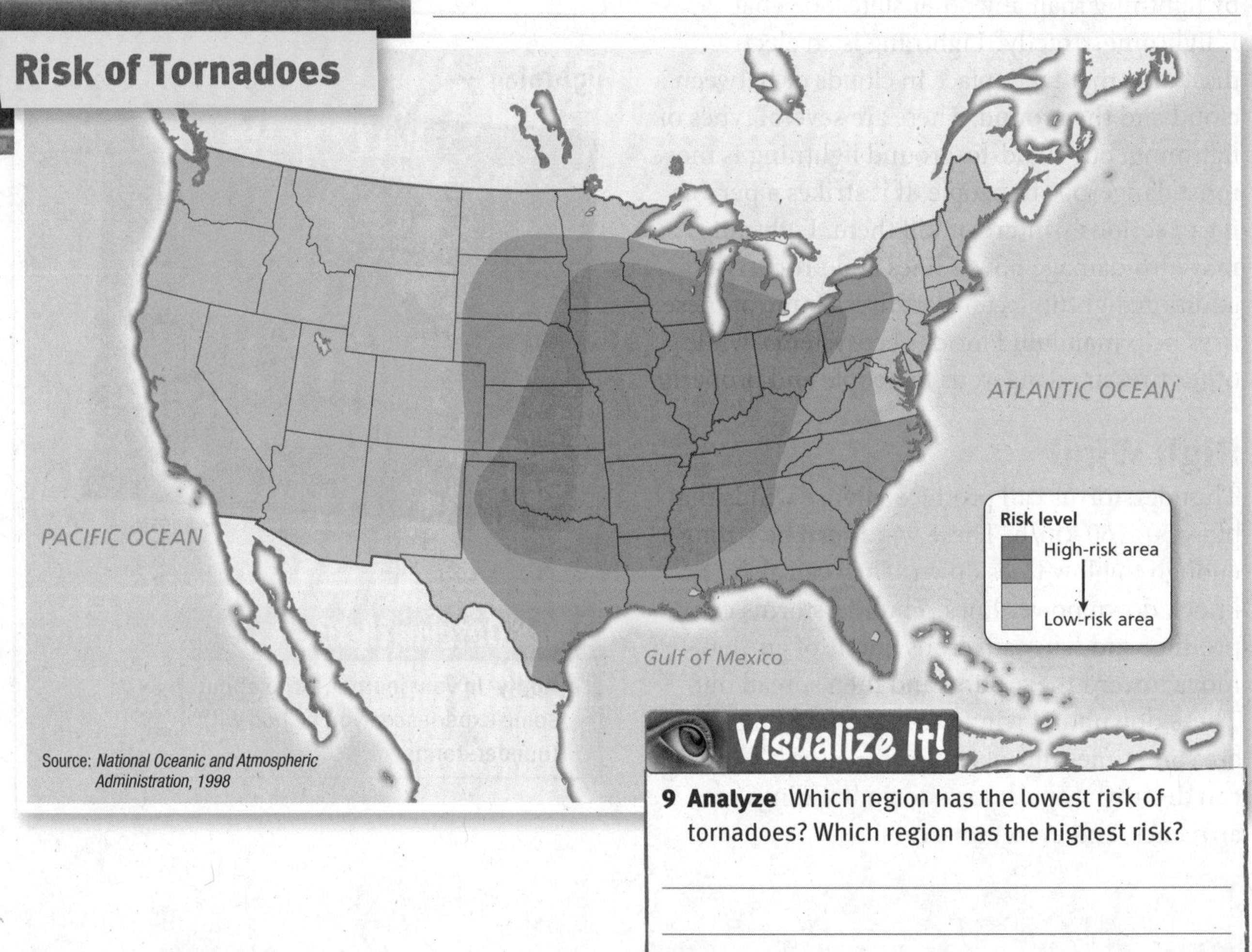

Source: *National Oceanic and Atmospheric Administration, 1998*

Visualize It!

9 Analyze Which region has the lowest risk of tornadoes? Which region has the highest risk?

What are the effects of floods?

Floods are very common in Florida because the state is relatively flat, a great deal of rainfall is received, , and, in some areas, the rock layer under the soil doesn't let water through easily. When heavy rain occurs, low-lying areas can become flooded. Any homes and buildings in these areas may be threatened by rising water, which can cause millions of dollars in property damage. In addition, flooded roads are very dangerous to drive on, and fast-moving water can sweep people away. Finally, floodwater can enter the drinking-water supply and contaminate the water with pollutants. Contaminated water is unsafe to drink.

In addition to inland flooding, much of Florida is at risk from flooding from the ocean. During hurricanes, water from the ocean can be pushed up onto land when a storm surge hits. A *storm surge* is a swell of water that builds up in the ocean due to a hurricane's heavy winds. A storm surge can be especially devastating when the tide is high. It can also cause rivers to back up and flood. Coastal areas and islands can be totally covered by ocean water. Because of this, the Florida Keys are especially at risk from storm surges. You will learn more about storm surges later in this lesson.

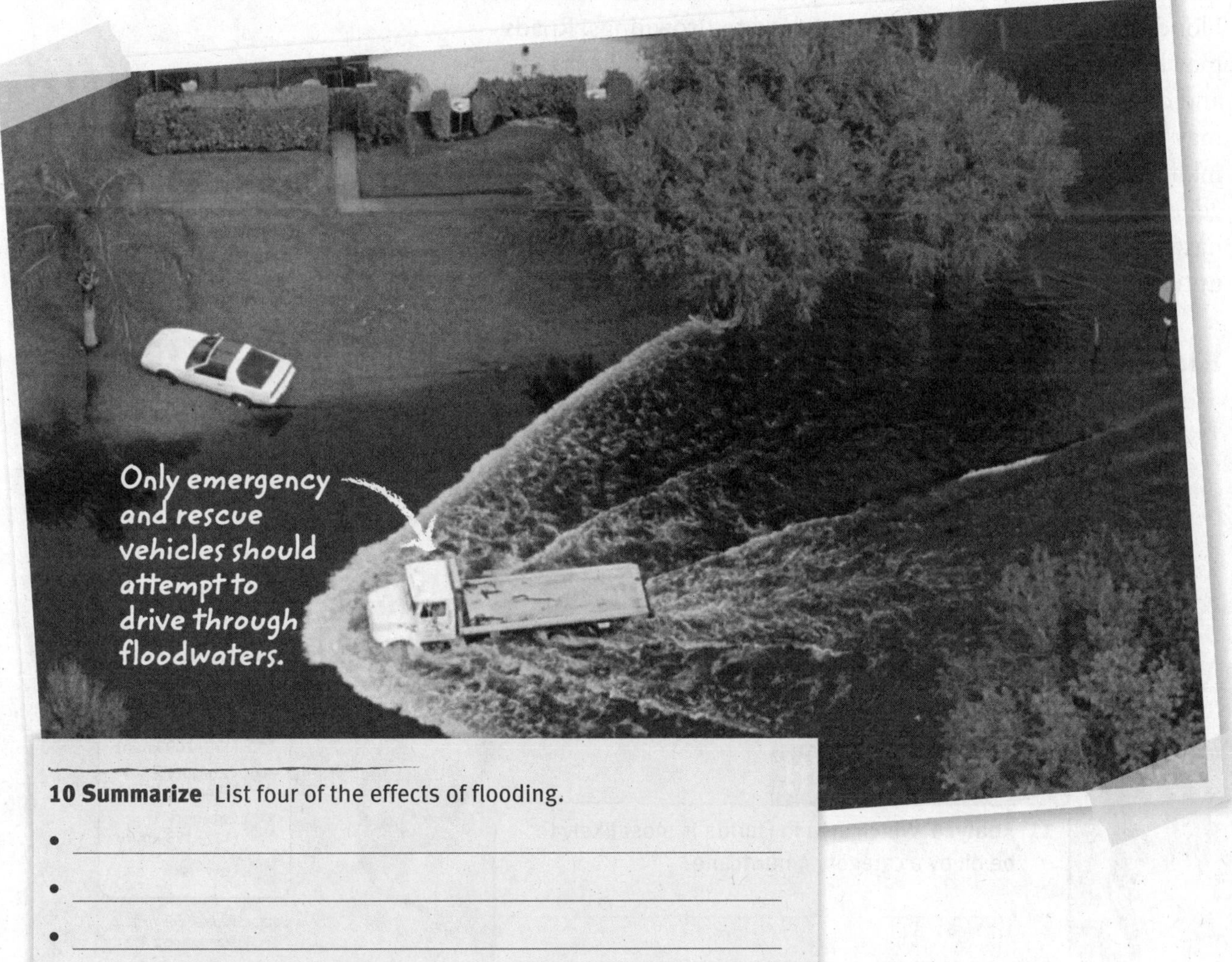

Only emergency and rescue vehicles should attempt to drive through floodwaters.

10 Summarize List four of the effects of flooding.

- ______________________
- ______________________
- ______________________
- ______________________

Weathering the Storm

What are the effects of hurricanes?

Hurricanes are low-pressure systems with thunderstorms and winds that circle around a central "eye." The winds circling the eye must sustain speeds of at least 119 km/h for the storm to be classified as a hurricane.

Hurricanes form over warm ocean water. If a hurricane travels over cold water, it will die out. Hurricanes usually occur in summer in the northern hemisphere. Hurricane season runs from June 1 to November 30. Because Florida is near the warm waters of the Gulf of Mexico, the Atlantic Ocean, and the Caribbean Sea, Florida is hit by more hurricanes than any other state.

Hazards to People

Hurricanes are the most violent storms on Earth. They can be deadly. Because of this danger, government officials often order citizens to evacuate when a hurricane is about to strike. However, the area still may not be safe even after the hurricane has ended. Floodwaters from the hurricane can lead to drownings. Roads may be covered by debris, causing car accidents. Broken tree limbs and damaged structures can fall on people. Broken electric lines may lead to electrocution. Because of widespread power outages, many people use generators for electricity. If not used properly, generators can cause carbon monoxide poisoning. Due to all these hazards, you should not return to an area affected by a hurricane until officials say it is safe to do so.

Risk of Hurricane Strike

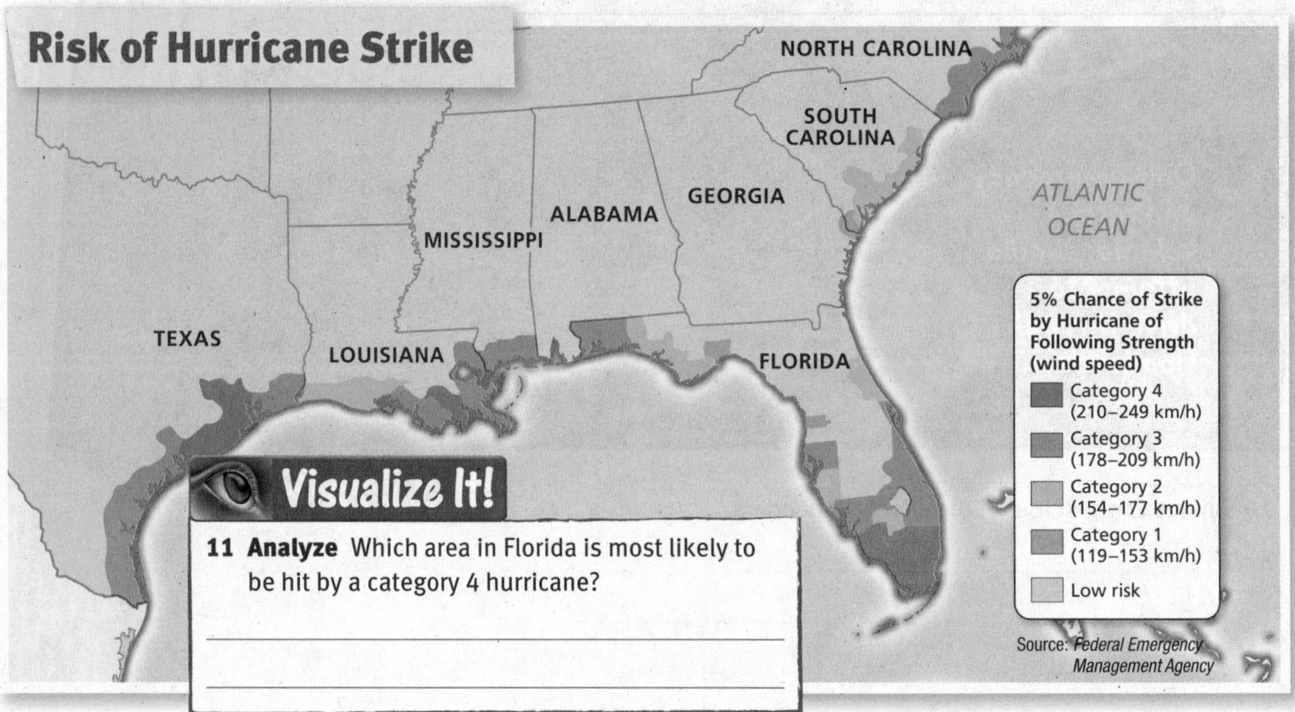

Visualize It!

11 Analyze Which area in Florida is most likely to be hit by a category 4 hurricane?

____

____

Damage to Property

Florida's flat land makes it vulnerable to the full force of hurricane winds. Because of this, hurricanes striking Florida can cause an enormous amount of property damage. For major hurricanes, it typically costs several billion dollars to repair the damage.

Larger hurricanes can affect more areas than smaller hurricanes, but the destructive power of a hurricane is also related to its strength. Category 1 hurricanes are the weakest because they have the slowest winds (119–153 km/h). Category 5 hurricanes have the fastest winds (greater than 250 km/h). Winds can rip roofs off buildings or slam objects against structures. In addition, a great deal of damage can be caused by a storm surge because of the power of rising ocean water. The impact of a storm surge depends on the direction of the wind and whether the tide is high when a hurricane hits.

12 Explain How do hurricane winds affect property?

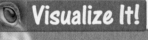

Visualize It!

During a regular high tide, the waters don't cause floods or damage.

Storm surges push waters far above the high tide level and cause severe flooding.

13 Apply When a hurricane approaches land, people living directly on the coast should always evacuate when told to do so by authorities. Use the information in the diagram to explain why.

More Recipes for Disaster

These strawberry plants have been covered in ice to protect them from cold weather.

What are the effects of cold weather?

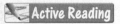

Active Reading

14 Identify Underline the two main ways Florida's economy can be hurt by cold weather spells.

We don't often think about cold weather in many parts of Florida. But when cold weather does strike, it can damage crops, harm the tourism industry, and be dangerous to people. Cold weather can also make the roads icy and hazardous to drive on.

In Florida, farmers may protect crops from freezing weather by covering them or spraying them with water. The water freezes and forms a layer of ice, which traps some heat in the plant. This process keeps the developing fruit from freezing. However, if temperatures stay too low for too long, the crop will be damaged.

Because Florida usually has mild weather, many homes do not have adequate heating and insulation. As a result, people in Florida may have trouble staying warm during cold weather. Electricity can be disrupted by an ice storm, which may result in near-freezing temperatures inside houses. People who are exposed to cold weather for a long time may fall dangerously ill. If the weather gets too cold, wear several layers of dry clothing and use safe heating devices.

What are the effects of sinkholes?

15 Identify Underline at least five effects of sinkholes.

Sinkholes are a danger in some parts of Florida. **Sinkholes** are holes in the ground that form when a cave collapses. In Florida, sinkholes often form where limestone is eroded by ground water, making a cave. The cave's roof falls in when ground water supporting the roof drains away. The map below shows that sinkholes are one of the major landforms in the state.

Sinkholes can swallow cars, damage homes, and even destroy whole city blocks! People can be killed when sinkholes form. Look at the photo of the sinkhole below. Nobody was killed when this sinkhole formed, but a road caved in. Sinkholes can cause millions of dollars of damage. In addition, sinkholes can disrupt services by breaking underground telephone lines, sewer lines, and more.

Sinkholes can lead to the contamination of a town's water supply. Anything that goes into a sinkhole can enter the ground water, which is used for drinking water by many Floridians. So, trash should not be dumped in a sinkhole. And because sinkholes can collapse further, you should stay away from them.

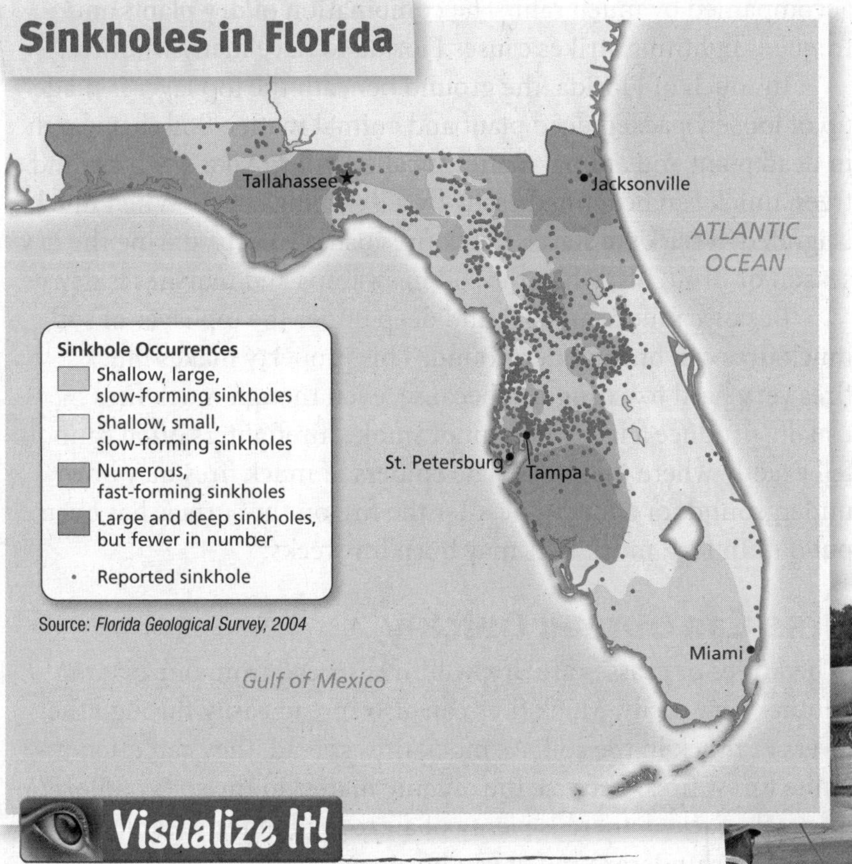

Visualize It!

16 Analyze What type of sinkholes would you expect to find around Jacksonville?

____

____

A sinkhole in Plant City, Florida

Up in Flames

What do we know about wildfires?

Wildfires are uncontrolled fires burning in natural areas. Every 3 to 5 years, there is an increase in the number of wildfires that burn in Florida. This cycle of wildfires coincides with the state's natural climatic cycles. Wildfires increase during periods of dry weather and drought.

Active Reading **17 Identify** Underline the sentences below that describe how a muck fire typically starts.

Fires Are Often Caused by Lightning

Wildfires usually start when lightning ignites dry trees or grasses. After the dry season, dry grass and trees may catch fire easily. Florida has frequent, intense lightning storms that may not be accompanied by much rain. The combination of dry plants and frequent lightning strikes causes Florida to have many wildfires.

In much of Florida, the ground beneath the top layer is made up of loosely packed dead plant and animal matter. Soil that is rich in dead plant and animal matter is called *muck.* Like dry grass and trees, muck can be ignited easily by a lightning strike. When muck is ignited, a **muck fire** starts. Muck fires usually occur during the dry season or droughts, when the soil in swamps and marshes is dry.

Because muck can be found deep under the top layer of soil, muck fires can burn underground. This property makes muck fires very hard to extinguish because, even though muck fires usually produce a large amount of smoke, firefighters often cannot tell exactly where the fire is. The embers of muck fires may burn underground for a long time after the fire on the surface has been put out. In fact, muck fires may burn for weeks.

Fires Can Spread Quickly

When trees or grasses are dry, wildfires spread from one plant to another very easily. Muck fires can also spread easily through the layers of muck in the soil. As muck fires spread, they can often re-ignite forest fires. Because the organic matter in the soils of Florida is loosely packed, there is plenty of air to feed muck fires. As the fire spreads underground, it can burn tree roots. When the trees fall, the underground fire may restart a surface fire.

Wildfires in the Continental United States, 1980–2003

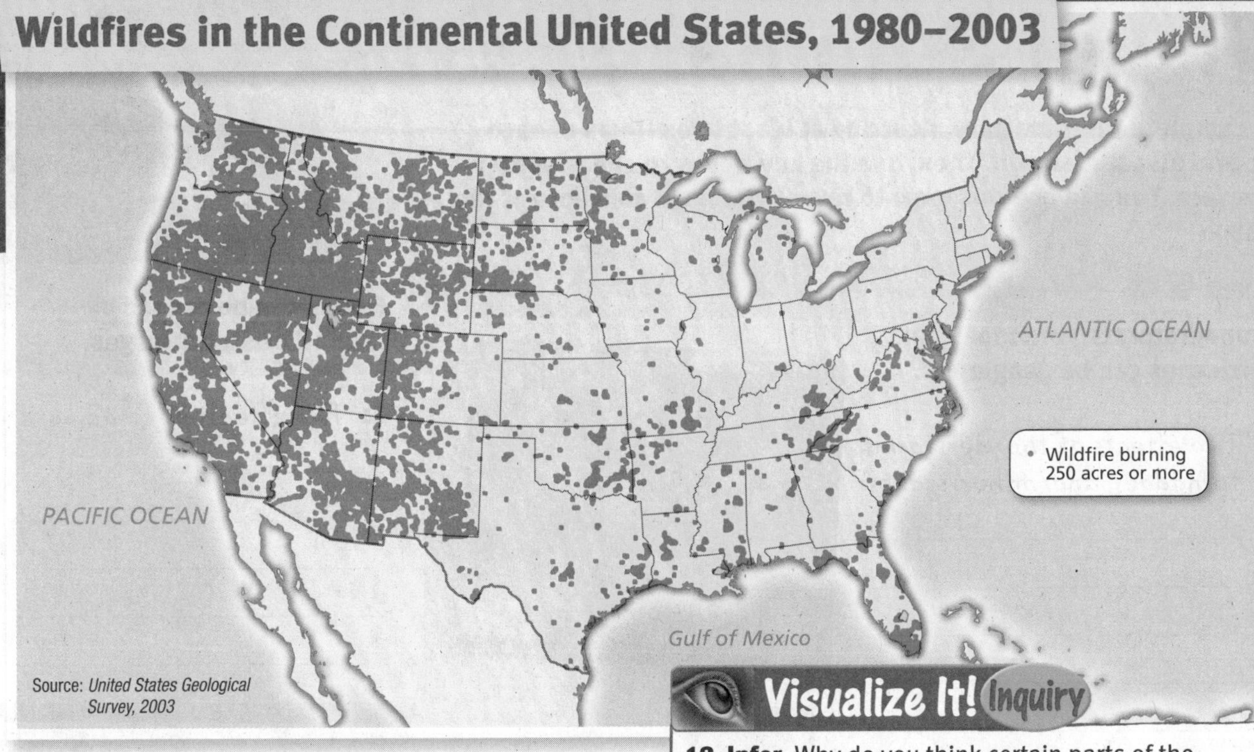

Source: *United States Geological Survey, 2003*

Fires Destroy Property

More and more homes in Florida are built in wilderness areas that are prone to fires. Most of the Florida developments in rural areas or near wilderness have burned in the last 100 years. In 1998, about 45,000 people were evacuated from their homes because of fires. Thanks to firefighters, though, only 337 houses and 33 businesses were damaged. However, 500,000 acres were burned. These fires temporarily destroyed the habitats of many animals, but the fires added nutrients to the soil and helped renew the plant life in the ecosystems.

There are several things you can do to stay safe from fires. First, know whether your home is in a fire-prone area. Second, many plants are resistant to fire. Plant these near your home. Third, have a disaster plan and supplies in your home and car. Last, if a wildfire is occuring in your area, listen to local radio or TV stations for the latest information and evacuation instructions.

Visualize It! Inquiry

18 Infer Why do you think certain parts of the country are more susceptible to wildfires than other parts?

____

____

This truck was caught in a wildfire.

19 Summarize Make a checklist of safety measures you can take to protect yourself and your family from wildfires.

____

____

____

____

____

____

Visual Summary

To complete this summary, describe at least two effects of each natural disaster shown. Then, use the key below to check your answers. You can use this page to review the main concepts of the lesson.

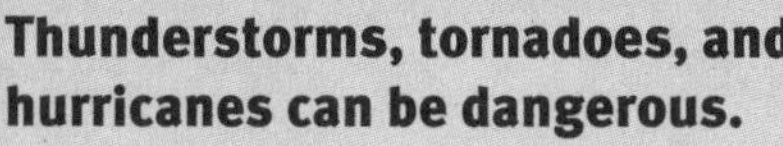

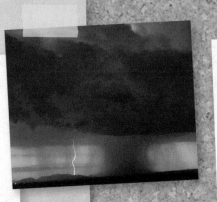

Thunderstorms, tornadoes, and hurricanes can be dangerous.

20 Two effects of thunderstorms, tornadoes, and/or hurricanes:

Floods can be caused by rainfall or storm surges.

21 Two effects of flooding:

Natural Disasters

Cold weather can impact Florida's economy.

22 Two effects of cold weather:

Sinkholes are common in Florida.

23 Two effects of sinkholes:

Fires can spread quickly with little warning.

24 Two effects of fires:

Sample answers: 20 flooding; property damage from hail, wind, and lightning; 21 damage to property, cars and people carried away; 22 crop damage, car accidents; 23 contaminated ground water, disrupted utilities; 24 buildings destroyed, forests burned

25 Explain How can thunderstorms lead to both flooding and fires?

Lesson Review

Vocabulary

Fill in the blank with the term that best completes the following sentences.

1 A(n) ____________________ can form when water supporting the roof of a cavern drains and the roof falls.

2 A fire burning uncontrolled in a natural area is called a(n) ____________________

Key Concepts

3 Identify What are the dangers associated with thunderstorms?

4 Describe Describe how a tornado can endanger property and people.

5 State How can floodwater affect the public drinking water supply?

6 Explain Why is Florida susceptible to sinkholes?

7 Summarize How can you protect yourself from the cold?

Critical Thinking

Use the table to answer the following questions.

Top Six Deadliest U.S. Hurricanes				
Rank	**Name** (Landfall location)	**Year**	**Category**	**Deaths**
1	Unnamed (Galveston, TX)	1900	4	8,000–12,000
2	Unnamed (West Palm Beach, FL)	1928	4	2,500–3,000
3	Katrina (Florida and Louisiana)	2005	3	1,800
4	Audrey (Texas and Louisiana)	1957	4	419
5	Unnamed (Florida Keys)	1935	5	408
6	Unnamed (Miami, FL)	1926	4	372

8 Analyze Where have the majority of the hurricanes listed made landfall? What is the likely reason for this?

9 Infer Did the deadliest hurricane happen recently or in the past? Why do you think this is the case?

10 Relate Which area would be most likely to experience wildfires: a wet area with many lightning strikes, a dry area with few lightning strikes, or a dry area with many lightning strikes? Explain.

People in Science

J. Marshall Shepherd

METEOROLOGIST AND CLIMATOLOGIST

J. Marshall Shepherd

Dr. Marshall Shepherd, who works at the University of Georgia, has been interested in weather since he made his own weather-collecting instruments for a school science project. Although the instruments he uses today, like computers and satellites, are much larger and much more powerful than the ones he made in school, they give him some of the same information.

In his work, Dr. Shepherd tries to understand weather events, such as hurricanes and thunderstorms, and relate them to current weather and climate change. He once led a team that used space-based radar to measure rainfall over urban areas. The measurements confirmed that the areas downwind of major cities experience more rainfall in summer than other areas in the same region. He explained that the excess heat retained by buildings and roads changes the way the air circulates, and this causes rain clouds to form.

While the most familiar field of meteorology is weather forecasting, research meteorology is also used in air pollution control, weather control, agricultural planning, climate change studies, and even criminal and civil investigations.

Social Studies Connection

An almanac is a type of calendar that contains various types of information, including weather forecasts and astronomical data, for every day of the year. Many people used almanacs before meteorologists started to forecast the weather. Use an almanac from the library or the Internet to find out what the weather was on the day that you were born.

JOB BOARD

Atmospheric Scientist

What You'll Do: Collect and analyze data on Earth's air pressure, humidity, and winds to make short-range and long-range weather forecasts. Work around the clock during weather emergencies like hurricanes and tornadoes.

Where You Might Work: Weather data collecting stations, radio and television stations, or private consulting firms.

Education: A bachelor's degree in meteorology, or in a closely related field with courses in meteorology, is required. A master's degree is necessary for some jobs.

Airplane Pilot

What You'll Do: Fly airplanes containing passengers or cargo, or for crop dusting, search and rescue, or fire-fighting. Before flights, check the plane's control equipment and weather conditions. Plan a safe route. Pilots communicate with air traffic control during flight to ensure a safe flight and fill out paperwork after the flight.

Where You Might Work: Flying planes for airlines, the military, radio and tv stations, freight companies, flight schools, farms, national parks, or other businesses that use airplanes.

Education: Most pilots will complete a four-year college degree before entering a pilot program. Before pilots become certified and take to the skies, they need a pilot license and many hours of flight time and training.

Snow Plow Operator

What You'll Do: In areas that receive snowfall, prepare the roads by spreading a mixture of sand and salt on the roads when snow is forecast. After a snowfall, drive snow plows to clear snow from roads and walkways.

Where You Might Work: For public organizations or private companies in cities and towns that receive snowfall.

Education: In most states, there is no special license needed, other than a driver's license.

Lesson 6

Climate

ESSENTIAL QUESTION

How is climate affected by energy from the sun and variations on Earth's surface?

By the end of this lesson, you should be able to describe the main factors that affect climate and explain how scientists classify climates.

Earth has a wide variety of climates, including polar climates like the one shown here. What kind of climate do you live in?

Sunshine State Standards

SC.6.E.7.2 Investigate and apply how the cycling of water between the atmosphere and hydrosphere has an effect on weather patterns and climate.

SC.6.E.7.5 Explain how energy provided by the sun influences global patterns of atmospheric movement and the temperature differences between air, water, and land.

SC.6.E.7.6 Differentiate between weather and climate.

Engage Your Brain

1 Predict Check T or F to show whether you think each statement is true or false.

T	F	
☐	☐	Locations in Florida and Oregon receive the same amount of sunlight on any given day.
☐	☐	Temperature is an important part of determining the climate of an area.
☐	☐	The climate on even the tallest mountains near the equator is too warm for glaciers to form.
☐	☐	Winds can move rain clouds from one location to another.

2 Infer Volcanic eruptions can send huge clouds of gas and dust into the air. These dust particles can block sunlight. How might the eruption of a large volcano affect weather for years to come?

Active Reading

3 Synthesize You can often define an unknown word if you know the meaning of its word parts. Use the word parts and sentence below to make an educated guess about the meaning of the word *topography*.

Word part	Meaning
topos-	place
-graphy	writing

Example sentence

The topography of the area is varied, because there are hills, valleys, and flat plains all within a few square miles.

topography:

Vocabulary Terms

- **weather**
- **climate**
- **latitude**
- **topography**
- **elevation**
- **surface currents**

4 Apply As you learn the definition of each vocabulary term in this lesson, create your own definition or sketch to help you remember the meaning of the term.

How's the **Climate?**

What determines climate?

Active Reading

5 Identify As you read, underline two elements of weather that are important in determining climate.

Weather conditions change from day to day. **Weather** is the condition of Earth's atmosphere at a particular time and place. **Climate**, on the other hand, describes the weather conditions in an area over a long period of time. For the most part, climate is determined by temperature and precipitation (pree•SIP•uh•tay•shuhn). But what factors affect the temperature and precipitation rates of an area? Those factors include latitude, wind patterns, elevation, locations of mountains and large bodies of water, and nearness to ocean currents.

Temperature

Temperature patterns are an important feature of climate. Although the average temperature of an area over a period of time is useful information, using only average temperatures to describe climate can be misleading. Areas that have similar average temperatures may have very different temperature ranges.

A temperature range includes all of the temperatures in an area, from the coldest temperature extreme to the warmest temperature extreme. Organisms that thrive in a region are those that can survive the temperature extremes in that region. Temperature ranges provide more information about an area and are unique to the area. Therefore, temperature ranges are a better indicator of climate than are temperature averages.

Visualize It!

6 Infer How might the two different climates shown below affect the daily lives of the people who live there?

Precipitation

Precipitation, such as rain, snow, or hail, is also an important part of climate. As with temperature, the average yearly precipitation alone is not the best way to describe a climate. Two places that have the same average yearly precipitation may receive that precipitation in different patterns during the year. For example, one location may receive small amounts of precipitation throughout the year. This pattern would support plant life all year long. Another location may receive all of its precipitation in a few months of the year. These months may be the only time in which plants can grow. So, the pattern of precipitation in a region can determine the types of plants that grow there and the length of the growing season. Therefore, the pattern of precipitation is a better indicator of the local climate than the average precipitation alone.

Think Outside the Book Inquiry

8 Apply With a classmate, discuss what condition, other than precipitation, is likely related to better plant growth in the temperate area shown directly below than in the desert on the bottom right.

Visualize It!

7 Interpret Match the climates represented in the bar graph below to the photos by writing *A*, *B*, or *C* in the blank circles.

◯ There are enough resources in the area for plants to thickly cover the ground.

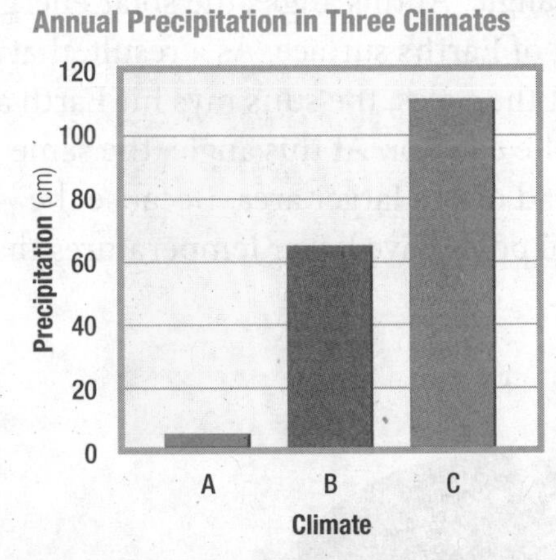

Some plants that grow in deserts have long roots to reach the water deep underground.

Conditions in a tropical forest allow lots of plants to grow quickly and closely together.

Here Comes the Sun!

How is the sun's energy related to Earth's climate?

Active Reading

9 Identify As you read, underline how solar energy affects the climate of an area.

The climate of an area is directly related to the amount of energy from the sun, or *solar energy*, that the area receives. This amount depends on the latitude (LAHT•ih•tood) of the area. **Latitude** is the angular distance in degrees north and south from the equator. Different latitudes receive different amounts of solar energy. The available solar energy powers the water cycle and winds, which affect the temperature, precipitation, and other factors that determine the local climate.

Latitude Affects the Amount of Solar Energy an Area Receives and that Area's Climate

Latitude helps determine the temperature of an area, because latitude affects the amount of solar energy an area receives. The figure below shows how the amount of solar energy reaching Earth's surface varies with latitude. Notice that the sun's rays travel in lines parallel to one another. Near the equator, the sun's rays hit Earth directly, at almost a 90° angle. At this angle, the solar energy is concentrated in a small area of Earth's surface. As a result, that area has high temperatures. At the poles, the sun's rays hit Earth at a lesser angle than they do at the equator. At this angle, the same amount of solar energy is spread over a larger area. Because the energy is less concentrated, the poles have lower temperatures than areas near the equator do.

Visualize It!

10 Analyze What is the difference between the sun's rays that strike at the equator and the sun's rays that strike at the poles?

____

____

____

____

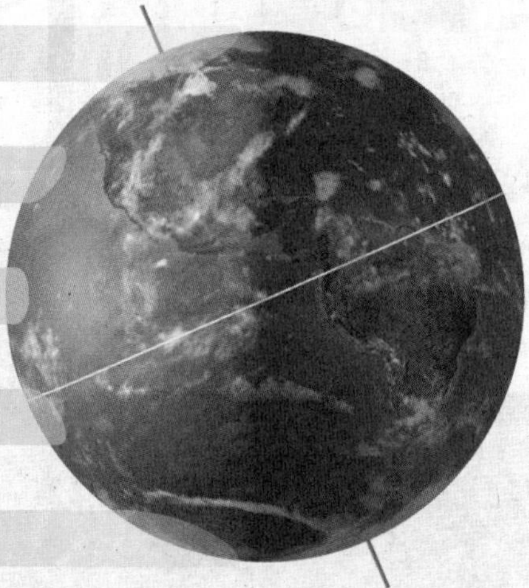

The amount of solar energy an area receives depends on latitude.

Drawing is not to scale.

The Sun Powers the Water Cycle

It is easy to see how the water cycle affects weather and climate. For example, when it rains or snows, you see precipitation. In the water cycle, energy from the sun warms the surface of the ocean or other body of water. Some of the liquid water evaporates, becoming invisible water vapor, a gas. When cooled, some of the vapor condenses, turning into droplets of liquid water and forming clouds. Some water droplets collide, becoming larger. Once large enough, they fall to Earth's surface as precipitation.

Visualize It!

11 Apply Using the figure below, explain how the water cycle affects the climate of an area.

____

____

____

____

____

Clouds
Condensation
Precipitation
Water vapor
Water storage in ice and snow
Surface runoff
Evaporation

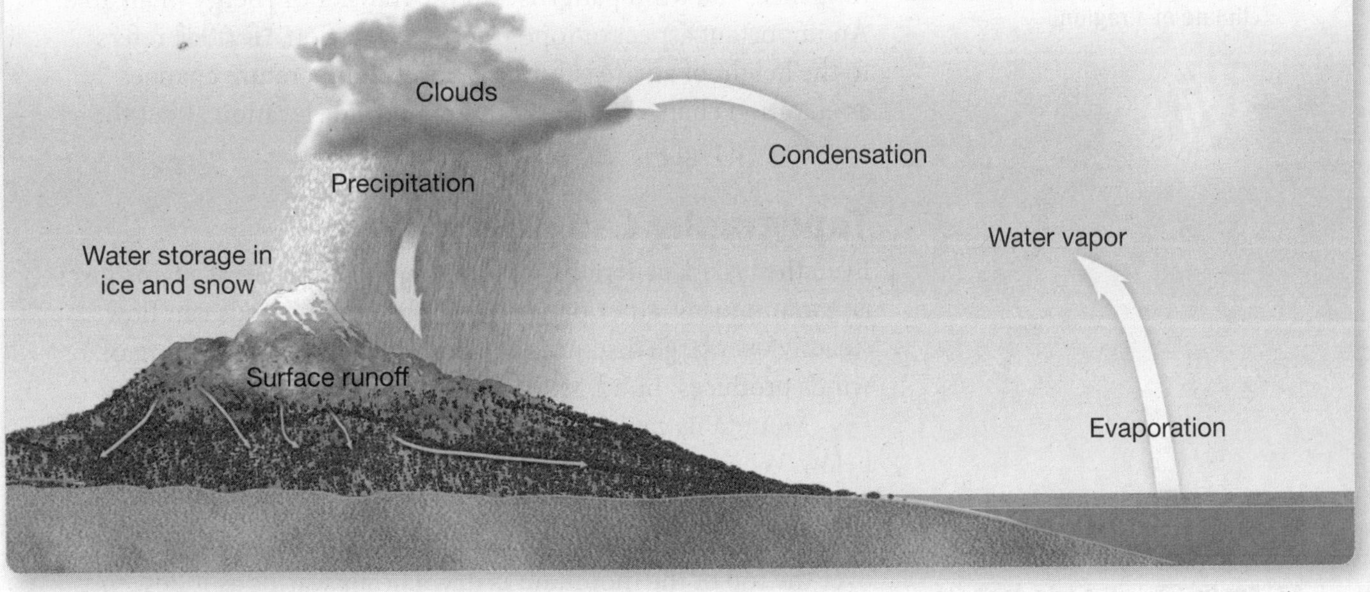

The Sun Powers Wind

The sun warms Earth's surface unevenly, creating areas of different air pressure. As air moves from areas of higher pressure to areas of lower pressure, it is felt as wind, as shown below. Global and local wind patterns transfer energy around Earth's surface, affecting global and local temperatures. Winds also carry water vapor from place to place. If the air cools enough, the water vapor will condense and fall as precipitation. The speed, direction, temperature, and moisture content of winds affect the climate and weather of the areas they move through.

Warm, less dense air rises, creating areas of low pressure.
Cold, more dense air sinks, creating areas of high pressure.
Wind forms when air moves from a high-pressure area to a low-pressure area.
Warm surface
Cool surface

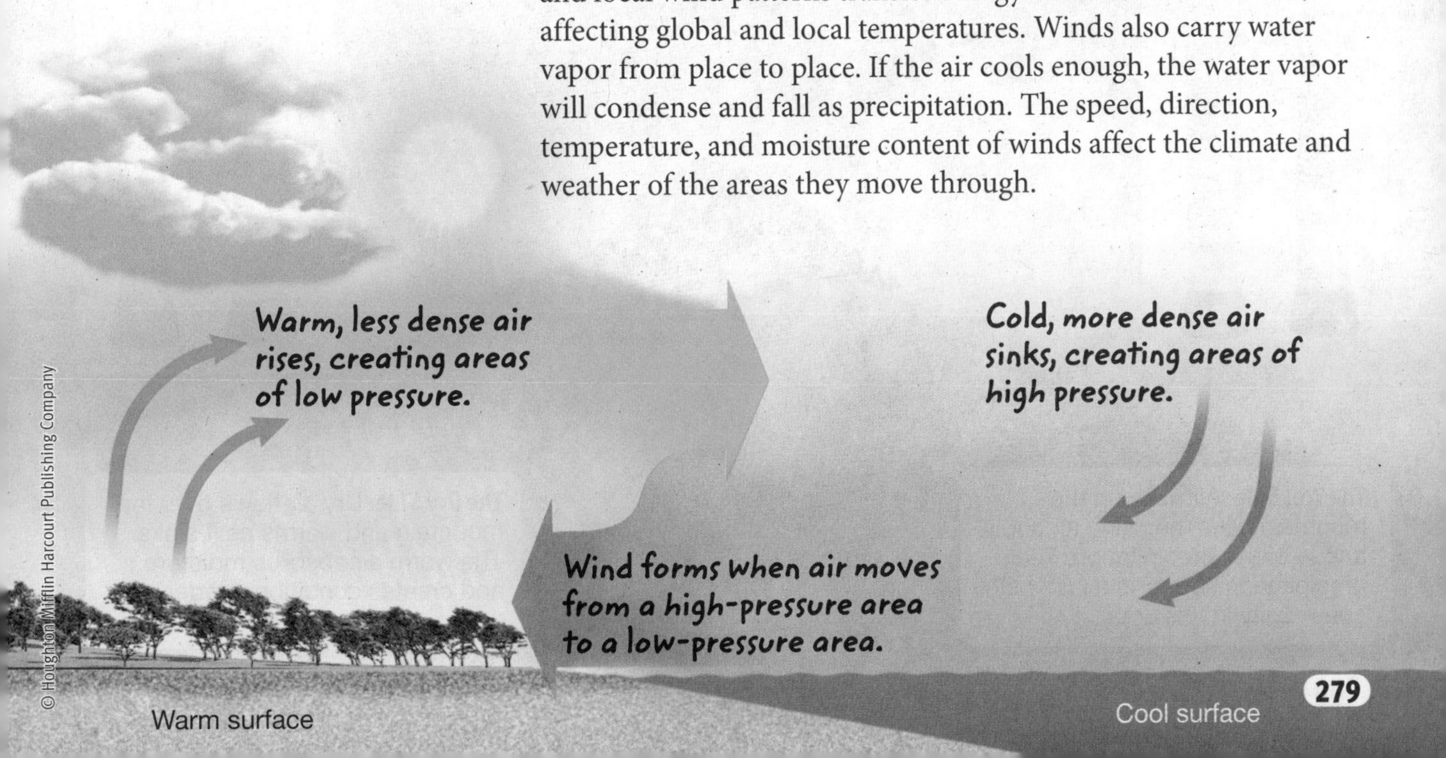

Latitude Isn't Everything

How do Earth's features affect climate?

12 Identify As you read, underline how topography affects the climate of a region.

On land, winds have to flow around or over features on Earth's surface, such as mountains. The surface features of an area combine to form its **topography** (tuh•POG•ruh•fee). Topography influences the wind patterns and the transfer of energy in an area. An important aspect of topography is elevation. **Elevation** refers to the height of an area above sea level. Temperature changes as elevation changes. Thus, topography and elevation affect the climate of a region.

Topography Can Affect Winds

Even the broad, generally flat topography of the Great Plains gives rise to unique weather patterns. On the plains, winds can flow steadily over large distances before they merge. This mixing of winds produces thunderstorms and even tornadoes.

Mountains can also affect the climate of an area, as shown below. When moist air hits a mountain, it is forced to rise up the side of the mountain. The rising air cools and often releases rain, which supports plants on the mountainside. The air that moves over the top of the mountain is dry. The air warms as it descends, creating a dry climate, which supports desert formation. Such areas are said to be in a *rain shadow,* because the air has already released all of its water by the time that it reaches this side of the mountain.

Visualize It!

13 Apply Circle the rain gauge in each set that corresponds to how much rain each side of the mountain is likely to receive.

The Wet Side Air rises up the mountainside. The rising air cools and releases precipitation. The precipitation supports a lush plant community in this area.

The Dry Side Dry air flows over the mountain and warms as it sinks. The warm air absorbs moisture and creates conditions under which deserts may develop.

Elevation Influences Temperature

Elevation has a very strong effect on the temperature of an area. If you rode a cable car up a mountain, the temperature would decrease by about 6.5 °C (11.7 °F) for every kilometer you rose in elevation. Why does it get colder as you move higher up? Because the lower atmosphere is mainly warmed by Earth's surface that is directly below it. The warmed air lifts to higher elevations, where it expands and cools. Even close to the equator, temperatures at high elevations can be very cold. For example, Mount Kilimanjaro in Tanzania is close to the equator, but it is still cold enough at the peak to support a permanent glacier. The example below shows how one mountain can have several types of climates.

Visualize It!

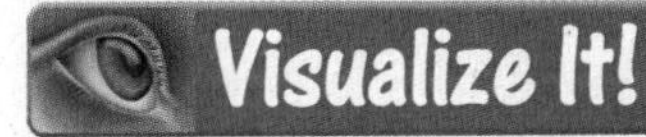

14 Apply Circle the thermometer that shows the most likely temperature for each photo at different elevations.

Effects of Elevation

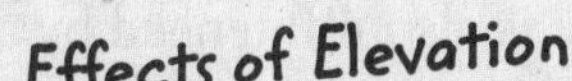

Haleakala, Maui
Elevation: 3,048 m (10,000 ft)

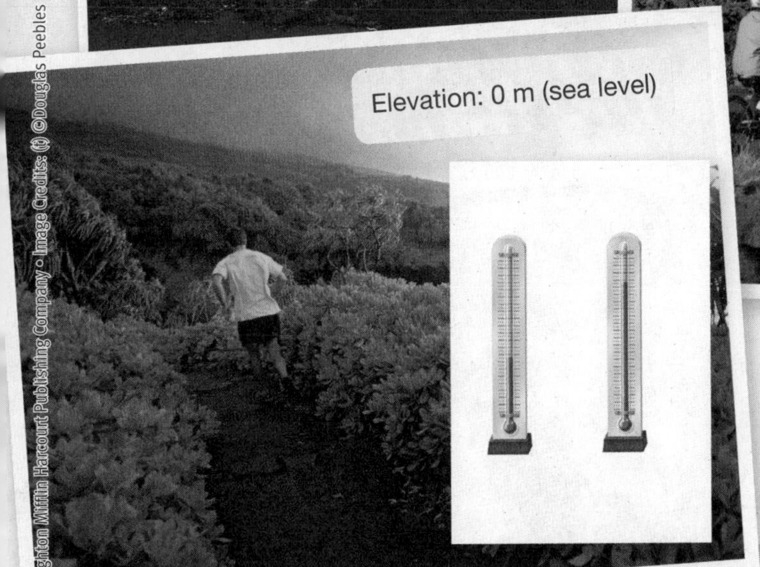

Elevation: 0 m (sea level)

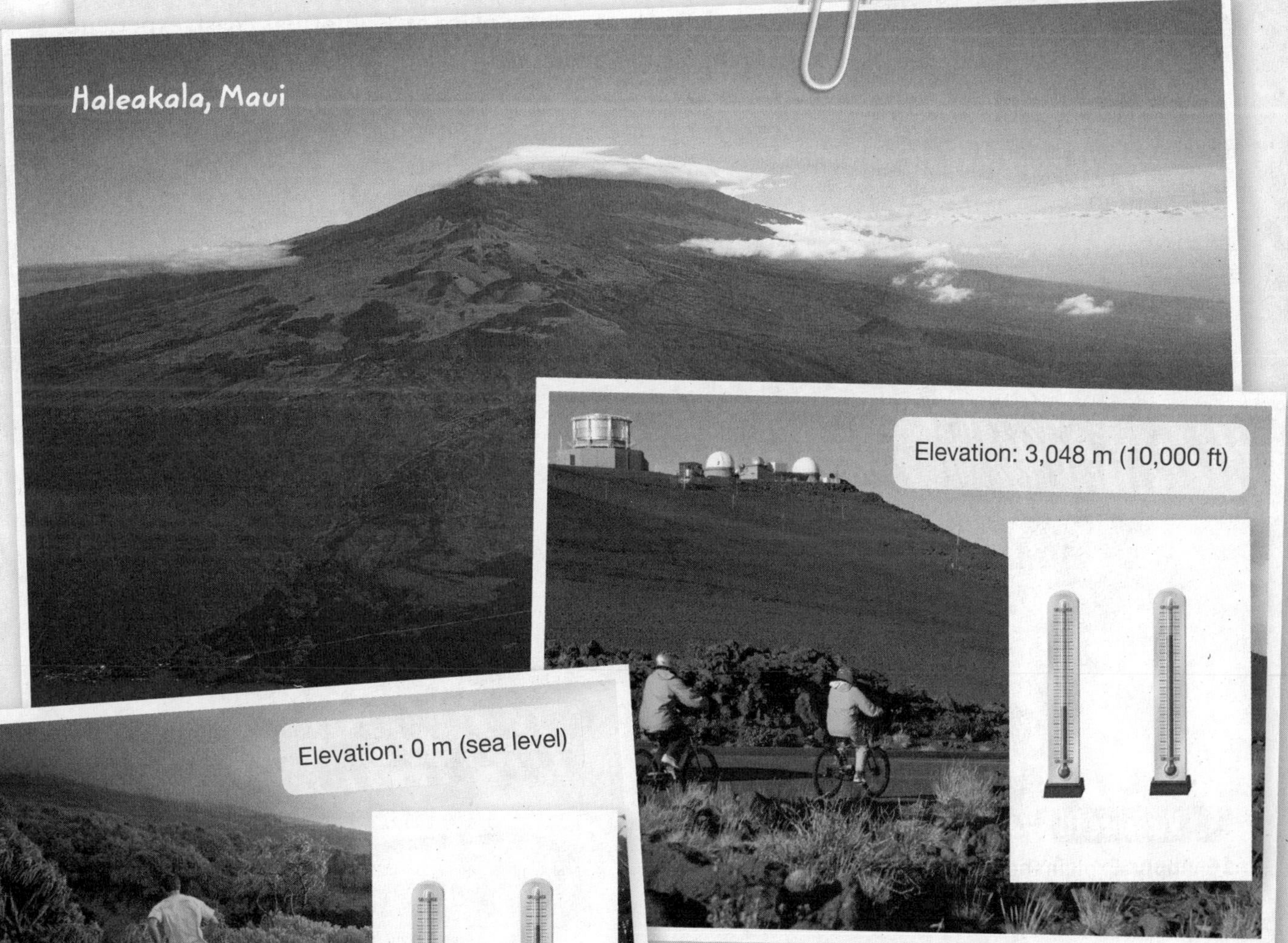

15 Infer Generally, why are there no trees above a certain elevation on very tall mountains?

____

____

Waterfront Property

How do large bodies of water affect climate?

Large bodies of water, such as the ocean, can influence an area's climate. Water absorbs and releases energy as heat more slowly than land does. So, water helps moderate the temperature of nearby land. Sudden or extreme temperature changes rarely take place on land near large bodies of water. The state of Michigan, which is nearly surrounded by the Great Lakes, has more moderate temperatures than places far from large bodies of water at the same latitude. California's coastal climate is also influenced by a large body of water—the ocean. Places that are inland, but that are at the same latitude as a given place on California's coast, experience wider ranges of temperature.

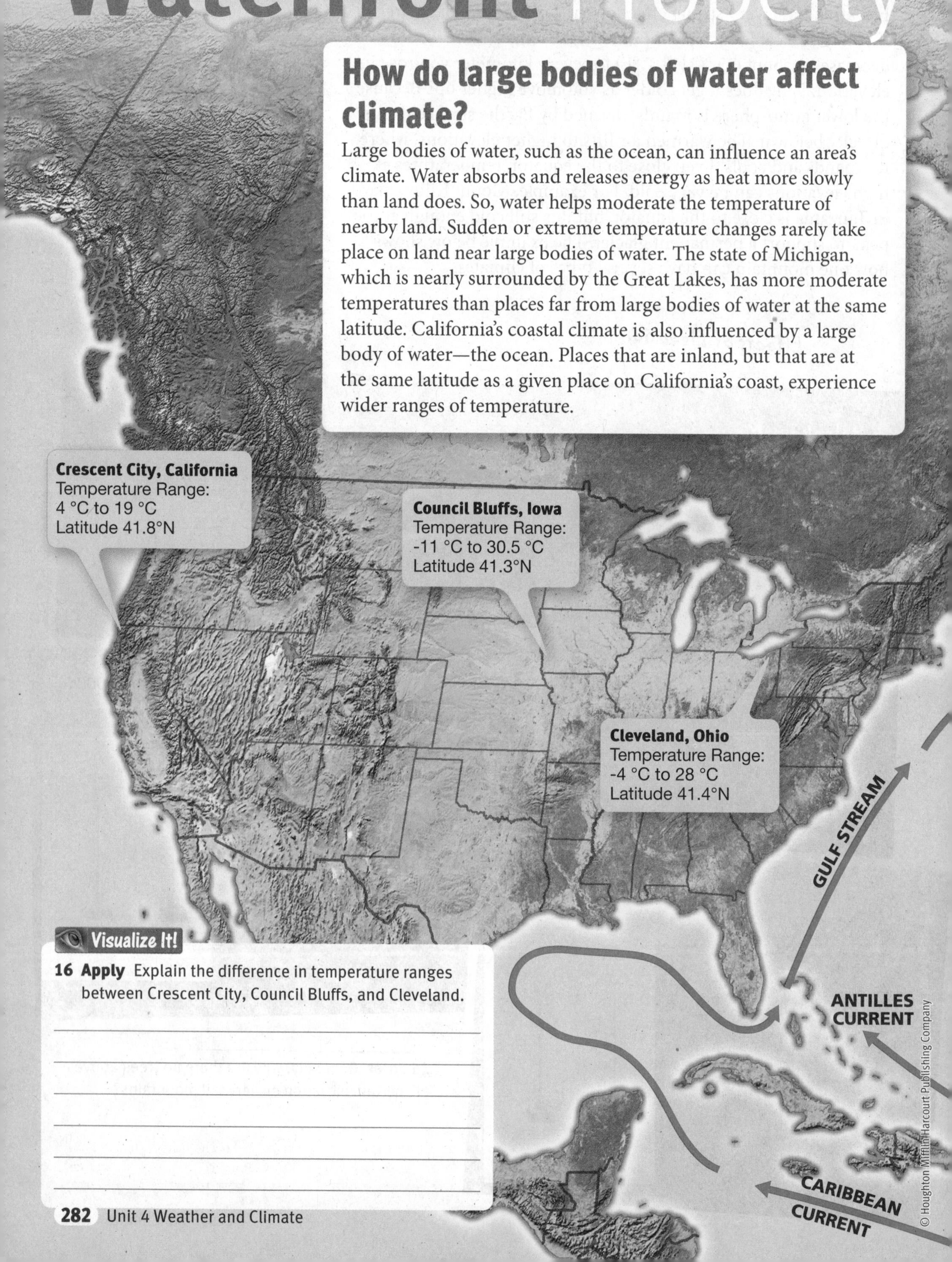

Visualize It!

16 Apply Explain the difference in temperature ranges between Crescent City, Council Bluffs, and Cleveland.

How do ocean currents affect climate?

An *ocean current* is the movement of water in a certain direction. There are many different currents in the oceans. Ocean currents move water and distribute energy and nutrients around the globe. The currents on the surface of the ocean are called **surface currents.** Surface currents are driven by winds and carry warm water away from the equator and carry cool water away from the poles.

Cold currents cool the air in coastal areas, while warm currents warm the air in coastal areas. Thus, currents moderate global temperatures. For example, the Gulf Stream is a surface current that moves warm water from the Gulf of Mexico northeastward, toward Great Britain and Europe. The British climate is mild because of the warm Gulf Stream waters. Polar bears do not wander the streets of Great Britain, as they might in Natashquan, Canada, which is at a similar latitude.

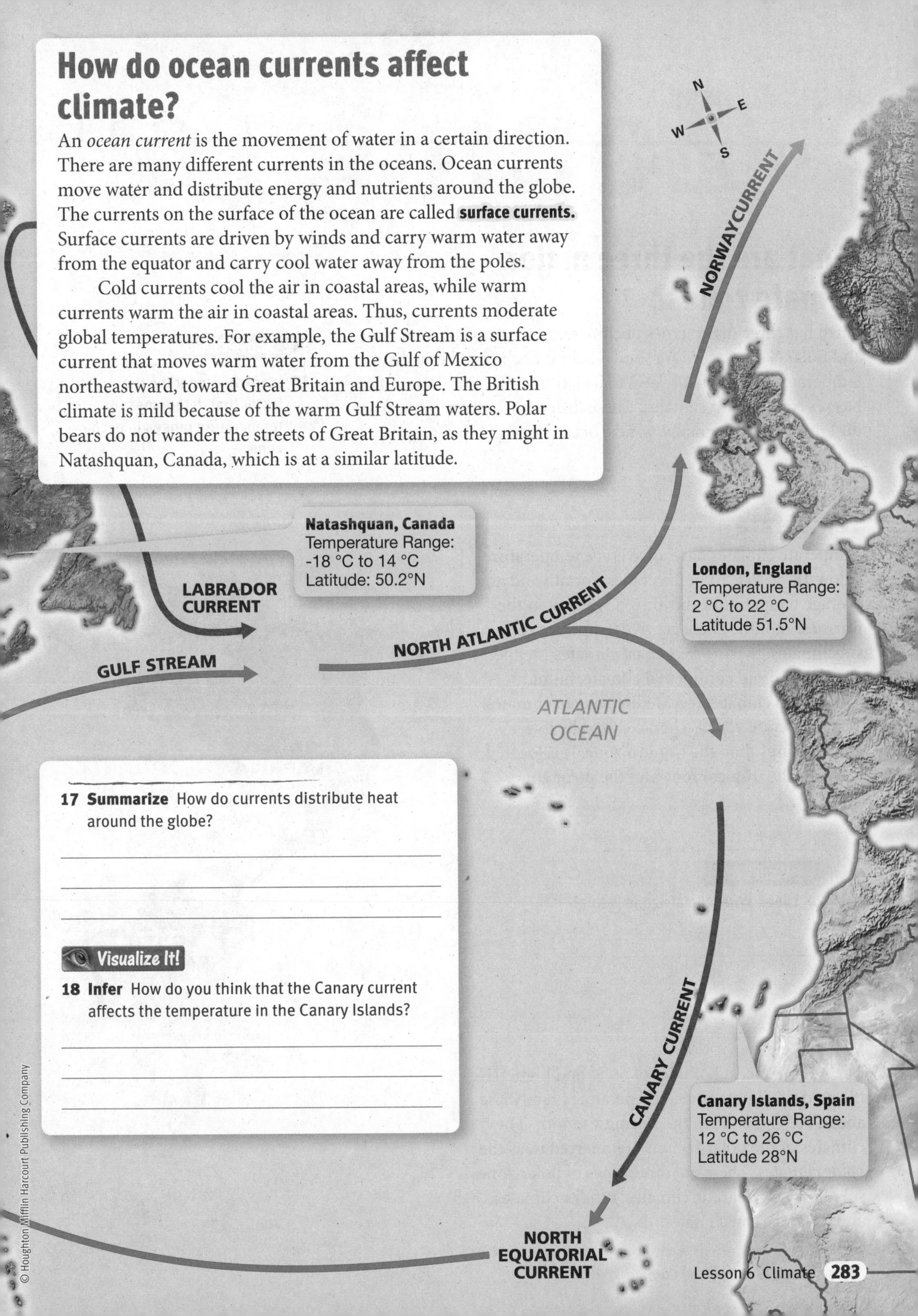

17 Summarize How do currents distribute heat around the globe?

Visualize It!

18 Infer How do you think that the Canary current affects the temperature in the Canary Islands?

Zoning Out

What are the three major climate zones?

Earth has three major types of climate zones: tropical, temperate, and polar. These zones are shown below. Each zone has a distinct temperature range that relates to its latitude. Each of these zones has several types of climates. These different climates result from differences in topography, winds, ocean currents, and geography.

Active Reading

19 Identify Underline the factor that determines the temperature ranges in each zone.

Temperate

Temperate climates have an average temperature below 18 °C (64 °F) in the coldest month and an average temperature above 10 °C (50 °F) in the warmest month. There are five temperate zone subclimates: marine west coast climates, steppe climates, humid continental climate, humid subtropical climate, and Mediterranean climate. The temperate zone is characterized by lower temperatures than the tropical zone. It is located between the tropical zone and the polar zone.

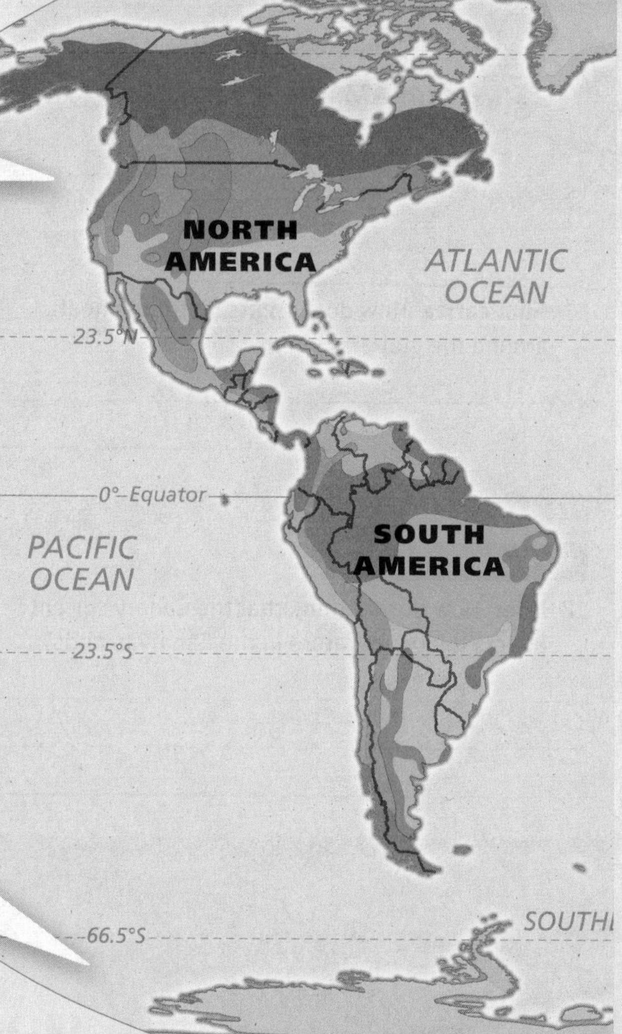

Visualize It!

20 Label What climate zone is this?

___

Polar

The polar zone, at latitudes of 66.5° and higher, is the coldest climate zone. Temperatures rarely rise above 10 °C (50 °F) in the warmest month. The climates of the polar regions are referred to as the *polar climates*. There are three types of polar zone subclimates: subarctic climates, tundra climates, and polar ice cap climates.

21 Summarize Fill in the table for either the factor that affects climate or the effect on climate the given factor has.

Factor	Effect on climate
Latitude	
	Cooler temperatures as you travel up a tall mountain
Winds	
	Moderates weather so that highs and lows are less extreme
Surface ocean currents	
	Impacts wind patterns and the transfer of energy in an area

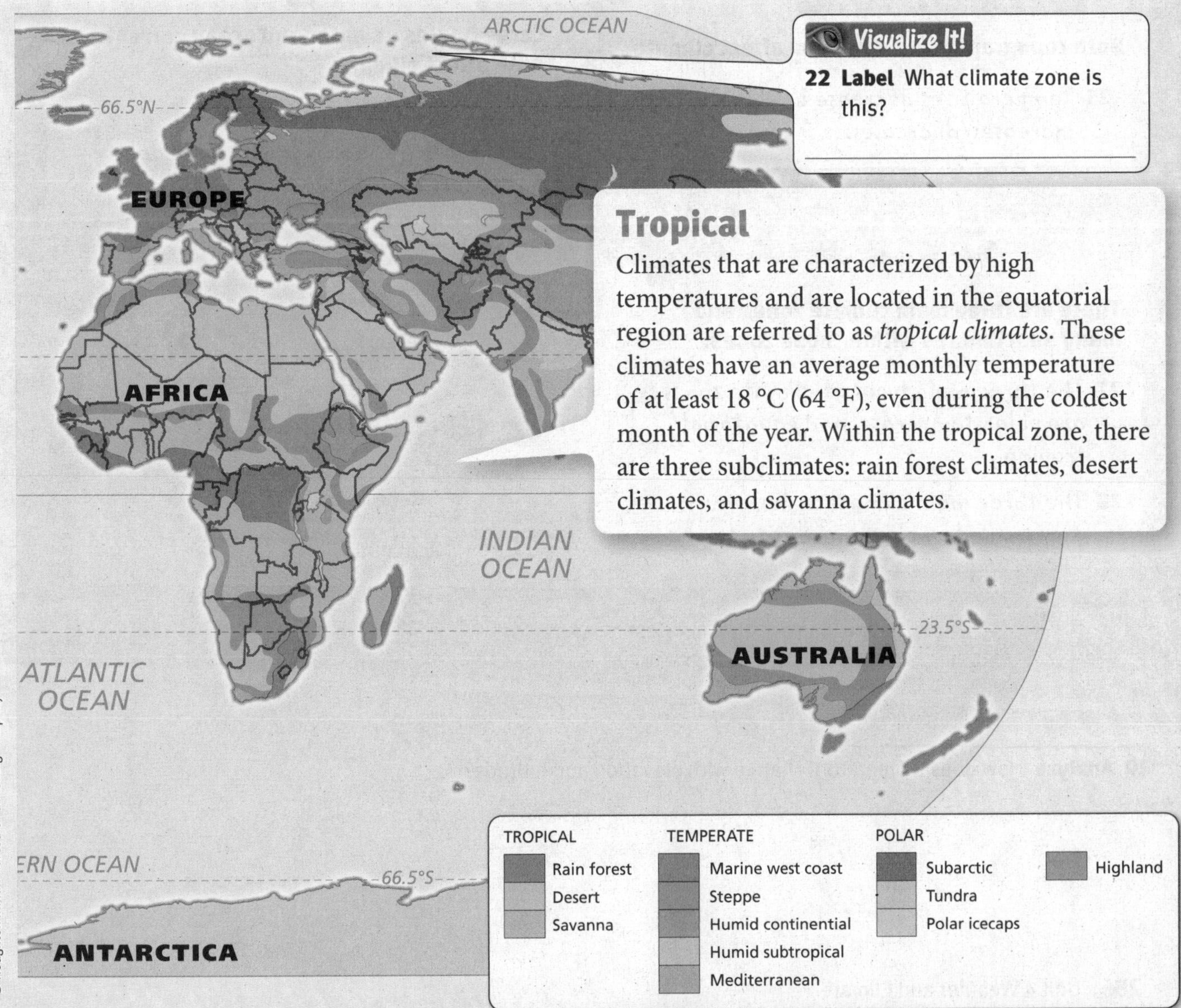

Visualize It!

22 Label What climate zone is this?

____

Tropical

Climates that are characterized by high temperatures and are located in the equatorial region are referred to as *tropical climates*. These climates have an average monthly temperature of at least 18 °C (64 °F), even during the coldest month of the year. Within the tropical zone, there are three subclimates: rain forest climates, desert climates, and savanna climates.

Visual Summary

To complete this summary, circle the correct word or phrase. Then, use the key below to check your answers. You can use this page to review the main concepts of the lesson.

Climate

Temperature and precipitation are used to describe climate.

23 Climate is the characteristic weather conditions in a place over a short/long period.

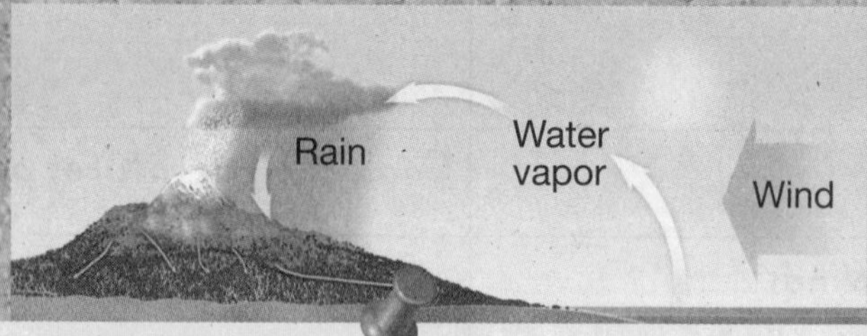

Winds transfer energy and moisture to new places.

24 Winds can affect the amount of precipitation in/elevation of an area.

Both topography and elevation affect climate.

25 Temperatures decrease as elevation increases/decreases.

Large bodies of water and ocean currents both affect climate.

26 Large bodies of water affect the climate of nearby land when cool waters absorb energy as heat from the warm air/cold land.

There are three main climate zones and many subclimates within those zones.

27 The three main types of climate zones are polar, temperate, and equatorial/tropical.

28 The three main climate zones are determined by elevation/latitude.

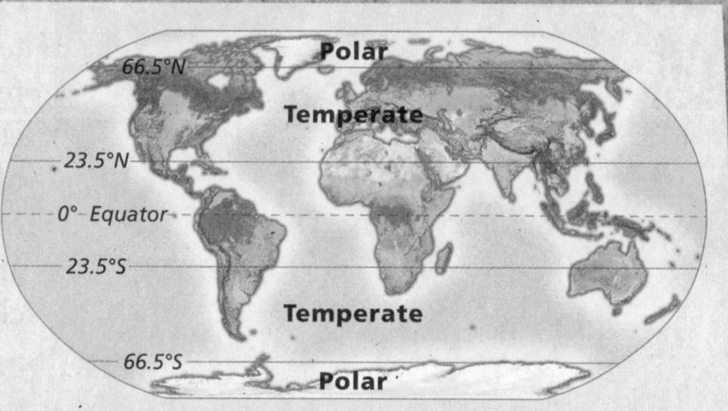

Answers: 23 long; 24 precipitation; 25 increases; 26 warm air; 27 tropical; 28 latitude

29 Analyze How does temperature change with elevation and latitude?

Lesson Review

Vocabulary

In your own words, define the following terms.

1 topography

____

____

2 climate

____

____

Key Concepts

Fill in the table below.

Factor	Effect on Climate
3 Identify Latitude	
4 Identify Elevation	
5 Identify Large bodies of water	
6 Identify Wind	

7 Explain What provides Great Britain with a moderate climate? How?

____

____

____

8 Identify What are two characteristics used to describe the climate of an area?

____

Critical Thinking

Use the image below to answer the following question.

9 Explain Location A receives nearly 200 cm of rain each year, while Location B receives only 30 cm. Explain why Location A gets so much more rain. Use the words *rain shadow* and *precipitation* in your answer.

____

____

____

____

____

____

____

10 Analyze What climate zone are you in if the temperatures are always very warm? Where is this zone located on Earth?

____

11 Analyze How does the sun's energy affect the climate of an area?

____

____

____

____

____

____

My Notes

Unit 4 Summary

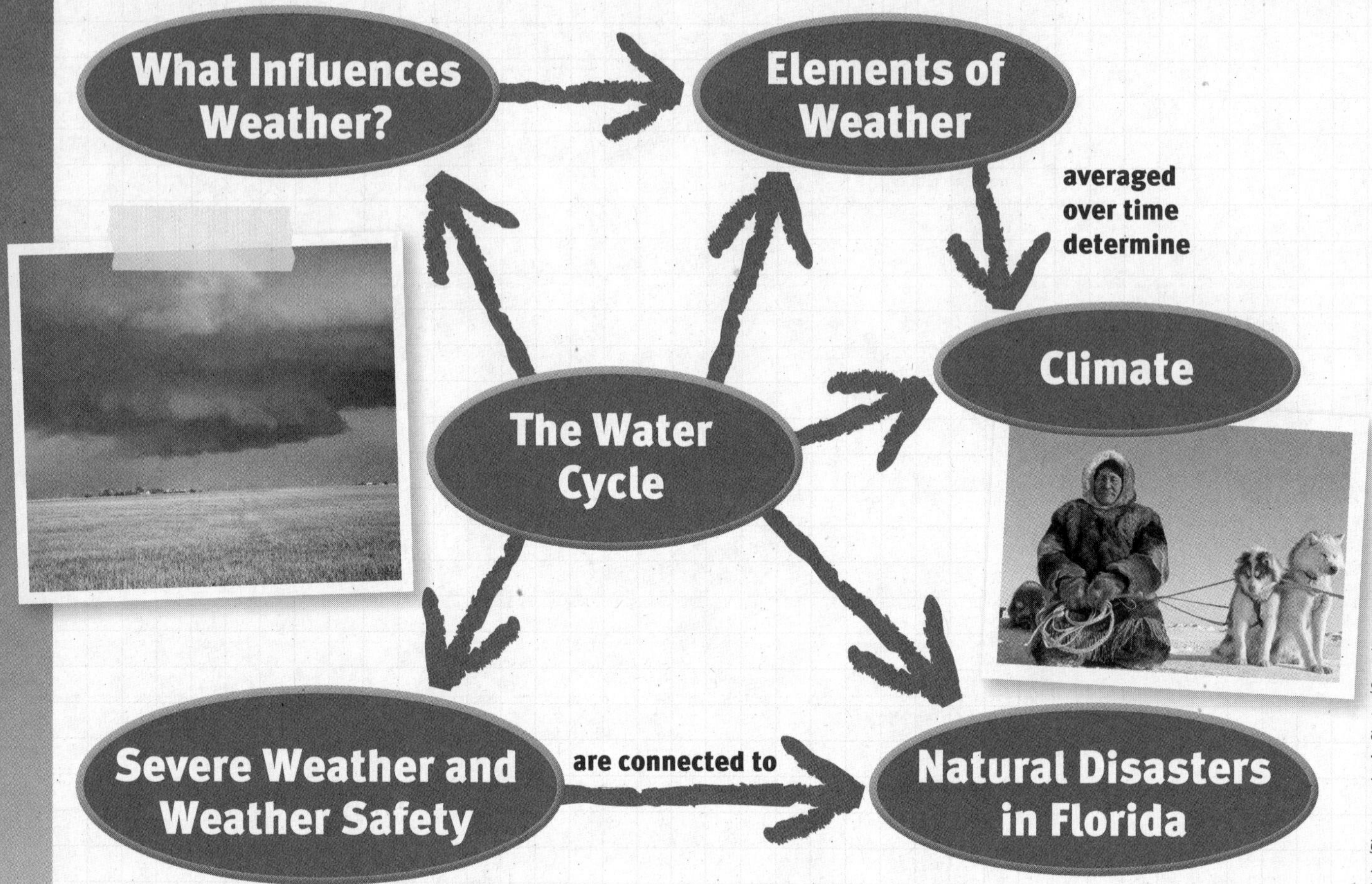

What Influences Weather?

Elements of Weather

averaged over time determine

Climate

The Water Cycle

Severe Weather and Weather Safety

are connected to

Natural Disasters in Florida

1 Interpret The Graphic Organizer above shows that the water cycle influences weather and climate. Explain why this is true.

2 Explain Why is knowing about hurricane safety particularly important to Florida residents?

3 Distinguish Describe the difference between weather and climate.

4 Justify *Weather safety* means that people should be prepared for certain types of good weather. Explain why this is true.

How are kinetic energy and potential energy different?

Kinetic energy and potential energy both have the ability to cause change. But they have some important differences. Kinetic energy is the energy of motion, but potential energy is stored energy that can be converted into motion. It is easy to know whether an object has kinetic energy because it is moving. It may not be easy to know how much potential energy an object has, because there are many kinds of potential energy. It is hard to see how much chemical energy an object has. However, you can usually know if an object has gravitational potential energy because it will be above the ground and can fall.

Many objects have both kinetic and potential energy. For example, an object can be both moving and above the ground. There are many examples of this: a helicopter flying through the air, a bumblebee whizzing past your head, or a baseball thrown to a catcher. The skydivers in the air have both kinetic and potential energy. They have kinetic energy because they are moving as they fall through the air. They also have gravitational potential energy because they are above the ground and can continue to fall.

9 Classify Determine whether the three scenarios in the chart below are examples of kinetic energy, gravitational potential energy, or both.

Scenario	Kind of energy
Speeding boat	
Flying bird	
Diver at the top of a diving board	

Think Outside the Book Inquiry

10 Classify Keep a journal of ten examples of kinetic and potential energy that you see in one day. Are they examples of kinetic energy, gravitational potential energy, or both?

Add It Up!

What is mechanical energy?

The skater in the picture has both kinetic energy and potential energy. There are many times when these two types of energy are found together. **Mechanical energy** (meh•KAN•ih•kuhl) is the kinetic energy plus the potential energy due to position.

Gravitational potential energy is one type of energy of position. An object compressing a spring also has potential energy of position. Both of these are mechanical potential energies. Add together an object's mechanical potential energies and its kinetic energy to get its mechanical energy. Often, you can add just the object's kinetic and gravitational potential energies.

At any point on the half-pipe shown in the photograph, the mechanical energy of the skater is equal to the sum of his kinetic energy and his gravitational potential energy. At any point where his kinetic energy is zero, then his mechanical energy is equal to potential energy. When he is both moving and above his lowest point, his mechanical energy is the sum of both kinds of energy.

(D) As the skater moves up the ramp, he gains height but loses speed. The kinetic energy he loses is equal to the potential energy that he gains.

(C) At the bottom of the ramp, the skater's kinetic energy is greatest because he is going the fastest. His potential energy is at its lowest because he is closer to the ground than at any other point on the ramp.

What is the law of conservation of energy?

The **law of conservation of energy** states that energy can be neither created nor destroyed. It can only be transformed. The mechanical energy of an object always remains the same unless some of it is transformed into other forms of energy, such as heat through friction. If no energy is transformed, the mechanical energy of an object stays the same.

As a skater rolls down the ramp, the amounts of kinetic and potential energy change. However, the law of conservation of energy requires that the total—or mechanical energy—stays the same, assuming no energy is converted into other forms. In order for the mechanical energy to stay the same, some potential energy changes into kinetic energy. At other times, some kinetic energy changes into potential energy. The picture below shows the skater's mechanical energy at four key places: the top of the ramp, between the top and the bottom of the ramp, the bottom of the ramp, and between the bottom and top of the ramp.

Active Reading

11 Identify As you read, underline examples in the text where kinetic energy changes into potential energy or where potential energy changes into kinetic energy.

At the top of the ramp, the skater has potential energy because gravity can pull him downward. He has no speed, so he has no kinetic energy.

(A)

As the skater moves closer to the ground, he loses potential energy, but gains the same amount of kinetic energy. As he rolls down the ramp, his potential energy decreases because his distance from the ground decreases. His kinetic energy increases because his speed increases.

(B)

12 Analyze Do you think that the skater has any gravitational potential energy at point C? Why?

Visual Summary

To complete this summary, fill in the blanks with the correct word or phrase. Then, use the answer key to check your answers. You can use this page to review the main concepts of the lesson.

Energy is the ability to cause change.

13 *Kinetic energy is the energy of* ____________________

14 *Potential energy is the energy of* ____________________

Kinetic and Potential Energy

Mechanical energy is conserved. Ball A has the most potential energy. As it rolls down the hill, its potential energy is converted to kinetic energy. Ball B has both kinetic and potential energy. At the bottom of the hill, most of the ball's energy is kinetic.

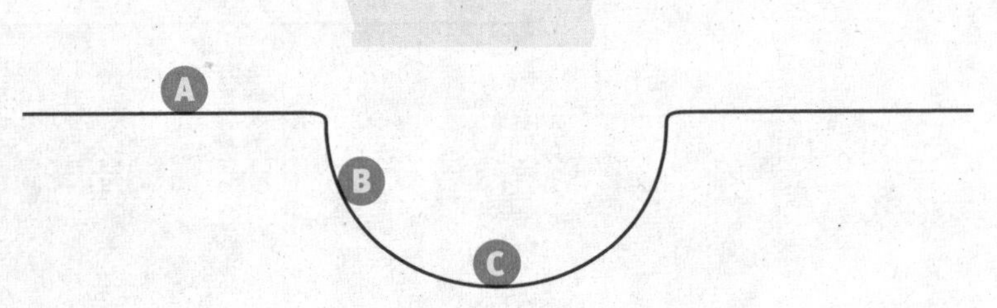

15 *Mechanical energy is the sum of* ____________________

Answers: 13 motion; 14 position or chemical composition; 15 kinetic energy and potential energy

16 Apply Explain how the law of conservation of energy might apply to energy use that you observe in your daily life.

Lesson Review

Vocabulary

Fill in the blank with the term that best completes the following sentences.

1 Energy is the ability to ____________________

____

2 ____________________ is an object's total kinetic and potential energy.

3 The law of conservation of energy states that

____

____

____

Key Concepts

4 Describe List two ways you use energy. How does each example involve a change?

____

____

____

____

____

5 Identify What are two factors that determine an object's kinetic energy?

____

____

6 Identify What are two factors that determine an object's gravitational potential energy?

____

____

7 Describe How does the law of conservation of energy affect the total amount of energy in any process?

____

____

____

____

____

Critical Thinking

Use the illustration below to answer the following questions.

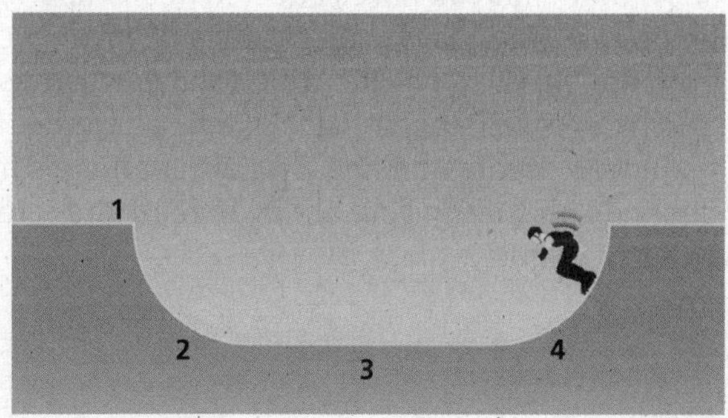

8 Apply At which position would the skater have the most kinetic energy?

____

9 Apply At which position would the skater have the most potential energy?

____

10 Synthesize At which position would the skater's kinetic energy begin to change into potential energy? Explain.

____

____

____

____

11 Incorporate How have your ideas about energy and its forms changed after reading this lesson? Provide an example to describe how you would have thought about energy compared to how you think about it now.

____

____

____

____

____

____

____

Think Science

Interpreting Graphs

Sunshine State Standards

SC.6.N.1.1 Define a problem from the sixth grade curriculum, use appropriate reference materials to support scientific understanding, plan and carry out scientific investigation of various types, such as systematic observations or experiments, identify variables, collect and organize data, interpret data in charts, tables, and graphics, analyze information, make predictions, and defend conclusions.

A visual display, such as a graph or table, is a useful way to show data that you have collected in an experiment. The ability to interpret graphs is a necessary skill in science, and it is also important in everyday life. You will come across various types of graphs in newspaper articles, medical reports, and, of course, textbooks. Understanding a report or article's message often depends heavily on your ability to read and interpret different types of graphs.

Tutorial

Ask yourself the following questions when studying a graph.

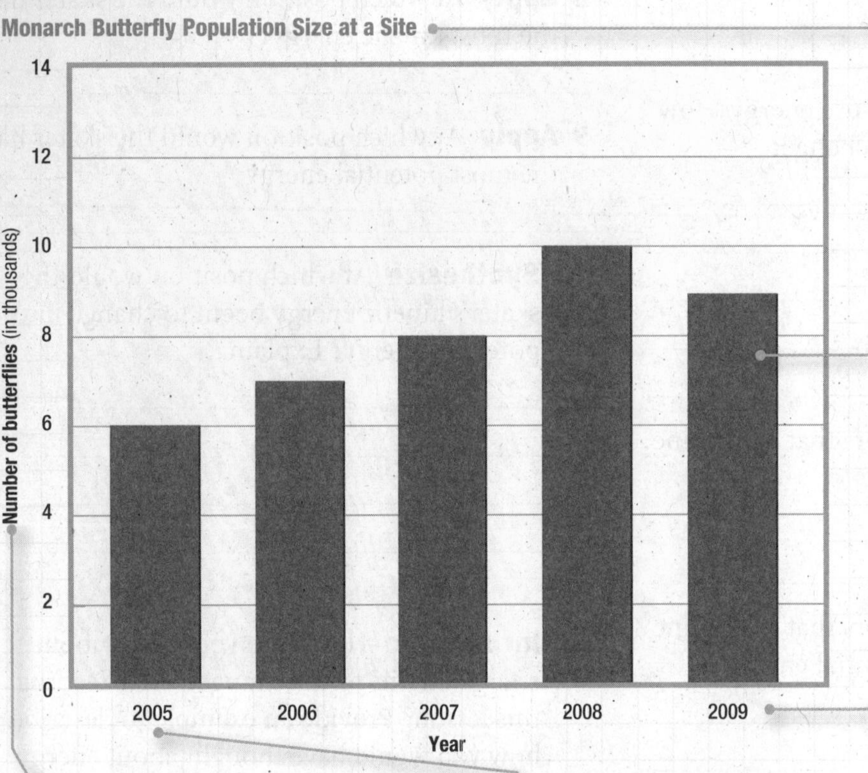

What is the title of the graph? Reading the title can tell you the subject or main idea of the graph. The subject here is monarch butterfly population.

What type of graph is it? Bar graphs, like the one here, are useful for comparing categories or total values. The lengths of the bars are proportional to the value they represent.

Do you notice any trends in the graph? After you understand what the graph is about, look for patterns. For example, here the monarch butterfly population increased each year from 2005 to 2008. But in 2009, the monarch butterfly population decreased.

What are the labels and headings in the graph? What is on each axis of the graph? Here, the vertical axis shows the population in thousands. Each bar represents a different year from 2005 to 2009. So from 2005 to 2009, the monarch butterfly population ranged from 6,000 to 10,000.

Can you describe the data in the graph? Data can be numbers or text. Analyze the information you read at specific data points. For example, the graph here tells us that there were 6,000 monarch butterflies in 2005.

You Try It!

A member of your research group has made the graph shown below about an object in motion. Study the graph, then answer the questions that follow.

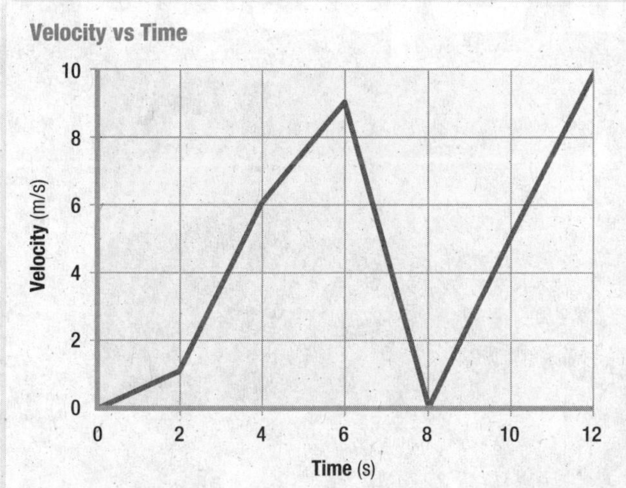

1 Interpreting Graphs Study the graph shown above. Identify the title of this graph, the *x*-axis, the *y*-axis, and the type of graph.

A title of graph ______

B *x*-axis ______

C *y*-axis ______

D type of graph ______

2 Identify Study the graph shown above and record the velocity at the indicated times.

Time (s)	Velocity (m/s)
2	
4	
6	
8	
10	

3 Using Graphs Use the graph to answer the following questions.

A What is the approximate velocity of the object at 5 seconds?

______

B During what time interval is the object slowing down? Explain how you can tell.

______

C At what time or times was the velocity of the object about 40 m/s?

______

4 Communicating Results In a short paragraph, describe the motion of the object.

______

Take It Home

Find a newspaper or magazine article that has a graph. What type of graph is it? Study the graph and determine its main message. Bring the graph to class and be prepared to discuss your interpretation of the graph.

Lesson 2

Motion and Speed

ESSENTIAL QUESTION

How are distance, time, and speed related?

By the end of this lesson, you should be able to analyze how distance, time, and speed are related.

The personal watercraft in this photo is going fast. How can we measure how fast it is going?

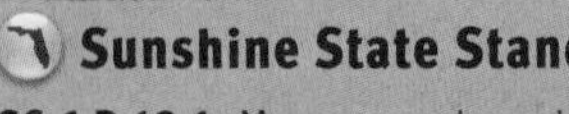

Sunshine State Standards

SC.6.P.12.1 Measure and graph distance versus time for an object moving at a constant speed. Interpret this relationship.

MA.6.A.3.6 Construct and analyze tables, graphs, and equations to describe linear functions and other simple relations using both common language and algebraic notation.

Engage Your Brain

1 Predict Circle the correct words in the paragraph below to make true statements.

A dog usually moves faster than a bug. That means that if I watch them move for one minute, then the dog would have traveled a *greater/ smaller* distance than the bug. However, a car usually goes *faster/slower* than a dog. If the car and the dog both traveled to the end of the road, then the *car/dog* would get there first.

2 Explain Draw or sketch something that you might see move. Write a caption that answers the following questions: How would you describe its motion? Is it moving at a constant speed, or does it speed up and slow down?

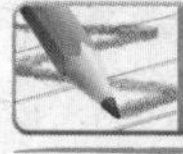

Active Reading

3 Define Fill in the blank with the word that best completes the following sentences.

If an object changes its position, then it is

____

The speed of a car describes

____

____

Vocabulary Terms

- position
- reference point
- motion
- speed
- vector
- velocity

4 Apply As you learn the definition of each vocabulary term in this lesson, make your own definition or sketch to help you remember the meaning of the term.

Location, location,

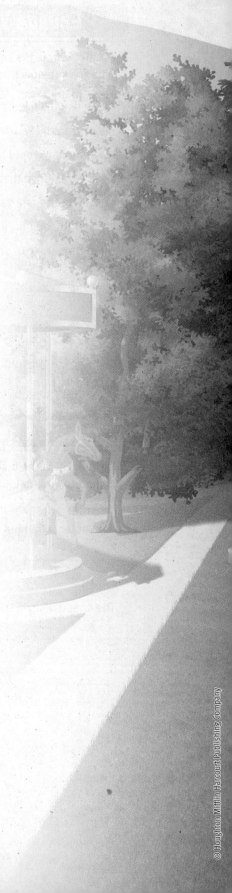

How can you describe the location of an object?

Have you ever gotten lost while looking for a specific place? If so, you probably know that the description of the location can be very important. Imagine that you are trying to describe your location to a friend. How would you explain where you are? You need two pieces of information: a position and a reference point.

With a Position

Position describes the location of an object. Often, you describe where something is by comparing its position with where you currently are. For example, you might say that a classmate sitting next to you is two desks to your right, or that a mailbox is two blocks south of where you live. Each time you identify the position of an object, you are comparing the location of the object with the location of another object or place.

With a Reference Point

When you describe a position by comparing it to the location of another object or place, you are using a reference point. A **reference point** is a location to which you compare other locations. In the example above of a mailbox that is two blocks south of where you live, the reference point is "where you live."

Imagine that you are at a zoo with some friends. If you are using the map to the right, you could describe your destination using different reference points. Using yourself as the reference point, you might say that the red panda house is one block east and three blocks north of your current location. Or you might say the red panda house is one block north and one block east of the fountain. In this example, the fountain is your reference point.

Active Reading **5 Apply** How would you describe where this question is located on the page? Give two different answers using two different reference points.

___

___

___

___

location

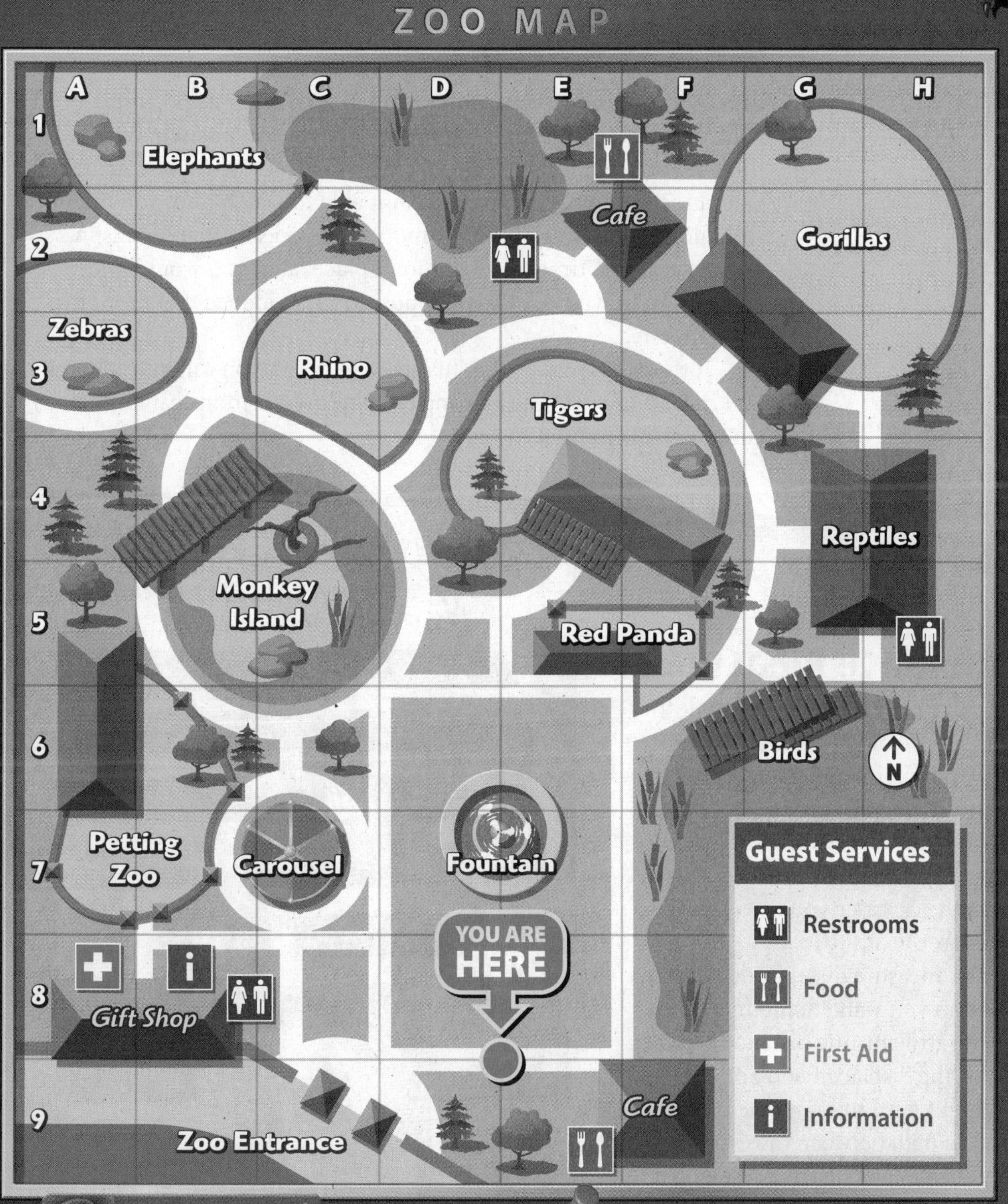

ZOO MAP

A B C D E F G H

1 2 3 4 5 6 7 8 9

Elephants

Cafe

Gorillas

Zebras

Rhino

Tigers

Reptiles

Monkey Island

Red Panda

Birds

N

Petting Zoo

Carousel

Fountain

YOU ARE HERE

Gift Shop

Cafe

Zoo Entrance

Guest Services

- Restrooms
- Food
- First Aid
- Information

Visualize It!

6 Apply One of your friends is at the southeast corner of Monkey Island. He would like to meet you. How would you describe your location to him?

7 Apply You need to go visit the first aid station. How would you describe how to get there?

MOVE It!

What is motion?

An object moves, or is in motion, when it changes its position relative to a reference point. **Motion** is a change in position over time. If you were to watch the biker pictured to the right, you would see him move. If you were not able to watch him, you might still know something about his motion. If you saw that he was in one place at one time and a different place later, you would know that he had moved. A change in position is evidence that motion has happened.

If the biker returned to his starting point, you might not know that he had moved. The starting and ending positions cannot tell you everything about motion.

How is distance measured?

Suppose you walk from one building to another building that is several blocks away. If you could walk in a straight line, you might end up 500 meters from where you started. The actual distance you travel, however, would depend on the exact path you take. If you take a route that has many turns, the distance you travel might be 900 meters or more.

The way you measure distance depends on the information you want. Sometimes you want to know the straight-line distance between two positions, or the displacement. Sometimes, however, you might need to know the total length of a certain path between those positions.

When measuring any distances, scientists use a standard unit of measurement. The standard unit of length is the meter (m), which is about 3.3 feet. Longer distances can be measured in kilometers (km), and shorter distances in centimeters (cm). In the United States, distance is often measured in miles (mi), feet (ft), or inches (in).

The distance from point A to point B depends on the path you take.

Visualize It!

8 Illustrate Draw a sample path on the maze that is a different distance than the one in red but still goes from the start point, "A," to the finish point, "B."

This biker is in motion.

What is speed?

A change in an object's position tells you that motion took place, but it does not tell you how quickly the object changed position. The **speed** of an object is a measure of how far something moves in a given amount of time. In other words, speed measures how quickly or slowly the object changes position. In the same amount of time, a faster object would move farther than a slower moving object would.

What is average speed?

The speed of an object is rarely constant. For example, the biker in the photo above may travel quickly when he begins a race but may slow down as he gets tired at the end of the race. *Average speed* is a way to calculate the speed of an object that may not always be moving at a constant speed. Instead of describing the speed of an object at an exact moment in time, average speed describes the speed over a stretch of time.

Active Reading **9 Compare** What is the difference between speed and average speed?

____

____

____

Think Outside the Book Inquiry

10 Analyze Research the top speeds of a cheetah, a race car, and a speed boat. How do they rank in order of speed? Make a poster showing which is fastest and which is slowest. How do the speeds of the fastest human runners compare to the speeds you found?

Speed It Up!

How is average speed calculated?

11 Identify As you read, underline sentences that relate distance and time.

Speed can be calculated by dividing the distance an object travels by the time it takes to cover the distance. Speed is shown in the formula as the letter *s*, distance as the letter *d*, and time as the letter *t*. The formula shows how distance, time, and speed are related. If two objects travel the same distance, the object that took a shorter amount of time will have the greater speed. An object with a greater speed will travel a longer distance in the same amount of time than an object with a lower speed will.

The following equation can be used to find average speed:

$$\text{average speed} = \frac{\text{distance}}{\text{time}}$$

$$s = \frac{d}{t}$$

The standard unit for speed is meters per second (m/s). Speed can also be given in kilometers per hour (km/h). In the United States, speeds are often given in miles per hour (mi/h or mph). One mile per hour is equal to 0.45 m/s.

Do the Math **Sample Problem**

A penguin swimming underwater goes 20 meters in 8 seconds. What is its average speed?

Identify

A. What do you know? $d = 20$ m, $t = 8$ s

B. What do you want to find out? average speed

Plan

C. Draw and label a sketch: 20 m / 8 sec

D. Write the formula: $s = d/t$

E. Substitute into the formula: $s = \frac{20 \text{ m}}{8 \text{ s}}$

Solve

F. Calculate and simplify: $s = \frac{20 \text{ m}}{8 \text{ s}} = 2.5 \text{ m/s}$

G. Check that your units agree: Unit is m/s. Unit of speed is distance/time. Units agree.

Answer: 2.5 m/s

Do the Math You Try It

12. Calculate This runner completed a 100-meter race with a time of 13.75 seconds. What was her average speed?

Identify

A. What do you know?

B. What do you want to find out?

Plan

C. Draw and label a sketch:

D. Write the formula:

E. Substitute into the formula:

Solve

F. Calculate and simplify:

G. Check that your units agree:

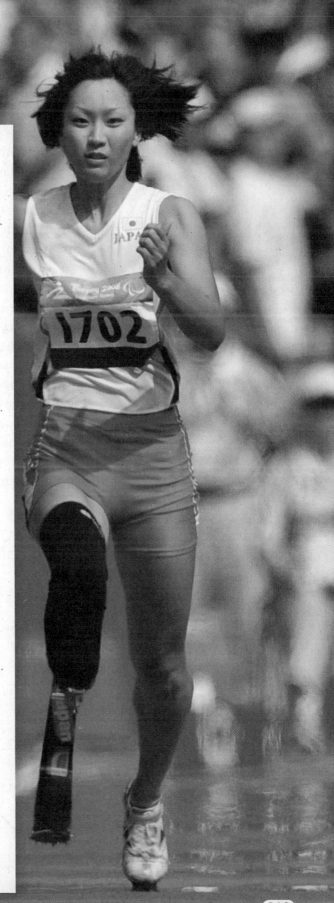

Answer:

Fast Graphs

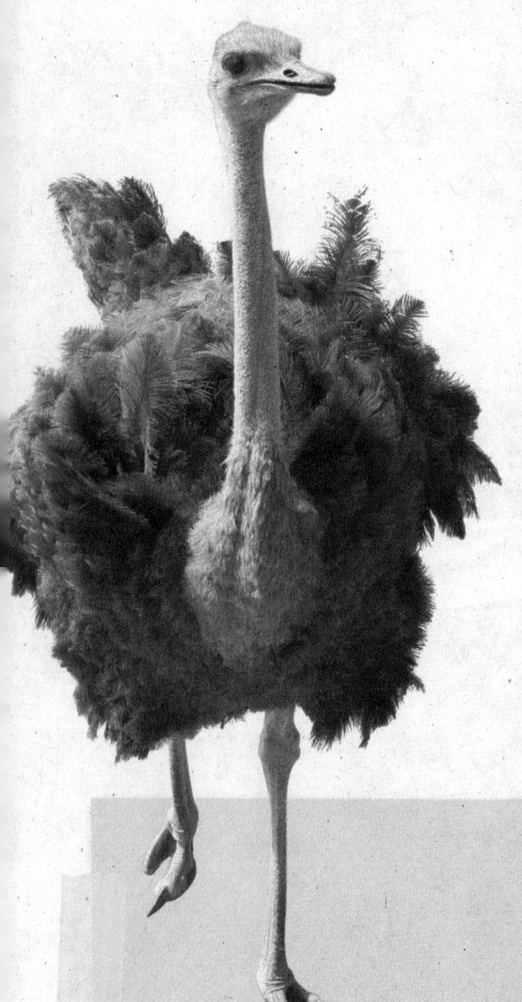

How is constant speed graphed?

A convenient way to show the motion of an object is by using a graph that plots the distance the object has traveled against time. This type of graph is called a distance-time graph. You can use it to see how both distance and speed change with time.

How far away the object is from a reference point is plotted on the *y*-axis. So the *y*-axis expresses distance in units such as meters, centimeters, or kilometers. Time is plotted on the *x*-axis, and can display units such as seconds, minutes, or hours. If an object moves at a constant speed, the graph is a straight line.

You can use a distance-time graph to determine the average speed of an object. The slope, or steepness, of the line is equal to the average speed of the object. You calculate the average speed for a time interval by dividing the change in distance by the change in time for that time interval.

Suppose that an ostrich is running at a constant speed. The distance-time graph of its motion is shown below. To calculate the speed of the ostrich, choose two data points from the graph below and calculate the slope of the line. The calculation of the slope is shown below. Since we know that the slope of a line on a distance-time graph is its average speed, then we know that the ostrich's speed is 14 m/s.

How can you calculate slope?

$$\text{slope} = \frac{\text{change in } y}{\text{change in } x}$$

$$= \frac{140\text{ m} - 70\text{ m}}{10\text{ s} - 5\text{ s}}$$

$$= \frac{70\text{ m}}{5\text{ s}}$$

$$= 14\text{ m/s}$$

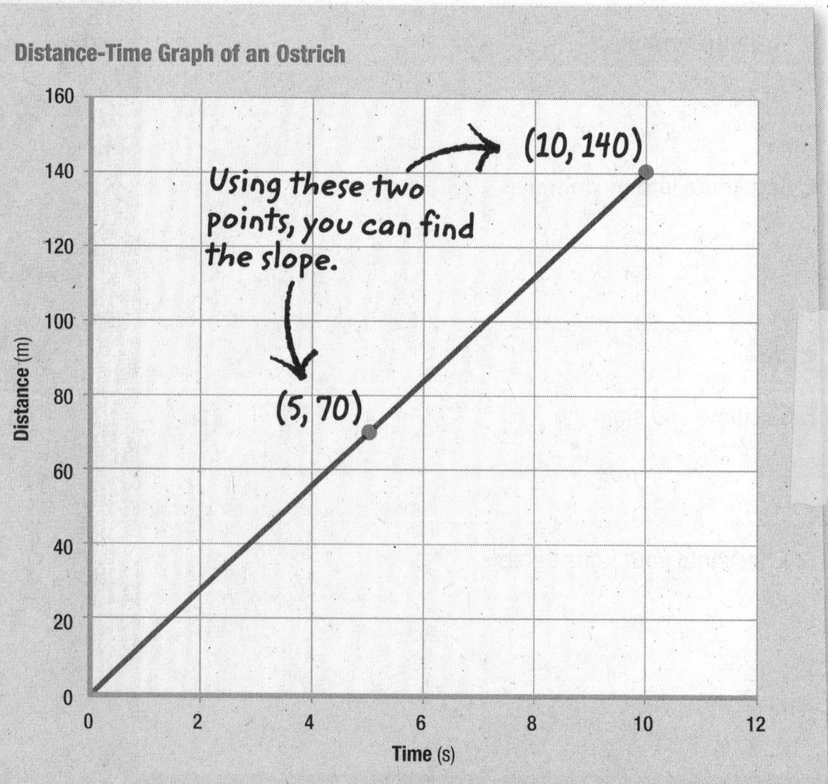

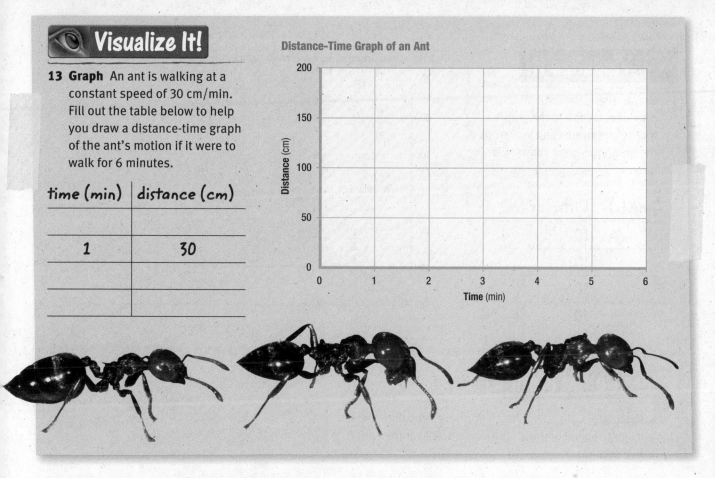

Visualize It!

13 Graph An ant is walking at a constant speed of 30 cm/min. Fill out the table below to help you draw a distance-time graph of the ant's motion if it were to walk for 6 minutes.

time (min)	distance (cm)
1	30

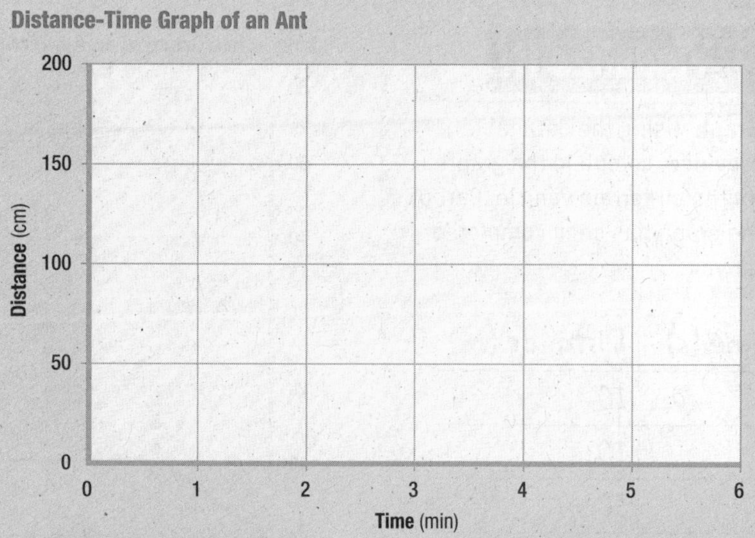

Distance-Time Graph of an Ant

How are changing speeds graphed?

Some distance-time graphs show the motion of an object with a changing speed. In these distance-time graphs, the change in the slope of a line indicates that the object has either sped up, slowed down, or stopped.

As an object moves, the distance it travels increases with time. The motion can be seen as a climbing line on the graph. The slope of the line indicates speed. Steeper lines show intervals where the speed is greater than intervals with less steep lines. If the line gets steeper, the object is speeding up. If the line gets less steep, the object is slowing. If the line becomes flat, or horizontal, the object is not moving. In this interval, the speed is zero meters per second.

For objects that change speed, you can calculate speed for a specific interval of time. You would choose two points close together on the graph. Or, you can calculate the average speed over a long interval of time. You would choose two points far apart on the graph to calculate an average over a long interval of time.

Active Reading **14 Analyze** If a line on a distance-time graph becomes steeper, what has happened to the speed of the object? What if it becomes a flat horizontal line?

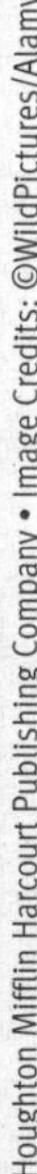

Visualize It!

15. Graph Using the data table provided, complete the graph for the all-terrain vehicle. Part of the graph has been completed for you.

Time (s)	Distance (m)
1	10
3	10
4	30
5	50

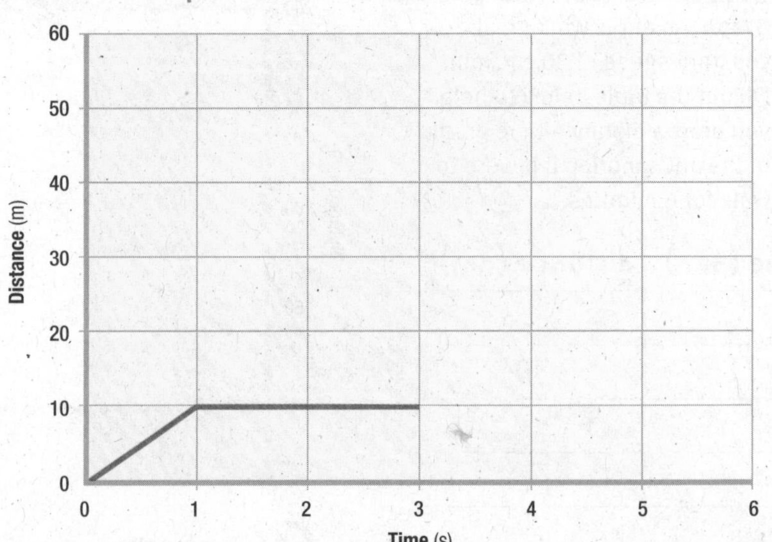

Do the Math You Try It

16. Calculate Using the data given above, calculate the average speed of the all-terrain vehicle over the entire five seconds.

Identify

A. What do you know?

B. What do you want to find out?

Plan

C. Draw and label a sketch:

D. Write the formula:

E. Substitute into the formula:

Solve

F. Calculate and simplify:

G. Check that your units agree:

Answer:

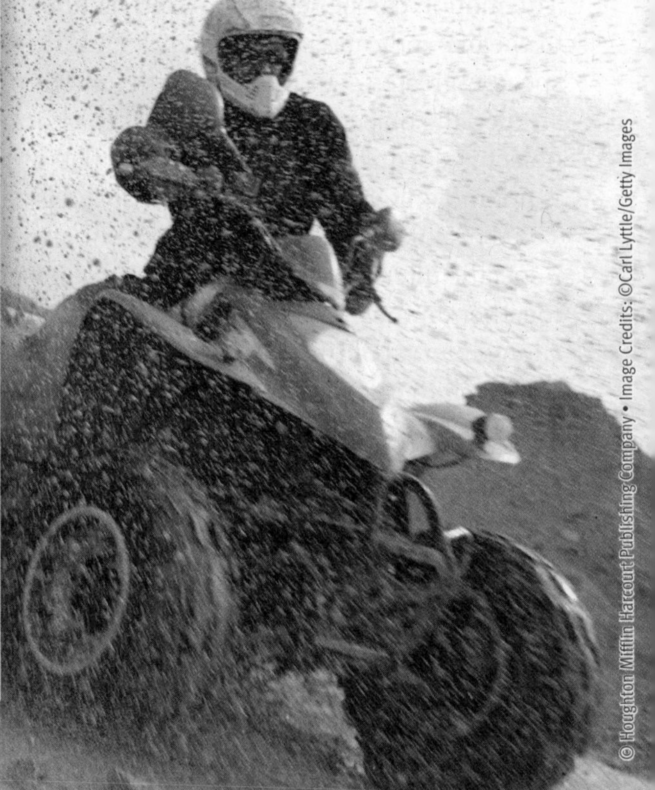

What would the distance-time graph of this ATV's motion look like?

Follow Directions

What is velocity?

Suppose that two birds start from the same place and fly at 10 km/h for 5 minutes. Why might they not end up at the same place? Because the birds were flying in different directions! There are times when the direction of motion must be included in a measurement. A **vector** is a quantity that has both size and direction.

In the example above, the birds' speeds were the same, but their velocities were different. **Velocity** [vuh•LAHS•ih•tee] is speed in a specific direction. If a police officer gives a speeding ticket for a car traveling 100 km/h, the ticket does not list a velocity. But it would list a velocity if it described the car traveling south at 100 km/h.

These chair lifts have opposite velocities because they are going at the same speed but in opposite directions.

Because velocity includes direction, it is possible for two objects to have the same speed but different velocities. In the picture to the right, the chair lifts are going the same speed but in opposite directions: some people are going up the mountain while others are going down the mountain.

Average velocity is calculated in a different way than average speed. Average speed depends on the total distance traveled along a path. Average velocity depends on the straight-line distance from the starting point to the final point, or the displacement. A chair lift might carry you up the mountain at an average speed of 5 km/h, giving you an average velocity of 5 km/h north. After a round-trip ride, your average traveling speed would still be 5 km/h. Your average velocity, however, would be 0 km/h because you ended up exactly where you started.

17. Compare Fill in the Venn diagram to compare and contrast speed and velocity.

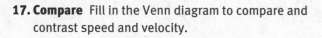

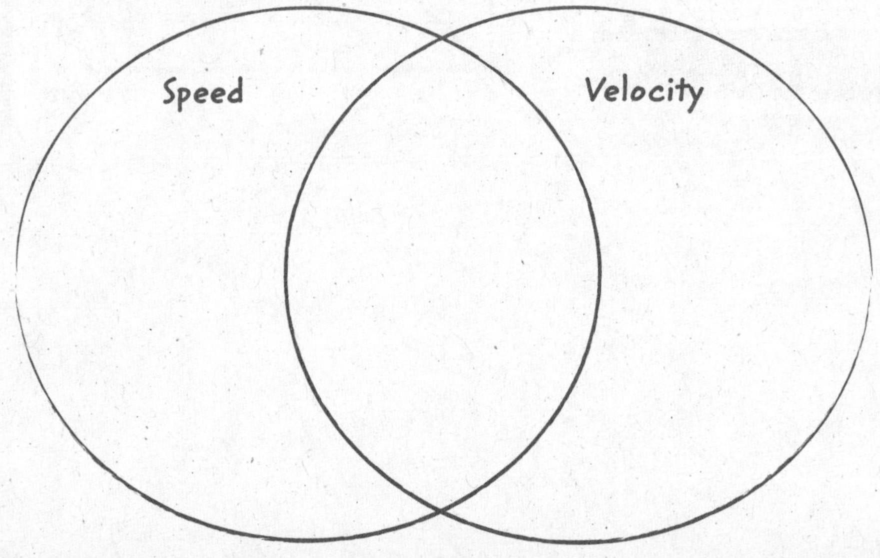

Visual Summary

To complete this summary, check the box that indicates true or false. Then use the key below to check your answers. You can use this page to review the main concepts of the lesson.

Motion is a change in position over time.

T F

18 ☐ ☐ A reference point is a location to which you compare other locations.

19 ☐ ☐ Distance traveled does not depend on the path you take.

Speed measures how far something moves in a given amount of time.

$$s = \frac{d}{t}$$

T F

20 ☐ ☐ To calculate speed, you first need to find the mass of an object.

21 ☐ ☐ Average speed is a way to describe the speed of an object that may not always be moving at a constant speed.

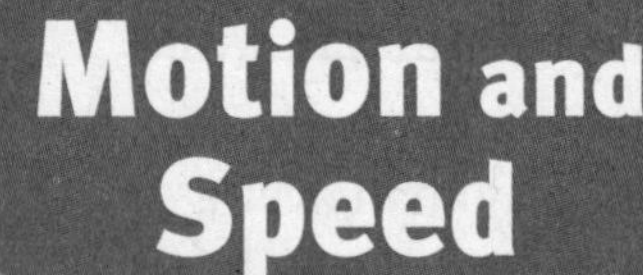

A distance-time graph plots the distance traveled by an object and the time it takes to travel that distance.

T F

22 ☐ ☐ In the graph at the right, the object is moving at a constant speed.

Answers: 18 T; 19 F; 20 F; 21 T; 22 T

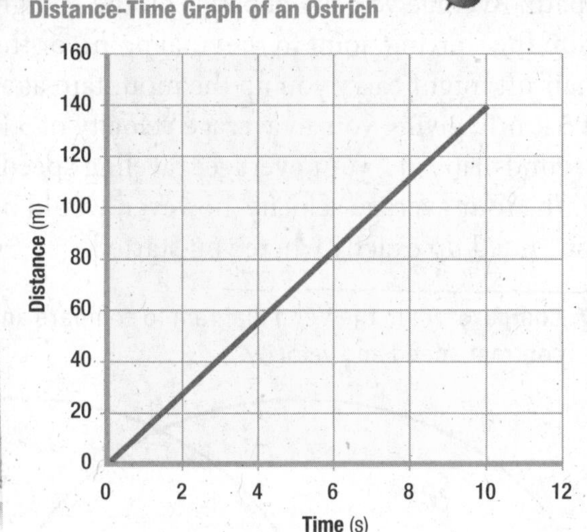

23 Predict Amy and Ellie left school at the same time. Amy lives farther away than Ellie, but she and Ellie arrived at their homes at the same time. Compare the girls' speeds.

Lesson Review

Vocabulary

Draw a line to connect the following terms to their definitions.

1 velocity	**A** describes the location of an object
2 reference point	**B** speed in a specific direction
3 speed	**C** a location to which you compare other locations
4 position	**D** a measure of how far something moves in a given amount of time

Key Concepts

5 Describe What information do you need to describe an object's location?

6 Predict How would decreasing the time it takes you to run a certain distance affect your speed?

7 Calculate Juan lives 100 m away from Bill. What is Juan's average speed if he reaches Bill's home in 50 s?

8 Describe What do you need to know to describe the velocity of an object?

Use this graph to answer the following questions.

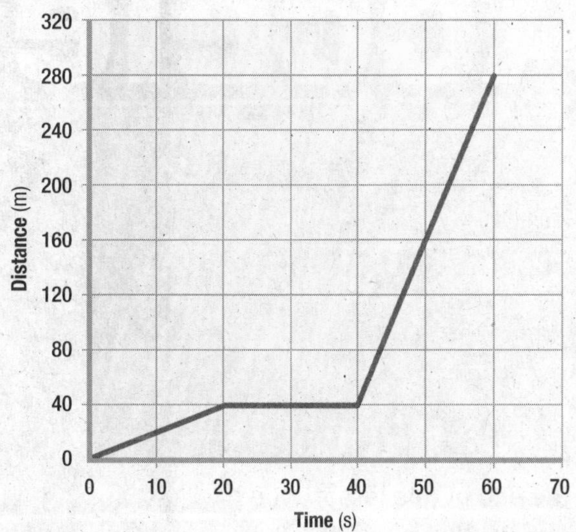

9 Analyze When is the zebra in motion? When is it not moving?

In motion: ______

Not moving: ______

10 Calculate What is the average speed of the zebra during the time between 0 s and 40 s?

Critical Thinking

11 Apply Look around you to find an object in motion. Describe the object's motion by discussing its position and direction of motion in relation to a reference point. Then explain how you could determine the object's speed.

Lesson 3

Acceleration

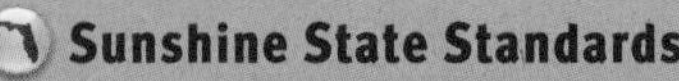

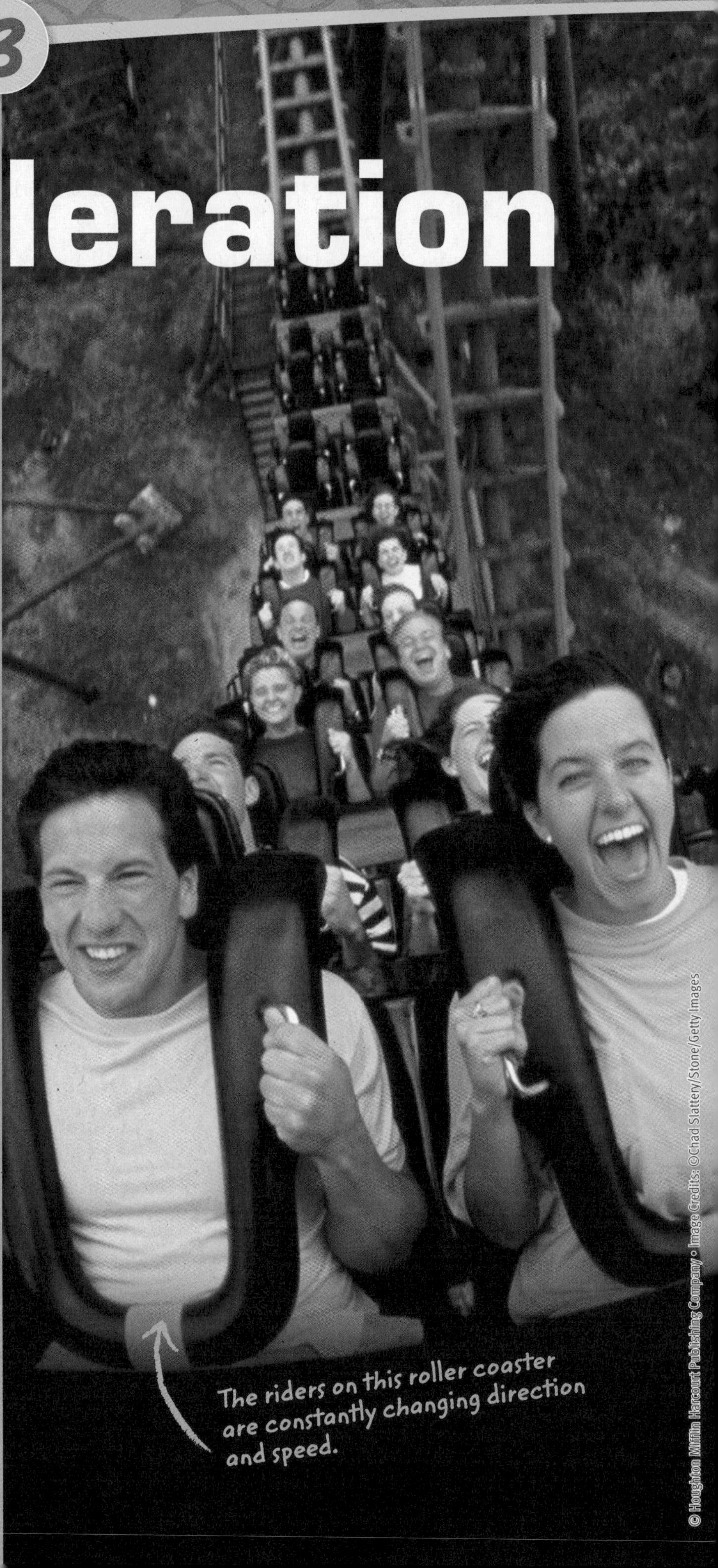

The riders on this roller coaster are constantly changing direction and speed.

ESSENTIAL QUESTION

How does motion change?

By the end of this lesson, you should be able to analyze how acceleration is related to time and velocity.

Sunshine State Standards

MA.6.A.3.6 Construct and analyze tables, graphs, and equations to describe linear functions and other simple relations using both common language and algebraic notation.

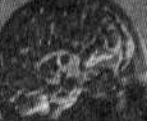

Engage Your Brain

1 Predict Check T or F to show whether you think each statement is true or false.

T	F	
☐	☐	A car taking a turn at a constant speed is accelerating.
☐	☐	If an object has low acceleration, it isn't moving very fast.
☐	☐	An accelerating car is always gaining speed.

2 Identify The names of the two things that can change when something accelerates are scrambled together below. Unscramble them!

PEDSE

___

CDEIINORT

___

Active Reading

3 Synthesize You can often define an unknown word if you know the meaning of its word parts. Use the word parts and sentence below to make an educated guess about the meaning of the word *centripetal*.

Word part	Meaning
centri-	center
pet-	tend toward

Example Sentence:
Josephina felt the centripetal force as she spun around on the carnival ride.

centripetal:

___

___

___

Vocabulary Terms

- **acceleration**
- **centripetal acceleration**

4 Distinguish As you read, draw pictures or make a chart to help remember the relationship between distance, velocity, and acceleration.

Getting up to

How do we measure changing velocity?

Imagine riding a bike as in the images below. You start off not moving at all, then move slowly, and then faster and faster each second. Your velocity is changing. You are accelerating.

Active Reading **5 Identify** Underline the two components of a vector.

Acceleration Measures a Change in Velocity

Just as velocity measures a rate of change in position, acceleration measures a rate of change in velocity. **Acceleration** (ack•SELL•uh•ray•shuhn) is the rate at which velocity changes. Velocity is a vector, having both a magnitude and direction, and if either of these change, then the velocity changes. So, an object accelerates if its speed, its direction of motion, or both change.

Keep in mind that acceleration depends not only on how much velocity changes, but also on how much time that change takes. A small change in velocity can still be a large acceleration if the change happens quickly, and a large change in velocity can be a small acceleration if it happens slowly. Increasing your speed by 5 m/s in 5 s is a smaller acceleration than to do the same in 1 s.

Each second, the cyclist's southward velocity increases by 1 m/s south.

Speed

How is average acceleration calculated?

Acceleration is a change in velocity as compared with the time it takes to make the change. You can find the average acceleration experienced by an accelerating object using the following equation.

$$\text{average acceleration} = \frac{(\text{final velocity} - \text{starting velocity})}{\text{time}}$$

Velocity is expressed in meters per second (m/s) and time is measured in seconds (s). So acceleration is measured in meters per second per second, or meters per second squared (m/s^2).

As an example, consider an object that starts off moving at 8 m/s west, and then 16 s later is moving at 48 m/s west. The average acceleration of this object is found by in the following equation.

$$a = \frac{(48\ m/s - 8\ m/s)}{16\ s}$$

$$a = 2.5\ m/s^2 \text{ west}$$

6 Identify Underline the units of acceleration.

This formula is often abbreviated as

$$a = \frac{(v_2 - v_1)}{t}$$

Visualize It!

7 Analyze What is the change in velocity of the biker below as he travels from point *B* to point *C*? What is his acceleration from point *B* to point *C*?

8 Calculate Find the average acceleration of the cyclist moving from point *A* to point *B*, and over the whole trip (from point *A* to point *D*).

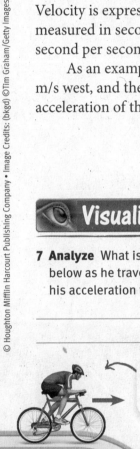

The cyclist is riding at 4 m/s. One second later, at the bottom of the hill, he is riding at 8 m/s. After going up a small incline, he has slowed to 7 m/s.

What a Drag!

How can accelerating objects change velocity?

Like velocity, acceleration is a vector, with a magnitude and a direction.

Accelerating Objects Change Speed

Although the word *acceleration* is commonly used to mean an increasing speed, in scientific use, the word applies to both increases and decreases in speed.

When you slide down a hill, you go from a small velocity to a large one. An increase in velocity like this is called *positive acceleration*. When a race car slows down, it goes from a high velocity to a low velocity. A decrease in velocity like this is called *negative acceleration*.

What is the acceleration when an object decreases speed? Because the initial velocity is larger than the final velocity, the term $(v_2 - v_1)$ will be negative. So the acceleration $a = \frac{(v_2 - v_1)}{t}$ will be a negative.

When acceleration and velocity (rate of motion) are in the same direction, the speed will increase. When acceleration and velocity are in opposing directions, the acceleration works against the initial motion in that direction, and the speed will decrease.

Active Reading

9 Identify Underline the term for an increase in velocity and the term for a decrease in velocity.

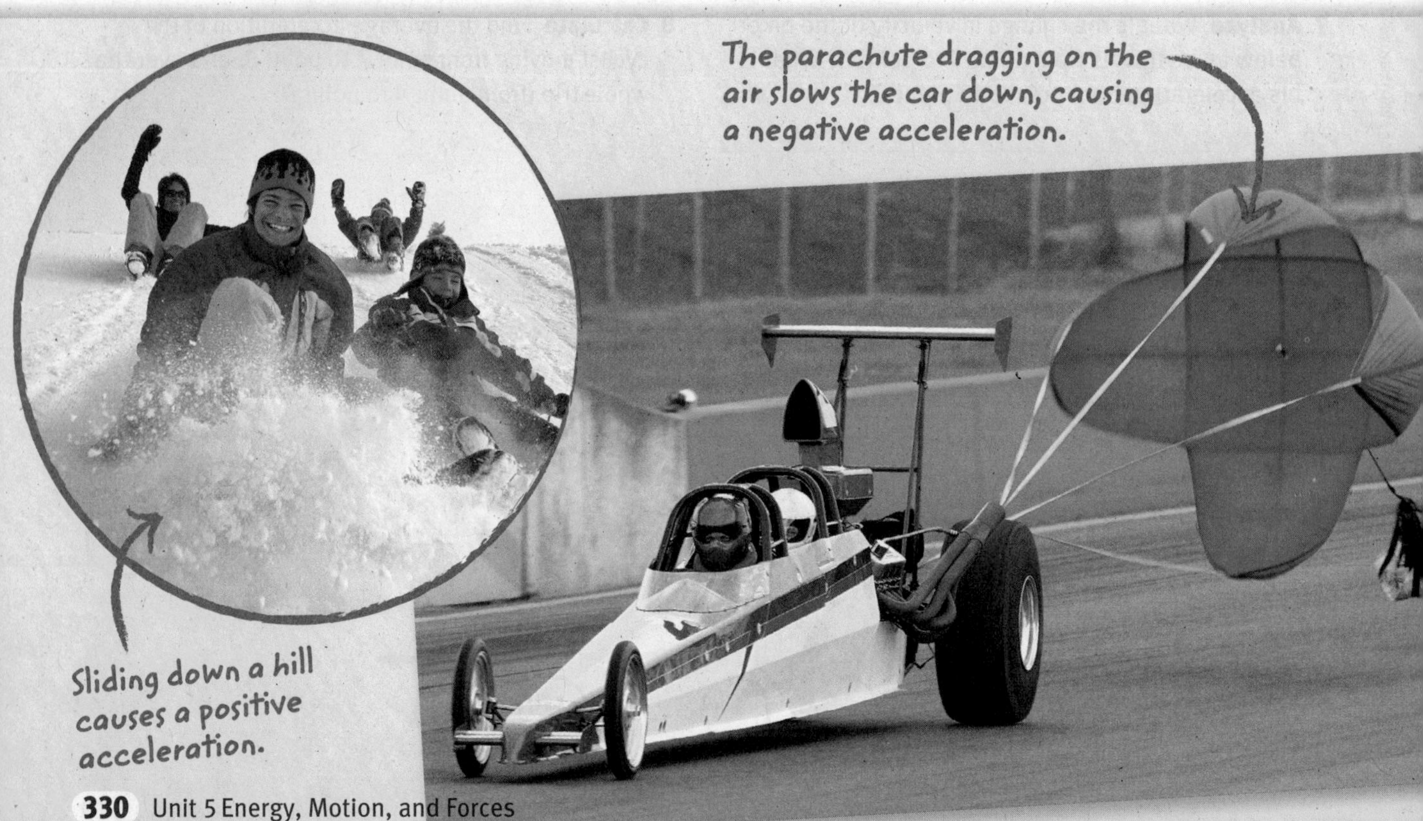

The parachute dragging on the air slows the car down, causing a negative acceleration.

Sliding down a hill causes a positive acceleration.

Accelerating Objects Change Direction

An object changing direction of motion experiences acceleration even when it does not speed up or slow down. Think about a car that makes a sharp left turn. The direction of velocity changes from “forward” to “left.” This change in velocity is an acceleration, even if the speed does not change. As the car finishes the turn, the acceleration drops to zero.

What happens, however, when an object is *always* turning? An object traveling in a circular motion is always changing its direction, so it always experiences acceleration. Acceleration in circular motion is known as **centripetal acceleration**. (sehn•TRIP•ih•tahl ack•SELL•uh•ray•shuhn)

A skater rounding a curve experiences centripetal acceleration.

Inquiry

10 Conclude An acceleration in the direction of motion increases speed, and an acceleration opposite to the direction of motion decreases speed. What direction is the acceleration in centripetal acceleration, where speed does not change but direction does?

____

____

____

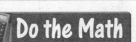

Do the Math

11 Calculate The horse is galloping at 13 m/s. Five seconds later, after climbing the hill, the horse is moving at 5.5 m/s. Find the acceleration that describes this change in velocity.

$$a = \frac{(v_2 - v_1)}{t}$$

Running uphill is tough to do without slowing down!

Visual Summary

To complete this summary, complete the statements below by filling in the blanks. You can use this page to review the main concepts of the lesson.

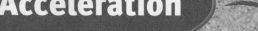

Acceleration

Acceleration measures a change in velocity.

12 The formula for calculating average acceleration is

____

Acceleration can be a change in speed or a change in direction of motion.

13 When acceleration and velocity are in the same direction, the speed will _______________

14 When acceleration and velocity are in opposing directions, the speed will _______________

15 Objects traveling in _______________ motion experience centripetal acceleration.

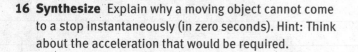

Answers: 12 $a = \frac{(v_2 - v_1)}{t}$; 13 increase; 14 decrease; 15 circular

16 Synthesize Explain why a moving object cannot come to a stop instantaneously (in zero seconds). Hint: Think about the acceleration that would be required.

Lesson Review

Vocabulary

Fill in the blank with the term that best completes the following sentences.

1 Acceleration is a change in ______________

2 ______________ occurs when an object travels in a curved path.

3 A decrease in the magnitude of velocity is called ______________

4 An increase in the magnitude of velocity is called ______________

Key Concepts

5 State The units for acceleration are

____

6 Label In the equation $a = \frac{(v_2 - v_1)}{t}$, what do v_1 and v_2 represent?

____

____

7 Calculate What is the acceleration experienced by a car that takes 10 s to reach 27 m/s from rest?

8 Identify Acceleration can be a change in speed or ______________

9 Identify A helicopter flying west begins experiencing an acceleration of 3 m/s^2 east. Will the magnitude of its velocity increase or decrease?

____

Critical Thinking

10 Model Describe a situation when you might travel at a high velocity, but with low acceleration.

____

____

____

Use this graph to answer the following questions. Assume Jenny's direction did not change.

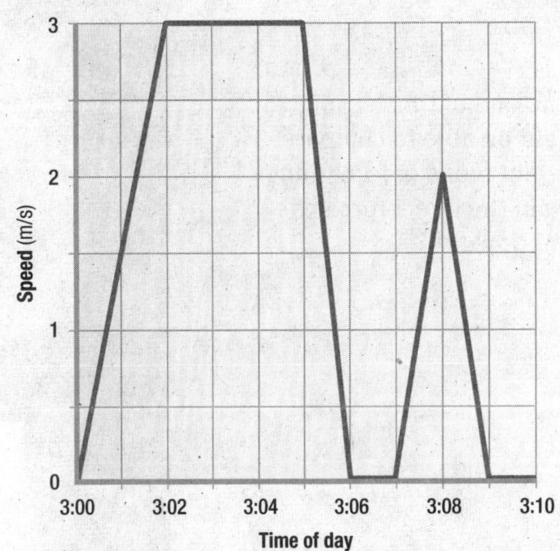

11 Analyze During what intervals was Jenny negatively accelerating?

____

____

12 Analyze During what intervals was Jenny positively accelerating?

____

____

13 Analyze During what intervals was Jenny not accelerating at all?

____

____

____

Lesson 4

Forces

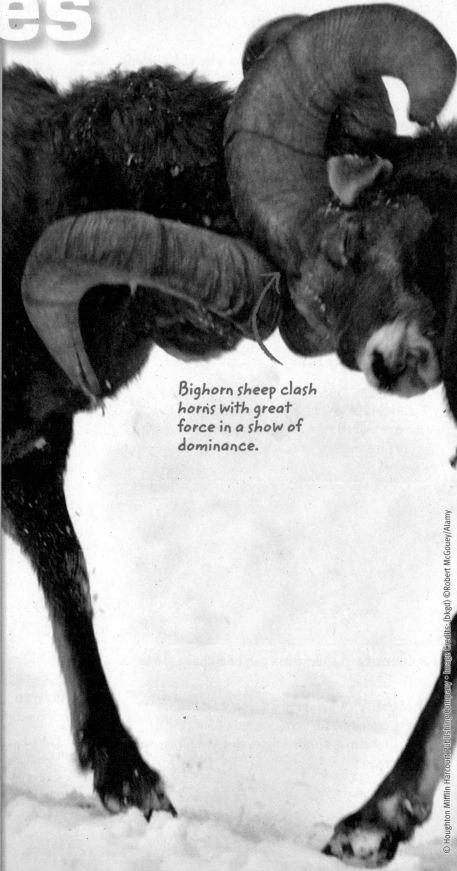

ESSENTIAL QUESTION

What causes motion?

By the end of this lesson, you should be able to compare different types of forces and explain the effect force has on motion.

Bighorn sheep clash horns with great force in a show of dominance.

Sunshine State Standards

SC.6.N.3.3 Give several examples of scientific laws.

SC.6.P.13.1 Investigate and describe types of forces including contact forces and forces acting at a distance, such as electrical, magnetic, and gravitational.

SC.6.P.13.3 Investigate and describe that an unbalanced force acting on an object changes its speed, or direction of motion, or both.

MA.6.A.3.6 Construct and analyze tables, graphs, and equations to describe linear functions and other simple relations using both common language and algebraic notation.

Engage Your Brain

1 Identify Draw an example of a force acting on an object.

2 Explain Imagine that you have two marbles on a table. You roll one marble toward another. When the marbles collide, the marble at rest begins to roll. What do you think caused the second marble to move? What do you think causes the marbles to stop rolling?

Active Reading

3 Apply Many scientific words, such as *force*, also have everyday meanings. Use context clues to write your own definition for each underlined word.

Example Sentence
Alena tried to force her brother to leave her bedroom.

force:

Example Sentence
The hammer hit the nail with a great deal of force.

force:

Vocabulary Terms

- **force**
- **net force**
- **inertia**

4 Identify This list contains the key terms you'll learn in this section. As you read, underline the definition of each term.

Force of Nature

What is a force?

You have probably heard the word *force* in everyday conversation. People say things such as, "Our football team is a force to be reckoned with." But what exactly is a force, as it is used in science?

A Force Is a Push or Pull

In science, a **force** is simply a push or a pull. Forces are vectors, meaning that they have both a magnitude and a direction. A force can cause an object to accelerate, and thereby change the speed or direction of motion. In fact, when you see a change in an object's motion, you can infer that one or more forces acted on the object. The unit that measures force is the newton (N). One newton is equal to one kilogram-meter per second squared ($kg \cdot m/s^2$).

All forces act on objects. Forces exist only when there is something for them to act on! However, a force can act on an object without causing a change in motion. For example, when you sit on a chair, the downward force you exert on the chair doesn't cause the chair to move, because the floor exerts a counteracting upward force on the chair.

Active Reading **5 Name** What units are used to measure force?

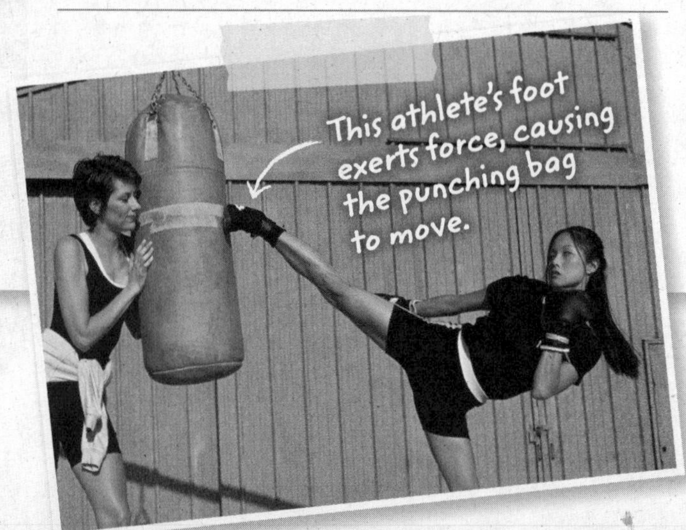

This athlete's foot exerts force, causing the punching bag to move.

Visualize It!

6 List What are some of the forces affecting each of these rock climbers?

How can forces act?

Forces affect us at all times. Whether you are moving or staying still, many different forces may affect you. How are forces classified, and what do forces do when they act on objects?

Forces Can Act in Direct Contact or at a Distance

It is not always easy to tell what is exerting a force or what is being acted on by a force. Forces can be contact forces, as when one object touches or bumps into another. But forces can also act at a distance. When you jump up, a force called gravity pulls you back to the ground even though you are separated from Earth. Magnetic force is another example of a force that can act at a distance. The magnet does not have to be directly touching the metal to be held to it. This is useful: magnetic force can hold a magnet to a refrigerator even when there is something in the way, like paper or a photograph.

Active Reading **7 Identify** What is the force that holds things to the Earth's surface?

____

Magnetic force pulls the magnets to the refrigerator, holding the paper in place.

Forces Can Transfer Energy

Forces can be used to transfer energy from one object to another. Unless balanced by another force, when a force acts on an object, it changes the object's motion. The force accelerates the object. If the speed changes, then the kinetic energy of the object is changed by the force. For example, when wind pushes the blades of a windmill, some of the kinetic energy of the moving air is transferred to the blades, which begin to turn.

Sometimes a force slows an object's motion. One such force is called *friction,* which happens when an object moves while touching another object. Friction causes some of the kinetic energy to become heat energy. You can feel the energy as warmth when you rub your hands together quickly. So, a force transfers energy when it converts kinetic energy to heat energy.

A force provides energy for this radio.

Inquiry

8 Explain Describe how force enables the hand-powered radio to work.

____

____

____

In the Balance

How do multiple forces interact?

Usually, more than one force is acting on an object. The **net force** is the combination of all the forces acting on an object. How do we determine net force? The answer depends on the directions of the forces involved.

When forces act in the same direction, they are simply added together to determine the net force. When forces act in opposite directions, the smaller force is subtracted from the larger force to determine the net force.

Active Reading

9 Determine How do you determine the net force on an object if all forces act in the same direction?

These dogs are pulling with equal force on the toy. The net force is 0 N, and the toy will not move.

Balanced Forces Do Not Change Motion

When the forces on an object produce a net force of 0 N, the forces are balanced. Balanced forces will not cause a change in the motion of a moving object, and will not cause a nonmoving object to start moving. Many objects around you have only balanced forces acting on them. A light hanging from the ceiling does not move because the force of gravity pulling down on the light is balanced by the force of the cord pulling upward.

One of these dogs is pulling with more force on the toy. The toy will move in the direction of the larger dog.

Unbalanced Forces Combine to Produce Acceleration

When the net force is not 0 N, the forces on the object are unbalanced. Unbalanced forces produce a change in motion, such as a change in speed or direction. This change in motion is acceleration. The acceleration is always in the direction of the net force.

Net Force Is a Combination of Forces

When the forces on an object are unbalanced, the object will begin to move. But in which direction?

The forces on an object can be unbalanced, but not perfectly opposite in direction. When this occurs, the net force will be in a direction that is a combination of the directions of the individual forces. For example, when a dog walker experiences a 20 N force pulling her east and another 20 N force pulling her south, the resulting force will have a direction of southeast.

When the forces are not of equal strength, the direction will be closer to the direction of the stronger force.

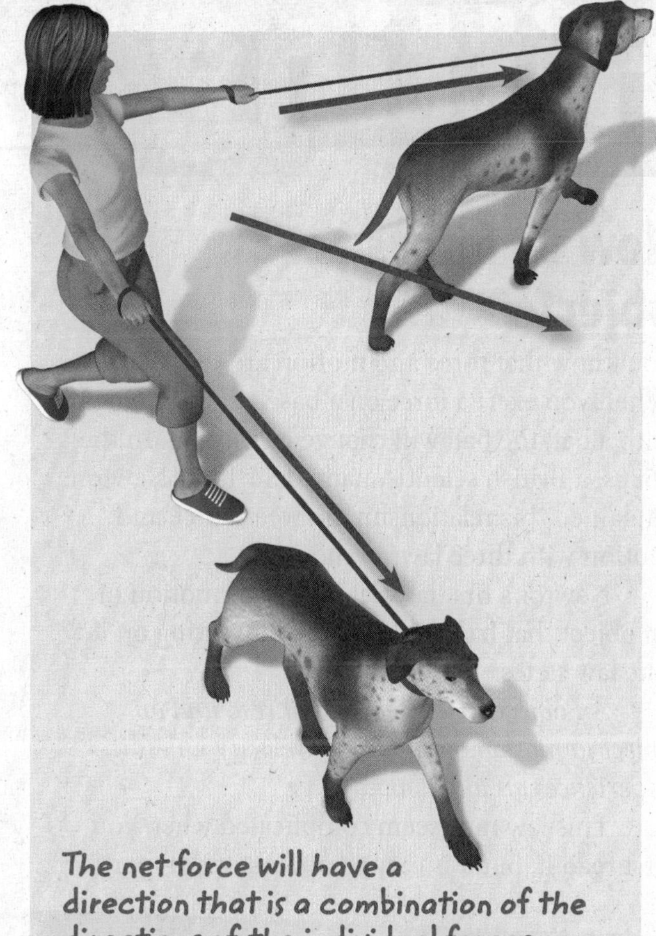

The net force will have a direction that is a combination of the directions of the individual forces.

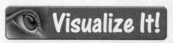

Visualize It!

10 Illustrate Both players kick the ball with equal strength. Draw arrows to show the forces on the ball, and if the forces are unbalanced, draw an arrow to show which direction the ball will move.

Hitting *the* Brakes

How do forces act on objects?

You know that force and motion are related. When you exert a force on a baseball by hitting it with a bat, the ball will change its motion. In the 1680s, a British scientist named Sir Isaac Newton explained this relationship between force and motion with three laws of motion.

Newton's first law describes the motion of an object that has a net force of 0 N acting on it. The law states:

An object at rest remains at rest, and an object in motion maintains its velocity unless it experiences an unbalanced force.

This law may seem complicated when you first read it, but it is easy to understand in parts.

Even though the car has stopped moving, the test dummy does not stop until it hits the airbag and seat belt.

On the moon, there is no atmosphere and virtually no erosion to move the dust. With nothing to move it, this footprint left by an astronaut could remain unchanged for millions of years.

Forces Can Start Objects Moving

An object at rest remains at rest . . . unless it experiences an unbalanced force.

An object that is not moving is said to be at rest. A chair on the floor or a golf ball on a tee are examples of objects at rest. Newton's first law says that objects at rest will stay at rest unless acted on by an unbalanced force. An object will not start moving until a push or a pull is exerted upon it. So, a chair won't slide across the floor unless a force pushes the chair, and a golf ball won't move off the tee until a force pushes it off. Nothing at rest starts moving until a force makes it move.

Forces Can Bring Objects to Rest

An object in motion maintains its velocity unless it experiences an unbalanced force.

The second part of Newton's first law is about objects with a certain velocity. Such objects will continue to move forever with the same velocity unless an unbalanced force acts on them. Think about coming to a sudden stop while driving in a car. The car comes to a stop when the brakes are applied. But you continue to move forward until the force from your seat belt stops you.

These two parts of the law are really stating the same thing. After all, an object at rest has a velocity—its velocity is zero!

With little matter in space, there is nearly no friction or air resistance. Without a force to stop it, the satellite will stay in motion indefinitely.

Smooth ice does not have much friction, so a hockey puck can slide a long way without changing direction.

Forces Can Change the Motion of Objects

Newton's first law is also called the law of inertia. **Inertia** (ih•NER•shuh) is the tendency of all objects to resist any change in motion. Because of inertia, an object at rest will remain at rest until a force makes it move. Likewise, inertia is why a moving object will maintain its velocity until a force changes its speed or direction. Inertia is why it is impossible for a plane, a car, or a bicycle to stop immediately.

Active Reading **12 Identify** What is another name for Newton's first law?

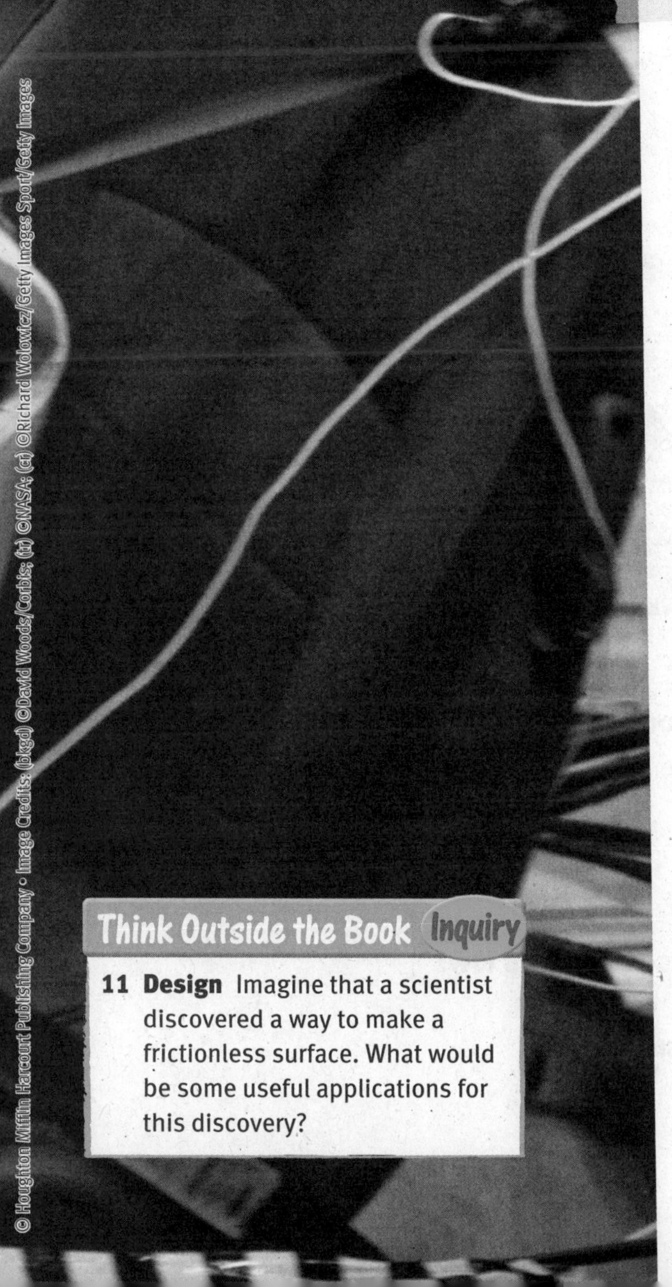

Think Outside the Book Inquiry

11 Design Imagine that a scientist discovered a way to make a frictionless surface. What would be some useful applications for this discovery?

Forces Can Accelerate Objects

When an unbalanced force acts on an object, the object moves with accelerated motion. Newton's second law describes the motion:

The acceleration of an object depends on the mass of the object and the amount of force applied.

This law links force, mass, and acceleration. This relationship can be expressed mathematically:

$$F = ma$$

From this equation, we see that a given force applied to a large mass will have only a small acceleration. When the same force is applied to a small mass, the acceleration will be large.

Imagine pushing a grocery cart. When the cart is empty, it has less mass. Your force accelerates the cart quickly. But when it is full, the same push accelerates the cart much more slowly.

13 Relate What three quantities does Newton's second law relate?

F_{net} = 150 N

F_{net} = 150 N

Do the Math

Sample Problem

These players train by pushing a massive object. If the players produce a net force of 150 N, and the object has a mass of 75 kg, what is the object's acceleration?

Use Newton's law:

$F = ma$

$150\text{ N} = (75\text{ kg})(a)$

$a = \dfrac{150\text{ N}}{75\text{ kg}}$

$a = 2\text{ m/s}^2$

You Try It!

14 Calculate For a more difficult training session, the mass to be pushed is increased to 300 kg. If the players still produce a net force of 150 N, what is the acceleration of the 300 kg mass?

Use Newton's law:

$F = ma$

150 N =

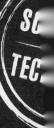

Why It Matters

A Wearable Robot?

Scientists and engineers are working on developing powered exoskeletons for people to wear. These special suits have many useful applications.

Feats of Strength

The suits have sensors that detect a person's muscle movements, and they typically have an air pump that increases lifting force.

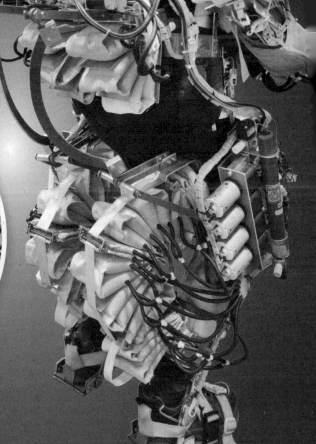

Giving a Hand Up

These suits were designed to help in nursing care. Here, the suit lets a nurse lift a patient out of a wheelchair with ease.

Extend

Inquiry

15 **Analyze** How does the extra force from a power suit make moving a mass easier?

16 **Predict** What do you think are some of the difficulties in making a power suit work?

17 **Apply** Think of some other tasks that could benefit from the development of a cheaper, more durable power suit. Make a drawing showing how much easier the task would be with a power suit.

A Matching Pair

How do force pairs act?

Newton also devised a third law of motion:

Whenever one object exerts a force on a second object, the second object exerts an equal and opposite force on the first.

Newton's third law can be simply stated as follows: All forces act in pairs.

Forces Always Occur in Pairs

If a force is exerted, another force occurs that is equal in size and opposite in direction. The law itself addresses only forces. But the way that force pairs interact affects the motion of objects.

How do forces act in pairs? Action and reaction forces are present even when there is no motion. For example, you exert a force on a chair when you sit on it. Your weight pushing down on the chair is the action force. The reaction force is the force you feel exerted by the chair that pushes up on your body.

Active Reading

18 Identify What do we call the two forces in a force pair?

____

____

____

____

The bear's paw exerts a force on the water.
The water exerts a force on the bear's paw.

Force Pairs Do Not Act on the Same Object

A force is always exerted on one object by another object. This rule is true for all forces, including action and reaction forces. However, action and reaction forces in a pair do not act on the same object. If they did, the net force would always be 0 N and nothing would ever move!

To understand how force pairs act on different objects, consider the act of swimming. When a bear swims, the action force is the bear's paw pushing on the water. The reaction force is the water pushing on the bear's paw. The action force pushes the water backward, and the reaction force moves the bear forward. Each object exerts a force on the other. Instead of neither moving, both the bear and the water move!

Force Pairs Can Have Unequal Effects

Even though both the action force and the reaction force are equal in size, their effects are often different. The force of gravity is a force pair between two objects. If you drop a ball, gravity pulls the ball toward Earth. This force is the action force exerted by Earth on the ball. But gravity also pulls Earth toward the ball! This is the reaction force. It's easy to see the action force in this example. Why don't you notice the effect of the reaction force—Earth being pulled upward? Think about Newton's second law. The force on the ball is the same size as the force on the Earth, but the Earth has much, much more mass than the ball. So the Earth's acceleration is much, much smaller than that of the ball!

It is difficult to observe the effect of this reaction force due to Earth's large mass.

Active Reading **19 Explain** Why don't force pairs have equal effects?

____

____

____

Visualize It!

20 Apply Name one force pair that has not been pointed out in the picture of the baseball player below.

____

____

____

Forces Can Occur in Several Pairs

An object can have multiple forces acting on it at once. When this happens, each force is part of a force pair. When a baseball bat hits a baseball, the bat does not fly backward, because the player's hand is exerting another force on the bat. What keeps the player's hand from flying back? A force exerted on the hand by the bones and muscles in the player's arm, and so on.

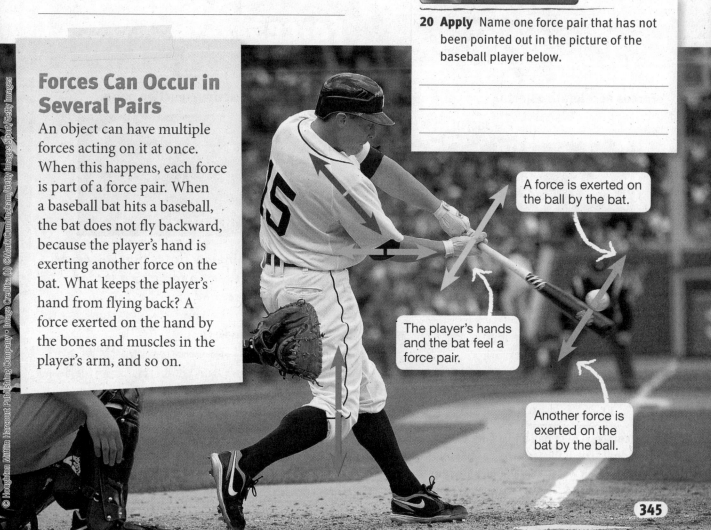

A force is exerted on the ball by the bat.

The player's hands and the bat feel a force pair.

Another force is exerted on the bat by the ball.

Visual Summary

To complete this summary, fill in the blanks with the correct word or phrase. Then use the key below to check your answers. You can use this page to review the main concepts of the lesson.

Balanced forces do not change motion. Unbalanced forces produce acceleration.

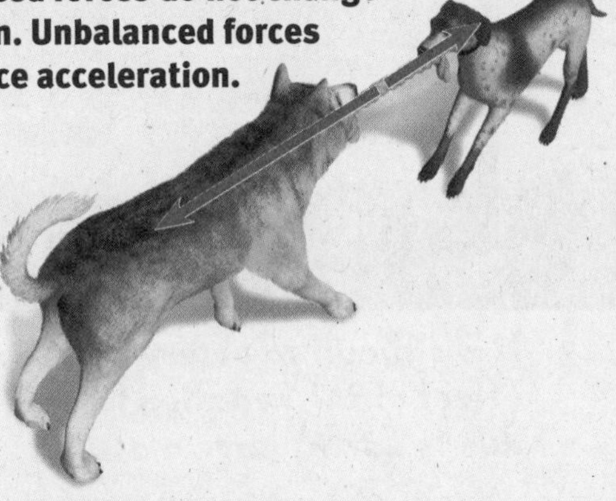

21 When the net force is not ____________ N, the forces on the object are unbalanced, and the object will accelerate in the direction of the ____________

Forces are required to change the motion of objects.

22 Newton's first law states that objects maintain their velocity unless

____

____

Forces

Forces accelerate objects.

23 Newton's second law states that force equals ____________ times ____________

Forces occur in action/reaction pairs.

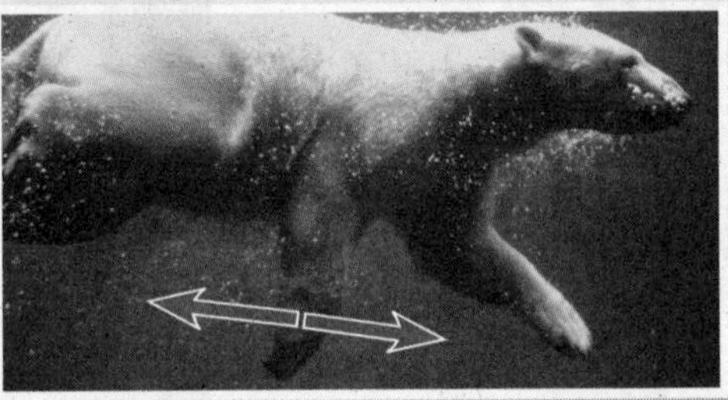

24 Newton's third law states that whenever one object exerts a force on a second object, the second object exerts an ____________ and ____________ force on the first.

Answers: 21. zero, net force; 22. they experience an unbalanced force; 23. mass, acceleration; 24. equal, opposite

25 Calculate A 6-kg ball and a 4-kg ball are acted on by forces of equal size. If the large ball accelerates at 2 m/s^2, what acceleration will the small ball undergo?

Lesson Review

Vocabulary

Draw a line to connect the following terms to their definitions.

1 force

2 inertia

3 net force

A a push or a pull exerted on an object

B the combination of all forces acting on an object

C the tendency of an object to resist a change in motion

Key Concepts

4 Identify Give an example of a contact force and an example of a force that acts at a distance.

5 Explain Two forces are applied on a soccer ball. Which of the following statements explains why the ball accelerates?

A The net force applied to the ball is 0 N.

B The ball resists one force but not the other.

C Newton's second law does not apply to round objects.

D The two forces are unbalanced.

6 Calculate What force is necessary to accelerate a 70-kg object at a rate of 4.2 m/s^2? Show your work below.

Critical Thinking

Use this diagram to answer the following questions.

7 Explain When the mover pushes the box, two equal forces result. Explain why the box moves even though the forces are equal and opposite.

8 Apply When the box is moving, it experiences a friction force of 20 N to the left, or toward the mover. What force does the mover need to apply in order to keep the box moving to the right at 1 m/s?

9 Conclude Use Newton's first law of motion to explain why air bags in cars are important during head-on collisions.

People in Science

Steve Okamoto

ROLLER COASTER DESIGNER

A day in the life of a roller coaster designer is filled with twists and turns—just ask designer Steve Okamoto. As a kid, he became interested in roller coasters after a trip to Disneyland. To become a product designer, Steve studied subjects like math and science. He later earned a degree in product design that involved studying mechanical engineering and studio art.

Before he starts designing roller coasters, Steve has to think about all of the parts of a roller coaster and how it will fit in the amusement park. It's like putting together a huge puzzle. Different parts of the puzzle include the safety equipment needed, what the roller coaster will be made out of, and how the track will fit in next to other rides. He also has to think about what visitors to the park will want to see and experience in a roller coaster ride.

As he is designing a roller coaster, Steve's math and science background comes in handy. For example, in order to make sure that a roller coaster's cars make it up each hill, he has to calculate the speed and acceleration of the cars on each part of the track. To create the curves, loops, and dips of the roller coaster track, he uses his knowledge of physics and geometry.

Acceleration from the downhill run provides the speed for the next climb.

JOB BOARD

Machinists

What You'll Do: Use machine tools, such as lathes, milling machines, and machining centers, to produce new metal parts.

Where You Might Work: Machine shops and manufacturing plants in industries including the automotive and aerospace industries.

Education: In high school, you should take math courses, especially trigonometry, and, if available, courses in blueprint reading, metalworking, and drafting. After high school, most people acquire their skills in an apprenticeship program. This gives a person a mix of classroom and on-the-job training.

Bicycle Mechanic

What You'll Do: Repair and maintain different kinds of bikes, from children's bikes to expensive road bikes.

Where You Might Work: Independent bicycle shops or large chain stores that carry bicycles; certain sporting events like Olympic and national trials.

Education: Some high schools and trade schools have shop classes that teach bicycle repair. Most bicycle mechanics get on-the-job training. To work as a mechanic at national and international cycling events, you will have to earn a bicycle mechanic's license.

PEOPLE IN SCIENCE NEWS

Mike Hensler

The Surf Chair

As a Daytona Beach lifeguard, Mike Hensler realized that the beach was almost impossible for someone in a wheelchair. Although he had never invented a machine before, Hensler decided to build a wheelchair that could be driven across sand without getting stuck. He began spending many evenings in his driveway with a pile of lawn-chair parts, designing the chair by trial and error.

The result looks very different from a conventional wheelchair. With huge rubber wheels and a thick frame of white PVC pipe, the Surf Chair not only moves easily over sandy terrain but also is weather resistant and easy to clean. The newest models of the Surf Chair come with optional attachments, such as a variety of umbrellas, detachable armrests and footrests, and even places to attach fishing rods.

Gravity and Motion

Overcoming the force of gravity is hard to do for very long!

ESSENTIAL QUESTION

How do objects move under the influence of gravity?

By the end of this lesson, you should be able to describe the effect that gravity, including Earth's gravity, has on matter.

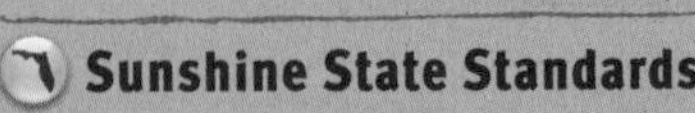

Sunshine State Standards

SC.6.P.13.1 Investigate and describe types of forces including contact forces and forces acting at a distance, such as electrical, magnetic, and gravitational.

SC.6.P.13.2 Explore the Law of Gravity by recognizing that every object exerts gravitational force on every other object and that the force depends on how much mass the objects have and how far apart they are.

Engage Your Brain

1 Predict Check *T* or *F* to show whether you think each statement is true or false.

T	F	
☐	☐	Earth's gravity makes heavy objects fall faster than light objects.
☐	☐	A person would weigh the same on other planets as on Earth.
☐	☐	Planets are round because of gravity.

2 Infer List some ways houses would be built differently if gravity were much stronger or much weaker.

Active Reading

3 Predict What do you think the phrase *free fall* might mean? Write your own definition. After reading the lesson, see how close you were!

Vocabulary Terms

- **gravity**
- **free fall**
- **orbit**

4 Apply This list contains the key terms you'll learn in this section. As you read, underline the definition of each term.

Down to EARTH

Gravity pulls the skydiver, his clothes, and his parachute toward the Earth, all with the same acceleration.

This stop-action photo shows that when there is no air resistance, a feather and a billiard ball fall at the same rate.

Active Reading

5 Analyze What has to happen for a feather and a ball to fall at the same rate?

What is gravity?

If you watch video of astronauts on the moon, you see them wearing big, bulky spacesuits and yet jumping lightly. Why is leaping on the moon easier than on Earth? The answer is gravity. **Gravity** is a force of attraction between objects due to their mass. Gravity is a noncontact force that acts between two objects at any distance apart. Even when a skydiver is far above the ground, Earth's gravity acts to pull him downward.

Gravity Is An Attractive Force

Earth's gravity pulls everything toward Earth's center. It pulls, but it does not push, so it is called an attractive force.

You feel the force due to Earth's gravity as the heaviness of your body, or your weight. Weight is a force, and it depends on mass. Greater mass results in greater weight. This force of gravity between Earth and an object is equal to the mass of the object *m* multiplied by a factor due to gravity *g*.

$$F = mg$$

On Earth, *g* is about 9.8 m/s². The units are the same as the units for acceleration. Does this mean that Earth's gravity accelerates all objects in the same way? The surprising answer is yes.

Suppose you dropped a heavy object and a light object at the same time. Which would hit the ground first? Sometimes an object experiences a lot of air resistance and falls slowly or flutters to the ground. But if you could take away air resistance, all objects would fall with the same acceleration. When gravity is the only force affecting the fall, a light object and a heavy object hit the ground at the same time.

Acceleration depends on both force and mass. The heavier object experiences a greater force, or weight. But the heavier object is also harder to accelerate, because it has more mass. The two effects cancel, and the acceleration due to gravity is the same for all masses.

Gravity Affects Mass Equally

All matter has mass. Gravity is a result of mass, so all matter is affected by gravity. Every object exerts a gravitational pull on every other object. Your pencil and shoes are gravitationally attracted to each other, each to your textbook, all three to your chair, and so on. So why don't objects pull each other into a big pile? The gravitational forces between these objects are too small. Other forces, such as friction, are strong enough to balance the gravitational pulls and prevent changes in motion. Gravity is not a very powerful force—you overcome the attraction of Earth's entire mass on your body every time you stand up!

However, when enough mass gathers together, its effect can be large. Gravity caused Earth and other planets to become round. All parts of the planet pulled each other toward the center of mass, resulting in a sphere.

Some astronomical bodies do not have enough mass to pull themselves into spheres. Small moons and asteroids can maintain a lumpy shape, but larger moons such as Earth's have enough mass to form a sphere.

Gravity also acts over great distances. It determines the motion of celestial bodies. The paths of planets, the sun, and other stars are determined by gravity. Even the motion of our galaxy through the universe is due to gravity.

Galaxies, made up of billions of stars, have characteristic shapes and motions that are due to gravity.

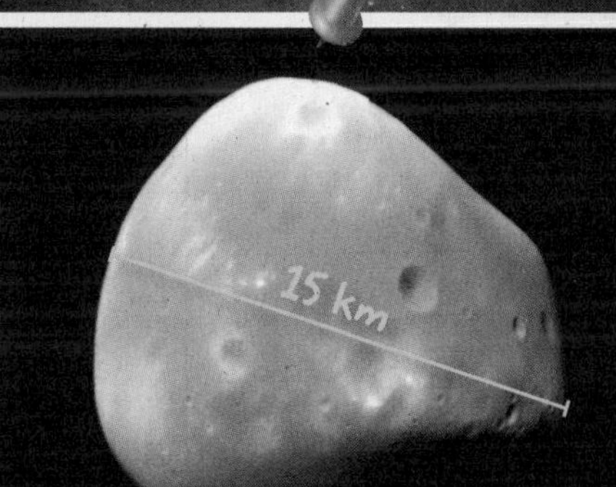

Deimos, one of the moons of Mars, is only about 15 km at its longest stretch. Deimos does not have enough mass to form a sphere.

Earth's moon has a diameter of more than 3,400 km. It has more than enough mass to pull itself into a sphere.

3,400 km

Think Outside the Book

6 Incorporate Write a short story about a time when you had to overcome the force of gravity to get something done.

A WEIGHTY Issue

What determines the force of gravity?

The law of universal gravitation relates gravitational force, mass, and distance. It states that all objects attract each other through gravitational force. The strength of the force depends on the masses involved and distance between them.

Gravity Depends on Distance

The gravitational force between two objects increases as the distance between their centers decreases. This means that objects far apart have a weaker attraction than objects close together. If two objects move closer, the attraction between them increases. For example, you can't feel the sun's gravity because it is so far away, but if you were able to stand on the surface of the sun, you would find it impossible to move due to the gravity!

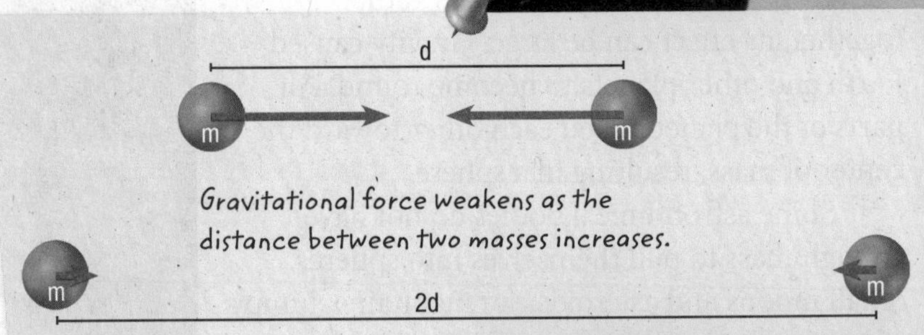

Gravitational force weakens as the distance between two masses increases.

Active Reading **7 Explain** How does distance affect gravitational force?

____

____

Gravity Depends on Mass

The gravitational force between two objects increases with the mass of each object. This means that objects with greater mass have more attraction between them. A cow has more mass than a cat, so there is more attraction between the Earth and the cow, and the cow weighs more.

This part of the law of universal gravitation explains why astronauts on the moon bounce when they walk. The moon has less mass than Earth, so the astronauts weigh less. The force of each step pushes an astronaut higher than it would on Earth.

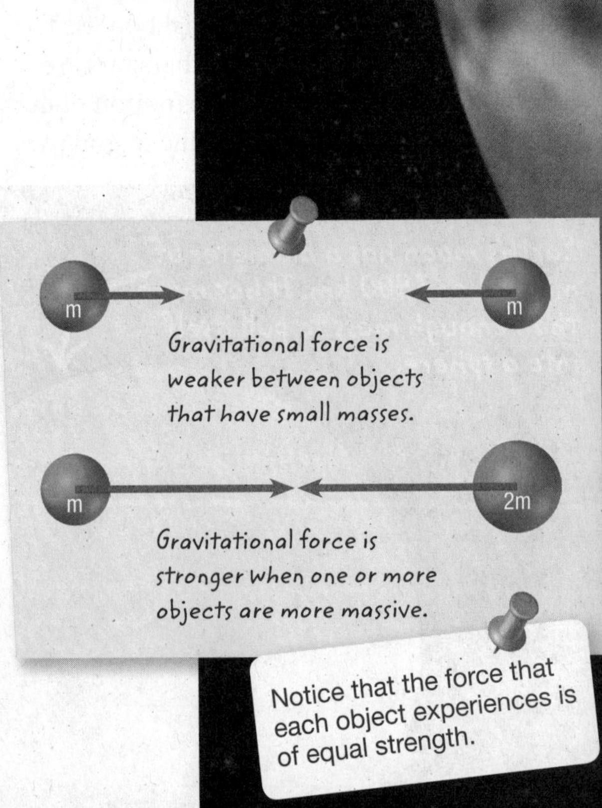

Gravitational force is weaker between objects that have small masses.

Gravitational force is stronger when one or more objects are more massive.

Notice that the force that each object experiences is of equal strength.

Active Reading **8 Explain** How does mass affect gravitational force?

____

____

Finding Gravity in Strange Places

The gravity of the moon is less than that of Earth, because the moon has much less mass than Earth.

The moon does not pull as hard on an astronaut, so the force of her weight on the scale is less. The astronaut weighs less on the moon than on Earth.

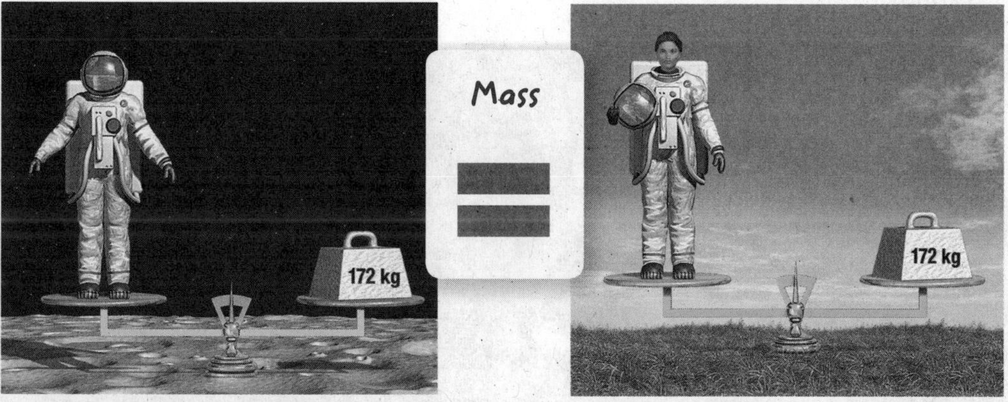

The astronaut has the same mass on the moon and Earth.

9 List This table lists the weights of a 80 kg person on different planets. List these planets in decreasing order of mass.

Planet	Weight of 80 kg
Venus	710 N
Earth	784 N
Mars	297 N
Jupiter	1983 N

10 Justify The weight of 80 kg of mass on Mercury is 296 N, almost identical to the weight of the same mass on Mars. But Mercury has much less mass than Mars! Explain how this can be. (What else could affect gravitational force?)

Don't Bring Me DOWN

How does gravity keep objects in orbit?

Something is in **free fall** when gravity is pulling it down and no other forces are acting on it. An object is in **orbit** when it travels around another object in space. When a satellite or spacecraft orbits Earth, it is moving forward. But it is also in free fall. The combination of the forward motion and downward motion due to gravity combine to cause orbiting.

A spacecraft in orbit is always falling, but never hits the ground! This happens because of forward motion. As the object falls, it moves forward far enough that the planet curves away under it, so it has exactly that much farther to fall. It never actually gets closer to Earth. In order to move forward far enough to counteract the fall, objects in orbit must travel very fast—as much as 8 kilometers per second!

Active Reading

11 Identify When is an object in free fall?

How Does a Satellite Stay in Orbit?

The satellite moves forward at a constant speed. If there were no gravity, the satellite would follow the path of the green line.

The satellite is in free fall because gravity pulls it toward Earth. The satellite would move straight down if it were not traveling forward.

12 Assess What would happen to an object in orbit without gravity pulling down?

The discovery of the planet Neptune (above) was predicted by observing the effect that its gravity had on the motions of the planet Uranus.

The path of the satellite follows the curve of Earth's surface. Following a path around Earth is known as orbiting.

Gravity Can Make Objects Move in Circles

Besides spacecraft and satellites, many other objects in the universe are in orbit. The moon orbits Earth. Planets orbit the sun. Many stars orbit large masses in the center of galaxies. These objects travel along circular or elliptical paths. As an object moves along a curve, it changes direction constantly. The change in motion is due to an unbalanced force. The direction of the force must change constantly to produce curved motion. The force must be directed inward, toward the center of the curve or circle.

Gravity provides the force that keeps objects in orbit. This force pulls one object into a path that curves around another object. Gravitational force is directed inward. For example, this inward force pulls the moon toward Earth and constantly changes the moon's motion.

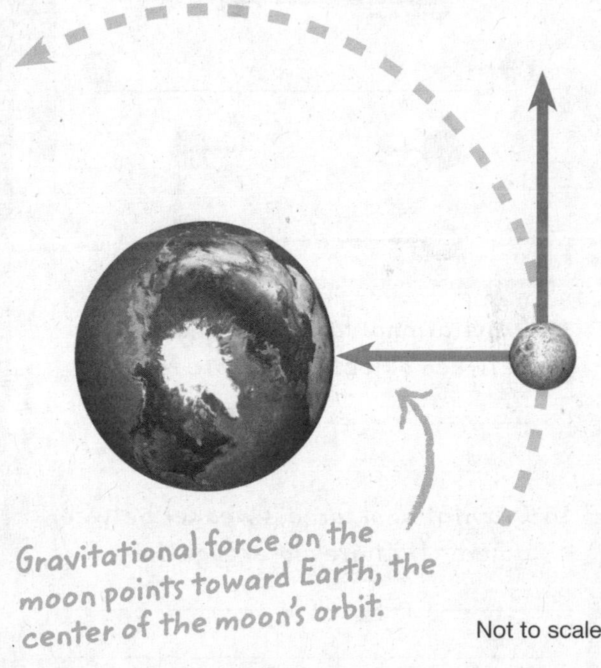

Gravitational force on the moon points toward Earth, the center of the moon's orbit.

13 Model Imagine tying a string to a ball and twirling it around you. How is this similar to the moon orbiting Earth? In this example, what is providing the constantly changing, inward force?

Visual Summary

To complete this summary, read the statements in the boxes below. Circle any that are true. Cross out any that are false, and correct the statement so that it is true. You can use this page to review the main concepts of the lesson.

Gravity and Motion

Gravity depends on mass and distance.

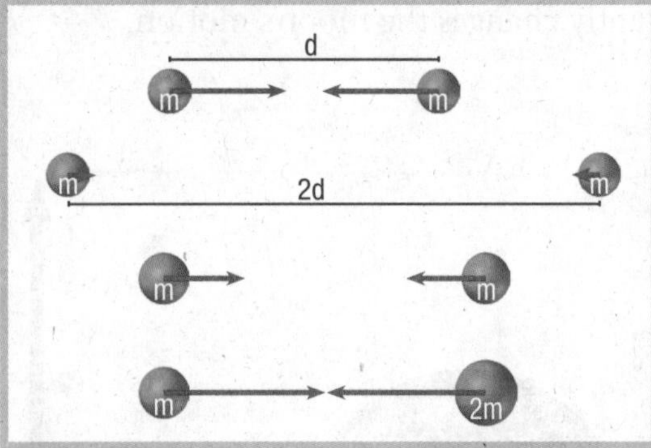

15 *Gravitational force is stronger between objects with more mass.*

16 *Gravitational force is weaker between objects that are closer together.*

Gravity is an attractive force that exists between all objects with mass.

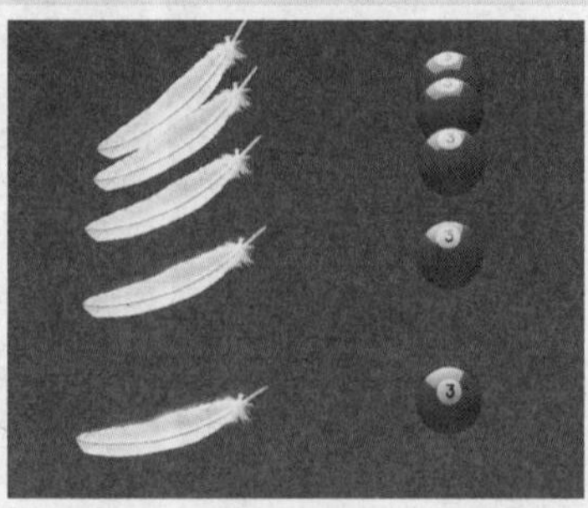

14 *The acceleration due to gravity is the same for all falling objects when there is no air resistance.*

Gravity keeps objects in orbit.

17 *The moon does not fall to Earth because of friction.*

Answers: 14 True; 15 True; 16 False, gravity is stronger when objects are closer; 17 False, the force keeping the moon orbiting the Earth is gravity.

18 **Justify** If Earth were replaced by an object with the same mass but much smaller in size, would the moon continue to orbit the new object, fall into it, or fly off into space? Why?

Lesson Review

Vocabulary

Fill in the blanks with the term that best completes the following sentences.

1 _______________ is a force that attracts all matter to each other.

2 When the only force affecting an object is gravity, that object is in _______________

3 An object traveling around another object in space is in _______________

Key Concepts

4 Relate The gravitational attraction between two objects will _______________ if one object acquires more mass.

5 Relate The gravitational attraction between two objects will _______________ if the objects move farther apart.

6 Explain Why are large astronomical bodies such as planets and stars round?

7 Identify What two motions combine to produce an orbit?

8 Distinguish Explain the difference between mass and weight.

Critical Thinking

9 Infer The weight of an object on a planet depends not only on its mass, but also on its distance from the planet's center. This table lists the weight of 80 kg on each planet in the solar system. Uranus has more than 14 times as much mass as Earth, yet the gravitational force is less. Explain how this could be.

Planet	Weight of 80 kg
Mercury	296 N
Venus	710 N
Earth	784 N
Mars	297 N
Jupiter	1983 N
Saturn	838 N
Uranus	708 N
Neptune	859 N

10 Apply Why don't satellites in orbit fall to the ground? Why don't they fly off into space?

My Notes

Unit 5 Summary

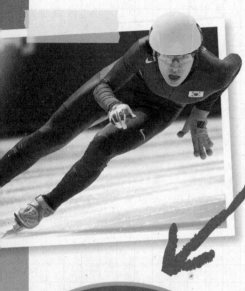

Kinetic and Potential Energy

Motion and Speed

Acceleration

Forces

Gravity and Motion

1 Interpret The Graphic Organizer above shows that force is related to acceleration and gravity. Explain.

2 Distinguish What is the difference between kinetic energy, potential energy, and mechanical energy?

3 Judge "An object will only change its motion if a force is directly applied to it." Is this a true statement? Explain why or why not.

4 Infer You are riding in a car that is traveling at a constant speed. Yet, the car is accelerating. Explain how this can be true.

Benchmark Review

Name ______________________________

Multiple Choice

Identify the choice that best completes the statement or answers the question.

1 In order for a space shuttle to leave Earth, it must produce a great amount of thrust. Its rocket boosters create this thrusting force by burning great amounts of fuel. However, once in space, the shuttle needs very little fuel. It circles Earth while gravity pulls it toward Earth. What term describes the circular path the shuttle makes in space?

A. orbit

B. gravity

C. free fall

D. weight

2 A weather station records the wind as blowing from the northeast at 12 km/h. Which statement explains why northeast at 12 km/h is a vector?

F. The speed is given in km/h.

G. The speed is a constant value.

H. An average speed is reported.

I. Speed and direction are given.

3 One ball rolls along a shelf at a steady rate. A second ball rolls off the shelf and gains speed as it falls in a curved path. Which must have an unbalanced force acting on it?

A. the ball that rolls along the shelf

B. the ball that falls

C. both balls

D. neither ball

Benchmark Review

4 Penny says that there is no gravitational force between dust particles because they have too little mass. Ella says that dust particles do pull on each other gravitationally and would move toward each other if they were in outer space instead of in air. Who has the better argument, and why?

F. Penny, because objects with only a little mass are not affected by gravity.

G. Penny, because any force on a dust particle would change its motion.

H. Ella, because any two objects exert a gravitational force on each other.

I. Ella, because objects with smaller mass have more gravity acting on them.

5 Luis is trying to push a box of new soccer balls across the floor. In the illustration, the arrow on the box represents the force that Luis exerts.

If the box is not moving, which of the following must be true?

A. The box is exerting a larger force on Luis than he is exerting on the box.

B. There is another force acting on the box that balances Luis's force.

C. Luis is applying a force that acts at a distance.

D. There is no force of friction acting on the box.

6 Ignacio uses a hammer to hit a nail into a board on the floor. How does gravity make it easier to hammer the nail?

F. Gravity pushes the board up to help the nail go in.

G. Gravity pulls the board and the nail toward each other.

H. Gravity pulls the hammer down so that it pushes on the nail.

I. Gravity pulls the nail down but does not pull on the hammer.

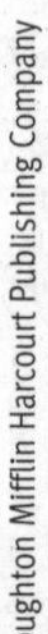

7 Every moving object has kinetic energy. This illustration shows four vehicles. Assume that they are all traveling at the same speed on a highway.

What do you know about the kinetic energy of the vehicles?

A. The motorcycle has the most kinetic energy because it is the vehicle with the least mass.

B. All of the vehicles have the same kinetic energy because they are moving at the same speed.

C. The delivery van has the greatest kinetic energy because its mass is greater than that of the other vehicles.

D. The delivery van has the greatest kinetic energy because it has the most tires in contact with the pavement.

8 Andre boarded a train at Lincoln Station. The train left the station at 9:10 p.m. and traveled, without stopping, 6 miles to Union Station. What additional information does Andre need to find the average speed of the train from Lincoln Station to Union Station?

F. the direction the train traveled

G. the time the train left Union Station

H. the initial and maximum speeds of the train

I. the time the train arrived at Union Station

9 Measuring acceleration requires the appropriate units. Scientists measure acceleration using a standardized set of units that are part of the SI system. Which are SI units for acceleration?

A. N

B. m/s

C. m/s^2

D. kg·m/s

Benchmark Review

10 Two identical space probes are orbiting Jupiter. Scientists determine that one of the space probes has a larger gravitational force acting on it than the other. Which of the following is the most likely reason for the difference?

F. One space probe reached Jupiter before the other.

G. One space probe has more air resistance than the other.

H. Only one space probe is exerting a gravitational force on the other.

I. One space probe is closer to Jupiter than the other.

11 Blair and Aaron competed in a 400-m running race. Blair finished the race in 55 s and came in first. Aaron finished the race in 58 s and came in second. Which of the following must have been greater for Blair than for Aaron?

A. maximum speed during the race

B. average speed for the entire race

C. speed for the last 100 m of the race

D. initial speed for the first 100 m the race

12 When a pendulum is released, it swings back and forth. The speed and position change throughout each swing. The illustration identifies three positions of the pendulum during its swing.

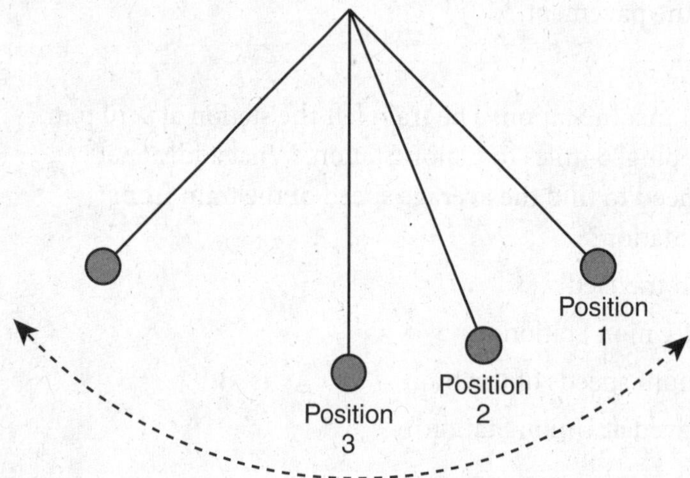

At which point does the pendulum weight have the greatest amount of mechanical energy?

F. Position 1

G. Position 2

H. Position 3

I. Mechanical energy does not change.

UNIT 6

The Cell

Big Idea 14

Organization and Development of Living Organisms

Big Idea 15

Diversity and Evolution of Living Organisms

Colorized picture of the organelles of a cell through a modern microscope

What do you think?

As microscopes have become more powerful, our understanding of cells and their functions has also increased. What kinds of questions would you use a microscope to answer?

Cells seen through an early microscope

Unit 6

The Cell

CITIZEN SCIENCE

Seeing through Microscopes

Microscopes have come a long way. Today, we can see the details of the surface of metals at the atomic level. Microscopes have allowed us to study our world at some of the smallest levels.

Circa 1000 CE

Although people may have used rock crystals to magnify things thousands of years ago, it wasn't until about 1000 CE that people were able to form and polish clear-glass partial spheres. Placing these reading stones on top of a page made it easier to read the words.

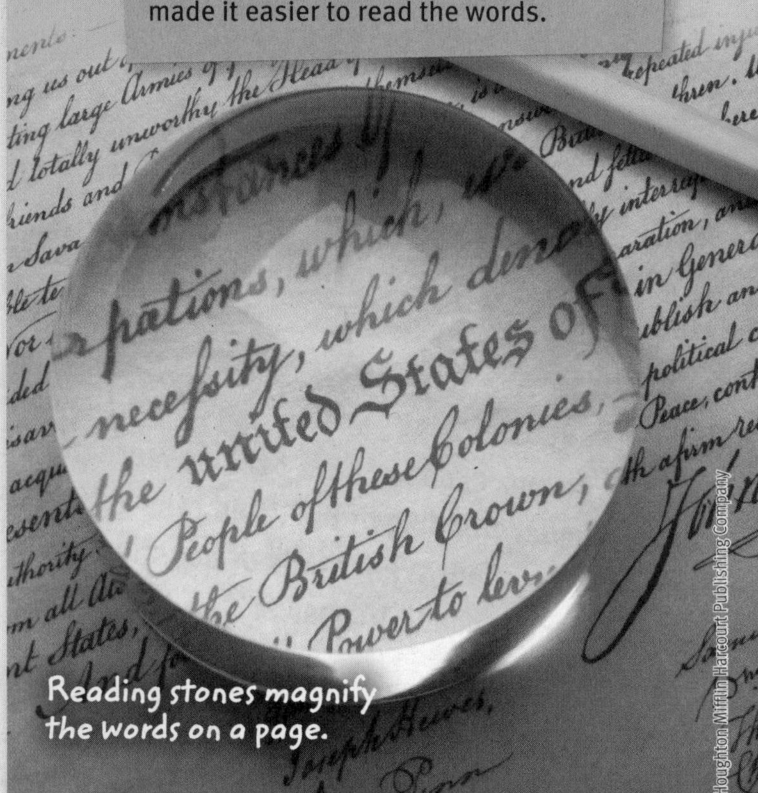

Reading stones magnify the words on a page.

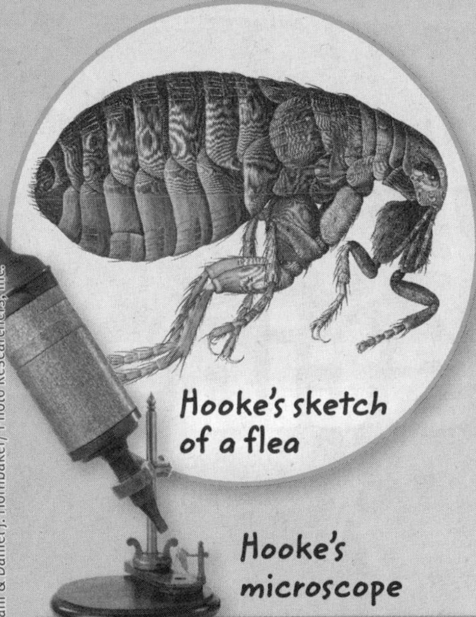
Hooke's sketch of a flea

Hooke's microscope

1665
Robert Hooke was interested in many areas of science. In 1665, Hooke invented a light microscope to look at small creatures like fleas. Hooke's microscope was similar to a telescope, but it also had a way to shine light on the object.

1931
Ernst Ruska developed the electron microscope, which shows much greater detail than light microscopes do. The electron microscope uses an electron beam instead of light to show things as small as the structure of viruses. Ruska received the Nobel Prize in Physics in 1986 for his breakthrough.

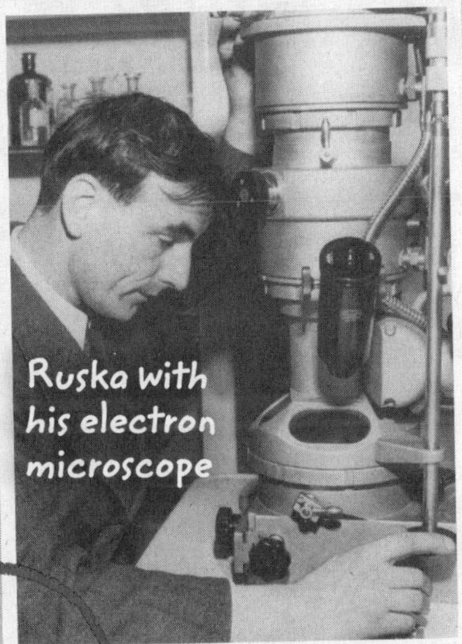
Ruska with his electron microscope

Atoms at platinum's surface

1981
The scanning tunneling microscope changed the way scientists look at things again. Using this microscope, we can look at images of surfaces at the atomic level. The microscope uses a beam of electrons to map a surface. This information is collected and processed so that it can be viewed on a computer screen.

What's in a Microscope?

1 Think About It

A What characteristics do different microscopes have?

B Why are they used?

2 Conduct Research

Choose a specific kind of microscope and research how it is used, whether it is used to view live or dead samples, and its range of magnification.

Take It Home

With an adult, prepare an oral presentation for your class on the microscope that you have researched.

Lesson 1

The Characteristics of Cells

ESSENTIAL QUESTION

What are living things made of?

By the end of this lesson, you should be able to explain the components of the scientific theory of cells.

People communicate to others through talking, signing, body language, and other methods. Inside your body, cells communicate too. Brain cells, like the ones shown here, control balance, posture, and muscle coordination.

Sunshine State Standards

SC.6.L.14.2 Investigate and explain the components of the scientific theory of cells (cell theory): all organisms are composed of cells (single-celled or multi-cellular), all cells come from pre-existing cells, and cells are the basic unit of life.

MA.6.A.3.6 Construct and analyze tables, graphs, and equations to describe linear functions and other simple relations using both common language and algebraic notation.

Engage Your Brain

1 Predict Check T or F to show whether you think each statement is true or false.

T	F	
☐	☐	All living things are made up of one or more cells.
☐	☐	Rocks are made up of cells.
☐	☐	All cells are the same size.
☐	☐	Cells perform life functions for living things.

2 Describe Sketch your idea of what a cell looks like. Label any parts you include in your sketch.

Active Reading

3 Synthesize Many English words have their roots in other languages. Use the Greek words below to make an educated guess about the meanings of the words *prokaryote* and *eukaryote*. Here *kernel* refers to the nucleus where genetic material is contained in some cells.

Word part	Meaning
pro-	before
eu-	true
karyon	kernel

prokaryote:

eukaryote:

Vocabulary Terms

- **cell**
- **organism**
- **cell membrane**
- **cytoplasm**
- **organelle**
- **nucleus**
- **prokaryote**
- **eukaryote**

4 Apply As you learn the definition of each vocabulary term in this lesson, create your own sketches of a prokaryotic cell and a eukaryotic cell and label the parts in each cell.

Cell-*ebrate!*

What is a cell?

Like all living things, you are made up of cells. A **cell** is the smallest functional and structural unit of all living organisms. An **organism** is any living thing. All organisms are made up of cells. Some organisms are just one cell. Others, like humans, contain trillions of cells. An organism carries out all of its own life processes.

Robert Hooke was the first person to describe cells. In 1665, he built a microscope to look at tiny objects. One day, he looked at a thin slice of cork from the bark of a cork tree. The cork looked as if it was made of little boxes. Hooke named these boxes *cells*, which means "little rooms" in Latin.

5 Identify As you read, underline the reasons why cells are important.

6 Compare Looking at the photos of the three different cells, what do the cells have in common?

____

____

____

____

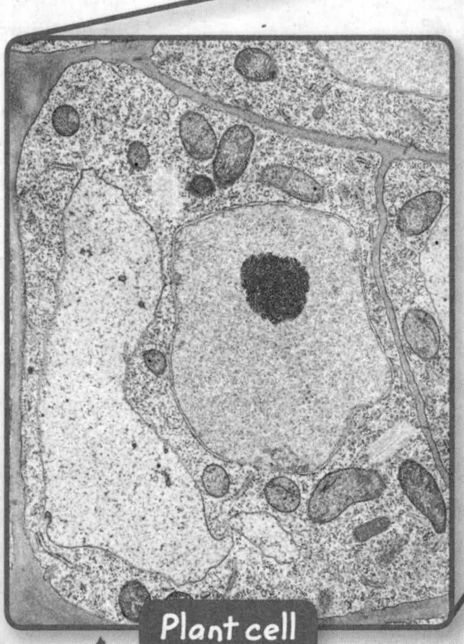

Plant cells range in size from 10 μm to 100 μm. They can be much larger than animal cells.

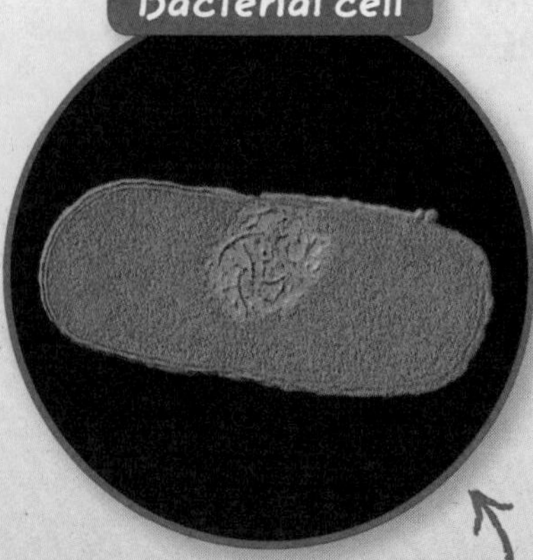

Bacterial cells are up to 1000 times smaller than human cells.

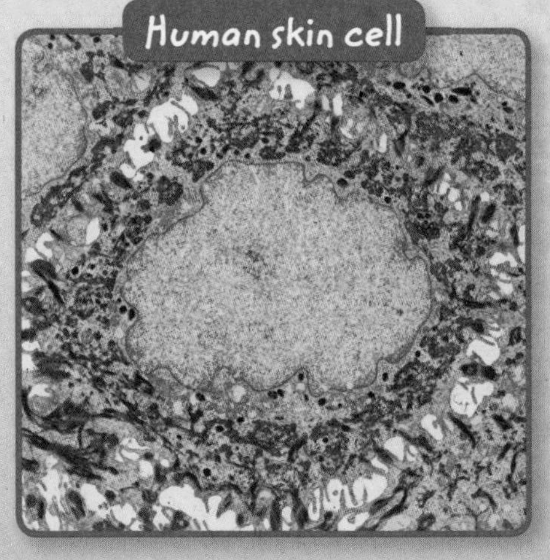

The average size of a human cell is 10 μm. It would take about 50 average human cells to cover the dot on this letter i.

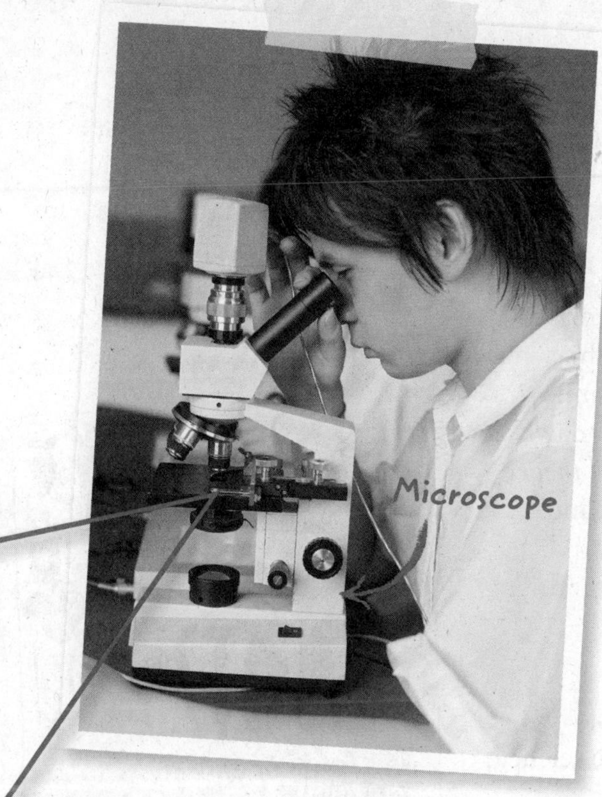

Why are most cells small?

Most cells are too small to be seen without a microscope. Cells are small because their size is limited by their outer surface area. Cells take in food and get rid of wastes through their outer surface. As a cell grows, it needs more food and produces more waste. Therefore, more materials pass through its outer surface. However, as a cell grows, the cell's volume increases faster than the surface area. If a cell gets too large, the cell's surface area will not be large enough to take in enough nutrients or pump out enough wastes. The ratio of the cell's outer surface area to the cell's volume is called the *surface area-to-volume ratio*. Smaller cells have a greater surface area-to-volume ratio than larger cells.

Do the Math

Here's an example of how to calculate the surface area-to-volume ratio of the cube shown at the right.

Sample Problem

A Calculate the surface area.

surface area of cube =

number of faces × area of one face

surface area of cube = 6(2 cm × 2 cm)

surface area of cube = 24 cm^2

B Calculate the volume.

volume of cube = side × side × side

volume of cube = 2 cm × 2 cm × 2 cm

volume of cube = 8 cm^3

C Calculate the surface area-to-volume ratio. A ratio is a comparison between numbers. It can be written by placing a colon between the numbers being compared.

surface area : volume = 24 cm^2 : 8 cm^3

surface area : volume = 3 cm^2 : 1 cm^3

You Try It

7 Calculate What is the surface area-to-volume ratio of a cube whose sides are 3 cm long?

A Calculate the surface area.

B Calculate the volume.

C Calculate the surface area-to-volume ratio.

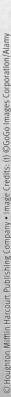

Cell *Hall of Fame*

What is the cell theory?

Scientific knowledge often results from combining the work of several scientists. For example, the discoveries of Matthias Schleiden (muh•THY•uhs SHLY•duhn), Theodor Schwann (THEE•oh•dohr SHVAHN), and Rudolf Virchow (ROO•dawlf VIR•koh) led to one very important theory called the *cell theory*. The cell theory lists three basic characteristics of all cells and organisms:

- All organisms are made up of one or more cells.
- The cell is the basic unit of all organisms.
- All cells come from existing cells.

The cell theory is fundamental to the study of organisms, medicine, heredity, evolution, and all other aspects of life science.

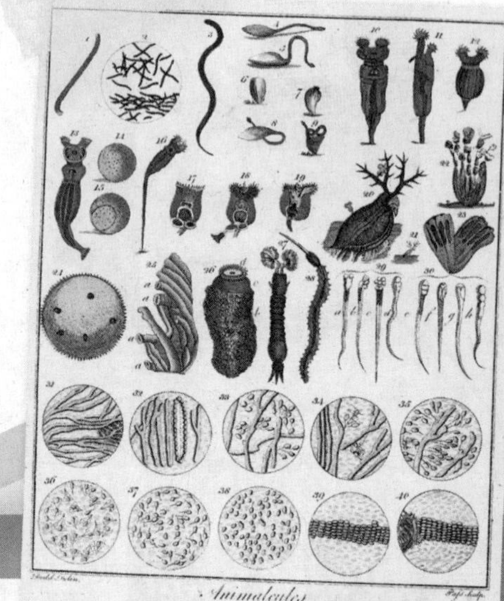

Visualize It!

8 Provide As you read, fill in the missing events on the timeline.

1673
Anton van Leeuwenhoek made careful drawings of the organisms he observed.

Model of Hooke's microscope

1665
Robert Hooke sees tiny, box-like spaces when using a microscope like this to observe thin slices of cork. He calls these spaces cells.

1858
Rudolf Virchow ______________
____
____
____

Think Outside the Book **Inquiry**

9 Explain How can microscopes help you see cells? First, think of a good place to collect a sample of cells. Then, in a paragraph, describe how to prepare a microscope slide to observe those cells.

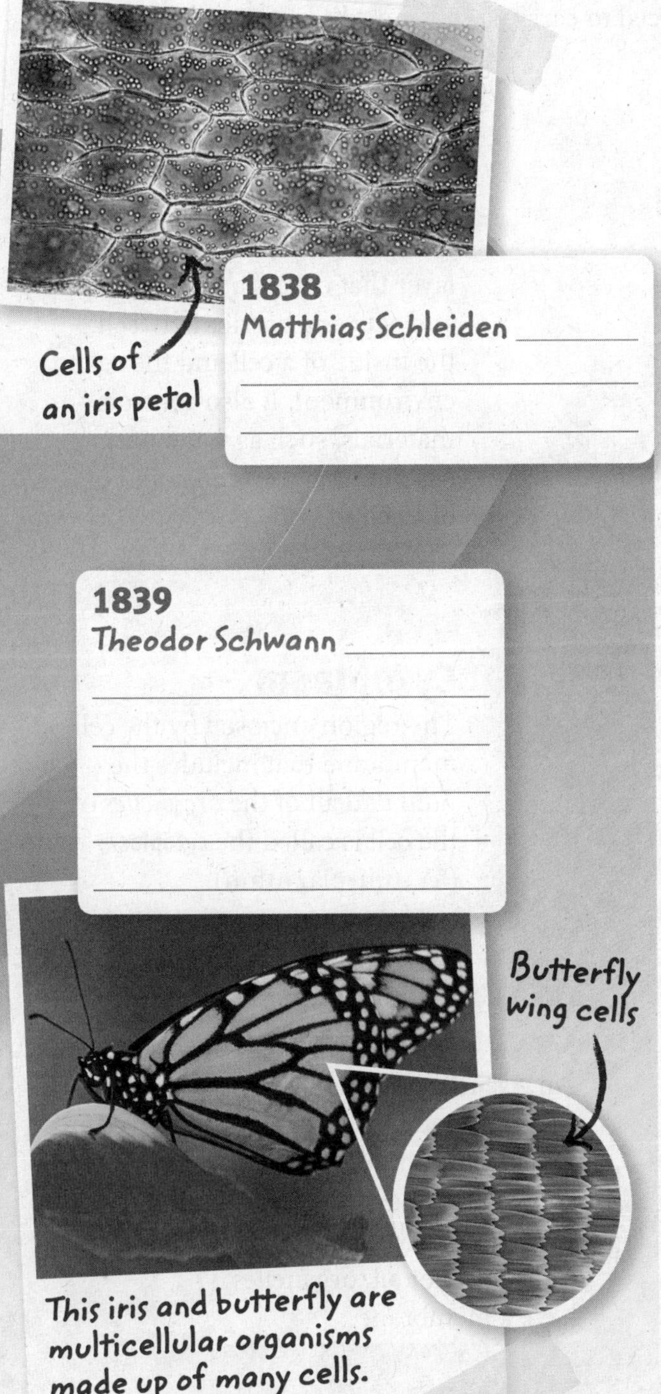

This iris and butterfly are multicellular organisms made up of many cells.

All Organisms Are Made Up of One or More Cells

Anton van Leeuwenhoek (AN•tahn VAN LAY•vuhn•huk) was the first person to describe actual living cells when he looked at a drop of pond water under a microscope. These studies made other scientists wonder if all living things were made up of cells. In 1838, Matthias Schleiden concluded that plants are made of cells. Then in 1839, Theodor Schwann determined that all animal tissues are made of cells. He concluded that all organisms are made up of one or more cells.

Organisms that are made up of just one cell are called *unicellular organisms*. The single cell of a unicellular organism must carry out all of the functions for life. Organisms that are made up of more than one cell are called *multicellular organisms*. The cells of multicellular organism often have specialized functions.

The Cell Is the Basic Unit of All Organisms

Based on his observations about the cellular make up of organisms, Schwann made another conclusion. He determined that the cell is the basic unit of all living things. Thus, Schwann wrote the first two parts of the cell theory.

All Cells Come from Existing Cells

In 1858, Rudolf Virchow, a doctor, proposed that cells could form only from the division of other cells. Virchow then added the third part of the cell theory that all cells come from existing cells.

Active Reading

10 Summarize What is the cell theory?

On the Cellular

What parts do all cells have in common?

Different cells vary in size and shape. However, all cells have some parts in common, including cell membranes, cytoplasm, organelles, and DNA. These different parts help the cell to carry out all the tasks needed for life.

11 Identify As you read, underline the function of cell membranes, organelles, and DNA.

Cell Membrane

A **cell membrane** is a protective layer that covers a cell's surface and acts as a barrier between the inside of a cell and the cell's environment. It also controls materials, such as water and oxygen, that move into and out of a cell.

Cytoplasm

The region enclosed by the cell membrane that includes the fluid and all of the *organelles* of the cell is called the **cytoplasm** (SY•tuh•plaz•uhm).

Organelles

An **organelle** is a small body in a cell's cytoplasm that is specialized to perform a specific function. Cells can have one or more types of organelles. Most, but not all, organelles have a membrane.

DNA

Deoxyribonucleic acid, or DNA, is genetic material that provides instructions for all cell processes. Organisms inherit DNA from their parent or parents. In some cells, the DNA is contained in a membrane-bound organelle called the **nucleus**. In other types of cells, the DNA is not contained in a nucleus.

What are the two types of cells?

Although cells have some basic parts in common, there are some important differences. The way that cells store their DNA is the main difference between the two cell types.

12 Define As you read, underline the differences between prokaryotes and eukaryotes.

Prokaryotic

A **prokaryote** (proh•KAIR•ee•oht) is a single-celled organism that does not have a nucleus or membrane-bound organelles. Its DNA is located in the cytoplasm. Prokaryotic cells contain organelles called *ribosomes* that do not have a membrane. Some prokaryotic cells have hairlike structures called *flagella* that help them move. Prokaryotes, which include all bacteria and archaea, are smaller than eukaryotes.

Eukaryotic

A **eukaryote** (yoo•KAIR•ee•oht) is an organism made up of cells that contain their DNA in a nucleus. Eukaryotic cells contain membrane-bound organelles, as well as ribosomes. Not all eukaryotic cells are the same. Animals, plants, protists, and fungi are eukaryotes. All multicellular organisms are eukaryotes. Most eukaryotes are multicellular. Some eukaryotes, such as amoebas and yeasts, are unicellular.

Visualize It!

13 Identify Use the list of terms below to fill in the blanks with the matching cell parts in each cell. Some terms are used twice.

DNA in cytoplasm
DNA in nucleus
Cytoplasm
Cell membrane
Organelles

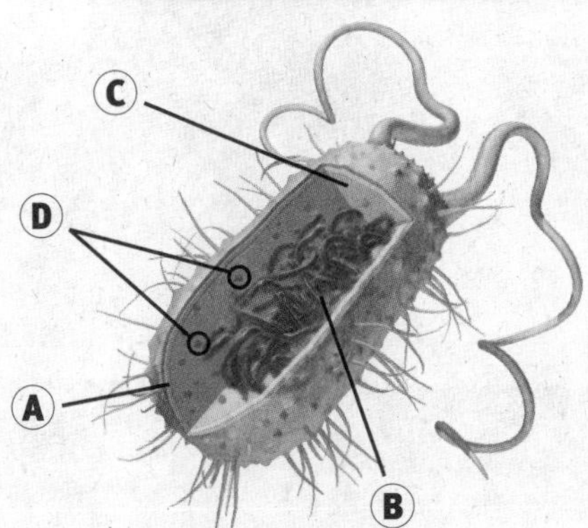

Prokaryotic

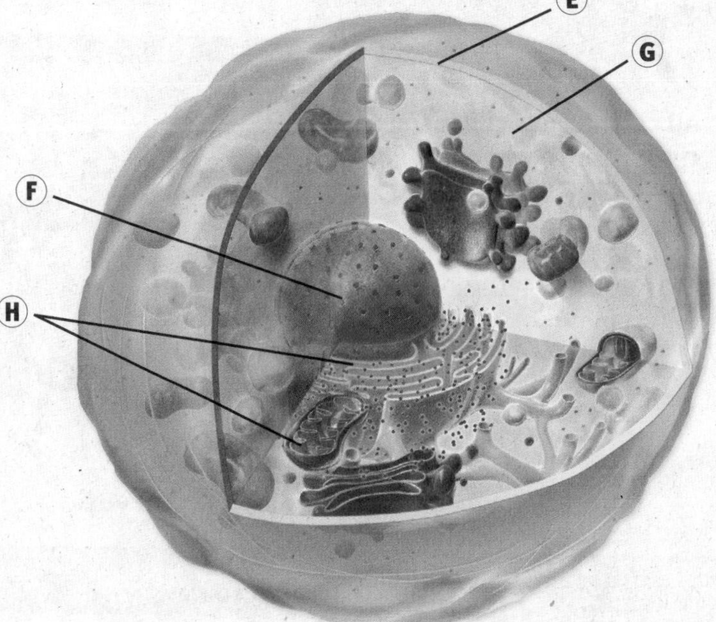

Eukaryotic

A ________________

B ________________

C ________________

D ________________

E ________________

F DNA in nucleus

G ________________

H ________________

Visual Summary

To complete this summary, fill in the blanks with the correct word or phrase. Then use the key below to check your answers. You can use this page to review the main concepts of the lesson.

Cells and Cell Theory

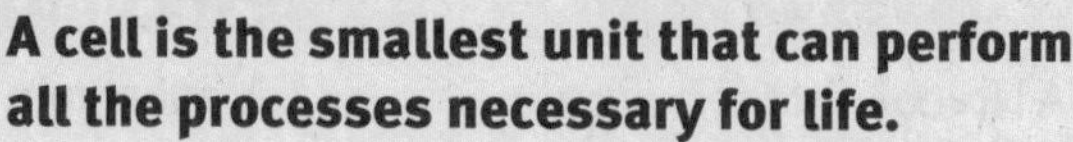

A cell is the smallest unit that can perform all the processes necessary for life.

14 The cell of a ________________ organism must carry out all of its life functions; an organism made up of more than one cell is called a ________________ organism.

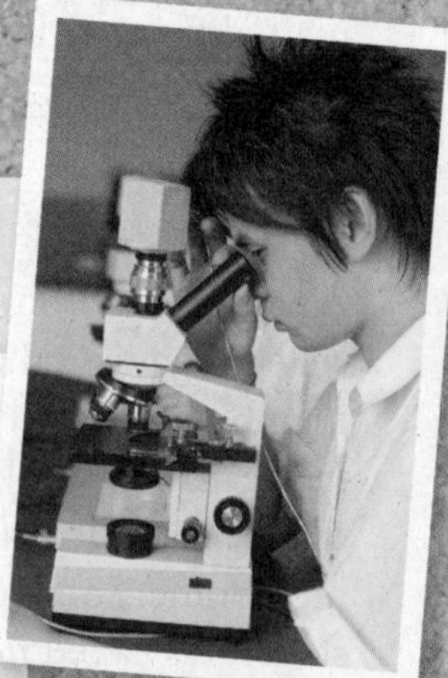

The cell theory lists three basic principles of all cells and organisms.

15 All cells come from existing ________________

All cells have a cell membrane, cytoplasm, organelles, and DNA.

16 The organelle that contains DNA in eukaryotic cells is called a ________________

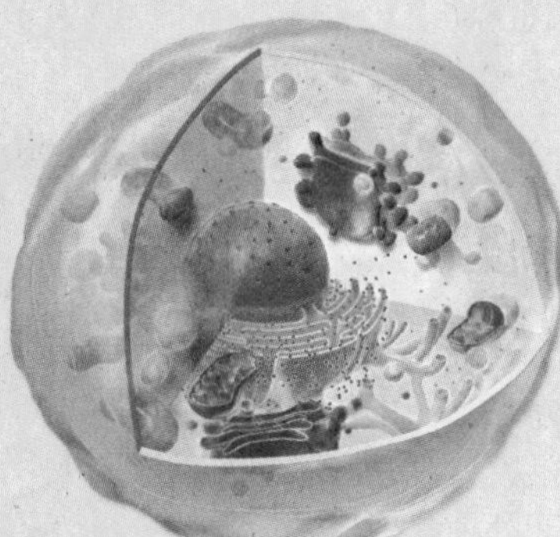

Eukaryotic

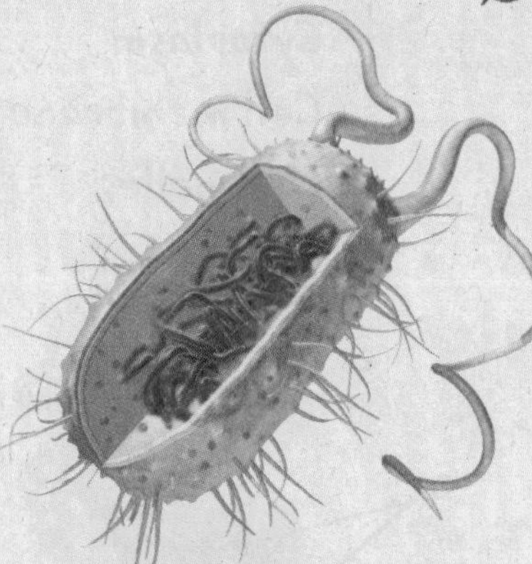

Prokaryotic

Answers: 14 unicellular, multicellular; 15 cells; 16 nucleus

17 Relate Choose an organism that you are familiar with, and explain how the three parts of the cell theory relate to that organism.

Lesson Review

Vocabulary

Fill in the blank with the term that best completes the following sentences.

1 The ______________________ is the smallest functional and structural unit of all living things.

2 All cells are surrounded by a(n) ______________________

3 A living thing is called a(n) ______________________

Key Concepts

4 Describe Discuss two ways that all cells are alike.

5 List What are the main ideas of the cell theory?

6 Compare How do prokaryotes differ from eukaryotes? How are they similar?

Critical Thinking

Use this figure to answer the following questions.

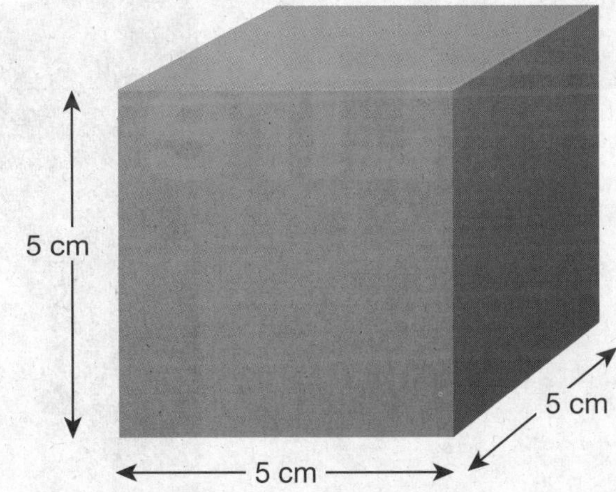

7 Apply What is the surface area-to-volume ratio of this cube?

8 Apply Cells are not as large as this cube. Explain why in terms of a cell's surface area-to-volume ratio.

9 Compare How is the structure of a unicellular organism different than the structure of a multicellular organism? How does this affect function?

Lesson 2

Chemistry of Life

ESSENTIAL QUESTION

What are the building blocks of organisms?

By the end of this lesson, you should be able to discuss the chemical makeup of living things.

Sunshine State Standards

SC.6.N.1.1 Define a problem from the sixth grade curriculum, use appropriate reference materials to support scientific understanding, plan and carry out scientific investigation of various types, such as systematic observations or experiments, identify variables, collect and organize data, interpret data in charts, tables, and graphics, analyze information, make predictions, and defend conclusions.

SC.6.L.14.1 Describe and identify patterns in the hierarchical organization of organisms from atoms to molecules and cells to tissues to organs to organ systems to organisms.

LA.6.4.2.2 The student will record information (e.g., observations, notes, lists, charts, legends) related to a topic, including visual aids to organize and record information and include a list of sources used.

These fungi are bioluminescent, which means they produce light from chemical reactions in their bodies. The light attracts insects that disperse the fungi's spores.

Engage Your Brain

1 Describe Fill in the blank with the word or phrase that you think correctly completes the following sentences.

The chemical formula for ______________

is H_2O. The *H* stands for hydrogen and the

______________ stands for oxygen.

If you don't get enough water, you might

____

____

2 Relate What do you think you are made of?

____

____

____

____

____

Active Reading

3 Synthesize You can often define an unknown word if you know the meaning of its word parts. Use the word parts and sentence below to make an educated guess about the meaning of the word *atom*.

Word part	Meaning
a–	not
tom	to cut

Example sentence
Air is mostly made up of oxygen and nitrogen <u>atoms</u>.

atom:

____

____

Vocabulary Terms

- atom
- molecule
- lipid
- protein
- carbohydrate
- nucleic acid
- phospholipid

4 Identify This list contains the key terms you'll learn in this lesson. As you read, circle the definition of each term.

It's Elementary

What are atoms and molecules?

Think about where you live. The streets are lined with many types of buildings. But these buildings are made from a lot of the same materials, such as bricks, glass, wood, and steel. Similarly, all cells are made from the same materials. The materials in cells are made up of atoms that can join together to form molecules.

Atoms Are the Building Blocks of Matter

The matter that you encounter every day, both living and nonliving, is made up of basic particles called **atoms.** Not all atoms are the same. There are nearly one hundred types of atoms that occur naturally on Earth. These different types of atoms are known as *elements.* Each element has unique properties. For example, oxygen is a colorless gas made up of oxygen atoms. The element gold is a shiny metal made up of gold atoms. Just six elements make up most of the human body. These and other elements are important for cell processes in all living things.

Active Reading

5 Relate How do atoms relate to cells?

____

____

____

____

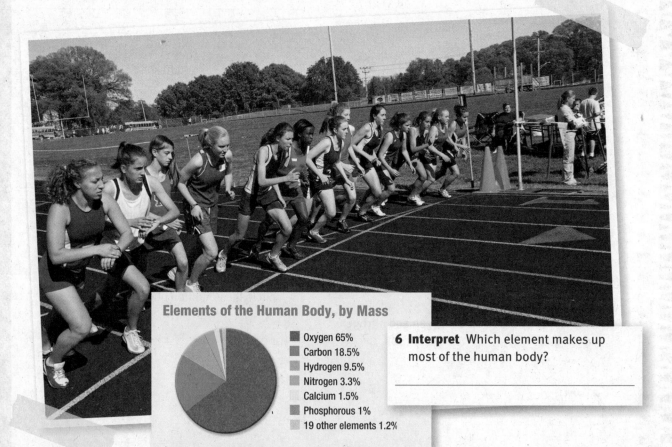

Elements of the Human Body, by Mass

- Oxygen 65%
- Carbon 18.5%
- Hydrogen 9.5%
- Nitrogen 3.3%
- Calcium 1.5%
- Phosphorous 1%
- 19 other elements 1.2%

6 Interpret Which element makes up most of the human body?

____

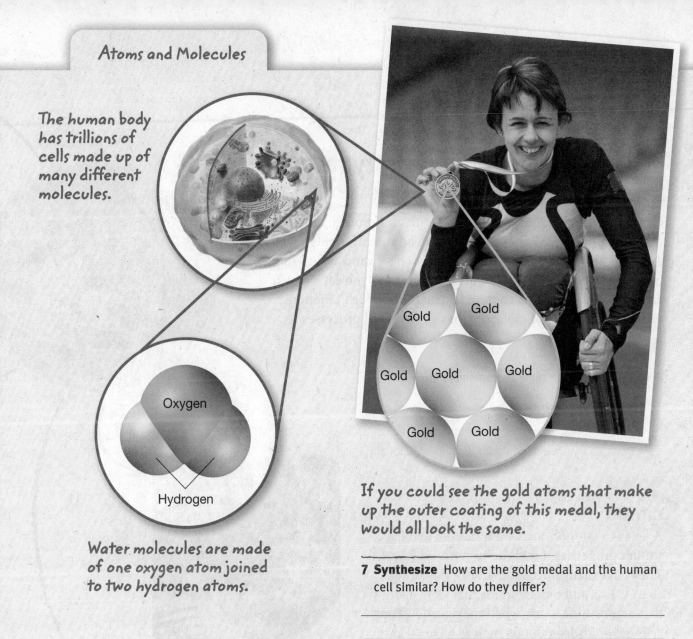

Atoms and Molecules

The human body has trillions of cells made up of many different molecules.

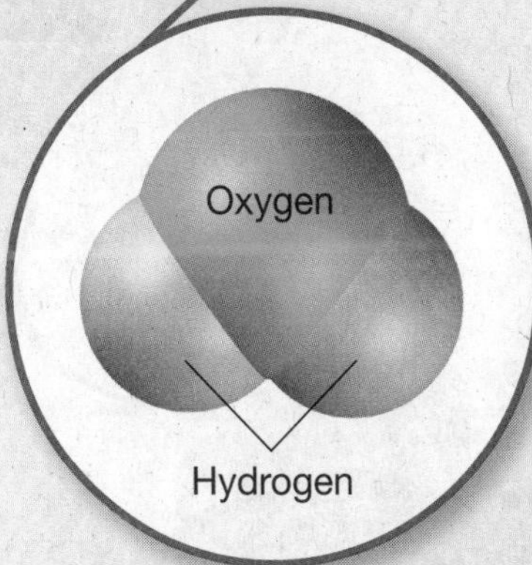

Oxygen

Hydrogen

Water molecules are made of one oxygen atom joined to two hydrogen atoms.

Gold
Gold
Gold
Gold
Gold
Gold
Gold

If you could see the gold atoms that make up the outer coating of this medal, they would all look the same.

7 Synthesize How are the gold medal and the human cell similar? How do they differ?

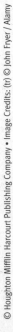

____

____

____

Molecules Are Made of Two or More Atoms

A **molecule** is a group of atoms that are held together by chemical bonds. For example, the molecule of water shown above is made of one oxygen atom bonded to two hydrogen atoms. If you separated the oxygen and hydrogen atoms, then you would no longer have a water molecule.

Some molecules are made up of only one type of atom. For example, a molecule of oxygen gas is made of two oxygen atoms. Other molecules contain different types of atoms. A substance made up of atoms of two or more elements joined by chemical bonds is called a *compound*. Most of the molecules found in cells are also compounds.

Cell Fuel

What are some important types of molecules in cells?

Organisms need certain types of molecules for growth, repair, and other life processes. For example, organisms use nutrients such as lipids, proteins, and carbohydrates for energy and as building materials. You get these nutrients from the food you eat. Nucleic acids are molecules that contain instructions for cell functions. Each of these types of molecules has a role in cell processes.

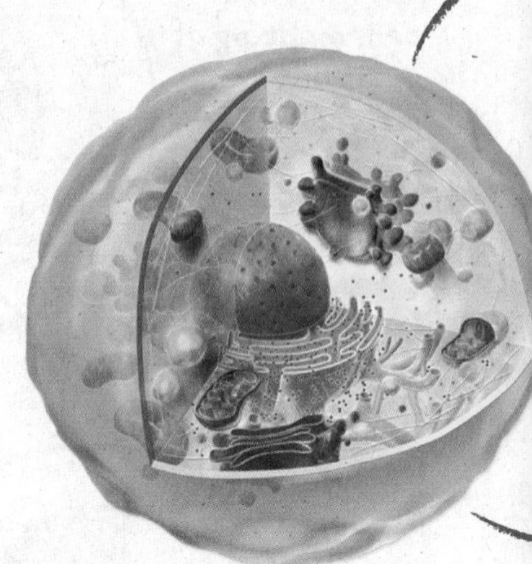

8 Identify What are some examples of nutrients?

____

____

____

Lipids

A **lipid** is a fat molecule or a molecule that has similar properties. Lipids do not mix with water. They have many jobs in cells, such as storing energy. Fats and oils are lipids that store energy that organisms can use when they need it. Your cells get lipids from foods such as olive oil and fish. Waxes and steroids are other types of lipids.

Proteins

A **protein** is a molecule made up of smaller molecules called *amino acids*. When you eat foods high in proteins, such as peanut butter and meat, the proteins are broken down into amino acids. Amino acids are used to make new proteins. Proteins are used to build and repair body structures and to regulate body processes. Proteins called *enzymes* (EHN•zymz) help chemical processes happen in cells.

9 Describe What are the building blocks of proteins?

____

Carbohydrates

Molecules that include sugars, starches, and fiber are called **carbohydrates**. Cells use carbohydrates as a source of energy and for energy storage. Cells break down carbohydrates to release the energy stored in them. Carbohydrates contain carbon, hydrogen, and oxygen atoms. Simple carbohydrates, such as table sugar, are made up of one sugar molecule or a few sugar molecules linked together. Complex carbohydrates, such as starch, are made of many sugar molecules linked together. Pasta, made from grains, is a good source of complex carbohydrates.

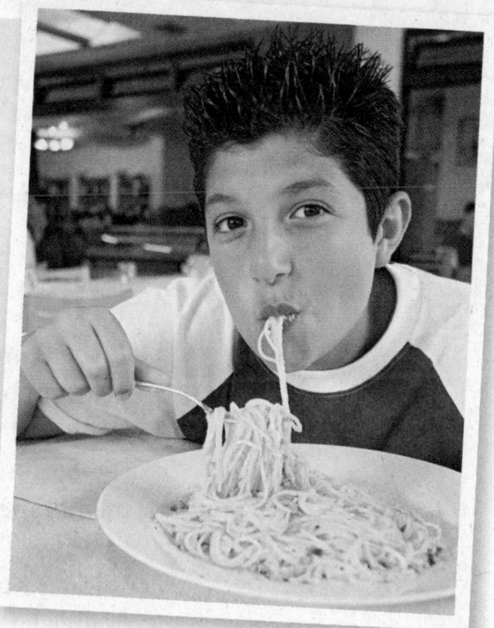

Nucleic Acids

A **nucleic acid** is a molecule that carries information in cells. Nucleic acids are made up of smaller molecules called *nucleotides* (NOO•klee•oh•TYDZ). Deoxyribonucleic acid, or DNA, is one type of nucleic acid that is found in all cells. DNA contains the information that cells need to make molecules, such as proteins. The order of nucleotides in DNA reads like a recipe. Each nucleotide tells the cell the order of amino acids needed to build a certain protein.

DNA

10 Summarize Fill in the table with a function of each nutrient in the cell.

Nutrient	Function in the cell
Lipids	
Proteins	
Carbohydrates	
Nucleic acids	

Waterworks

What are phospholipids?

All cells are surrounded by a cell membrane. The cell membrane helps protect the cell and keep the internal conditions of the cell stable. A lipid that contains phosphorus is called a **phospholipid** (FOSS•foh•LIH•pyd). Phospholipids form much of the cell membrane. The head of a phospholipid molecule is attracted to water. The tail repels water, or pushes it away. Because there is water inside and outside the cell, the phospholipids form a double layer. One layer lines up so that the heads face the outside of the cell. A second layer of phospholipids line up so the heads face the inside of the cell. The tails from both layers face each other, forming the middle of the cell membrane. Molecules, such as water, are regulated into and out of a cell through the cell membrane.

Active Reading **11 Explain** Describe how phospholipids form a barrier between water inside the cell and water outside the cell.

____

____

____

____

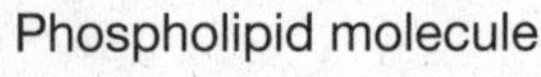

12 Identify Write *attracts* next to the end of the phospholipid that attracts water. Write *repels* next to the end that repels water.

Phospholipid molecule

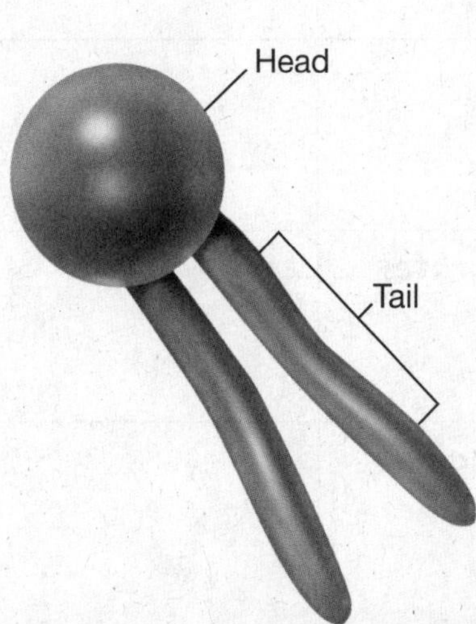

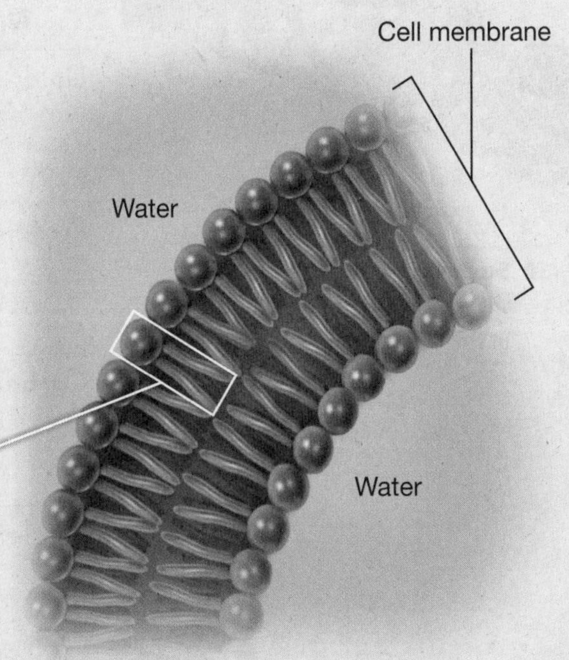

Why is water important?

Many cell processes require water, which makes up nearly two-thirds of the mass of the cell. Thus, water is an important nutrient for life. Water moves through the cell membrane by a process called *osmosis*. Osmosis depends on the concentration of the water inside and outside of the cell. Pure water has the highest concentration of water molecules. If the water concentration inside the cell is lower than the water concentration outside the cell, then water will move into the cell. If the environment outside a cell has a low concentration of water, such as in a salty solution, water will move out of the cell.

Think Outside the Book Inquiry

14 Associate Think of an object that could be an analogy to the cell membrane. Draw a picture of the object and explain how it is similar to and different from a cell membrane.

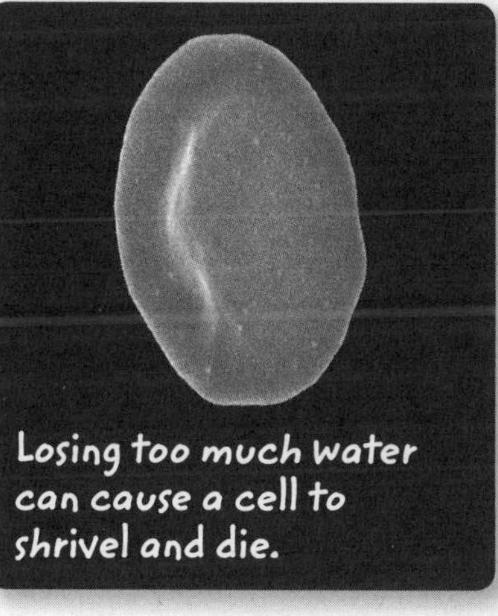
Losing too much water can cause a cell to shrivel and die.

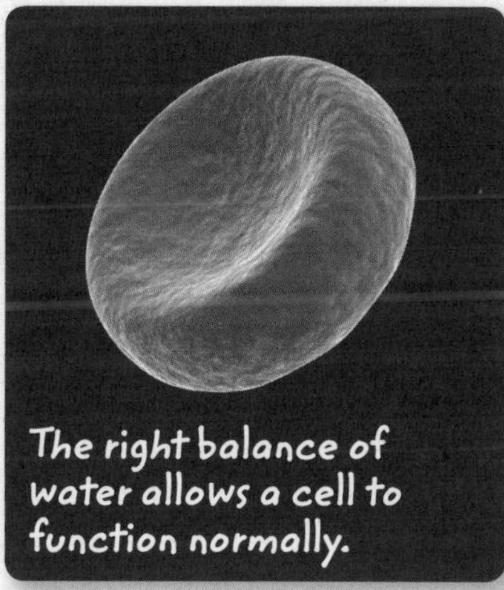
The right balance of water allows a cell to function normally.

If too much water enters a cell, it may swell up and burst.

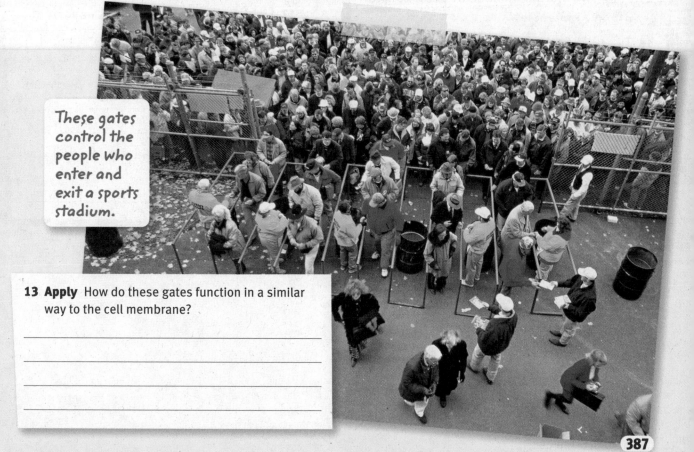

These gates control the people who enter and exit a sports stadium.

13 Apply How do these gates function in a similar way to the cell membrane?

Visual Summary

To complete this summary, circle the correct word and fill in the blanks with the correct word or phrase. Then, use the key below to check your answers. You can use this page to review the main concepts of the lesson.

Cell Chemistry

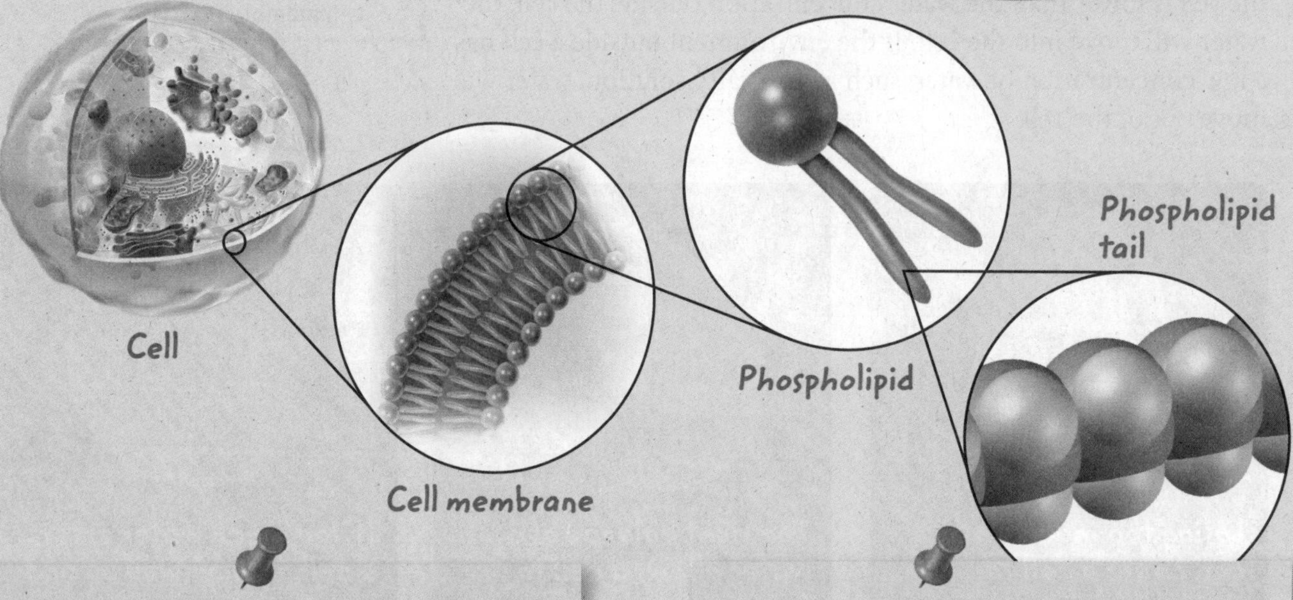

Cells are made up of atoms and molecules.

15 A cell membrane is made of phospholipid atoms / molecules.

16 The tail of the phospholipid is made up of carbon and hydrogen atoms / molecules.

Cells use different molecules for life processes.

17 List four types of molecules important for cell processes.

____

____

____

____

18 Water moves into and out of a cell through the

____

Answers: 15 molecules; 16 atoms; 17 lipids, carbohydrates, proteins, nucleic acids; 18 cell membrane

19 Relate Explain how atoms and molecules are important to cell processes.

Lesson Review

Vocabulary

Fill in the blank with the term that best completes the following sentences.

1 The smallest unit of an element is a(n) ____________________

2 A(n) ____________________ is a group of atoms joined by chemical bonds.

Key Concepts

3 Contrast What is the difference between atoms and molecules?

4 Identify What are the functions of proteins in organisms?

5 List Name four important types of molecules found in cells.

6 Describe How does the structure of the cell membrane help the cell regulate water?

Critical Thinking

Use this diagram to answer the following questions.

7 Identify Is this an atom or a molecule? Explain.

8 Recognize The red spheres represent oxygen atoms, and the blue spheres represent hydrogen atoms. Is this substance a compound? Explain.

9 Summarize Why is water important in cells?

Lesson 3

Cell Structure and Function

ESSENTIAL QUESTION

What are the different parts that make up a cell?

By the end of this lesson, you should be able to compare the structure and function of cell parts in plant and animal cells.

Cells have many parts. This part is called a Golgi complex. It functions like a shipping facility, packaging and distributing proteins and other materials for use in the cell.

Sunshine State Standards

SC.6.L.14.4 Compare and contrast the structure and function of major organelles of plant and animal cells, including cell wall, cell membrane, nucleus, cytoplasm, chloroplasts, mitochondria, and vacuoles.

Engage Your Brain

1 Predict Check T or F to show whether you think each statement is true or false.

T	F	
☐	☐	All cells have the same structure and function.
☐	☐	Prokaryotes do not have a nucleus.
☐	☐	Plant cells are the same as animal cells.
☐	☐	All organisms are multicellular.

2 Relate How does the structure of this umbrella relate to its function?

Active Reading

3 Synthesis You can often define an unknown word if you know the meaning of its word parts. Use the word parts and sentence below to make an educated guess about the meaning of the word *chloroplast*.

Word part	Meaning
chloro-	green
plast	structure

Example sentence
Plant cells have chloroplasts, which contain a green pigment used for making their own food.

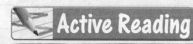

chloroplast:

Vocabulary Terms

- cytoskeleton
- mitochondrion
- ribosome
- endoplasmic reticulum
- Golgi complex
- cell wall
- vacuole
- chloroplast
- lysosome

4 Apply As you learn the definition of each vocabulary term in this lesson, create your own definition or sketch to help you remember the meaning of the term.

Being Eu-nique

What are the characteristics of eukaryotic cells?

Active Reading

5 Identify As you read, underline the characteristics of eukaryotic cells.

All organisms are made up of one or more cells, but what kinds of cells? There are two types of organisms: prokaryotes and eukaryotes. Prokaryotes are made up of a single prokaryotic cell. Eukaryotes are made up of one or more eukaryotic cells. Prokaryotic cells do not have a nucleus or membrane-bound organelles. Eukaryotic cells have membrane-bound organelles, including a nucleus.

Eukaryotic cells can differ from each other depending on their *structure* and *function*. A cell's structure is the arrangement of its parts. A cell's function is the activity the parts carry out. For example, plant cells and animal cells have different parts that have different functions for the organism. This is what make plants and animals so different from each other. Even cells within the same organism can differ from each other depending on their function. Most of the cells in multicellular organisms are specialized to perform a specific function. However, all eukaryotic cells share some characteristics. They all have a nucleus, membrane-bound organelles, and parts that protect and support the cell.

Visualize It!

6 Apply A euglena is a unicellular organism. Why is it a eukaryote like the plant and animal cells shown here?

______

______

______

______

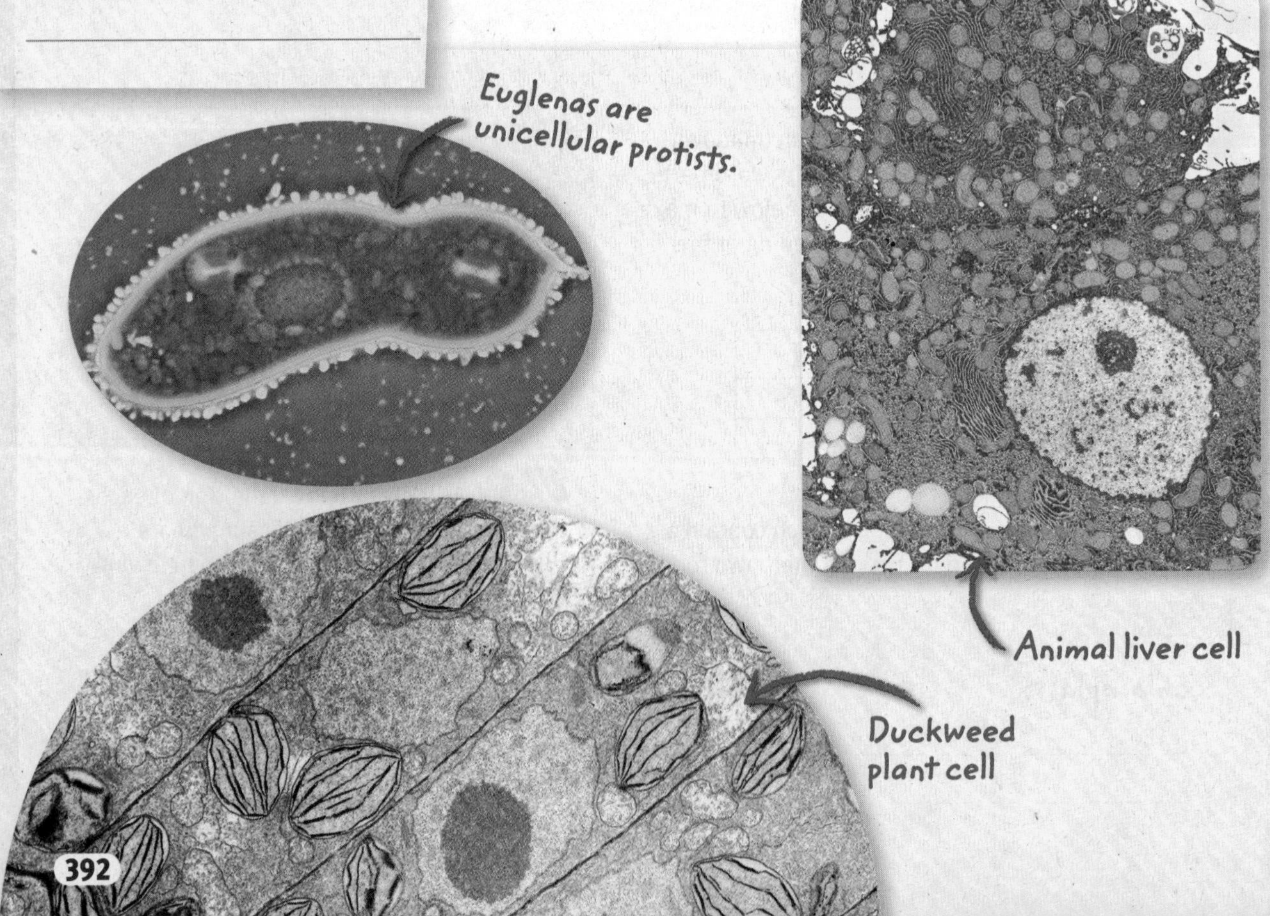

Parts that Protect and Support the Cell

Every cell is surrounded by a cell membrane. The cell membrane acts as a barrier between the inside of a cell and the cell's environment. The cell membrane protects the cell and regulates what enters and leaves the cell.

The cytoplasm is the region between the cell membrane and the nucleus that includes fluid and all of the organelles. Throughout the cytoplasm of eukaryotic cells is a **cytoskeleton**. The cytoskeleton is a network of protein filaments that gives shape and support to cells. The cytoskeleton is also involved in cell division and in movement. It may help parts within the cell to move. Or it may form structures that help the whole organism to move.

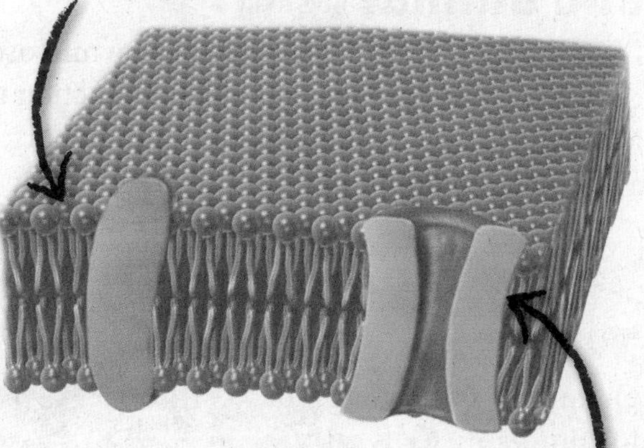

The cell membrane is a double layer of phospholipids. Water molecules and some gas molecules can pass through the cell membrane.
Other larger materials must pass through protein channels in the membrane.

7 Describe What are two functions of the cell membrane?

Genetic Material in the Nucleus

The nucleus is an organelle in eukaryotic cells that contains the cell's genetic material. Deoxyribonucleic acid, or DNA, is stored in the nucleus. DNA is genetic material that contains information needed for cell processes, such as making proteins. Proteins perform most actions of a cell. Although DNA is found in the nucleus, proteins are not made there. Instead, instructions for how to make proteins are stored in DNA. These instructions are sent out of the nucleus through pores in the nuclear membrane. The nuclear membrane is a double layer. Each layer is similar in structure to the cell membrane.

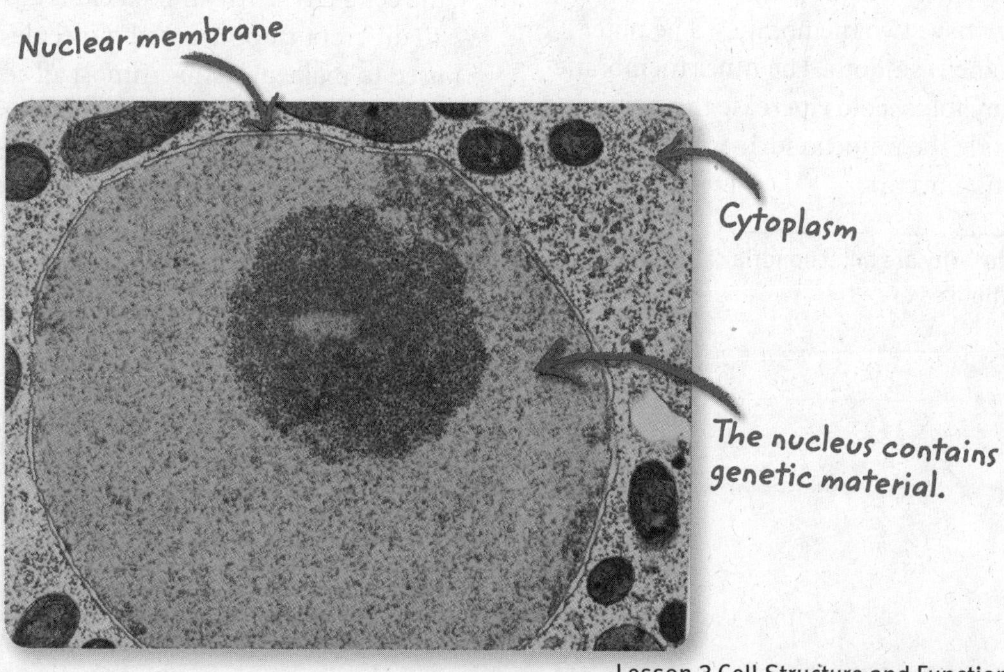

Part-iculars

What organelles are found in plant and animal cells?

Even though plant and animal cells are microscopic, they are very complex. They have many parts that function to keep the cell alive. Many of these parts are membrane-bound organelles that perform a specific function.

Mitochondria

Organisms need energy for life processes. Cells carry out such processes for growth and repair, movement of materials into and out of the cell, and chemical processes. Cells get energy by breaking down food using a process called *cellular respiration.* Cellular respiration occurs in an organelle called the **mitochondrion** (my•TOH•kahn•dree•ahn). In cellular respiration, cells use oxygen to release energy stored in food. For example, cells break down the sugar glucose to release the energy stored in the sugar. The mitochondria then transfer the energy released from the sugar to a molecule called adenosine triphosphate, or ATP. Cells use ATP to carry out cell processes.

Mitochondria have their own DNA and they have two membranes. The outer membrane is smooth. The inner membrane has many folds. Folds increase the surface area inside the mitochondria where cellular respiration occurs.

8 Explain Why are mitochondria called the powerhouses of cells?

____

____

____

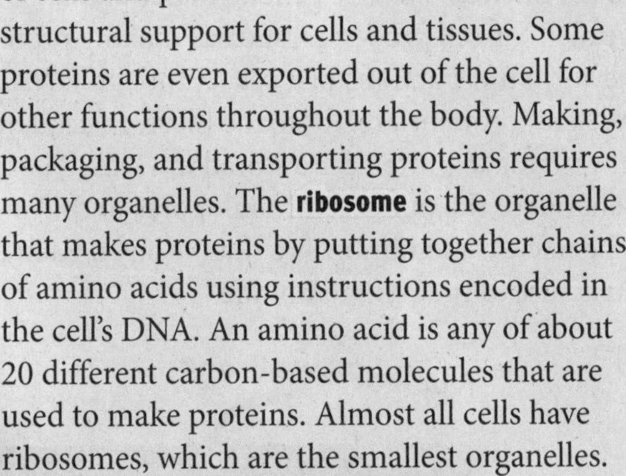

Ribosomes

Proteins control most chemical reactions of cells and provide structural support for cells and tissues. Some proteins are even exported out of the cell for other functions throughout the body. Making, packaging, and transporting proteins requires many organelles. The **ribosome** is the organelle that makes proteins by putting together chains of amino acids using instructions encoded in the cell's DNA. An amino acid is any of about 20 different carbon-based molecules that are used to make proteins. Almost all cells have ribosomes, which are the smallest organelles.

Ribosomes are not enclosed in a membrane. In prokaryotes, the ribosomes are suspended freely in the cytoplasm. In eukaryotes, some ribosomes are free, and others are attached to another organelle called the *endoplasmic reticulum.*

9 Describe How do ribosomes make proteins?

____

____

____

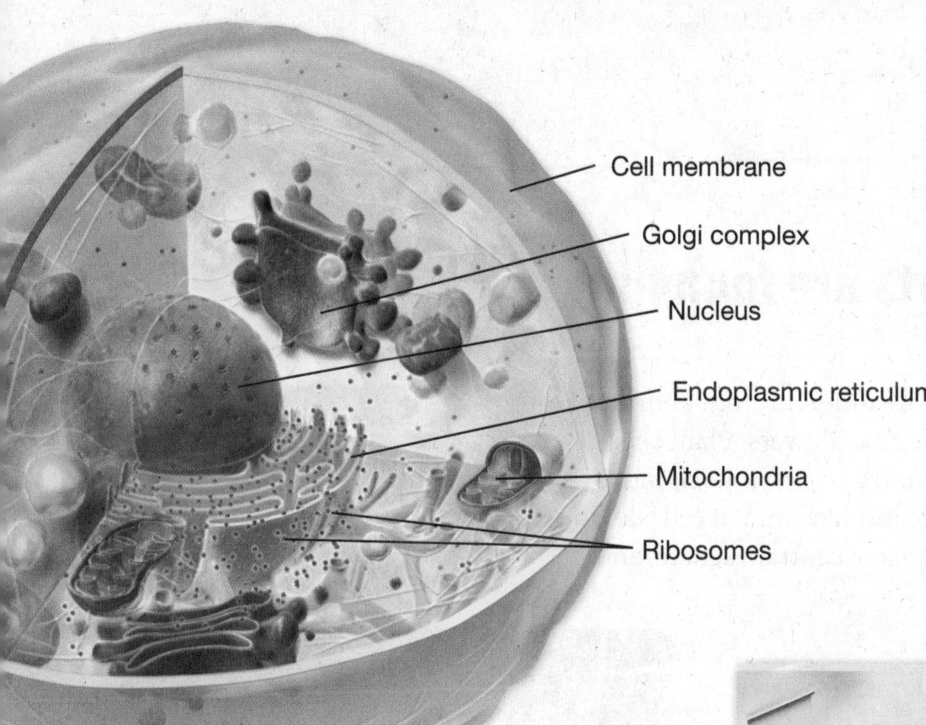

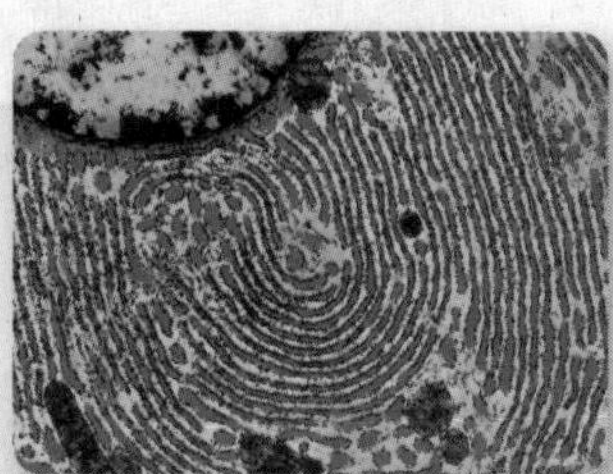

Endoplasmic Reticulum

In the cytoplasm is a system of membranes near the nucleus called the **endoplasmic reticulum** (ehn•doh•PLAHZ•mick rhett•ICK•yoo•luhm), or ER. The ER assists in the production, processing, and transport of proteins and in the production of lipids. The ER is either smooth or rough. Rough ER has ribosomes attached to its membrane, while smooth ER does not. Ribosomes on the rough ER make many of the cell's proteins. Some of these proteins move through the ER to different places in the cell. The smooth ER makes lipids and breaks down toxic materials that could damage the cell.

10 Compare How does rough ER differ from smooth ER in structure and function?

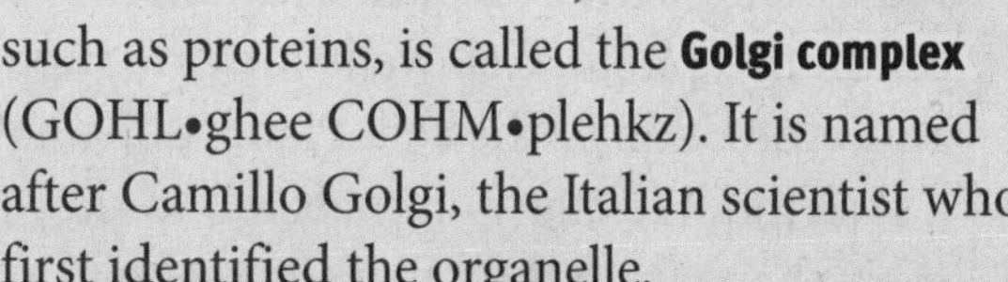

Golgi Complex

The membrane-bound organelle that packages and distributes materials, such as proteins, is called the **Golgi complex** (GOHL•ghee COHM•plehkz). It is named after Camillo Golgi, the Italian scientist who first identified the organelle.

The Golgi complex is a system of flattened membrane sacs. Lipids and proteins from the ER are delivered to the Golgi complex where they may be modified to do different jobs. The final products are enclosed in a piece of the Golgi complex's membrane. This membrane pinches off to form a small bubble, or vesicle. The vesicle transports its contents to other parts of the cell or out of the cell.

11 Describe What is the function of the Golgi complex?

Now Showing:

The Plant Cell

What additional parts are found in plant cells?

Think about some ways that plants are different from animals. Plants don't move around, and some have flowers. Plant cells do have a cell membrane, cytoskeleton, nucleus, mitochondria, ribosomes, ER, and a Golgi complex just like animal cells do. In addition, plant cells have a cell wall, large central vacuole, and chloroplasts.

12 Identify As you read, underline the functions of the cell wall, large central vacuole, and the chloroplasts.

Cell Wall

In addition to the cell membrane, plant cells have a **cell wall**. The cell wall is a rigid structure that surrounds the cell membrane, identified by the yellow line around the plant cell in this photo. Cell walls provide support and protection to the cell. Plants don't have a skeleton like many animals do, so they get their shape from the cell wall. The cells of fungi, archaea, bacteria, and some protists also have cell walls.

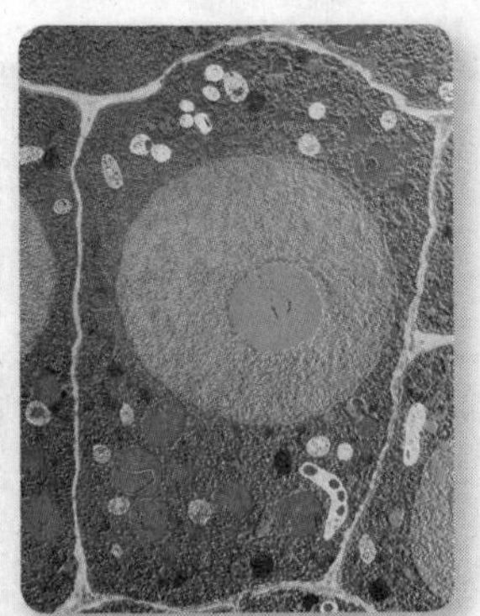

Large Central Vacuole

A **vacuole** (VAK•yoo•ohl) is a fluid-filled vesicle found in the cells of most animals, plants, and fungi. A vacuole may contain enzymes, nutrients, water, or wastes. Plant cells also have a large central vacuole that stores water. Central vacuoles full of water help support the cell. Plants may wilt when the central vacuole loses water.

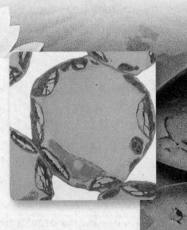

13 Compare How do large central vacuoles differ from vacuoles?

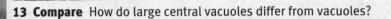

Visualize It!

14 Identify Label these cell parts on the plant cell shown here:

- Mitochondrion
- Golgi complex
- Nucleus
- Endoplasmic reticulum
- Ribosomes
- Cell wall
- Cell membrane
- Cytoskeleton

Large central vacuole

F ______

G ______

A ______

B ______

C ______

D ______

E ______

H ______

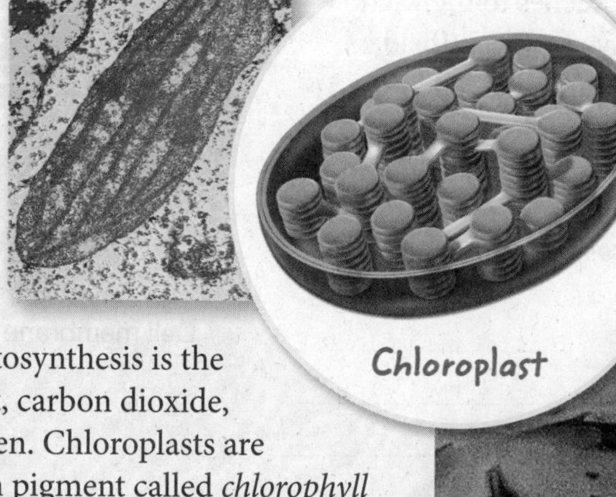

Chloroplast

Chloroplasts

Animals must eat food to provide their cells with energy. However, plants, and some protists, can make their own food using photosynthesis. These organisms have **chloroplasts** (KLOHR•oh•plahstz), organelles where photosynthesis occurs. Photosynthesis is the process by which cells use sunlight, carbon dioxide, and water to make sugar and oxygen. Chloroplasts are green because they contain a green pigment called *chlorophyll* (KLOHR•oh•fill). Chlorophyll absorbs the energy in sunlight. This energy is used to make sugar, which is then used by mitochondria to make ATP. Chloroplasts have two outer membranes.

15 Describe What is the role of chlorophyll inside chloroplasts?

______

______

______

Think Outside the Book *Inquiry*

16 Describe Cyanobacteria and green algae are similar to plants. Choose one of these organisms and explain why they are similar to plants but are not classified as plants.

Introducing:

The Animal Cell

What additional part is found in animal cells?

Animal cells are eukaryotic cells that contain a nucleus and are surrounded by a cell membrane. They contain many of the same organelles as most plant cells, including mitochondria, ribosomes, ER, and a Golgi complex. Most animal cells also contain a membrane-bound organelle called a *lysosome*.

Active Reading **17 Recognize** As you read, underline the function of lysosomes.

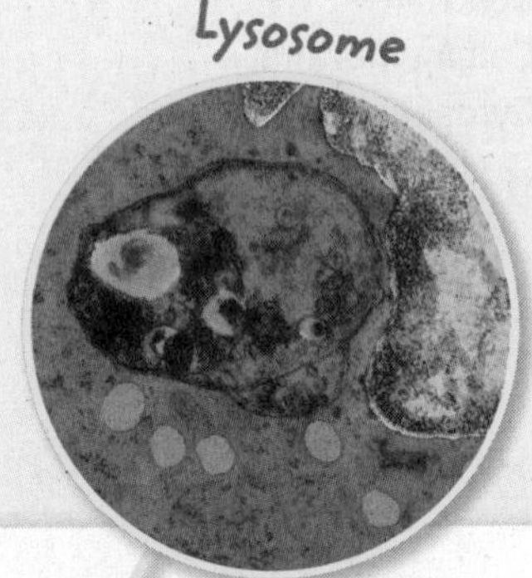

Lysosomes

Organelles called **lysosomes** (LY•soh•zohmz) contain digestive enzymes, which break down worn-out or damaged organelles, waste materials, and foreign invaders in the cell. Some of these materials are collected in vacuoles. A lysosome attaches to the vacuole and releases the digestive enzymes inside. Some of these materials are recycled and reused in the cell. For example, a human liver cell recycles half of its materials each week.

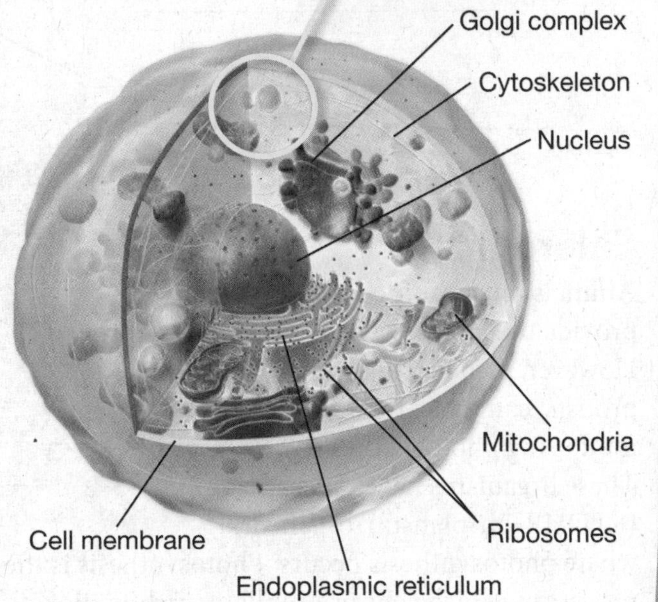

18 Compare How are lysosomes similar to vacuoles?

____

____

____

____

19 Compare Draw a sketch for each organelle identified in the *Structure* column. Put check marks in the last two columns to identify whether the cell structure can usually be found in plant cells, animal cells, or both.

Structure	Function	In plant cell?	In animal cell?
Nucleus	Contains the genetic material		
Endoplasmic reticulum	Processes and transports proteins and makes lipids		
Golgi complex	Packages and distributes materials within or out of the cell		
Ribosome	Makes proteins		
Chloroplast	Uses sunlight, carbon dioxide, and water to make food by photosynthesis		
Mitochondrion	Breaks down food molecules to release energy by cellular respiration		
Large central vacuole	Stores water and helps give shape to the cell		
Lysosome	Produces enzymes that digest wastes, cell parts, and foreign invaders		

Visual Summary

To complete this summary, fill in the blanks to identify the organelles in each cell. Then, use the key below to check your answers. You can use this page to review the main concepts of the lesson.

Compare Plant Cells and Animal Cells

Structures in plant cells

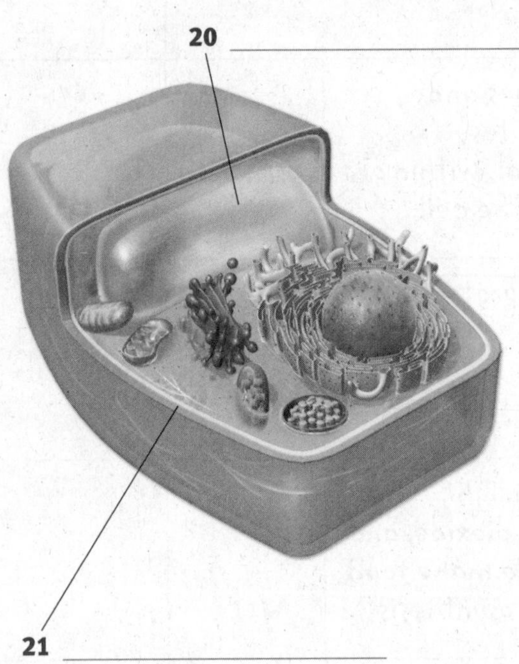

Structures in animal cells

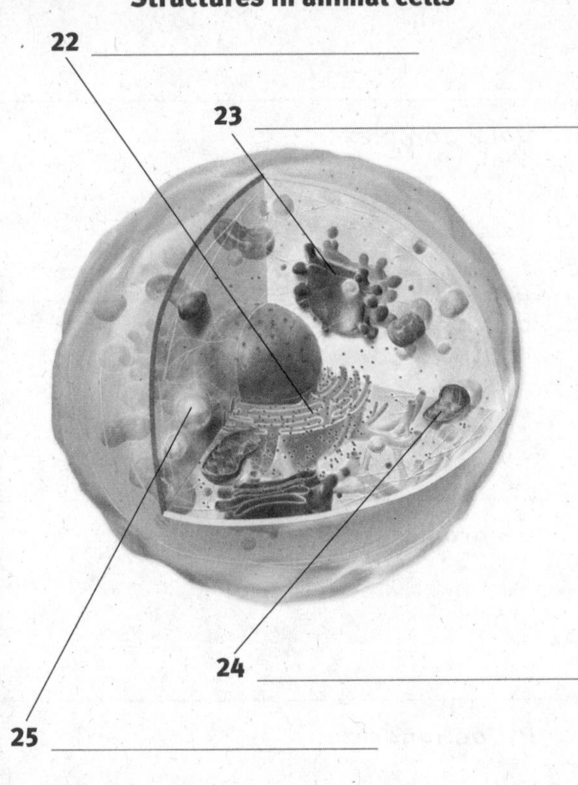

Plants and animals are eukaryotes. The structures inside a eukaryotic cell work together to keep the cell and the entire organism alive.

Answers: 20 large central vacuole; 21 cell wall; 22 endoplasmic reticulum; 23 Golgi complex; 24 mitochondrion; 25 lysosome

26 Summarize How do eukaryotic cells differ from each other?

Lesson Review

Vocabulary

Circle the term that best completes the following sentences.

1 A *Golgi complex* / *ribosome* makes proteins that are transported through the endoplasmic reticulum.

2 The *nucleus* / *large central vacuole* contains genetic material of a eukaryotic cell.

3 The *cell membrane* / *cytoplasm* acts as a barrier between the inside of a cell and the cell's environment.

4 The organelle in which photosynthesis takes place is the *cell wall* / *chloroplast*.

Key Concepts

5 Recognize What do all eukaryotic cells have in common?

6 Compare How are the functions of the cytoskeleton and the cell wall similar?

7 Contrast What structures are found in plant cells that are not found in animal cells?

Critical Thinking

Use this diagram to answer the following questions.

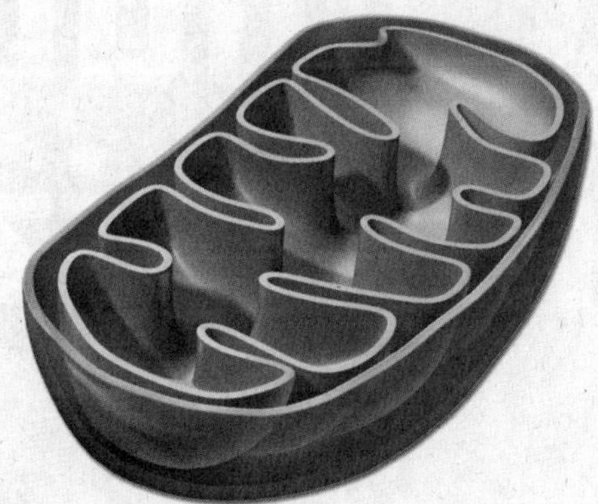

8 Identify What is this organelle?

9 Explain How does its structure affect its function?

10 Compare Which cells contain this organelle: plant cells, animal cells, or both?

11 Apply Explain the function of ribosomes and why cells need them.

Lesson 4

Levels of Cellular Organization

ESSENTIAL QUESTION

How are living things organized?

By the end of this lesson, you should be able to describe the different levels of organization in living things.

Eyes may seem like small and simple body parts, but they are organs made up of millions of cells and many layers of tissues.

Sunshine State Standards

SC.6.L.14.1 Describe and identify patterns in the hierarchical organization of organisms from atoms to molecules and cells to tissues to organs to organ systems to organisms.

LA.6.4.2.2 The student will record information (e.g., observations, notes, lists, charts, legends) related to a topic, including visual aids to organize and record information and include a list of sources used.

Engage Your Brain

1 Describe Fill in the blank with the word or phrase that you think correctly completes the following sentences.

Your body has many organs, such as a heart and ____________

Plant organs include stems and ____________

Animal and plant organs are organized into organ systems, much like you organize your homework in ____________

2 Explain How is the structure of a hammer related to its function?

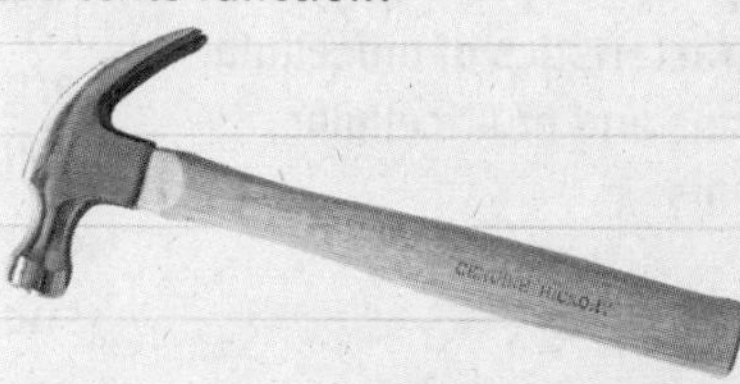

Active Reading

3 Relate Many scientific words, such as *organ* and *tissue,* also have everyday meanings. Use context clues to write your own definition for each underlined word.

It is helpful to use a <u>tissue</u> when sneezing to prevent the spread of droplets carrying bacteria.

tissue:

An <u>organ</u> can be very difficult to play.

organ:

Vocabulary Terms

- organism
- tissue
- organ
- organ system
- structure
- function

4 Apply As you learn the definition of each vocabulary term in this lesson, create your own definition or sketch to help you remember the meaning of the term.

Body Building

How are living things organized?

Active Reading

5 Identify As you read, underline the characteristics of unicellular organisms and multicellular organisms.

An **organism** is a living thing that can carry out life processes by itself. *Unicellular organisms* are made up of just one cell that performs all of the functions necessary for life. Unicellular organisms do not have levels of organization. Having only one cell has advantages and disadvantages. For example, unicellular organisms need fewer resources and can live in harsh conditions, such as hot springs and very salty water. However, unicellular organisms are very small, which means they may be eaten by larger organisms. Another disadvantage of being unicellular is that the entire organism dies if the single cell dies.

Cells

Multicellular organisms are made up of more than one cell. These cells are grouped into different levels of organization, including tissues, organs, and organ systems. The cells that make up a multicellular organism, such as humans and plants, may be specialized to perform specific functions. Different cells have different functions in the body. This specialization makes the multicellular organism more efficient. Other benefits of being multicellular are larger size and longer life span.

There are disadvantages to being multicellular, too. Multicellular organisms need more resources than unicellular organisms do. Also, the cells of multicellular organisms are specialized for certain jobs, which means that cells must depend on each other to perform all of the functions that an organism needs.

Humpback whales are multicellular organisms.
Diatoms are unicellular organisms that live in water.

Tissues

A **tissue** is a group of similar cells that perform a common function. Humans and many other animals are made up of four basic types of tissue: nervous, epithelial, connective, and muscle. Nervous tissue functions as a messaging system within the body. Epithelial tissue is protective and forms boundaries, such as skin. Connective tissue, including bones and blood, holds parts of the body together and provides support and nourishment to organs. Muscle tissue helps produce movement.

Plants have three types of tissues: transport, protective, and ground. Transport tissues move water and nutrients throughout the plant. Protective tissues protect the outside of the plant. Ground tissues provide support and storage. They absorb light energy to make food in photosynthesis (foh•toh•SYN•thuh•sys).

6 Explain FIll in the Venn diagram to compare the functions of animal tissues and plant tissues. What functions do they share?

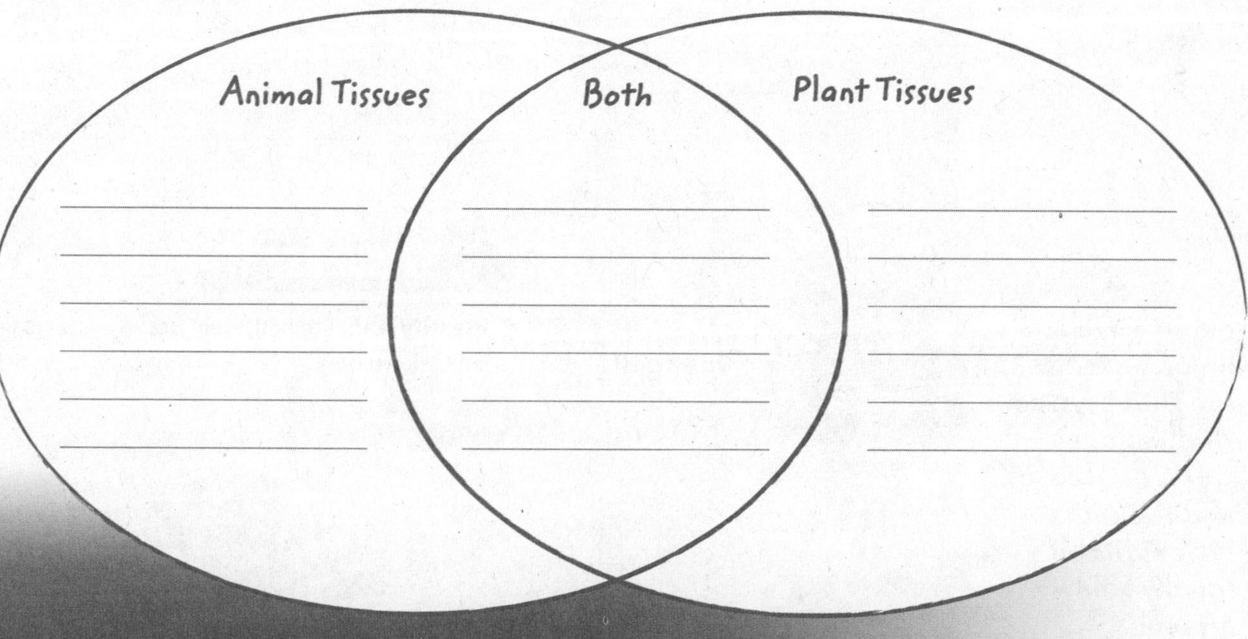

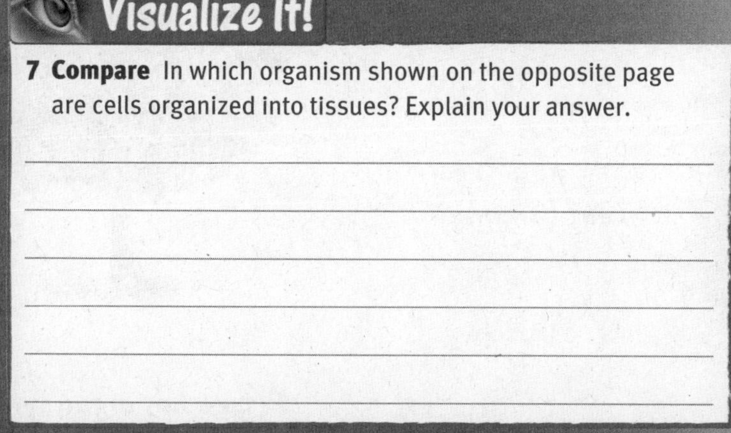

7 Compare In which organism shown on the opposite page are cells organized into tissues? Explain your answer.

Organs

A structure made up of a collection of tissues that carries out a specialized function is called an **organ**. The stomach is an organ that breaks down food for digestion. Different types of tissues work together to accomplish this function. For example, nervous tissue sends messages to muscle tissue to tell the muscle tissue to contract. When the muscle tissue contracts, food and stomach acids are mixed and the food breaks down.

Plants also have organs that are made up of different tissues working together. For example, a leaf is an organ that contains protective tissue to reduce water loss, ground tissue for photosynthesis, and transport tissue to distribute nutrients from leaves to stems. Stems and roots are organs that function to transport and store water and nutrients in the plant. The trunk of most trees is a stem. Roots are usually below ground.

8 Apply How do organs relate to cells and tissues?

____

____

____

Plants have two organ systems: the shoot system that includes stems and leaves, and the root system that is usually below ground.

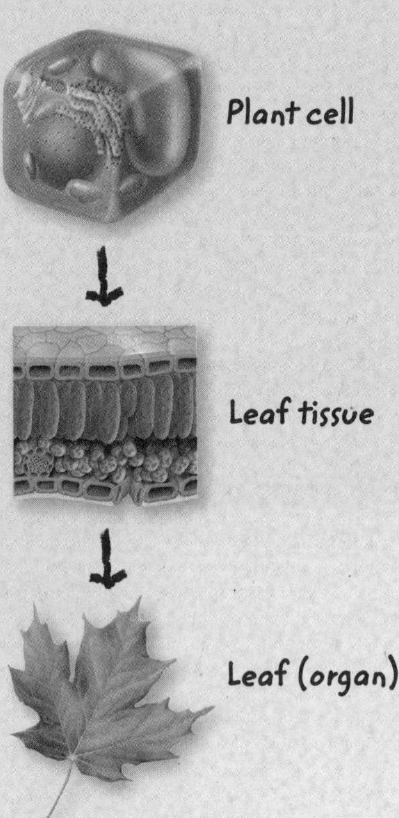

9 Identify Label the different organ systems on the tree shown here.

A tree has organ systems.

The digestive system is an organ system in many animals, including humans.

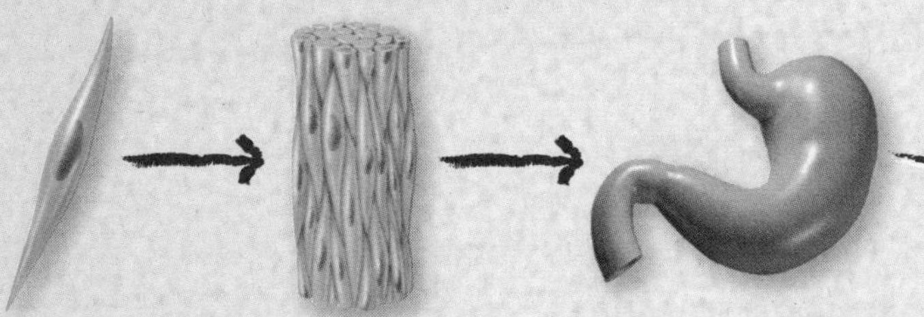

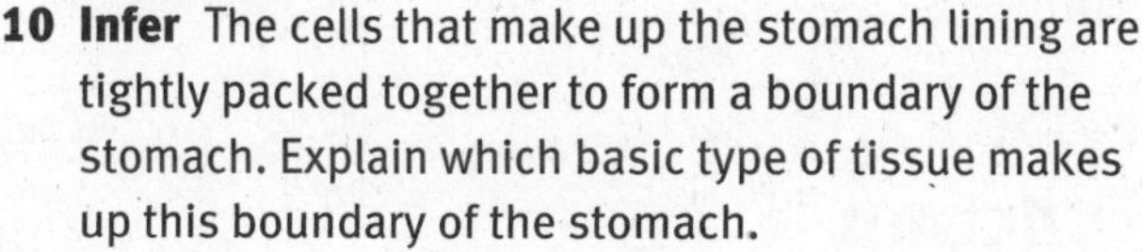

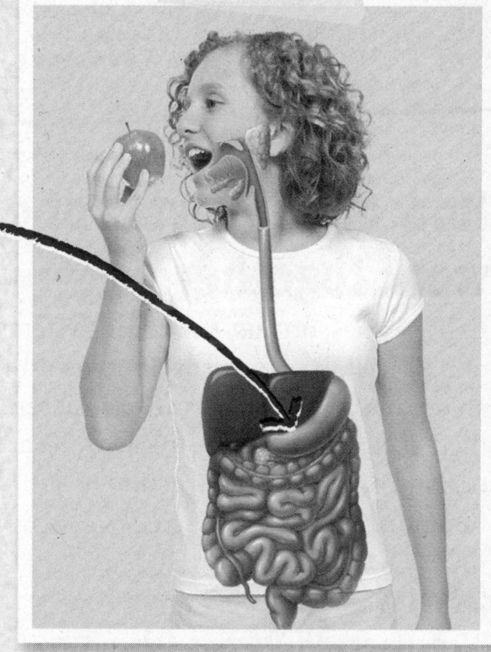

Digestive system in humans

10 Infer The cells that make up the stomach lining are tightly packed together to form a boundary of the stomach. Explain which basic type of tissue makes up this boundary of the stomach.

____

____

____

Organ Systems

An **organ system** is a group of organs that work together to perform body functions. Each organ system has a specific job to do for the organism. For example, the stomach works with other organs of the digestive system to digest and absorb nutrients from food. Other organs included in the digestive system are the esophagus and the small and large intestines.

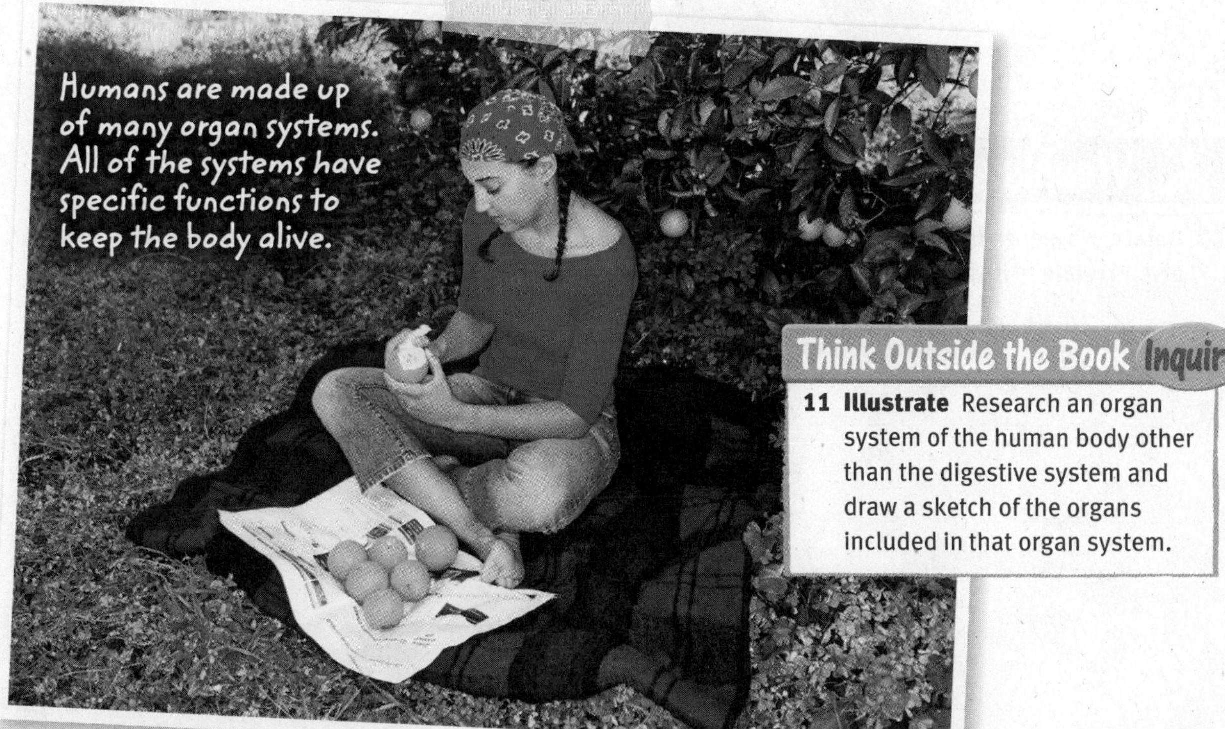

Humans are made up of many organ systems. All of the systems have specific functions to keep the body alive.

Think Outside the Book Inquiry

11 Illustrate Research an organ system of the human body other than the digestive system and draw a sketch of the organs included in that organ system.

What's Your Function?

How do the levels of organization work together?

Cells, tissues, organs, and organ systems make up the structure of multicellular organism. **Structure** is the arrangement of parts in an organism or an object. The structure of a cell, tissue, or organ then determines their **function**, or the activity of each part in an organism. In fact, the structure of any object can determine its function.

12 Recognize As you read, underline examples of cellular structures.

Structure

A sports car differs from a dump truck even though they are both vehicles. The structure of the parts in a sports car allow it to go fast. A dump truck is large and sturdy, which allows it to haul things. Cells, tissues, and organs also vary in structure. For example, bone cells look different than plant leaf cells. A lung differs from a stomach because they have different functions.

Function

The structure of each vehicle determines what function the vehicle performs.The relationship of structure and function is true for cells, too. Cells, tissues, and organs are specialized to perform specific functions. Those that have similar structures likely have similar functions. For example, a lung is an organ made up of cells and tissues that work together to help you breathe. The lungs are made up of millions of tiny air sacs called *alveoli* (ahl•VEE•oh•lye). The large number of alveoli increases the surface area of the lungs to allow enough oxygen and carbon dioxide to move between the lungs and the blood.

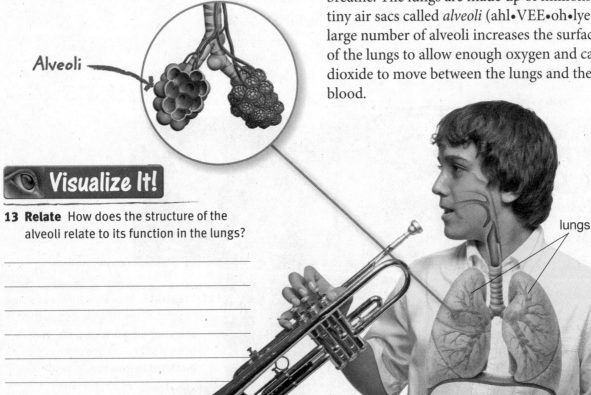

Alveoli

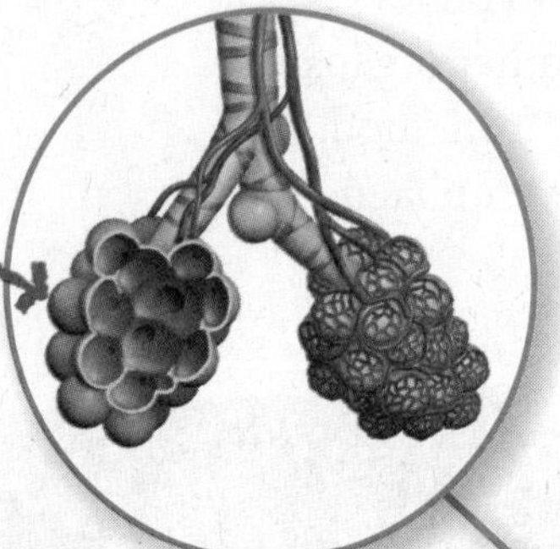

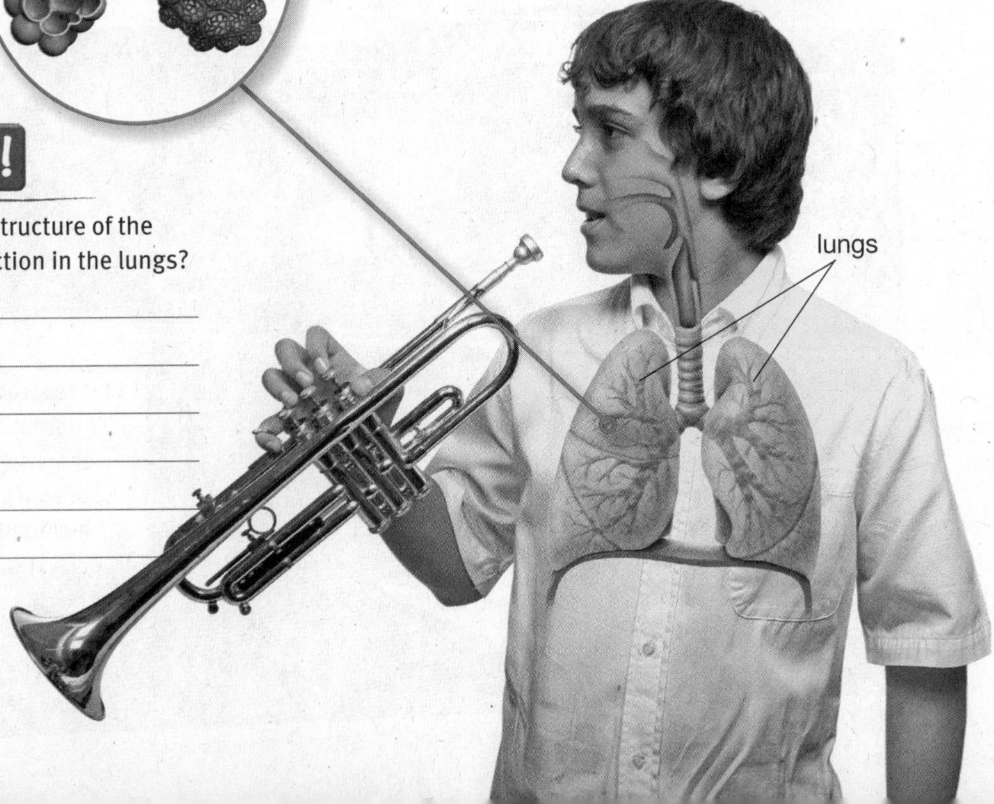

lungs

Visualize It!

13 Relate How does the structure of the alveoli relate to its function in the lungs?

Why It Matters

Odd Bodies

With the millions of different organisms that exist on Earth, it's no wonder there are so many different body structures. Some organisms have special structures that can help them eat or not be eaten!

Can't Touch This!

Named for its prickly body, the spiny katydid doesn't make much of a meal for its predator. Male katydids sing loudly at night to attract female katydids. The singing can also attract predators, such as bats, who hunt for food at night. Its spines provide the katydid with some protection from being eaten.

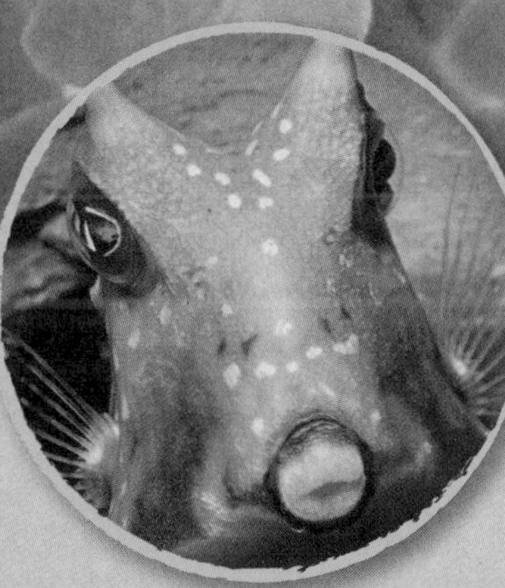

Blow on Your Food

The longhorn cowfish is a marine organism that lives on the sandy bottom at up to 50 m deep. Its permanently puckered mouth helps the cowfish find food. The cowfish blows jets of water into the sand to find and feed on tiny organisms.

Night Vision

The tarsier's huge eyes provide excellent vision for hunting insects at night. Its eyes average 16 mm in diameter, while the tarsier's overall body size ranges from 85 mm to 165 mm. If a tarsier were your height, its eyes would be about the size of apples! When the tarsier spots its prey, it leaps through the air to pounce on it. The tarsier's long fingers help it grasp branches when it's on the move.

Extend

Inquiry

14 Relate How does the body structure of each of these organisms contribute to a particular function?

15 Contrast How do structures in organisms compare with structures of nonliving things such as construction cranes, buildings, ships, airplanes, or bridges?

16 Imagine Describe an organism that might live in an extreme environment like inside a volcano, deep in the ocean, or in an icy cave. Is it a plant or an animal? What special structures would it have in order to survive in that environment?

Visual Summary

To complete this summary, check the box that indicates true or false. Then, use the key below to check your answers. You can use this page to review the main concepts of the lesson.

Cellular Organization

All organisms are made up of one or more cells.

T F

17 ☐ ☐ A plant is a unicellular organism.

The structures of cells, tissues, and organs determine their functions.

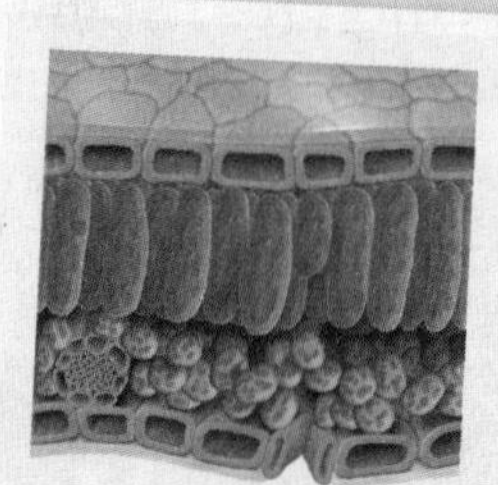

T F

18 ☐ ☐ The protective tissue on a leaf has a structure that keeps the plant from drying out.

Multicellular organisms are organized into tissues, organs, and organ systems.

T F

19 ☐ ☐ This leaf is an example of a plant organ.

T F

20 ☐ ☐ Organs form organ systems.

Answers: 17 F; 18 T; 19 T; 20 T

21 Synthesize How do cells, tissues, organs, and organ systems work together in a multicellular organism?

Lesson Review

Vocabulary

Fill in the blank with the term that best completes the following sentences.

1 Animals have four basic types of ______________: nervous, epithelial, muscle, and connective.

2 Together, the esophagus, stomach, and intestines are part of a(n) ______________

Key Concepts

3 Describe What are the levels of organization in multicellular organisms?

4 Analyze Discuss two benefits of multicellular organisms having some specialized cells rather than all the cells being the same.

5 Relate How do the structures in an organism relate to its function?

Critical Thinking

Use the figure to answer the next two questions.

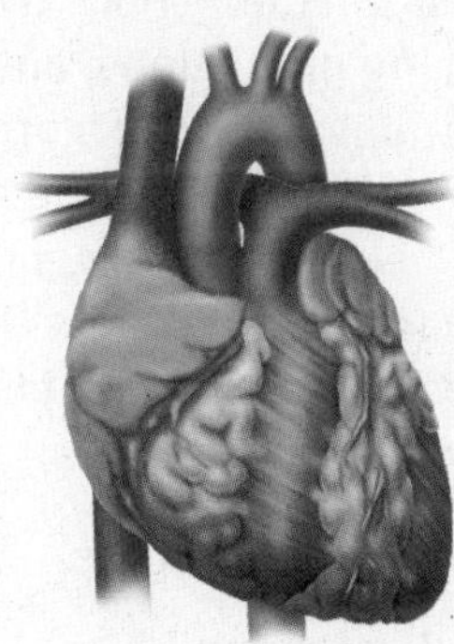

6 Apply What level of organization is shown here?

7 Relate How does this level of organization relate to cells? To organ systems?

8 Hypothesize Birds that fly have lightweight bones, some of which are hollow. How might this unique body structure benefit the bird?

Think Science

Making Predictions

Sunshine State Standards

MA.6.A.3.6 Construct and analyze tables, graphs, and equations to describe linear functions and other simple relations using both common language and algebraic notation.

Scientists try to answer questions about the world by developing hypotheses, making predictions, and conducting experiments to test those predictions. To make a prediction, a scientist will analyze a general idea and then predict specific results. Predictions often take the form of "if–then" statements. For example, "If living organisms are made of small units called cells, then we predict that we will see cells if we look at organisms up close under a microscope."

A dividing frog cell showing microtubules (green) and DNA (blue)

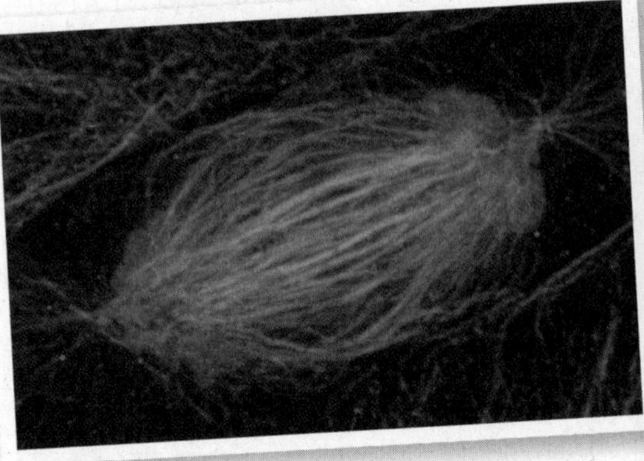

Tutorial

For an organism to grow and reproduce, chromosomes must replicate and cells must divide. The following steps will teach you how to make predictions from hypotheses about the role of protein fibers, called microtubules, in cell division.

Question: How do chromosomes move and separate during cell division?

Hypothesis: Microtubules play an important role in the movement of the chromosomes during cell division.

Prediction: If microtubules were inhibited during cell division, then chromosomes would not be able to move and separate from each other during cell division.

Observations: When microtubules are exposed to a drug that blocks microtubule formation, movement of chromosomes is inhibited and cell division stops.

What is the hypothesis? A hypothesis is a plausible answer to a scientific question. Form a hypothesis based on prior experience, background knowledge, or your own observations.

What would we expect or predict to see if the hypothesis were true? When scientists summarize their data, they look for observations and measurements that will support their hypothesis.

Does the prediction match the observations? If the data matches the predictions generated by the hypothesis, then the hypothesis is supported. Sometimes errors occur during the scientific investigation, which can lead to incorrect results. There is also the possibility that correct data will not match the hypothesis. When this happens, generate a new hypothesis.

You Try It!

Scientists often propose hypotheses about the causes of events they observe. Read the following scenario, and answer the questions that follow.

Scenario: A cell biologist has three cell cultures of human skin cells. The cells in each culture are taken from the same cell line. Each cell culture is placed in a solution for observation. The cells in culture A are growing faster than the cells in cultures B and C.

Question: Why are the cells in culture A growing at a faster rate than the cells in cultures B and C?

Hypothesis 1: The waste level is higher in cultures B and C than in culture A.

Hypothesis 2: The nutrient levels are higher in culture A than in cultures B and C.

1 Making Predictions Read each of the hypotheses above and then make a prediction for each about what might be observed.

Hypothesis 1:

____

____

____

Hypothesis 2:

____

____

____

2 Testing a Hypothesis Identify a possible experiment for each hypothesis that you can perform or observations that you can make to find out whether the hypothesis is supported.

Hypothesis 1:

____

____

____

Hypothesis 2:

____

____

____

____

3 Predicting Outcomes Fill in the two tables below with plausible data that supports each hypothesis.

Culture	Waste level	Rate of growth (cells/hour)
A		
B		
C		

Culture	Nutrient level	Rate of growth (cells/hour)
A		
B		
C		

Take It Home

Find a recent newspaper or magazine article that makes a conclusion based on a scientific study. Carefully evaluate the study and identify the predictions that were tested in the study. Bring the article to class and be prepared to discuss your analysis of the article.

Lesson 5

Homeostasis and Cell Processes

ESSENTIAL QUESTION

How do organisms maintain homeostasis?

By the end of this lesson, you should be able to explain the important processes that organisms undergo to maintain stable internal conditions.

These American alligators are warming themselves in the sun. Temperature is one factor that an organism can control to maintain stable internal conditions.

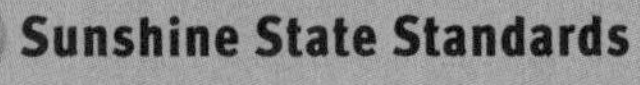

Sunshine State Standards

SC.6.L.14.3 Recognize and explore how cells of all organisms undergo similar processes to maintain homeostasis, including extracting energy from food, getting rid of waste, and reproducing.

Engage Your Brain

1 Explain How is this person able to stay on the skateboard?

____

____

2 Describe Fill in the blanks with the word or phrase that you think correctly completes the following sentences.

Eating _______________ provides your body with nutrients it needs for energy.

Cells can _______________ to make more cells.

Trucks, airplanes, and trains are used to _______________ people and supplies from one place to another.

Active Reading

3 Synthesis You can often define an unknown word if you know the meaning of its word parts. Use the word parts and sentence below to make an educated guess about the meaning of the word *photosynthesis*.

Word part	Meaning
photo-	light
synthesis	to make

Example sentence

Plants use a process called photosynthesis to make their own food.

photosynthesis:

____

____

Vocabulary Terms

- **homeostasis**
- **photosynthesis**
- **cellular respiration**
- **mitosis**
- **passive transport**
- **diffusion**
- **osmosis**
- **active transport**
- **endocytosis**
- **exocytosis**

4 Identify As you read, place a question mark next to any words that you don't understand. When you finish reading the lesson, go back and review the text that you marked. If the information is still confusing, consult a classmate or a teacher.

Stayin' Alive

What is homeostasis?

We all feel more comfortable when our surroundings are ideal—not too hot, not too cold, not too wet, and not too dry. Cells are the same way. However, a cell's environment is constantly changing. **Homeostasis** (hoh•mee•oh•STAY•sis) is the maintenance of a constant internal state in a changing environment. In order to survive, your cells need to be able to obtain and use energy, make new cells, exchange materials, and eliminate wastes. Homeostasis ensures that cells can carry out these tasks in a changing environment.

Active Reading **6 Summarize** What are four things that cells can do to maintain homeostasis?

Think Outside the Book Inquiry

5 Select Many mechanisms are used to regulate different things in our lives. Choose one of the following devices, and do some research to describe what it regulates and how it works:

- thermostat
- insulin pump
- dam

Visualize It!

7 Apply Think about how this girl is feeling after she exercises. What things can you see that are helping to keep her body temperature stable?

Balance in Organisms

All cells need energy and materials in order to carry out life processes. A unicellular organism exchanges materials directly with its environment. The cell membrane and other parts of the cell regulate what materials get into and out of the cell. This is one way that unicellular organisms maintain homeostasis.

Cells in multicellular organisms must work together to maintain homeostasis for the entire organism. For example, multicellular organisms have systems that transport materials to cells from other places in the organism. The main transport system in your body is your cardiovascular system. The cardiovascular system includes the heart, blood vessels, and blood. The heart pumps blood through branched blood vessels that come close to every cell in the body. Blood carries materials to the cells and carries wastes away from the cells. Other multicellular organisms have transport systems, too. For example, many plants have two types of vascular tissues that work together as a transport system. *Xylem* is the tissue that transports water and minerals from the roots to the rest of the plant. Another tissue called *phloem* transports food made within plant cells.

Active Reading

8 Compare As you read, underline how unicellular organisms and multicellular organisms exchange materials.

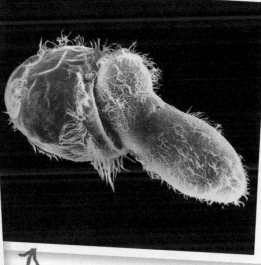

A unicellular organism, **Didinium**, is eating another unicellular organism, called a **Paramecium**.

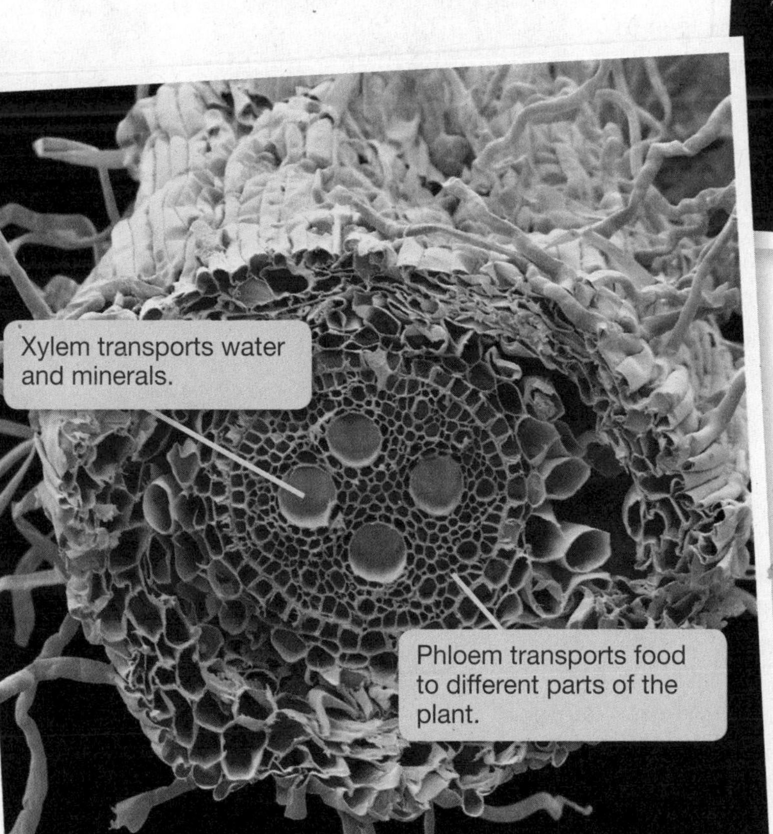
Xylem transports water and minerals.
Phloem transports food to different parts of the plant.

Plants have two types of vascular tissue that they use to transport materials.

Get Growing!

How do cells get energy?

Cells need energy to perform cell functions. Cells get energy by breaking down materials, such as food, in which energy is stored. Breaking down food also provides raw materials the cell needs to make other materials for cell processes.

Photosynthesis

The sun provides the energy for plants to grow and make food. Plants use sunlight to change carbon dioxide and water into sugar and oxygen. This process by which plants, algae, and some bacteria make their own food is called **photosynthesis**. Inside plant and algal cells are special organelles, called chloroplasts, where photosynthesis takes place.

Cellular Respiration

All living things need food to produce energy for cell processes. The process by which cells use oxygen to produce energy from food is called **cellular respiration**. Plants, animals, and most other organisms use cellular respiration to get energy from food.

Nearly all the oxygen around us is made by photosynthesis. Animals and plants use oxygen during cellular respiration to break down food. Cellular respiration also produces carbon dioxide. Plants need carbon dioxide to make sugars. So, photosynthesis and respiration are linked, each one depending on the products of the other.

Plants provide the food for nearly all living thing on land. Some organisms eat plants for food. Other organisms eat animals that eat plants.

9 Synthesize Fill in the blanks with the materials that are involved in photosynthesis and cellular respiration.

Photosynthesis	________ + carbon dioxide —sunlight→ ________ + oxygen
Cellular respiration	sugar + ________ ——→ water + ________ + energy

How do cells divide?

Cells grow, divide, and die. Some cells divide more often than others. For example, cells in the skin are constantly dividing to replace those that have died or are damaged. Some cells, such as nerve cells, cannot divide to produce new cells once they are fully formed. Multicellular organisms grow by adding more cells. These new cells are made when existing cells divide.

The Cell Cycle

Cell division in eukaryotes is a complex process. Before a cell can divide, its DNA is copied. Then, the DNA copies are sorted into what will become two new cells. In order to divide up the DNA evenly between the new cells, the DNA needs to be packaged. The packages are called *chromosomes* (croh•moh•SOHMS). Equal numbers of chromosomes are separated, and the nucleus splits to form two identical nuclei. This process is called **mitosis**. Then, the rest of the cell divides, resulting in two identical cells. Because the two new cells have DNA identical to that found in the original cell, all the cells in an organism have the same genetic material.

10 Explain Why is it important for DNA to be copied before cell division?

11 Compare How do new cells form in plants and animal?

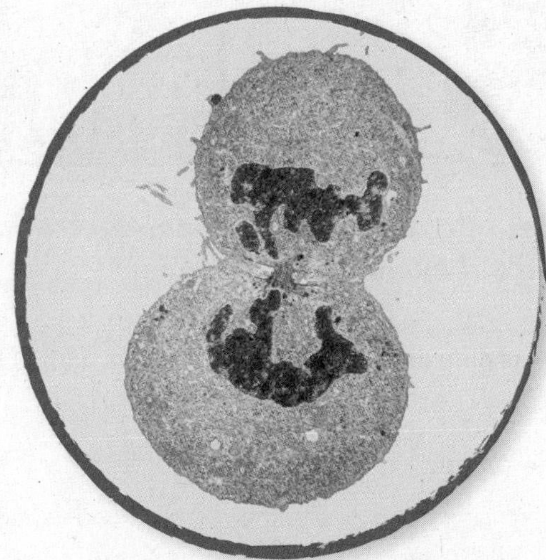

In animal cells, the cell membrane pinches inward through the cell to form two new cells.

When a plant cell divides, a cell plate forms and the cell splits into two cells.

Move It!

How do cells exchange materials?

What would happen to a factory if its supply of raw materials never arrived or it couldn't get rid of its garbage? Like a factory, an organism must be able to obtain materials for energy, make new materials, and get rid of wastes. The exchange of materials between a cell and its environment takes place at the cell's membrane. Cell membranes are *semi-permeable* because they allow only certain particles to cross into or out of the cell.

Active Reading

12 Relate As you read, underline the similarity between diffusion and osmosis.

Passive Transport

The movement of particles across a cell membrane without the use of energy by the cell is called **passive transport**. For example, when a tea bag is added to a cup of water, the molecules in the tea will eventually spread throughout the water. **Diffusion** is the movement of molecules from high concentrations to low concentrations. Some nutrients move into a cell by diffusion. Some waste products move out of the cell by diffusion. **Osmosis** is the diffusion of water through a semi-permeable membrane. Many molecules are too large to diffuse through the cell membrane. Some of these molecules enter and exit cells through protein channels embedded in the cell membrane. When molecules move through these protein channels from areas of higher concentration to areas of lower concentration, the process usually requires no energy.

The tea has a higher concentration of molecules in the tea bag than in the rest of the mug.

Tea moves into areas of lower concentration, spreading out evenly in the mug.

13 Apply How is diffusion related to smelling the odor of a skunk that is far away?

Active Transport

Cells often need to move materials across the cell membrane from areas of low concentration into areas of higher concentration. This is the opposite direction of passive transport. **Active transport** is the movement of particles against a concentration gradient and requires the cell to use energy. Some large particles that do not fit through the protein channels may require active transport across the cell membrane by processes called *endocytosis* and *exocytosis*.

Visualize It!

14 Identify Place a check mark next to the box that describes diffusion. Explain your answer.

____

____

____

____

Chemical energy
Passive transport moves materials into and out of a cell to areas of lower concentration. ☐
Active transport uses energy to move materials into and out of a cell to areas of higher concentration. ☐

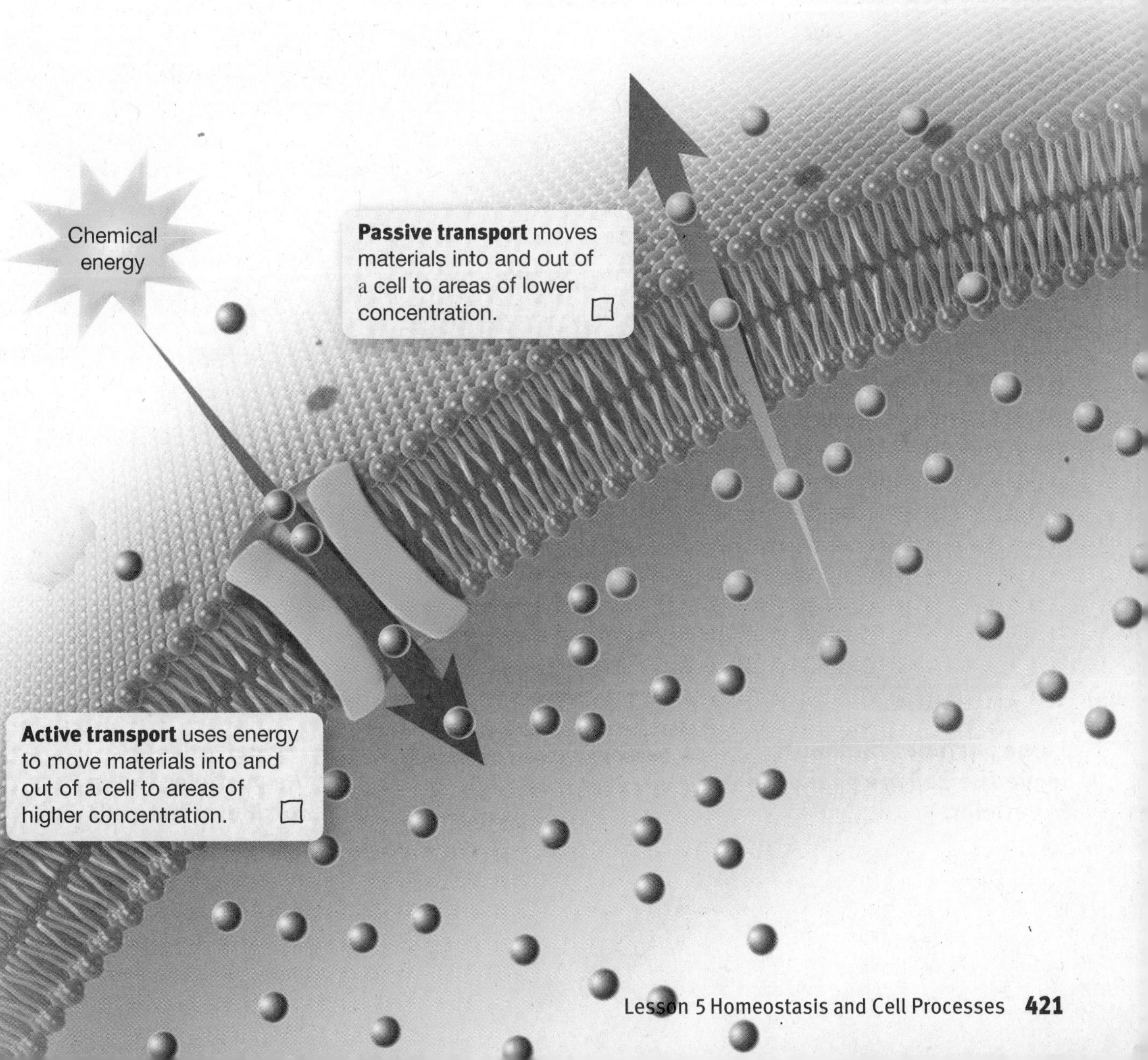

Endocytosis

The process by which a cell uses energy to surround a particle and enclose the particle in a vesicle to bring the particle into the cell is called **endocytosis** (en•doh•sye•TOH•sis). Vesicles are sacs formed from pieces of the cell membrane. Unicellular organisms, such as amoebas, use endocytosis to capture smaller organisms for food.

The cell comes into contact with a particle.

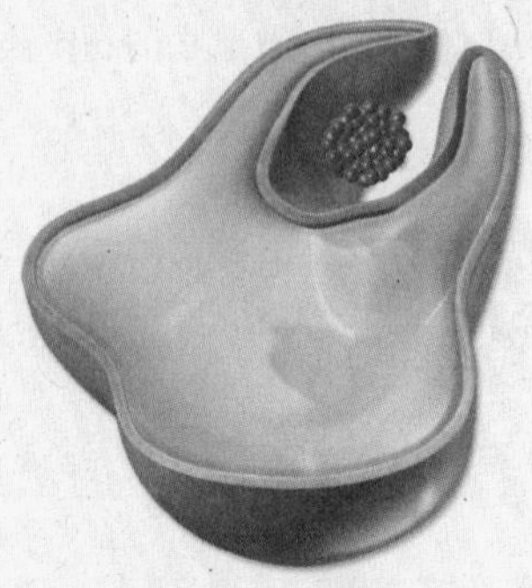

The cell membrane begins to wrap around the particle.

15 Describe What is happening in this step?

____

____

____

____

Exocytosis

When particles are enclosed in a vesicle and released from a cell, the process is called **exocytosis** (ek•soh•sye•TOH•sis). Exocytosis is the reverse process of endocytosis. Exocytosis begins when a vesicle forms around particles within the cell. The vesicle fuses to the cell membrane and the particles are released outside of the cell. Exocytosis is an important process in multicellular organisms.

Large particles that must leave the cell are packaged in vesicles.

16 Describe What is happening in this step?

____

____

____

____

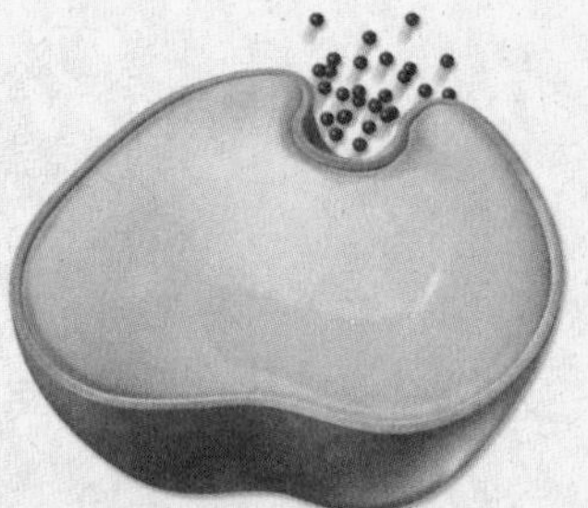

The cell releases the particles to the outside of the cell.

How do organisms maintain homeostasis?

As you have read, cells can obtain energy, divide, and transport materials to maintain stable internal conditions. In multicellular organisms, the cells must work together to maintain homeostasis for the entire organism. For example, when some organisms become cold, the cells respond in order to maintain a normal internal temperature. Muscle cells will contract to generate heat, a process known as shivering.

Some animals adapt their behavior to control body temperature. For example, many reptiles bask in the sun or seek shade to regulate their internal temperatures. When temperatures become extremely cold, some animals hibernate. Animals such as ground squirrels are able to conserve their energy during the winter when food is scarce.

Some trees lose all their leaves around the same time each year. This is a seasonal response. Having bare branches during the winter reduces the amount of water loss. Leaves may also change color before they fall. As autumn approaches, chlorophyll, the green pigment used for photosynthesis, breaks down. As chlorophyll is lost, other yellow and orange pigments can be seen.

Active Reading

17 Identify As you read, underline the different ways that organisms can respond to changes in the environment.

Visualize It!

18 Describe How is this boy's body responding to the cold weather?

____

____

____

The leaves of some trees change colors when the season changes.

Visual Summary

To complete this summary, fill in the blanks with the correct word or phrase. Then use the key below to check your answers. You can use this page to review the main concepts of the lesson.

Cells need energy to perform cell functions.

19 Food is made during ________________
Energy is produced from food during
____

Cell division allows organisms to grow and repair damaged parts.

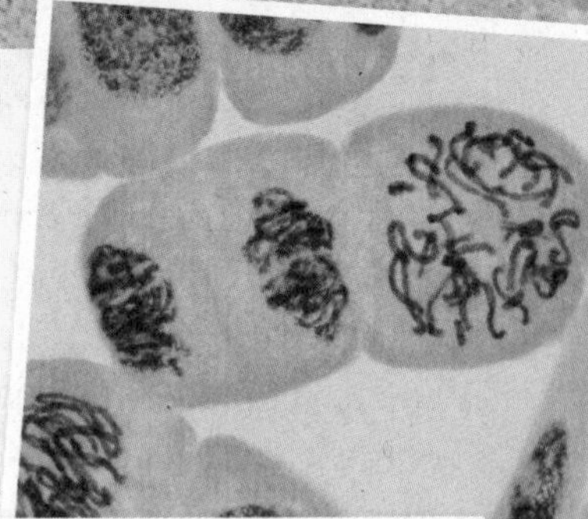

20 ________________ occurs when cells divide to form two new nuclei that are identical to each other.

Maintaining Homeostasis:
Balance In Organisms

Materials move into and out of cells through the cell membrane.

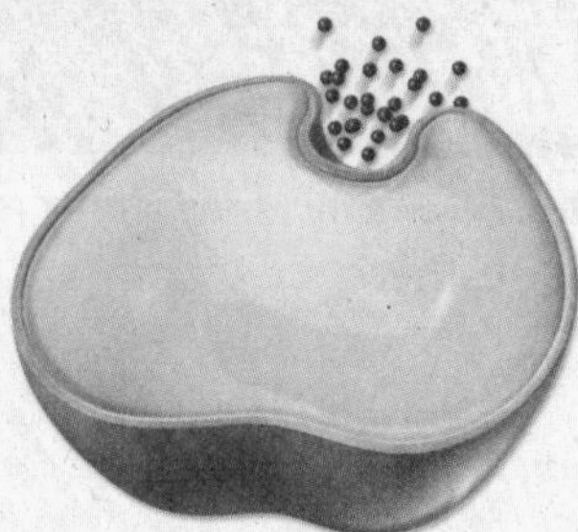

21 ________________ uses energy to release particles from a cell.

Organisms respond to changes in the environment.

22 The change in leaf color on these trees is one way the trees maintain ________________

Answers: 19 photosynthesis; cellular respiration; 20 Mitosis; 21 Active transport; 22 homeostasis

23 Summarize Explain why organisms need to maintain homeostasis.

Lesson Review

Vocabulary

In your own words, define the following terms.

1 homeostasis

2 endocytosis

Key Concepts

3 Compare What is the difference between passive and active transport?

4 List List four things that cells do to maintain homeostasis.

5 Describe What happens during mitosis?

6 Apply How do the cells in your body get energy?

Critical Thinking

Use the graphs to answer the next two questions.

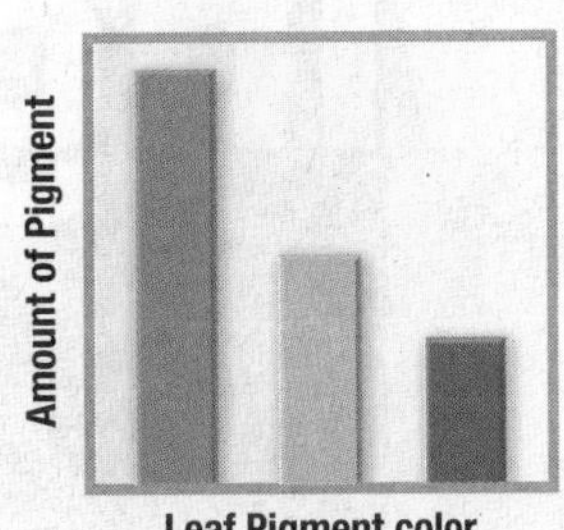

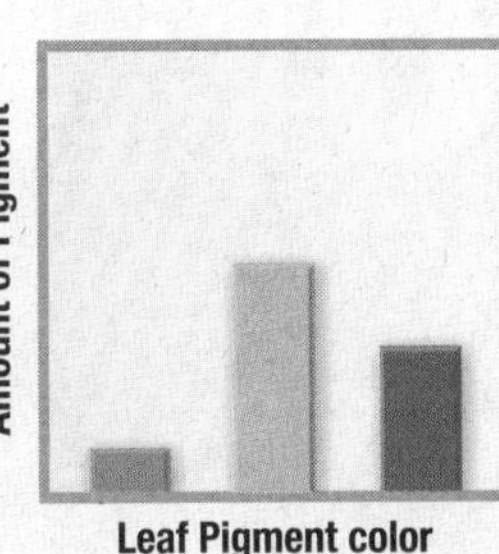

7 Compare How do the amounts of green pigment, chlorophyll, differ from summer to fall?

8 Infer How do you think the change in chlorophyll levels is a response to changes in the length of day from summer to fall?

9 Explain Why is homeostasis important for cells as well as for an entire organism?

Classification of Living Things

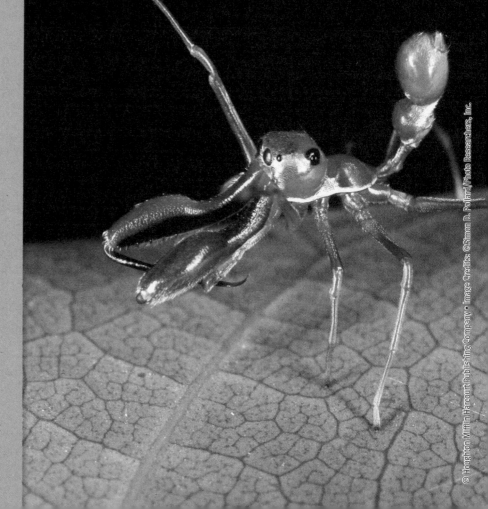

ESSENTIAL QUESTION

How are organisms classified?

By the end of this lesson, you should be able to describe how people sort living things into groups based on shared characteristics.

Scientists use physical and chemical characteristics to classify organisms. Is that an ant? Look again. It's an ant-mimicking jumping spider!

 **Sunshine State Standards**

SC.6.L.15.1 Analyze and describe how and why organisms are classified according to shared characteristics with emphasis on the Linnaean system combined with the concept of Domains.

Engage Your Brain

1 Predict Check T or F to show whether you think each statement is true or false.

T	F	
☐	☐	The classification system used today has changed very little since it was introduced.
☐	☐	To be classified as an animal, organisms must have a backbone.
☐	☐	Organisms can be classified by whether they have nuclei in their cells.
☐	☐	Scientists can study genetic material to classify organisms.
☐	☐	Organisms that have many physical similarities may be related.

2 Analyze The flowering plant shown above is called an Indian pipe. It could be mistaken for a fungus. Write down how the plant is similar to and different from other plants you know.

____

____

____

Active Reading

3 Synthesize Often, you can define an unknown word if you know the meaning of its word parts. Use the word parts and sentence below to make an educated guess about the meaning of the term *dichotomous key*.

Word part	Meaning
dich-	in two
-tomous	to cut

Example sentence

Sophie used the paired statements in a dichotomous key to identify the animal she found during the field trip.

dichotomous key:

____

____

____

Vocabulary Terms

- species
- genus
- domain
- Bacteria
- Archaea
- Eukarya
- Animalia
- Plantae
- Protista
- Fungi
- dichotomous key

4 Apply As you learn the definition of each vocabulary term in this lesson, write your own definition or make a sketch to help you remember the meaning of each term.

Sorting Things Out!

Why do we classify living things?

There are millions of living things on Earth. How do scientists keep all of these living things organized? Scientists *classify* living things based on characteristics that living things share. Classification helps scientists answer questions such as:

- How many kinds of living things are there?
- What characteristics define each kind of living thing?
- What are the relationships among living things?

Sharks have fins and gills.
Dolphins also have fins, but not gills.

Visualize It!

5 Analyze The photos below show two organisms. In the table, place a check mark in the box for each characteristic that the organisms have.

Miami blue butterfly

Scrub jay

	Wings	Antennae	Beak	Feathers
Miami blue butterfly				
Scrub jay				

6 Summarize What characteristics do Miami blue butterflies have in common with scrub jays? How do they differ?

How do scientists know living things are related?

If two organisms look similar, are they related? To classify organisms, scientists compare physical characteristics. For example, they may look at size or bone structure. Scientists also compare the chemical characteristics of living things.

Active Reading

7 Identify As you read this page, underline the characteristics used to classify living things.

Physical Characteristics

How are chickens similar to dinosaurs? If you compare dinosaur fossils and chicken skeletons, you'll see that chickens and dinosaurs share many physical characteristics. Scientists look at physical characteristics, such as skeletal structure. They also study how organisms develop from an egg to an adult. Organisms that have similar skeletons and development may be related.

Chemical Characteristics

Scientists can identify the relationships among organisms by studying genetic material such as DNA and RNA. They use mutations and genetic similarities to find relationships among organisms. Organisms that have very similar gene sequences or have the same mutations are likely related. Other chemicals, such as proteins and hormones, can also be studied to learn how organisms are related.

Kaibab squirrels live on the North Rim of the Grand Canyon.

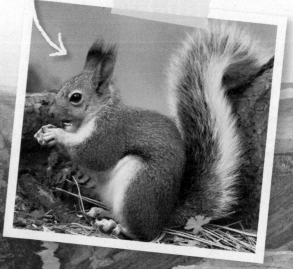

Abert's squirrels live on the South Rim of the Grand Canyon.

Kaibab squirrels and Abert's squirrels look different, and they are separated by the Grand Canyon. However, DNA testing showed that these squirrels are very closely related.

8 Synthesize In addition to canyons, what other kinds of geologic formations might separate similar organisms?

What's in a Name?

How are living things named?

Early scientists used names as long as 12 words to identify living things, and they also used common names. So, classification was confusing. In the 1700s, a scientist named Carolus Linnaeus (KAR•uh•luhs lih•NEE•uhs) simplified the naming of living things. He gave each kind of living thing a two-part *scientific name*.

HELLO
my name is
Carolus Linnaeus

Scientific Names

Each species has its own scientific name. A **species** (SPEE•sheez) is a group of organisms that are very closely related. They can mate and produce fertile offspring. Consider the scientific name for a mountain lion: *Puma concolor*. The first part, *Puma,* is the genus name. A **genus** (JEE•nuhs; plural, *genera*) includes similar species. The second part, *concolor,* is the specific, or species, name. No other species is named *Puma concolor*.

A scientific name always includes the genus name followed by the specific name. The first letter of the genus name is capitalized, and the first letter of the specific name is lowercase. The entire scientific name is written either in italics or underlined.

The A.K.A. Files

Some living things have many common names. Scientific names prevent confusion when people discuss organisms.

Scientific name:
Puma concolor

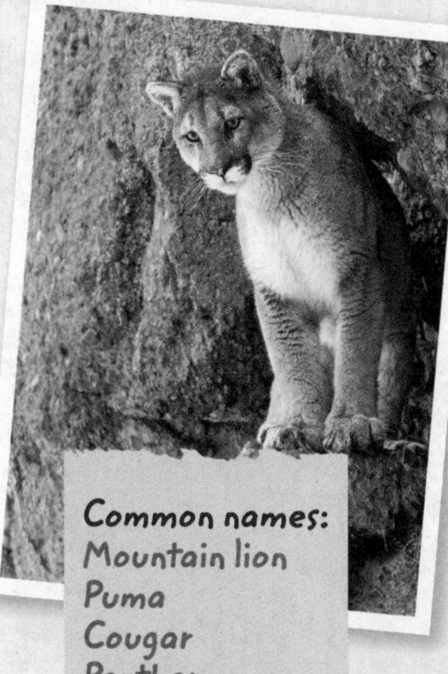

Common names:
Mountain lion
Puma
Cougar
Panther

Scientific name:
Acer rubrum

Common names:
Red maple
Swamp maple
Soft maple

9 Apply In the scientific names above, circle the genus name and underline the specific name.

What are the levels of classification?

Linnaeus's ideas became the basis for modern taxonomy (tak•SAHN•uh•mee). *Taxonomy* is the science of describing, classifying, and naming living things. At first, many scientists sorted organisms into two groups: plants and animals. But many organisms did not fit into either group.

Today, scientists use an eight-level system to classify living things. Each level gets more definite. Therefore, it contains fewer kinds of living things than the level before it. Living things in the lower levels are more closely related to each other than they are to organisms in the higher levels. From most general to most definite, the levels of classification are domain, kingdom, phylum (plural, *phyla*), class, order, family, genus, and species.

Think Outside the Book *Inquiry*

10 Analyze With a partner, investigate how Linnaeus's development of scientific names affected taxonomy. Make an informative brochure that describes your findings.

Classifying Organisms

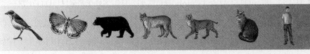

Domain **Domain Eukarya** includes all protists, fungi, plants, and animals.

Kingdom **Kingdom Animalia** includes all animals.

Phylum Animals in **Phylum Chordata** have a hollow nerve cord in their backs. Some have a backbone.

Class Animals in **Class Mammalia**, or mammals, have a backbone and nurse their young.

Order Animals in **Order Carnivora** are mammals that have special teeth for tearing meat.

Family Animals in **Family Felidae** are cats. They are carnivores that have retractable claws.

Genus Animals in **Genus *Felis*** are cats that cannot roar. They can only purr.

Species The **species *Felis domesticus***, or the house cat, has unique traits that other members of genus *Felis* do not have.

From domain to species, each level of classification contains a smaller group of organisms.

Visualize It!

11 Apply How does the shape of a pyramid relate to the number of organisms in each level of the classification system?

Triple Play

What are the three domains?

Once, kingdoms were the highest level of classification. Scientists used a six-kingdom system. But scientists noticed that organisms in two of the kingdoms differed greatly from organisms in the other four kingdoms. So, scientists added a new classification level: domains. A **domain** represents the largest differences among organisms. The three domains are Bacteria (bak•TIR•ee•uh), Archaea (ar•KEE•uh), and Eukarya (yoo•KEHR•ee•uh).

12 Identify As you read, underline the three domains of life.

Bacteria

All bacteria belong to domain Bacteria. Domain **Bacteria** is made up of prokaryotes that usually have a cell wall and reproduce by cell division. *Prokaryotes* are single-celled organisms that lack a nucleus in their cells. Bacteria live in almost any environment—soil, water, and even inside the human body!

Archaea

Domain **Archaea** is also made up of prokaryotes. They differ from bacteria in their genetics and in the makeup of their cell walls. Archaea were discovered living in harsh environments, such as hot springs and thermal vents, where other organisms could not survive. Some archaea are found in the open ocean and soil.

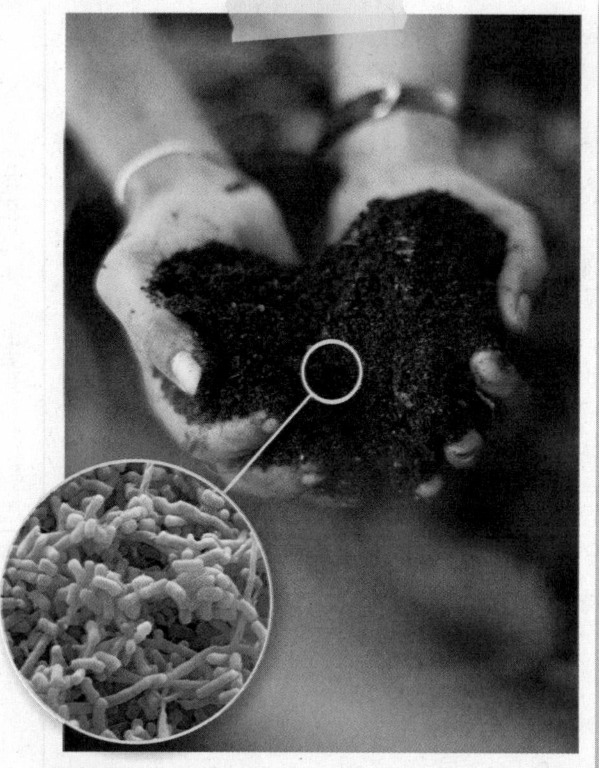

Bacteria from the genus *Streptomyces* are commonly found in soil.

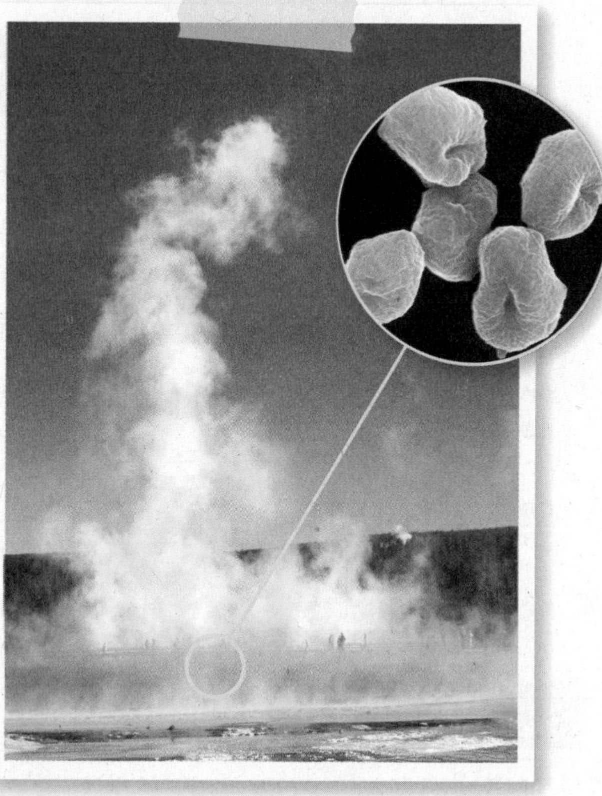

Archaea from genus *Sulfolobus* are found in hot springs.

Eukarya

What do algae, mushrooms, trees, and humans have in common? All of these organisms are *eukaryotes*. Eukaryotes are made up of cells that have a nucleus and membrane-bound organelles. The cells of eukaryotes are more complex than the cells of prokaryotes. For this reason, the cells of eukaryotes are usually larger than the cells of prokaryotes. Some eukaryotes, such as many protists and some fungi, are single-celled. Many eukaryotes are multicellular organisms. Some protists and many fungi, plants, and animals are multicellular eukaryotes. Domain **Eukarya** is made up of all eukaryotes.

It may look like a pinecone, but the pangolin is actually an animal from Africa. It is in domain Eukarya.

13 Analyze To demonstrate your understanding of domains, fill in the concept map below.

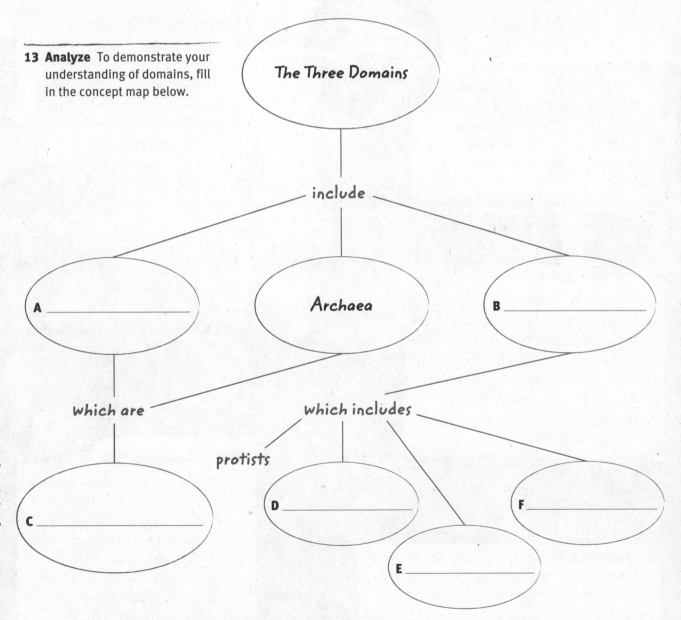

The Three Domains

include

A ________________

Archaea

B ________________

which are

which includes

protists

C ________________

D ________________

E ________________

F ________________

My Kingdom for a Eukaryote!

What kingdoms are in Eukarya?

Eukaryotes are found throughout the world. They vary in size from single-celled organisms, such as plankton, to multicellular organisms, such as blue whales. Currently, four kingdoms make up the domain Eukarya: Protista, Fungi, Plantae, and Animalia.

Kingdom Animalia

Kingdom **Animalia** contains multicellular organisms that lack cell walls, are usually able to move around, and have specialized sense organs. They eat other organisms for food. Birds, fish, reptiles, insects, and mammals are just a few examples of animals.

Kingdom Plantae

Kingdom **Plantae** consists of multicellular organisms that have cell walls, cannot move around, and make their own food. Plants are found on land and in water that light can pass through.

Kingdom Protista

Members of the kingdom **Protista**, called *protists*, are single-celled or simple multicellular organisms such as algae, protozoans, and slime molds. Protists are a very diverse group of organisms, with plantlike, animal-like, or funguslike characteristics.

Kingdom Fungi

The members of kingdom **Fungi** get energy by absorbing materials and have cells with cell walls but no chloroplasts. Fungi are single-celled or multicellular. Yeasts, molds, and mushrooms are fungi. Fungi use digestive juices to break down materials around them for food.

Visualize It!

14 Synthesize For which kingdom would you most likely need a magnifying lens or microscope to study the organisms?

____

How do classification systems change?

Thousands of organisms have been identified, but millions remain to be named. Many new organisms fit into the existing system. However, scientists often find organisms that don't fit. Not only do scientists identify new species, but they find new genera and even phyla. In fact, many scientists argue that protists are so different from each other that they should be classified into several kingdoms instead of one. Classification continues to change as scientists learn more about living things.

Active Reading

15 Predict How might the classification of protists change in the future?

How are classification relationships illustrated?

How do you organize your closet? What about your books? People organize things in many different ways. Scientists use different tools to organize information about classification. Among those tools are *branching diagrams*.

Branching Diagrams

Scientists often use a type of branching diagram called a *cladogram* (KLAD•uh•gram). A cladogram shows relationships among species. Organisms are grouped based on common characteristics. Usually, these characteristics are listed along a line that points to the right. Branches extend from this line. Organisms on branches to the right of each characteristic have the characteristic. Organisms on branches to the left lack the characteristic.

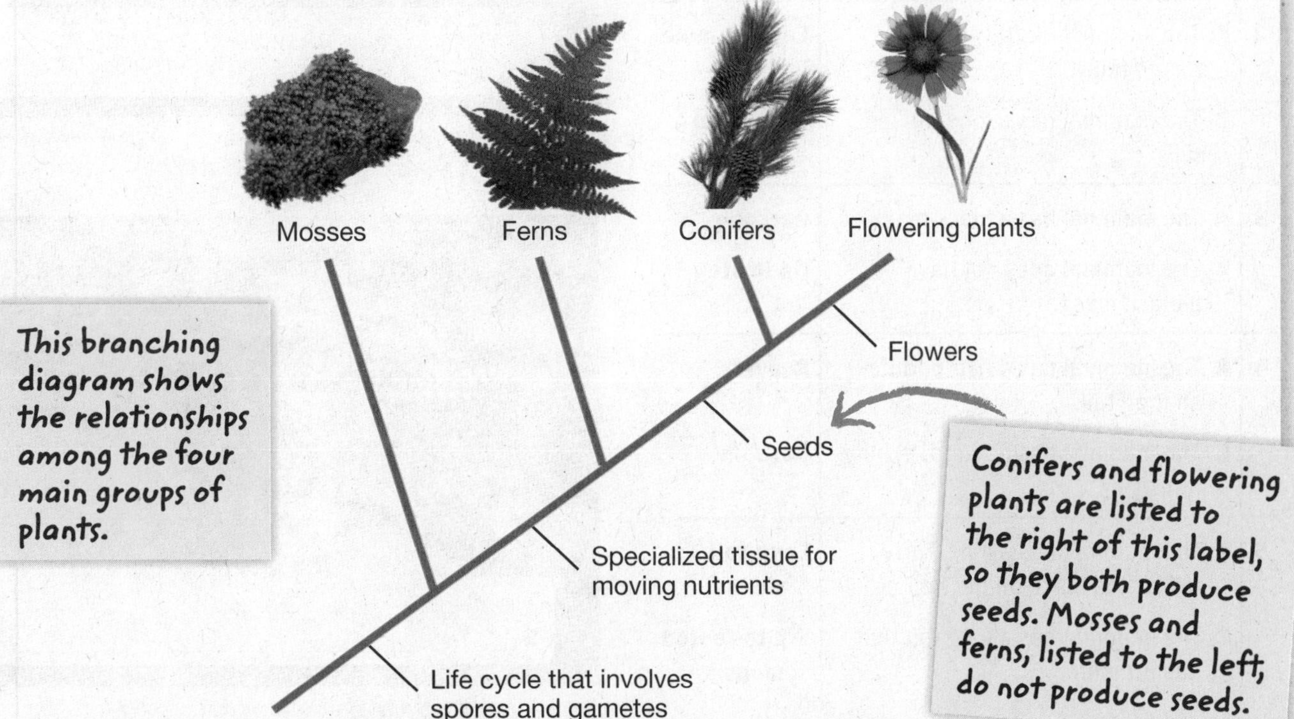

This branching diagram shows the relationships among the four main groups of plants.

Conifers and flowering plants are listed to the right of this label, so they both produce seeds. Mosses and ferns, listed to the left, do not produce seeds.

Keys to Success

How can organisms be identified?

Imagine walking through the woods. You see an animal sitting on a rock. It has fur, whiskers, and a large, flat tail. How can you find out what kind of animal it is? You can use a dichotomous key.

Dichotomous Keys

A **dichotomous key** (di•KOT•uh•muhs KEE) uses a series of paired statements to identify organisms. Each pair of statements is numbered. When identifying an organism, read each pair of statements. Then choose the statement that best describes the organism. Either the chosen statement identifies the organism or you will be directed to another pair of statements. By working through the key, you can eventually identify the organism.

16 Apply Use the dichotomous key below to identify the animals shown in the photographs.

Dichotomous Key to Six Mammals in the Eastern United States

1	**A** The mammal has no hair on its tail.	**Go to step 2**
	B The mammal has hair on its tail.	**Go to step 3**
2	**A** The mammal has a very short, naked tail.	**Eastern mole**
	B The mammal has a long, naked tail.	**Go to step 4**
3	**A** The mammal has a black mask.	**Raccoon**
	B The mammal does not have a black mask.	**Go to step 5**
4	**A** The mammal has a flat, paddle-shaped tail.	**Beaver**
	B The mammal has a round, skinny tail.	**Possum**
5	**A** The mammal has a long, furry tail that is black on the tip.	**Long-tail weasel**
	B The mammal has a long tail that has little fur.	**White-footed mouse**

A ____________

B ____________

Visualize It!

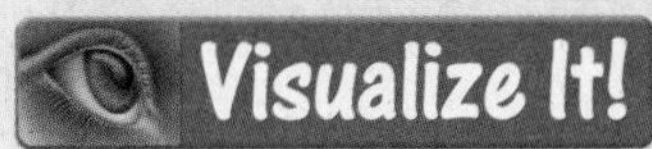

17 Apply Some dichotomous keys are set up as diagrams instead of tables. Work through the key below to identify the unknown plant.

?
Leaf has three or more main veins
Leaf has a single main vein
Maple
Leaf has no teeth, no lobes
Leaf has teeth or lobes
Leaf is somewhat lobed
Leaf is not lobed
Crabapple
Leaf has veins that end in teeth
Leaf has more teeth than side veins
American Beech
Apple
Leaf has a bristle on its tip
Leaf has no bristle
Shingle Oak
Leaf tapers at both ends
Leaf is heart shaped
Dogwood
Catalpa

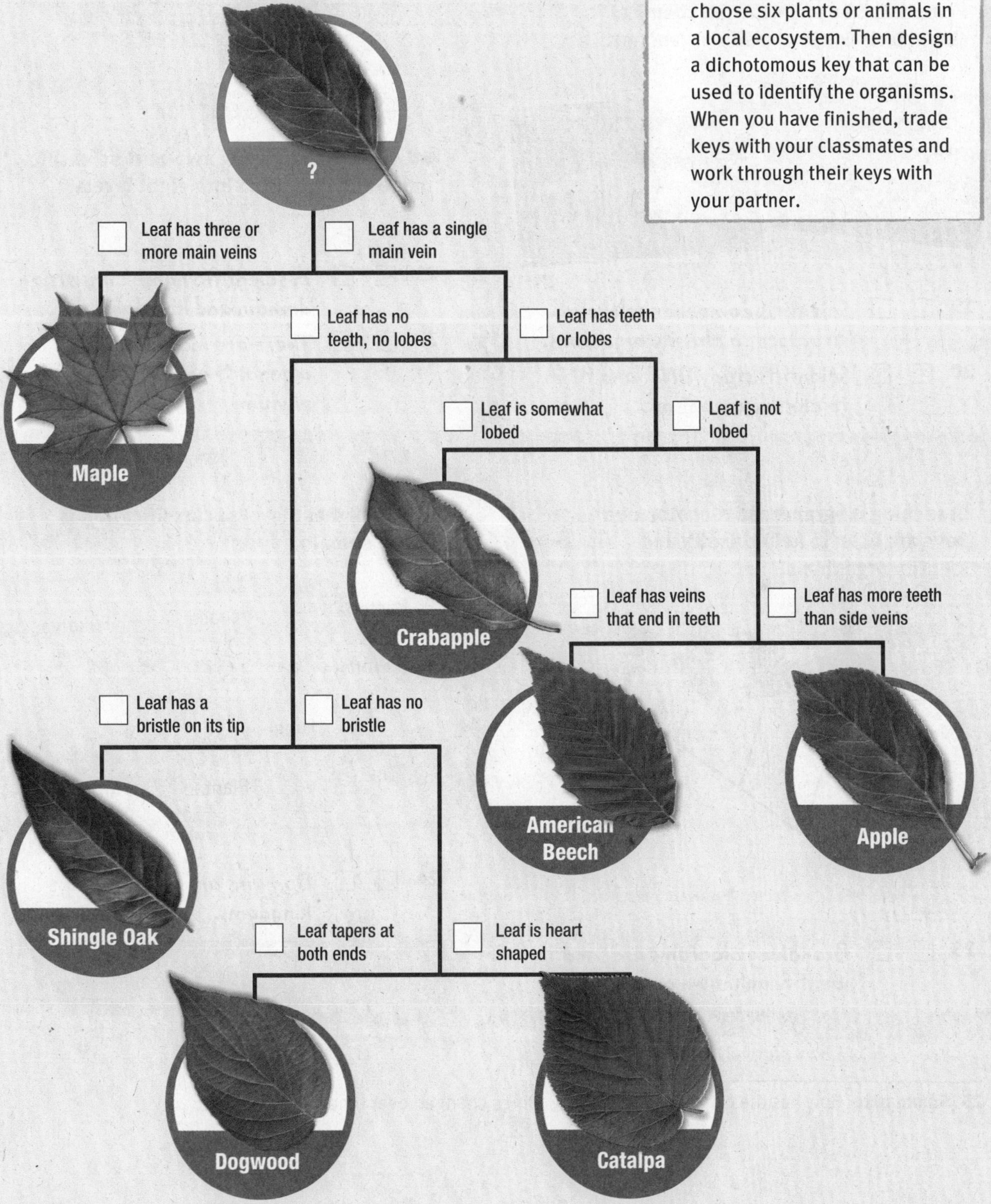

Think Outside the Book (Inquiry)

18 Summarize With a partner, choose six plants or animals in a local ecosystem. Then design a dichotomous key that can be used to identify the organisms. When you have finished, trade keys with your classmates and work through their keys with your partner.

Visual Summary

To complete this summary, check the box that indicates true or false. Then use the key below to check your answers. You can use this page to review the main concepts of the lesson.

Classification

Scientists use physical and chemical characteristics to classify organisms.

	T	F	
19	☐	☐	Scientists compare skeletal structure to classify organisms.
20	☐	☐	Scientists study DNA and RNA to classify organisms.

All species are given a two-part scientific name and classified into eight levels.

	T	F	
21	☐	☐	A scientific name consists of domain and kingdom.
22	☐	☐	There are more organisms in a genus than there are in a phylum.

Branching diagrams and dichotomous keys are used to help classify and identify organisms.

	T	F	
23	☐	☐	Branching diagrams are used to identify unknown organisms.

The highest level of classification is the domain.

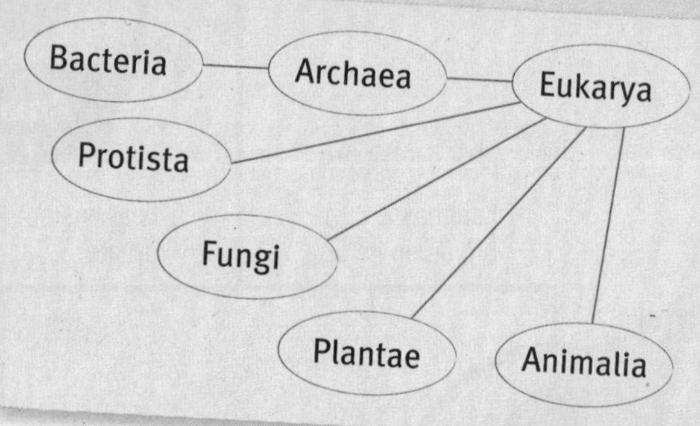

	T	F	
24	☐	☐	Domains are divided into kingdoms.

Answers: 19 T; 20 T; 21 F; 22 F; 23 F; 24 T

25 Summarize How has the classification of living things changed over time?

Lesson Review

Vocabulary

Fill in the blanks with the term that best completes the following sentences.

1 A ______________________ contains paired statements that can be used to identify organisms.

2 The kingdoms of eukaryotes are ______________________, Fungi, Plantae, and Animalia.

3 Domains ______________________ and ______________________ are made up of prokaryotes.

Key Concepts

4 List Name the eight levels of classification from most general to most definite.

5 Explain How did scientific names impact classification?

6 Identify What two types of evidence are used to classify organisms?

7 Compare Dichotomous keys and branching diagrams organize different types of information about classification. How are these tools used differently?

Critical Thinking

Use the figure to answer the following questions.

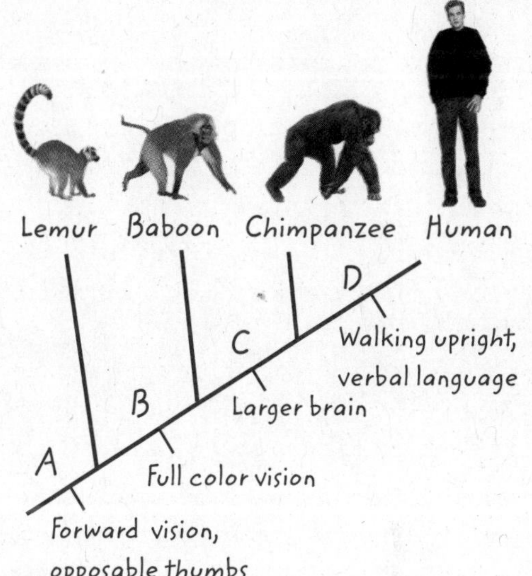

8 Identify Which traits do baboons have?

9 Analyze Which animal shares the most traits with humans?

10 Synthesize Do both lemurs and humans have the trait listed at point D? Explain.

11 Classify A scientist finds an organism that cannot move. It has many cells, produces spores, and gets food from its environment. In which kingdom does it belong? Explain.

My Notes

Unit 6 Summary

Chemistry of Life

is a component of the

Classification of Living Things

The Characteristics of Cells

Cell Structure and Function

Levels of Cellular Organization

Homeostasis and Cell Processes

1 Interpret The Graphic Organizer above shows that the characteristics of cells are related to cell structure and function. For example, all cells have a cell membrane. Explain the role of this characteristic in a cell's structure and function.

2 Distinguish Describe the difference between the four levels of cellular organization.

3 Infer Why is waste removal a necessary cellular process for a cell to maintain homeostasis?

4 Apply If two animals have almost identical physical characteristics, can you assume that they are related species? Why or why not?

Name ______________________________

Multiple Choice

Identify the choice that best completes the statement or answers the question.

1 Serena knows that scientists use physical characteristics to classify organisms. She studies the figures of four different organisms.

Which two organisms should Serena conclude are **most** closely related?

A. 1 and 2

B. 1 and 3

C. 2 and 3

D. 2 and 4

2 Eukaryotic cells and prokaryotic cells have some parts in common. Which of the following pairs of parts would you find in **both** types of cells?

F. cytoplasm and nucleus

G. cell membrane and cytoplasm

H. DNA and membrane-bound organelles

I. cell membrane and membrane-bound organelles

3 Robert Hooke was the first person to describe cells. Which of the following instruments did he use to make his observations?

A.

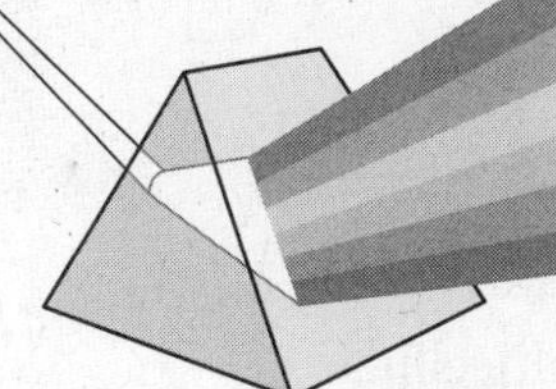

C.

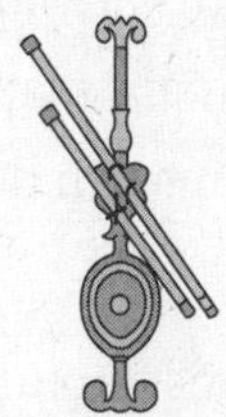

B.

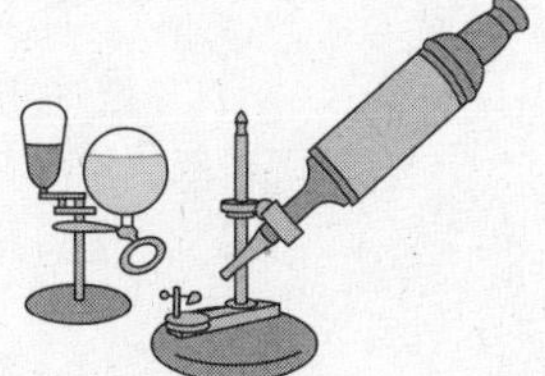

D.

Benchmark Review

4 Cells use energy to carry out various cell processes. Which of the following molecules stores energy for the cell to use?

F. ATP

G. DNA

H. water

I. chloroplast

5 In biology class, Zach observes cells. Each cell has a structure that separates the inside of the cell from the environment. Which structure is Zach observing?

A. nucleus

B. cytoskeleton

C. cell membrane

D. genetic material

6 Imagine a cell that has the shape of a cube with sides that are 3 cm long. What is the surface area-to-volume ratio of this cell?

F. 27 cm^3

G. 54 cm^2

H. 27 cm^3 : 54 cm^2

I. 54 cm^2 : 27 cm^3

7 Jemin made a poster to compare unicellular organisms with multicellular organisms. Which of the following statements that she included is **not** true?

A. Unicellular organisms live longer.

B. Multicellular organisms are larger.

C. Unicellular organisms are made of just one cell.

D. Multicellular organisms can have groups of cells that work together.

8 Gerard listed four levels of structural organization within multicellular organisms. He listed them in order from the smallest structure to the largest structure. Which of the following lists is correct?

F. cells, tissues, organ systems, organs

G. cells, tissues, organs, organ systems

H. tissues, cells, organ systems, organs

I. tissues, cells, organs, organ systems

Name ________________

9 The following picture shows a single cell.

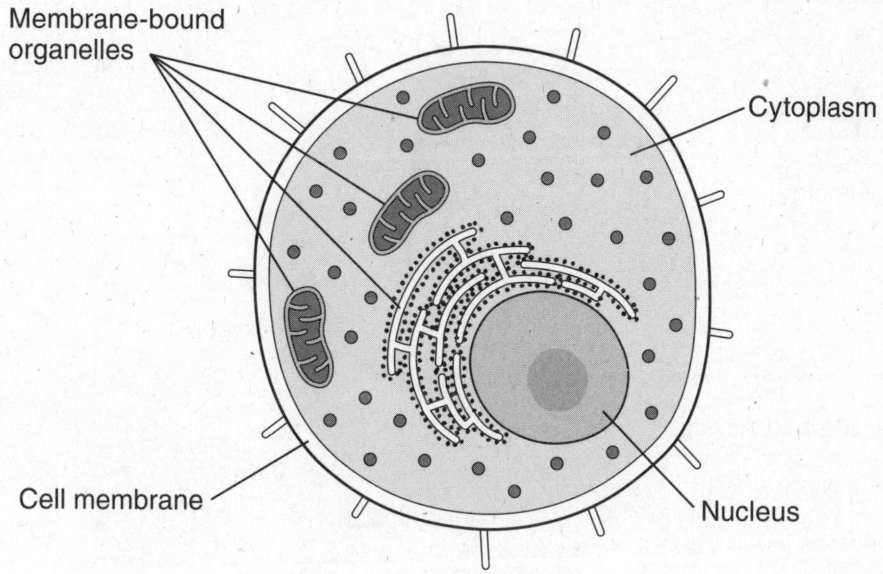

What is the function of the structure labeled *Nucleus*?

A. to hold the cell's DNA

B. to hold the cell's organelles

C. to hold the cell's cytoplasm

D. to hold the cell's cell membrane

10 Kayla summarizes the cell theory to her class. She states that all organisms are made up of one or more cells. Which pair of statements correctly completes her summary?

F. All cells come from existing cells, and all cells have the same parts.

G. All cells are the same size, and the cell is the basic unit of all organisms.

H. The cell is the basic unit of all organisms, and all cells have the same parts.

I. The cell is the basic unit of all organisms, and all cells come from existing cells.

Benchmark Review

11 The following diagram shows the basic steps of photosynthesis.

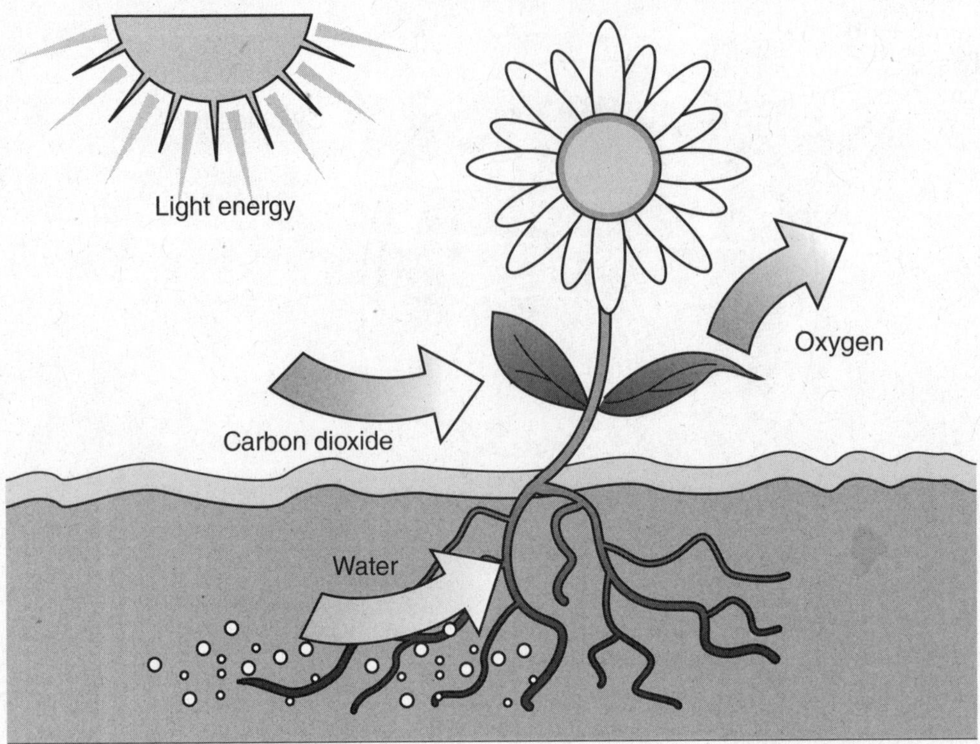

What label would you add to complete this illustration so that it shows the products of photosynthesis?

A. ATP
B. Fat
C. Protein
D. Sugar

12 Mariella is observing the cells of an organism that has ribosomes, mitochondria, and lysosomes. She notes that the cells do not have a cell wall. What type of organism is Mariella **most likely** observing?

F. a plant
G. a fungus
H. an animal
I. a prokaryote

13 Lilly is writing a report about nutrients. Which of the following is a **true** statement about nutrients that she could include in her report?

A. Some organisms do not need nutrients.
B. Lipids and carbohydrates are two types of nutrients.
C. Nutrients are cells in the bodies of animals but not plants.
D. Nutrients are chemical compounds that have no function in animals.

14 Tina looks in her science book at a diagram of a cellular organelle. The diagram is shown below.

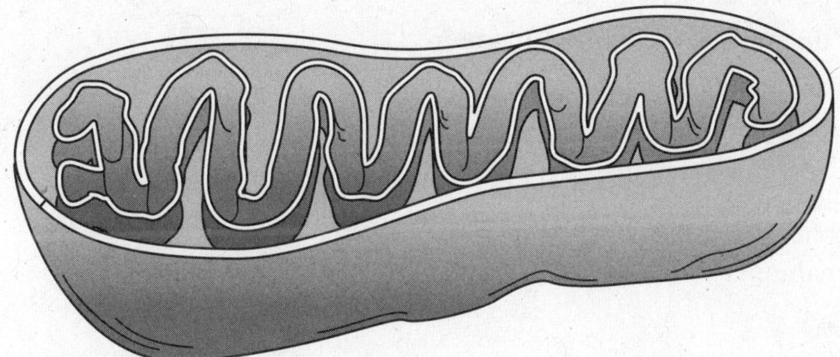

Which organelle is Tina observing?

F. cytoskeleton
G. large central vacuole
H. mitochondrion
I. ribosome

15 Plant cells use photosynthesis to make food. Plant cells also use cellular respiration to get energy from the food they make. How is cellular respiration **different** from photosynthesis?

A. Photosynthesis produces ATP, and cellular respiration produces sugars.
B. Photosynthesis requires oxygen, and cellular respiration requires carbon dioxide.
C. Photosynthesis produces oxygen, and cellular respiration produces carbon dioxide.
D. Photosynthesis requires energy from food, and cellular respiration requires energy from the sun.

Benchmark Review

16 Jelal subscribes to a nature magazine. An article about the classification of mammals included the following table.

	Mammal 1	Mammal 2	Mammal 3
Height at shoulder	42 cm	62 cm	77 cm
Length without tail	68 cm	81 cm	110 cm
Weight	22 lb	30 lb	80 lb
Scientific name	*Canis mesomelas*	*Canis latrans*	*Canis lupus*

Which of the following is a statement that Jelal might read in the article?

F. The organisms belong in the same genus.

G. The organisms do not have a common ancestor.

H. The organisms are members of the domain Archaea.

I. The organisms lack common chemical characteristics.

17 Mike is trying to explain scientific names to a classmate. What are the two parts of a scientific name?

A. genus and species

B. phylum and class

C. domain and genus

D. domain and kingdom

18 Roger explains to his sister the importance of water in cell processes. He describes the chemical structure of water to her. Which of the following is a **true** statement about water?

F. Water is an element.

G. Water is a molecule because it contains carbon.

H. Water is a molecule because it has two different elements.

I. Water is a molecule because it is made up of two or more atoms.

UNIT 7

Human Body Systems

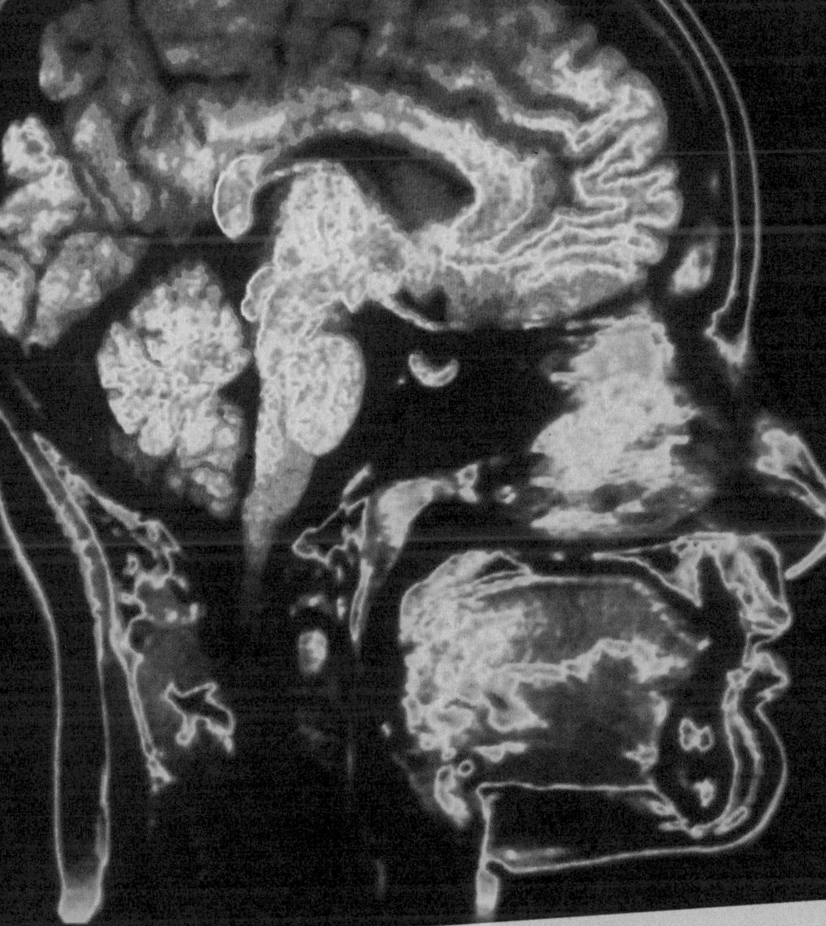

Big Idea 14

Organization and Development of Living Organisms

A brain scan can show whether the brain is functioning normally.

What do you think?

In the Middle Ages, people dug up the dead and operated on them to learn about the body. Today, technology like the MRI scanner allows us to study the living body. How does the living body work?

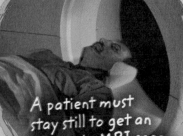

A patient must stay still to get an accurate MRI scan.

Unit 7

Human Body Systems

CITIZEN SCIENCE

Muscles at Work

Design a test for muscle endurance or strength.

1 Define the Problem

Unlike many things that wear out with use, our muscles actually get stronger the more often they are used. Doing different kinds of exercises helps different groups of muscles. But how can you tell if you are improving? How can you tell how strong a group of muscles are?

Muscles become larger as they become stronger.

Strength moves like this hold take practice and training.

2 Think About It

Design a test for a group of muscles.

Choose a group of muscles that you would like to work with. Then, come up with one or two simple exercises that can be done to show either how strong the muscles are or how well they are able to work continuously. Place a time limit on your tests so that the tests don't take too long.

Check off the points below as you use them to design your test.

- ☐ The kind of action the muscles can do.
- ☐ To do the test safely, remember to isolate the group of muscles. (Research how to do an exercise safely.)
- ☐ The equipment you will need for the test.

3 Plan and Test Your Design

A Write out how you will conduct your test in the space below. Check your plan with your teacher before proceeding.

____

____

____

____

____

____

B Conduct the test on yourself. Have a classmate time you, help you count, or make any other measurements that you might need help with. Briefly state your findings.

____

____

____

____

____

Take It Home

Do the same exercises at home throughout the week. Then conduct your test again. See if there is any improvement. Report your findings to the class.

Lesson 1

Introduction to Body Systems

ESSENTIAL QUESTION

How do the body systems work together to maintain homeostasis?

By the end of this lesson, you should be able to describe the functions of the human body systems, including how they work together to maintain homeostasis.

This image was made by a magnetic resonance imaging (MRI) scanner. The body's organs work together to ensure our bodies stay healthy and alive!

Sunshine State Standards

SC.6.L.14.5 Identify and investigate the general functions of the major systems of the human body (digestive, respiratory, circulatory, reproductive, excretory, immune, nervous, and musculoskeletal) and describe ways these systems interact with each other to maintain homeostasis.

HE.6.C.1.8 Explain how body systems are impacted by hereditary factors and infectious agents.

Engage Your Brain

1 Predict Check T or F to show whether you think each statement is true or false.

T	F	
☐	☐	Your muscles provide a framework that supports and protects your body.
☐	☐	When you breathe in and out, you're using your lungs.
☐	☐	Your nervous system gets rid of wastes from your body.
☐	☐	When you eat food, it enters your digestive system.

2 Identify Draw a diagram of your body showing at least four organs. As you read the lesson, write down the organ system that each organ is a part of.

Active Reading

3 Synthesize You can often define an unknown word if you know the meaning of its word parts. Use the word parts and sentence below to make an educated guess about the meaning of the word *homeostasis*.

Greek word	Meaning
homoios	same
stasis	standing

Example Sentence

In order to maintain homeostasis, the cardiovascular system and the respiratory system work together to move oxygen-carrying blood around the body.

homeostasis:

Vocabulary Terms

- **homeostasis**

4 Apply As you learn the definition of the vocabulary term in this lesson, make a sketch that shows the meaning of the term or an example of that term. Next to your drawing, write your own definition of the term.

What do the body systems do?

Humans and other organisms need to get energy. They need to use energy to run their bodies and move. They need to reproduce. They need to get rid of waste and protect their bodies. Body systems, also called *organ systems*, help organisms to do all of these things. They also coordinate all the functions of a body.

Groups of organs that work together form body systems. Nerves detect a stimulus in the environment and send a signal through the spinal cord to the brain. The brain sends a signal to respond. Without all the parts, the system would not work. Some organs work in more than one organ system.

Active Reading **5 Identify** As you read about body systems on these pages, underline the main function of each body system.

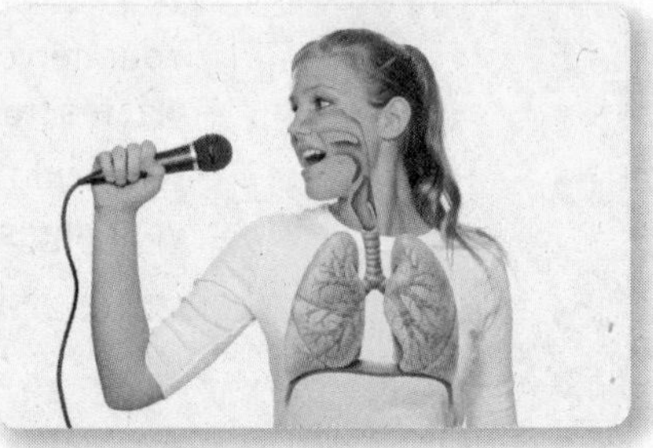

The respiratory system gathers oxygen from the environment and gets rid of carbon dioxide from the body. The exchange occurs in the lungs.

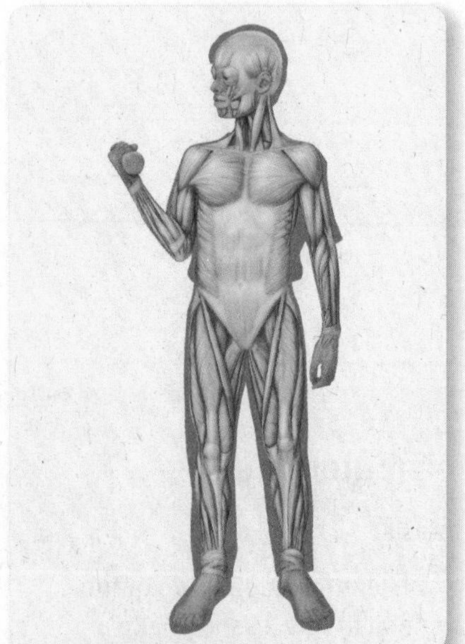

The muscular system allows movement of body parts. It works with the skeletal system to help you move.

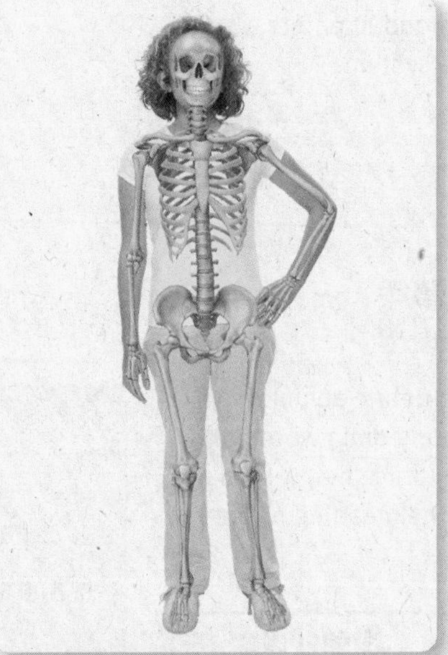

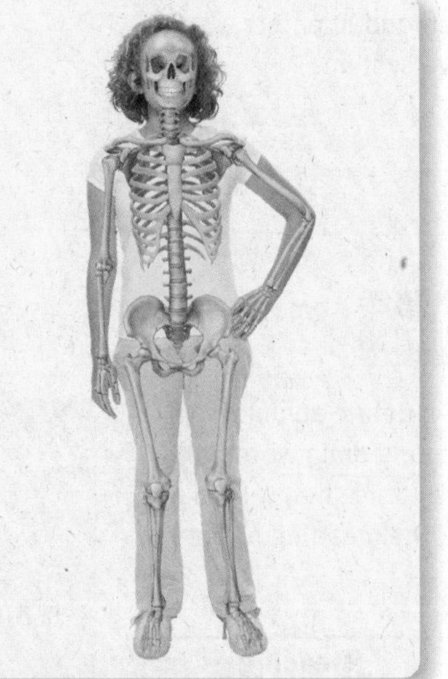

The skeletal system is made up of bones, ligaments, and cartilage. It supports the body and protects important organs. It also makes blood cells.

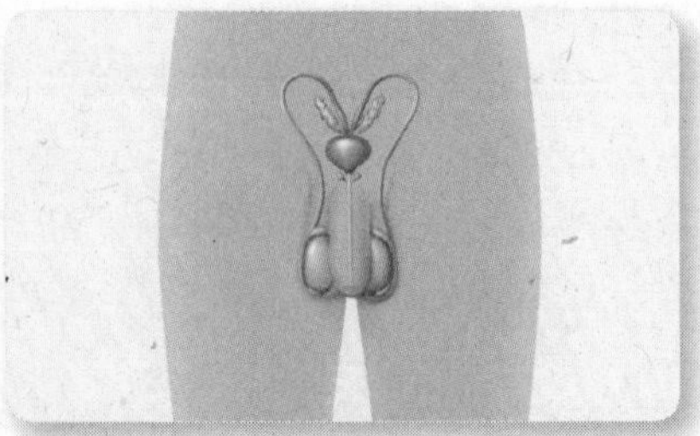

The male reproductive system produces sperm and delivers it to the female reproductive system.

The female reproductive system produces eggs and nourishes a developing fetus.

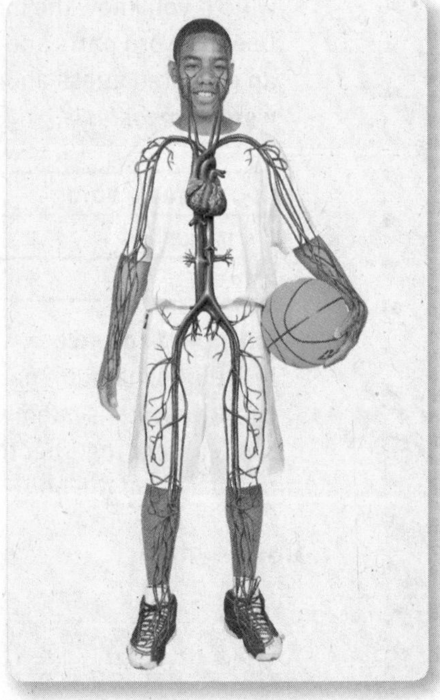

The cardiovascular system moves blood through the body. The heart is the pump for this system. Blood flows through blood vessels.

Visualize It!

6 Analyze Look closely at the body systems shown on these pages. Then circle the two systems that send messages around the body.

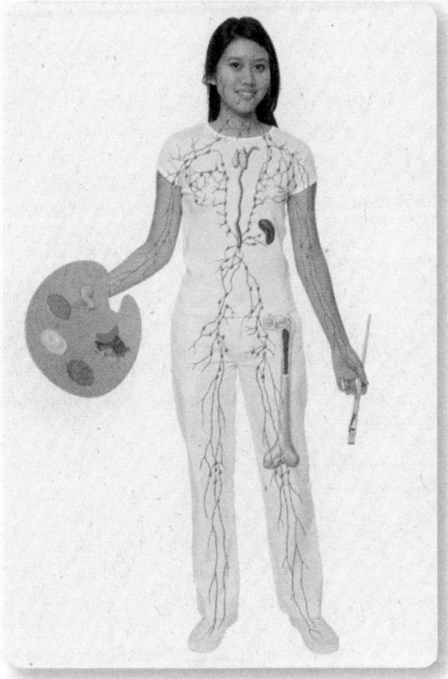

The lymphatic system returns leaked fluid back to the blood. As a major part of the immune system, it has cells that help get rid of invading bacteria and viruses.

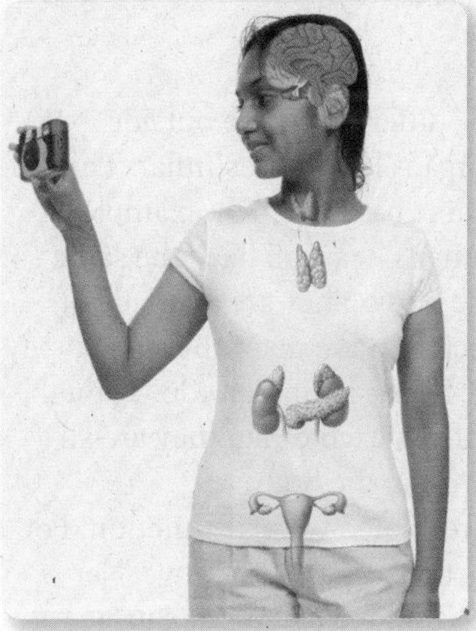

The endocrine system makes chemical messages. These messages help to regulate conditions inside the body. They also influence growth and development.

The integumentary system is the protective covering of the body. It includes the skin, hair, and nails. As part of the immune system, the skin acts as a barrier that protects the body from infection.

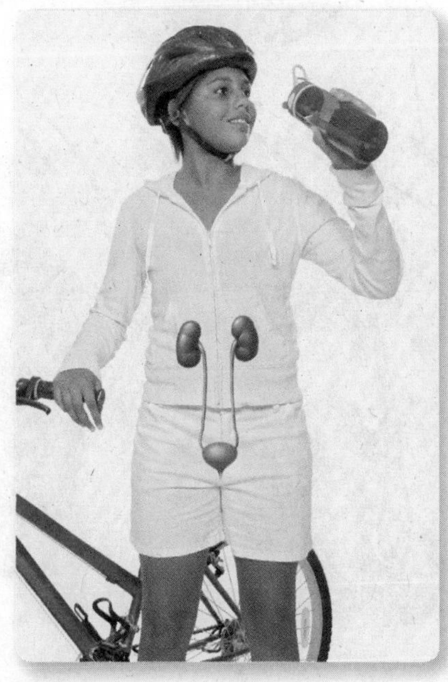

The excretory system gets rid of the body's wastes. The urinary system, shown here, removes wastes from blood. The skin, lungs, and digestive system also remove wastes from the body.

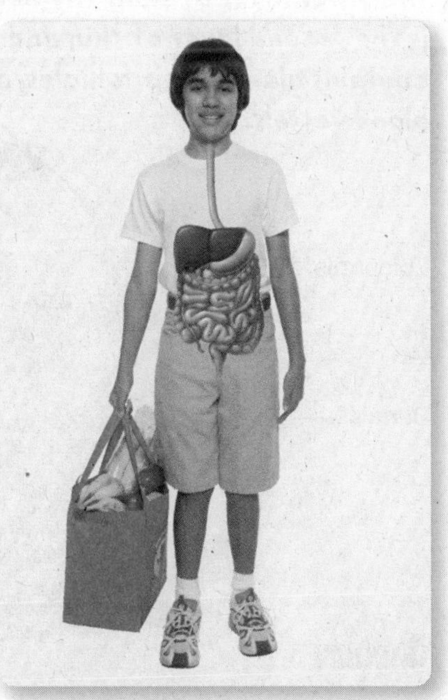

The digestive system breaks down food into nutrients that can be used by the body. The stomach breaks down food into tiny pieces. Nutrients are absorbed in the small intestine.

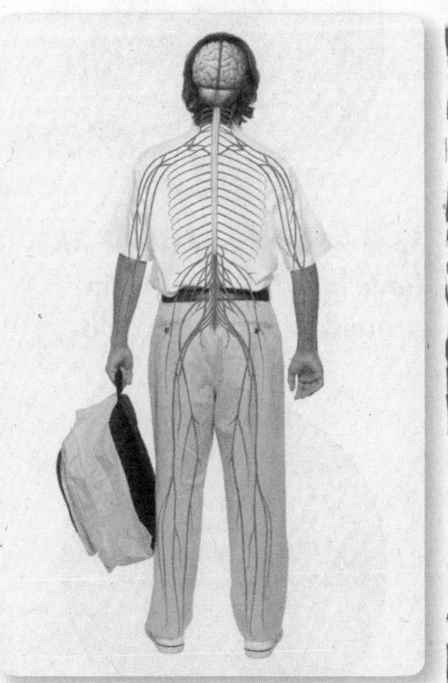

The nervous system collects information and responds to it by sending electrical messages. This information may come from outside or inside the body. The brain is the center of the nervous system.

A Closer Look

How are structure and function linked?

Even though animals may look very different on the outside, on the inside, their cells, tissues, and organs look very similar. This is because these structures do the same basic job. For example, a frog's heart, a bird's heart, and a human's heart all have the same function, to pump blood around the body. They are all made of the same type of muscle tissue, which is made up of the same type of muscle cells. The structure of the hearts is similar, too. Though their shape may be a little different from each other, they are all muscular pumps that push blood around the body.

The shapes and sizes of cells are related to their function. For example, sperm cells have long tails that are used to move. Nerve cells are long and thin to send messages long distances. Surface skin cells are broad and flat. The diagram below shows how skin cells form the skin, which covers and protects the body.

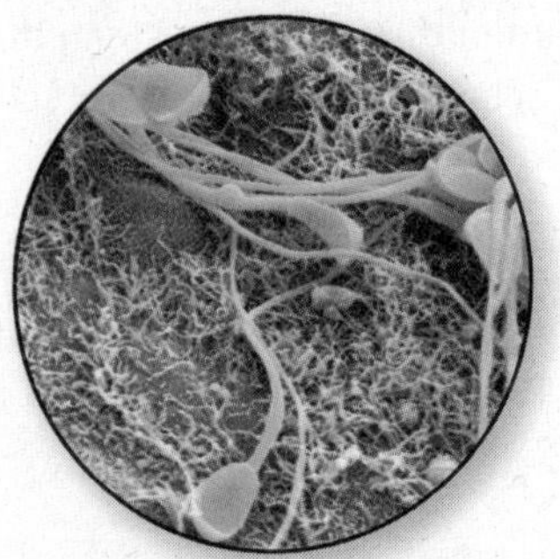

Sperm cells can "swim." They have long tails that whip around to move the cells.

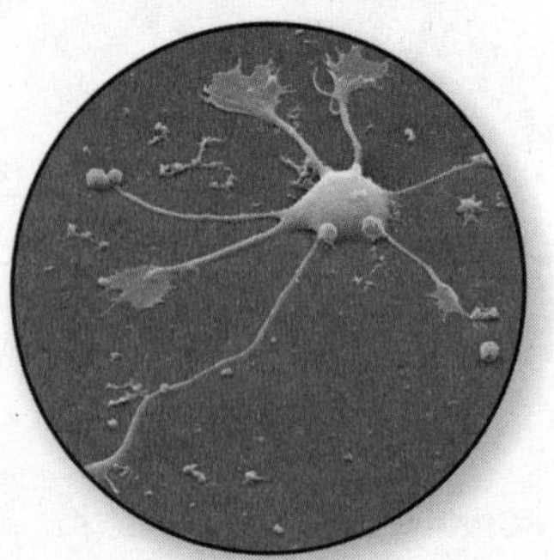

Nerve cells have long, thin branches to send electrical messages between the brain and far-away body parts.

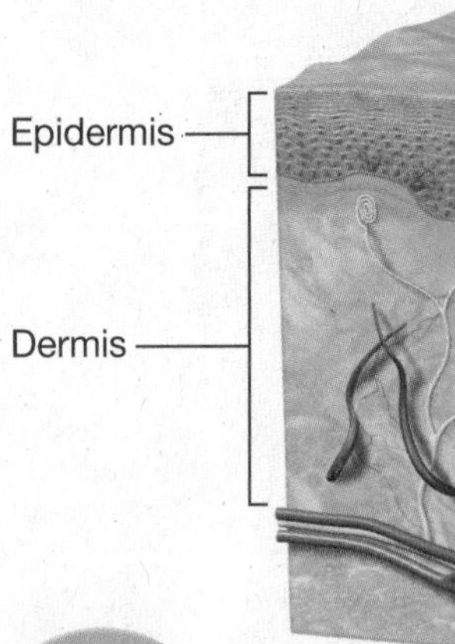

Skin is made up of different cells in many layers. The epidermis is the outer layer of skin. The dermis is the second layer of skin and contains glands, hair follicles, and blood vessels.

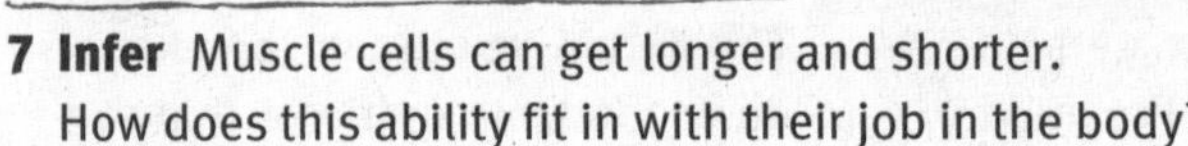

Inquiry

7 Infer Muscle cells can get longer and shorter. How does this ability fit in with their job in the body?

____

____

____

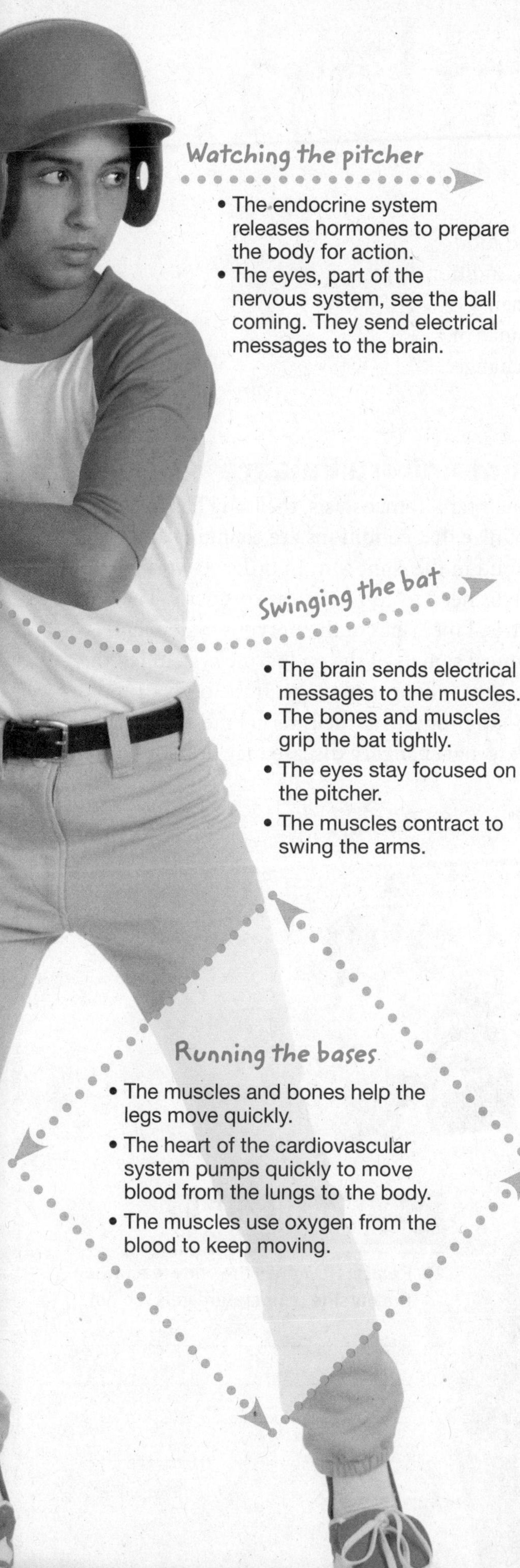

Watching the pitcher
• The endocrine system releases hormones to prepare the body for action.
• The eyes, part of the nervous system, see the ball coming. They send electrical messages to the brain.
Swinging the bat
• The brain sends electrical messages to the muscles.
• The bones and muscles grip the bat tightly.
• The eyes stay focused on the pitcher.
• The muscles contract to swing the arms.
Running the bases
• The muscles and bones help the legs move quickly.
• The heart of the cardiovascular system pumps quickly to move blood from the lungs to the body.
• The muscles use oxygen from the blood to keep moving.

How do body systems work together?

Our body systems can do a lot, but they can't work alone! Almost everything we need for our bodies to work properly requires many body systems to work together. For example, the nervous system may sense danger. The endocrine system releases hormones that cause the heart to beat faster to deliver more oxygen through the circulatory system to muscles. The muscular system and skeletal system work together to run away from danger.

Active Reading **8 Identify** As you read the captions on the left, underline examples of body systems working together.

Body Systems Share Organs

Many organs are part of several body systems. Reproductive organs are part of the reproductive system and part of the endocrine system. The liver works in the digestive system but also is part of the excretory system. The heart is part of the muscular system and the cardiovascular system. Blood vessels too are shared. For example, blood vessels transport chemical messages from the endocrine system and cells from the lymphatic and cardiovascular systems.

Body Systems Communicate

There are two basic ways cells communicate: by electrical messages and by chemical messages. Nerve cells transfer information between the body and the spinal cord and brain. Nerves pass electrical messages from one cell to the next along the line. The endocrine system sends chemical messages through the bloodstream to certain cells.

9 Apply When you are finished running the bases, you are sweating and you feel thirsty. What body systems are interacting in this case?

Keeping the Balance

What is homeostasis?

Cells need certain conditions to work properly. They need food and oxygen and to have their wastes taken away. If body conditions were to change too much, cells would not be able to do their jobs. **Homeostasis** (hoh•mee•oh•STAY•sis) is the maintenance of a constant internal environment when outside conditions change. Responding to change allows all systems to work properly.

Responding to Change

If the external environment changes, body systems work together to keep conditions stable within the body. For example, if body cells were to get too cold, they would not work properly and they could die. So, if the brain senses the body temperature is getting too low, it tells the muscles to shiver. Shivering muscles release energy as heat which warms the body. Your brain will also tell you to put on a sweater!

Maintaining a Balance

To maintain homeostasis, the body has to recognize that conditions are changing and then respond in the right way. In order to work, organ systems need to communicate properly. The electrical messages of the nervous system and chemical signals of the endocrine system tell the body what changes to make. If the body cannot respond properly to the internal messages or to an external change, a disease may develop.

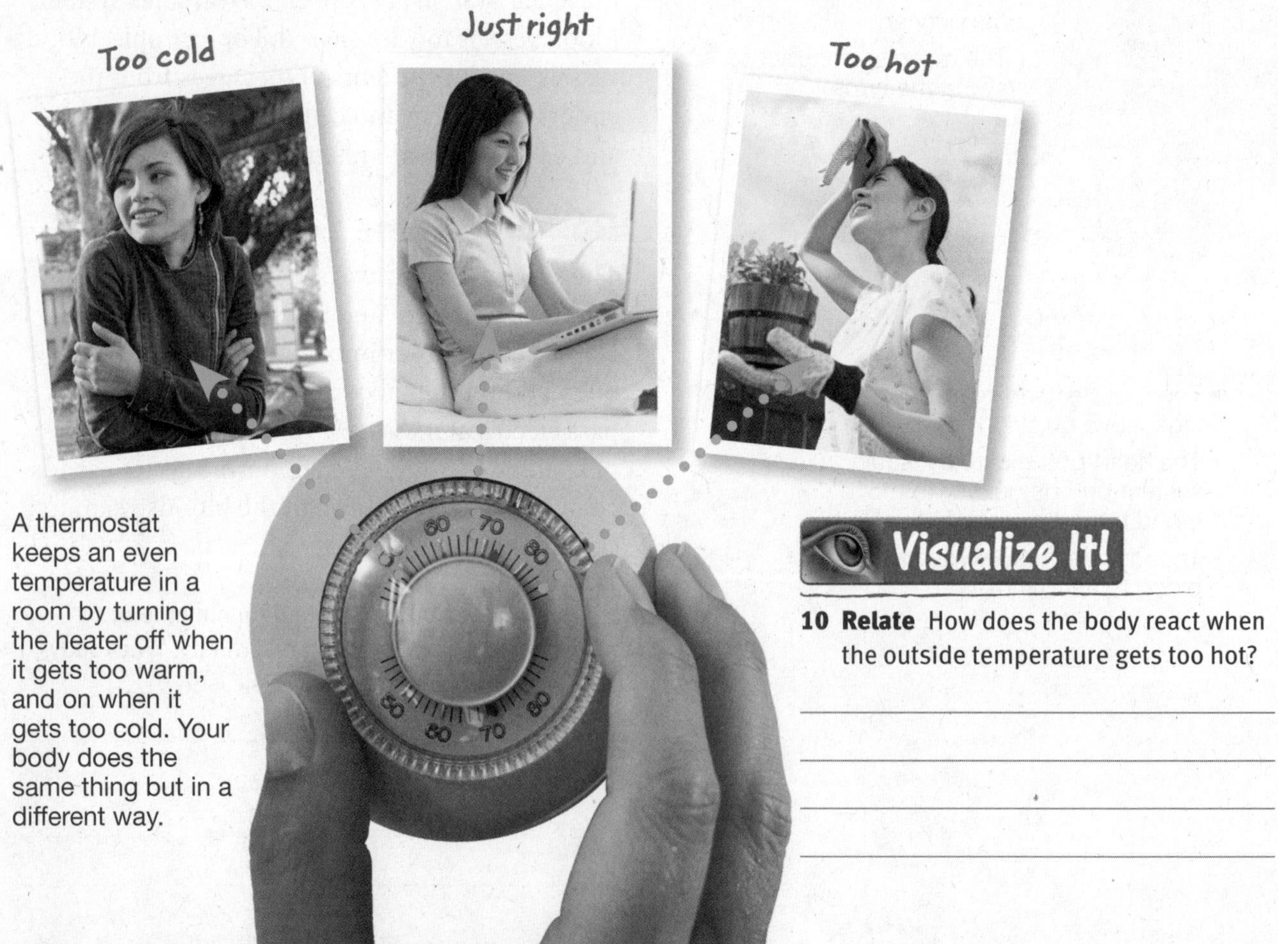

A thermostat keeps an even temperature in a room by turning the heater off when it gets too warm, and on when it gets too cold. Your body does the same thing but in a different way.

Visualize It!

10 Relate How does the body react when the outside temperature gets too hot?

____

____

____

____

What can go wrong with homeostasis?

If one body system does not work properly, other body systems can be affected. For example, body cells that do not get enough energy or nutrients cannot work properly. A lack of food harms many systems and may cause disease or even death. The presence of toxins or pathogens also can disrupt homeostasis. Toxins can prevent cells from carrying out life processes and pathogens can break down cells. Problems also occur if the body's messages do not work, or they are not sent when or where they are needed. Many diseases which affect homeostasis are hereditary.

11 Identify As you read this page, underline what can happen if homeostasis is disrupted.

Structure or Function Diseases

Problems with the structure or function of cells, tissues, or organs can affect the body. For example, diabetes is a disease that affects cell function. Certain changes in body cells stop them from taking glucose in from the blood as they normally do. If cells cannot get energy in the form of glucose, they cannot work properly.

Pathogens and Disease

When the body cannot maintain homeostasis, it is easier for pathogens to invade the body. Pathogens can also cause a disruption in homeostasis. For example, tuberculosis is a lung disease caused by bacteria. It weakens the lungs and body. Weakened lungs cannot take in oxygen well. Low oxygen levels affect the whole body.

12 Apply Alcoholism is a disease that disrupts homeostasis. Below are three body systems that are affected by alcohol. The effects on the nervous system are filled in. In the space provided, predict what might happen when the function of the two remaining systems is affected.

Body systems affected	What are the effects?
Nervous system	Disrupts proper functioning of the brain. The brain cannot respond properly to internal or external messages.
Digestive system	
Reproductive system	

Alcoholism can damage the structure and function of the liver and reduce its ability to remove toxins from the blood.

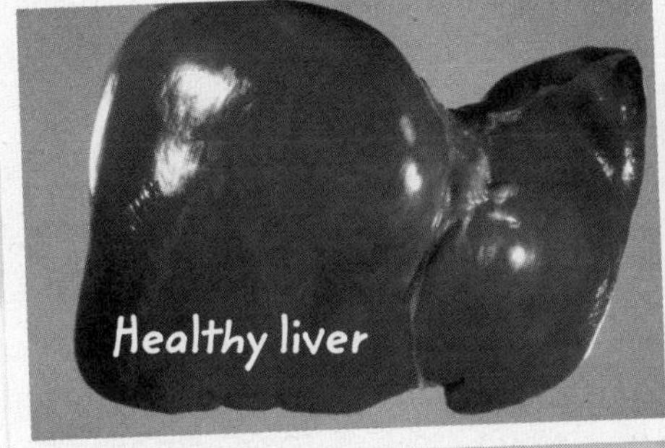

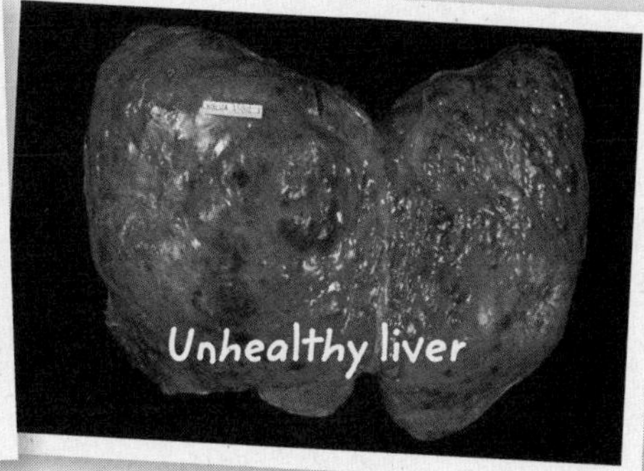

Visual Summary

To complete this summary, fill in the blanks with the correct word or phrase. Then use the key below to check your answers. You can use this page to review the main concepts of the lesson.

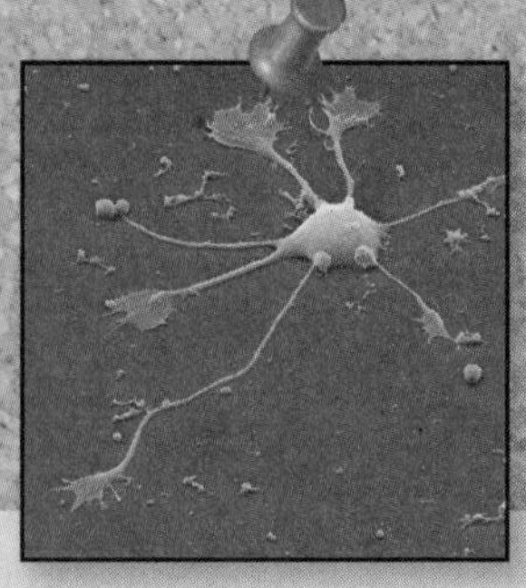

Body Systems and Homeostasis

Body systems each have specific jobs.

13 The ____________ system brings oxygen into the blood and releases carbon dioxide from the body.

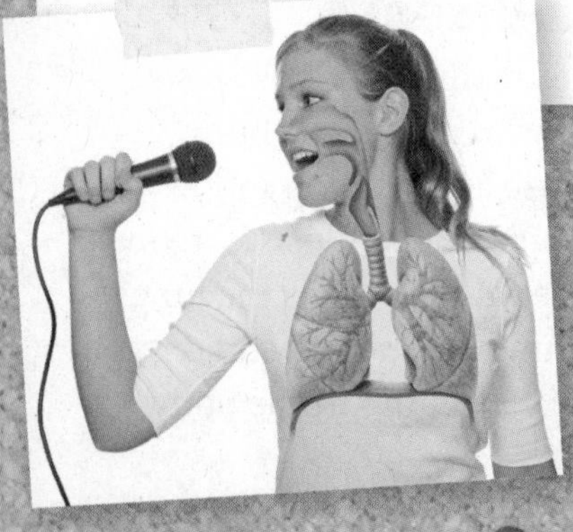

The structure of cells, tissues, and organs are linked to their functions.

14 The long, thin cells of the ____________ system help transmit messages around the body. The muscular heart pushes ____________ around the body.

Body systems work together, which allows the body to work properly.

15 The ____________ and ____________ systems work together to allow the player to swing the bat.

The body maintains homeostasis by adjusting to change.

16 If body temperature goes up, the ____________ senses the change and will work to reduce the body temperature to normal.

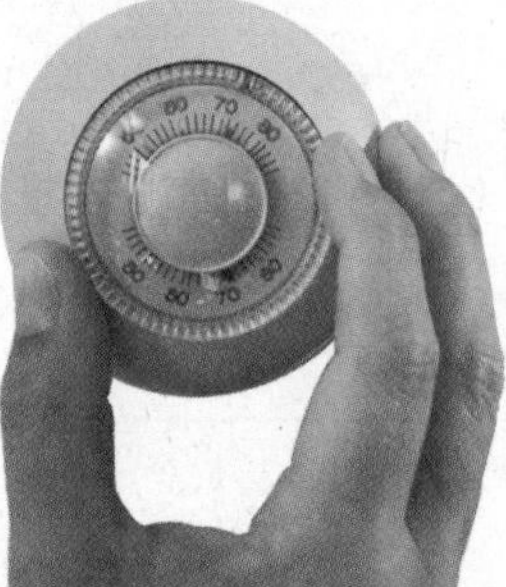

Answers: 13 respiratory; 14 nervous; blood; 15 nervous; muscular (either order); 16 brain

17 Explain How might disruption of the respiratory system affect homeostasis of the body?

Lesson Review

Vocabulary

Use a term from the lesson to complete each sentence below.

1 ________________________ is maintaining stable conditions inside the body.

2 A group of organs that work together is called a(n) ________________________ .

Key Concepts

3 **Compare** How are the functions of the skeletal and muscular systems related?

4 **Identify** What body system receives information from inside and outside the body and responds to that information?

5 **Explain** How is skin part of the integumentary system and the excretory system?

6 **Describe** What are the basic needs of all cells in the body?

7 **Relate** Give an example of how a cell's structure relates to its function in the body.

Critical Thinking

Use the graph to answer the following questions.

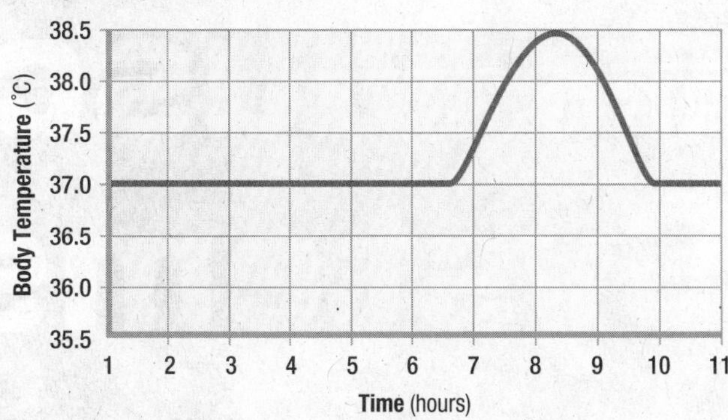

8 **Analyze** Is the body in homeostasis during the entire time shown in the graph? Explain your answer.

9 **Predict** What would happen to the body if the graph continued to decrease during the tenth hour instead of leveling off?

10 **Apply** The body loses water and salts in sweat. Explain why drinking large volumes of plain water after exercising may affect the salt balance in the body.

Lesson 2

The Skeletal and Muscular Systems

ESSENTIAL QUESTION

How do your skeletal and muscular systems work?

By the end of this lesson, you should be able to explain how the skeletal and muscular systems work together to allow movement of the body.

By working together, your muscular and skeletal systems allow you to do many things such as stand up, sit down, type a note, or run a race.

Sunshine State Standards

SC.6.L.14.5 Identify and investigate the general functions of the major systems of the human body (digestive, respiratory, circulatory, reproductive, excretory, immune, nervous, and musculoskeletal) and describe ways these systems interact with each other to maintain homeostasis.

HE.6.C.1.8 Explain how body systems are impacted by hereditary factors and infectious agents.

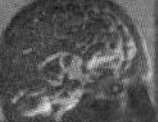

Engage Your Brain

1 **Identify** Circle the terms that best complete the following sentences.

The *skeletal / muscular* system is responsible for supporting the body.

Bones are part of your *skeletal / muscular* system.

Your heart is made up of *bone / muscle* tissue.

You can increase your flexibility by stretching your *bones / muscles*.

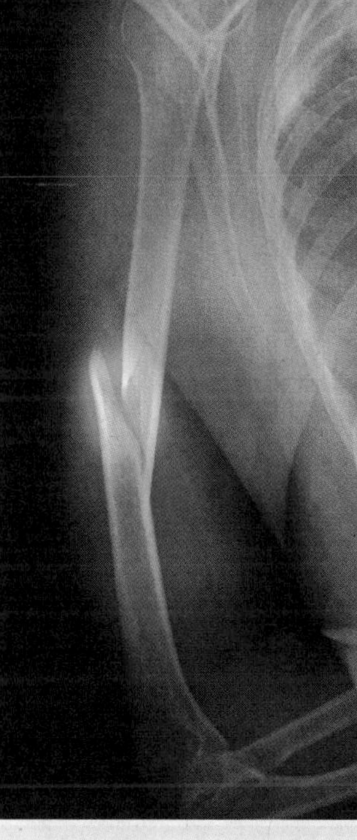

2 **Infer** This x-ray shows a broken arm. How might this injury affect your ability to move?

Active Reading

3 **Synthesize** You can often identify functions of a body part if you know what its name means. Use the Latin words below and context clues to make an educated guess about a function of *ligaments* and *tendons*.

Latin word	Meaning
ligare	to tie
tendere	to stretch

Example Sentence
Ligaments are found at the ends of bones.

ligament:

Example Sentence
Tendons connect muscles to bones.

tendon:

Vocabulary Terms

- **skeletal system**
- **muscular system**
- **ligament**
- **tendon**
- **joint**

4 **Apply** As you learn the definition of each vocabulary term in this lesson, create your own definition or sketch it to help you remember the meaning of the term.

What's Inside?

What are the main functions of the skeletal system?

When you hear the word *skeleton*, you might think of the dry, white bones that you see in the models in your science class. You might think your bones are lifeless, but they are very much alive. The **skeletal system** is the organ system that supports and protects the body and allows it to move. Its other jobs include storing minerals and producing red blood cells. A human's skeleton is inside the body, so it is called an *endoskeleton*.

5 Identify As you read, underline the main functions of the skeletal system.

Visualize It!

6 Relate How might a suit of armor be a good analogy for a function of the skeletal system?

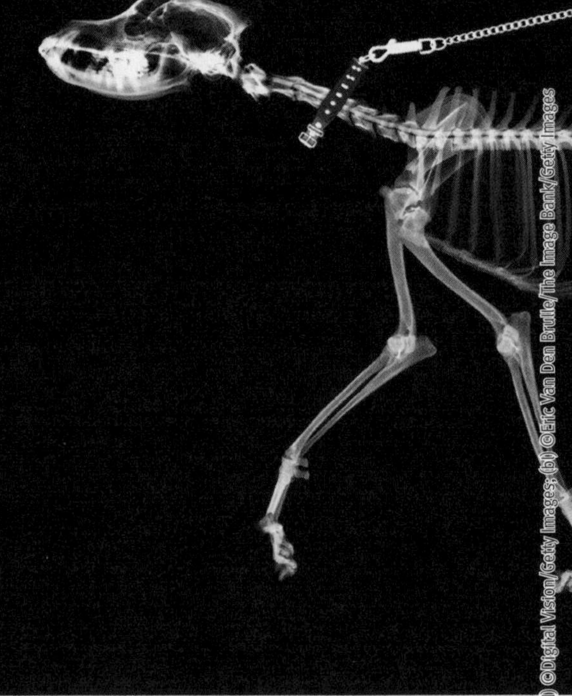

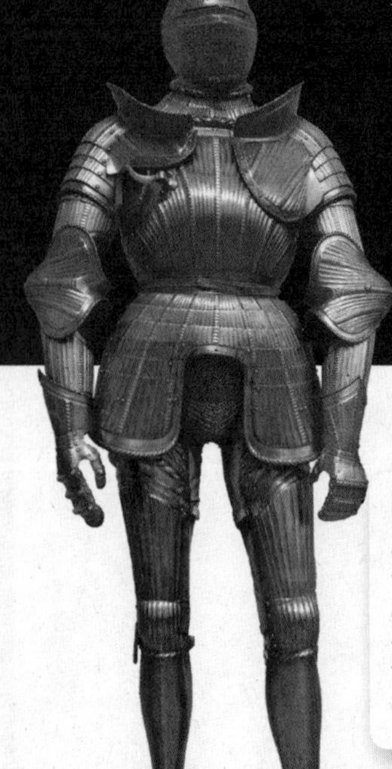

Protection

Bones provide protection to organs. For example, your ribs protect your heart and lungs, your vertebrae protect your spinal cord, and your skull protects your brain.

Storage

The hard outer layer of bone, called *compact bone*, stores important minerals such as calcium. These minerals are necessary for nerves and muscles to work properly.

Support

Bones provide support for your body and make it possible for you to sit or stand upright. If you did not have bones you would be a mass of soft tissue, like a slug. However, unlike a slug, you would not be able to move around without your bones.

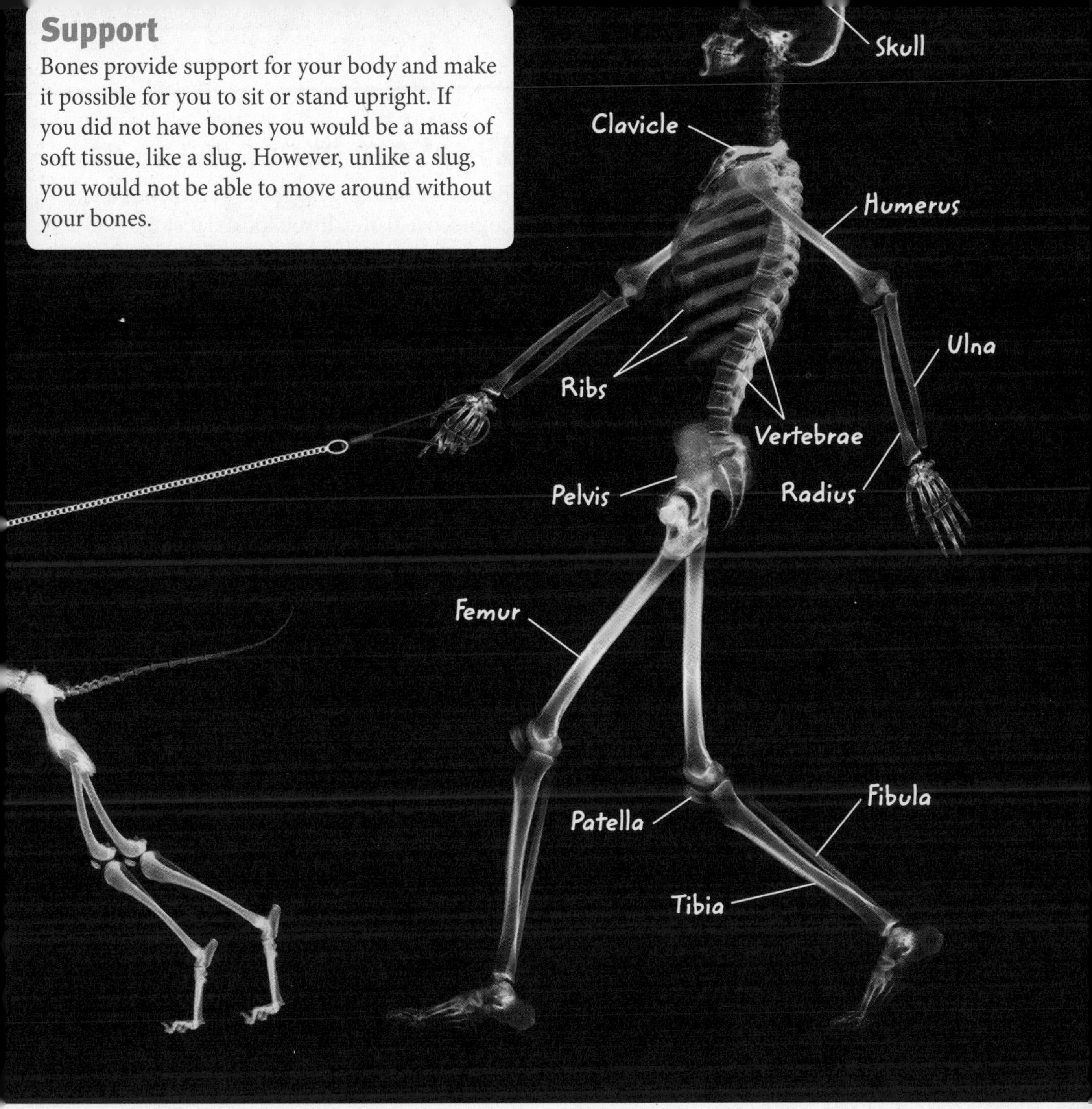

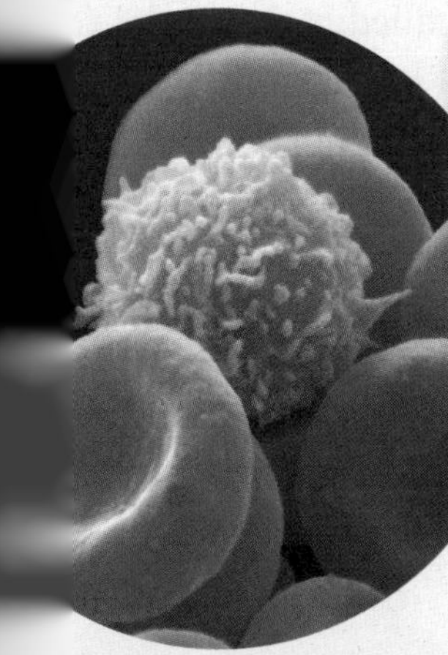

Blood Cell Production

At the center of bones, such as the long bones in the man's and dog's legs, is soft tissue called *marrow*. Red marrow, a type of marrow that makes blood cells, is found mostly in flat bones such as the ribs, pelvis and skull. The red and white blood cells shown here are made in the red bone marrow.

Movement

Bones play an important role in movement by providing a place for muscles to attach. Muscles pull on bones to move the body. Without bones, muscles could not do their job of moving the body.

No Bones About It!

What are the parts of the skeletal system?

Bones, ligaments, and cartilage make up your skeletal system. The skeletal system is divided into two parts. The skull, vertebrae, and ribs make up the *axial skeleton*, which supports the body's weight and protects internal organs. The arms, legs, shoulders, and pelvis make up the *appendicular skeleton*, which allows for most of the body's movement.

Bones

Bones are alive! They have blood vessels which supply nutrients and nerves which signal pain. The body of a newborn baby has about 300 bones, but the average adult has only 206 bones. As a child grows, some bones fuse together.

Ligaments

The tough, flexible strand of connective tissue that holds bones together is a **ligament**. Ligaments allow movement, and are found at the end of bones. Some ligaments, such as the ones on your vertebrae, prevent too much movement of bones.

7 Compare How does the axial skeleton differ from the appendicular skeleton?

Cartilage

Cartilage is a strong, flexible, and smooth connective tissue found at the end of bones. It allows bones to move smoothly across each other. The tip of your nose and your ears are soft and bendy because they contain only cartilage. Cartilage does not contain blood vessels.

What are bones made of?

Bones are hard organs made of minerals and connective tissue. If you looked inside a bone, you would notice two kinds of bone tissue. One kind, called *compact bone*, is dense and does not have any visible open spaces. Compact bone makes bones rigid and hard. Tiny canals within compact bone contain blood capillaries. The other kind of bone tissue, called *spongy bone*, has many open spaces. Spongy bone provides most of the strength and support for a bone. In long bones, such as those of the arm or the leg, an outer layer of compact bone surrounds spongy bone and another soft tissue called *marrow*.

Active Reading **8 Identify** As you read, underline the name of a protein found in bone.

Minerals

Calcium is the most plentiful mineral in bones. The minerals in bones are deposited by bone cells called *osteoblasts*. Minerals such as calcium make the bones strong and hard.

Connective Tissue

The connective tissue in bone is made mostly of a protein called *collagen*. Minerals make the bones strong and hard, but the collagen in bones allows them to be flexible enough to withstand knocks and bumps. Otherwise, each time you bumped a bone, it would crack like a china cup.

Marrow

Bones also contain a soft tissue called *marrow*. There are two types of marrow. Red marrow is the site of platelet and red and white blood cell production. Red marrow is in the center of flat bones such as the ribs. Yellow marrow, which is found in the center of long bones such as the femur, stores fat.

Visualize It!

Bones, such as the femur shown here, are made mostly of connective tissue. They also contain minerals such as calcium.

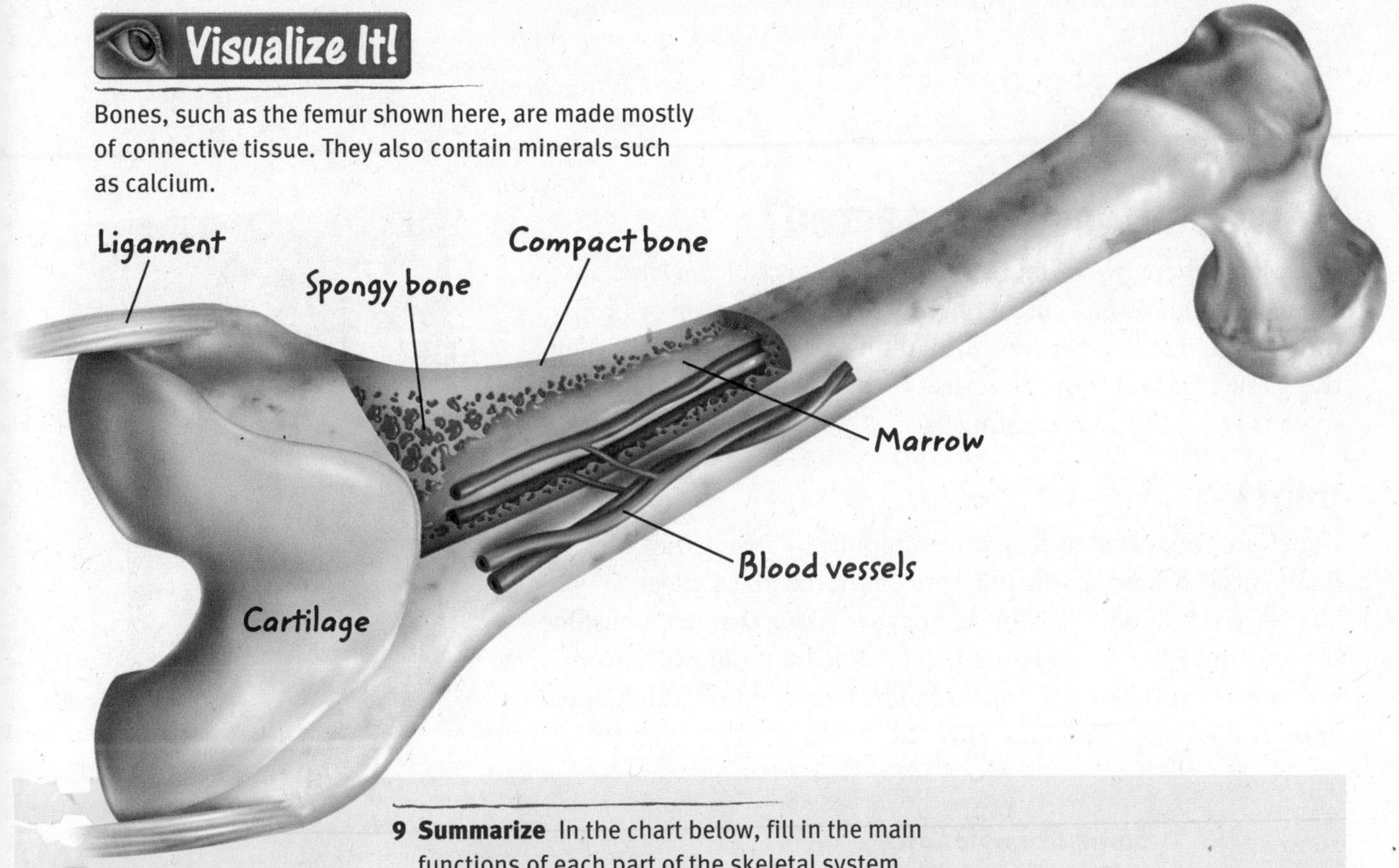

Ligament

Spongy bone

Compact bone

Marrow

Blood vessels

Cartilage

9 **Summarize** In the chart below, fill in the main functions of each part of the skeletal system.

Structure	Function
Spongy bone	
Compact bone	
Cartilage	
Ligaments	

How do bones grow?

The skeleton of a fetus growing inside its mother's body does not contain hard bones. Instead, most bones start out as flexible cartilage. When a baby is born, it still has a lot of cartilage. As the baby grows, most of the cartilage is replaced by bone.

The bones of a child continue to grow. The long bones lengthen at their ends, in areas called *growth plates*. Growth plates are areas of cartilage that continue to make new cells. Bone cells called *osteocytes* move into the cartilage, hardening it and changing it into bone. Growth continues into adolescence and sometimes even into early adulthood. Most bones harden completely after they stop growing. Even after bones have stopped growing, they can still repair themselves if they break.

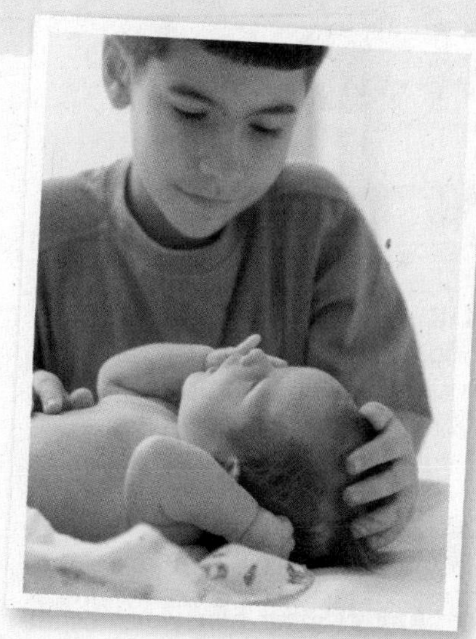

This baby's skeleton has more cartilage than his older brother's skeleton has.

Bone Connections

How are bones connected?

The place where two or more bones connect is called a **joint**. Some joints allow movement of body parts, others stop or limit movement. Just imagine how difficult it would be to do everyday things such as tying your shoelaces if you could not bend the joints in your arms, legs, neck, or fingers!

Your joints allow you to do everyday tasks easily.

Joints

Bones are connected to each other at joints by strong, flexible ligaments. The ends of the bone are covered with cartilage. Cartilage is a smooth, flexible connective tissue that helps cushion the area in a joint where bones meet. Some joints allow little or no movement. These *fixed joints* can be found in the skull. Other joints, called *movable joints*, allow movement of the bones.

Some Examples of Movable Joints

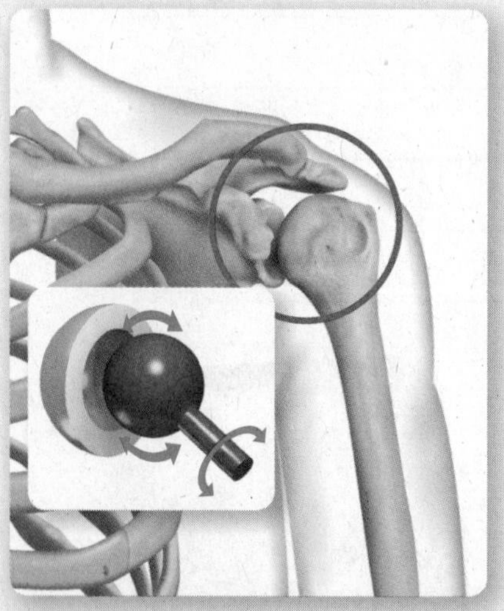

Ball and Socket joint
Shoulders and hips are ball-and-socket joints. Ball-and-socket joints allow one of the bones of the joint to rotate in a large circle.

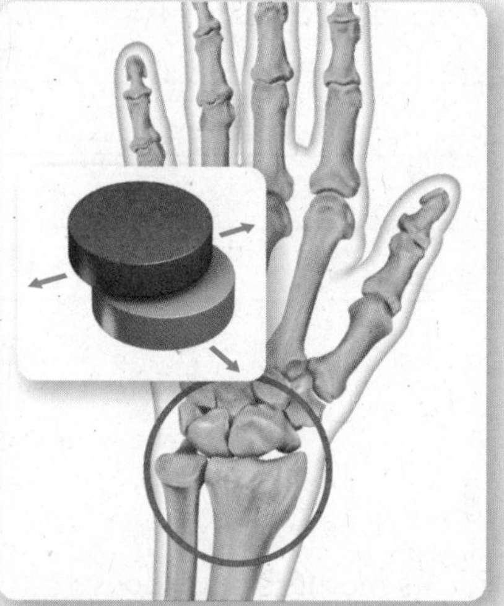

Gliding joint
Wrists and ankles are gliding joints. Gliding joints allow a great deal of flexibility in many directions.

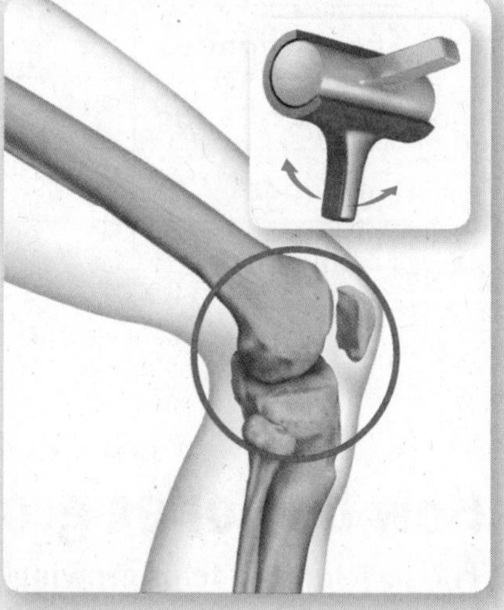

Hinge joint
Knees and elbows are hinge joints. Hinge joints work like door hinges, allowing bones to move back and forth.

10 Apply Some joints, such as the ones in your skull, do not move at all. Why do you think it is important that skull joints cannot move?

What are some injuries and disorders of the skeletal system?

Sometimes the skeletal system can become injured or diseased. Injuries and diseases of the skeletal system affect the body's support system and ability to move. Hereditary factors may play a role in the incidence of diseases such as osteoporosis and arthritis.

11 Identify As you read, underline the characteristics of each injury and disease.

Fractures

Bones may be fractured, or broken. Bones can be broken by a high-force impact such as a fall from a bike. A broken bone usually repairs itself in six to eight weeks.

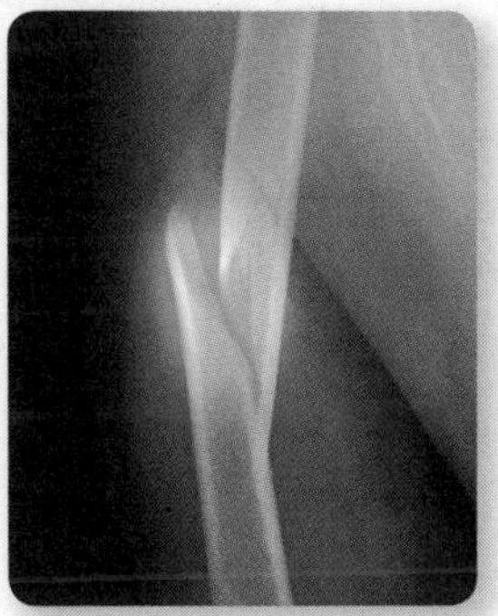

Sprains

A sprain is an injury to a ligament that is caused by stretching a joint too far. The tissues in the sprained ligament can tear and the joint becomes swollen and painful to move. Sprains are common sports injuries.

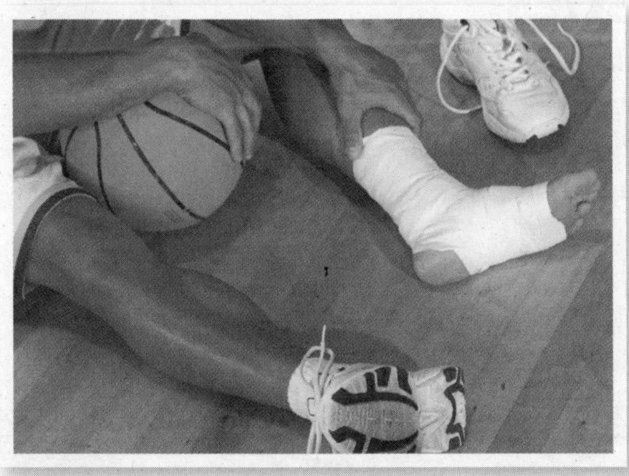

12 Apply How could someone sprain a ligament?

Osteoporosis

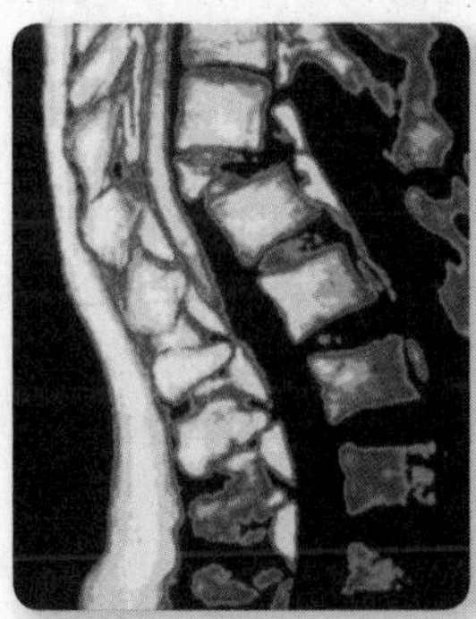

Osteoporosis is a disease that causes bone tissue to become thin. The bones become weak and break more easily. It is most common among adults who do not get enough calcium in their diet. What you eat now can affect your risk of developing osteoporosis later in life.

13 Infer Why is it important to get enough calcium in your diet?

Arthritis

Arthritis is a disease that causes joints to swell, stiffen, and become painful. It may also cause the joint to become misshapen, as shown in the photo. A person with arthritis finds it difficult to move the affected joint. Arthritis can be treated with drugs that reduce swelling.

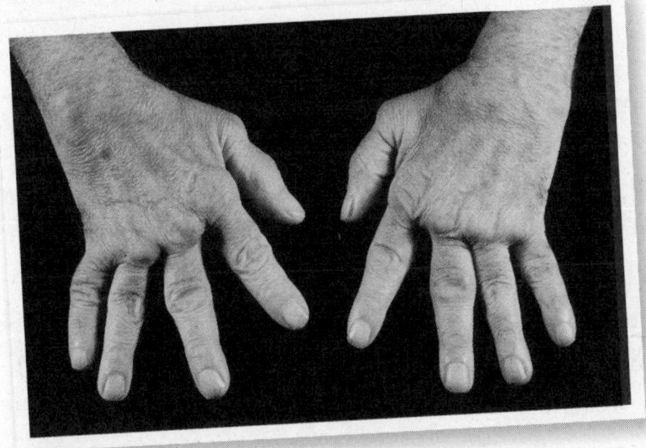

Keep Moving!

What are the main functions of the muscular system?

Muscles pump blood through your body, enable you to breathe, hold you upright, and allow you to move. All animals except the simplest invertebrates have muscles for movement. The **muscular system** is mostly made of the muscles that allow your body to move and be flexible. Other muscles move materials inside your body. *Muscle* is the tissue that contracts and relaxes, making movement possible. Muscle tissue is made up of muscle cells. Muscle cells contain special proteins that allow them to shorten and lengthen.

Active Reading **14 Identify** How do muscles make movement possible?

____

____

____

What are the three types of muscles?

Your body has three kinds of muscle tissue: *skeletal muscle, smooth muscle*, and *cardiac muscle*. Each muscle type has a specific function in your body.

You are able to control the movement of skeletal muscle, so it is called *voluntary muscle*. You are not able to control the movement of smooth muscle and cardiac muscles. Muscle action that is not under your control is *involuntary*. Smooth muscle and cardiac muscle are called *involuntary muscles*.

Smooth Muscle

Smooth muscle is found in internal organs and blood vessels. It helps move materials through the body. Arteries and veins contain a layer of smooth muscle that can contract and relax. This action controls blood flow through the blood vessel. Smooth muscle movement in your digestive system helps move food through your intestines. Smooth muscle is involuntary muscle.

Smooth muscle cells are spindle shaped. They are fat in the middle with thin ends.

Cardiac muscle cells are long, thin, and branched.

Cardiac Muscle

Cardiac muscle is the tissue that makes up the heart. Your heart never gets tired like your skeletal muscle can. This is because cardiac muscle cells are able to contract and relax without ever getting tired. In order to supply lots of energy to the cells, cardiac muscle cells contain many mitochondria. Your cardiac muscles do not stop moving your entire lifetime!

The contractions of cardiac muscle push blood out of the heart and pump it around the body. Cardiac muscle is involuntary; you cannot consciously stop your heart from pumping.

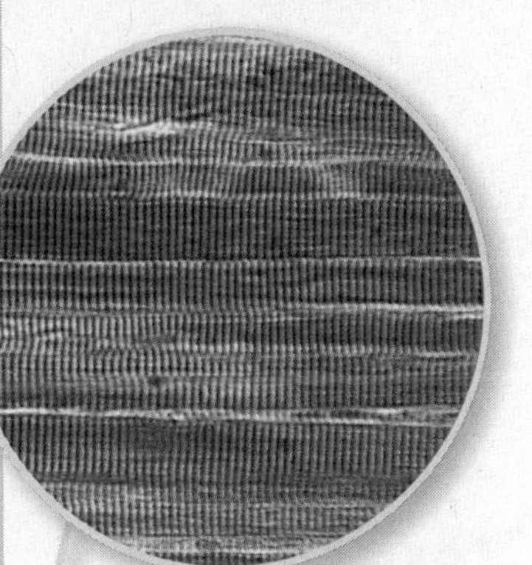

Skeletal muscle cells are long and thin with stripes, or striations.

Skeletal Muscle

Skeletal muscle is attached to your bones and allows you to move. You have control over your skeletal muscle. For example, you can bring your arm up to your mouth to take a bite from an apple. The tough strand of tissue that connects a muscle to a bone is called a **tendon**. When a muscle contracts, or shortens, the attached bones are pulled closer to each other. For example, when the bicep muscle shortens, the arm bends at the elbow.

Most skeletal muscles work in pairs around a joint, as shown below. One muscle in the pair, called a *flexor*, bends a joint. The other muscle, the *extensor*, straightens the joint. When one muscle of a pair contracts, the other muscle relaxes to allow movement of the body part. Muscle pairs are found all around the body.

Visualize It!

15 Apply What would happen to the arm if the flexor was not able to contract?

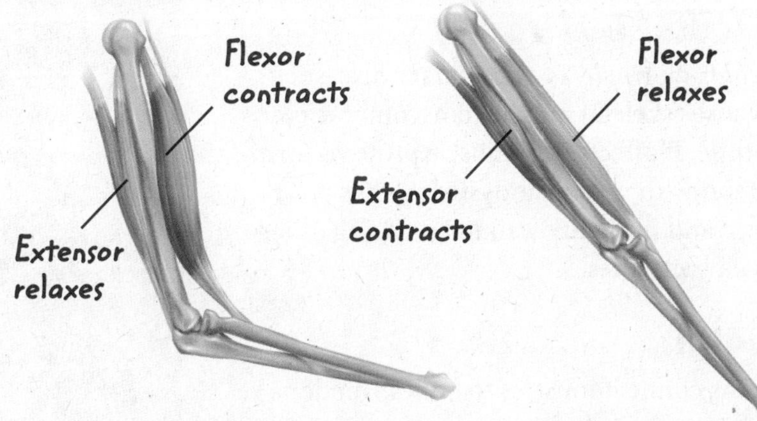

The biceps muscle is the flexor that contracts to bend the arm.

The triceps muscle is the extensor that contracts to straighten the arm.

16 Compare How do the three muscle tissue types look similar and different?

Move It or Lose It!

What are some injuries and disorders of the muscular system?

Like other systems, the muscular system can suffer injury or disease. As a result, muscles may lose normal function. Some muscle diseases are hereditary. Diseases that affect muscle function can also affect other body systems. For example, myocarditis is an inflammation of the heart muscle that can cause heart failure and harm the cardiovascular system.

Muscle Strain and Tears

A *strain* is a muscle injury in which a muscle is overstretched or torn. This can happen when muscles have not been stretched properly or when they are overworked. Strains cause the muscle tissue to swell and can be painful. Strains and tears need rest to heal.

Muscular Dystrophy

Muscular dystrophy is a hereditary disease that causes skeletal muscle to become weaker over time. It affects how muscle proteins form. A person with muscular dystrophy has poor balance and difficulty walking or doing other everyday activities.

Tendinitis

Tendons connect muscles to bones. Tendons can become inflamed or even torn when muscles are overused. This painful condition is called *tendinitis*. Tendinitis needs rest to heal. It may also be treated with medicines that reduce swelling.

17 Contrast What is the difference between a muscle strain and tendinitis?

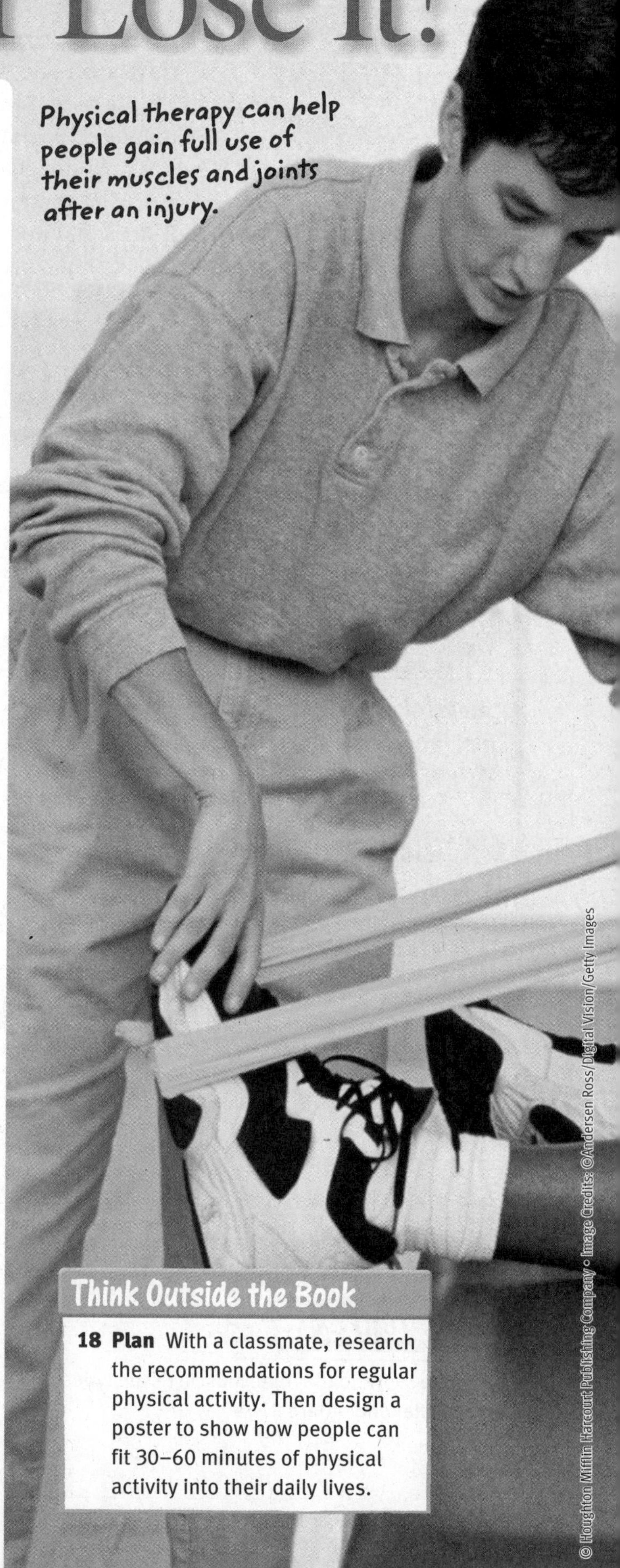

Physical therapy can help people gain full use of their muscles and joints after an injury.

Think Outside the Book

18 Plan With a classmate, research the recommendations for regular physical activity. Then design a poster to show how people can fit 30–60 minutes of physical activity into their daily lives.

What are some benefits of exercise?

Exercising is one of the best things you can do to keep your body healthy. *Exercise* is any activity that helps improve physical fitness and health. Exercise benefits the muscular system by increasing strength, endurance, and flexibility. Exercise helps other body systems, too. It helps keep your heart, blood vessels, lungs, and bones healthy. Exercise also reduces stress, helps you sleep well, and makes you feel good.

Exercises that raise your heart rate to a certain level for at least 60 minutes improve the fitness of the heart. A fit heart is a more efficient pump. It can pump more blood around the body with each beat. It is also less likely to develop heart disease. Good muscle strength and joint flexibility may help a person avoid injuries. Weight training helps bones stay dense and strong. Dense, strong bones are less likely to break. Thirty to sixty minutes of physical activity every day can help improve the health of people of all ages, from children to older adults.

19 Identify As you read, underline the characteristics of anaerobic and aerobic exercise.

Muscle Strength

Resistance exercise helps improve muscle strength by building skeletal muscle and increasing muscle power. Resistance exercise involves short bursts of intense effort lasting no more than a few minutes. Resistance exercises are also called *anaerobic exercises* because the muscle cells contract without using oxygen. Lifting weights and doing pushups are examples of anaerobic exercises.

Muscle Endurance

Endurance exercises allow muscles to contract for a longer time without getting tired. Endurance exercises are also called *aerobic exercises* because the muscle cells use oxygen when contracting. Aerobic exercises involve moderately intense activity from about 30 to 60 minutes at a time. Some examples of aerobic exercises are walking, jogging, bicycling, skating, and swimming.

Flexibility

Can you reach down and touch your toes? If a joint can move through a wide range of motions, it has good flexibility. *Flexibility* refers to the full range of motion of a joint. Stretching exercises help improve flexibility of a joint. Having good flexibility can help prevent ligament, tendon, and muscle injuries. Stretching after aerobic or anaerobic exercises may also help prevent injuries.

Visual Summary

To complete this summary, fill in the blanks with the correct word or phrase. Then, use the key below to check your answers. You can use this page to review the main concepts of the lesson.

The Skeletal and Muscular Systems

The skeletal system supports and protects the body and allows for movement.

20 The three main parts of the skeletal system are bones, ________________, and ________________.

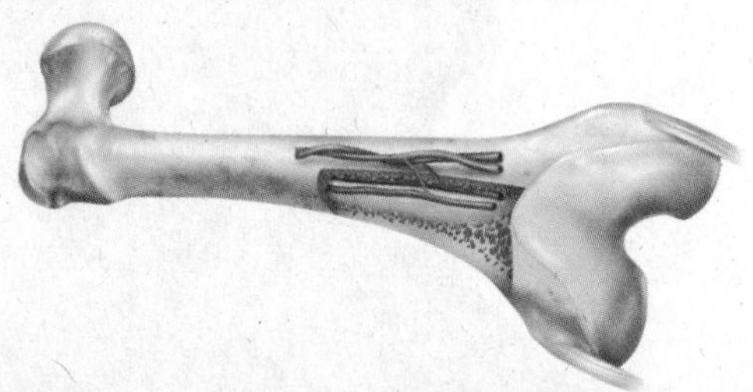

Joints connect two or more bones.

21 The shoulder is an example of a ________________ joint.

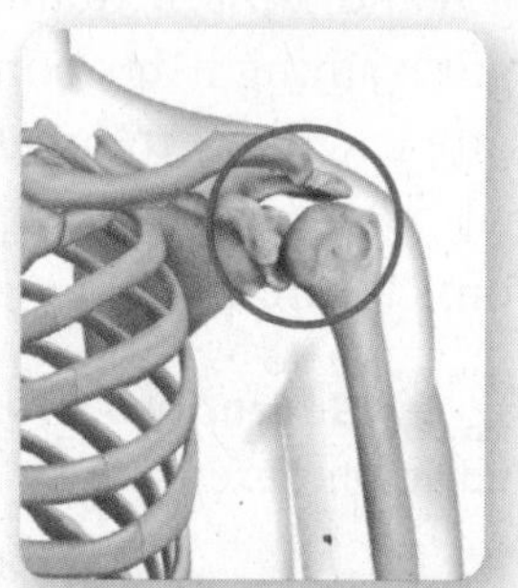

The muscular system allows for movement and flexibility.

22 Muscles work in ________________ to move body parts.

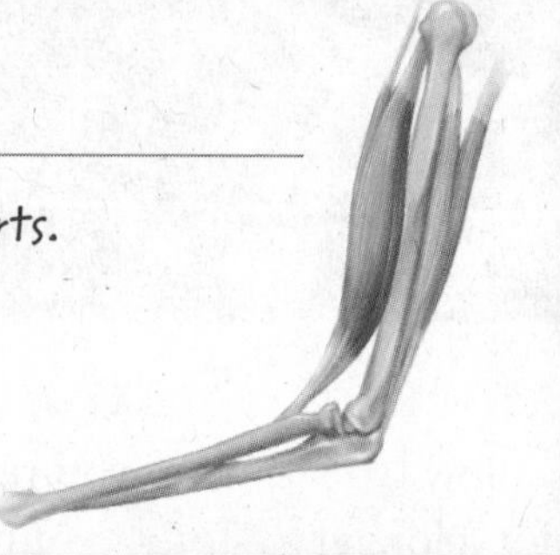

Exercise benefits the body in many ways.

23 Aerobic exercises improve muscle ________________.
Anaerobic exercises improve muscle ________________.

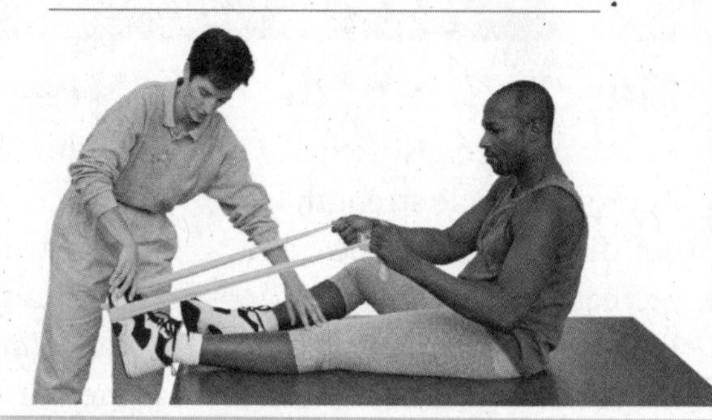

Answers: 20 cartilage; ligaments; 21 ball and socket; 22 pairs; 23 endurance; strength

24 Synthesize Explain why you need both muscles and bones to move your body.

Lesson Review

Vocabulary

Draw a line to connect the following terms to their definitions.

1 skeletal system	**A** groups of muscles that allow you to move and that move materials inside your body
2 ligament	**B** a place where two or more bones connect
3 muscular system	**C** bones, cartilage, and the ligaments that hold bones together
4 joint	**D** tough strands of tissue that connect muscles to bones
5 tendon	**E** a type of tough, flexible connective tissue that holds bones together

Key Concepts

6 List What are the functions of the skeletal system?

7 Analyze What are bones made of?

8 Explain How do muscles work in pairs to move the body?

9 Identify What bone disease is caused by a lack of calcium in the diet?

Critical Thinking

Use this graph to answer the following questions.

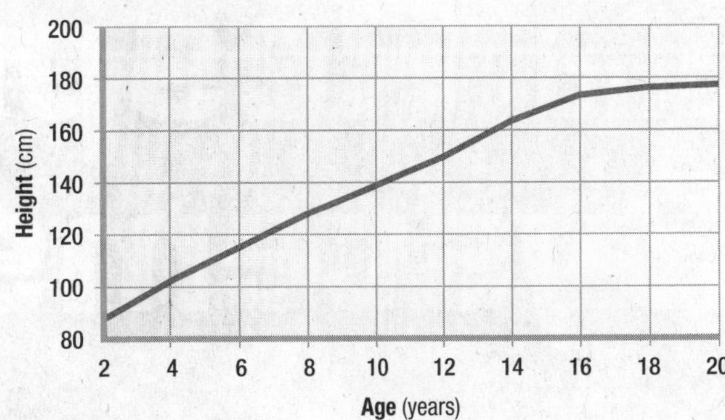

10 Analyze At which points in this graph is bone growing at the fastest rate?

11 Infer At which times on this graph would you expect that the boy's growth plates have stopped creating new bone?

12 Apply If aerobic exercise improves heart strength so that it pumps more blood with each beat, what likely happens to the heart rate as the cardiac muscle gets stronger? Explain your answer.

Lesson 3

The Circulatory and Respiratory Systems

ESSENTIAL QUESTION

How do the circulatory and respiratory systems work?

By the end of this lesson, you should be able to relate the structures of the circulatory and respiratory systems to their functions in the human body.

Sunshine State Standards

SC.6.L.14.5 Identify and investigate the general functions of the major systems of the human body (digestive, respiratory, circulatory, reproductive, excretory, immune, nervous, and musculoskeletal) and describe ways these systems interact with each other to maintain homeostasis.

LA.6.4.2.2 The student will record information (e.g., observations, notes, lists, charts, legends) related to a topic, including visual aids to organize and record information and include a list of sources used.

HE.6.C.1.3 Identify environmental factors that affect personal health.

HE.6.C.1.8 Explain how body systems are impacted by hereditary factors and infectious agents.

This micrograph shows red blood cells inside a blood vessel in the lung. The blood cells are picking up oxygen to bring to the rest of the body.

Engage Your Brain

1 Identify Check T or F to show whether you think each statement is true or false.

T	F	
☐	☐	Air is carried through blood vessels.
☐	☐	The cardiovascular system does not interact with any other body system.
☐	☐	The respiratory system gets rid of carbon dioxide from the body.
☐	☐	Smoking cigarettes can lead to lung disease.

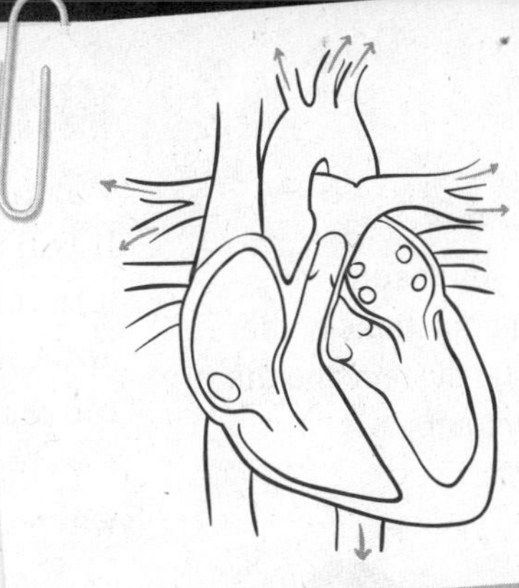

2 Identify What is the name of the organ, shown here, that makes the "lub-dub" sound in your chest?

3 Infer What is the function of this organ?

Active Reading

4 Synthesize You can sometimes tell a lot about the structure of an unknown object by understanding the meaning of its name. Use the meaning of the Latin word and the sentence below to write your own definition of *capillary*.

Latin word	Meaning
capillaris	thin and hairlike

Example Sentence
Oxygen that is carried by blood cells moves across the capillary wall and into body cells.

capillary:

Vocabulary Terms

- cardiovascular system
- blood
- lymphatic system
- lymph
- lymph node
- artery
- capillary
- vein
- respiratory system
- pharynx
- larynx
- trachea
- bronchi
- alveoli

5 Apply As you learn the definition of each vocabulary term in this lesson, create your own definition or sketch to help you remember the meaning of the term.

Go with the Flow!

What is the circulatory system?

Active Reading

6 Identify As you read, underline the functions of the cardiovascular system and the lymphatic system.

When you hear the term *circulatory system,* what do you think of? If you said "heart, blood, and blood vessels," you are half right. The term circulatory system describes both the cardiovascular system and the lymphatic system. Both systems work closely together to move fluids around your body and protect it from disease. Your moving blood helps to keep all parts of your body warm. In these ways the two systems help maintain homeostasis.

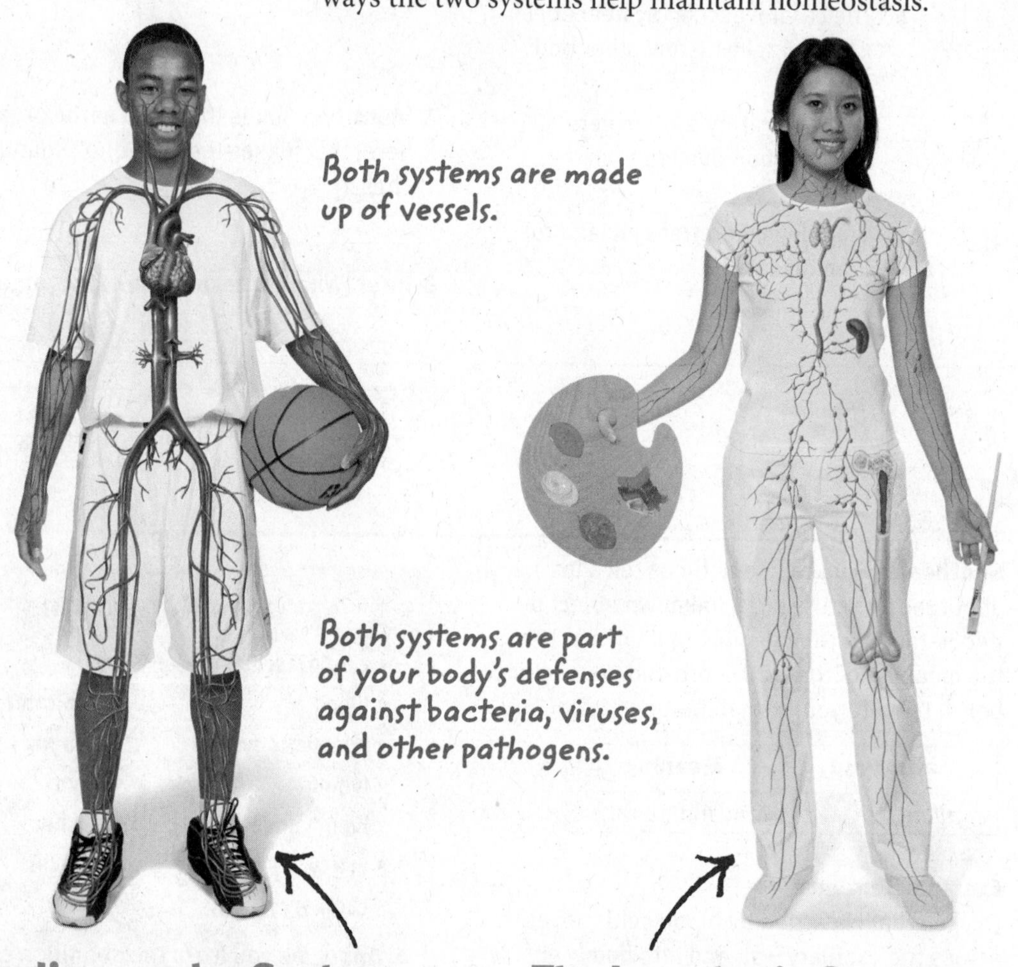

Both systems are made up of vessels.
Both systems are part of your body's defenses against bacteria, viruses, and other pathogens.

The Cardiovascular System

Your heart, blood, and blood vessels make up your **cardiovascular system**, which transports blood around your body. **Blood** is the fluid that carries gases, nutrients, and wastes through the body. The cardiovascular system is a closed circulatory system; the blood is carried in vessels that form a closed loop. The blood maintains homeostasis by transporting hormones, nutrients, and oxygen to cells and by carrying wastes away from cells.

The Lymphatic System

The **lymphatic system** is a group of organs and tissues that collect the fluid that leaks from blood and returns it to the blood. The leaked fluid is called **lymph**. The lymphatic system is an open circulatory system, and lymph can move in and out of the vessels. The lymphatic system is also part of the body's defenses against disease. Certain lymph vessels in the abdomen move fats from the intestine and into the blood.

7 Compare Fill in the Venn diagram to compare the structures and functions of both these systems. You can add more details as you read more about these systems in this lesson.

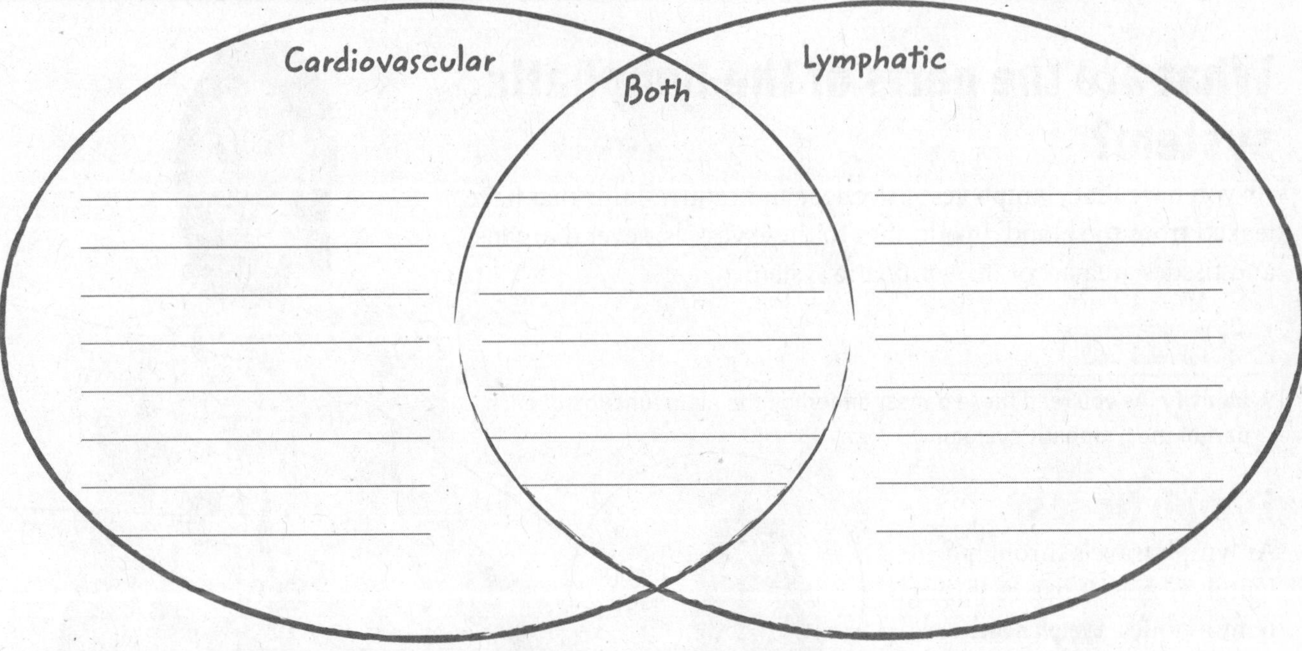

How do the systems work together?

Every time your heart pumps, a little fluid is forced out of the thin walls of the tiniest blood vessels, called *capillaries.* Most of this fluid is reabsorbed by the capillaries, and the remaining fluid is collected by lymph capillaries. *Lymph capillaries* absorb fluid, particles such as dead cells, and pathogens from around body cells. The lymph capillaries carry the fluid, now called *lymph,* to larger lymph vessels. Lymph is returned to the cardiovascular system when it drains into blood vessels at the base of the neck.

The lymphatic system is the place where certain blood cells, called *white blood cells,* mature. Some of these white blood cells stay in the lymphatic system where they attack invading pathogens.

8 Synthesize How does returning leaked fluid from the blood help maintain homeostasis?

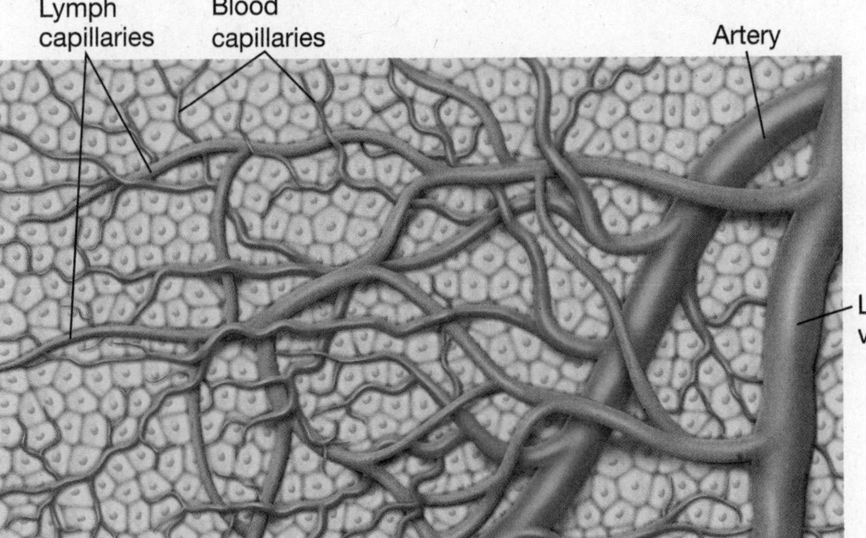

The fluid that leaks from blood capillaries moves into lymph capillaries and is eventually returned to the blood.

Node Doubt!

What are the parts of the lymphatic system?

As you have read, lymph vessels collect and return fluids that have leaked from the blood. In addition to these vessels, several organs and tissues are part of the lymphatic system.

Active Reading

9 Identify As you read these pages, underline the main function of each part of the lymphatic system.

Lymph node

Lymph Nodes

As lymph travels through lymph vessels, it passes through lymph nodes. **Lymph nodes** are small, bean-shaped organs that remove pathogens and dead cells from lymph. Lymph nodes are concentrated in the armpits, neck, and groin. Infection-fighting blood cells, called *white blood cells,* are found in lymph nodes. When bacteria or other pathogens cause an infection, the number of these blood cells may multiply greatly. The lymph nodes fill with white blood cells that are fighting the infection. As a result, some lymph nodes may become swollen and painful. Swollen lymph nodes might be an early clue of an infection.

Lymph Vessels

Lymph vessels are the thin-walled vessels of the lymphatic system. They carry lymph back to lymph nodes. From the lymph nodes, the fluid is returned to the cardiovascular system through the lymph vessels. The vessels have valves inside them to stop lymph from flowing backward.

Bone Marrow

Bones—part of your skeletal system—are very important to your lymphatic system. *Bone marrow* is the soft tissue inside of bones where blood cells are produced.

Tonsils

Tonsils are small lymphatic organs at the back of the throat and tongue. The tonsils at the back of the throat are the most visible. Tonsils help defend the body against infection. White blood cells in the tonsil tissues trap pathogens. Tonsils in the throat sometimes get infected. An infection of the tonsils is called *tonsillitis*. When tonsils get infected, they may become swollen, as shown here.

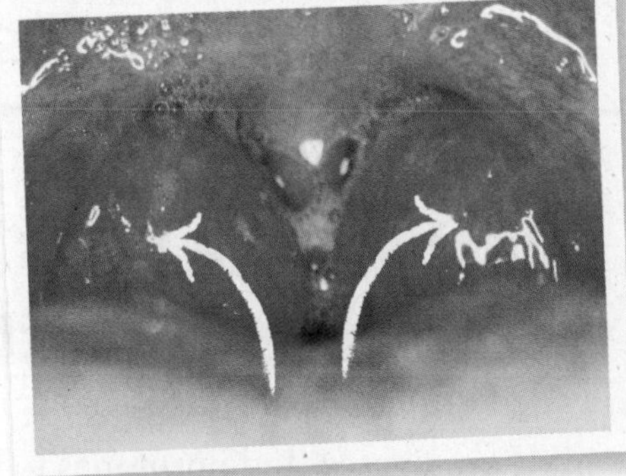

Swollen tonsils

10 Predict A bad case of tonsillitis can sometimes affect a person's breathing. How is this possible?

____

____

____

Thymus

The *thymus* is an organ in the chest. Some white blood cells made in the bone marrow finish developing in the thymus. From the thymus, the white blood cells travel through the lymphatic system to other areas of the body. The thymus gets smaller as a person gets older. This organ is also a part of the endocrine system.

Spleen

The *spleen* is the largest lymphatic organ. It stores white blood cells and also allows them to mature. As blood flows through the spleen, white blood cells attack or mark pathogens in the blood. If pathogens cause an infection, the spleen may also release white blood cells into the bloodstream.

What are some disorders of the lymphatic system?

11 Identify As you read, underline the names of the lymphatic system diseases discussed here.

Lymphoma is a type of cancer that often begins in a lymph node. It can cause a swelling in the node called a *tumor*. There are many different types of lymphomas. Another disorder of the lymph system is lymphedema (lim•fih•DEE•muh). Lymphedema is a swelling of body tissues caused by a blockage or injury to lymph vessels. Lymph vessels are unable to drain lymph from a certain area, and that area becomes swollen. Filariasis is a disease caused by threadlike worms called *nematodes*. The nematodes may enter lymphatic vessels and block them, preventing lymph from moving around the body. Bubonic plague is a bacterial infection of the lymphatic system. The bacteria can enter the body through the bite of an infected flea. The bacteria grow inside lymph nodes, causing the nodes to swell.

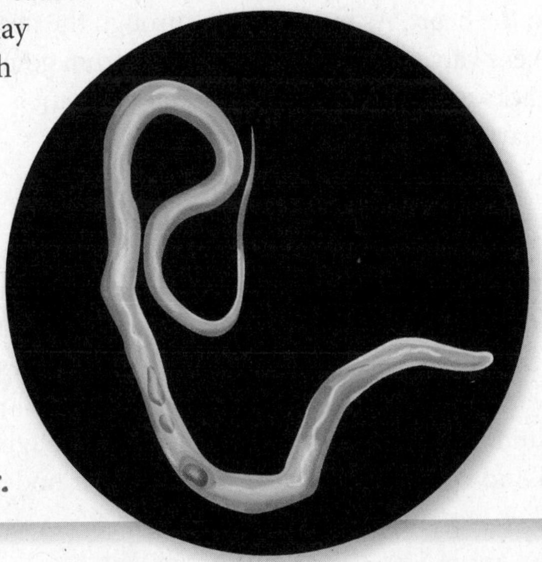

A person gets infected with filarial worms by being bitten by an infected fly. Filariasis is rare in the United States, but is common in developing countries.

The Heart of the Matter

What are the parts of the cardiovascular system?

Your cardiovascular system is the organ system that carries nutrients, gases, and hormones to body cells and waste products from body cells. It also helps keep the different parts of your body at an even temperature. Your cardiovascular system is made up of the heart, blood vessels, and blood.

Active Reading

12 Identify As you read this page, underline the parts of the heart that stop the blood from flowing backward.

Heart

The heart is the pump that sends blood around the body. Your heart is about the size of your fist and is almost in the center of your chest. When heart muscle contracts, it squeezes the blood inside the heart. This squeezing creates a pressure that pushes blood through the body.

Your heart has a left side and a right side. The two sides are separated by a thick wall. The right side of the heart pumps oxygen-poor blood to the lungs. The left side pumps oxygen-rich blood to the body. Each side has an upper chamber and a lower chamber. Each upper chamber is called an *atrium*. Each lower chamber is called a *ventricle*. Blood enters the atria and is pumped down to the ventricles. Flaplike structures called *valves* are located between the atria and the ventricles and in places where large vessels are attached to the heart. As blood moves through the heart, these valves close to prevent blood from going backward. The "lub-dub" sound of a beating heart is caused by the valves closing.

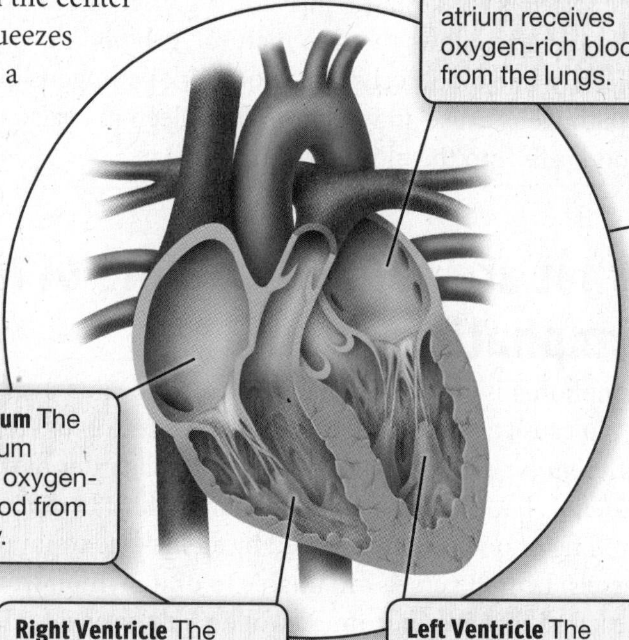

Left Atrium The left atrium receives oxygen-rich blood from the lungs.

Right Atrium The right atrium receives oxygen-poor blood from the body.

Right Ventricle The right ventricle pumps oxygen-poor blood to the lungs.

Left Ventricle The left ventricle pumps oxygen-rich blood to the body.

Blood

Blood is a type of connective tissue that is part of the cardiovascular system. It serves as a transport system, providing supplies for cells, carrying chemical messages, and removing wastes so cells can maintain homeostasis. Blood contains cells, fluid, and other substances. It travels through miles and miles of blood vessels to reach every cell in your body.

13 Infer Why is it important for your heart to keep oxygen-rich blood separate from oxygen-poor blood?

Blood Vessels

Blood travels throughout your body in tubes called *blood vessels*. The three types of blood vessels are arteries, capillaries, and veins.

An **artery** is a blood vessel that carries blood away from the heart. Arteries have thick walls with a layer of smooth muscle. Each heartbeat pumps blood into your arteries at high pressure, which is your *blood pressure*. This pressure pushes blood through the arteries. Artery walls are strong and stretch to withstand the pressure. Nutrients, oxygen, and other substances must leave the blood to get to your body's cells. Carbon dioxide and other wastes leave body cells and are carried away by blood. A **capillary** is a tiny blood vessel that allows these exchanges between body cells and the blood. The gas exchange can take place because capillary walls are only one cell thick. Capillaries are so narrow that blood cells must pass through them in single file! No cell in the body is more than three or four cells away from a capillary.

Capillaries lead to veins. A **vein** is a blood vessel that carries blood back to the heart. Blood in veins is not under as much pressure as blood in arteries is. Valves in the veins keep the blood from flowing backward. The contraction of skeletal muscles around veins can help blood move in the veins.

Arteries carry oxygen-rich blood away from the heart.

Veins carry oxygen-poor blood back to the heart.

Capillaries deliver oxygen-rich blood to body cells and take oxygen-poor blood away from body cells.

14 Apply Complete the table below by naming the blood vessels and by sketching their function. Your sketch may be a symbol, as shown here.

Type of blood vessel		Vein	
Sketch of function			

It's in the Blood

What is blood made of?

An adult human body has about 5 liters of blood. Your body probably has a little less than that. Blood is made up of plasma, platelets, and red and white blood cells. Blood is a tissue because it is made of at least two different cell types. If you looked at blood under a microscope, you would see these differently shaped cells and platelets.

White blood cell

Red blood cell

Platelet

The Blood Files

Plasma

The fluid part of the blood is called *plasma.* Plasma is a mixture of water, minerals, nutrients, sugars, proteins, and other substances. This fluid also carries waste. Red blood cells, white blood cells, and platelets are found in plasma.

Platelets

Platelets are tiny pieces of larger cells found in bone marrow. Platelets last for only five to ten days, but they have an important role. When you cut or scrape your skin, you bleed because blood vessels have been cut open. As soon as bleeding starts, platelets begin to clump together in the cut area. They form a plug that helps reduce blood loss. Platelets also release chemicals that react with proteins in plasma. The reaction causes tiny fibers to form. The fibers help create a blood clot.

White Blood Cells

White blood cells help keep you healthy by fighting pathogens such as bacteria and viruses. Some white blood cells squeeze out of blood vessels to search for pathogens. When they find one they destroy it. Other white blood cells form antibodies. *Antibodies* are chemicals that identify pathogens. White blood cells also keep you healthy by destroying body cells that have died or been damaged.

Red Blood Cells

Most blood cells are red blood cells. *Red blood cells* are disk-shaped cells that do not have a nucleus. They bring oxygen to every cell in your body. Cells need oxygen to carry out life functions. Each red blood cell has hemoglobin. *Hemoglobin* is an oxygen-carrying protein; it clings to the oxygen molecules you inhale. Red blood cells can then transport oxygen to cells in every part of the body. The disk shape of red blood cells helps them squeeze into capillaries.

15 Predict How would the body be affected if red blood cells had low levels of hemoglobin?

How does blood move through the body?

Blood is pumped from the right side of the heart to the lungs. From the lungs it returns to the left side of the heart. The blood is then pumped from the left side of the heart to the body. It flows to the tiny capillaries around the body before returning to the right side of the heart. Blood in the arteries that come out of the heart is under great pressure because of the force from the pumping action of the heart. Blood in veins is under much less pressure than arterial blood because veins have larger internal diameters than arteries do. Veins carry larger volumes of blood more slowly.

Blood Moves in Circuits

Blood moves in two loops or circuits around the body. The beating heart moves blood to the lungs and also around the body. The flow of blood between the heart and the lungs is called the *pulmonary circulation.* As blood passes through the lungs, carbon dioxide leaves the blood and oxygen is picked up. The oxygen-rich blood then flows back to the heart, where it is pumped around the rest of the body. The circulation of blood between the heart and the rest of the body is called *systemic circulation.* Oxygen-poor blood returns to the heart from body cells in the systemic circulation.

Active Reading **16 Compare** What is the difference between the pulmonary and systemic circulations?

In pulmonary circulation, blood is pumped to the lungs where carbon dioxide leaves the blood and oxygen enters the blood.

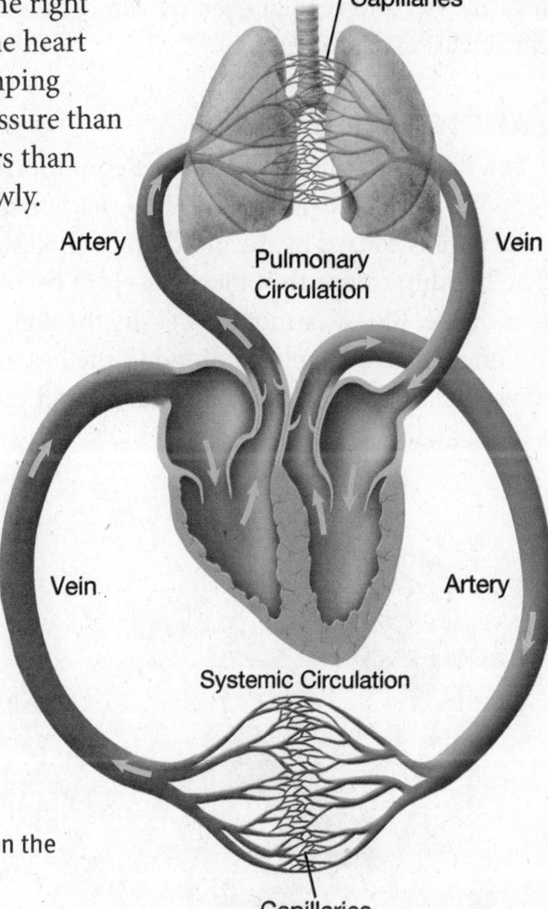

In systemic circulation, blood moves around the body.

Visualize It!

17 Apply Put a box around the part of the diagram that shows the pulmonary circulation. Where in the diagram would you find oxygen-poor blood?

How does circulation help maintain body temperature?

The circulation of blood also helps homeostasis. When the brain senses that body temperature is rising, it signals blood vessels in the skin to widen. As the vessels get wider, heat from the blood is transferred to the air around the skin. This transfer helps lower body temperature. When the brain senses that body temperature is normal, it signals the blood vessels to return to normal. When the brain senses the body temperature is getting too low, it signals the blood vessels near the skin to get narrower. This allows the blood to stay close to internal organs to keep them warm.

What are some problems that affect the cardiovascular system?

Cardiovascular disease is the leading cause of death in the United States. Cardiovascular disease can be caused by smoking, poor diet, stress, physical inactivity, or in some cases, heredity. Eating a healthy diet and regular exercise can reduce the risk of developing cardiovascular problems.

Atherosclerosis

A major cause of heart disease is a condition called *atherosclerosis* (ath•uh•roh•skluh•ROH•sis). Atherosclerosis is a hardening of artery walls caused by the build up of cholesterol and other lipids. The buildup causes the blood vessels to become narrower and less elastic. Blood cannot flow easily through a narrowed artery. When an artery supplying blood to the heart becomes blocked, oxygen cannot reach the heart muscle and the person may have a heart attack.

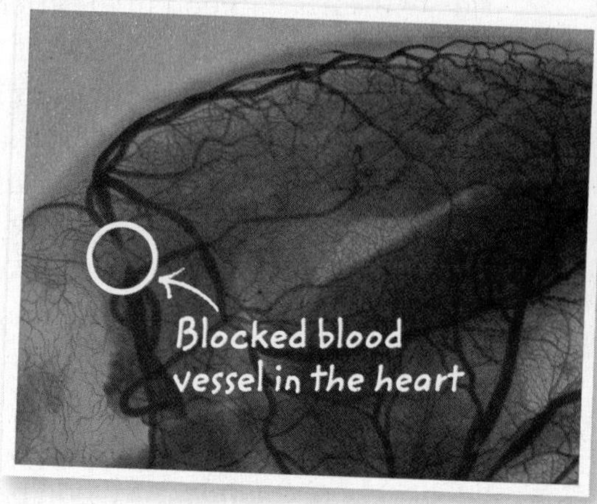
Blocked blood vessel in the heart

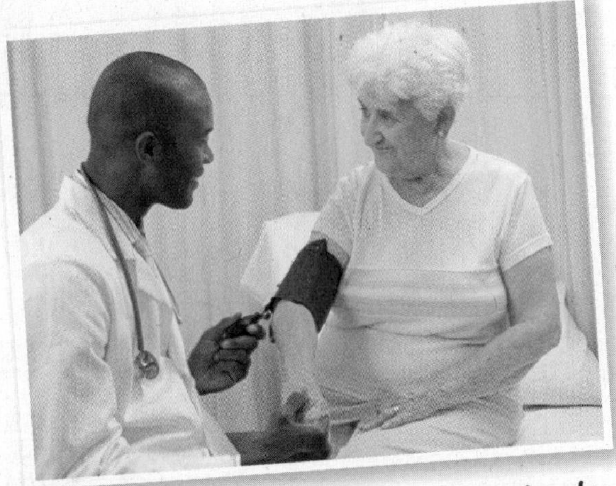
Blood pressure checks can help detect illness.

Hypertension

Hypertension is abnormally high blood pressure. Atherosclerosis may be caused in part by hypertension. The higher a person's blood pressure is, the greater their risk of developing cardiovascular problems such as heart attacks and strokes. Hypertension that is not treated can also cause kidney damage and shorten life expectancy. Regular check ups can help detect problems with blood pressure. Hypertension can be controlled with diet and sometimes with medication.

Heart Attacks and Strokes

A heart attack happens when an artery that supplies blood to the heart becomes blocked and the heart muscle tissue that depends on that blood supply does not get oxygen. Cells and tissues that do not get oxygen get damaged and can die. If enough heart muscle cells are damaged, the heart may stop beating.

A stroke can happen when a blood vessel in the brain becomes blocked or bursts. As a result, that part of the brain receives no oxygen. Without oxygen, brain cells die. Brain damage that occurs during a stroke can affect many parts of the body. People who have had a stroke may experience paralysis or difficulty in speaking.

Think Outside the Book Inquiry

18 Research Doctors often use an electrocardiogram (EKG) reading to see if there is something wrong with how a person's heart is beating. An EKG is a type of graph that "draws" the pumping activity of the heart. How might graphing the heartbeat help a doctor tell if there is a problem?

Take a Deep Breath

What are the functions of the respiratory system?

Your cells need a constant supply of oxygen to stay alive. Your cells must also be able to get rid of the waste product carbon dioxide, which is toxic to them. Breathing takes care of both of these needs. The **respiratory system** is the group of organs that takes in oxygen and gets rid of carbon dioxide. *Respiration,* or breathing, is the transport of oxygen from outside the body to cells and tissues, and the transport of carbon dioxide and wastes away from cells and to the environment.

19 Identify As you read this page, underline the gas that is needed by your body for cellular respiration.

Takes in Oxygen

When a person inhales, air is drawn into the lungs. Oxygen in the air moves into the blood from the lungs. The oxygen-rich blood flowing away from the lungs is carried to all the cells in the body. Oxygen leaves the capillaries and enters the body cells. Inside each cell, oxygen is used for cellular respiration. During cellular respiration, the energy that is stored in food molecules is released. Without oxygen, body cells would not be able to survive.

Releases Carbon Dioxide

When a person exhales, carbon dioxide is released from the body. Carbon dioxide is a waste product of cellular respiration, and the body needs to get rid of it. Carbon dioxide moves from body cells and into capillaries where it is carried in the blood all the way to the lungs. Blood that flows to the lungs contains more carbon dioxide than oxygen. The carbon dioxide moves out of the lung capillaries and into the lungs where it is exhaled.

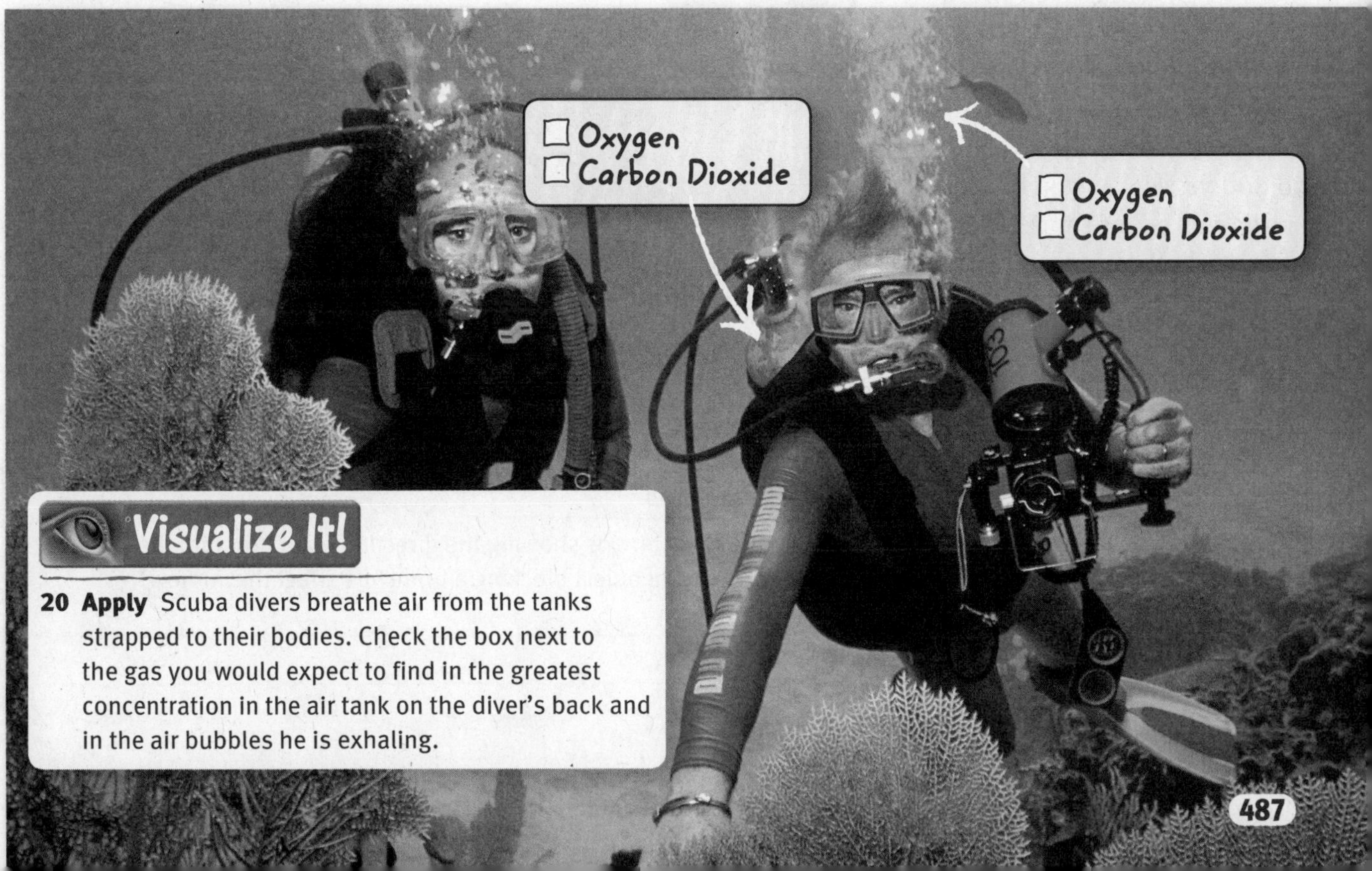

☐ Oxygen
☐ Carbon Dioxide

☐ Oxygen
☐ Carbon Dioxide

Visualize It!

20 Apply Scuba divers breathe air from the tanks strapped to their bodies. Check the box next to the gas you would expect to find in the greatest concentration in the air tank on the diver's back and in the air bubbles he is exhaling.

Breathe Easy

What are the parts of the respiratory system?

Breathing is made possible by your respiratory system. Air enters your respiratory system through your nose or mouth when you breathe in. From there, the air moves through a series of tubes to get to your lungs.

Nose, Pharynx, and Larynx

Air enters your respiratory system through your nose and your mouth. From the nose, air flows into the **pharynx** (FAIR•ingks), or throat. The pharynx branches into two tubes. One tube, the *esophagus*, leads to the stomach. The other tube, called the *larynx,* leads to the lungs. The **larynx** (LAIR•ingks) is the part of the throat that holds the vocal cords. When air passes across the vocal cords, they vibrate, making the voice.

Trachea

The larynx is connected to a large tube called the **trachea** (TRAY•kee•uh), or windpipe. Air flows from the larynx through the trachea to the lungs. The trachea splits into two branches called **bronchi** (singular, *bronchus*). One bronchus connects to each lung. Each bronchus branches into smaller tubes called *bronchioles*.

Bronchioles and Alveoli

In the lungs, the bronchioles lead to tiny sacs called **alveoli** (singular, *alveolus*). Alveoli are surrounded by blood vessels. Gases in the air move across the thin walls of the alveoli and blood vessels. As you breathe, air is sucked into and forced out of alveoli. Breathing is carried out by the diaphragm and rib muscles. The *diaphragm* is a dome-shaped muscle below the lungs. As you inhale, the diaphragm contracts and moves down. The volume of the chest increases. As a result, a vacuum is created and air is sucked in. Exhaling reverses this process.

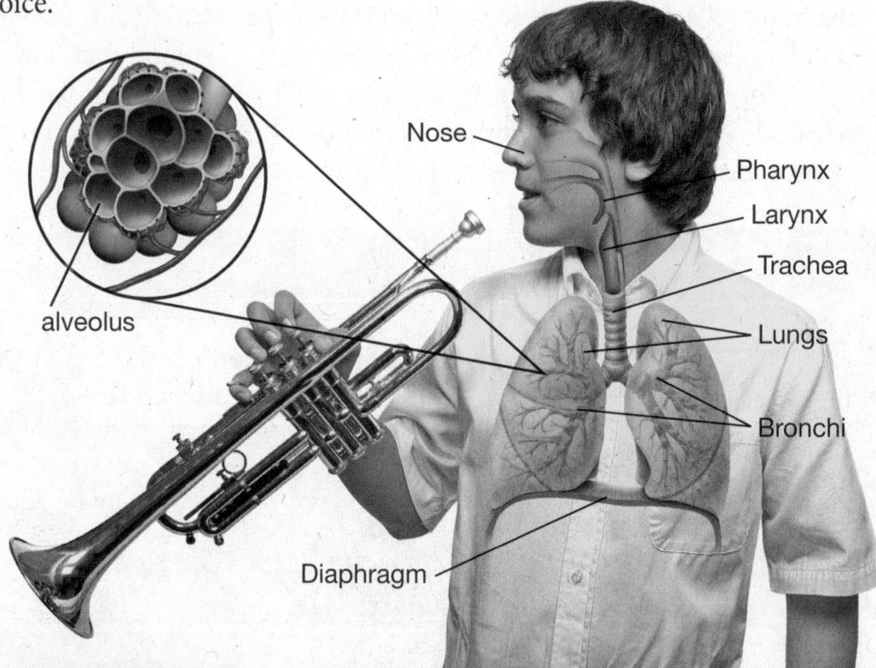

Visualize It!

21 Apply Draw arrows showing the direction of air flow into the lungs. How would an object blocking a bronchus affect this airflow?

What are some disorders of the respiratory system?

Millions of people suffer from respiratory disorders. These disorders include asthma, pneumonia, emphysema, and lung cancer. Some respiratory problems such as emphysema and lung cancer are strongly linked to cigarette smoke. Other respiratory disorders such as pneumonia are caused by pathogens, and some are genetic disorders. Depending on the cause, there are many different ways to treat respiratory diseases.

Active Reading

22 Identify As you read, underline the characteristics of the different respiratory disorders.

Asthma

Asthma is a condition in which the airways are narrowed due to inflammation of the bronchi. During an asthma attack, the muscles in the bronchi tighten and the airways become inflamed. This reduces the amount of air that can get into or out of the lungs. Asthma is treated with medicines that open the bronchioles.

Pneumonia

Pneumonia (noo•MOHN•yuh) is an inflammation of the lungs that is usually caused by bacteria or viruses. Inflamed alveoli may fill with fluid. If the alveoli are filled with too much fluid, the person cannot take in enough oxygen and he or she may suffocate. Pneumonia can be treated with medicines that kill the pathogens.

Emphysema

Emphysema (em•fuh•SEE•muh) occurs when the alveoli have been damaged. As a result, oxygen cannot pass across into the blood as well as it could in a normal alveolus. People who have emphysema have trouble getting the oxygen they need and removing carbon dioxide from the lungs. This condition is often linked to long-term use of tobacco.

Visualize It!

23 Compare How are these two lungs different? How can you tell the diseased lung from the healthy lung?

Think Outside the Book

24 Imagine Pretend you are a lung. The behavior of your body has not been very healthy, and as a result you are sick. Write a plea to your body to help you improve your health. Be sure to include the important functions that you perform and what the body can do to make you healthier.

Visual Summary

To complete this summary, fill in the blanks with the correct word or phrase. Then use the key below to check your answers. You can use this page to review the main concepts of the lesson.

Circulatory and Respiratory Systems

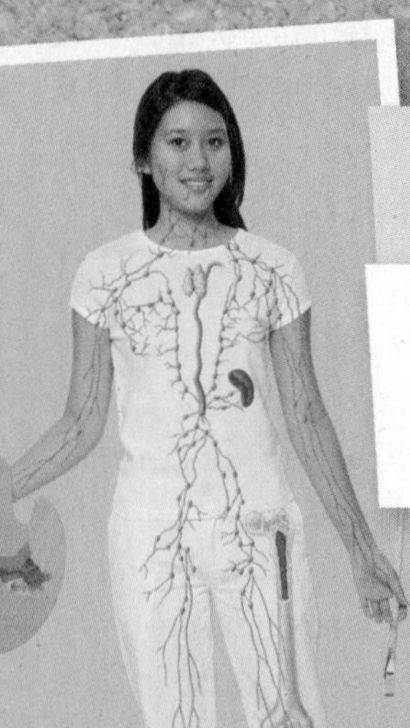

The lymphatic system returns fluid to the blood.

25 The lymph organs found in your throat are called

________________________.

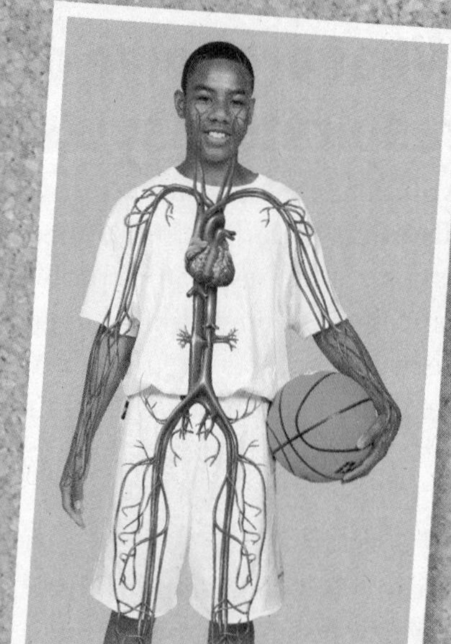

The cardiovascular system moves blood throughout the body and carries nutrients and oxygen to body cells.

26 The two gases that the blood carries around the body are

________________________ and

________________________.

The respiratory system takes oxygen into the body and releases carbon dioxide.

27 Oxygen enters the blood and carbon dioxide leaves the blood in the

____________________ of the lungs.

Answers: 25 tonsils; 26 oxygen, carbon dioxide; 27 alveoli

28 Relate Describe how a problem with the respiratory system could directly affect the cardiovascular system.

Lesson Review

Vocabulary

In your own words, define the following terms.

1 Blood

2 Lymph

3 Alveoli

Key Concepts

Fill in the table below.

System	Structures
4 Identify What are the main structures of the lymphatic system?	
5 Identify What are the main structures of the cardiovascular system?	
6 Identify What are the main structures of the respiratory system?	

7 Explain How does blood help maintain homeostasis in the body?

8 Contrast How are arteries and veins different?

9 Relate How might a blockage of the lymph vessels affect the function of the cardiovascular system?

Critical Thinking

Use this image to answer the following questions.

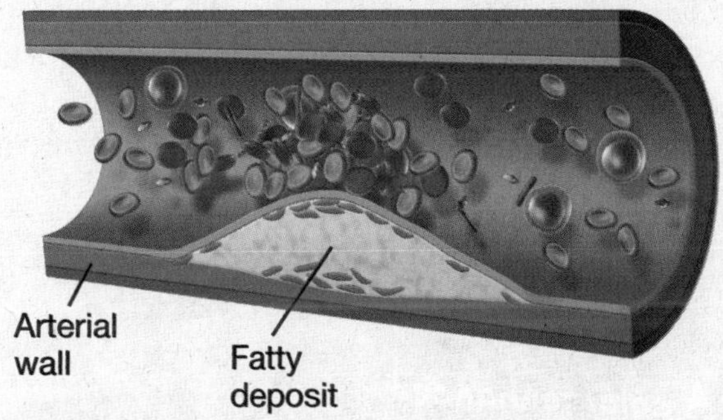

10 Relate To what body system does this structure belong?

11 Predict How might what is happening in this image affect the nervous system?

12 Infer Why is it important that lymph vessels are spread throughout the body?

People in Science

Olufunmilayo Falusi Olopade

MEDICAL DOCTOR

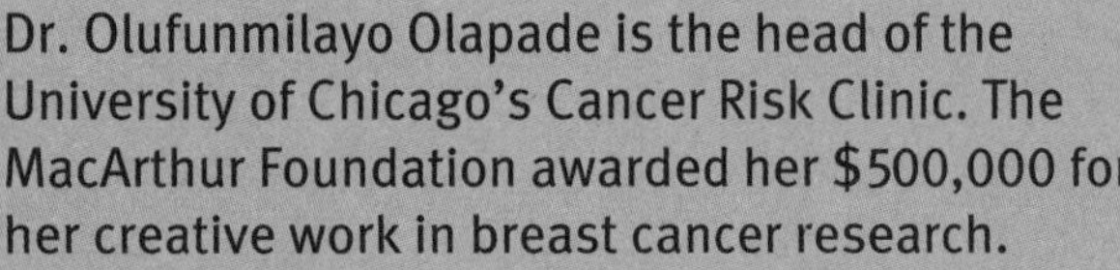

Dr. Olufunmilayo Olapade is the head of the University of Chicago's Cancer Risk Clinic. The MacArthur Foundation awarded her $500,000 for her creative work in breast cancer research.

Born in Nigeria, Dr. Olopade began her career as a medical officer at the Nigerian Navy Hospital in Lagos. She later came to Chicago to do cancer research. She became a professor at the University of Chicago in 1991. She founded the Cancer Risk Clinic shortly after this.

Dr. Olopade has found that tumors in African-American women often come from a different group of cells than they do in Caucasian women. These tumors, therefore, need different treatment. Dr. Olopade designs treatments that address the source of the tumor. More importantly, her treatments try to address the particular risk factors of each patient. These can include diet, heredity, age, and activity. The MacArthur Foundation recognized Dr. Olopade for designing such new and practical treatment plans for patients. Studying cells has provided Dr. Olopade with clues on how to improve the lives of millions of African-American women.

A color-enhanced scanning electron micrograph (SEM) of a breast cancer cell

JOB BOARD

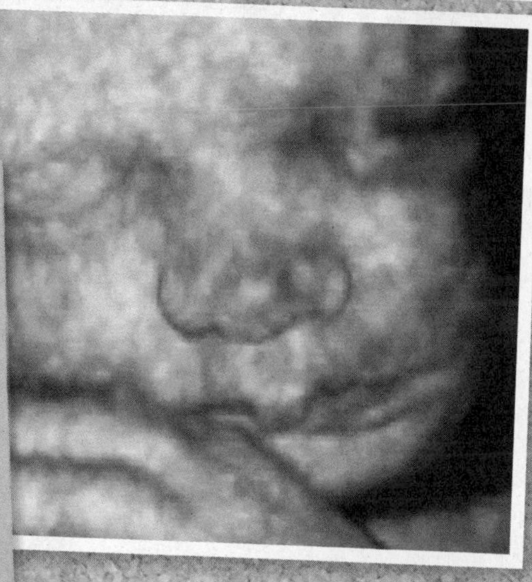

Diagnostic Medical Sonographer

What You'll Do: Operate and take care of the sonogram equipment that uses sound waves to create pictures of inside human bodies that a doctor can interpret.

Where You Might Work: Hospitals, clinics, and private offices that have sonogram equipment.

Education: A two- or four-year undergraduate degree or a special certification program is necessary.

Physical Therapist

What You'll Do: Use exercise, ultrasound, heat, and other treatments when working with patients to help them improve their muscular strength, endurance, and flexibility.

Where You Might Work: Hospitals, clinics, and private physiotherapy offices, as well as some gyms and yoga studios.

Education: A master's degree from an accredited physical therapy program is required.

Prosthetics Technician

What You'll Do: Create, test, fit, maintain, and repair artificial limbs and other prosthetic devices for people who need them.

Where You Might Work: Hospitals with prosthetic divisions and private companies.

Education: Technicians must have an associate, bachelor's, or post-graduate degree in orthotics and prosthetics. Some companies may require additional certification.

Language Arts Connection

Find one report of a new discovery in cancer prevention. Summarize the key points of the discovery in a paragraph. Be sure to include information about what the discovery is, who made it, how the discovery was made, and how it changes what we know about cancer.

Lesson 4

The Digestive and Excretory Systems

ESSENTIAL QUESTION

How do your body's digestive and excretory systems work?

By the end of this lesson, you should be able to relate the parts of the digestive and excretory systems to their roles in the human body.

Sunshine State Standards

SC.6.L.14.5 Identify and investigate the general functions of the major systems of the human body (digestive, respiratory, circulatory, reproductive, excretory, immune, nervous, and musculoskeletal) and describe ways these systems interact with each other to maintain homeostasis.

HE.6.C.1.8 Explain how body systems are impacted by hereditary factors and infectious agents.

Your digestive system works to get all of the nutrients out of the food you eat.

Engage Your Brain

1 Fill in the blanks with the words that you think best complete the following sentences.

Inside your ________________, food is chewed and broken down by teeth and saliva.

The ____________________________ is a muscle inside your mouth that helps you to swallow food and liquids.

If you eat too much food too quickly, you may get a __________________ache.

2 Imagine How is a blender like your stomach?

Active Reading

3 Synthesize You can often define an unknown word if you see it used in a sentence. Use the sentence below to make an educated guess about the meaning of the word *enzyme*.

Example sentence
Enzymes in the mouth, stomach, and small intestine help in the chemical digestion of food.

enzyme:

Vocabulary Terms

- **digestive system**
- **enzyme**
- **esophagus**
- **stomach**
- **small intestine**
- **large intestine**
- **pancreas**
- **liver**
- **excretory system**
- **kidney**
- **nephron**
- **urine**

4 Apply As you learn the meaning of each vocabulary term in this lesson, create your own definition or sketch to help you remember the meaning of the term.

You are what you eat!

What is the digestive system?

5 Identify As you read, underline the ways that your body uses nutrients.

Your cells need a lot of energy for their daily activities. Cells use nutrients, which are substances in food, for energy, growth, maintenance, and repair. The **digestive system** breaks down the food you eat into nutrients that can be used as building materials and that can provide energy for cells.

The digestive system interacts with other body systems to obtain and use energy from food. Blood, part of the circulatory system, transports nutrients to other tissues. In order to extract energy from nutrients, cells need oxygen. The respiratory system is responsible for obtaining this oxygen from the environment. The nervous system controls and regulates the functioning of the digestive system.

What are the two types of digestion?

Digestion is the process of breaking down food into a form that can pass from the digestive system into the bloodstream. There are two types of digestion: mechanical and chemical.

The Stomach

The deep pits and grooves in the stomach lining help grind food.

Inquiry

6 Infer The stomach lining is made up of deep muscular grooves. How do you think these structures help the stomach to break down food?

Mechanical Digestion

Mechanical digestion is the breaking, crushing, and mashing of food. Chewing is a type of mechanical digestion. Chewing creates small pieces of food that are easier to swallow and digest than large pieces are. Mechanical digestion increases the surface area of food for the action of chemical digestion.

Chemical Digestion

Chemical digestion is the process in which large molecules of food are broken down into smaller molecules so that they can pass into the bloodstream. An **enzyme** (EN•zym) is a chemical that the body uses to break down large molecules into smaller molecules. Enzymes act like chemical scissors. They "cut up" large molecules into smaller pieces. Mechanical digestion breaks up food and increases surface area so that enzymes can break nutrients into smaller molecules. Without mechanical digestion, chemical digestion would take days instead of hours!

7 Categorize Decide whether each of these steps in digestion is an example of mechanical digestion or chemical digestion. Then put a check in the correct box.

In your mouth, teeth grind food.

- ☐ mechanical
- ☐ chemical

Salivary glands release a liquid called saliva, which helps to break food down.

- ☐ mechanical
- ☐ chemical

In the stomach, muscles contract to grind food into a pulpy mixture.

- ☐ mechanical
- ☐ chemical

In the small intestine, most nutrients are broken down by enzymes.

- ☐ mechanical
- ☐ chemical

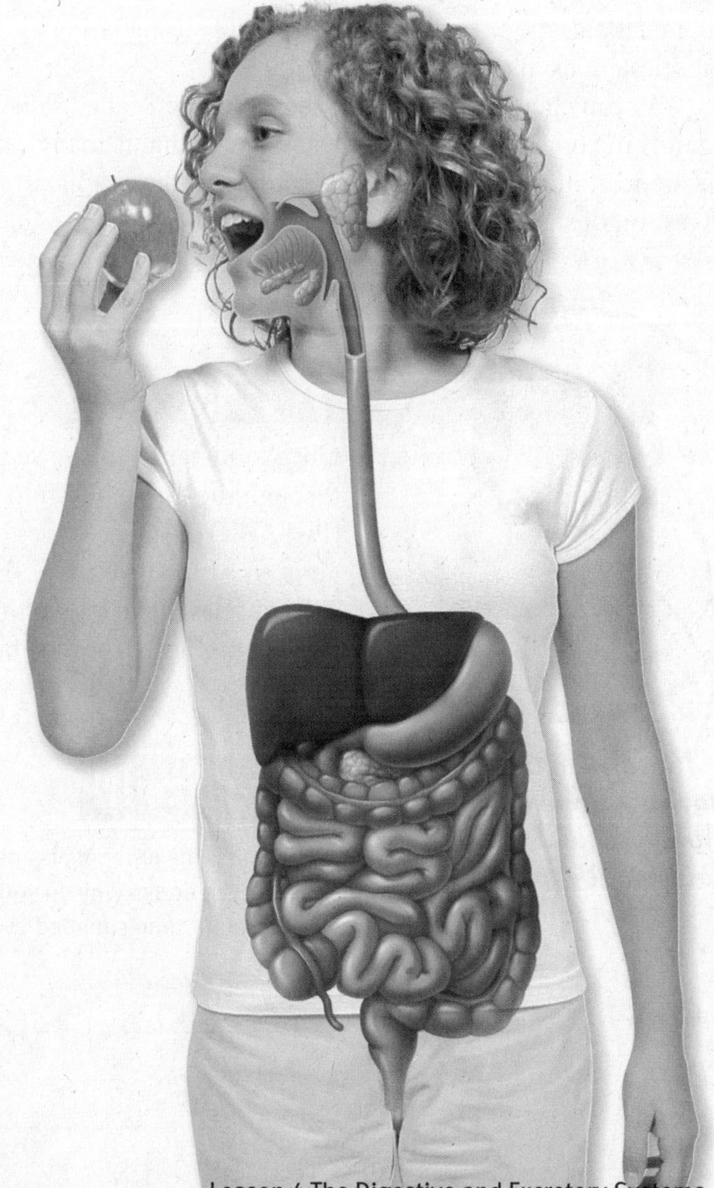

Chew on this

What are the parts of the digestive system?

8 As you read, underline the function of each organ of the digestive system.

Has anyone ever reminded you to chew your food? Chewing food is the first part of digestion. After food is chewed and swallowed, pieces of that food move through other organs in the digestive system, where the food is broken down even more.

The Mouth

Digestion begins in the mouth with both mechanical and chemical digestion. Teeth, with the help of strong jaw muscles, break and crush food.

As you chew, food is moistened by a liquid called *saliva*. Glands in your mouth make saliva. Saliva contains many substances, including an enzyme that begins the chemical digestion of starches in food.

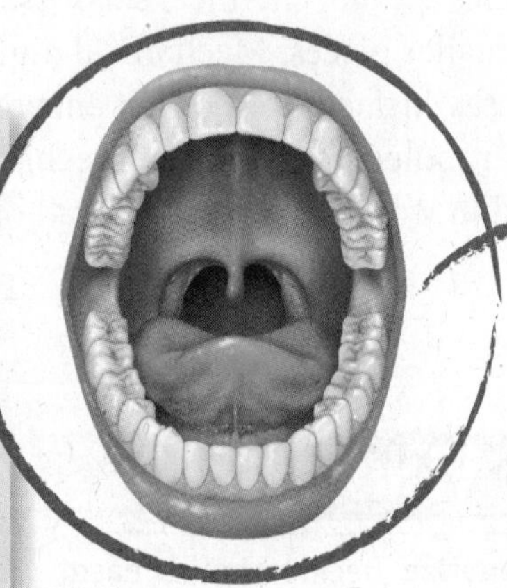

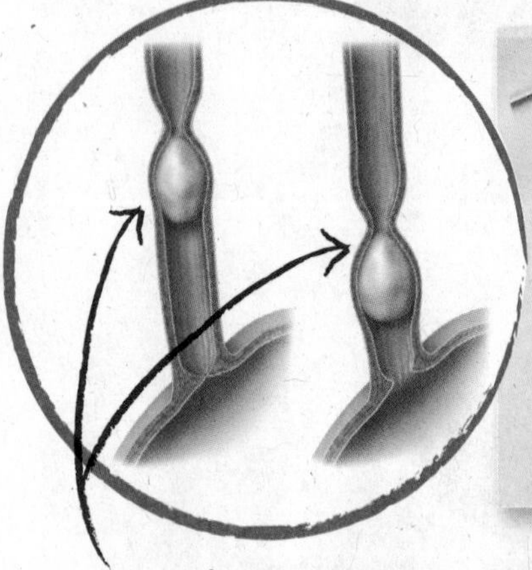

Muscles in the esophagus move this clump of food from your mouth to your stomach.

The Esophagus

Once food has been chewed, it is swallowed. The food moves through the throat and into a long tube called the **esophagus** (ih•SAWF•uh•gus). Waves of muscle contractions called *peristalsis* (per•ih•STAWL•sis) move the food into the stomach. The muscles move food along in much the same way as you move toothpaste from the bottom of the tube with your thumbs.

9 Infer Consider the order of organs in the digestive system and their positions in the body. Why do you think digestion is more efficient if you are sitting up, rather than slumped over or lying down?

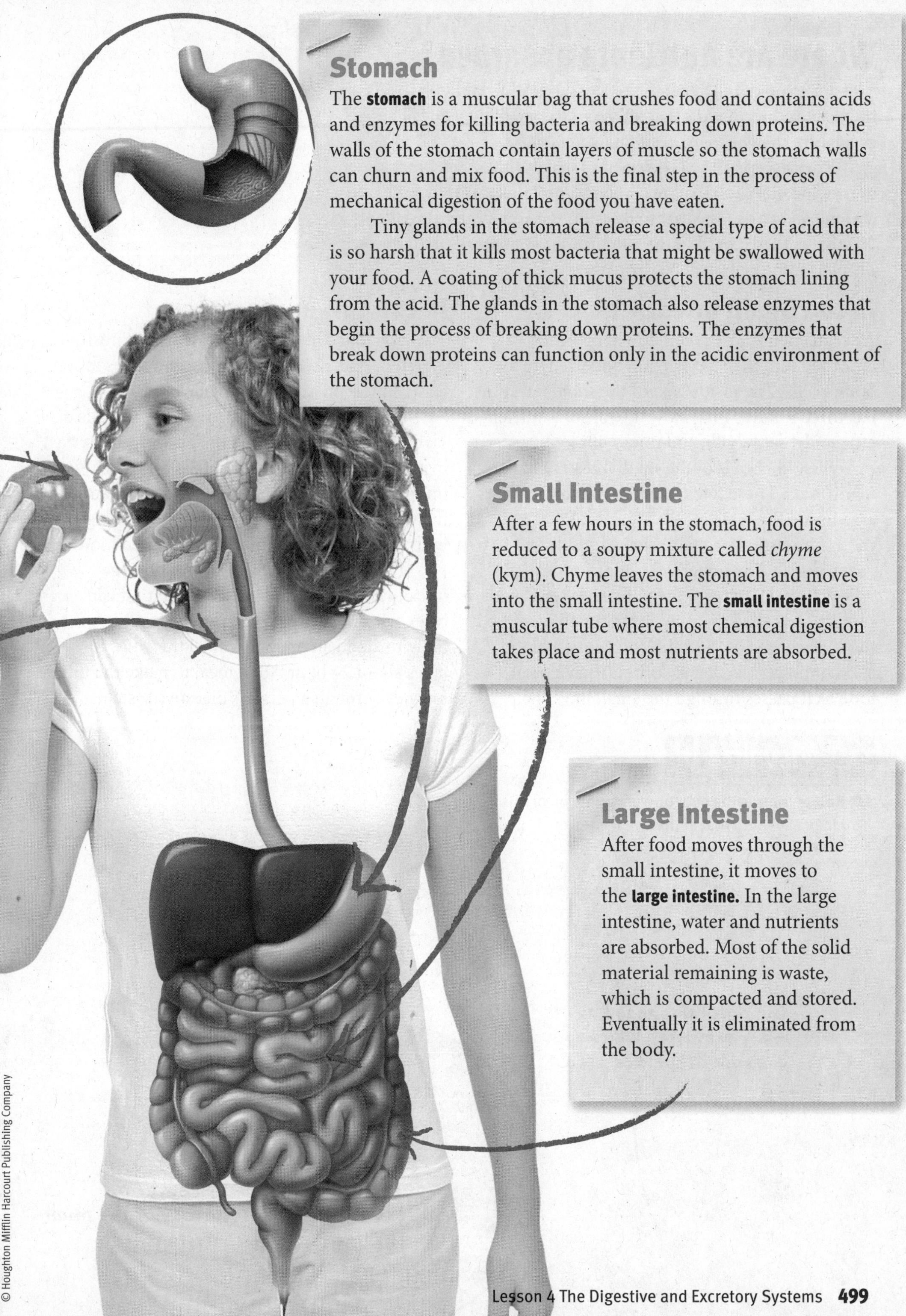

Stomach

The **stomach** is a muscular bag that crushes food and contains acids and enzymes for killing bacteria and breaking down proteins. The walls of the stomach contain layers of muscle so the stomach walls can churn and mix food. This is the final step in the process of mechanical digestion of the food you have eaten.

Tiny glands in the stomach release a special type of acid that is so harsh that it kills most bacteria that might be swallowed with your food. A coating of thick mucus protects the stomach lining from the acid. The glands in the stomach also release enzymes that begin the process of breaking down proteins. The enzymes that break down proteins can function only in the acidic environment of the stomach.

Small Intestine

After a few hours in the stomach, food is reduced to a soupy mixture called *chyme* (kym). Chyme leaves the stomach and moves into the small intestine. The **small intestine** is a muscular tube where most chemical digestion takes place and most nutrients are absorbed.

Large Intestine

After food moves through the small intestine, it moves to the **large intestine.** In the large intestine, water and nutrients are absorbed. Most of the solid material remaining is waste, which is compacted and stored. Eventually it is eliminated from the body.

Where are nutrients absorbed?

The digestion of nutrients in the small intestine takes place with the help of three organs that attach to the small intestine. These organs are the *pancreas*, *liver*, and *gall bladder*.

The **pancreas** (PANG•kree•uhz) makes fluids that break down every type of material found in foods: proteins, carbohydrates, fats, and nucleic acids. The **liver** makes and releases a mixture called *bile* that is then stored in the gall bladder. Bile breaks up large fat droplets into very small fat droplets.

In the Small Intestine

After nutrients are broken down, they are absorbed into the bloodstream and used by the body's cells. The inside wall of the small intestine has three features that allow it to absorb nutrients efficiently: folds, villi, and microvilli.

First, the walls of the small intestine have many folds. These folds increase the surface area inside the intestine wall, creating more room for nutrients to be absorbed. Each fold is covered with tiny fingerlike projections called *villi* (VIL•eye). In turn, the villi are covered with projections called microvilli. Microvilli increase the surface area of the villi. Villi contain blood and lymph vessels that absorb nutrients from food as it passes through the small intestine.

In the Large Intestine

The large intestine removes water from mostly-digested food, absorbs vitamins, and turns food waste into semi-solid waste called feces.

Some parts of food, such as the cell walls of plants, cannot be absorbed by the body. Bacteria live in the large intestine that feed off of this undigested food. The bacteria produce vitamins that are absorbed by the large intestine along with most of the water in the undigested food.

The *rectum* is the last part of the large intestine. The rectum stores feces until it can be expelled. Feces pass to the outside of the body through an opening called the *anus*. It takes about 24 hours for a meal to make the full journey through a person's digestive system.

Visualize It!

10 Relate How is the structure and function of this sponge similar to that of the small intestine?

____

____

____

____

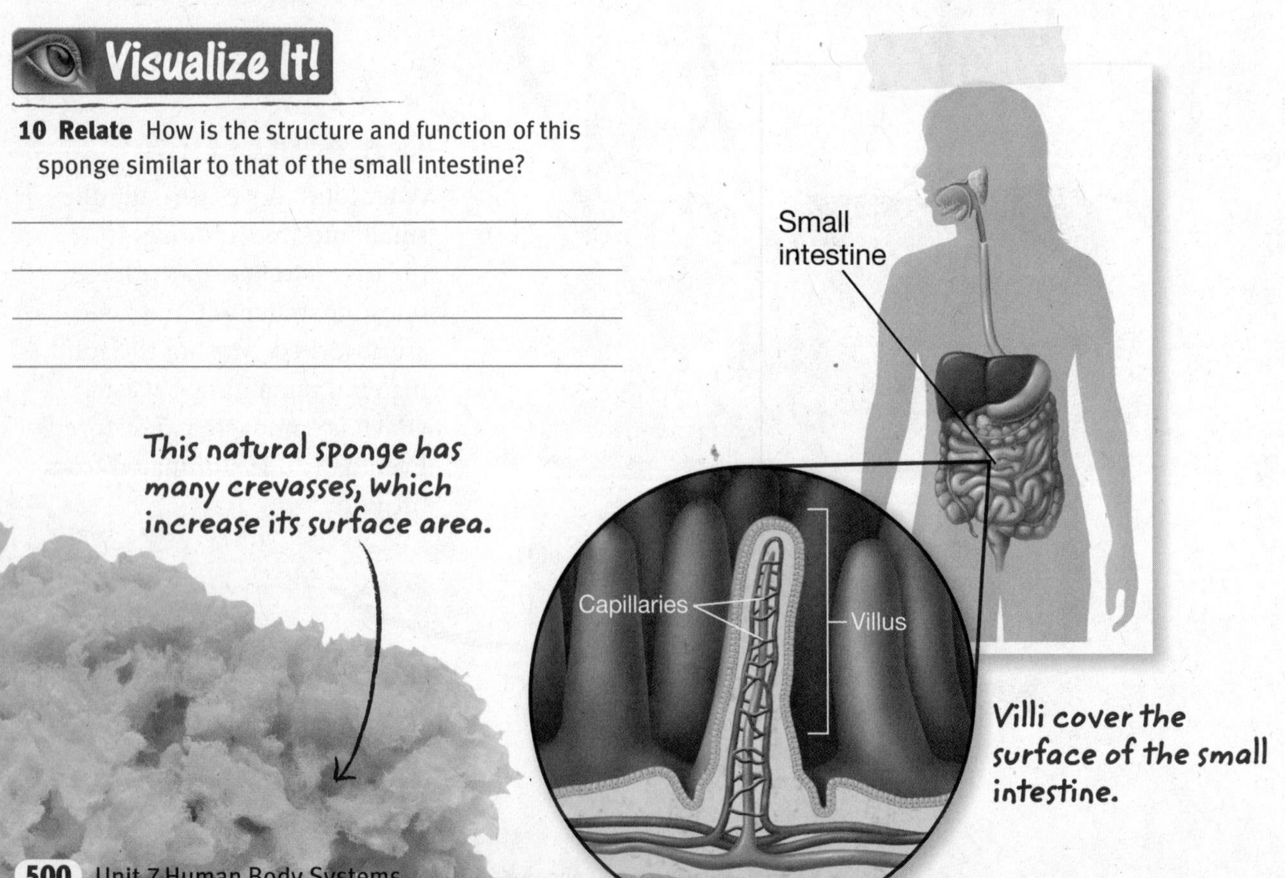

This natural sponge has many crevasses, which increase its surface area.

Villi cover the surface of the small intestine.

Toxic Waste!

What are the functions of the excretory system?

You have toxic waste in your body! As your cells perform the chemical activities that keep you alive, waste products, such as carbon dioxide and ammonia, are made. These waste products are toxic to cells. If waste builds up in a cell, homeostasis will be disrupted and the cell may die. The **excretory system** eliminates cellular wastes from the body through the lungs, skin, kidneys, and digestive system.

Waste Removal

After you read the text, answer the associated questions below.

To Sweat

Your skin is part of the excretory and the integumentary systems. Waste products such as excess salts are released through your skin when you sweat.

11 Identify Sweat releases wastes through your ______________

To Exhale

Your lungs are part of the excretory and respiratory systems. Lungs release water and toxic carbon dioxide when you exhale.

12 List Two waste products that are released when you exhale are ______________ and ______________

To Produce Urine and Feces

Kidneys, part of the urinary system, remove all types of cellular waste products from your blood. Your digestive system eliminates feces from your body.

13 Identify The urinary system filters waste out of your ______________

Cleanup crew

What organs are in the urinary system?

The urinary system collects cellular waste and eliminates it from the body in the form of liquid waste. Waste products enter the urinary system through the kidneys.

Active Reading

14 Identify As you read, underline the functions of the organs in the urinary system.

Kidneys

The **kidney** is one of a pair of organs that remove waste from the blood. Inside each kidney are more than 1 million microscopic structures called **nephrons** (NEF•rahnz). Fluid is filtered from the blood into the nephron through a structure called the glomerulus (gloh•MEHR•yuh•luhs). Filtered blood leaves the glomerulus and circulates around the tubes that make up the nephron. These structures return valuable salts and ions to the blood. Tubes in the kidneys collect the wastes from the nephrons. Water and the wastes filtered out of the blood form a liquid known as **urine.**

Ureters

Urine forms in the kidneys. From the kidneys, urine travels through the *ureters*. The ureters are tubes that connect the kidneys to the bladder.

Bladder

The urine is transported from the kidneys to the bladder. The bladder is a saclike organ that stores urine. Voluntary muscles hold the urine until it is ready to be released. At that time, the muscles contract and squeeze urine out of the bladder.

Urethra

Urine exits the bladder through a tube called the urethra.

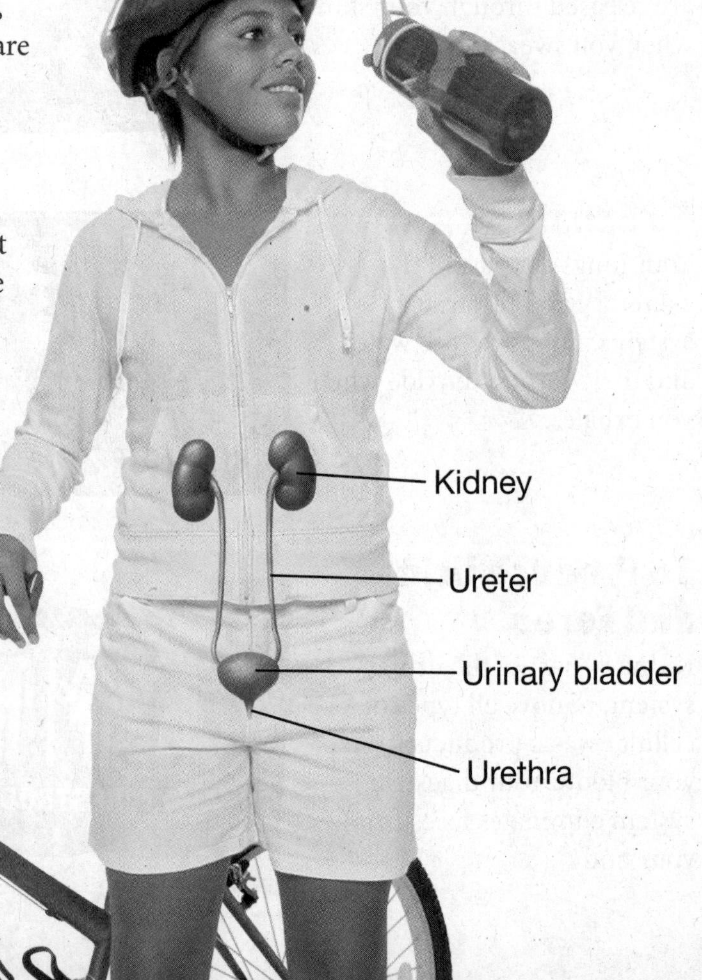

Filtering Blood

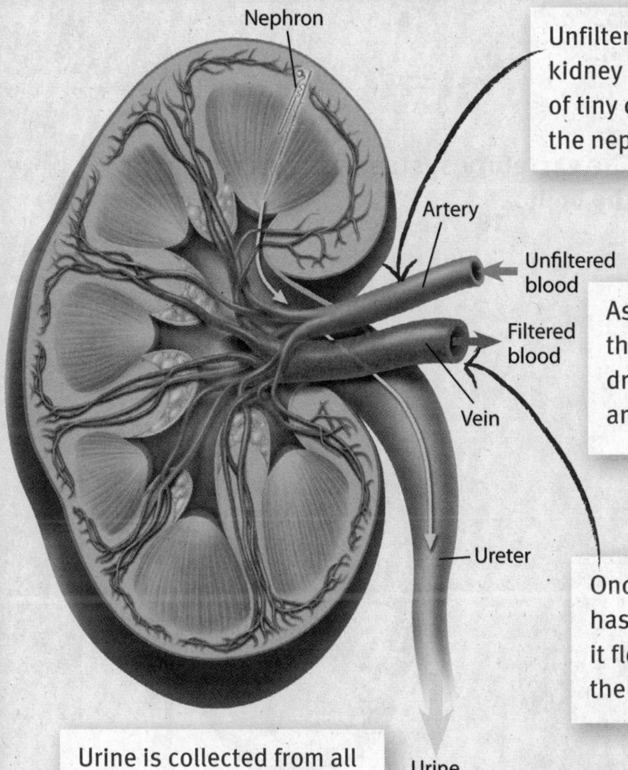

Nephron

Artery

Unfiltered blood

Filtered blood

Vein

Ureter

Urine

Unfiltered blood enters the kidney and flows into millions of tiny capillaries attached to the nephrons.

As blood flows through the capillaries, wastes are drawn out of the blood and into the nephron.

Once the blood has been filtered, it flows back out of the kidney.

Urine is collected from all of the nephrons and then flows out of the kidney through the ureter.

Visualize It!

15 Identify After blood enters the kidneys, name the two paths the fluid takes.

How does the urinary system maintain homeostasis?

Your cells have to maintain a certain level of water and salt in order to function properly. The excretory system works with the endocrine system to help maintain homeostasis. Chemical messengers called *hormones* signal the kidneys to filter more or less water or salt, depending on the levels of water and salt in the body. For example, when you sweat a lot the water content of your blood can drop. When this happens, a hormone is released that signals the kidneys to conserve more water and make less urine. When your blood has too much water, less of the hormone is released. As a result, the nephrons conserve less water, and more urine is produced by the kidneys.

Household or environmental toxins that enter the body through the skin, lungs, or mouth eventually end up in the bloodstream. When the kidneys are damaged, many toxins can accumulate in the blood. Infections can also affect the kidneys. Bacterial infections can occur when bacteria around the opening of the urethra travels up to the bladder and possibly the kidneys.

Active Reading

16 Explain How does exercise affect the balance of salt and water in your body?

Visual Summary

To complete this summary, fill in the blanks with the correct word or phrase. Then, use the answer key to check your answers. You can use this page to review the main concepts of the lesson.

The digestive system breaks down the food you eat into nutrients that provide energy and building materials for cells.

17 The two types of digestion that take place in the mouth are ______________ and ______________

The excretory system removes waste from the body.

18 The ______________ remove waste from the blood.

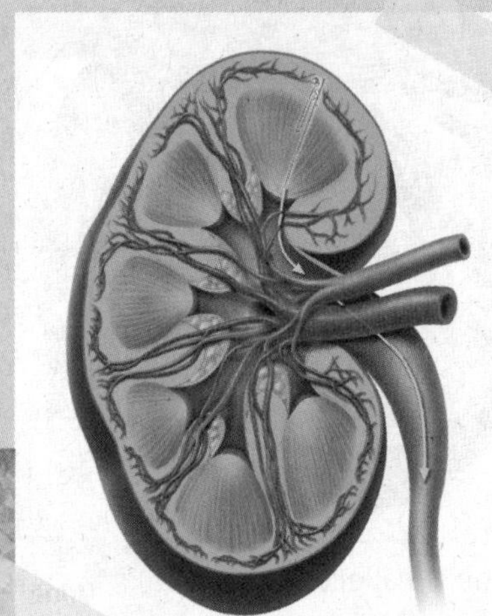

Digestion and Excretion

The digestive and excretory sytems work together to process the food that you eat.

19 To process this salad, food is broken down by the ______________ ______________ and wastes are removed by the ______________

Answers: 17 mechanical, chemical; 18 kidneys; 19 digestive system, excretory system

20 Summarize What types of wastes does the excretory system remove?

Lesson 4

Lesson Review

Vocabulary

Fill in the blank with the term that best completes the following sentences.

1 The ________________ system helps the body maintain homeostasis by giving it the nutrients it needs to perform different functions.

2 The ______________ system eliminates cellular waste through the lungs, skin, and kidneys.

3 The _______________ is the name for the hollow muscular organ that stores urine.

Key Concepts

4 Compare What is the difference between mechanical digestion and chemical digestion in the mouth?

5 Describe Starting with the mouth, describe the pathway that food takes through the digestive system.

6 Explain How does the circulatory system interact with the digestive system?

7 Identify Where does urine go after it exits the kidneys?

8 Summarize How do kidneys work with other body systems to maintain homeostasis?

Use the diagram to answer the following question.

9 Apply Identify the organs numbered below.

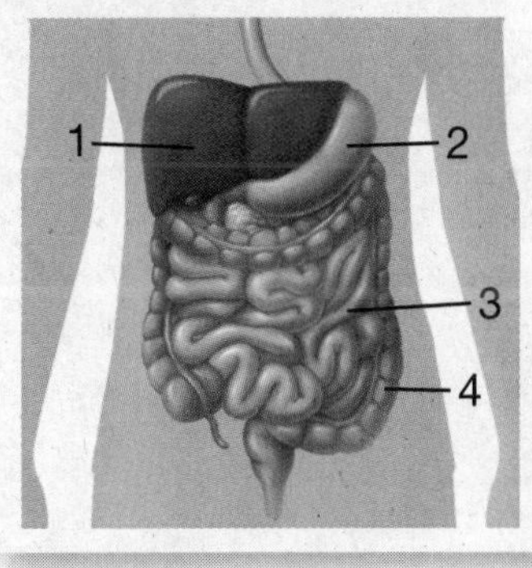

Critical Thinking

10 Relate Why would damaged kidneys affect your health?

11 Infer Suppose a person has a small intestine that has fewer villi than normal. Would the person most likely be overweight or underweight? Explain.

Lesson 5

The Nervous and Endocrine Systems

ESSENTIAL QUESTION

How do the nervous and endocrine systems work?

By the end of this lesson, you should be able to relate the structures of the nervous and endocrine systems to their functions in the human body.

This sky diver can sense his surroundings and feel the rush of excitement with the help of his nervous and endocrine systems.

Sunshine State Standards

SC.6.L.14.5 Identify and investigate the general functions of the major systems of the human body (digestive, respiratory, circulatory, reproductive, excretory, immune, nervous, and musculoskeletal) and describe ways these systems interact with each other to maintain homeostasis.

HE.6.C.1.8 Explain how body systems are impacted by hereditary factors and infectious agents.

Engage Your Brain

1 Predict Check T or F to show whether you think each statement is true or false.

T	F	
☐	☐	The central nervous system allows us to sense the environment.
☐	☐	The endocrine system functions by sending chemical signals.
☐	☐	The spinal cord is part of the peripheral nervous system.
☐	☐	The endocrine system helps regulate our blood sugar after we eat a meal.

2 Describe Think about a situation that makes you feel very nervous or anxious. Describe how this makes you feel inside. What do you think is going on in your body?

____

____

____

____

____

Active Reading

3 Apply You can often understand the meaning of a word if you use it in a sentence. Use the following definition to write your own sentence that has the word *gland*.

Definition
gland: a group of cells that make special chemicals for the body

gland:

____

____

____

____

____

Vocabulary Terms

- **nervous system**
- **brain**
- **spinal cord**
- **neuron**
- **axon**
- **dendrite**
- **endocrine system**
- **hormone**
- **gland**

4 Apply As you learn the definition of each vocabulary term in this lesson, create your own definition or sketch to help you remember the meaning of the term.

Brainiac!

What is the function of the nervous system?

The **nervous system** is made of the structures that control the actions and reactions of the body in response to stimuli from the environment. Your nervous system has two parts: the central nervous system (CNS) and the peripheral (puh•RIFF•uh•rahl) nervous system (PNS).

The CNS Processes Information

The brain and the spinal cord make up the CNS. The **brain** is the body's central command organ. It constantly receives impulses from all over the body. Your **spinal cord** allows your brain to communicate with the rest of your body. Your nervous system is mostly made up of specialized cells that send and receive electrical signals.

The PNS Connects the CNS to Muscles and Organs

Your PNS connects your CNS to the rest of your body. The PNS has two main parts—the sensory part and the motor part. Many processes that the brain controls happen automatically—you have no control over them. These processes are called *involuntary*. For example, you could not stop your heart from beating even if you tried. However, some of the actions of your brain you can control—these are *voluntary*. Moving your arm is a voluntary action.

The CNS is shown in yellow.

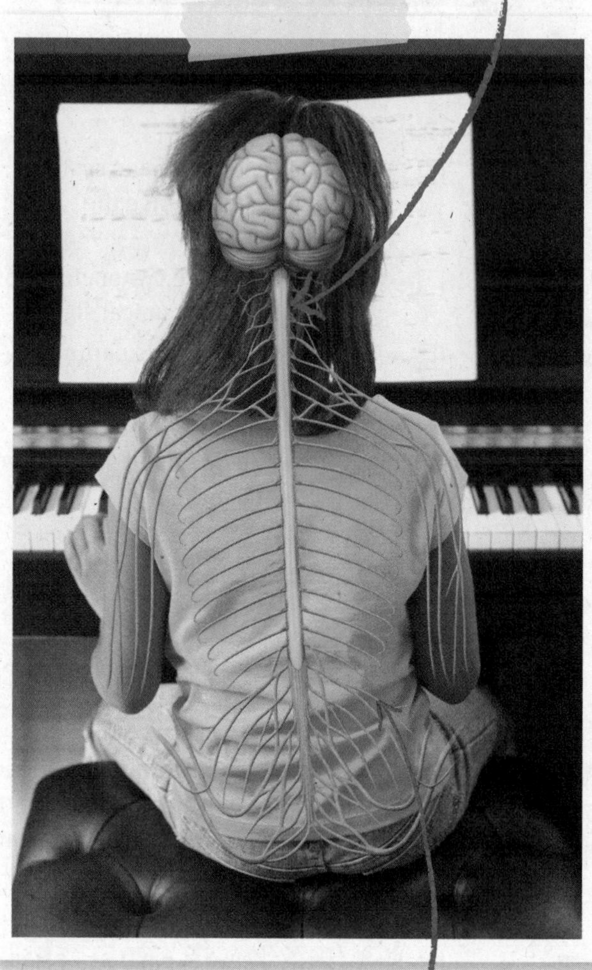

The PNS is shown in green.

Parts of the CNS

____

and

____

The CNS and PNS are both made of

____

Parts of the PNS

____

and

____

5 Compare Fill in the Venn diagram to compare and contrast the structure of the CNS and the PNS.

What are the parts of the CNS?

The CNS is made up of the brain and the spinal cord.

The Brain

The three main areas of the brain are the cerebrum, the cerebellum, and the brain stem. The largest part of the brain is the cerebrum. The cerebrum is where you think and problem-solve, and where most of your memories are stored. It controls voluntary movements and allows you to sense touch, light, sound, odors, taste, pain, heat, and cold. The second largest part of your brain is the cerebellum. It processes information from your body. This allows the brain to keep track of your body's position and coordinate movements. The brain stem connects your brain to your spinal cord. The medulla is part of the brain stem. It controls involuntary processes, such as blood pressure, body temperature, heart rate, and involuntary breathing.

6 Identify List a function of each part of the brain shown here.

Cerebrum

____

Cerebellum

____

Brain stem

____

The Spinal Cord

The spinal cord is made of bundles of nerves. A *nerve* is a collection of nerve cell extensions bundled together with blood vessels and connective tissue. Nerves are everywhere in your body. The spinal cord is surrounded by protective bones called *vertebrae.*

Special cells in your skin and muscles carry sensory information to the spinal cord. The spinal cord carries these impulses to the brain. The brain interprets these impulses as warmth, pain, or other sensations and sends information back to the spinal cord. Different cells in the spinal cord then send impulses to the rest of the body to create a response.

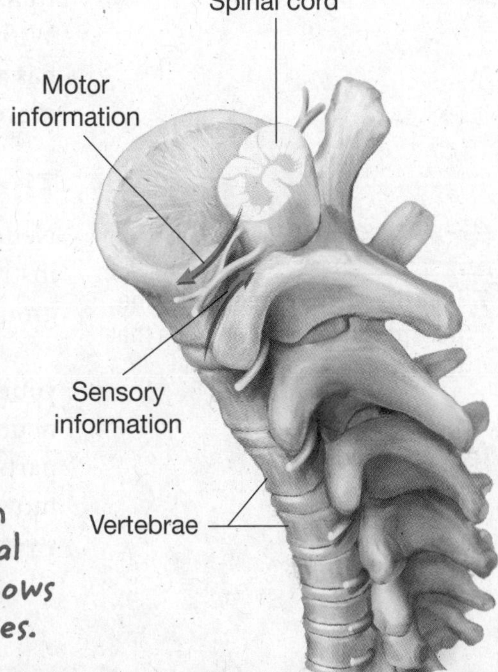

Sensory information (red) flows in from the environment to the spinal cord. Motor information (blue) flows out from the spinal cord to muscles.

You've Got Nerves!

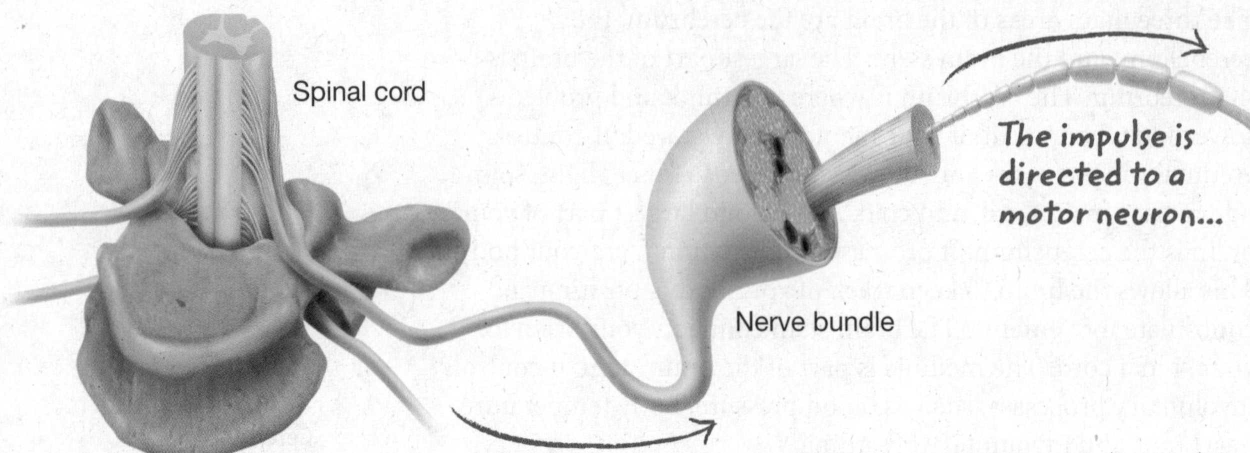

If you notice that your shoe is untied, your brain interprets this information and sends an impulse down the spinal cord.

How do signals move through the nervous system?

Your nervous system works by receiving information from the environment and translating that information into electrical signals. Those electrical signals are sent from the brain to the rest of the body by special cells called *neurons*. A **neuron** is a cell that moves messages in the form of fast-moving electrical energy. These electrical messages are called *impulses*.

Signals move through the central and peripheral nervous systems with the help of glial (GLEE•uhl) cells. Glial cells do not transmit nerve impulses, but they protect and support neurons. Without glial cells, neurons would not work properly. Your brain has about 100 billion neurons, but there are about 10 to 50 times more glial cells in your brain.

Through Sensory and Motor Neurons

Active Reading

7 Identify As you read, underline the special types of neurons that receive and send messages.

Neurons carry information from the body to the brain, and carry instructions from the brain back to the rest of the body. The two groups of neurons are sensory neurons and motor neurons.

Sensory neurons gather information from in and around your body. They then move this information to the brain. Motor neurons move impulses from the brain and spinal cord to other parts of the body. For example, when you are hot, motor neurons move messages from your brain to your sweat glands to tell the sweat glands to make sweat. Sweating cools your body.

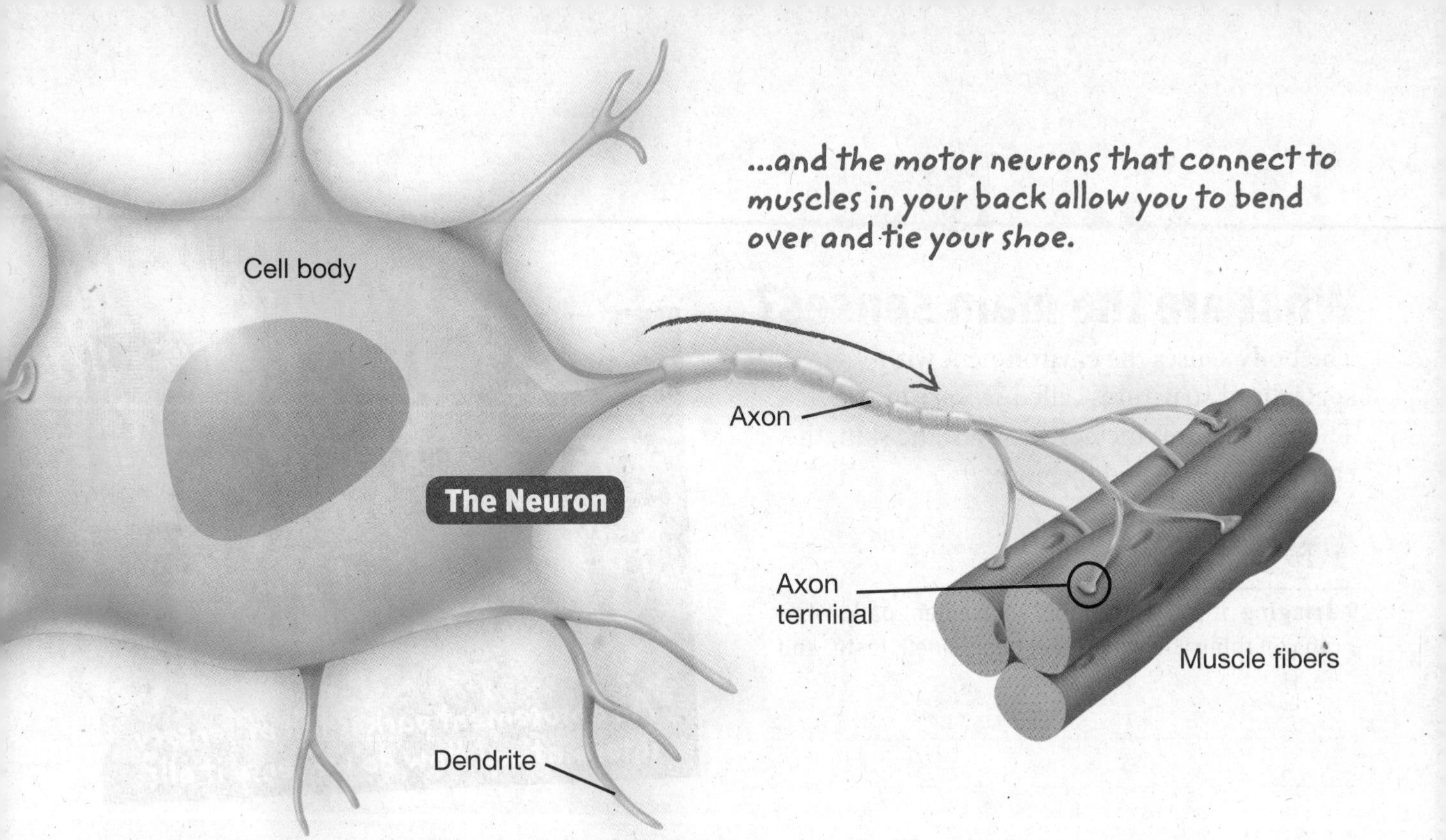

...and the motor neurons that connect to muscles in your back allow you to bend over and tie your shoe.

The Neuron

Cell body

Axon

Axon terminal

Muscle fibers

Dendrite

What are the parts of a neuron?

A neuron is made up of a large region called the *cell body,* a long extension called the *axon*, and short branches called *dendrites*. At the end of the axon is the *axon terminal.*

Like other cells, a neuron's cell body has a nucleus and organelles. But neurons have other structures that allow them to communicate with other cells. A **dendrite** (DEHN•dryt) is a usually short, branched extension of the cell body. A neuron may have one, two, or many dendrites. Neurons with many dendrites can receive impulses from thousands of cells at a time. The cell body gathers information from the dendrites and creates an impulse.

Impulses are carried away from the cell body by extensions of the neuron, called an **axon**. A neuron has only one axon, and they can be very short or quite long. Some long axons extend almost 1 m from your lower back to your toes! Impulses move in one direction along the axon.

At the end of an axon is the axon terminal, where a signal is changed from an electrical signal to a chemical signal. This chemical signal, called a *neurotransmitter,* is released into the gap between the neuron and other cells.

8 Apply In the boxes below, fill in the appropriate neuron parts, structures, or functions.

NEURON PART	STRUCTURE	FUNCTION
Cell body	region containing nucleus and organelles	
	branches of the cell body	gathers information from other cells
Axon		sends impulse away from cell body
	end of an axon	changes electrical signal to chemical signal

That Makes Sense!

What are the main senses?

The body senses the environment with specialized structures called *sensory organs*. These structures include the eyes, the skin, the ears, the mouth, and the nose.

9 Imagine If you were at this amusement park, what do you think you would see, hear, smell, taste, and feel?

An amusement park is full of sensory information! How do we sense it all?

Sight

Your eye allows you to see the size, shape, motion, and color of objects around you. The front of the eye is covered by a clear membrane called the *cornea*. Light from an object passes through an opening called the *pupil*. Light hits the eye's lens, an oval-shaped piece of clear, curved material. Eye muscles change the shape of the lens to focus light onto the retina. The *retina* (RET•nuh) is a layer of light-sensitive photoreceptor cells that change light into electrical impulses. These cells, called *rods* and *cones*, generate nerve impulses that are sent to the brain.

Rays form an upside-down image on the retina at the back of the eye. This image is translated by the brain.

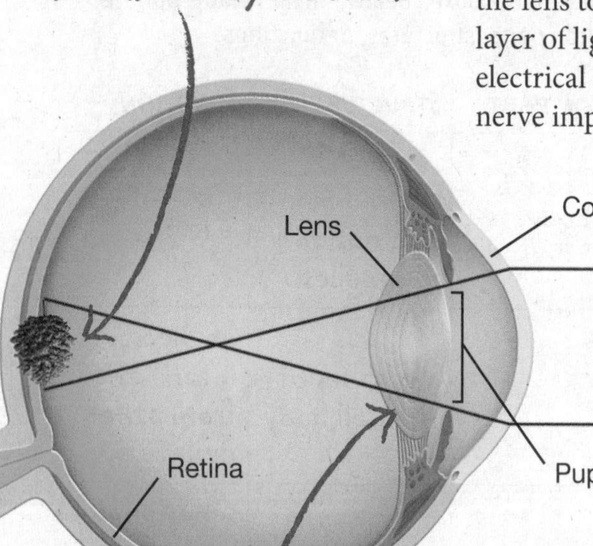

Light enters the eye through the lens. Light rays are bent by the cornea.

Visualize It!

10 Identify What part of the eye focuses light on to the retina?

Touch

You feel a tap on your shoulder. The tap produces impulses in sensory receptors on your shoulder. These impulses travel to your brain. Once the impulses reach your brain, they create an awareness called a *sensation*. In this case, the sensation is that of your shoulder being touched. The skin has different kinds of receptors that detect pressure, temperature, pain, and vibration.

Hearing

Ears pick up sound wave vibrations. These sound waves push air particles, creating a wave of sound energy. The sensory cells of your ears turn sound waves into electrical impulses. These electrical impulses then travel to your brain. Each ear has an outer, a middle, and an inner portion. Sound waves reaching the outer ear are funneled toward the middle ear. There, the waves make the eardrum vibrate. The *eardrum* is a thin membrane separating the outer ear from the middle ear. The vibrating eardrum makes three tiny bones in the middle ear vibrate. The last of these bones vibrates against the *cochlea* (KOH•klee•uh), a fluid-filled organ of the inner ear. Inside the cochlea, the vibrations make waves in the fluid. Sensory receptors called *hair cells* move about in the fluid. Movement of the hair cells causes neurons in the cochlea to send electrical impulses. These impulses travel to the brain via the auditory nerve and are interpreted as sound.

The ears also help you maintain balance. Special fluid-filled canals in the inner ear are filled with hair cells that respond to changes in head orientation. These hair cells then send signals to the brain about the position of the head with respect to gravity.

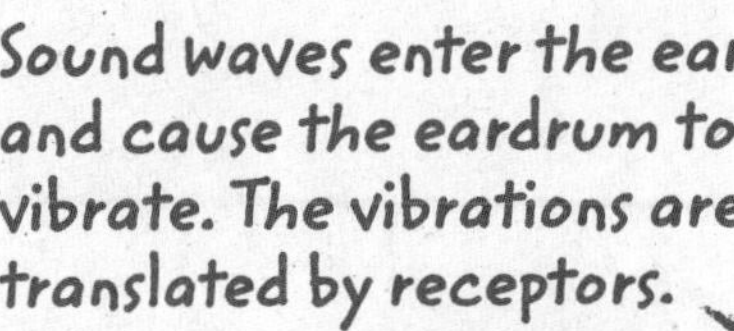

Sound waves enter the ear and cause the eardrum to vibrate. The vibrations are translated by receptors.

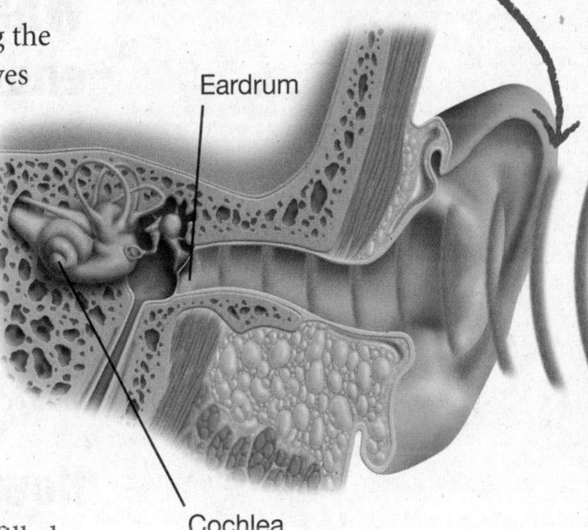

Taste

Your tongue is covered with taste buds. These taste buds contain clusters of *taste cells* that respond to signals in dissolved molecules in food. Taste cells react to five basic tastes: sweet, sour, salty, bitter, and savory. Your sense of taste can protect you from eating something that could be harmful.

Smell

The nose is your sense organ for smell. Receptors for smell are located in the upper part of your nasal cavity. Sensory receptors called *olfactory cells* react to chemicals in the air. These molecules dissolve in the moist lining of the nasal cavity and trigger an impulse in the receptors. The nerve impulses are sent to the brain, where they are interpreted as an odor. Your senses of taste and smell work together to allow you to taste a variety of food flavors. Both senses detect chemical cues in the environment.

11 Apply If you have a cold that causes congestion in your sinuses, how might that affect your sense of smell?

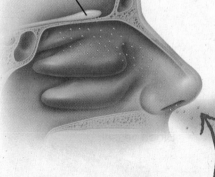

Olfactory cells

Molecules in the air enter your nose. There, they bind to receptors in the top of your nasal cavity.

Keep Your Cool!

What is the function of the endocrine system?

Your **endocrine system** controls body functions and helps maintain homeostasis by using hormones. A **hormone** is a chemical messenger made in one cell or tissue that causes a change in another cell or tissue in a different part of the body. Hormones are produced by endocrine glands or tissues. A **gland** is a group of cells that make special chemicals for your body. Unlike direct signals of the nervous system, the signals sent by the endocrine system are indirect because they cycle through the whole body.

12 Identify As you read, underline the structure which allows hormones to affect only certain cells.

How do hormones work?

Hormones travel through the bloodstream. They travel from the endocrine gland where they are made and can reach every cell in the body. However, hormones affect only the cells that have specific *receptors.* Each hormone has its own receptor and affects only cells that have that receptor. These cells are called *target cells.* Many cells throughout the body have the same receptors, so hormones are able to perform many functions at the same time in different cells.

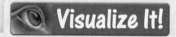

13 Apply Explain the difference between an endocrine cell and a target cell.

____

____

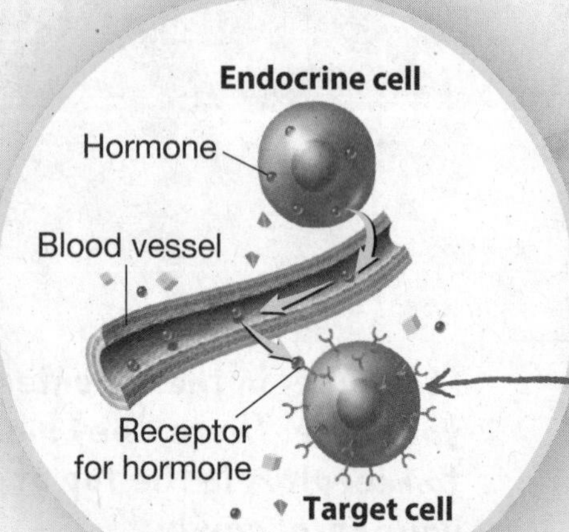

Hormones are released from an endocrine cell and travel through the bloodstream to bind to a receptor on a target cell. Sometimes a target cell is very far away!

What glands make up the endocrine system?

Your body has several endocrine glands or tissues that make up the endocrine system.

- Your pituitary gland is very important because it secretes hormones that affect other glands. It also stimulates growth and sexual development.
- The hypothalamus is a gland in the brain that controls the release of hormones from the pituitary gland.
- The pineal gland, also in the brain, produces hormones essential in the control of sleep, aging, reproduction, and body temperature.
- Hormones from the thyroid control your metabolism.
- The parathyroid gland controls calcium levels in the blood.
- Hormones made in the reproductive organs (ovaries or testes) control reproduction.
- Other endocrine glands include the pancreas and adrenal glands. The pancreas regulates blood sugar levels and the adrenal glands control the body's fight or flight response in dangerous situations.

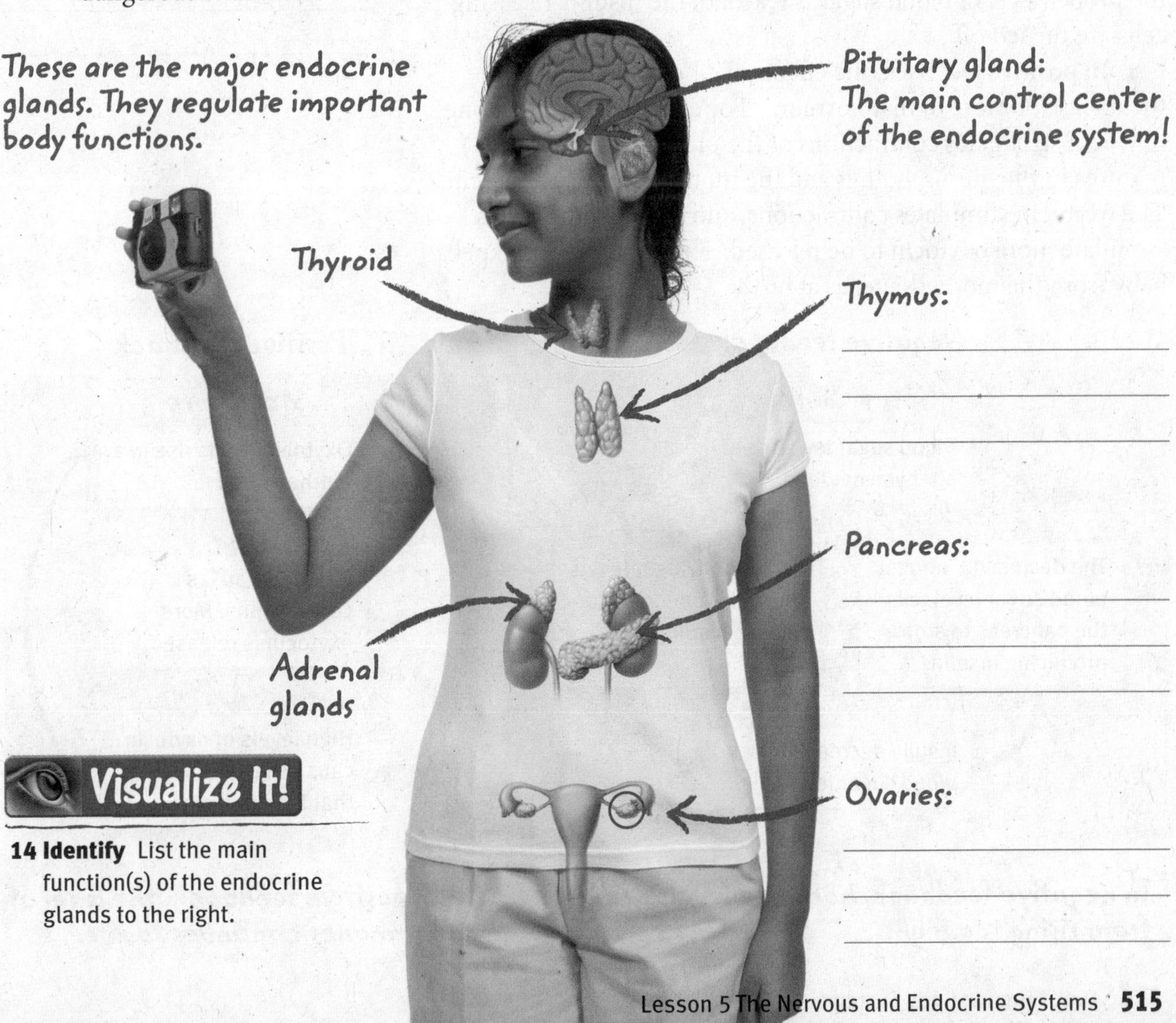

These are the major endocrine glands. They regulate important body functions.
Pituitary gland: The main control center of the endocrine system!
Thyroid
Thymus:
Pancreas:
Adrenal glands
Ovaries:

Visualize It!

14 Identify List the main function(s) of the endocrine glands to the right.

Feed←Back

How are hormone levels controlled?

The endocrine system keeps the body's internal environment in homeostasis. It does this by increasing or decreasing the amount of hormones in the bloodstream, some of which may have opposite effects on body cells. Such a process is called a feedback mechanism. A *feedback mechanism* is a cycle of events in which information from one step controls or affects a previous step.

By Feedback Mechanisms

There are two types of feedback, positive and negative. In negative feedback, the effects of a hormone in the body cause the release of that hormone to be turned down. For example, when you eat food, your blood sugar levels go up. Insulin is released and blood sugar levels are lowered. Once this happens, the lower blood sugar levels tell the pancreas to stop releasing insulin. In other words, when the proper level of blood sugar is reached, the insulin-releasing cells are turned off.

In positive feedback, the effects of a hormone stimulate the release of more of that hormone. For example, the hormone oxytocin stimulates contractions of the uterus. When a fetus matures in the uterus, both it and the mother produce oxytocin. The oxytocin stimulates contractions, and these contractions stimulate more oxytocin to be released. The contractions expel a baby from the mother's uterus at birth.

Active Reading

15 Compare Describe the difference between negative and positive feedback.

______

______

______

______

______

Negative Feedback

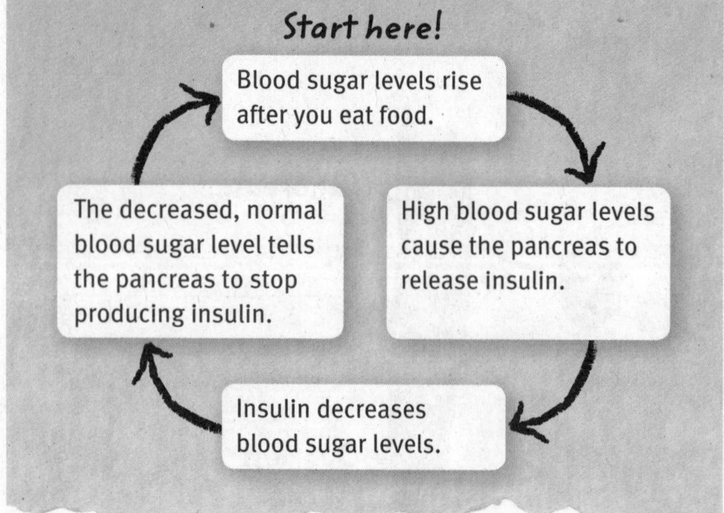

In negative feedback, hormone levels are kept from rising too high.

Positive Feedback

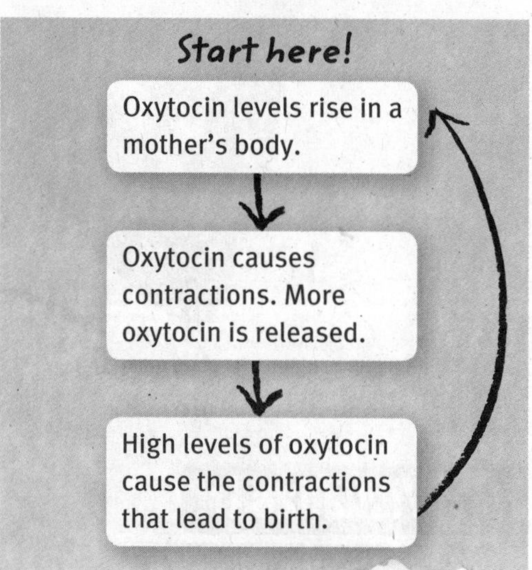

In positive feedback, the level of hormones continues to rise.

What are disorders of the endocrine and nervous systems?

The endocrine system and nervous system are both responsible for sending messages around our bodies. If a problem developed with one or more of these systems, other systems of the body would need to adjust to compensate for this loss.

Think Outside the Book

16 Compare Many systems you use every day send messages, such as e-mail, a thermostat, and TV remote controls. Research how one of these systems sends and receives messages. Make a chart to compare this system to the endocrine system.

Hormone Imbalances

Disorders of the endocrine system occur when an endocrine gland makes too much or not enough of a hormone. For example, a person whose pancreas does not make enough insulin has a condition called type 1 diabetes. This condition causes an imbalance of the blood sugar. A person who has diabetes may need daily injections of insulin to keep blood sugar levels within safe limits. Some patients receive their insulin automatically from a small pump worn next to the body. New technology allows people with type 1 diabetes to intake insulin using an inhaler.

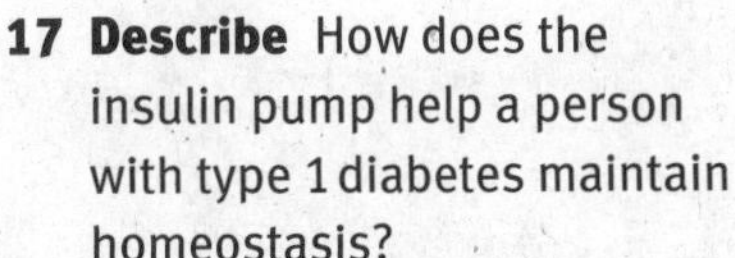

17 Describe How does the insulin pump help a person with type 1 diabetes maintain homeostasis?

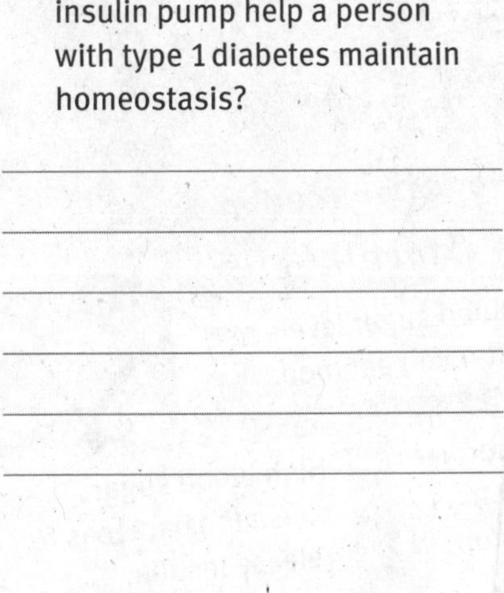

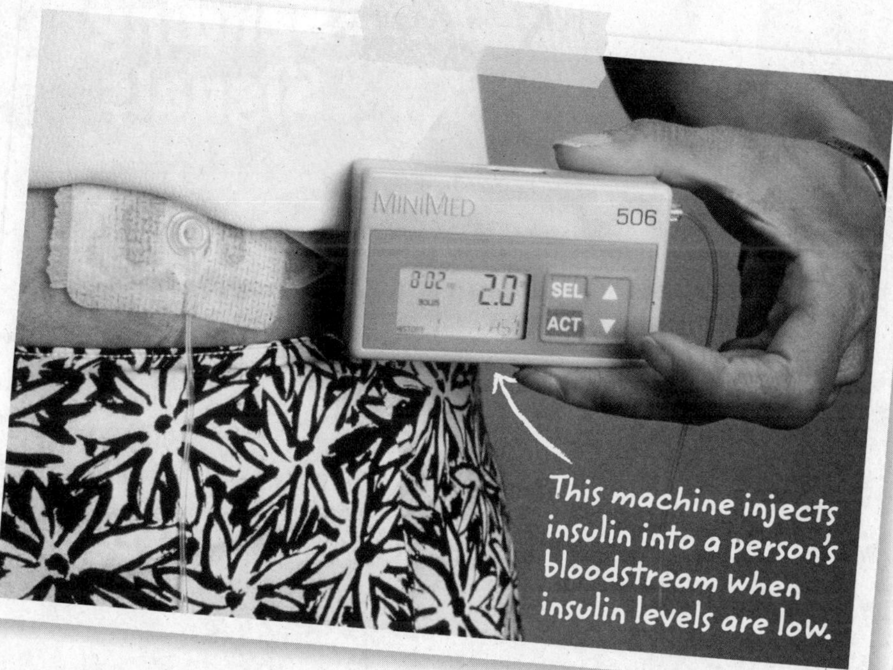

This machine injects insulin into a person's bloodstream when insulin levels are low.

Nerve Damage

Disorders of the nervous system include Parkinson's disease, multiple sclerosis, and spinal cord injury. In Parkinson's disease, the cells that control movement are damaged. Multiple sclerosis affects the brain's ability to send signals to the rest of the body.

A spinal cord injury may block information to and from the brain. For example, impulses coming from the feet and legs may be blocked. People with such an injury cannot sense pain in their legs. The person would also not be able to move his or her legs, because impulses from the brain could not get past the injury site.

Visual Summary

To complete this summary, fill in the blank to answer the question. Then, use the key below to check your answers. You can use this page to review the main concepts of the lesson.

The nervous system gathers information and responds by sending electrical signals.

18 Nerve cells called ______________ carry electrical messages called ______________

The endocrine system controls conditions in your body by sending chemical messages.

19 Hormones have specific actions by attaching to ______________ on target cells.

Hormones are controlled by feedback mechanisms.

20 ______________ feedback is when higher levels of a hormone turn off the production of that hormone.

Negative Feedback

Start here!

Blood sugar levels rise after you eat food.

High blood sugar cause the pancreas to release insulin.

Insulin decreases blood sugar levels.

The decreased, normal blood sugar level tells the pancreas to stop producing insulin.

Answers: 18 neurons, impulses; 19 receptors; 20 Negative

21 Apply Describe how both your nervous and endocrine systems would be involved if you walked into a surprise party and were truly surprised.

Lesson Review

Vocabulary

Use a term from the section to complete each sentence below.

1 The ____________________ is made up of the brain and spinal cord.

2 Glands in the ____________________ send messages to target cells.

3 Use *gland* and *hormone* in the same sentence.

4 Use *hormone* and *feedback mechanism* in the same sentence.

Key Concepts

5 Identify Describe the function of the PNS and the CNS.

6 Apply What are the parts of a neuron?

7 Identify How are the messages of the endocrine system moved around the body?

8 Identify What is the main sense organ for each of the five senses?

Critical Thinking

The images below show how an eye responds to different light levels. Use the image to answer the following question.

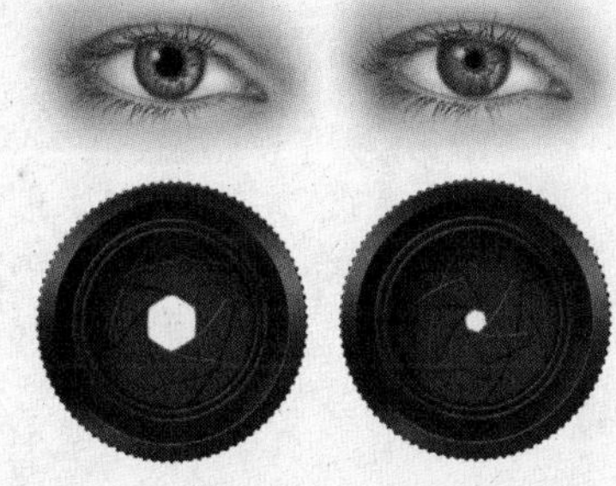

9 Interpret The pupil opens and closes automatically in response to light. What part of your nervous system controls this response?

10 Infer Explain whether this is a voluntary or involuntary action.

11 Predict How would your body be affected if your pituitary gland was not working properly?

Lesson 6

The Reproductive System

ESSENTIAL QUESTION

How does your reproductive system work?

By the end of this lesson, you should be able to relate the structure of the reproductive system to its function in the human body.

Many pregnant women do exercises such as yoga or other stretches to stay healthy as their baby develops.

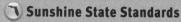

Sunshine State Standards

SC.6.N.3.4 Identify the role of models in the context of the sixth grade science benchmarks.

SC.6.L.14.5 Identify and investigate the general functions of the major systems of the human body (digestive, respiratory, circulatory, reproductive, excretory, immune, nervous, and musculoskeletal) and describe ways these systems interact with each other to maintain homeostasis.

MA.6.A.3.6 Construct and analyze tables, graphs, and equations to describe linear functions and other simple relations using both common language and algebraic notation.

HE.6.C.1.8 Explain how body systems are impacted by hereditary factors and infectious agents.

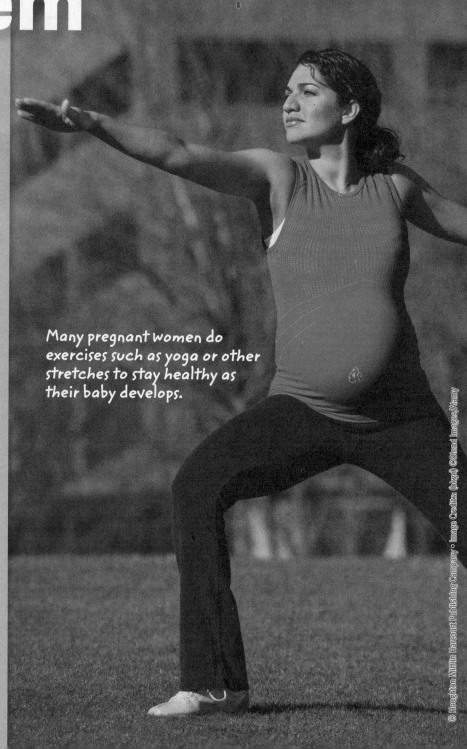

Engage Your Brain

1 Predict Have you met a woman who was pregnant? Write a short answer describing what type of development you think is going on inside a pregnant woman.

2 Apply Name five things that have changed about you from your fifth to your tenth birthday.

Active Reading

3 Explain You may be familiar with the eggs that farmers collect from chickens. Females of many species, including humans, produce eggs as part of the reproductive cycle. How do you think a human egg is similar to a chicken egg? How do you think they are different?

Vocabulary Terms

- **sperm**
- **testes**
- **penis**
- **egg**
- **ovary**
- **uterus**
- **vagina**
- **embryo**
- **placenta**
- **umbilical cord**
- **fetus**

4 Apply As you learn the definition of each vocabulary term in this lesson, create your own definition or sketch to help you remember the meaning of the term.

Reproduction

What are the main functions of the male reproductive system?

Active Reading

5 Identify As you read, underline the functions of the main hormones in the male and female reproductive systems.

The male reproductive system functions to produce sperm and deliver sperm to the female reproductive system. **Sperm** are the male cells that are used for reproduction. Each sperm cell carries 23 chromosomes, half of the chromosomes of other body cells. The male reproductive system also produces hormones.

Hormones are chemical messengers that control many important body functions such as growth, development, and sex-cell production. The **testes** (singular, *testis*) are the main organs of the male reproductive system. These organs produce *testosterone,* the male sex hormone. Testosterone causes male characteristics to develop, such as facial hair and a deep voice.

The testes also make sperm. After sperm mature, they are stored in the *epididymis* (EH•puh•DIH•duh•miss). They leave the epididymis through a tube called the *vas deferens* and mix with fluids from several glands. This mixture of sperm and fluids is called *semen.* To leave the body, semen passes through the *urethra,* the tube that runs through the penis. The **penis** is the organ that delivers semen into the female reproductive system.

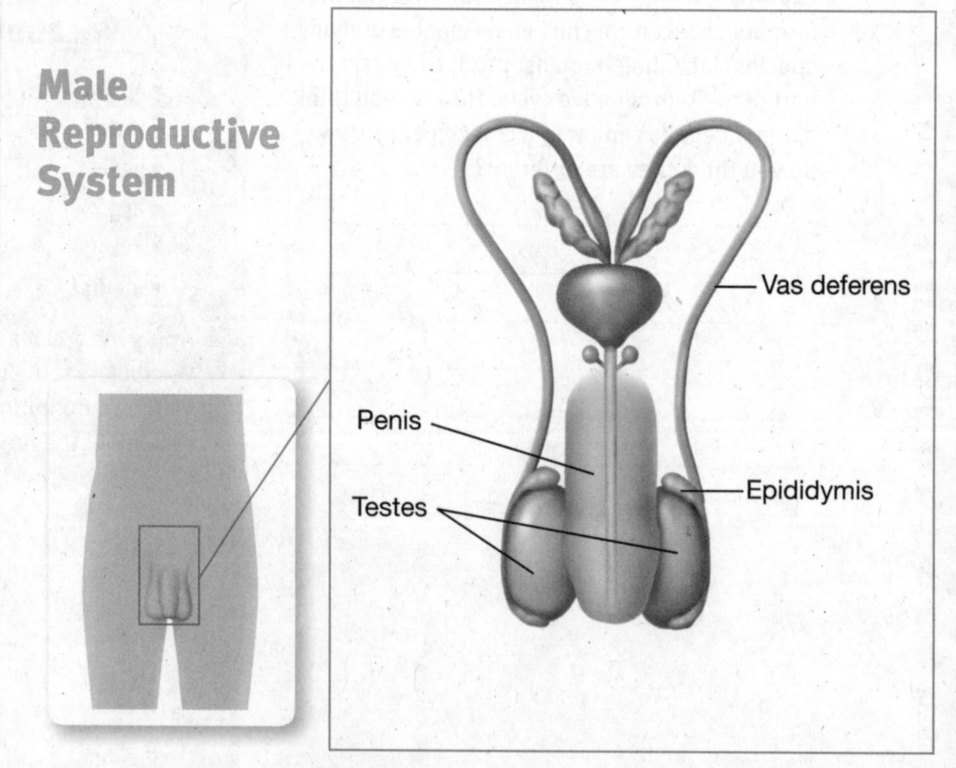

What are the main functions of the female reproductive system?

The female reproductive system produces hormones and eggs, and provides a place to nourish a developing human. An **egg** is the female sex cell. Like sperm, egg cells have 23 chromosomes, only half the number of other body cells.

The female reproductive system produces the sex hormones *estrogen* and *progesterone*. These hormones control the development of female characteristics, such as breasts and wider hips. They also regulate the development and release of eggs, and they prepare the body for pregnancy.

An **ovary** is the reproductive organ that produces eggs. At sexual maturity, females have hundreds of thousands of immature eggs in their ovaries. Like sperm, eggs are produced through the process of meiosis. During a female's lifetime, usually about 400 of her eggs will mature and be released from the ovaries.

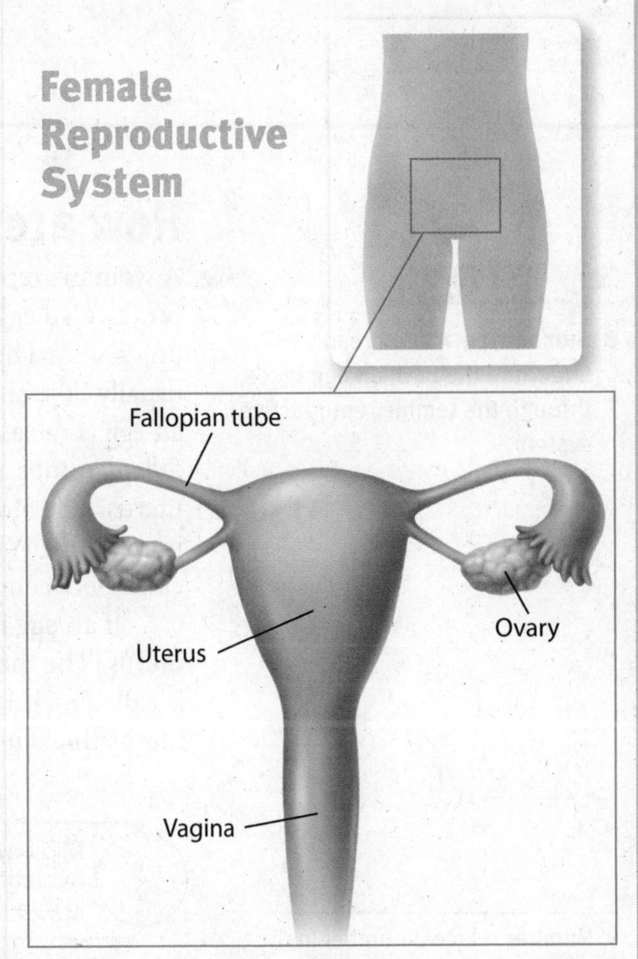

6 Summarize Fill in the chart below to summarize the structures of the male and female reproductive systems.

Sex	Sex cell	Organ that produces sex cell	Other reproductive organs
Male			
Female			

7 Contrast What makes sperm cells and egg cells different from almost all other types of body cells?

____

____

____

Fertile ground

How are eggs released?

Active Reading

8 Summarize As you read, underline the path an egg takes through the female reproductive system.

A woman's reproductive system goes through changes that produce an egg, release the egg, and prepare the body for pregnancy. These changes are called the *menstrual cycle* and usually take about one month. About halfway through the cycle, an egg is released from the ovary. The egg travels through the *fallopian tube,* a pair of tubes that connect each ovary to the uterus. The **uterus** is the organ in which a fertilized egg develops into a baby. When a baby is born, it passes through the **vagina**, the canal between the uterus and the outside of the body.

If an egg is not fertilized, it is shed with the lining of the uterus. The monthly discharge of blood and tissue from the uterus is called *menstruation.* When menstruation ends, the lining of the uterus thickens and the cycle begins again.

9 Number Place a number in the circles to order the steps of the menstrual cycle.

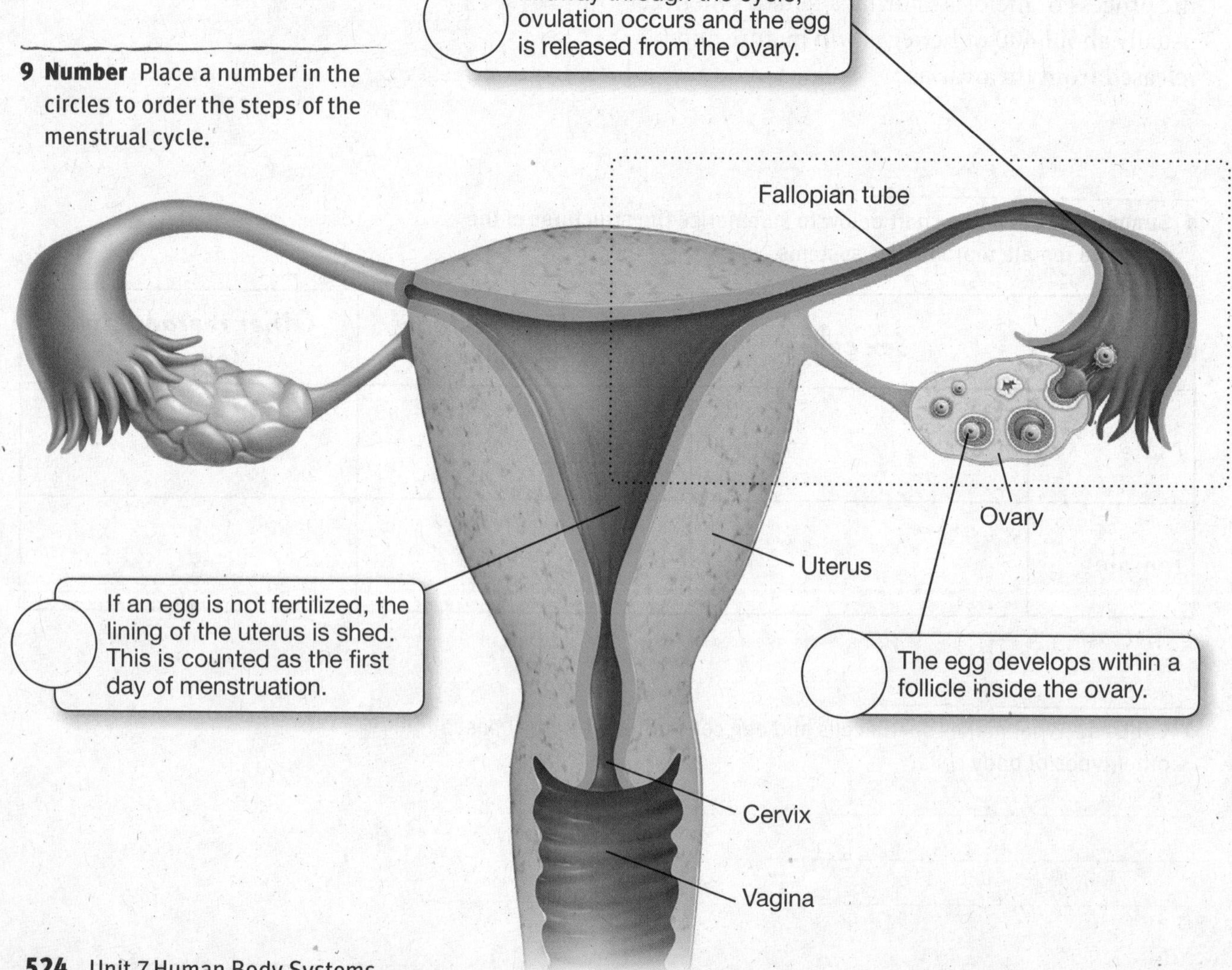
Midway through the cycle, ovulation occurs and the egg is released from the ovary.
Fallopian tube
Ovary
Uterus
If an egg is not fertilized, the lining of the uterus is shed. This is counted as the first day of menstruation.
The egg develops within a follicle inside the ovary.
Cervix
Vagina

How are eggs fertilized?

When sperm enter the female reproductive system, a few hundred make it through the uterus into a fallopian tube. There, the sperm release enzymes that help dissolve the egg's outer covering.

When a sperm enters an egg, the egg's membrane changes to stop other sperm from entering. During fertilization, the egg and sperm combine to form one cell. Once cell division occurs, the fertilized egg becomes an **embryo**. The genetic material from the father and the mother combine and a unique individual begins to develop. Usually, only one sperm gets through the outer covering of the egg. If more than one sperm enter the egg, multiple identical embryos can form. After fertilization, the embryo travels from the fallopian tube to the uterus over five to six days, and attaches to the thickened and nutrient-rich lining of the uterus.

Inquiry

10 Infer Sometimes more than one egg is released at a time. What do you think would happen if two eggs were released and both were fertilized? Explain your answer.

______

______

______

______

______

11 Summarize Determine what happens if an egg is fertilized and if it is not fertlized, and fill in both of the boxes below.

Was the egg fertilized?

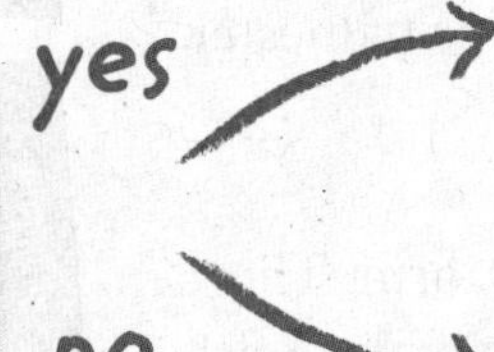
yes
no

______

______

______

______

______

______

______

______

Steps of Fertilization

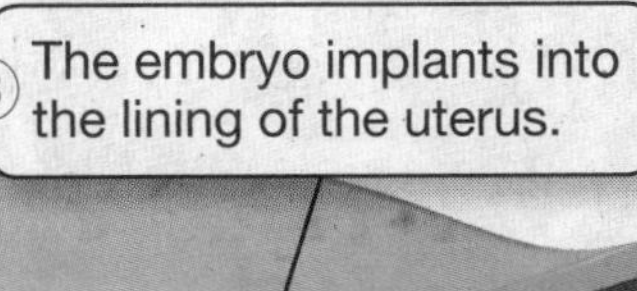
2 The egg is fertilized in the fallopian tube by a sperm.
3 The embryo implants into the lining of the uterus.
1 The egg is released from the ovary.

Happy Birthday!

What are the stages of pregnancy?

A normal pregnancy lasts about nine months. These nine months are broken down into three 3-month periods, called *trimesters*.

Active Reading **12 Identify** Underline three things that take place during each trimester.

First Trimester

Soon after implantation, the placenta begins to grow. The **placenta** is a network of blood vessels that provides the embryo with oxygen and nutrients from the mother's blood and carries away wastes. The embryo is surrounded by the *amnion*, a sac filled with fluid that protects the embryo. The embryo connects to the placenta by the **umbilical cord**. After week 10, the embryo is called a **fetus**. Many organs such as the heart, liver and brain form. Arms and legs as well as fingers and toes also form during this trimester.

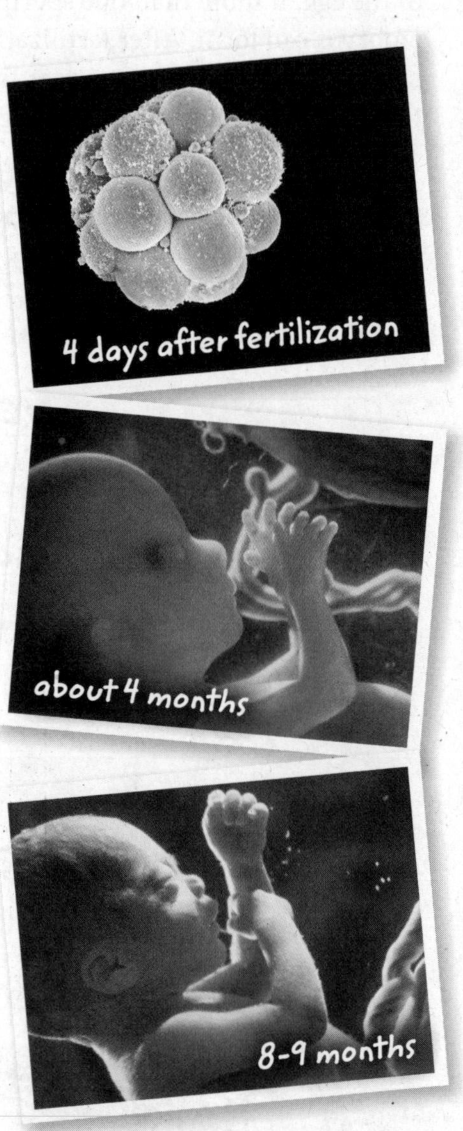

Second Trimester

During the second trimester, joints and bones start to form. The fetus's muscles grow stronger. As a result, the fetus can make a fist and begins to move. The fetus triples its size within a month and its brain begins to grow rapidly. Eventually, the fetus can make faces. The fetus starts to make movements the mother can feel. Toward the end of the trimester, the fetus can breathe and swallow.

Third Trimester

During the third trimester, the fetus can respond to light and sound outside the uterus. The brain develops further, and the organs become fully functional. Bones grow and harden, and the lungs completely develop. By week 32, the fetus's eyes can open and close. By the third trimester the fetus can also dream. After 36 weeks, the fetus is almost ready to be born. A full-term pregnancy usually lasts about 40 weeks.

How are babies born?

As birth begins, the mother's uterus starts a series of muscular contractions called *labor*. Usually, these contractions push the fetus through the mother's vagina, and the baby is born. The umbilical cord is tied and cut. All that will remain of the place where the umbilical cord was attached is the navel. Finally, the mother pushes out the placenta, and labor is complete.

What changes occur during infancy and childhood?

Development during infancy and childhood includes gaining control of skeletal muscles and learning to speak. Generally, infancy is the stage from birth to age 2. During infancy, babies grow quickly and baby teeth appear. The nervous system develops, and babies become more coordinated and start to walk. Many babies begin to say words by age 1. During this time, the body is growing rapidly. Childhood lasts from age 2 to puberty. Baby teeth are replaced by permanent teeth. Children learn to speak fluently and their muscles become more coordinated, allowing them to run, jump, and perform other activities.

What changes occur during adolescence and adulthood?

The stage from puberty to adulthood is *adolescence*. During adolescence, a person's reproductive system becomes mature. In most boys, puberty takes place between the ages of 9 and 16. During this time, the young male's body becomes more muscular, his voice becomes deeper, and body and facial hair appear. In most girls, puberty takes place between the ages of 9 and 15. During this time, the amount of fat in the hips and thighs increases, the breasts enlarge, body hair appears, and menstruation begins.

During adulthood, a person reaches physical and emotional maturity. A person is considered a young adult from about age 20 to age 40. Beginning around age 30, changes associated with aging begin. The aging process continues into middle age (between 40 and 65 years old). During this time, hair may turn gray, athletic abilities will decline, and skin may wrinkle. A person more than 65 years old is considered an older adult. Exercising and eating well-balanced diets help people stay healthy as they grow older.

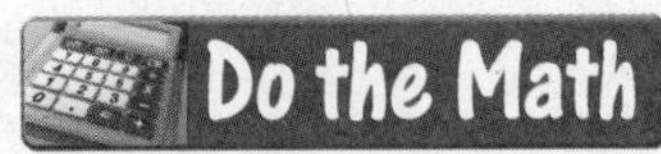

Do the Math

Everyone grows as they age, but does the amount you grow change as you get older?

Sample Problem

To calculate growth rate, divide the difference in height by the difference in age. For example, the growth rate between the ages of one and five for the girl shown below is:

(102 cm − 71 cm) ÷ (5 years − 1 year) = 8 cm/year

You Try It

13 Calculate Determine the growth rate for the girl between the ages of 14 and 19. Is the amount of growth greater between ages 1 and 5 or between ages 14 and 19?

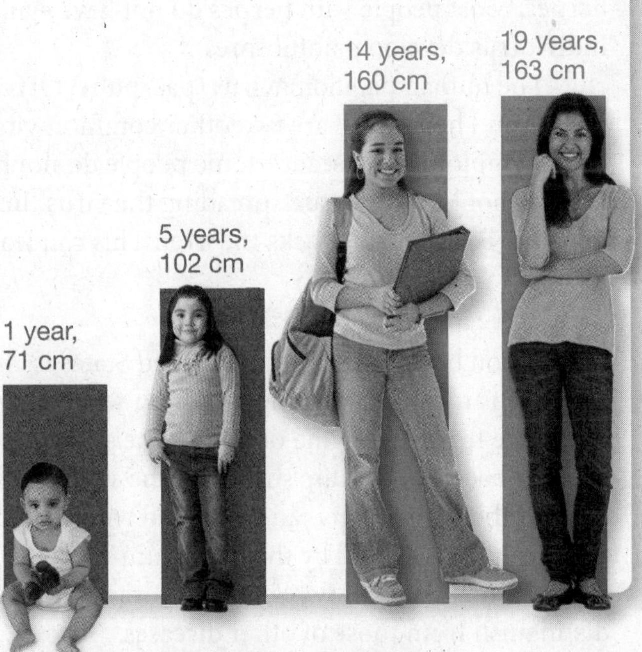

Think Outside the Book

14 Research Learning a new language can be easier for young children. This phenomenon is known as a "critical period." Research critical periods for language and write a short report describing what you learned.

Infections

What causes STIs?

Sexually transmitted infections (STIs) are infections that are passed from one person to another during sexual contact. STIs can be caused by viruses, bacteria, or parasites.

Active Reading **15 Identify** As you read, underline the symptoms of each STI listed below.

Viruses

Acquired immunodeficiency syndrome (AIDS) is caused by the human immunodeficiency virus (HIV). This virus infects and destroys immune system cells. As a result, people with AIDS usually show symptoms of many other illnesses that the immune system of a healthy person usually can fight. Most HIV infections are transmitted through sexual contact.

A much more common, but less deadly, viral STI is genital herpes. Most people with herpes do not have symptoms, but some individuals develop painful sores.

The human papillomavirus (paa•puh•LOH•muh•vy•russ) (HPV) and hepatitis B are two other common viral STIs that are often symptomless. Because some people do not have symptoms, they do not know they are spreading the virus. In the case of hepatitis B, the virus attacks the liver. This can lead to death.

Bacteria and Parasites

A common bacterial STI in the United States is chlamydia. Symptoms include a burning sensation when urinating or a discharge from the vagina or penis. The symptoms for gonorrhea, another bacterial STI, are similar to the symptoms of chlamydia. Both of these infections can be treated with antibiotics. Another STI, syphilis, is caused by the bacterium *Treponema pallidum.* Its symptoms, such as swollen glands, rash and fever, are hard to distinguish from those of other diseases.

Some STIs are caused by parasites. For example, the STI trichomoniasis is caused by the protozoan *Trichomonas vaginalis.* It is the most common curable STI for young women. Symptoms are more common in women and may include a genital discharge and pain during urination. Another parasitic STI is a pubic lice infestation. Pubic lice are tiny insects that feed on blood. The most common symptom of a pubic lice infection is genital itching.

16 Label For each photo below, label the type of infection as a virus, a bacterium, or a parasite.

Chlamydia cell

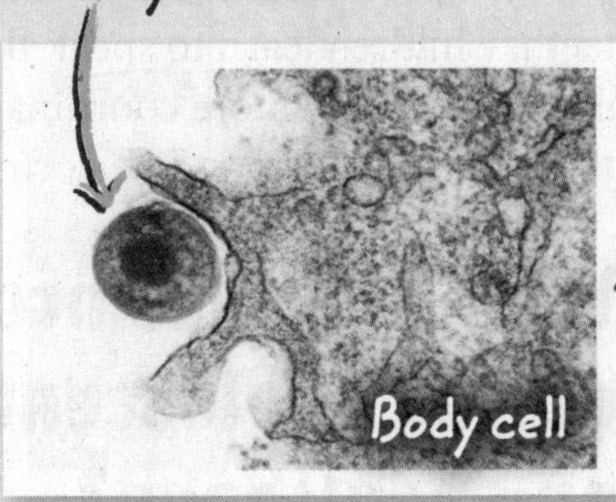

____

Herpes-infected immune cells

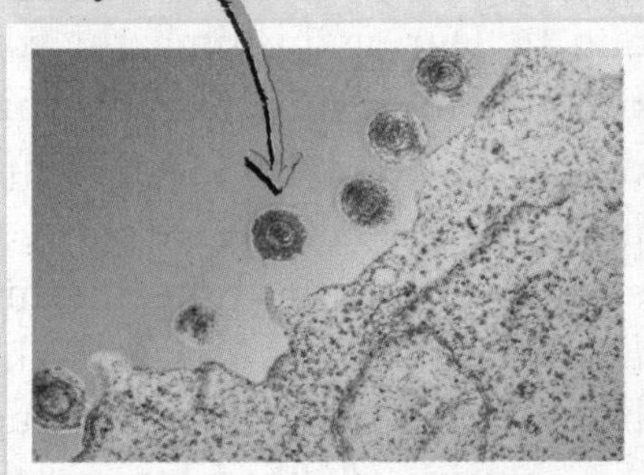

____

Syphilis cell

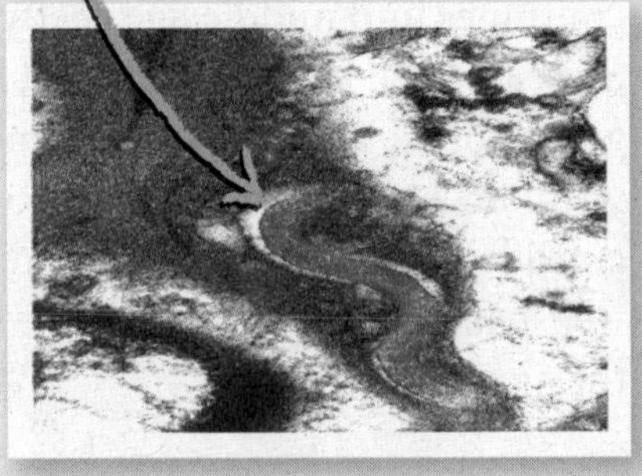

____

Why It Matters

Seeing Double

HEALTH WATCH

Multiple births occur when two or more babies are carried during the same pregnancy. In humans, the most common type of multiple births occurs when the mother gives birth to two children, or twins. About 3% of all births in the United States result in twins.

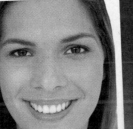

Identical Twins

Identical twins form when a single sperm fertilizes a single egg. The developing embryo then divides in two. Identical twins are always the same gender and are genetically identical.

Fraternal Siblings

Fraternal siblings form when two sperm fertilize two or more separate eggs. Fraternal siblings can be the same gender or different genders and are as different genetically as any ordinary siblings.

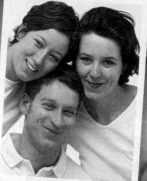

Triplets

While twinning is the most common type of multiple birth, other multiples still occur. About 0.1% of all births are triplets.

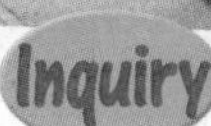

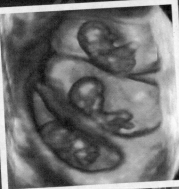

Extend

Inquiry

17 Infer Based on how identical twins form, infer how identical triplets could develop.

18 Research Describe some shared behavioral traits or language between twins and give an example.

19 Create Illustrate how fertilized eggs develop into fraternal triplets. You may choose to make a poster, make a model, or write a short story.

Visual Summary

To complete this summary, circle the correct word. Then, use the key below to check your answers. You can use this page to review the main concepts of the lesson.

Reproduction and Development

The male reproductive system makes hormones and sperm cells.

20 Sperm are produced in the penis / testes.

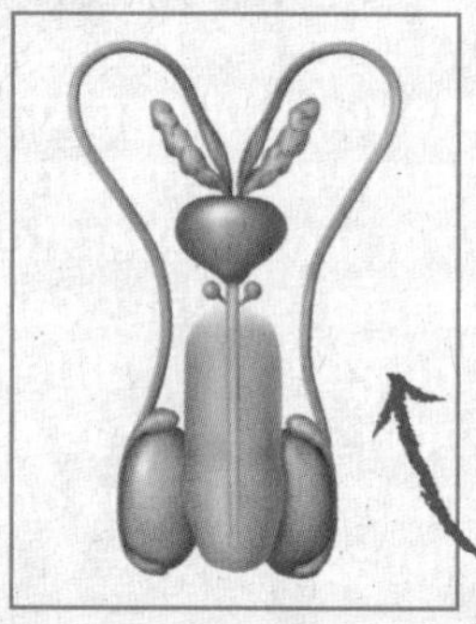

The female reproductive system makes hormones and egg cells, and protects a developing baby if fertilization occurs.

21 Eggs are produced in the ovary / vagina.

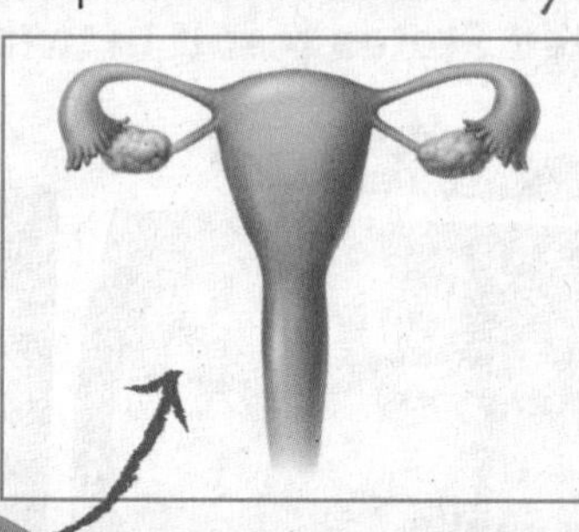

A baby goes through many changes as it develops into an adult.

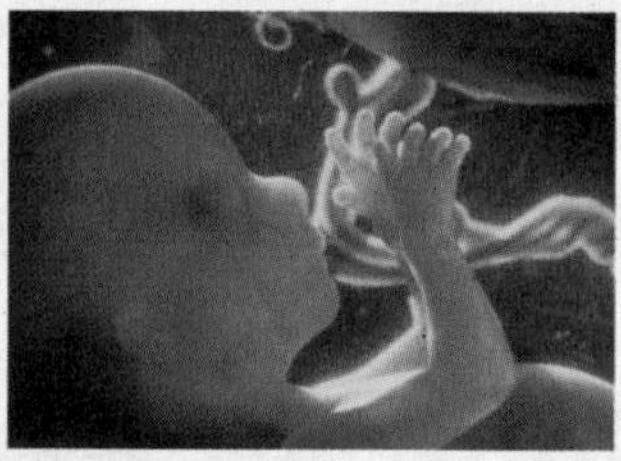

22 During pregnancy, a growing baby gets oxygen and nourishment from an organ called the embryo / placenta.

Sexually transmitted infections (STIs) are caused by viruses, bacteria, and parasites.

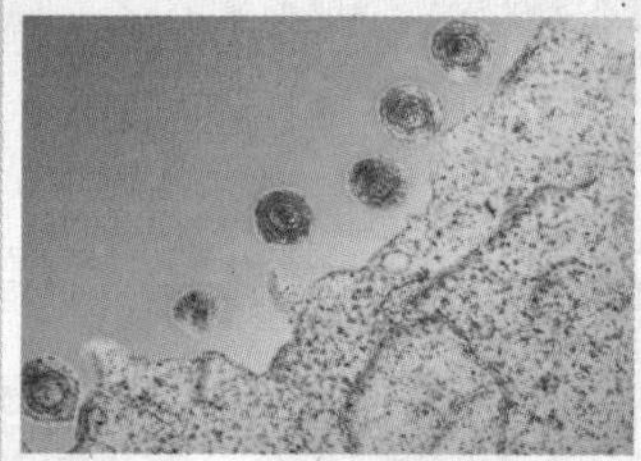

23 STIs are spread through the air / sexual contact.

Answers: 20 testes; 21 ovary; 22 placenta; 23 sexual contact

24 Applying Concepts Why does the egg's covering change after a sperm has entered the egg?

Lesson Review

Vocabulary

1 Use *uterus* and *vagina* in the same sentence.

2 Use *sperm* and *egg* in the same sentence.

Key Concepts

3 Compare Compare the functions of the male and female reproductive systems.

4 Summarize Summarize the processes of fertilization and implantation.

5 Identify Explain what causes STIs and how they are transmitted.

6 Explain How does a fetus get nourishment up until the time it is born?

Use the graph to answer the following question.

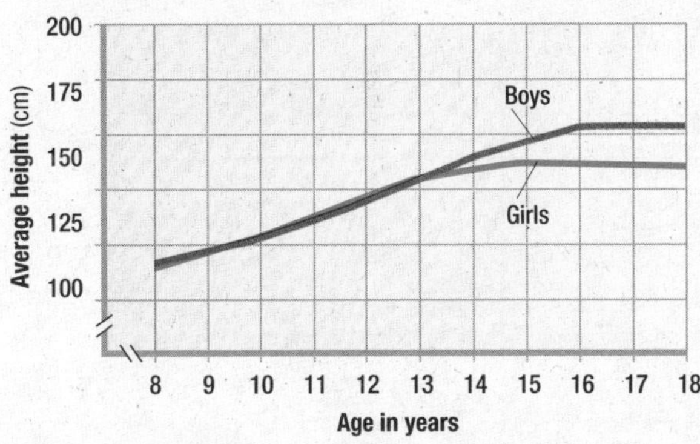

7 Interpret At what age is the difference between the average height of boys and girls greatest? Estimate this difference to the nearest centimeter.

Critical Thinking

8 Predict How might cancer of the testes affect a man's ability to make sperm?

9 Apply Explain the difference beween identical twins and fraternal twins. Include in your answer how they form and their genetic makeup.

My Notes

Unit 7 **Summary**

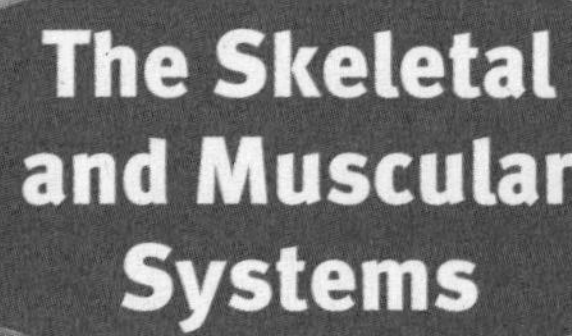

The Circulatory and Respiratory Systems

Introduction to Body Systems

The Nervous and Endocrine Systems

The Reproductive System

The Digestive and Excretory Systems

1 Interpret The Graphic Organizer above shows the systems that must function well for a body to remain healthy. Describe what state the body is in when all of these systems are working well.

2 Apply Provide an example for each system that describes how the nervous system and the endocrine system can affect other parts of the body.

3 Analyze Describe the two parts of the circulatory system, and explain how they work together.

4 Compare Name the two types of digestion, and describe how they are similar and different.

Name ______________________

Multiple Choice

Identify the choice that best completes the statement or answers the question.

1 It is important for conditions inside the body to be stable as the external environment changes. The endocrine system helps the body do this through feedback mechanisms. Which of the following describes a feedback mechanism of the endocrine system?

A. an involuntary reaction that controls the way an organ works

B. a way to remove waste in response to more food being digested

C. a change in the amount of hormones that affect certain body cells

D. an increase in electrical signals from the nerves to the brain

2 Pierre is studying the organs in the human digestive system. He looks at a diagram of the intestines, similar to the one that follows.

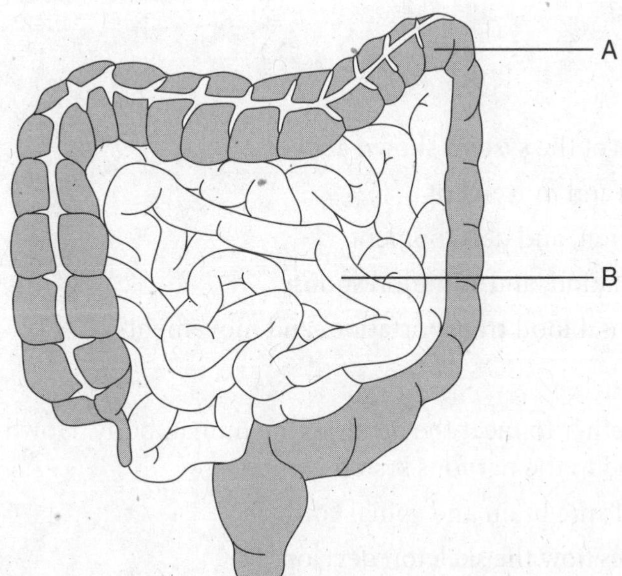

Which of the following **correctly** describes the diagram?

F. Structure A is the small intestine, and structure B connects the mouth to the stomach.

G. Structure A is the small intestine, and structure B absorbs water from digested material.

H. Structure A is the large intestine, and structure B absorbs nutrients from digested material.

I. Structure A is the large intestine, and structure B produces bile and stores it temporarily.

Benchmark Review

3 In science class, Rupert learns about the different systems of the human body.

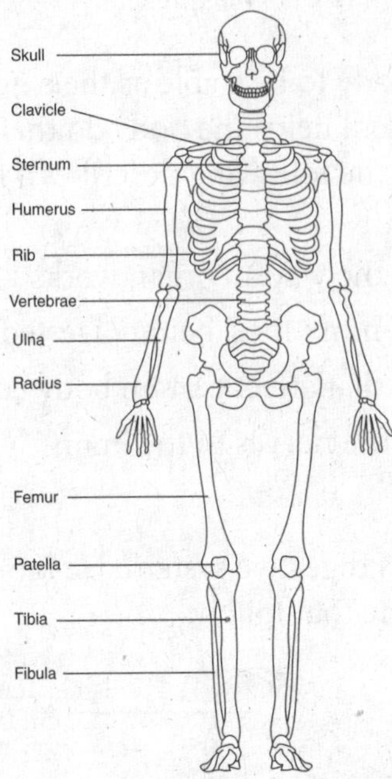

What are three functions of the system shown above?

A. support, protection, and movement
B. gas exchange, digestion, and development
C. waste removal, regulation, and stimuli response
D. removal of pathogens, blood transportation, and movement

4 Organ systems work together to meet the needs of the human body. How is the skeletal system related to the nervous system?

F. The skeleton protects the brain and spinal cord.
G. The brain determines how the skeleton develops.
H. The brain and spinal cord hold the skeleton together.
I. The skeletal system works as a part of the nervous system.

5 Groups of organs in the body work together as organ systems. Each organ system has a special role in the body. Organ systems include the nervous system, immune system, and endocrine system. What is the role of the endocrine system in the body?

A. It gets rid of wastes that the body produces.
B. It uses electrical signals to control body functions.
C. It uses chemical messages to control body functions.
D. It gets rid of pathogens that invade the body.

Name ______________________

6 Kim is studying certain blood vessels in the body. Blood travels from the heart to the muscles in the upper arms. Which type of vessels is Kim studying?

F. veins

G. arteries

H. capillaries

I. lymph ducts

7 Muscles often work together to produce movement, as shown below.

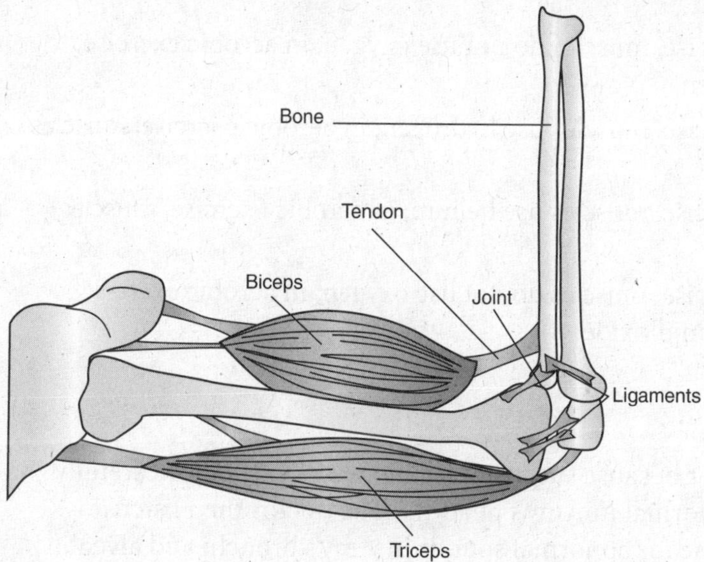

When the bicep contracts and gets shorter, what does the tricep do?

A. It relaxes and gets longer.

B. It relaxes and gets shorter.

C. It contracts and gets longer.

D. It contracts and gets shorter.

8 The human muscular system can suffer injury or disease. Which of the following is an example of a genetic disease that affects the muscular system?

F. tendonitis

G. muscular dystrophy

H. a muscle strain

I. a muscle tear

Benchmark Review

9 The environment can affect a person's health. Which of the following diseases would be most adversely affected by cigarette smoke?

A. emphysema and Parkinson's disease

B. asthma and gonorrhea

C. asthma and Parkinson's disease

D. emphysema and asthma

10 Anaerobic exercise is an intense activity that lasts a short period of time. This kind of exercise increases muscle power. Aerobic exercise is a moderate activity that lasts a longer period of time. This kind of exercise strengthens the heart. Which of the following is another difference between anaerobic and aerobic exercise?

F. In anaerobic exercise, muscles do not use oxygen; in aerobic exercise, muscles use oxygen.

G. In anaerobic exercise, muscles use hydrogen; in aerobic exercise, muscles use nitrogen.

H. In anaerobic exercise, muscles use helium; in aerobic exercise, muscles uses methane.

I. In anaerobic exercise, muscles do not use oxygen; in aerobic exercise, muscles use carbon dioxide.

11 Amy goes to the doctor because she is not feeling well. The doctor carefully looks for anything abnormal in Amy's pharynx. The doctor then listens through his stethoscope for abnormal sounds in Amy's bronchi and alveoli. Which body system is the doctor examining?

A. the lymphatic system

B. the respiratory system

C. the circulatory system

D. the cardiovascular system

12 When he eats, Eli chews his food carefully. Which of these explains what Eli is doing as his teeth mash and crush the food into small pieces?

F. He is performing peristalsis.

G. He is chemically digesting his food.

H. He is mechanically digesting his food.

I. He is mixing his saliva with bile.

13 Sexually transmitted infections, called STIs, are illnesses that are transferred by sexual contact. STIs can be caused by viruses, bacteria, or parasites. Which of the following is an STI that is caused by a virus?

A. syphilis

B. pubic lice

C. gonorrhea

D. genital herpes

14 Alice feels pain in her chest after she eats a big meal. Her doctor tells her that the pain is from stomach acid being pushed up into the tube that leads from her mouth to her stomach. To which structure is Alice's doctor referring?

F. liver

G. esophagus

H. large intestine

I. small intestine

15 Sergey runs a mile in gym class. After running, Sergey breathes heavily, pulling air into his lungs. Which statement **best** describes the path that the oxygen takes from his lungs to cells in his body?

A. Oxygen first enters his systemic circulation, then his heart, then his pulmonary circulation.

B. Oxygen first enters his pulmonary circulation, then his heart, then his systemic circulation.

C. Oxygen first enters his heart, then his systemic circulation, then his pulmonary circulation.

D. Oxygen first enters his heart, then his pulmonary circulation, then his systemic circulation.

16 Some diseases cause a person's kidneys to not function properly. A dialysis machine is a device that does the work of a person's kidneys. What does a dialysis machine do?

F. breaks down nutrients

G. filters waste from the blood

H. regulates the digestive system

I. delivers oxygen to the blood

Benchmark Review

17 At puberty, hormones trigger the development of sexual characteristics. Hormones also aid in reproduction. Which of the following are female sex hormones?

A. corpus and luteum
B. gonads and gametes
C. estrogen and progesterone
D. androgens and testosterone

18 The diagram shows the two main parts of the nervous system. The part labeled A processes and sends messages. The part labeled B transports the messages to and from the rest of the body.

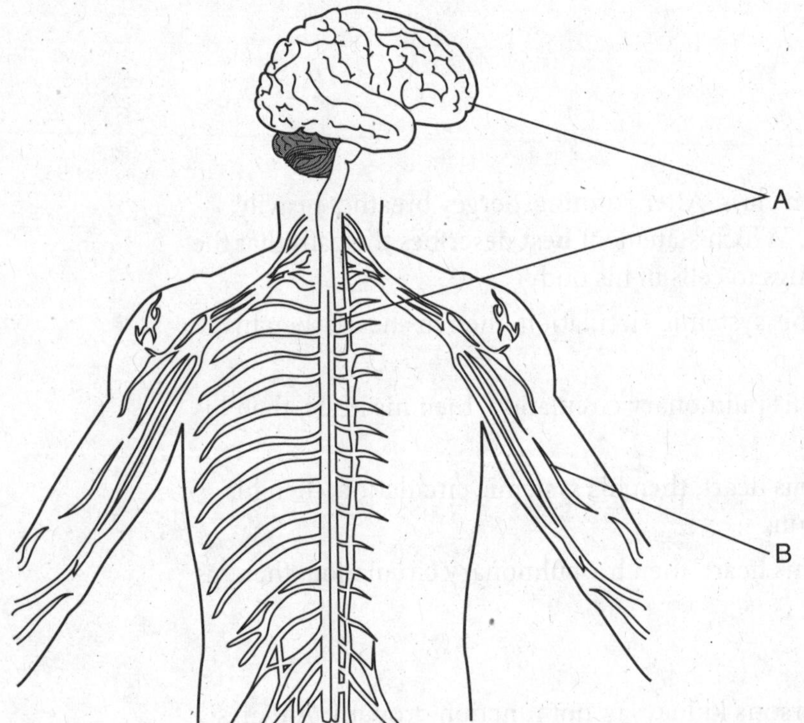

What structures make up the part of the nervous system labeled B?

F. the spinal cord only
G. the brain and spinal cord
H. blood vessels and muscle cells
I. motor nerves and sensory nerves

UNIT 8

Immunity, Disease, and Disorders

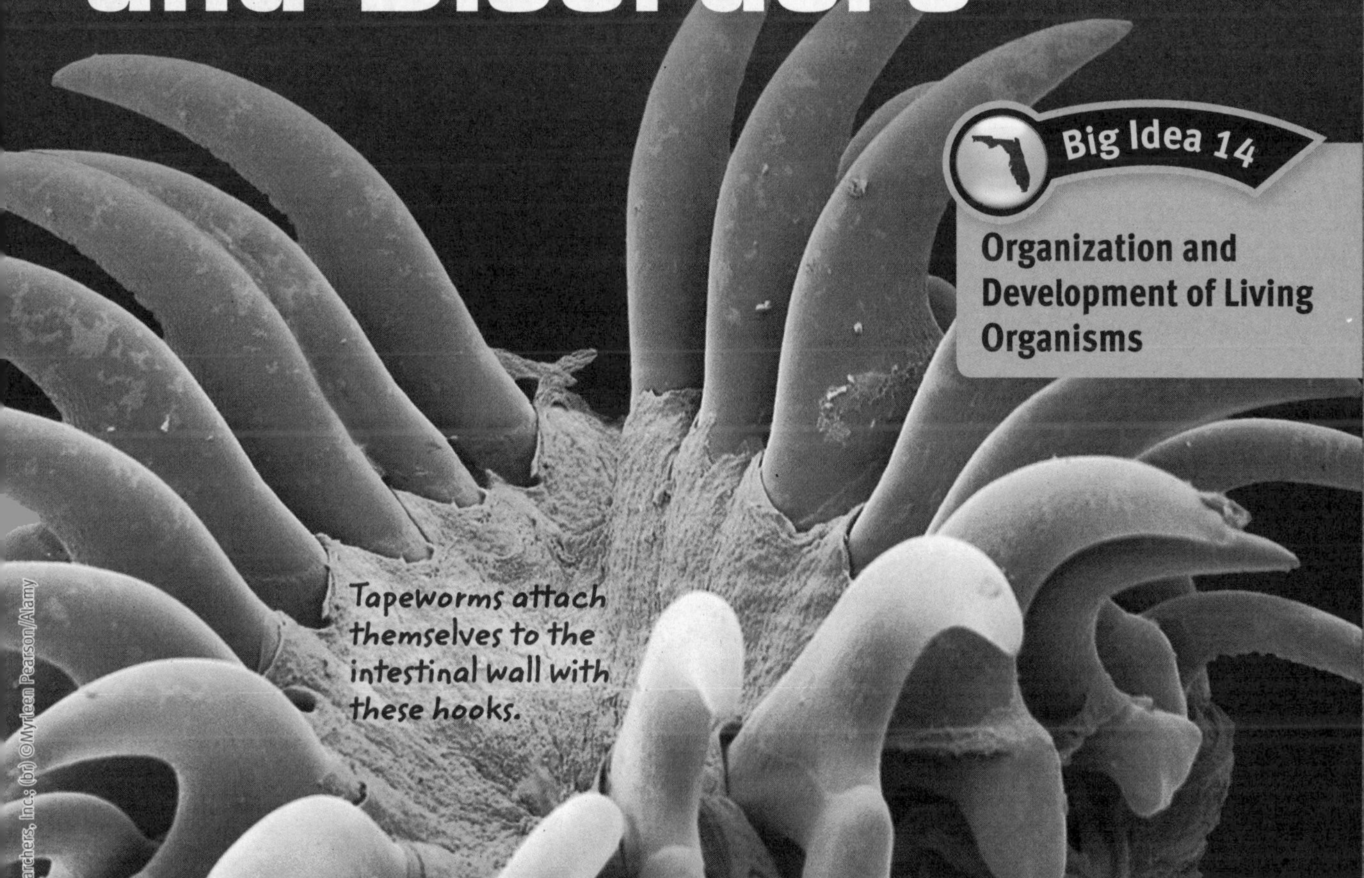

Big Idea 14

Organization and Development of Living Organisms

Tapeworms attach themselves to the intestinal wall with these hooks.

What do you think?

Tapeworms can be passed between infected animals and people. Tapeworms make organisms sick by absorbing nutrients more quickly than their host can. How does your body respond to infectious disease?

Keeping your pets healthy can help keep you healthy.

Unit 8

Immunity, Disease, and Disorders

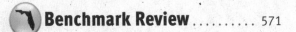

CITIZEN SCIENCE

Stop the Flu!

Many diseases spread through contact between infected people. Simple measures can help stop diseases from spreading.

1 Think About It

A Take a quick survey of the students in your class to find out how many had the flu in the past year. Record your findings here.

____

____

____

B Ask students who have had the flu to describe the symptoms they had. Record the symptoms below.

____

____

____

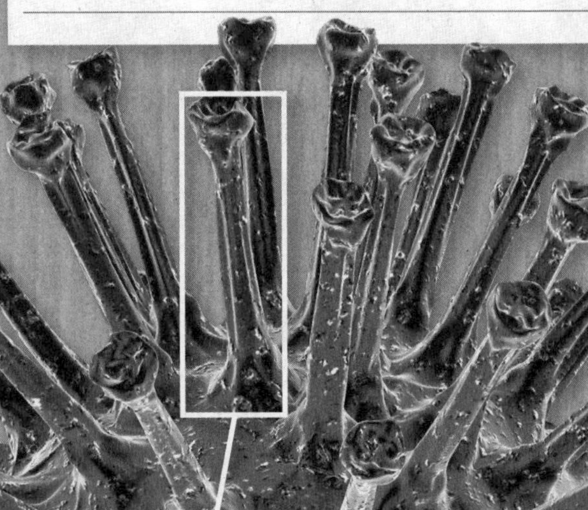

Each of the long thin objects on the surface of this cell is a single flu virus.

2 Ask a Question

How do you fight a flu?

The flu is caused by a family of viruses. Viruses are tiny particles that attach to the surface of the cells in the body. But how do they get there? With your class, conduct research to answer the questions below:

A How is the flu spread?

B What are common ways to prevent the spread of the flu?

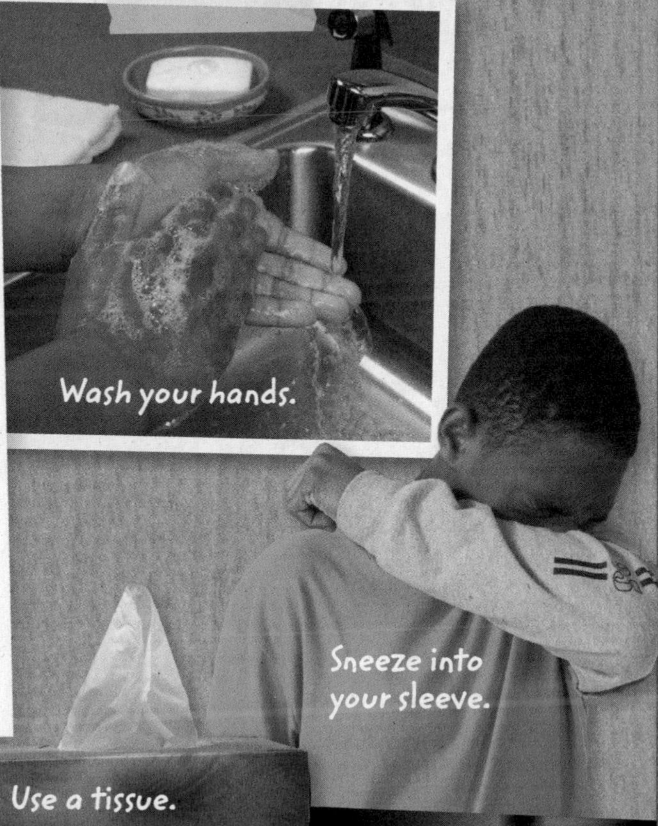
Wash your hands.
Sneeze into your sleeve.
Use a tissue.

3 Make a Plan

A Choose one or two of the ways to fight the flu that you would like your whole school to do.

B In the space below, sketch out a design for a poster or pamphlet that would inform students of how they can avoid the flu.

C Once you have created your pamphlets or posters, write down how you plan to give out the pamphlets or where you would place the posters.

Take It Home

Take your pamphlet or poster home. Use the pamphlet or poster to explain to everyone at home how they too can avoid the flu.

Lesson 1

The Immune System

ESSENTIAL QUESTION

How does your body's defense system work?

By the end of this lesson, you should be able to explain how the immune system fights infection.

Sunshine State Standards

SC.6.N.1.1 Define a problem from the sixth grade curriculum, use appropriate reference materials to support scientific understanding, plan and carry out scientific investigation of various types, such as systematic observations or experiments, identify variables, collect and organize data, interpret data in charts, tables, and graphics, analyze information, make predictions, and defend conclusions.

SC.6.L.14.5 Identify and investigate the general functions of the major systems of the human body (digestive, respiratory, circulatory, reproductive, excretory, immune, nervous, and musculoskeletal) and describe ways these systems interact with each other to maintain homeostasis.

MA.6.A.3.6 Construct and analyze tables, graphs, and equations to describe linear functions and other simple relations using both common language and algebraic notation.

HE.6.C.1.8 Explain how body systems are impacted by hereditary factors and infectious agents.

Parasitic worm

Macrophage

This parasitic worm can enter your body through the bite of an infected mosquito and cause disease. Fortunately your body has special cells that can destroy disease-causing agents such as this worm. Here you see a type of white blood cell, called a macrophage, attacking the parasitic worm.

Engage Your Brain

1 Infer What happens when a computer gets a virus?

VIRUS!

2 Predict Check T or F to show whether you think each statement is true or false.

T	F	
☐	☐	Your body has cells that can help fight against disease.
☐	☐	Most microscopic organisms are harmless.
☐	☐	Skin can protect against infection.
☐	☐	Fever is always harmful to the body.

Active Reading

3 Synthesize You can often define an unknown word if you know the meaning of its word parts. Use the word parts and sentence below to make an educated guess about the meaning of the word *pathogen*.

Word part	Meaning
patho-	disease
-gen	to bring forth

Example sentence

Your body is constantly protecting itself against pathogens.

pathogen:

Vocabulary Terms

- pathogen
- immune system
- macrophage
- T cell
- B cell
- antibody
- immunity
- vaccine

4 Apply As you learn the definition of each vocabulary term in this lesson, create your own definition or sketch to help you remember the meaning of the term.

Playing DEFENSE

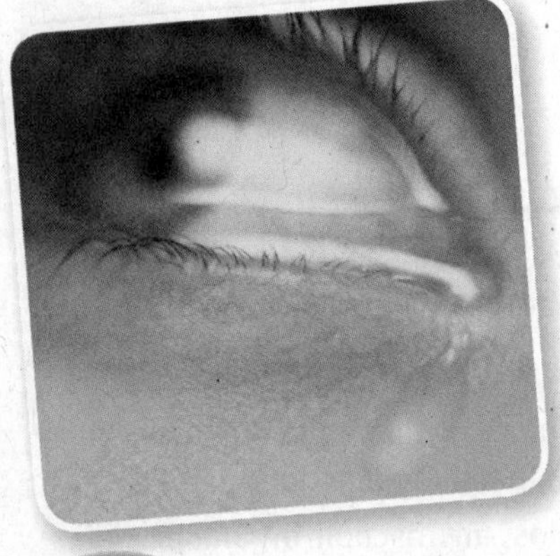

Inquiry

5 Describe How might watery eyes be a defensive response?

What is your body's defense system?

Microscopic organisms and particles, such as bacteria and viruses, are all around you. Most are harmless, but some can make you sick. A **pathogen** is an organism, a virus, or a protein that causes disease. Fortunately, your body has many ways to protect you from pathogens.

External Defenses

Your skin provides external protection against pathogens that may enter the body. Skin also has structures, such as hair, nails, and sweat and oil glands, that help provide protection. For example, glands in your skin secrete oil that can kill pathogens. Mucous produced by mucous membranes in your nose and saliva in your mouth wash pathogens down into your stomach, where most are quickly digested. Hair, such as eyelashes and ear hairs, keep many particles in the air from entering the body. Nails protect your fingertips and toes. The skin and all of these structures make up the *integumentary system*.

External Defense Example

Your body loses and replaces approximately 1 million skin cells every 40 min. In the process, countless pathogens are removed.

6 Apply Why is it important to clean and care for cuts on your skin?

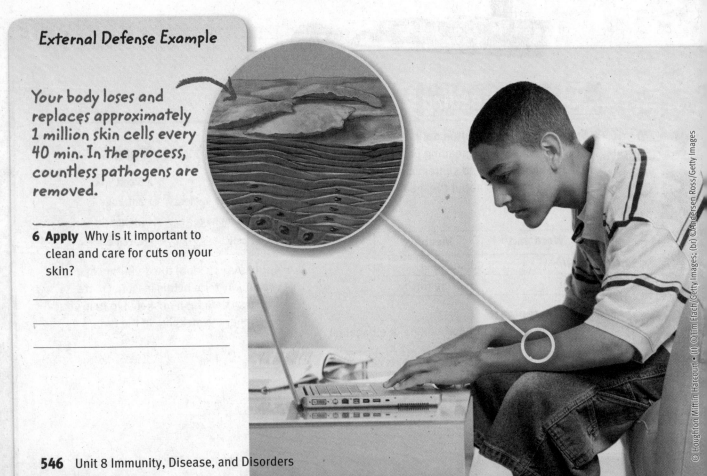

Internal Defenses

Most of the time, pathogens cannot get past external defenses. Sometimes, skin is cut and pathogens can enter the body. The body responds quickly to keep out as many pathogens as possible. Blood flow increases to the injured area, causing it to swell and turn red. This swelling and redness is called *inflammation*. Cell pieces in the blood, called *platelets*, help seal the open wound so that no more pathogens can enter.

Your body may also respond by raising your body temperature. This response is called *fever*, which slows the growth of bacteria and some other pathogens. Both inflammation and fever are a part of the body's internal defenses. If a pathogen is not destroyed by inflammation or fever, then the immune system responds.

The **immune system** is made up of tissues and specialized white blood cells that recognize and attack foreign substances in the body. These white blood cells function in a coordinated way to identify and destroy pathogens.

7 Recognize List some of the body's external and internal defenses.

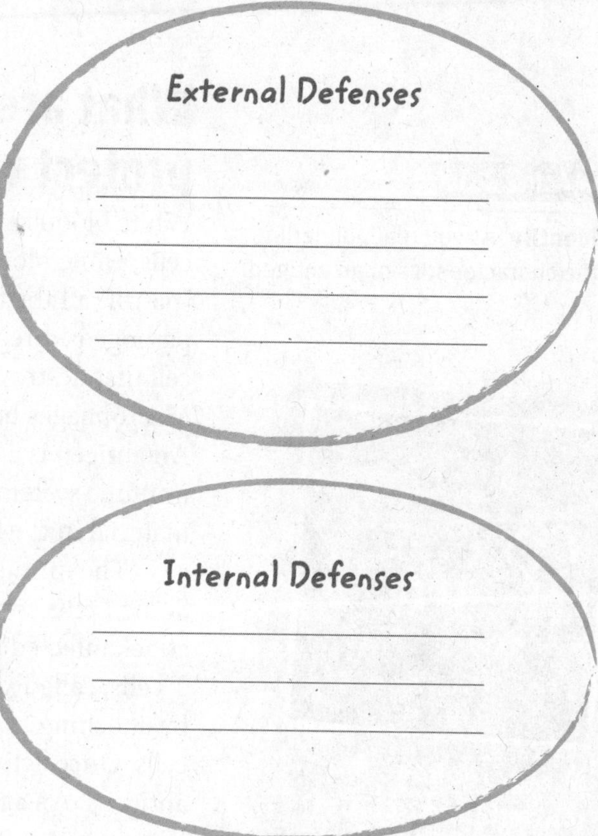

Do the Math

We usually measure temperature in degrees Fahrenheit (°F), but the standard scientific scale is in degrees Celsius (°C).

Sample Problems

To convert from °F to °C, first subtract 32 from the °F temperature, then multiply by 5, then divide by 9.

Normal body temperature is 98.6 °F. What is this temperature in °C?

$$(98.6\ ^\circ F - 32) \times 5 \div 9 = 37\ ^\circ C$$

To convert from °C to °F, first multiply the °C temperature by 9, then divide by 5, then add 32.

$$(37\ ^\circ C \times 9) \div 5 + 32 = 98.6\ ^\circ F$$

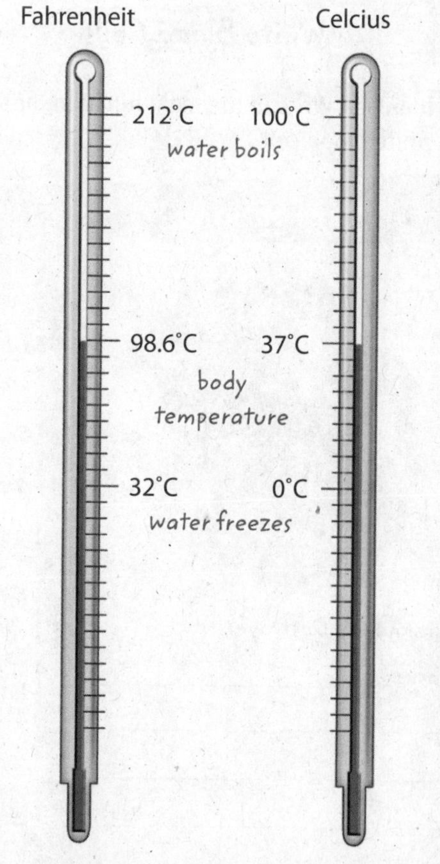

You Try It

8 Calculate If you have a fever, and your temperature is 39 °C, what is your temperature in °F?

Search and DESTROY

What are some white blood cells that protect the body?

9 Identify As you read, underline the characteristics of an antigen.

White blood cells destroy invading pathogens. Unlike red blood cells, white blood cells can move out of the blood vessels and "patrol" all the tissues of the body. Some of these cells attack pathogens directly. A **macrophage** (MAK•ruh•faj) is a white blood cell that destroys pathogens by engulfing and digesting them. Macrophages help start the body's immune response to *antigens*. An antigen is a substance that stimulates a response by the immune system. An antigen can be a pathogen or any foreign material in the body.

The immune system consists mainly of *T cells* and *B cells*. Some **T cells** coordinate the body's immune response, while others attack infected cells. T cells known as *helper T cells* activate other T cells, called *killer T cells*. Killer T cells attack infected body cells by attaching to specific antigens. Helper T cells also activate B cells. Once activated, **B cells** make antibodies that attach to specific antigens. An **antibody** is a specialized protein that binds to a specific antigen to tag it for destruction.

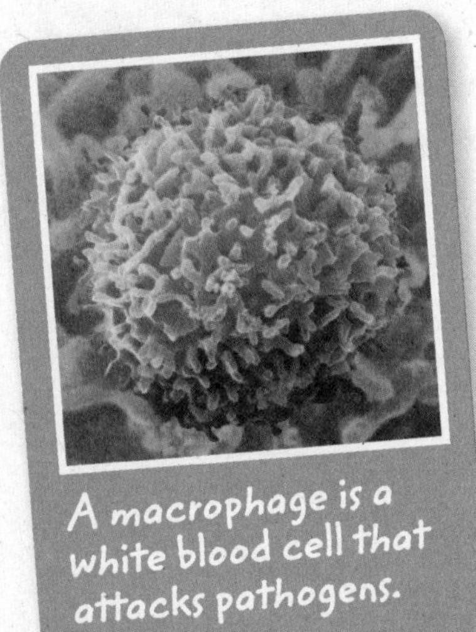

A macrophage is a white blood cell that attacks pathogens.

White Blood Cells

10 Identify Write in the main function, or task, of each white blood cell.

Macrophage	T cell	B cell
		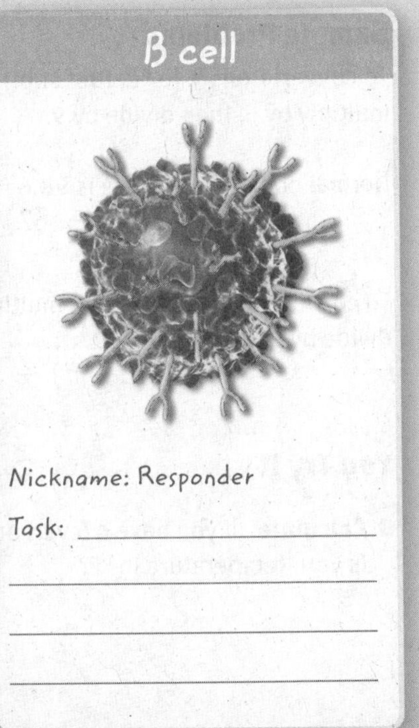
Nickname: Destroyer	Nickname: Activator/Attacker	Nickname: Responder
Task: ______	Task: ______	Task: ______

Visualize It!

The Immune Response

11 Diagram Trace the path of the B cell response using a solid line. Trace the path of the T cell response using a dashed line.

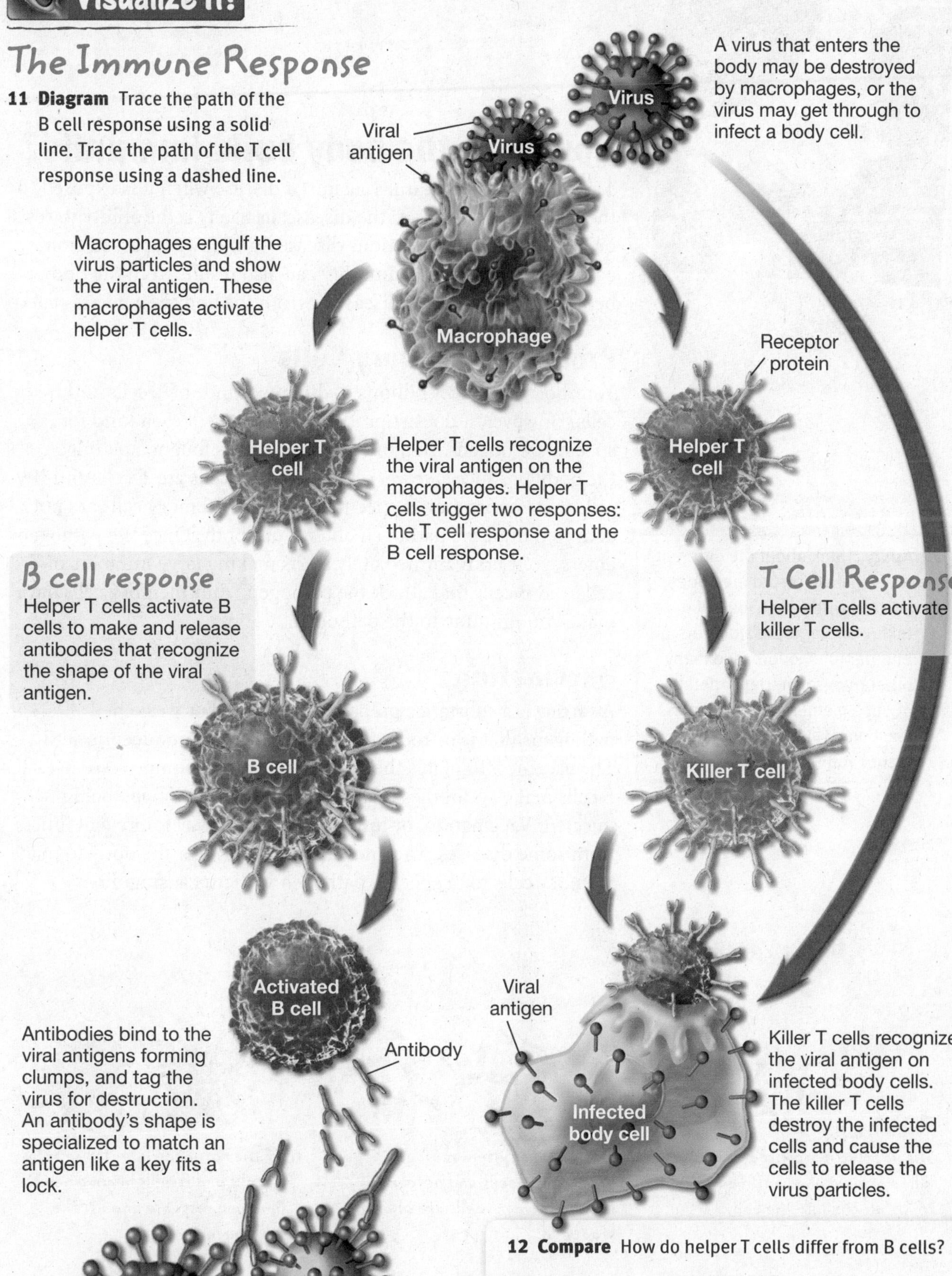

A virus that enters the body may be destroyed by macrophages, or the virus may get through to infect a body cell.
Virus
Viral antigen
Virus
Macrophages engulf the virus particles and show the viral antigen. These macrophages activate helper T cells.
Macrophage
Receptor protein
Helper T cell
Helper T cells recognize the viral antigen on the macrophages. Helper T cells trigger two responses: the T cell response and the B cell response.
Helper T cell
B cell response
Helper T cells activate B cells to make and release antibodies that recognize the shape of the viral antigen.
T Cell Response
Helper T cells activate killer T cells.
B cell
Killer T cell
Activated B cell
Viral antigen
Antibody
Antibodies bind to the viral antigens forming clumps, and tag the virus for destruction. An antibody's shape is specialized to match an antigen like a key fits a lock.
Infected body cell
Killer T cells recognize the viral antigen on infected body cells. The killer T cells destroy the infected cells and cause the cells to release the virus particles.
Virus

12 Compare How do helper T cells differ from B cells?

____

____

____

Shields UP!

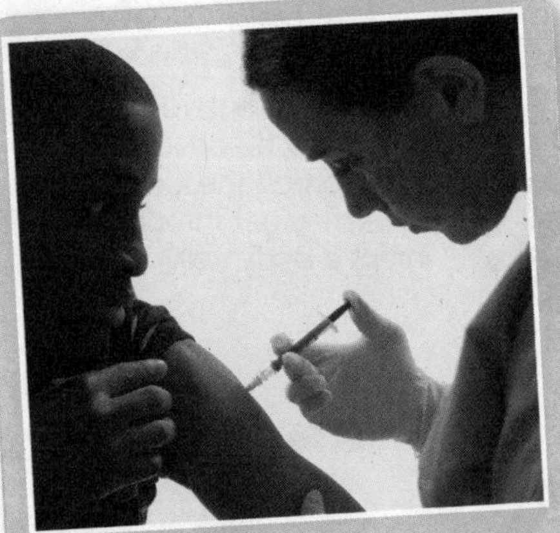

Vaccinations build immunity. This young person is receiving a vaccination shot.

How does the body build immunity?

The body builds immunity against a disease when it is exposed to the pathogen that causes the disease. **Immunity** is the ability to resist or recover from an infectious disease. Immunity is passed from a mother to her fetus. Immunity can also results from the body being infected with the disease or from the body being vaccinated.

Producing Memory Cells

Your body produces billions of different kinds of T cells and B cells. However, it doesn't produce very many of each kind for specific pathogens. But, once your body has fought a pathogen, the body produces *memory cells*. Memory cells are T cells and B cells that "remember" a specific pathogen. Memory cells are not activated until the pathogen enters your body. Once the pathogen enters, your body immediately starts making large numbers of T cells and B cells that attack the pathogen. Your memory cells have made you immune to the pathogen.

Think Outside the Book

13 Apply Think about the different ways that we record memories, such as writing in a journal or taking photographs. Journals, photographs, odors, and many other things can trigger details about a memory. Describe at least one way in which you record your memories.

Vaccination

A **vaccine** is a substance prepared from killed or weakened pathogens that is introduced into the body to produce immunity. The vaccine stimulates the body to make an immune response. B cells make antibodies to attack the specific pathogen being injected. Vaccination, or immunization, is a way to prevent illness from some diseases. Vaccines are used to trigger the body to make memory cells for a specific pathogen without causing illness.

How a Vaccine Works

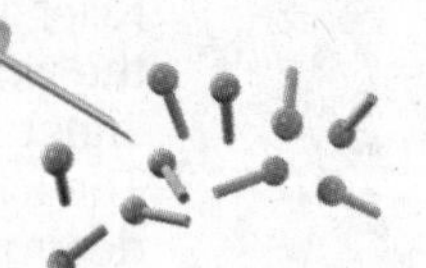

The vaccine is prepared from a killed or weakened pathogen and is introduced into the body.

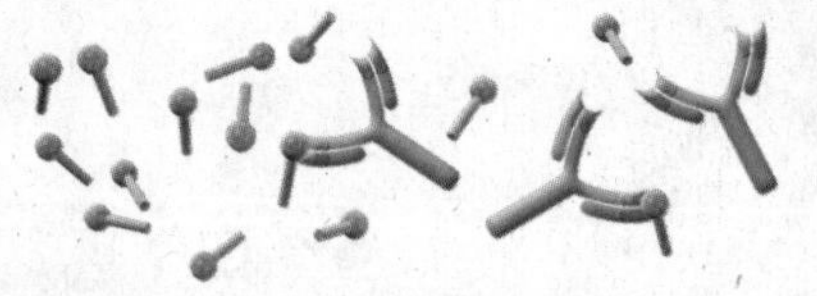

The immune system responds, producing T cells and activated B cells. Memory cells are also produced.

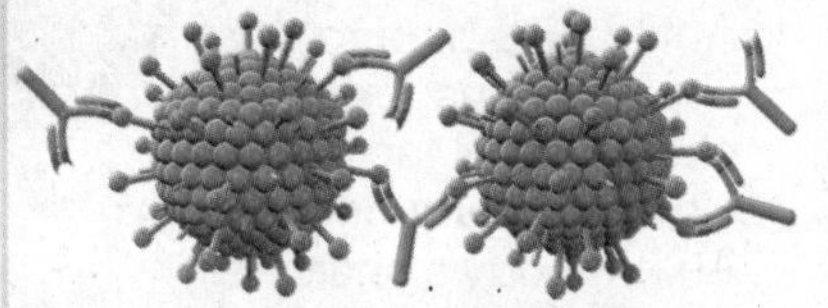

If the pathogen infects the body, T cells and B cells begin a new immune response against the pathogen.

14 Synthesize How are vaccines related to memory cells?

What can challenge the immune system?

The immune system is a very effective body defense system. However, sometimes the immune system doesn't work properly and disease results. This can occur when a person inherits a gene that prevents the immune system from developing properly. It can also happen as a result of some kinds of infection.

Challenges to Immune System

Allergies

Sometimes, a person's immune system reacts to foreign antigens that are not dangerous to most people. An immune system reaction to a harmless or common substance is called an *allergy*. Allergies can be caused by certain foods such as peanuts, medicines such as penicillin, or certain types of pollen and molds.

15 Relate List different allergies that you or someone you know may have.

____

____

____

Cancer

Healthy cells divide at a carefully controlled rate. Sometimes, cells don't respond to the body's controls. *Cancer* is a group of diseases in which cells divide at an uncontrolled rate. The immune system may not be able to stop the cancer cells from growing. Skin cancer is often caused by exposure to ultraviolet rays from sunlight, which can affect the cells that make pigment.

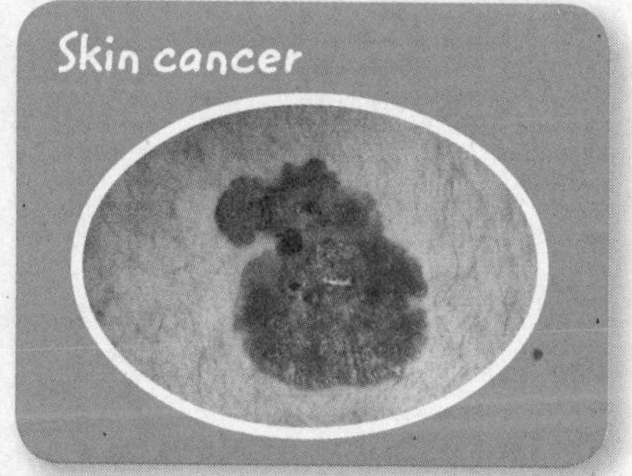
Skin cancer

Immune Deficiency

The immune system sometimes fails to develop properly or becomes weakened, resulting in an *immune deficiency disorder*. Acquired immune deficiency syndrome (AIDS) is caused by human immunodeficiency virus (HIV). This virus specifically infects the helper T cells. When the number of helper T cells becomes very low, neither T cell nor B cell immune responses can be activated. People who have AIDS can become very ill from pathogens that a healthy body can easily control.

16 Relate What is the relationship between HIV and AIDS?

____

____

____

____

____

____

Autoimmune Diseases

A disease in which the immune system attacks the body's own cells is called an *autoimmune disease*. In an autoimmune disease, immune system cells mistake body cells for foreign antigens. For example, rheumatoid arthritis (ROO•muh•toid ahr•THRY•tis) is a disease in which the immune system attacks the joints, most commonly the joints of the hands, as shown here.

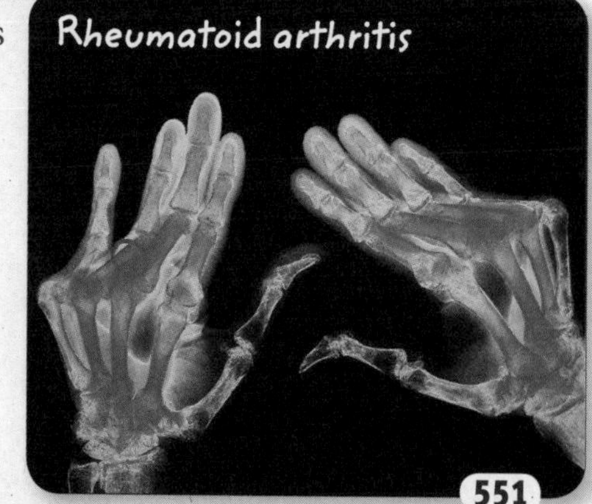
Rheumatoid arthritis

Visual Summary

To complete this summary, circle the correct word. Then use the key below to check your answers. You can use this page to review the main concepts of the lesson.

The Immune System

The human body has external and internal defenses.

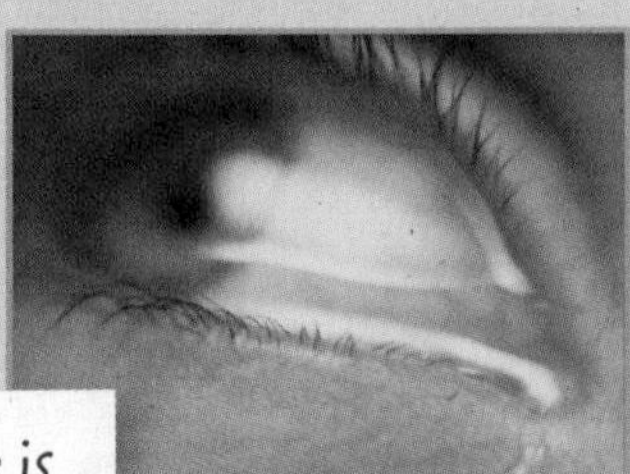

17 This type of defense is external / internal.

39 °C

Celcius

18 This type of defense is external / internal.

The immune system has a specialized internal immune response when pathogens invade the body.

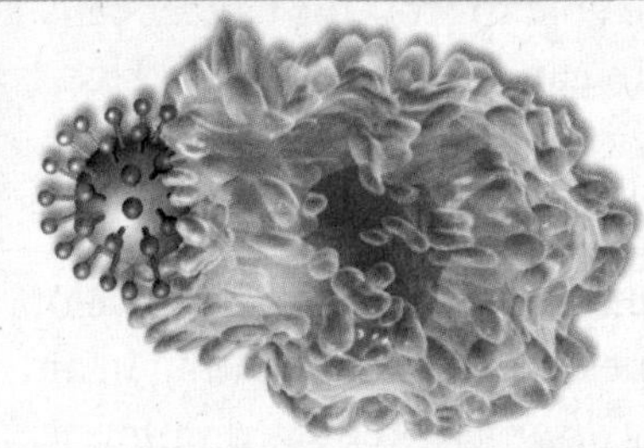

19 This is a macrophage/B cell engulfing a pathogen.

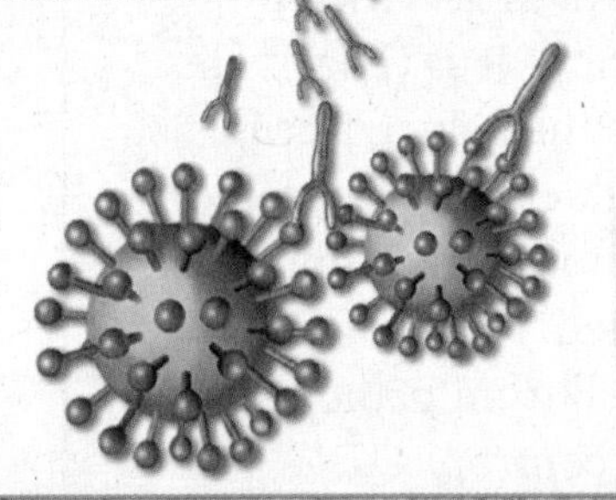

20 This is a(n) antibody / macrophage attaching to an antigen.

Answers: 17 external; 18 internal; 19 macrophage; 20 antibody

21 Summarize Explain three ways that your body can defend itself against pathogens.

Lesson Review

Vocabulary

In your own words, define the following terms.

1 pathogen

2 immune system

Key Concepts

3 List What are some of your body's external defenses against pathogens?

4 Summarize Explain how an immune response starts after a macrophage attacks a pathogen.

5 Compare How do T cells differ from B cells?

Critical Thinking

Use the graph to answer the following question.

T Cell Count of a Person with AIDS

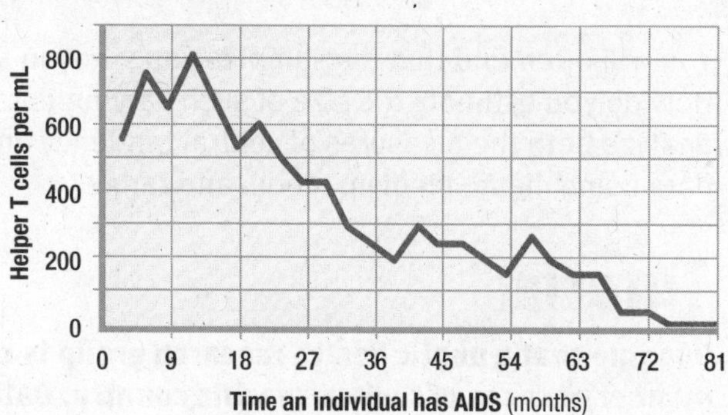

6 Interpret Over time, people with AIDS become very sick and are unable to fight off infection. Use the information in the graph to explain why this occurs.

7 Explain How does your body respond differently the second time it is exposed to a pathogen than the first time it was exposed to the same pathogen?

8 Infer Can your body make antibodies for pathogens that you have never been in contact with? Why or why not?

Think Science

Mean, Median, Mode, and Range

Sunshine State Standards

MA.6.S.6.2 Select and analyze the measures of central tendency or variability to represent, describe, analyze, and/or summarize a data set for the purposes of answering questions appropriately.

You will often find that the samples you study in science vary in size. How do you estimate the size of such varying data sets? You can analyze both the measures of central tendency and the variability of data using mean, median, mode, and range.

Tutorial

Imagine that a public health research group is comparing the number of cases of flu in a specific country. Data has been collected for the last five years.

When working with numerical data, it is helpful to find a value that describes the data set. These representative values can describe a typical data value, or describe how spread out the data values are.

Number of Cases of Flu

Year	Number of Cases
2004	800
2005	300
2006	150
2007	300
2008	200

Mean The mean is the sum of all of the values in a data set divided by the total number of values in the data set. The mean is also called the *average*.	$\frac{800 + 300 + 150 + 300 + 200}{5}$ **mean** = 350 cases/year
Median The median is the value of the middle item when data are arranged in numerical order. If there is an odd number of values, the median is the middle value. If there is an even number of values, the median is the mean of the two middle values.	If necessary, reorder the values from least to greatest: 150, 200, 300, 300, 800 → ← 300 is the middle value **median** = 300 cases/year
Mode The mode is the value or values that occur most frequently in a data set. If all values occur with the same frequency, the data set is said to have no mode. Values should be put in order to find the mode.	If necessary, reorder the values from least to greatest: 150, 200, 300, 300, 800 The value 300 occurs most frequently. **mode** = 300 cases/year
Range Range is another way to measure data. It measures how variable, or spread out, the data are. The range is the difference between the greatest value and the least value of a data set.	800 – 150 = 650 **range** = 650

You Try It!

The data table below shows the reported number of flu cases in four different countries.

Reported Number of Cases of Flu				
Year	**Country 1**	**Country 2**	**Country 3**	**Country 4**
2004	800	none	650	750
2005	300	350	450	450
2006	150	450	500	400
2007	300	200	550	350
2008	200	350	600	600

(1)

Using Formulas Find the mean, median, and mode of the data for Country 2.

(2)

Using Formulas Find the mean, median, and mode of the data for Country 3.

(3)

Analyzing Data Find the mean number of reported flu cases for only years in which cases were reported in Country 2. Compare this with the mean value for all years in Country 2. What conclusion can you draw about the effect of zeros on the mean of a data set?

Mean number of cases for years in which cases were reported: ________

Mean number of cases for all years: ________

Effect of zeros on the mean:

(4)

Evaluating Data Would the country with the greatest total number of flu cases from 2004 to 2008 have the greatest mean? Explain your reasoning.

(5)

Analyzing Methods Calculate the range for Country 3.

When do you think you might need to use range instead of mean, median or mode?

Lesson 2

Infectious Disease

ESSENTIAL QUESTION

What causes disease?

By the end of this lesson, you should be able to compare types of infectious agents that may infect the human body.

Sunshine State Standards

SC.6.L.14.6 Compare and contrast types of infectious agents that may infect the human body, including viruses, bacteria, fungi, and parasites.

HE.6.C.1.3 Identify environmental factors that affect personal health.

HE.6.C.1.8 Explain how body systems are impacted by hereditary factors and infectious agents.

This may look like a spaceship landing and taking off of a planet. In fact, this is a virus injecting its DNA into a bacterial cell. The bacteria will copy the viral DNA, making more viruses.

Engage Your Brain

1 **Predict** Check T or F to show whether you think each statement is true or false.

T	F	
☐	☐	Diseases cannot be treated.
☐	☐	Handwashing can help prevent the spread of disease.
☐	☐	Only bacteria and viruses cause disease.
☐	☐	All diseases can be spread from one person to another.

2 **Explain** Explain what you think the term *infection* means.

Active Reading

3 **Synthesize** You can often define an unknown word if you know the meaning of its word parts. Use the word parts and sentence below to make an educated guess about the meaning of the word *antibiotic*.

Word part	Meaning
anti-	against
bio-	life

Example sentence

Antibiotics are used to treat bacterial illnesses such as strep throat.

antibiotic:

Vocabulary Terms

- **noninfectious disease**
- **infectious disease**
- **antibiotic**
- **antiviral drug**

4 **Identify** This list contains the key terms you'll learn in this lesson. As you read, circle the definition of each term.

Getting Through Security

What is a noninfectious disease?

When you have a disease, your body does not function normally. You may feel tired, or have a sore throat, or have pain in your joints. Diseases have specific *symptoms,* or changes in how a person feels because of an illness. While there are many different kinds of diseases, all diseases can be categorized as either *noninfectious disease* or *infectious disease.*

Diseases that are caused by hereditary or environmental factors are called **noninfectious diseases**. For example, type I diabetes is caused by hereditary factors. Type 1 diabetes destroys cells that produce insulin. This makes it difficult for the body to use sugar for energy. Hemophilia is also caused by hereditary factors. The blood of people who have hemophilia does not clot properly when they get a cut. Some noninfectious diseases can be caused by environmental factors. *Mutagens* are environmental factors that cause mutations, or changes, in DNA. Sometimes, the changes cause a cell to reproduce uncontrollably. This results in a disease called *cancer.* X-rays, cigarette smoke, some air pollutants, and UV rays in sunlight can cause cancer. Cancer can have both hereditary and environmental causes.

Active Reading

5 List Name two types of factors that cause noninfectious disease.

____

____

____

X-RAYS
CONTROLLED
AREA

No
unauthorised entry

People who work around radiation, such as x-ray technicians, must protect themselves from overexposure.

Air pollution can cause respiratory disease.

Think Outside the Book Inquiry

6 Relate Think about a job that requires protection against some type of contamination. Then do the following:

- Explain why protection is necessary for that job.
- Draw the method of protection used for that job.

What is an infectious disease?

A disease that is caused by a *pathogen* is called an **infectious disease**. Pathogens include bacteria, fungi, and parasites, which are all alive. Pathogens also include viruses, which are noncellular particles that depend on living things to reproduce. Viruses cannot function on their own, so they are not considered to be alive.

Pathogens that cause disease can be picked up from the environment or passed from one living thing to another. Some pathogens travel through the air. Sneezing and coughing can release thousands of tiny droplets that may carry pathogens. If a person inhales these droplets, he or she may become infected. Some pathogens can be passed from nonliving things. A rusty nail can carry tetanus bacteria that may cause disease if a person is scratched by the nail. Pathogens can also be passed by other living things. Many diseases are carried by fleas, ticks, and mosquitoes.

A sneeze can force out thousands of droplets from your mouth and nose at speeds up to 160 km/h.

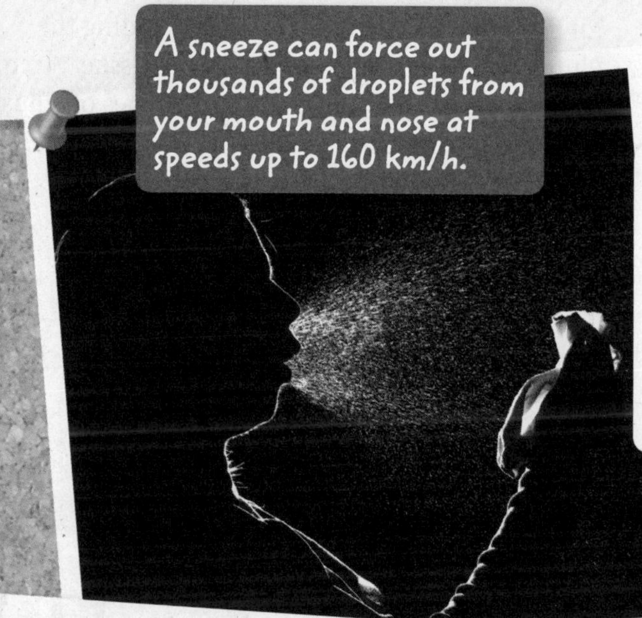

7 Apply What can you do to reduce the spread of droplets when you sneeze or cough?

____

____

____

8 Categorize Determine whether each disease is infectious or noninfectious, and put a check mark in the correct box.

Example	Noninfectious Disease	Infectious Disease
Emphysema caused by cigarette smoke		
Strep throat that's been going around school		
Skin cancer caused by too much sun exposure		
The flu that you and your family members have		

That's Sick!

What can cause infectious disease?

Each type of pathogen causes a specific infectious disease. But diseases caused by similar types of pathogens share some common characteristics. Knowing what type of pathogen causes a disease helps doctors know how to treat the disease.

Viruses

Viruses are tiny particles that have their own genetic material but depend on living things to reproduce. Viruses insert their genetic material into a cell, and then the cell makes more viruses. Many viruses cause disease. Some, such as cold and flu viruses, are spread through the air or by contact. Others, such as the human immunodeficiency virus, or HIV, are spread through the transfer of body fluids. There are many types of cold and flu viruses, so preventing a cold or flu can be difficult.

Visualize It!

9 Apply Once inside, what part of the cell do the viral particles go to? What do they do there?

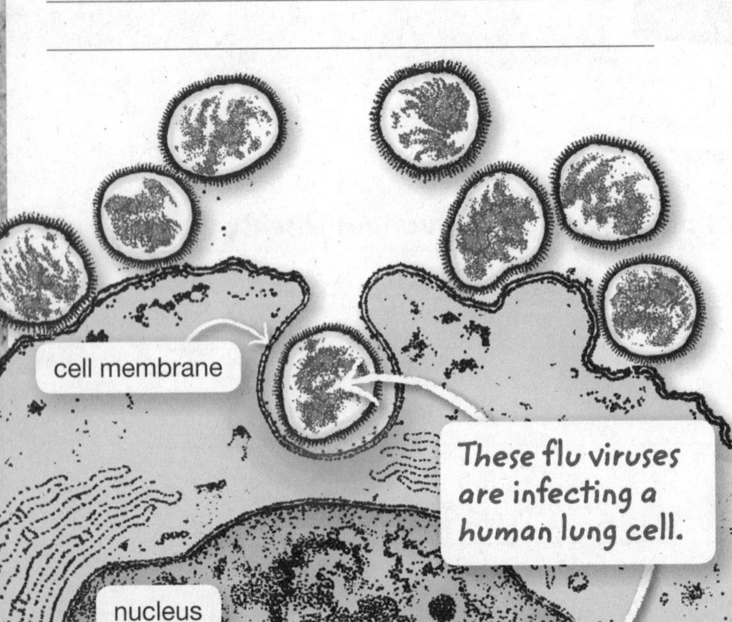

These flu viruses are infecting a human lung cell.

Bacteria

Most bacteria are beneficial to other living things. However, some bacteria cause disease. For example, the bacterium that causes tuberculosis infects about one-third of the world's population. It can infect a variety of organs, including the lungs, where it slowly destroys lung tissue. Strep throat, diarrheal illness, and some types of sinus infections are also caused by bacteria.

10 List Name some diseases caused by bacteria.

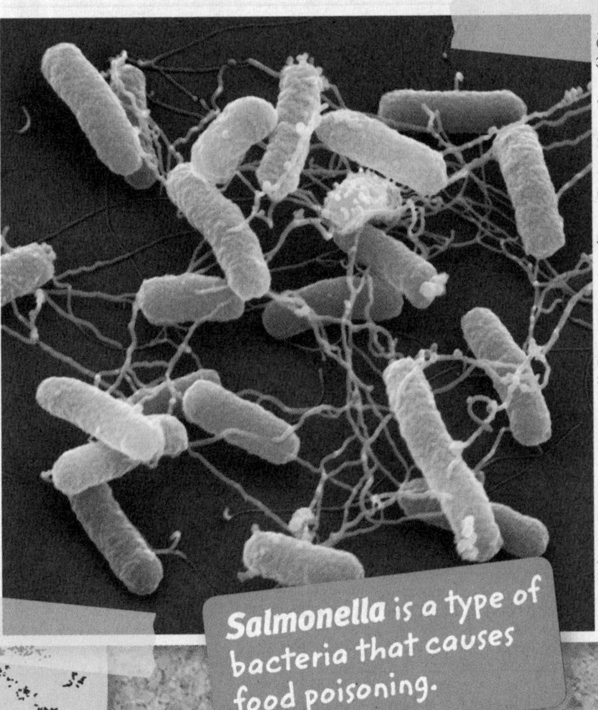

Salmonella is a type of bacteria that causes food poisoning.

Fungi

Most fungi are beneficial because they decompose, or break down, dead plants and animals into materials that other organisms use. However, some fungi are pathogens. The most common fungal diseases are skin infections. Two of the most common fungal skin infections are athlete's foot and ringworm of the body and scalp. These fungal skin infections can be passed on through contact with an infected person or contact with items such as socks, shoes, and shower surfaces where the fungus can grow.

11 Explain Why are most fungi beneficial?

Parasites

A *parasite* is an organism that lives on and feeds on another organism, called a *host*. Parasites usually harm the host. Some of the most common parasites in humans are certain types of single-celled organisms called *protists*. For example, the protists that cause malaria infect as many as 500 million people each year. Another disease, called giardiasis, occurs when people consume water or food contaminated with the protist *Giardia lamblia*. Worms can also be parasites. The roundworm *Ascaris lumbricoides* is the most common cause of parasitic worm infections. It is spread in contaminated food, such as unwashed fruits and vegetables.

Active Reading **12 Define** What is a parasite?

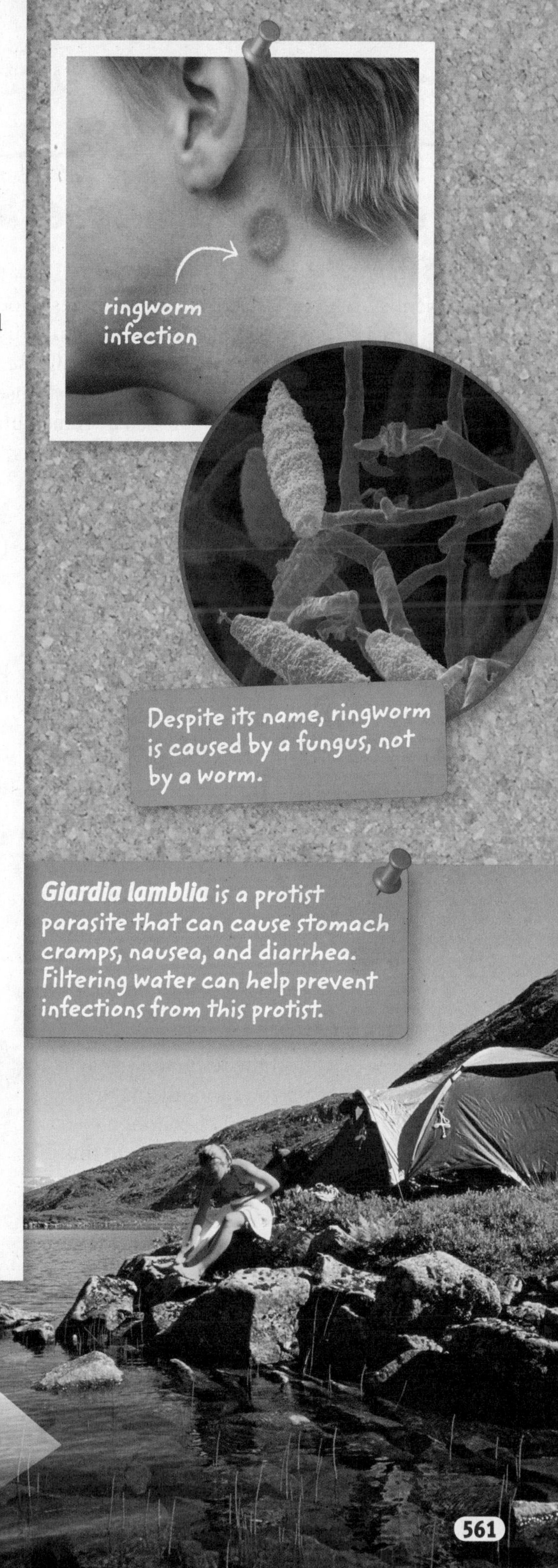

Despite its name, ringworm is caused by a fungus, not by a worm.

Giardia lamblia is a protist parasite that can cause stomach cramps, nausea, and diarrhea. Filtering water can help prevent infections from this protist.

Don't Pass It On

How can infectious diseases be transmitted?

Some scientists who investigate infectious diseases focus on the ways that diseases are passed on, or transmitted. A disease that spreads from person to person is a *contagious* disease. A person is also considered to be contagious if he or she has a disease that can spread to other people. Diseases can also be transmitted to people by other organisms and by contaminated food, water, or objects.

Water and Food

Drinking water in the United States is generally safe. But if a water treatment system fails, the water could become contaminated. Untreated water, such as rivers and streams, can also carry pathogens. Bacteria in foods can cause illness, too. For example, cattle and chickens often carry *Salmonella* bacteria. Raw beef, chicken, and eggs should be handled carefully during preparation to avoid contaminating food.

13 Infer Why should raw meats be kept separate from other foods?

Person to Person

Many diseases that affect the respiratory system are passed from one person to another through the air by a sneeze or cough. The common cold, the flu, and tuberculosis are usually spread this way. Pathogens can also be passed when an infected person touches another person. Other diseases, such as acquired immune deficiency syndrome, or AIDS, and hepatitis C can be passed during sexual contact.

14 Recognize List three ways that disease can be transmitted from one person to another.

Deer tick that can transmit Rocky Mountain spotted fever

Animals to People

Quite a few human diseases are transmitted to humans by animals, especially insects and ticks. For example, humans can become infected with malaria when they are bitten by a mosquito infected with the malaria parasite. In a similar way, certain species of ticks can transmit diseases such as Rocky Mountain spotted fever and Lyme disease. Animals infected with the rabies virus can pass the disease on to other animals or people through a bite that cuts the skin.

Contaminated Objects

Objects that are handled by sick people or that come in contact with infected animals or contaminated food can pick up pathogens. Drinking glasses, utensils, doorknobs, towels, keyboards, and many other objects can transfer pathogens from one person to another. People who inject illegal drugs, such as heroin, can easily pick up pathogens from contaminated needles and related items. Traces of contaminated blood on a needle can infect a person who shares that needle.

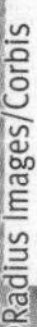

15 Predict Read the scenario in the table below, and explain how disease could be transmitted to other people.

Scenario	How could disease be transmitted?
A person with a cold sneezes in a bus full of people.	
A person with a skin fungus shares a towel with another person.	

End Transmission

refrigeration
pasteurization
pickling
A variety of technologies used today allow some foods to be stored longer.

16 Apply Which methods of food preservation do you use at home?

______

______

______

How can diseases be reduced?

Several important changes have helped decrease the occurrence of infectious disease. These changes include improved personal hygiene and improved technology used in medical procedures and food preservation.

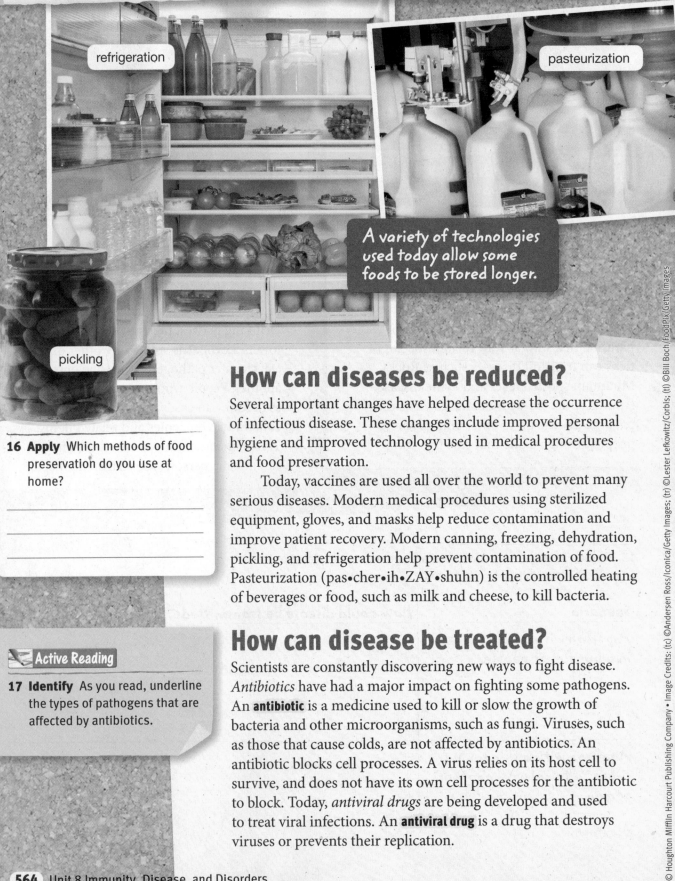

Today, vaccines are used all over the world to prevent many serious diseases. Modern medical procedures using sterilized equipment, gloves, and masks help reduce contamination and improve patient recovery. Modern canning, freezing, dehydration, pickling, and refrigeration help prevent contamination of food. Pasteurization (pas•cher•ih•ZAY•shuhn) is the controlled heating of beverages or food, such as milk and cheese, to kill bacteria.

Active Reading

17 Identify As you read, underline the types of pathogens that are affected by antibiotics.

How can disease be treated?

Scientists are constantly discovering new ways to fight disease. *Antibiotics* have had a major impact on fighting some pathogens. An **antibiotic** is a medicine used to kill or slow the growth of bacteria and other microorganisms, such as fungi. Viruses, such as those that cause colds, are not affected by antibiotics. An antibiotic blocks cell processes. A virus relies on its host cell to survive, and does not have its own cell processes for the antibiotic to block. Today, *antiviral drugs* are being developed and used to treat viral infections. An **antiviral drug** is a drug that destroys viruses or prevents their replication.

Why It Matters

HEALTH WATCH

Resisting ARREST

A microscopic world of organisms exists all around us. Bacteria live in your mouth, on your skin, and on many objects that you touch every day. Most bacteria are harmless. However, some strains of bacteria that cause disease are no longer affected by antibiotics.

Tough guys
Some strains of *Staphylococcus aureus* bacteria have developed a resistance to antibiotics.

The Value of Money
Your money may carry more than just value. At least 93 different types of bacteria have been identified on dollar bills. Think of all the places each bill has traveled!

Soap It Up
Being in contact with different people and objects increases your exposure to a variety of microscopic organisms. Washing your hands throughout the day can help reduce your risk for some infections.

Extend

Inquiry

18 Identify What is the name and type of pathogen discussed in this article?

19 Research *Salmonella* is a pathogen that can be transmitted by contaminated food. Research and describe how *Salmonella* could be transmitted from a food processing factory to you.

20 Apply Find an object in your school that you and your classmates come in contact with nearly every day. How can you protect yourself and others from pathogens that may be on the object?

Visual Summary

To complete this summary, fill in the blanks with the correct word or phrase. Then, use the key below to check your answers. You can use this page to review the main concepts of the lesson.

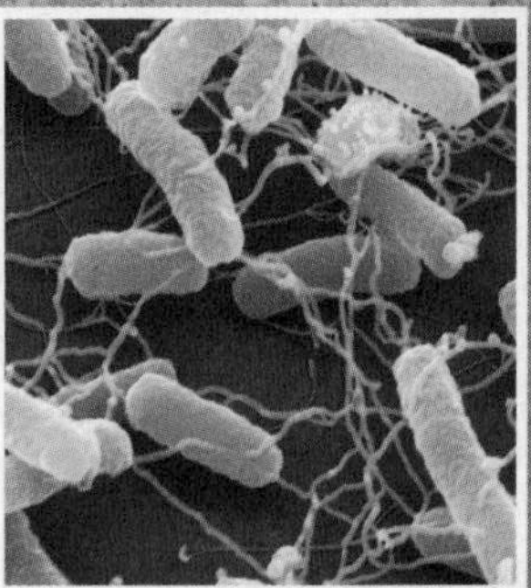

Diseases are categorized as noninfectious disease or infectious disease.

21 A disease that can be passed from one person to another is a(n)

____

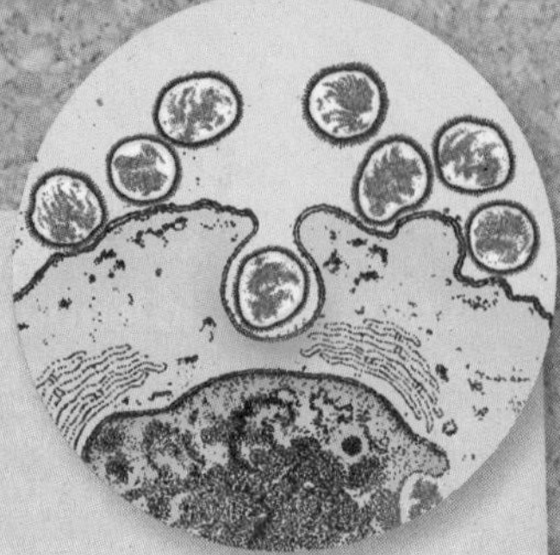

Infectious disease can be caused by different types of pathogens.

22 A type of pathogen that depends on living organisms to reproduce is a

____

Infectious Disease

Infectious disease can be transmitted in many different ways.

23 List four ways an infectious disease can be transmitted.

____

____

____

____

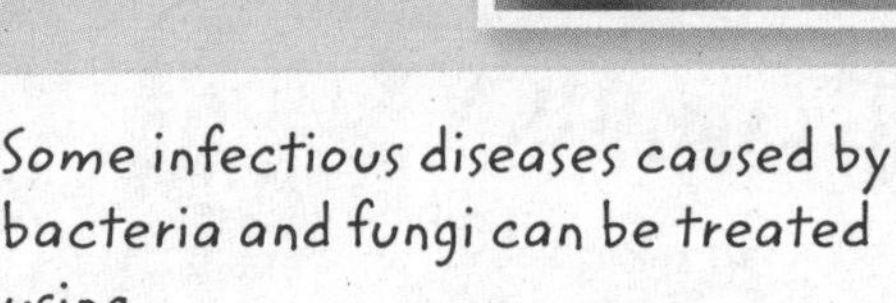

The spread of infectious diseases can be reduced, and some diseases can be treated.

24 Some infectious diseases caused by bacteria and fungi can be treated using

____

Answers: 21 infectious disease; 22 virus; 23 another person, some animals, water and food, contaminated objects; 24 antibiotics

25 Synthesis Explain why antibiotics cannot be used to treat noninfectious disease.

Lesson Review

Vocabulary

In your own words, define the following terms.

1 noninfectious disease

2 infectious disease

Key Concepts

3 Identify Name four types of pathogens that could cause infectious disease.

4 Justify How has technology helped to reduce the spread of infectious disease?

5 Compare How do viruses differ from bacteria, fungi, and parasites?

Critical Thinking

Use the graph to answer the following questions.

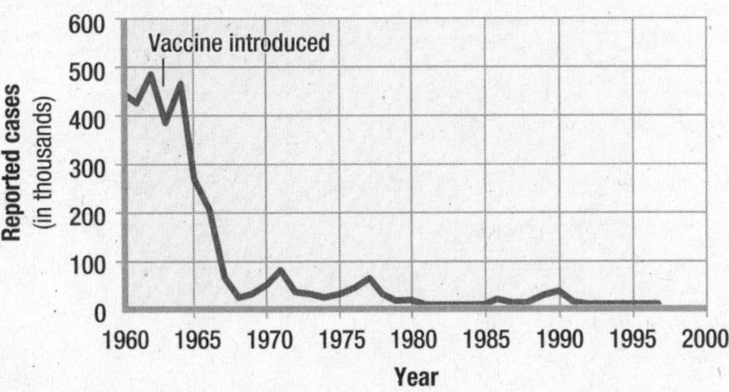

6 Compare How many cases of measles were reported in the United States in 1962, the year before the measles vaccine was licensed? How many cases were reported 5 years later?

7 Infer How many cases of measles would you predict were reported last year?

8 Hypothesize How can infectious and noninfectious diseases affect personal health?

9 Apply Why might the risk of infectious disease be high in a community that has no water treatment facility?

My Notes

Unit 8 **Summary**

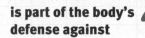

Immunity, Disease, and Disorders

involve

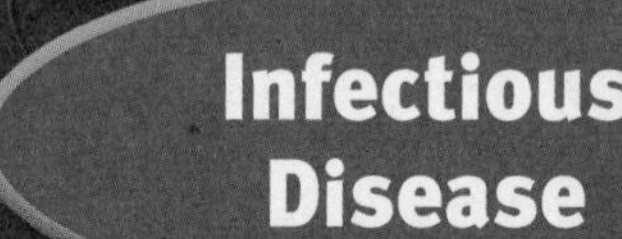

The Immune System

is part of the body's defense against

Infectious Disease

1 **Interpret** The Graphic Organizer above shows that the immune system defends against infectious disease. What other defenses, not shown on this organizer, protect your body against disease?

2 **Apply** Name two differences between infectious disease and noninfectious disease.

3 **Describe** What are three ways that your body builds immunity?

4 **Classify** Name the category of pathogen that causes each of the following diseases: (1) athlete's foot, (2) influenza, (3) strep throat, and (4) malaria.

Name ____________________

Multiple Choice

Identify the choice that best completes the statement or answers the question.

1 Sha-ree had been ill for 5 days. When her mother took her to the doctor, the doctor decided not to prescribe an antibiotic. He said Sha-ree had a virus. Why did the doctor **not** prescribe an antibiotic?

- **A.** Antibiotics target only white blood cells.
- **B.** Antibiotics are not used to fight any infections.
- **C.** Antibiotics cause fevers that make viruses stronger.
- **D.** Antibiotics kill some bacteria and fungi, not viruses.

2 Vaccinations can help build immunity. Vaccines stimulate the body to make an immune response. What is in a vaccine that causes the immune system to respond?

- **F.** antibiotic
- **G.** antiviral drug
- **H.** memory cells
- **I.** killed or weakened pathogen

3 The body's defense system uses cells that have different functions to fight against pathogens. Which of the cells pictured below engulfs pathogens and other foreign particles?

A. 

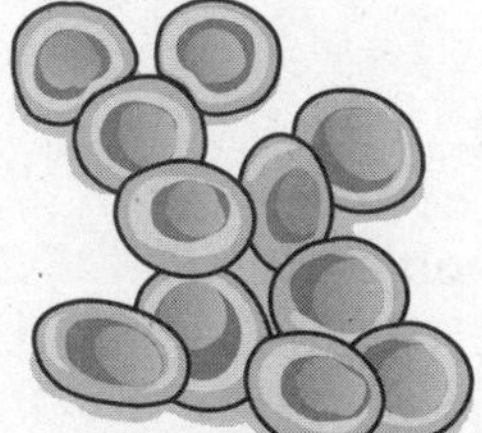

Red blood cells

C. 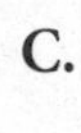

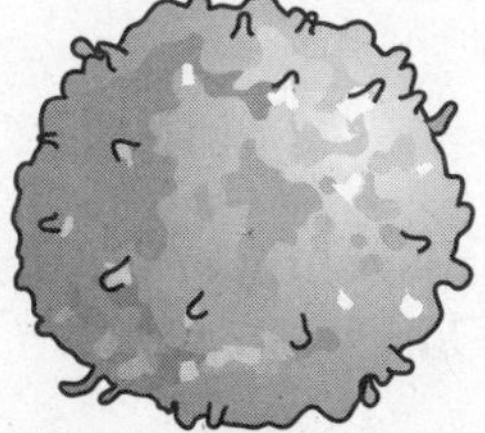

T cell

B. 

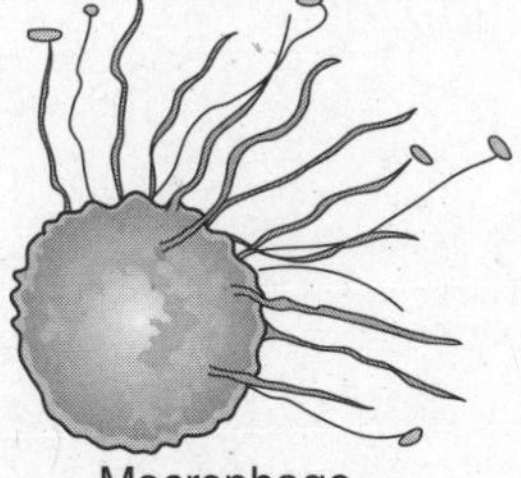

Macrophage

D.

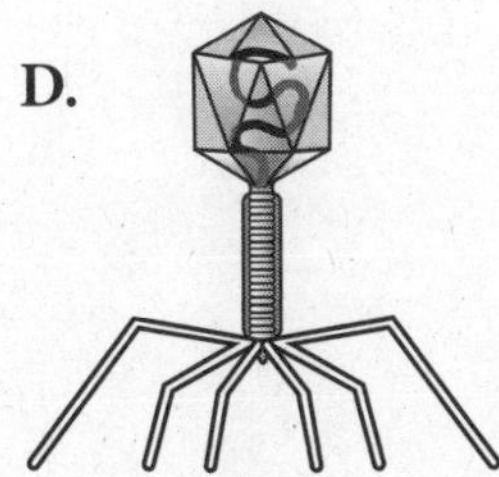

Virus

Benchmark Review

4 Mazie visited the school nurse because she felt ill. The nurse suggested that she might have a virus. Which of these words **best** describes a virus?

F. antibody

G. pathogen

H. antibiotic

I. macrophage

5 If a person eats food containing tapeworm eggs or larvae, the tapeworm can enter the intestines and grow there. The following picture shows a tapeworm.

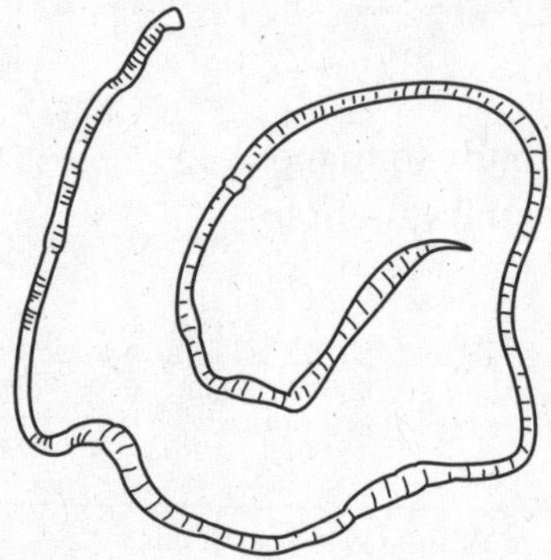

Which type of organism is a tapeworm?

A. bacterium

B. fungus

C. parasite

D. virus

6 Jill is recovering from the flu. At lunchtime, she shares her water bottle with her friend Dara. The next day, Dara is sick. Which type of disease is the flu?

F. autoimmune

G. environmental

H. infectious

I. parasitic

Name ______________________________

7 Insulin is a hormone that helps to control blood sugar levels in the body. Type 1 diabetes is a hereditary disease in which the body destroys the cells that produce insulin. What type of disease is type 1 diabetes?

A. infectious

B. autoimmune

C. allergy

D. virus

8 Jake has been sneezing a lot. Which defense is related to Jake's sneezing?

F. mucus

G. tears

H. skin

I. fever

9 Erik wants to avoid overexposure to mutagens as much as possible. Which strategy can **best** help him do this?

A. eat a balanced diet

B. exercise several days a week

C. wear sunscreen outdoors

D. wash his hands regularly

10 Jorge has a cold but feels well enough to study with his friends Lisa and Jin. Lisa and Jin become sick. Which term describes Jorge's condition when he was studying with his friends?

F. noninfectious

G. contagious

H. mutagen

I. pathogen

11 The human body has both internal and external defenses against disease. Which of these is an internal defense?

A. hair

B. tears

C. T cells

D. skin cells

Benchmark Review

12 The bacteria *Escherichia coli*, also called *E. coli*, are shown in the following picture.

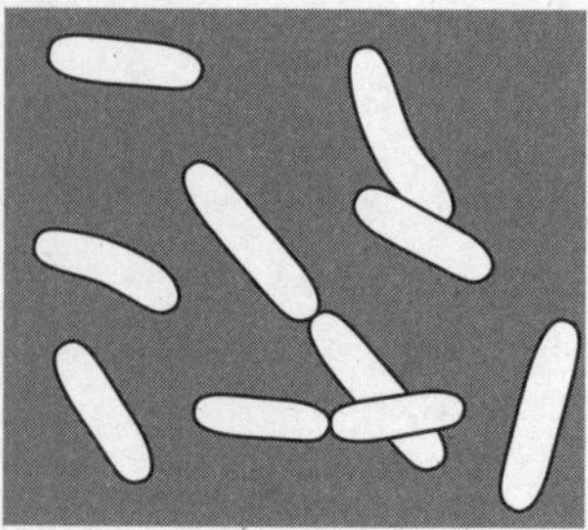

Some strains of these bacteria cause disease. Which term describes these organisms?

F. genetic factors

G. mutagens

H. pathogens

I. viruses

Look It Up!

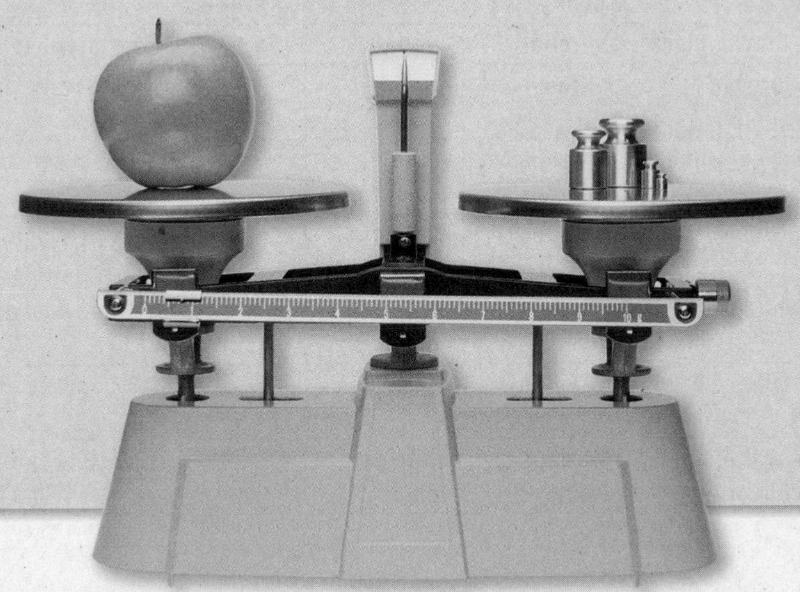

Reference Tables

Mineral Properties

Here are five steps to take in mineral identification:

1 Determine the color of the mineral. Is it light-colored, dark-colored, or a specific color?

2 Determine the luster of the mineral. Is it metallic or non-metallic?

3 Determine the color of any powder left by its streak.

4 Determine the hardness of your mineral. Is it soft, hard, or very hard? Using a glass plate, see if the mineral scratches it.

5 Determine whether your sample has cleavage or any special properties.

TERMS TO KNOW	DEFINITION
adamantine	a non-metallic luster like that of a diamond
cleavage	how a mineral breaks when subject to stress on a particular plane
luster	the state or quality of shining by reflecting light
streak	the color of a mineral when it is powdered
submetallic	between metallic and nonmetallic in luster
vitreous	glass-like type of luster

Silicate Minerals

Mineral	Color	Luster	Streak	Hardness	Cleavage and Special Properties
Beryl	deep green, pink, white, bluish green, or yellow	vitreous	white	7.5–8	1 cleavage direction; some varieties fluoresce in ultraviolet light
Chlorite	green	vitreous to pearly	pale green	2–2.5	1 cleavage direction
Garnet	green, red, brown, black	vitreous	white	6.5–7.5	no cleavage
Hornblende	dark green, brown, or black	vitreous	none	5–6	2 cleavage directions
Muscovite	colorless, silvery white, or brown	vitreous or pearly	white	2–2.5	1 cleavage direction
Olivine	olive green, yellow	vitreous	white or none	6.5–7	no cleavage
Orthoclase	colorless, white, pink, or other colors	vitreous	white or none	6	2 cleavage directions
Plagioclase	colorless, white, yellow, pink, green	vitreous	white	6	2 cleavage directions
Quartz	colorless or white; any color when not pure	vitreous or waxy	white or none	7	no cleavage

Nonsilicate Minerals					
Mineral	**Color**	**Luster**	**Streak**	**Hardness**	**Cleavage and Special Properties**
Native Elements					
Copper	copper-red	metallic	copper-red	2.5–3	no cleavage
Diamond	pale yellow or colorless	adamantine	none	10	4 cleavage directions
Graphite	black to gray	submetallic	black	1–2	1 cleavage direction
Carbonates					
Aragonite	colorless, white, or pale yellow	vitreous	white	3.5–4	2 cleavage directions; reacts with hydrochloric acid
Calcite	colorless or white to tan	vitreous	white	3	3 cleavage directions; reacts with weak acid; double refraction
Halides					
Fluorite	light green, yellow, purple, bluish green, or other colors	vitreous	none	4	4 cleavage directions; some varieties fluoresce
Halite	white	vitreous	white	2.0–2.5	3 cleavage directions
Oxides					
Hematite	reddish brown to black	metallic to earthy	dark red to red-brown	5.6–6.5	no cleavage; magnetic when heated
Magnetite	iron-black	metallic	black	5.5–6.5	no cleavage; magnetic
Sulfates					
Anhydrite	colorless, bluish, or violet	vitreous to pearly	white	3–3.5	3 cleavage directions
Gypsum	white, pink, gray, or colorless	vitreous, pearly, or silky	white	2.0	3 cleavage directions
Sulfides					
Galena	lead-gray	metallic	lead-gray to black	2.5–2.8	3 cleavage directions
Pyrite	brassy yellow	metallic	greenish, brownish, or black	6–6.5	no cleavage

Classification of Living Things

Domains and Kingdoms

All organisms belong to one of three domains: Domain Archaea, Domain Bacteria, or Domain Eukarya. Some of the groups within these domains are shown below. (Remember that genus names are italicized.)

Domain Archaea

The organisms in this domain are single-celled prokaryotes, many of which live in extreme environments.

Archaea		
Group	**Example**	**Characteristics**
Methanogens	*Methanococcus*	produce methane gas; can't live in oxygen
Thermophiles	*Sulpholobus*	require sulphur; can't live in oxygen
Halophiles	*Halococcus*	live in very salty environments; most can live in oxygen

Domain Bacteria

Organisms in this domain are single-celled prokaryotes and are found in almost every environment on Earth.

Bacteria		
Group	**Example**	**Characteristics**
Bacilli	*Escherichia*	rod shaped; some fix nitrogen; some cause disease
Cocci	*Streptococcus*	spherical shaped; cause diseases; can form spores
Spirilla	*Treponema*	spiral shaped; cause diseases, such as syphilis

Domain Eukarya

Organisms in this domain are single-celled or multicellular eukaryotes.

Kingdom Protista Many protists resemble fungi, plants, or animals, but are smaller and simpler in structure. Most are single-celled.

Protists		
Group	**Example**	**Characteristics**
Sarcodines	*Amoeba*	radiolarians; single-celled consumers
Ciliates	*Paramecium*	single-celled consumers
Flagellates	*Trypanosoma*	single-celled parasites
Sporozoans	*Plasmodium*	single-celled parasites
Euglenas	*Euglena*	single celled; photosynthesize
Diatoms	*Pinnularia*	most are single celled; photosynthesize
Dinoflagellates	*Gymnodinium*	single celled; some photosynthesize
Algae	*Volvox*	single celled or multicellular; photosynthesize
Slime molds	*Physarum*	single celled or multicellular; consumers or decomposers
Water molds	powdery mildew	single celled or multicellular; parasites or decomposers

Kingdom Fungi Most fungi are multicellular. Their cells have thick cell walls. Fungi absorb food from their environment.

Fungi		
Group	**Examples**	**Characteristics**
Bread molds	black bread mold	decomposers
Sac fungi	yeast; morels	saclike; parasites and decomposers
Club fungi	mushrooms; rusts; smuts	club shaped; parasites and decomposers
Chytrids	chytrid frog fungus	usually aquatic; can be decomposers or parasites

Kingdom Plantae Plants are multicellular and have cell walls made of cellulose. Plants make their own food through photosynthesis. Plants are classified into divisions instead of phyla.

Plants		
Group	**Examples**	**Characteristics**
Bryophytes	mosses, peat moss	no vascular tissue; reproduce by spores
Anthocerotophytes	hornworts	no vascular tissue; reproduce using horn-like structures
Hepatophytes	liverworts	no vascular tissue; live in moist environments
Lycophytes	*Lycopodium;* ground pine	grow in wooded areas; reproduce by spores
Pterophytes	horsetails; ferns	seedless, vascular tissue; reproduce by spores
Conifers	pines; spruces; firs	needlelike leaves; reproduce by seeds made in cones
Cycads	*Zamia*	slow-growing; reproduce by seeds made in large cones
Ginkgoes	*Ginkgo*	only one living species; reproduce by seeds
Angiosperms	all flowering plants	reproduce by seeds made in flowers; fruit

Kingdom Animalia Animals are multicellular. Their cells do not have cell walls. Most animals have specialized tissues and complex organ systems. Animals get food by eating other organisms.

Animals		
Group	**Examples**	**Characteristics**
Sponges	glass sponges	no symmetry or true segmentation; aquatic
Cnidarians	jellyfish; coral	radial symmetry; aquatic
Flatworms	planaria; tapeworms; flukes	bilateral symmetry; organ systems
Roundworms	*Trichina;* hookworms	bilateral symmetry; organ systems
Annelids	earthworms; leeches	bilateral symmetry; organ systems
Mollusks	snails; octopuses	bilateral symmetry; organ systems
Echinoderms	sea stars; sand dollars	radial symmetry; organ systems
Arthropods	insects; spiders; lobsters	bilateral symmetry; organ systems
Chordates	fish; amphibians; reptiles; birds; mammals	bilateral symmetry; complex organ systems

Periodic Table of the Elements

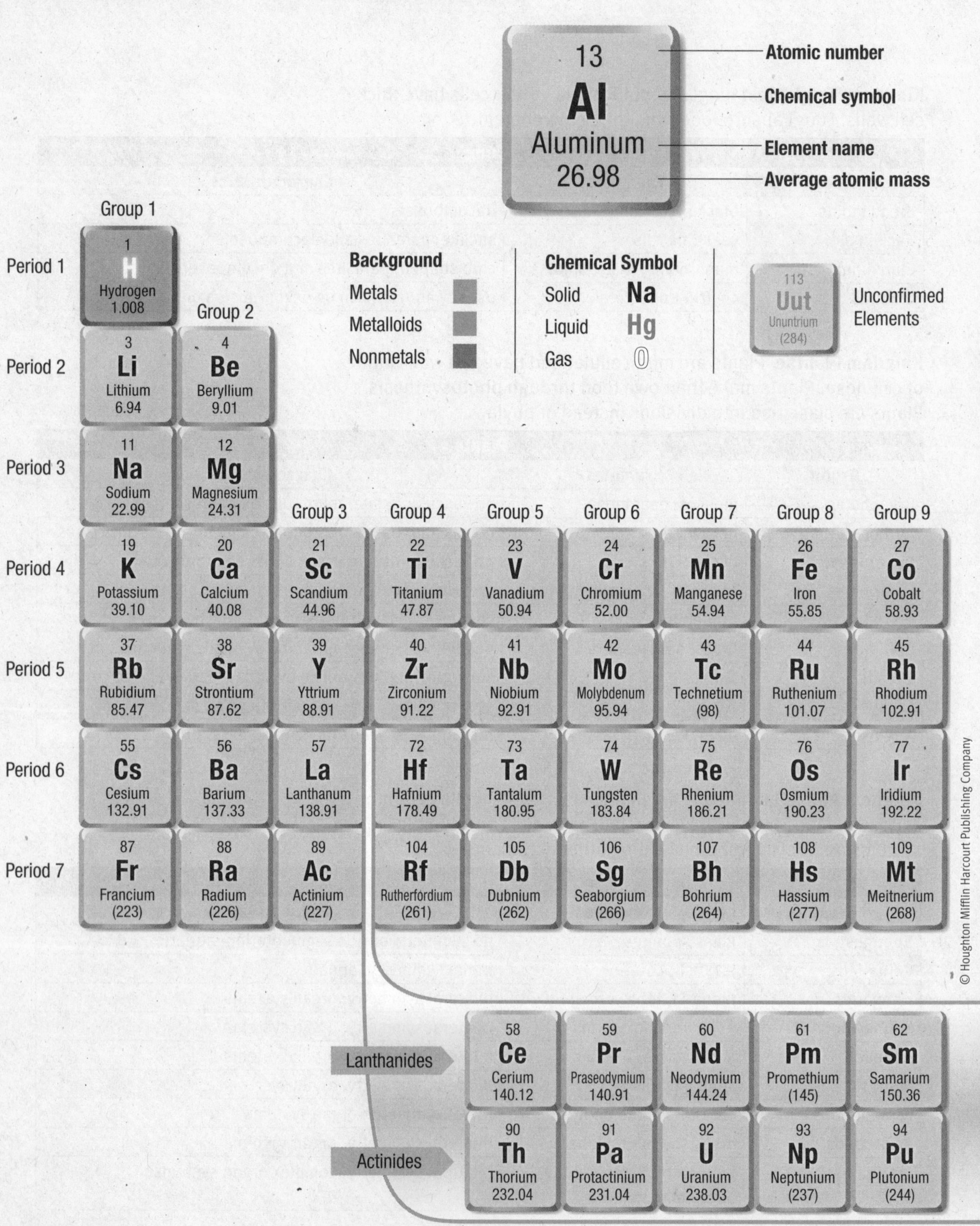

Key	
13	Atomic number
Al	Chemical symbol
Aluminum	Element name
26.98	Average atomic mass

Background	Chemical Symbol
Metals	Solid: Na
Metalloids	Liquid: Hg
Nonmetals	Gas: O

113 Uut Ununtrium (284) — Unconfirmed Elements

	Group 1	Group 2	Group 3	Group 4	Group 5	Group 6	Group 7	Group 8	Group 9
Period 1	1 H Hydrogen 1.008								
Period 2	3 Li Lithium 6.94	4 Be Beryllium 9.01							
Period 3	11 Na Sodium 22.99	12 Mg Magnesium 24.31							
Period 4	19 K Potassium 39.10	20 Ca Calcium 40.08	21 Sc Scandium 44.96	22 Ti Titanium 47.87	23 V Vanadium 50.94	24 Cr Chromium 52.00	25 Mn Manganese 54.94	26 Fe Iron 55.85	27 Co Cobalt 58.93
Period 5	37 Rb Rubidium 85.47	38 Sr Strontium 87.62	39 Y Yttrium 88.91	40 Zr Zirconium 91.22	41 Nb Niobium 92.91	42 Mo Molybdenum 95.94	43 Tc Technetium (98)	44 Ru Ruthenium 101.07	45 Rh Rhodium 102.91
Period 6	55 Cs Cesium 132.91	56 Ba Barium 137.33	57 La Lanthanum 138.91	72 Hf Hafnium 178.49	73 Ta Tantalum 180.95	74 W Tungsten 183.84	75 Re Rhenium 186.21	76 Os Osmium 190.23	77 Ir Iridium 192.22
Period 7	87 Fr Francium (223)	88 Ra Radium (226)	89 Ac Actinium (227)	104 Rf Rutherfordium (261)	105 Db Dubnium (262)	106 Sg Seaborgium (266)	107 Bh Bohrium (264)	108 Hs Hassium (277)	109 Mt Meitnerium (268)

Lanthanides	58 Ce Cerium 140.12	59 Pr Praseodymium 140.91	60 Nd Neodymium 144.24	61 Pm Promethium (145)	62 Sm Samarium 150.36
Actinides	90 Th Thorium 232.04	91 Pa Protactinium 231.04	92 U Uranium 238.03	93 Np Neptunium (237)	94 Pu Plutonium (244)

Group 10	Group 11	Group 12	Group 13	Group 14	Group 15	Group 16	Group 17	Group 18
								2 He Helium 4.003
			5 B Boron 10.81	6 C Carbon 12.01	7 N Nitrogen 14.01	8 O Oxygen 16.00	9 F Fluorine 19.00	10 Ne Neon 20.18
			13 Al Aluminum 26.98	14 Si Silicon 28.09	15 P Phosphorus 30.97	16 S Sulfur 32.07	17 Cl Chlorine 35.45	18 Ar Argon 39.95
28 Ni Nickel 58.69	29 Cu Copper 63.55	30 Zn Zinc 65.41	31 Ga Gallium 69.72	32 Ge Germanium 72.64	33 As Arsenic 74.92	34 Se Selenium 78.96	35 Br Bromine 79.90	36 Kr Krypton 83.80
46 Pd Palladium 106.42	47 Ag Silver 107.87	48 Cd Cadmium 112.41	49 In Indium 114.82	50 Sn Tin 118.71	51 Sb Antimony 121.76	52 Te Tellurium 127.6	53 I Iodine 126.9	54 Xe Xenon 131.29
78 Pt Platinum 195.08	79 Au Gold 196.97	80 Hg Mercury 200.59	81 Tl Thallium 204.38	82 Pb Lead 207.2	83 Bi Bismuth 208.98	84 Po Polonium (209)	85 At Astatine (210)	86 Rn Radon (222)
110 Ds Darmstadtium (271)	111 Rg Roentgenium (272)	112 Cn Copernicium (285)	113 Uut Ununtrium (284)	114 Uuq Ununquadium (289)	115 Uup Ununpentium (288)	116 Uuh Unhexium (292)		118 Uuo Ununoctium (294)

63 Eu Europium 151.96	64 Gd Gadolinium 157.25	65 Tb Terbium 158.93	66 Dy Dysprosium 162.5	67 Ho Holmium 164.93	68 Er Erbium 167.26	69 Tm Thulium 168.93	70 Yb Ytterbium 173.04	71 Lu Lutetium 174.97
95 Am Americium (243)	96 Cm Curium (247)	97 Bk Berkelium (247)	98 Cf Californium (251)	99 Es Einsteinium (252)	100 Fm Fermium (257)	101 Md Mendelevium (258)	102 No Nobelium (259)	103 Lr Lawrencium (262)

A How-To Manual for Active Reading

This book belongs to you, and you are invited to write in it. In fact, the book won't be complete until you do. Sometimes you'll answer a question or follow directions to mark up the text. Other times you'll write down your own thoughts. And when you're done reading and writing in the book, the book will be ready to help you review what you learned and prepare for the Sunshine State Benchmark tests.

Active Reading Annotations

Before you read, you'll often come upon an Active Reading prompt that asks you to underline certain words or number the steps in a process. Here's an example.

Marking the text this way is called **annotating,** and your marks are called **annotations.** Annotating the text can help you identify important concepts while you read.

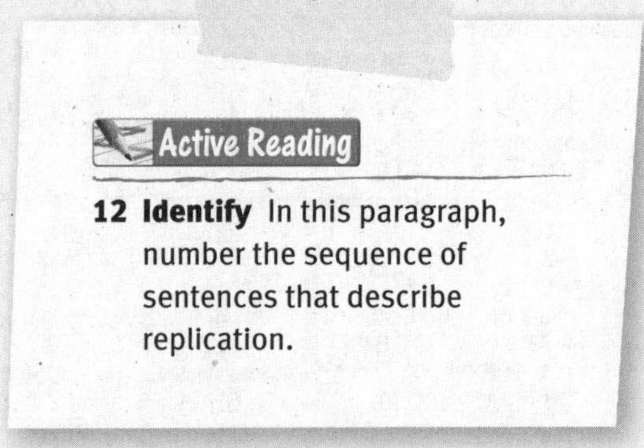

Active Reading
12 Identify In this paragraph, number the sequence of sentences that describe replication.

There are other ways that you can annotate the text. You can draw an asterisk (*) by vocabulary terms, mark unfamiliar or confusing terms and information with a question mark (?), and mark main ideas with a double underline. And you can even invent your own marks to annotate the text!

Other Annotating Opportunities

Keep your pencil, pen, or highlighter nearby as you read, so you can make a note or highlight an important point at any time. Here are a few ideas to get you started.

- Notice the headings in red and blue. The blue headings are questions that point to the main idea of what you're reading. The red headings are answers to the questions in the blue ones. Together these headings outline the content of the lesson. After reading a lesson, you could write your own answers to the questions.

- Notice the bold-faced words that are highlighted in yellow. They are highlighted so that you can easily find them again on the page where they are defined. As you read or as you review, challenge yourself to write your own sentence using the bold-faced term.
- Make a note in the margin at any time. You might
  - Ask a "What if" question
  - Comment on what you read
  - Make a connection to something you read elsewhere
  - Make a logical conclusion from the text

Use your own language and abbreviations. Invent a code, such as using circles and boxes around words to remind you of their importance or relation to each other. Your annotations will help you remember your questions for class discussions, and when you go back to the lesson later, you may be able to fill in what you didn't understand the first time you read it. Like a scientist in the field or in a lab, you will be recording your questions and observations for analysis later.

Active Reading Questions

After you read, you'll often come upon Active Reading questions that ask you to think about what you've just read. You'll write your answer underneath the question. Here's an example.

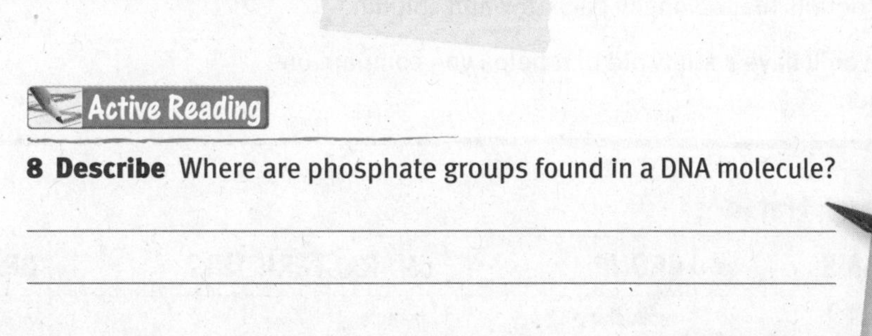

Active Reading
8 Describe Where are phosphate groups found in a DNA molecule?

This type of question helps you sum up what you've just read and pull out the most important ideas from the passage. In this case the question asks you to **describe** the structure of a DNA molecule that you have just read about. Other times you may be asked to do such things as **apply** a concept, **compare** two concepts, **summarize** a process, or **identify a cause-and-effect** relationship. You'll be strengthening those critical thinking skills that you'll use often in learning about science.

Using Graphic Organizers to Take Notes

Graphic organizers help you remember information as you read it for the first time and as you study it later. There are dozens of graphic organizers to choose from, so the first trick is to choose the one that's best suited to your purpose. Following are some graphic organizers to use for different purposes.

To remember lots of information	To relate a central idea to subordinate details	To describe a process	To make a comparison
• Arrange data in a Content Frame • Use Combination Notes to describe a concept in words and pictures	• Show relationships with a Mind Map or a Main Idea Web • Sum up relationships among many things with a Concept Map	• Use a Process Diagram to explain a procedure • Show a chain of events and results in a Cause-and-Effect Chart	• Compare two or more closely related things in a Venn Diagram

Content Frame

1 Make a four-column chart.

2 Fill the first column with categories (e.g., snail, ant, earthworm) and the first row with descriptive information (e.g., group, characteristic, appearance).

3 Fill the chart with details that belong in each row and column.

4 When you finish, you'll have a study aid that helps you compare one category to another.

Invertebrates

NAME	GROUP	CHARACTERISTICS	DRAWING
snail	mollusks	mangle	
ant	arthropods	six legs, exoskeleton	
earthworm	segmented worms	segmented body, circulatory and digestive systems	
heartworm	roundworms	digestive system	
sea star	echinoderms	spiny skin, tube feet	
jellyfish	cnidarians	stinging cells	

Combination Notes

1 Make a two-column chart.

2 Write descriptive words and definitions in the first column.

3 Draw a simple sketch that helps you remember the meaning of the term in the second column.

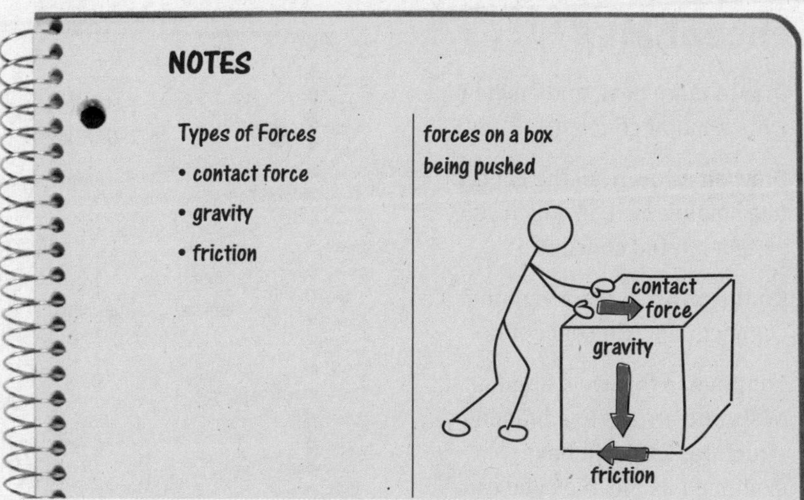

forces on a box

Mind Map

1 Draw an oval, and inside it write a topic to analyze.

2 Draw two or more arms extending from the oval. Each arm represents a main idea about the topic.

3 Draw lines from the arms on which to write details about each of the main ideas.

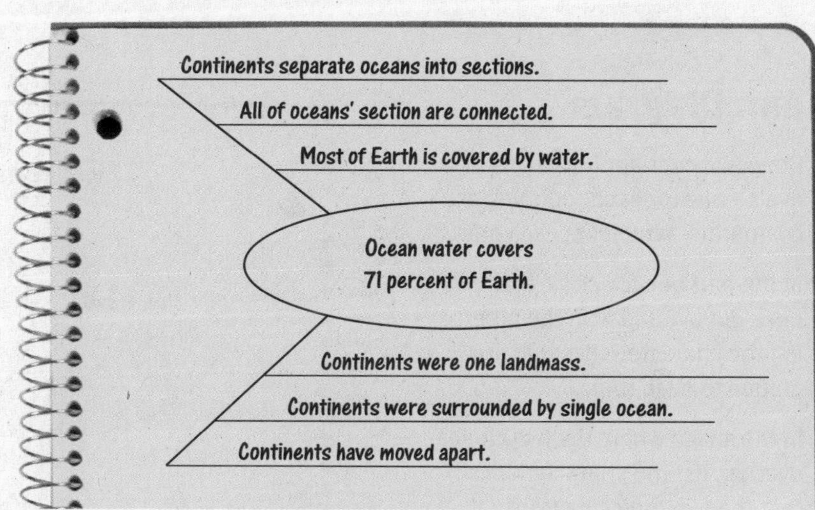

Continents separate oceans into sections.
All of oceans' section are connected.
Most of Earth is covered by water.
Ocean water covers 71 percent of Earth.
Continents were one landmass.
Continents were surrounded by single ocean.
Continents have moved apart.

Main Idea Web

1 Make a box and write a concept you want to remember inside it.

2 Draw boxes around the central box, and label each one with a category of information about the concept (e.g., definition, formula, descriptive details)

3 Fill in the boxes with relevant details as you read.

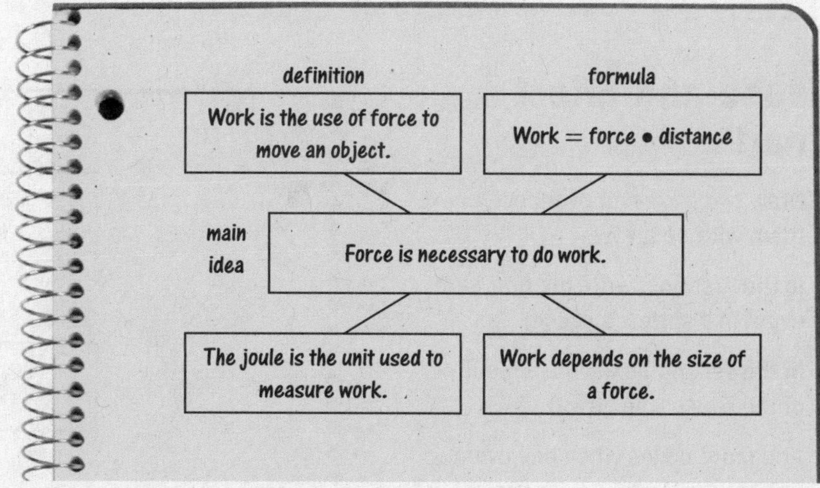

definition
Work is the use of force to move an object.
formula
Work = force • distance
main idea
Force is necessary to do work.
The joule is the unit used to measure work.
Work depends on the size of a force.

Reading and Study Skills

Concept Map

1 Draw a large oval, and inside it write a major concept.

2 Draw an arrow from the concept to a smaller oval, in which you write a related concept.

3 On the arrow, write a verb that connects the two concepts.

4 Continue in this way, adding ovals and arrows in a branching structure, until you have explained as much as you can about the main concept.

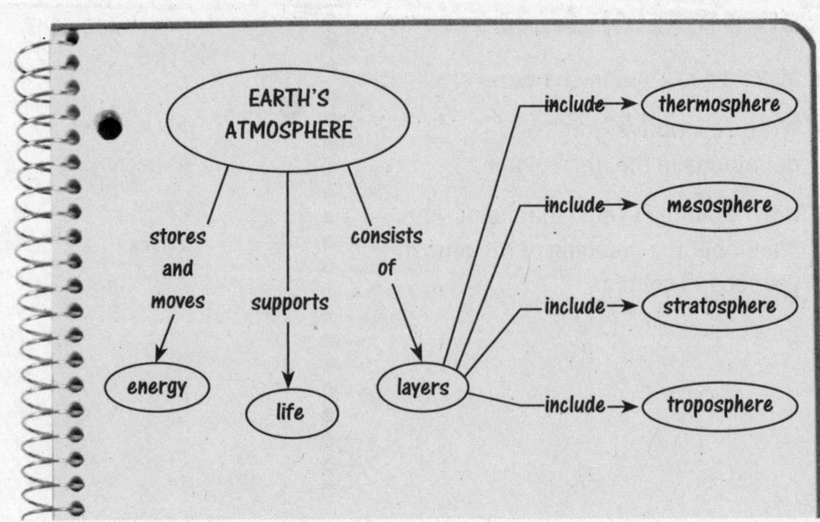

Venn Diagram

1 Draw two overlapping circles or ovals—one for each topic you are comparing—and label each one.

2 In the part of each circle that does not overlap with the other, list the characteristics that are unique to each topic.

3 In the space where the two circles overlap, list the characteristics that the two topics have in common.

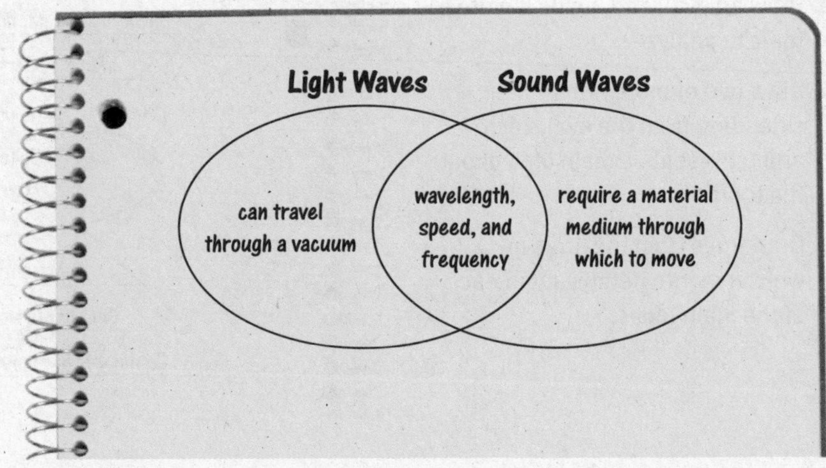

Cause-and-Effect Chart

1 Draw two boxes and connect them with an arrow.

2 In the first box, write the first event in a series (a cause).

3 In the second box, write a result of the cause (the effect).

4 Add more boxes when one event has many effects, or vice versa.

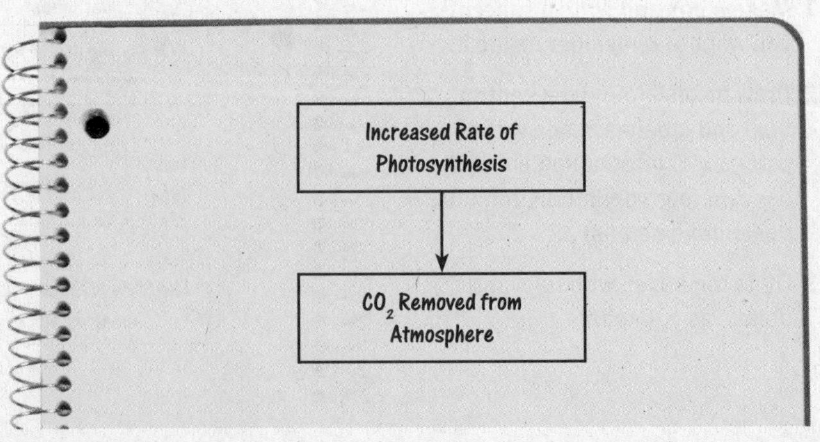

Process Diagram

A process can be a never-ending cycle. As you can see in this technology design process, engineers may backtrack and repeat steps, they may skip steps entirely, or they may repeat the entire process before a useable design is achieved.

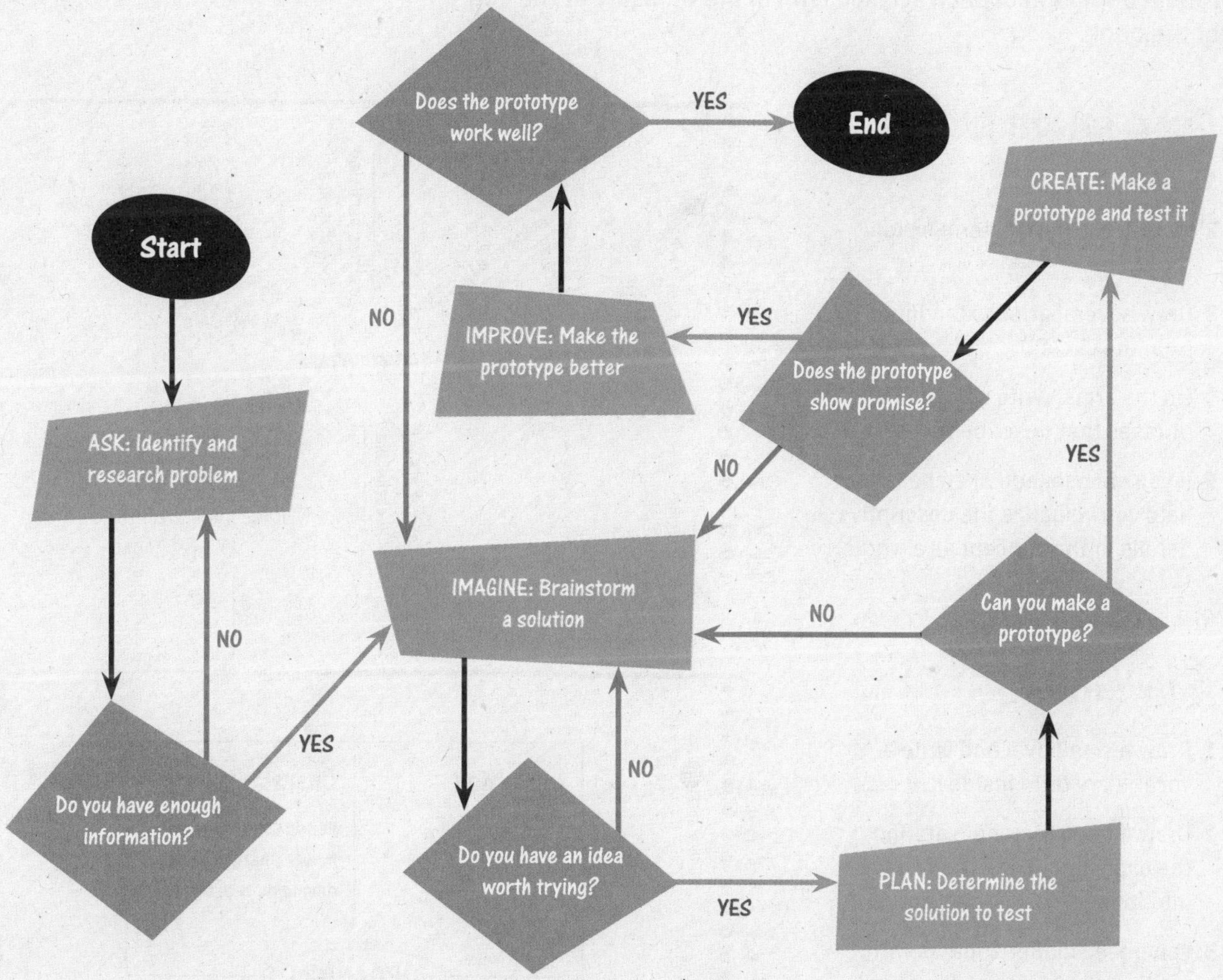

Using Vocabulary Strategies

Important science terms are highlighted where they are first defined in this book. One way to remember these terms is to take notes and make sketches when you come to them. Use the strategies on this page and the next for this purpose. You will also find a formal definition of each science term in the Glossary at the end of the book.

Description Wheel

1 Draw a small circle.

2 Write a vocabulary term inside the circle.

3 Draw several arms extending from the circle.

4 On the arms, write words and phrases that describe the term.

5 If you choose, add sketches that help you visualize the descriptive details or the concept as a whole.

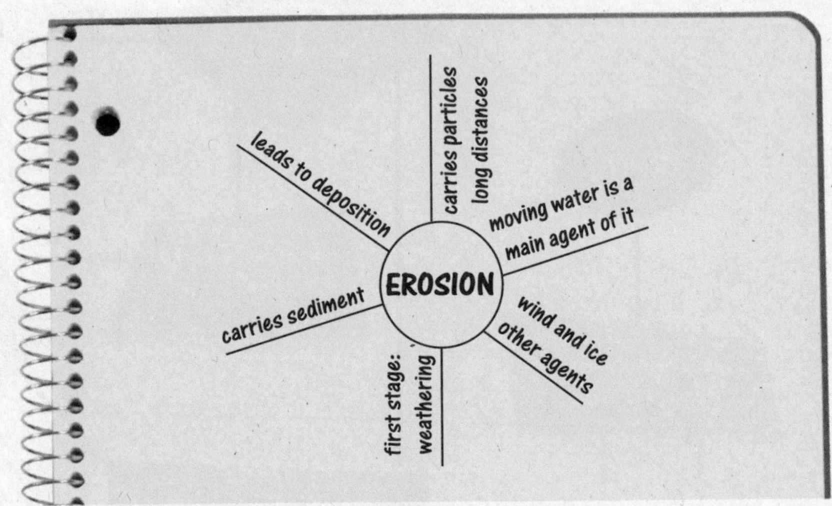

Four Square

1 Draw a small oval and write a vocabulary term inside it.

2 Draw a large rectangle around the oval, and divide the rectangle into four smaller squares.

3 Label the smaller squares with categories of information about the term, such as: definition, characteristics, examples, non-examples, appearance, and root words.

4 Fill the squares with descriptive words and drawings that will help you remember the overall meaning of the term and its essential details.

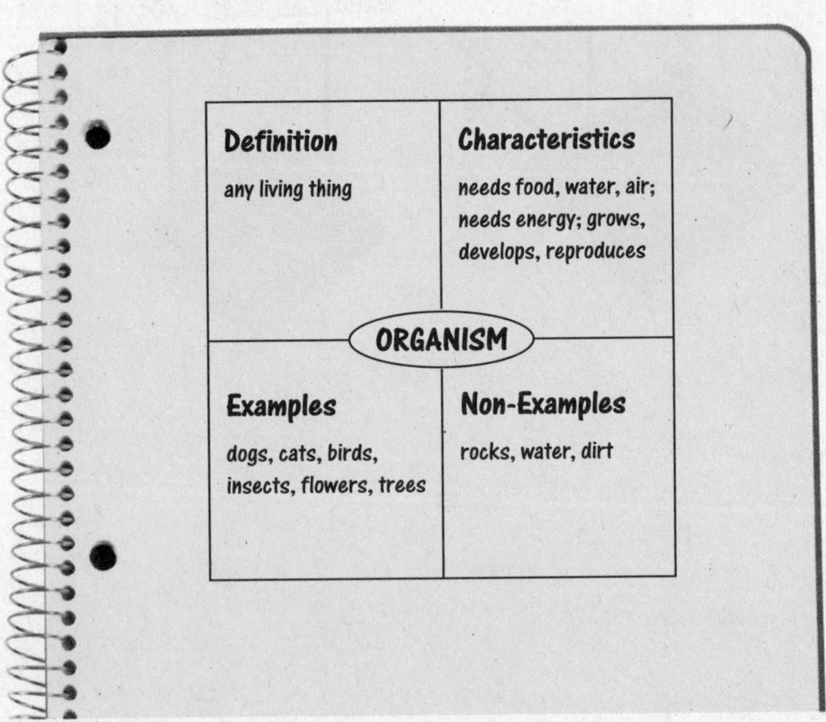

Frame Game

1 Draw a small rectangle, and write a vocabulary term inside it.

2 Draw a larger rectangle around the smaller one. Connect the corners of the larger rectangle to the corners of the smaller one, creating four spaces that frame the word.

3 In each of the four parts of the frame, draw or write details that help define the term. Consider including a definition, essential characteristics, an equation, examples, and a sentence using the term.

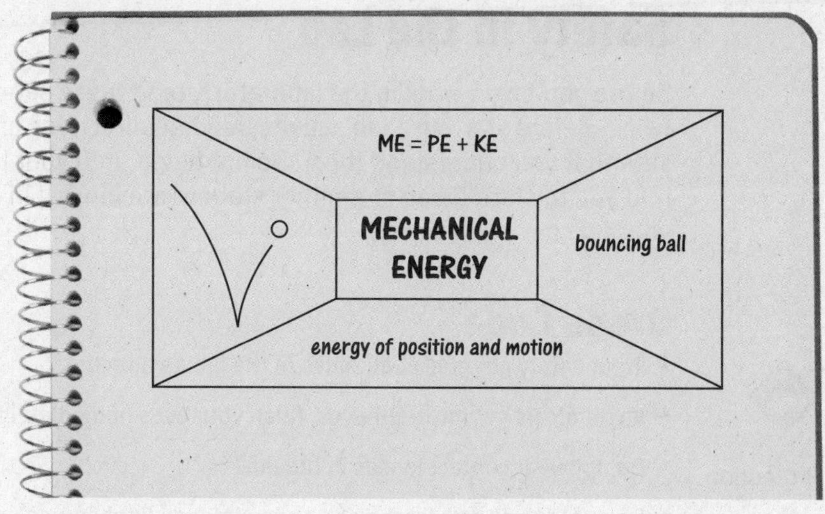

Magnet Word

1 Draw horseshoe magnet, and write a vocabulary term inside it.

2 Add lines that extend from the sides of the magnet.

3 Brainstorm words and phrases that come to mind when you think about the term.

4 On the lines, write the words and phrases that describe something essential about the term.

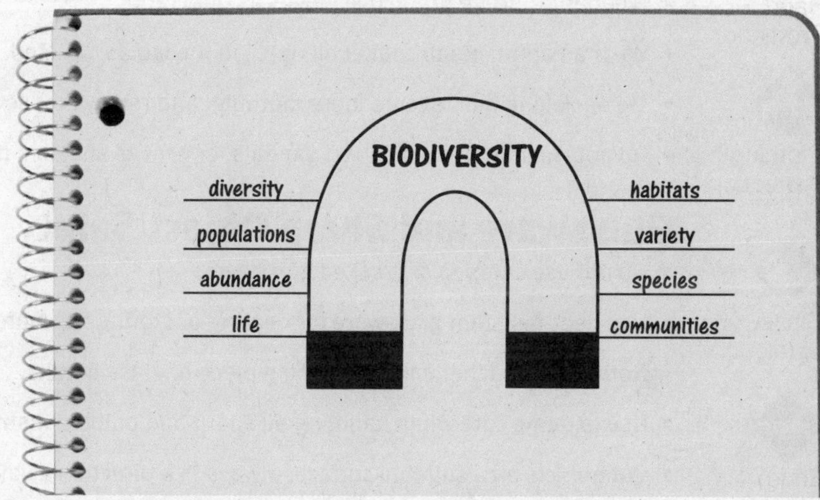

Word Triangle

1 Draw a triangle, and add lines to divide it into three parts.

2 Write a term and its definition in the bottom section of the triangle.

3 In the middle section, write a sentence in which the term is used correctly.

4 In the top section, draw a small picture to illustrate the term.

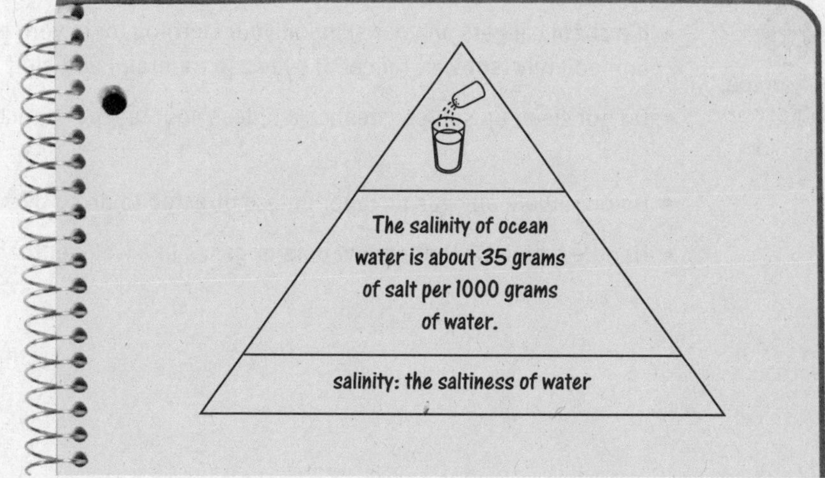

The salinity of ocean water is about 35 grams of salt per 1000 grams of water.
salinity: the saltiness of water

Safety in the Lab

Before you begin work in the laboratory, read these safety rules twice. Before starting a lab activity, read all directions and make sure that you understand them. Do not begin until your teacher has told you to start. If you or another student are injured in any way, tell your teacher immediately.

Dress Code

Eye Protection

Hand Protection

Clothing Protection

- Wear safety goggles at all times in the lab as directed.
- If chemicals get into your eyes, flush your eyes immediately.
- Do not wear contact lenses in the lab.
- Do not look directly at the sun or any intense light source or laser.
- Do not cut an object while holding the object in your hand.
- Wear appropriate protective gloves as directed.
- Wear an apron or lab coat at all times in the lab as directed.
- Tie back long hair, secure loose clothing, and remove loose jewelry.
- Do not wear open-toed shoes, sandals, or canvas shoes in the lab.

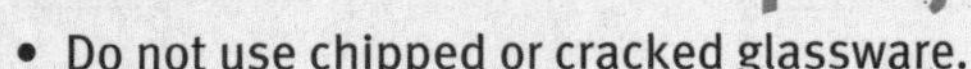

Glassware and Sharp Object Safety

Glassware Safety

Sharp Objects Safety

- Do not use chipped or cracked glassware.
- Use heat-resistant glassware for heating or storing hot materials.
- Notify your teacher immediately if a piece of glass breaks.
- Use extreme care when handling all sharp and pointed instruments.
- Cut objects on a suitable surface, always in a direction away from your body.

Chemical Safety

Chemical Safety

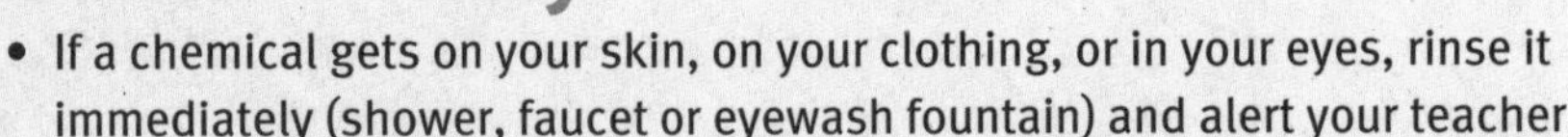

- If a chemical gets on your skin, on your clothing, or in your eyes, rinse it immediately (shower, faucet or eyewash fountain) and alert your teacher.
- Do not clean up spilled chemicals unless your teacher directs you to do so.
- Do not inhale any gas or vapor unless directed to do so by your teacher.
- Handle materials that emit vapors or gases in a well-ventilated area.

Electrical Safety

Electrical Safety

- Do not use equipment with frayed electrical cords or loose plugs.
- Do not use electrical equipment near water or when clothing or hands are wet.
- Hold the plug housing when you plug in or unplug equipment.

Heating and Fire Safety

Heating Safety

- Be aware of any source of flames, sparks, or heat (such as flames, heating coils, or hot plates) before working with any flammable substances.
- Know the location of lab fire extinguishers and fire-safety blankets.
- Know your school's fire-evacuation routes.
- If your clothing catches on fire, walk to the lab shower to put out the fire.
- Never leave a hot plate unattended while it is turned on or while it is cooling.
- Use tongs or appropriate insulated holders when handling heated objects.
- Allow all equipment to cool before storing it.

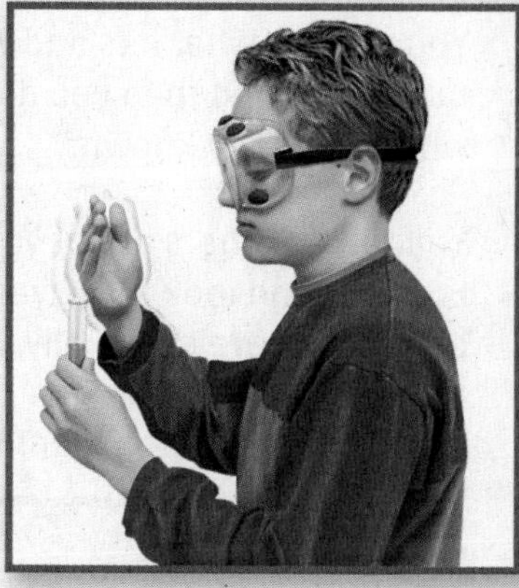
Wafting

Plant and Animal Safety

Plant Safety

Animal Safety

- Do not eat any part of a plant.
- Do not pick any wild plants unless your teacher instructs you to do so.
- Handle animals only as your teacher directs.
- Treat animals carefully and respectfully.
- Wash your hands thoroughly after handling any plant or animal.

Cleanup

Proper Waste Disposal

Hygienic Care

- Clean all work surfaces and protective equipment as directed by your teacher.
- Dispose of hazardous materials or sharp objects only as directed by your teacher.
- Keep your hands away from your face while you are working on any activity.
- Wash your hands thoroughly before you leave the lab or after any activity.

Designing an Experiment

An **experiment** is an organized procedure to study something under controlled conditions. Use the following steps of the scientific method when designing or conducting an experiment.

1 Identify a Research Problem

Every day you make **observations** by using your senses to gather information. Careful observations lead to good **questions,** and good questions can lead you to a purpose, or problem, for an experiment.

Imagine, for example, that you pass a pond every day on your way to school, and you notice green scum beginning to form on top of it. You wonder what it is and why it seems to be growing. You list your questions, and then you do a little preliminary research to find out what is already known.

You talk to others about your observations, learn that the scum is algae, and look for relvant information in books, journals, and online. You are especially interested in the data and conclusions from earlier experiments. Finally, you write the problem that you want to investigate. Your notes might look like these.

Area of Interest	Research Questions	Research Problem
Algae growth in lakes and ponds	• How do algae grow? • How do people measure algae? • What kind of fertilizer would affect the growth of algae? • Can fertilizer and algae be used safely in a lab? How?	How does fertilizer affect the presence of algae in a pond?

2 Make a Prediction

A **prediction** is a statement of what you expect will happen in your experiment. Before making a prediction, you need to decide in a general way what you will do in your procedure. You may state your prediction in an if-then format.

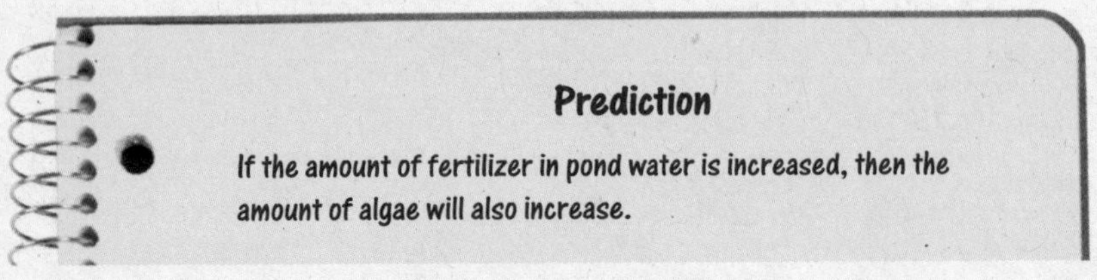
Prediction
If the amount of fertilizer in pond water is increased, then the amount of algae will also increase.

3 Form a Hypothesis

Many experiments are designed to test a hypothesis. A **hypothesis** is a tentative explanation for an expected result. You have predicted that additional fertilizer will cause additional algae growth in pond water; your hypothesis goes beyond your prediction to explain why fertilizer has that effect.

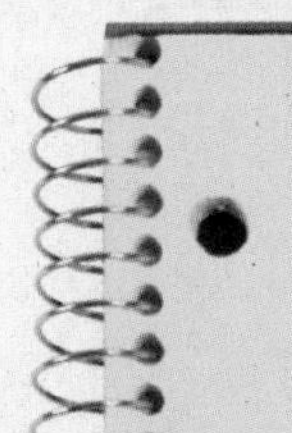

Hypothesis

If the amount of fertilizer in pond water is increased, then the amount of algae will also increase because fertilizers provide nutrients that algae need to grow.

4 Identify Variables to Test the Hypothesis

The next step is to design an experiment to test the hypothesis. The experiment may or may not support the hypothesis. Either way, the information that results from the experiment may be useful for future investigations.

Experimental Group and Control Group

An experiment to determine how two factors are related has a control group and an experimental group. The two groups are the same, except that the experimenter changes a single factor in the experimental group and does not change it in the control group.

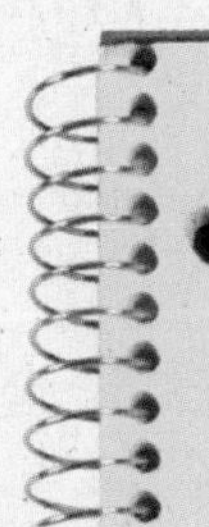

Experimental Group: *two containers of pond water with one drop of fertilizer solution added to each*

Control Group: *two containers of the same pond water sampled at the same time but with no fertilizer solution added*

Variables and Constants

In a controlled experiment, a **variable** is any factor that can change. **Constants** are all of the variables that are kept the same in both the experimental group and the control group.

The **independent variable** is the factor that is manipulated or changed in order to test the effect of the change on another variable. The **dependent variable** is the factor that the experimenter measures to gather data about the effect.

Independent Variable	Dependent Variable	Constants
Amount of fertilizer in pond water	Amount of algae that grow	• Where and when the pond water is obtained • The type of container used • Light and temperature conditions where the water is stored

5 Write a Procedure

Write each step of your procedure. Start each step with a verb, or action word, and keep the steps short. Your procedure should be clear enough for someone else to use as instructions for repeating your experiment.

Procedure

1. Put on your gloves. Use the large container to obtain a sample of pond water.
2. Divide the water sample equally among the four smaller containers.
3. Use the eyedropper to add one drop of fertilizer solution to two of the containers.
4. Use the masking tape and the marker to label the containers with your initials, the date, and the identifiers "Jar 1 with Fertilizer," "Jar 2 with Fertilizer," "Jar 1 without Fertilizer," and "Jar 2 without Fertilizer."
5. Cover the containers with clear plastic wrap. Use the scissors to punch ten holes in each of the covers.
6. Place all four containers on a window ledge. Make sure that they all receive the same amount of light.
7. Observe the containers every day for one week.
8. Use the ruler to measure the diameter of the largest clump of algae in each container, and record your measurements daily.

6 Experiment and Collect Data

Once you have all of your materials and your procedure has been approved, you can begin to experiment and collect data. Record both quantitative data (measurements) and qualitative data (observations), as shown below.

Fertilizer and Algae Growth

	Experimental Group		Control Group		
Date and Time	Jar 1 with Fertilizer (diameter of algae in mm)	Jar 2 with Fertilizer (diameter of algae in mm)	Jar 1 without Fertilizer (diameter of algae in mm)	Jar 2 without Fertilizer (diameter of algae in mm)	Observations
5/3 4:00 P.M.	0	0	0	0	condensation in all containers
5/4 4:00 P.M.	0	3	0	0	tiny green blobs in jar 2 with fertilizer
5/5 4:15 P.M.	4	5	0	3	green blobs in jars 1 and 2 with fertilizer and jar 2 without fertilizer
5/6 4:00 P.M.	5	6	0	4	water light green in jar 2 with fertilizer
5/7 4:00 P.M.	8	10	0	6	water light green in jars 1 and 2 with fertilizer and jar 2 without fertilizer
5/8 3:30 P.M.	10	18	0	6	cover off jar 2 with fertilizer
5/9 3:30 P.M.	14	23	0	8	drew sketches of each container

Drawings of Samples Viewed Under Microscope on 5/9 at 100x

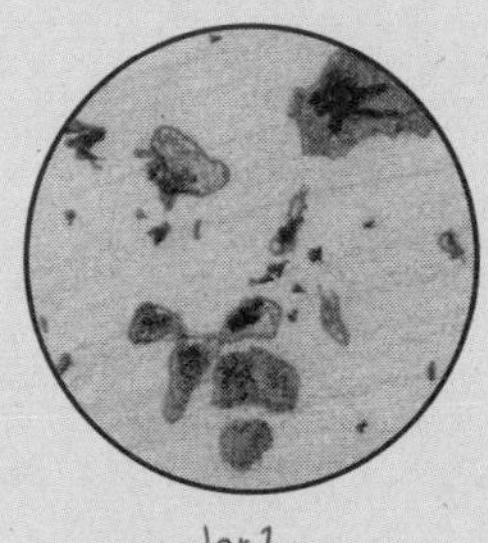
Jar 1 with Fertilizer

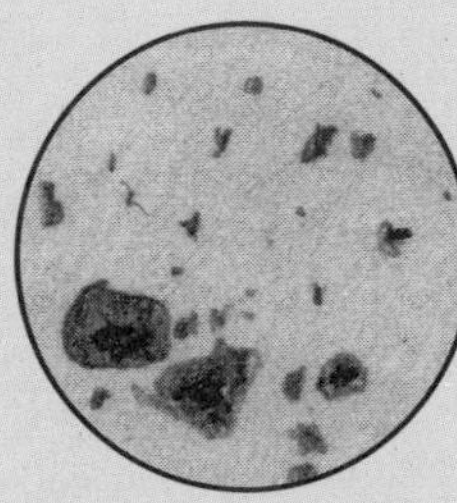
Jar 2 with Fertilizer

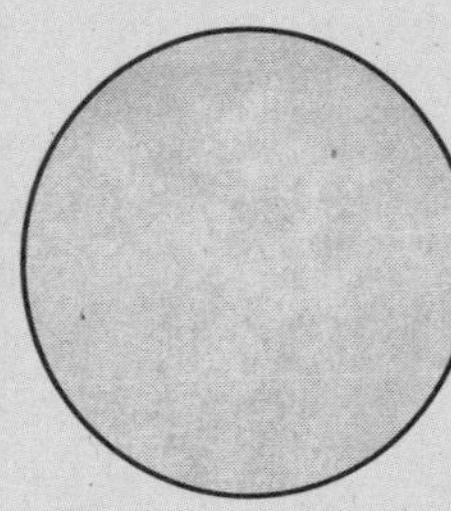
Jar 1 without Fertilizer

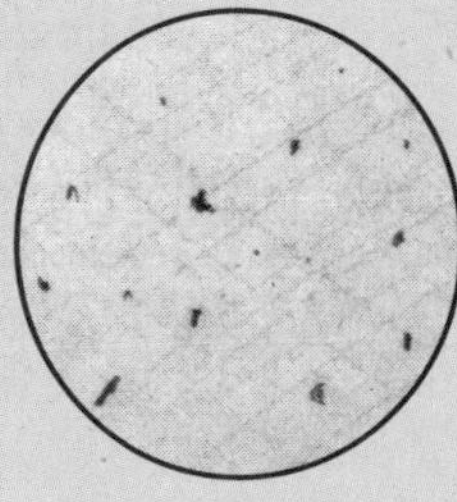
Jar 2 without Fertilizer

7 Analyze Data

After you have completed your experiments, made your observations, and collected your data, you must analyze all the information you have gathered. Tables, statistics, and graphs are often used in this step to organize and analyze the data.

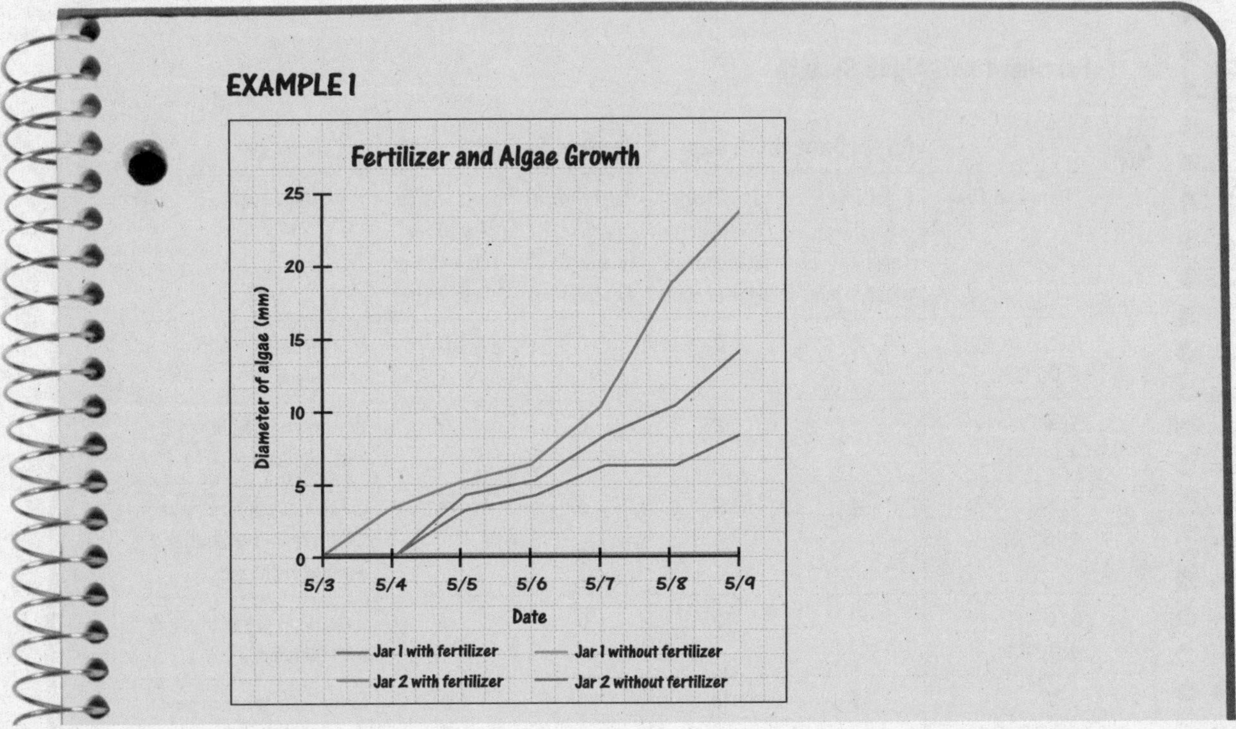

8 Make Conclusions

To draw conclusions from your experiment, first write your results. Then compare your results with your hypothesis. Do your results support your hypothesis?

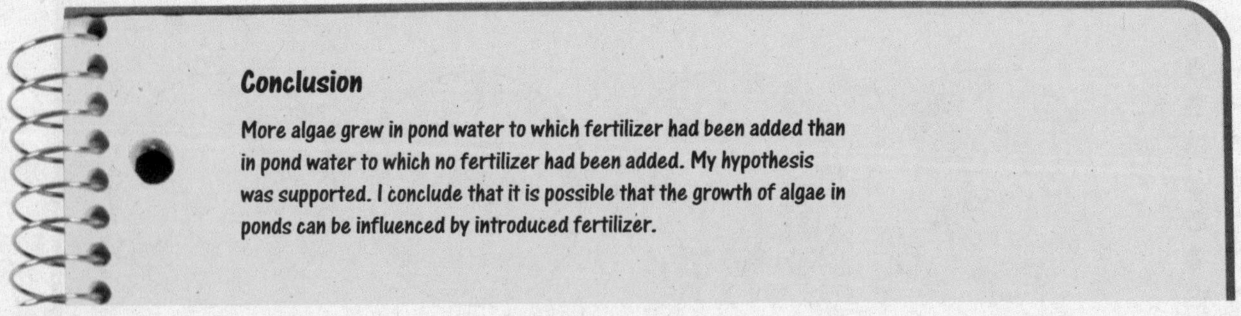

Conclusion
More algae grew in pond water to which fertilizer had been added than in pond water to which no fertilizer had been added. My hypothesis was supported. I conclude that it is possible that the growth of algae in ponds can be influenced by introduced fertilizer.

Using a Microscope

Scientists use microscopes to see very small objects that cannot easily be seen with the eye alone. A microscope magnifies the image of an object so that small details may be observed. A microscope that you may use can magnify an object 400 times—the object will appear 400 times larger than its actual size.

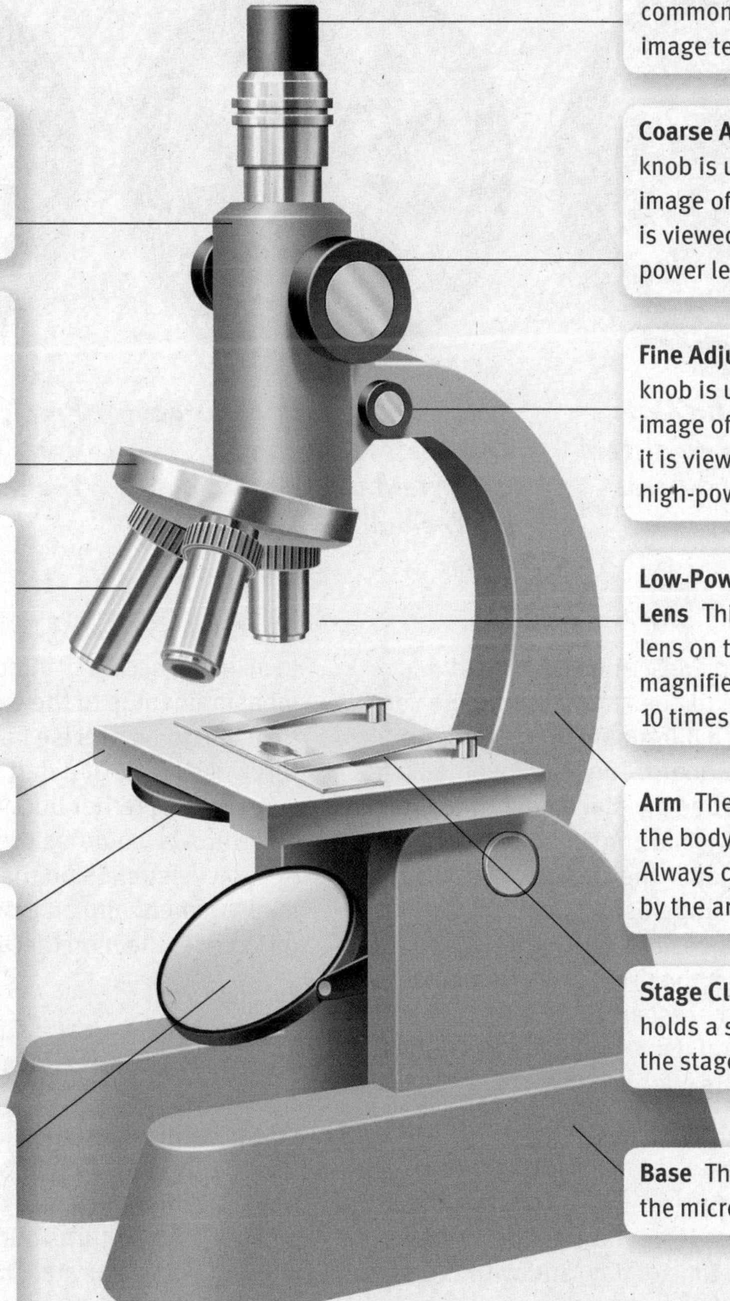

Eyepiece Objects are viewed through the eyepiece. The eyepiece contains a lens that commonly magnifies an image ten times.

Body The body separates the lens in the eyepiece from the objective lenses below.

Coarse Adjustment This knob is used to focus the image of an object when it is viewed through the low-power lens.

Nosepiece The nosepiece holds the objective lenses above the stage and rotates so that all lenses may be used.

Fine Adjustment This knob is used to focus the image of an object when it is viewed through the high-power lens.

High-Power Objective Lens This is the largest lens on the nosepiece. It magnifies an image approximately 40 times.

Low-Power Objective Lens This is the smallest lens on the nosepiece. It magnifies images about 10 times.

Stage The stage supports the object being viewed.

Arm The arm supports the body above the stage. Always carry a microscope by the arm and base.

Diaphragm The diaphragm is used to adjust the amount of light passing through the slide and into an objective lens.

Stage Clip The stage clip holds a slide in place on the stage.

Mirror or Light Source Some microscopes use light that is reflected through the stage by a mirror. Other microscopes have their own light sources.

Base The base supports the microscope.

Measuring Accurately

Precision and Accuracy

When you do a scientific investigation, it is important that your methods, observations, and data be both precise and accurate.

Low precision: The darts did not land in a consistent place on the dartboard.

Precision, but not accuracy: The darts landed in a consistent place, but did not hit the bull's eye.

Precision and accuracy: The darts landed consistently on the bull's eye.

Precision

In science, *precision* describes how close measurements are to one another. Imagine you threw five darts at a dart board, and the darts landed all over the board. The result would have low precision because the placement of the five darts on the board is not consistent. Another indicator of precision is the care taken to make sure that methods and observations are as exact and consistent as possible. Every time a particular experiment is done, the same procedure should be used. Precision is necessary because experiments are repeated several times and if the procedure changes, the results might change.

Example

Suppose you are measuring temperatures over a two-week period. Your precision will be greater if you measure each temperature at the same place, at the same time of day, and with the same thermometer than if you change any of these factors from one day to the next.

Accuracy

In science, *accuracy* indicates how close a measurement is to the expected result. It is possible to be precise but not accurate. If you threw five darts at a dart board and they landed very close together but not where you aimed, your throws would be precise but not accurate. Accuracy depends on the difference between a measurement and an actual value. The smaller the difference, the more accurate the measurement.

Example

Suppose you look at a stream and estimate that it is about 1 meter wide at a particular place. You decide to check your estimate by measuring the stream with a meter stick, and you determine that the stream is 1.32 meters wide. However, because it is difficult to measure the width of a stream with a meter stick, it turns out that your measurement was not very accurate. The stream is actually 1.14 meters wide. Therefore, even though your estimate of about 1 meter was less precise than your measurement, your estimate was actually more accurate.

Graduated Cylinders

How to Measure the Volume of a Liquid with a Graduated Cylinder

- Be sure that the graduated cylinder is on a flat surface so that your measurement will be accurate.
- When reading the scale on a graduated cylinder, be sure to have your eyes at the level of the surface of the liquid.
- The surface of the liquid will be curved in the graduated cylinder. Read the volume of the liquid at the bottom of the curve, or meniscus (muh-NIHS-kuhs).
- You can use a graduated cylinder to find the volume of a solid object by measuring the increase in a liquid's level after you add the object to the cylinder.

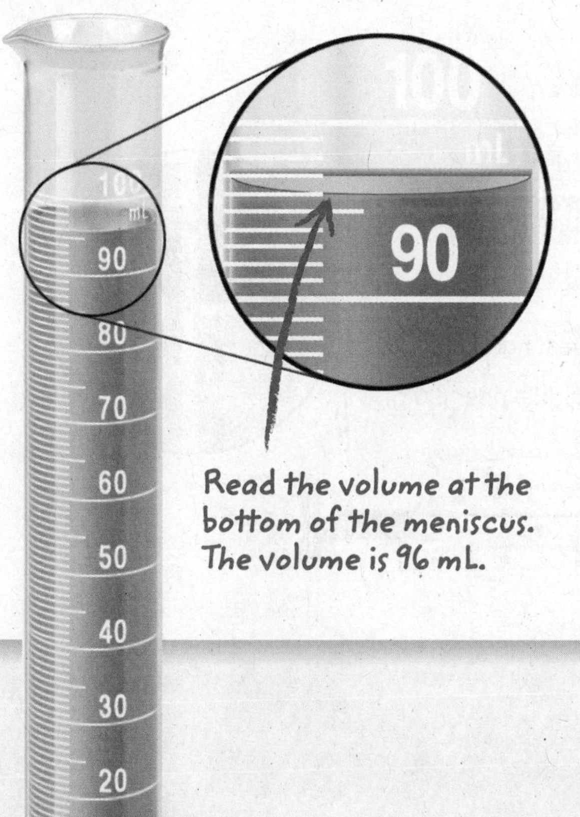

Metric Rulers

How to Measure the Length of a Leaf with a Metric Ruler

1 Lay a ruler flat on top of the leaf so that the 1-centimeter mark lines up with one end. Make sure the ruler and the leaf do not move between the time you line them up and the time you take the measurement.

2 Look straight down on the ruler so that you can see exactly how the marks line up with the other end of the leaf.

3 Estimate the length by which the leaf extends beyond a marking. For example, the leaf below extends about halfway between the 4.2-centimeter and 4.3-centimeter marks, so the apparent measurement is about 4.25 centimeters.

4 Remember to subtract 1 centimeter from your apparent measurement, since you started at the 1-centimeter mark on the ruler and not at the end. The leaf is about 3.25 centimeters long (4.25 cm − 1 cm = 3.25 cm).

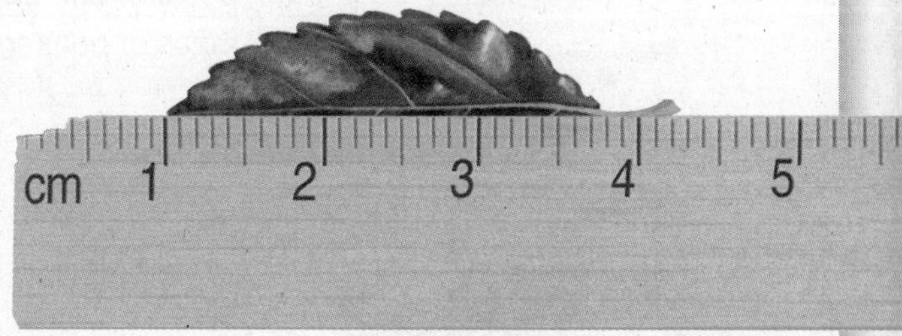

Triple Beam Balance

This balance has a pan and three beams with sliding masses, called riders. At one end of the beams is a pointer that indicates whether the mass on the pan is equal to the masses shown on the beams.

How to Measure the Mass of an Object

1 Make sure the balance is zeroed before measuring the mass of an object. The balance is zeroed if the pointer is at zero when nothing is on the pan and the riders are at their zero points. Use the adjustment knob at the base of the balance to zero it.

2 Place the object to be measured on the pan.

3 Move the riders one notch at a time away from the pan. Begin with the largest rider. If moving the largest rider one notch brings the pointer below zero, begin measuring the mass of the object with the next smaller rider.

4 Change the positions of the riders until they balance the mass on the pan and the pointer is at zero. Then add the readings from the three beams to determine the mass of the object.

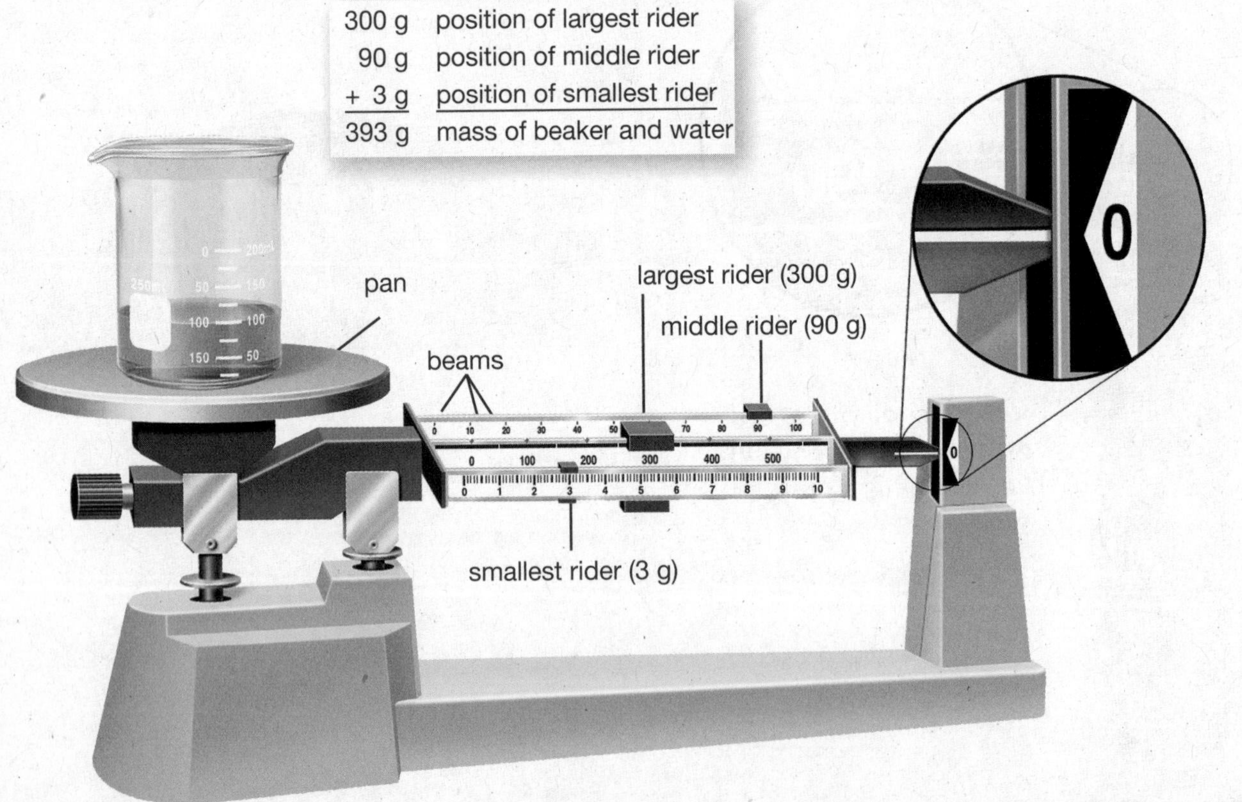

Using the Metric System and SI Units

Scientists use International System (SI) units for measurements of distance, volume, mass, and temperature. The International System is based on powers of ten and the metric system of measurement.

Basic SI Units		
Quantity	**Name**	**Symbol**
length	meter	m
volume	liter	L
mass	gram	g
temperature	kelvin	K

SI Prefixes		
Prefix	**Symbol**	**Power of 10**
kilo-	k	1000
hecto-	h	100
deca-	da	10
deci-	d	0.1 or $\frac{1}{10}$
centi-	c	0.01 or $\frac{1}{100}$
milli-	m	0.001 or $\frac{1}{1000}$

Changing Metric Units

You can change from one unit to another in the metric system by multiplying or dividing by a power of 10.

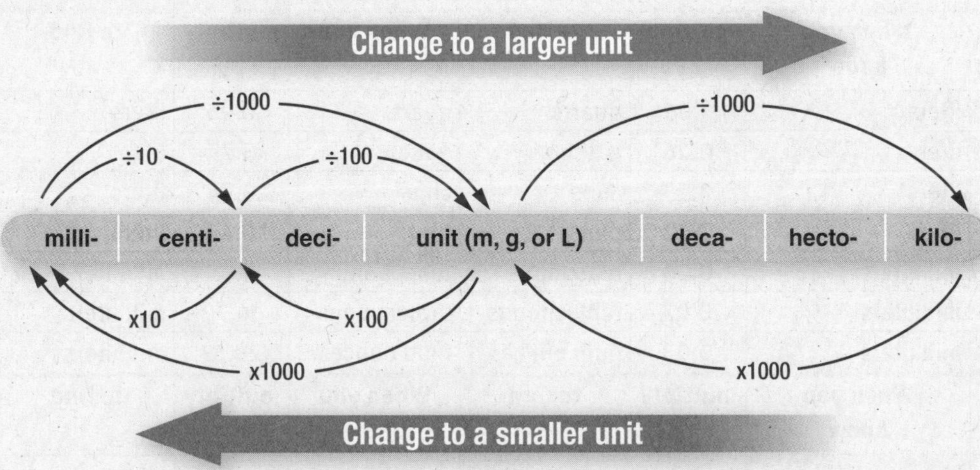

Example

Change 0.64 liters to milliliters.

1 *Decide whether to multiply or divide.*

2 *Select the power of 10.*

Change to a smaller unit by multiplying

mL ← x 1000 — L

0.64 x 1000 = 640.

ANSWER *0.64 L = 640 mL*

Example

Change 23.6 grams to kilograms.

1 *Decide whether to multiply or divide.*

2 *Select the power of 10.*

Change to a larger unit by dividing

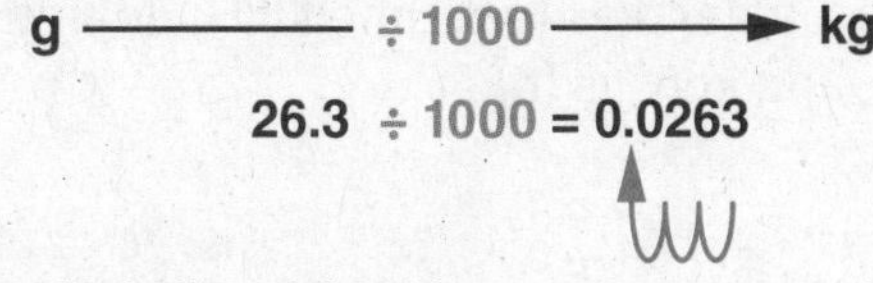

ANSWER *23.6 g = 0.0236 kg*

Converting Between SI and U.S. Customary Units

Use the chart below when you need to convert between SI units and U.S. customary units.

SI Unit	From SI to U.S. Customary			From U.S. Customary to SI		
Length	**When you know**	**multiply by**	**to find**	**When you know**	**multiply by**	**to find**
kilometer (km) = 1000 m	kilometers	0.62	miles	miles	1.61	kilometers
meter (m) = 100 cm	meters	3.28	feet	feet	0.3048	meters
centimeter (cm) = 10 mm	centimeters	0.39	inches	inches	2.54	centimeters
millimeter (mm) = 0.1 cm	millimeters	0.04	inches	inches	25.4	millimeters
Area	**When you know**	**multiply by**	**to find**	**When you know**	**multiply by**	**to find**
square kilometer (km^2)	square kilometers	0.39	square miles	square miles	2.59	square kilometers
square meter (m^2)	square meters	1.2	square yards	square yards	0.84	square meters
square centimeter (cm^2)	square centimeters	0.155	square inches	square inches	6.45	square centimeters
Volume	**When you know**	**multiply by**	**to find**	**When you know**	**multiply by**	**to find**
liter (L) = 1000 mL	liters	1.06	quarts	quarts	0.95	liters
	liters	0.26	gallons	gallons	3.79	liters
	liters	4.23	cups	cups	0.24	liters
	liters	2.12	pints	pints	0.47	liters
milliliter (mL) = 0.001 L	milliliters	0.20	teaspoons	teaspoons	4.93	milliliters
	milliliters	0.07	tablespoons	tablespoons	14.79	milliliters
	milliliters	0.03	fluid ounces	fluid ounces	29.57	milliliters
Mass	**When you know**	**multiply by**	**to find**	**When you know**	**multiply by**	**to find**
kilogram (kg) = 1000 g	kilograms	2.2	pounds	pounds	0.45	kilograms
gram (g) = 1000 mg	grams	0.035	ounces	ounces	28.35	grams

Temperature Conversions

Even though the kelvin is the SI base unit of temperature, the degree Celsius will be the unit you use most often in your science studies. The formulas below show the relationships between temperatures in degrees Fahrenheit (°F), degrees Celsius (°C), and kelvins (K).

$^\circ C = \frac{5}{9}\,(^\circ F - 32)$ $\quad ^\circ F = \frac{9}{5}\,^\circ C + 32$ $\quad K = {}^\circ C + 273$

Examples of Temperature Conversions		
Condition	**Degrees Celsius**	**Degrees Fahrenheit**
Freezing point of water	0	32
Cool day	10	50
Mild day	20	68
Warm day	30	86
Normal body temperature	37	98.6
Very hot day	40	104
Boiling point of water	100	212

Math Refresher

Performing Calculations

Science requires an understanding of many math concepts. The following pages will help you review some important math skills.

Mean

The mean is the sum of all values in a data set divided by the total number of values in the data set. The mean is also called the *average*.

Example

Find the mean of the following set of numbers: 5, 4, 7, and 8.

Step 1 Find the sum.

$5 + 4 + 7 + 8 = 24$

Step 1 Divide the sum by the number of numbers in your set. Because there are four numbers in this example, divide the sum by 4.

$24 \div 4 = 6$

Answer The average, or mean, is 6.

Median

The median of a data set is the middle value when the values are written in numerical order. If a data set has an even number of values, the median is the mean of the two middle values.

Example

To find the median of a set of measurements, arrange the values in order from least to greatest. The median is the middle value.

13 mm 14 mm 16 mm 21 mm 23 mm

Answer The median is 16 mm.

Mode

The mode of a data set is the value that occurs most often.

Example

To find the mode of a set of measurements, arrange the values in order from least to greatest and determine the value that occurs most often.

13 mm, 14 mm, 14 mm, 16 mm,
21 mm, 23 mm, 25 mm

Answer The mode is 14 mm.

A data set can have more than one mode or no mode. For example, the following data set has modes of 2 mm and 4 mm:

2 mm 2 mm 3 mm 4 mm 4 mm

The data set below has no mode, because no value occurs more often than any other.

2 mm 3 mm 4 mm 5 mm

Math Refresher

Ratios

A **ratio** is a comparison between numbers, and it is usually written as a fraction.

Example

Find the ratio of thermometers to students if you have 36 thermometers and 48 students in your class.

Step 1 Write the ratio.

$$\frac{36 \text{ thermometers}}{48 \text{ students}}$$

Step 2 Simplify the fraction to its simplest form.

$$\frac{36}{48} = \frac{36 \div 12}{48 \div 12} = \frac{3}{4}$$

The ratio of thermometers to students is 3 to 4 or 3:4.

Proportions

A **proportion** is an equation that states that two ratios are equal.

$$\frac{3}{1} = \frac{12}{4}$$

To solve a proportion, you can use cross-multiplication. If you know three of the quantities in a proportion, you can use cross-multiplication to find the fourth.

Example

Imagine that you are making a scale model of the solar system for your science project. The diameter of Jupiter is 11.2 times the diameter of the Earth. If you are using a plastic-foam ball that has a diameter of 2 cm to represent the Earth, what must the diameter of the ball representing Jupiter be?

$$\frac{11.2}{1} = \frac{x}{2 \text{ cm}}$$

Step 1 Cross-multiply.

$$\frac{11.2}{1} = \frac{x}{2}$$

$$11.2 \times 2 = x \times 1$$

Step 2 Multiply.

$$22.4 = x \times 1$$

$$x = 22.4 \text{ cm}$$

You will need to use a ball that has a diameter of 22.4 cm to represent Jupiter.

Rates

A **rate** is a ratio of two values expressed in different units. A unit rate is a rate with a denominator of 1 unit.

Example

A plant grew 6 centimeters in 2 days. The plant's rate of growth was $\frac{6 \text{ cm}}{2 \text{ days}}$.

To describe the plant's growth in centimeters per day, write a unit rate.

Divide numerator and denominator by 2:

$$\frac{6 \text{ cm}}{2 \text{ days}} = \frac{6 \text{ cm} \div 2}{2 \text{ days} \div 2}$$

Simplify:

$$= \frac{3 \text{ cm}}{1 \text{ day}}$$

Answer The plant's rate of growth is 3 centimeters per day.

Percent

A **percent** is a ratio of a given number to 100. For example, 85% = 85/100. You can use percent to find part of a whole.

Example

What is 85% of 40?

Step 1 Rewrite the percent as a decimal by moving the decimal point two places to the left.

0.85

Step 2 Multiply the decimal by the number that you are calculating the percentage of.

$0.85 \times 40 = 34$

85% of 40 is 34.

Decimals

To **add** or **subtract decimals,** line up the digits vertically so that the decimal points line up. Then, add or subtract the columns from right to left. Carry or borrow numbers as necessary.

Example

Add the following numbers: 3.1415 and 2.96.

Step 1 Line up the digits vertically so that the decimal points line up.

$$\begin{array}{r} 3.1415 \\ +\,2.96 \\ \hline \end{array}$$

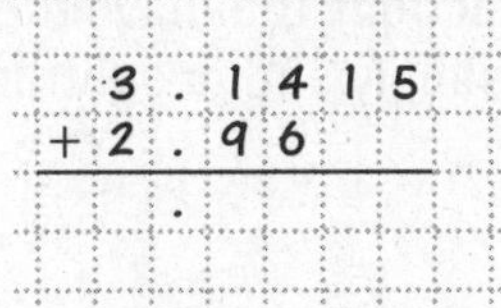

Step 2 Add the columns from right to left, and carry when necessary.

$$\begin{array}{r} 3.1415 \\ +\,2.96 \\ \hline 6.1015 \end{array}$$

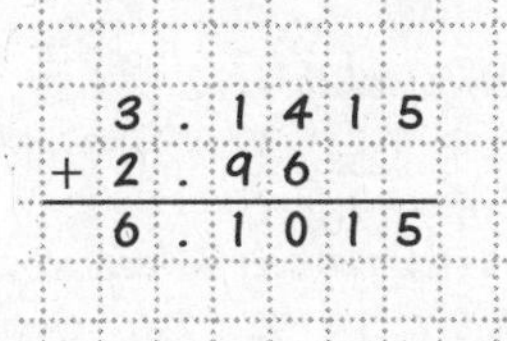

The sum is 6.1015.

Fractions

A **fraction** is a ratio of two nonzero whole numbers.

Example

Your class has 24 plants. Your teacher instructs you to put 6 plants in a shady spot. What fraction of the plants in your class will you put in a shady spot?

Step 1 In the denominator, write the total number of parts in the whole.

$$\frac{?}{24}$$

Step 2 In the numerator, write the number of parts of the whole that are being considered.

$$\frac{6}{24}$$

So, $\frac{6}{24}$ of the plants will be in the shade.

Math Refresher

Simplifying Fractions

It is usually best to express a fraction in its simplest form. Expressing a fraction in its simplest form is called **simplifying a fraction.**

Example

Simplify the fraction $\frac{30}{45}$ to its simplest form.

Step 1 Find the largest whole number that will divide evenly into both the numerator and denominator. This number is called the greatest common factor (GCF).

Factors of the numerator 30:
1, 2, 3, 5, 6, 10, **15**, 30

Factors of the denominator 45:
1, 3, 5, 9, **15**, 45

Step 2 Divide both the numerator and the denominator by the GCF, which in this case is 15.

$$\frac{30}{45} = \frac{30 \div 15}{45 \div 15} = \frac{2}{3}$$

Thus, $\frac{30}{45}$ written in its simplest form is $\frac{2}{3}$.

Adding and Subtracting Fractions

To **add** or **subtract fractions** that have the same denominator, simply add or subtract the numerators.

Examples

$\frac{3}{5} + \frac{1}{5} = ?$ and $\frac{3}{4} - \frac{1}{4} = ?$

Step 1 Add or subtract the numerators.

$\frac{3}{5} + \frac{1}{5} = \frac{4}{\ }$ and $\frac{3}{4} - \frac{1}{4} = \frac{2}{\ }$

Step 2 Write the sum or difference over the denominator.

$\frac{3}{5} + \frac{1}{5} = \frac{4}{5}$ and $\frac{3}{4} - \frac{1}{4} = \frac{2}{4}$

Step 3 If necessary, write the fraction in its simplest form.

$\frac{4}{5}$ cannot be simplified, and $\frac{2}{4} = \frac{1}{2}$.

To **add** or **subtract fractions** that have **different denominators,** first find the least common denominator (LCD)

Examples

$\frac{1}{2} + \frac{1}{6} = ?$ and $\frac{3}{4} - \frac{2}{3} = ?$

Step 1 Write the equivalent fractions that have a common denominator.

$\frac{3}{6} + \frac{1}{6} = ?$ and $\frac{9}{12} - \frac{8}{12} = ?$

Step 2 Add or subtract the fractions.

$\frac{3}{6} + \frac{1}{6} = \frac{4}{6}$ and $\frac{9}{12} - \frac{8}{12} = \frac{1}{12}$

Step 3 If necessary, write the fraction in its simplest form.

$\frac{4}{6} = \frac{2}{3}$, and $\frac{1}{12}$ cannot be simplified.

Multiplying Fractions

To **multiply fractions,** multiply the numerators and the denominators together, and then change the fraction to its simplest form.

Example

$\frac{5}{9} \times \frac{7}{10} = ?$

Step 1 Multiply the numerators and denominators.

$$\frac{5}{9} \times \frac{7}{10} = \frac{5 \times 7}{9 \times 10} = \frac{35}{90}$$

Step 2 Simplify the fraction.

$$\frac{35}{90} = \frac{35 \div 5}{90 \div 5} = \frac{7}{18}$$

Dividing Fractions

To **divide fractions,** first exchange the numerator and the denominator of the divisor (the number you divide by). This number is called the reciprocal of the divisor. Then multiply and simplify if necessary.

Example

$\frac{5}{8} \div \frac{3}{2} = ?$

Step 1 Rewrite the divisor as its reciprocal.

$\frac{3}{2} \rightarrow \frac{2}{3}$

Step 2 Multiply the fractions.

$\frac{5}{8} \times \frac{2}{3} = \frac{5 \times 2}{8 \times 3} = \frac{10}{24}$

Step 3 Simplify the fraction.

$\frac{10}{24} = \frac{10 \div 2}{24 \div 2} = \frac{5}{12}$

Using Significant Figures

The **significant figures** in a decimal are the digits that are warranted by the accuracy of a measuring device.

When you perform a calculation with measurements, the number of significant figures to include in the result depends in part on the number of significant figures in the measurements. When you multiply or divide measurements, your answer should have only as many significant figures as the measurement with the fewest significant figures.

Examples

Using a balance and a graduated cylinder filled with water, you determined that a marble has a mass of 8.0 grams and a volume of 3.5 cubic centimeters. To calculate the density of the marble, divide the mass by the volume.

Write the formula for density: Density $= \frac{\text{mass}}{\text{volume}}$

Substitute measurements: $= \frac{8.0 \text{ g}}{3.5 \text{ cm}^3}$

Use a calculator to divide: $\approx 2.285714286 \text{ g/cm}^3$

Answer Because the mass and the volume have two significant figures each, give the density to two significant figures. The marble has a density of 2.3 grams per cubic centimeter.

Using Scientific Notation

Scientific notation is a shorthand way to write very large or very small numbers. For example, 73,500,000,000,000,000,000,000 kg is the mass of the Moon. In scientific notation, it is 7.35×10^{22} kg. A value written as a number between 1 and 10, times a power of 10, is in scientific notation.

Examples

You can convert from standard form to scientific notation.

Standard Form	Scientific Notation
720,000 5 decimal places left	7.2×10^5 Exponent is 5.
0.000291 4 decimal places right	2.91×10^{-4} Exponent is –4.

You can convert from scientific notation to standard form.

Scientific Notation	Standard Form
4.63×10^7 Exponent is 7.	46,300,000 7 decimal places right
1.08×10^{-6} Exponent is –6.	0.00000108 6 decimal places left

Math Refresher

Making and Interpreting Graphs

Circle Graph

A circle graph, or pie chart, shows how each group of data relates to all of the data. Each part of the circle represents a category of the data. The entire circle represents all of the data. For example, a biologist studying a hardwood forest in Wisconsin found that there were five different types of trees. The data table at right summarizes the biologist's findings.

Wisconsin Hardwood Trees	
Type of tree	**Number found**
Oak	600
Maple	750
Beech	300
Birch	1,200
Hickory	150
Total	3,000

How to Make a Circle Graph

1 To make a circle graph of these data, first find the percentage of each type of tree. Divide the number of trees of each type by the total number of trees, and multiply by 100%.

$$\frac{\text{600 oak}}{\text{3,000 trees}} \times 100\% = 20\%$$

$$\frac{\text{750 maple}}{\text{3,000 trees}} \times 100\% = 25\%$$

$$\frac{\text{300 beech}}{\text{3,000 trees}} \times 100\% = 10\%$$

$$\frac{\text{1,200 birch}}{\text{3,000 trees}} \times 100\% = 40\%$$

$$\frac{\text{150 hickory}}{\text{3,000 trees}} \times 100\% = 5\%$$

A Community of Wisconsin Hardwood Trees

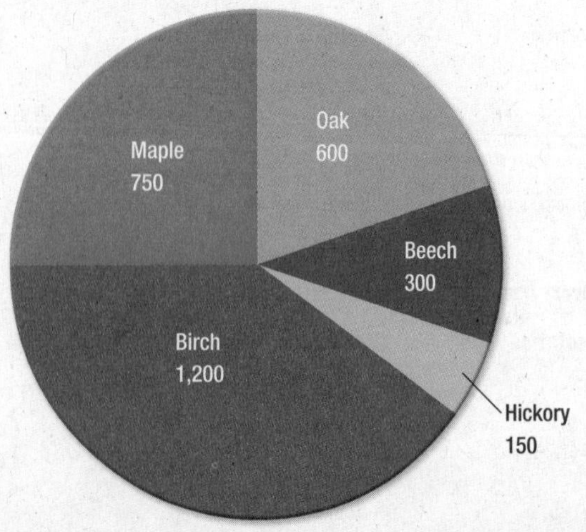

2 Now, determine the size of the wedges that make up the graph. Multiply each percentage by 360°. Remember that a circle contains 360°.

$20\% \times 360° = 72°$ $\quad$ $25\% \times 360° = 90°$

$10\% \times 360° = 36°$ $\quad$ $40\% \times 360° = 144°$

$5\% \times 360° = 18°$

3 Check that the sum of the percentages is 100 and the sum of the degrees is 360.

$$20\% + 25\% + 10\% + 40\% + 5\% = 100\%$$

$$72° + 90° + 36° + 144° + 18° = 360°$$

4 Use a compass to draw a circle and mark the center of the circle.

5 Then, use a protractor to draw angles of 72°, 90°, 36°, 144°, and 18° in the circle.

6 Finally, label each part of the graph, and choose an appropriate title.

Line Graphs

Line graphs are most often used to demonstrate continuous change. For example, Mr. Smith's students analyzed the population records for their hometown, Appleton, between 1910 and 2010. Examine the data at right.

Because the year and the population change, they are the variables. The population is determined by, or dependent on, the year. Therefore, the population is called the **dependent variable,** and the year is called the **independent variable**. Each year and its population make a **data pair.** To prepare a line graph, you must first organize data pairs into a table like the one at right.

Population of Appleton, 1910–2010	
Year	**Population**
1910	1,800
1930	2,500
1950	3,200
1970	3,900
1990	4,600
2010	5,300

How to Make a Line Graph

1 Place the independent variable along the horizontal (x) axis. Place the dependent variable along the vertical (y) axis.

2 Label the x-axis "Year" and the y-axis "Population." Look at your greatest and least values for the population. For the y-axis, determine a scale that will provide enough space to show these values. You must use the same scale for the entire length of the axis. Next, find an appropriate scale for the x-axis.

3 Choose reasonable starting points for each axis.

4 Plot the data pairs as accurately as possible.

5 Choose a title that accurately represents the data.

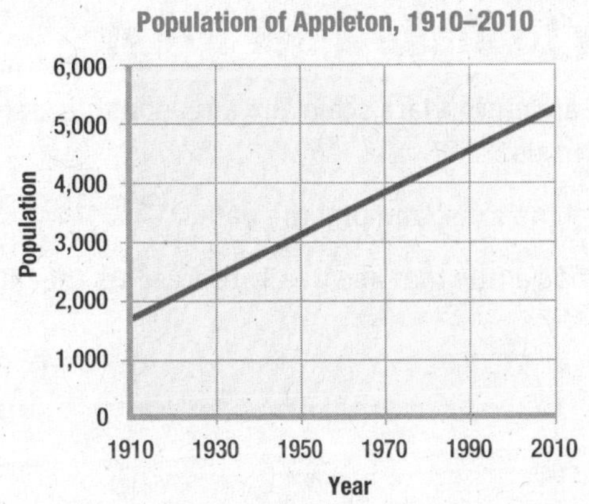

How to Determine Slope

Slope is the ratio of the change in the y-value to the change in the x-value, or "rise over run."

1 Choose two points on the line graph. For example, the population of Appleton in 2010 was 5,300 people. Therefore, you can define point A as (2010, 5,300). In 1910, the population was 1,800 people. You can define point B as (1910, 1,800).

2 Find the change in the y-value.
(y at point A) − (y at point B) =
5,300 people − 1,800 people =
3,500 people

3 Find the change in the x-value.
(x at point A) − (x at point B) =
2010 − 1910 = 100 years

4 Calculate the slope of the graph by dividing the change in y by the change in x.

$$slope = \frac{change\ in\ y}{change\ in\ x}$$

$$slope = \frac{3{,}500 \text{ people}}{100 \text{ years}}$$

$$slope = 35 \text{ people per year}$$

In this example, the population in Appleton increased by a fixed amount each year. The graph of these data is a straight line. Therefore, the relationship is **linear.** When the graph of a set of data is not a straight line, the relationship is **nonlinear.**

Bar Graphs

Bar graphs can be used to demonstrate change that is not continuous. These graphs can be used to indicate trends when the data cover a long period of time. A meteorologist gathered the precipitation data shown here for Summerville for April 1–15 and used a bar graph to represent the data.

Precipitation in Summerville, April 1–15			
Date	Precipitation (cm)	Date	Precipitation (cm)
April 1	0.5	April 9	0.25
April 2	1.25	April 10	0.0
April 3	0.0	April 11	1.0
April 4	0.0	April 12	0.0
April 5	0.0	April 13	0.25
April 6	0.0	April 14	0.0
April 7	0.0	April 15	6.50
April 8	1.75		

How to Make a Bar Graph

1 Use an appropriate scale and a reasonable starting point for each axis.

2 Label the axes, and plot the data.

3 Choose a title that accurately represents the data.

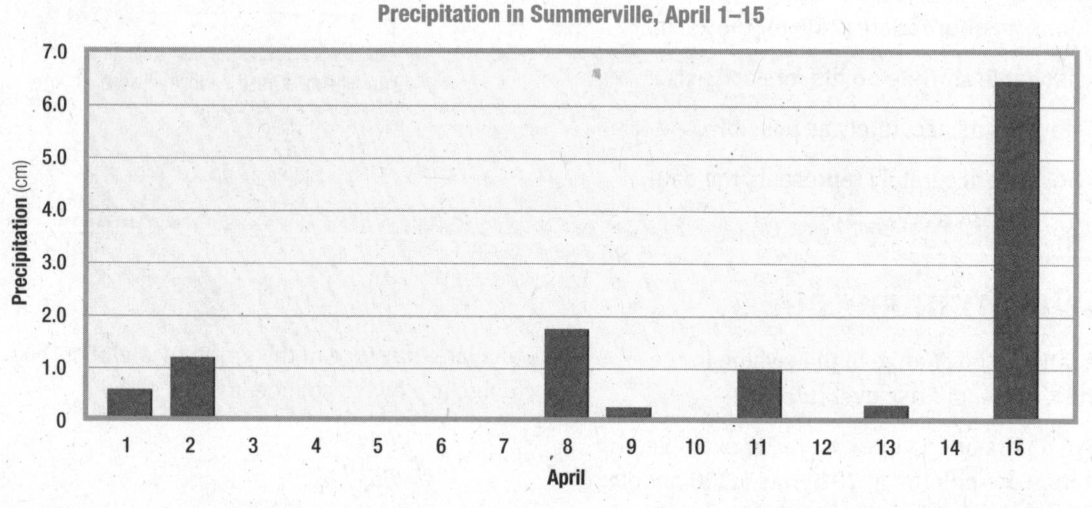

Glossary

Pronunciation Key

Sound	Symbol	Example	Respelling
ă	a	pat	PAT
ā	ay	pay	PAY
âr	air	care	KAIR
ä	ah	father	FAH•ther
är	ar	argue	AR•gyoo
ch	ch	chase	CHAYS
ĕ	e	pet	PET
ĕ (at end of a syllable)	eh	settee lessee	seh•TEE leh•SEE
ĕr	ehr	merry	MEHR•ee
ē	ee	beach	BEECH
g	g	gas	GAS
ĭ	i	pit	PIT
ĭ (at end of a syllable)	ih	guitar	gih•TAR
ī	y eye (only for a complete syllable)	pie island	PY EYE•luhnd
îr	ir	hear	HIR
j	j	germ	JERM
k	k	kick	KIK
ng	ng	thing	THING
ngk	ngk	bank	BANGK

Sound	Symbol	Example	Respelling
ŏ	ah	bottle	BAHT'l
ō	oh	toe	TOH
ô	aw	caught	KAWT
ôr	ohr	roar	ROHR
oi	oy	noisy	NOYZ•ee
ŏŏ	u	book	BUK
o͞o	oo	boot	BOOT
ou	ow	pound	POWND
s	s	center	SEN•ter
sh	sh	cache	CASH
ŭ	uh	flood	FLUHD
ûr	er	bird	BERD
z	z	xylophone	ZY•luh•fohn
z	z	bags	BAGZ
zh	zh	decision	dih•SIZH•uhn
ə	uh	around broken focus	uh•ROWND BROH•kuhn FOH•kuhs
ər	er	winner	WIN•er
th	th	thin they	THIN THAY
w	w	one	WUHN
wh	hw	whether	HWETH•er

Glossary

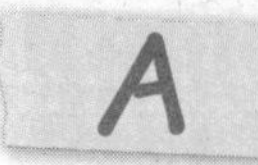

abrasion (uh•BRAY•zhuhn) the process by which rock is reduced in size by the scraping action of other rocks driven by water, wind, and gravity (75)
abrasión proceso por el cual se reduce el tamaño de las rocas debido al efecto de desgaste de otras rocas arrastradas por el agua, el viento o la gravedad

acceleration (ack•SELL•uh•ray•shuhn) the rate at which velocity changes over time; an object accelerates if its speed, direction, or both change (328)
aceleración la tasa a la que la velocidad cambia con el tiempo; un objeto acelera si su rapidez cambia, si su dirección cambia, o si tanto su rapidez como su dirección cambian

acid precipitation (AS•id prih•sip•ih•TAY•shun) precipitation, such as rain, sleet, or snow, that contains a high concentration of acids, often because of the pollution of the atmosphere (76)
precipitación ácida precipitación tal como lluvia, aguanieve o nieve, que contiene una alta concentración de ácidos debido a la contaminación de la atmósfera

active transport the movement of chemical substances, usually across the cell membrane, against a concentration gradient; requires cells to use energy (421)
transporte activo el movimiento de sustancias químicas, normalmente a través de la membrana celular, en contra de un gradiente de concentración; requiere que la célula gaste energía

air mass a large body of air throughout which temperature and moisture content are similar (232)
masa de aire un gran volumen de aire, cuya temperatura y cuyo contenido de humedad son similares en toda su extensión

air pressure the measure of the force with which air molecules push on a surface (147, 224)
presión del aire la medida de la fuerza con la que las moléculas del aire empujan contra una superficie

alluvial fan a fan-shaped mass of rock material deposited by a stream when the slope of the land decreases sharply (85)
abanico aluvial masa en forma de abanico de materiales depositados por un arroyo cuando la pendiente del terreno disminuye bruscamente

alveolus tiny, thin-walled, capillary-rich sac in the lungs where the exchange of oxygen and carbon dioxide takes place; also called air sac (488)
alveolo saco diminuto ubicado en los pulmones, de paredes delgadas y rico en capilares, en donde ocurre el intercambio de oxígeno y dióxido de carbono

Animalia a kingdom made up of complex, multicellular organisms that lack cell walls, can usually move around, and quickly respond to their environment (434)
Animalia un reino formado por organismos pluricelulares complejos que no tienen pared celular, normalmente son capaces de moverse y reaccionan rápidamente a su ambiente

antibiotic medicine used to kill bacteria and other microorganisms (564)
antibiótico medicina utilizada para matar bacterias y otros microorganismos

antibody a protein made by B cells that binds to a specific antigen (548)
anticuerpo una proteína producida por las células B que se une a un antígeno específico

antiviral drug a drug that destroys viruses or prevents their growth or replication (564)
medicamento antiviral un medicamento que destruye a los virus o que evita que crezcan o se reproduzcan

Archaea a domain made up of prokaryotes most of which are known to live in extreme environments that are distinguished from other prokaryotes by differences in their genetics and in the makeup of their cell wall (432)
Archaea un dominio compuesto por procariotes la mayoría de los cuales viven en ambientes extremos que se distinguen de otros procariotes por su genética y por la composición de su pared celular

artery a blood vessel that carries blood away from the heart to the body's organs (483)
arteria un vaso sanguíneo que transporta sangre del corazón a los órganos del cuerpo

atmosphere a mixture of gases that surrounds a planet, moon, or other celestial body (136, 146)
atmósfera una mezcla de gases que rodea un planeta, una luna, u otras cuerpos celestes

atom the smallest unit of an element that maintains the properties of that element (382)
átomo la unidad más pequeña de un elemento que conserva las propiedades de ese elemento

axon an elongated extension of a neuron that carries impulses away from the cell body (511)
axón una extensión alargada de una neurona que transporta impulsos hacia fuera del cuerpo de la célula

B

B cell a white blood cell that makes antibodies (548)
célula B un glóbulo blanco de la sangre que fabrica anticuerpos

Bacteria a domain made up of prokaryotes that usually have a cell wall and that usually reproduce by cell division (432)
Bacteria un dominio compuesto por procariotes que por lo general tienen pared celular y se reproducen por división celular

barrier island a long ridge of sand or narrow island that lies parallel to the shore (90)
isla barrera un largo arrecife de arena o una isla angosta ubicada paralela a la costa

beach an area of the shoreline that is made up of deposited sediment (90)
playa un área de la costa que está formada por sedimento depositado

biosphere the part of Earth where life exists; includes all of the living organisms on Earth (137)
biosfera la parte de la Tierra donde existe la vida; comprende todos los seres vivos de la Tierra

blood (BLUHD) the fluid that carries oxygen and nutrients to the body and that is made up of platelets, white blood cells, red blood cells, and plasma (478)
sangre el líquido que le lleva oxígeno y nutrientes al cuerpo y que está hecho de plaquetas, glóbulos blancos, glóbulos rojos y plasma

brain the organ that is the main control center of the nervous system (509)
encéfalo el órgano que es el centro principal de control del sistema nervioso

bronchus one of the two main branches of the trachea that lead directly to the lungs plural, bronchii (488)
bronquio una de las dos ramificaciones principales de la tráquea que conducen directamente a los pulmones

C

capillary a tiny blood vessel that allows an exchange between blood and cells in tissue (483)
capilar diminuto vaso sanguíneo que permite el intercambio entre la sangre y las células de los tejidos

carbohydrate a class of molecules that includes sugars, starches, and fiber; contains carbon, hydrogen, and oxygen (385)
carbohidrato una clase de moléculas entre las que se incluyen azúcares, almidones y fibra; contiene carbono, hidrógeno y oxígeno

cardiovascular system a collection of organs that transport blood throughout the body; the organs in this system include the heart, the arteries, and the veins (478)
aparato cardiovascular un conjunto de órganos que transportan la sangre a través del cuerpo; los órganos de este sistema incluyen al corazón, las arterias y las venas

cell (SEL) in biology, the smallest unit that can perform all life processes; cells are covered by a membrane and contain DNA and cytoplasm (372)
célula en biología, la unidad más pequeña que puede realizar todos los procesos vitales; las células están cubiertas por una membrana y tienen ADN y citoplasma

cell membrane a phospholipid layer that covers a cell's surface and acts as a barrier between the inside of a cell and the cell's environment (376)
membrana celular una capa de fosfolípidos que cubre la superficie de la célula y funciona como una barrera entre el interior de la célula y el ambiente de la célula

cellular respiration the process by which cells use oxygen to produce energy from food (418)
respiración celular el proceso por medio del cual las células utilizan oxígeno para producir energía a partir de los alimentos

cell wall a rigid structure that surrounds the cell membrane and provides support to the cell (396)
pared celular una estructura rígida que rodea la membrana celular y le brinda soporte a la célula

centripetal acceleration (sehn•TRIP•ih•tahl ack•SELL•uh•ray•shuhn) the acceleration directed toward the center of a circular path (331)
aceleración centrípeta la aceleración que se dirige hacia el centro de un camino circular

chemical weathering (KEM•ih•kuhl WETH•er•ing) the chemical breakdown and decomposition of rocks by natural processes in the environment (76)
desgaste químico la descomposición química que sufren las rocas por procesos naturales del entorno

chloroplast (KLOHR•oh•plahstz) an organelle found in plant and algae cells where photosynthesis occurs (397)
cloroplasto un organelo que se encuentra en las células vegetales y en las células de las algas, en el cual se lleva a cabo la fotosíntesis

climate the weather conditions in an area over a long period of time (276)
clima las condiciones del tiempo en un área durante un largo período de tiempo

coastline (KOHST•lyn) a location where land and ocean surface meet (116)
costa el lugar donde se encuentran la superficie del terreno y la del océano

condensation (kahn•den•SAY•shuhn) the change of state from a gas to a liquid (211)
condensación el cambio de estado de gas a líquido

conduction (kuhn•DUHK•shuhn) the transfer of energy as heat through a material (164)
conducción la transferencia de energía en forma de calor a través del contacto directo

convection (kun•DUHK•shuhn) the movement of matter due to differences in density that are caused by temperature variations; can result in the transfer of energy as heat (162)
convección el movimiento de la materia debido a diferencias en la densidad que se producen por variaciones en la temperatura; puede resultar en la transferencia de energía en forma de calor

convection current (kuhn•VEK•shuhn) any movement of matter that results from differences in density; may be vertical, circular, or cyclical (189)
corriente de convección cualquier movimiento de la materia que se produce como resultado de diferencias en la densidad; puede ser vertical, circular o cíclico

Coriolis effect (kawr•ee•OH•lis ih•FEKT) the curving of the path of a moving object from an otherwise straight path due to Earth's rotation (171, 185)
efecto de Coriolis la desviación de la trayectoria recta que experimentan los objetos en movimiento debido a la rotación de la Tierra

creep the slow downhill movement of weathered rock material (104)
arrastre el movimiento lento y descendente de materiales rocosos desgastados

cryosphere (KRY•oh•sfir) one of Earth's spheres where water is in solid form, including snow cover, floating ice, glaciers, ice caps, ice sheets, and frozen ground permafrost (135)
criosfera una de las esferas de la Tierra donde el agua se encuentra en estado sólido en forma de capas de nieve, hielos flotantes, glaciares, campos de hielo, capas de hielo continentales y porciones de suelo permanentemente congeladas permafrost

cytoplasm (SY•tuh•plaz•uhm) the region of the cell within the membrane that includes the fluid, the cytoskeleton, and all of the organelles except the nucleus (376)
citoplasma la región de la célula dentro de la membrana, que incluye el líquido, el citoesqueleto y los organelos, pero no el núcleo

cytoskeleton (KRY•oh•sfir) the cytoplasmic network of protein filaments that plays an essential role in cell movement, shape, and division (393)
citoesqueleto la red citoplásmica de filamentos de proteínas que juega un papel esencial en el movimiento, forma y división de la célula

D

data (DAY•tuh) information gathered by observation or experimentation that can be used in calculating or reasoning (29)
datos la información recopilada por medio de la observación o experimentación que puede usarse para hacer cálculos o razonar

deep current a streamlike movement of ocean water far below the surface (188)
corriente profunda un movimiento del agua del océano que es similar a una corriente y ocurre debajo de la superficie

delta (DEL•tuh) a mass of material deposited in a triangular or fan shape at the mouth of a river or stream (85, 115)
delta un depósito de materiales en forma de triángulo o abanico ubicado en la desembocadura de un río

dendrite (DEN•dryt) branchlike extension of a neuron that receives impulses from neighboring neurons (511)
dendrita la extensión ramificada de una neurona que recibe impulsos de las neuronas vecinas

deposition the process in which material is laid down (82)
deposición el proceso por medio del cual un material se deposita

dew point at constant pressure and water vapor content, the temperature at which the rate of condensation equals the rate of evaporation (221)
punto de rocío a presión y contenido de vapor de agua constantes, la temperatura a la que la tasa de condensación es igual a la tasa de evaporación

dichotomous key (di•KOT•uh•muhs KEE) an aid that is used to identify organisms and that consists of the answers to a series of questions (436)
clave dicotómica una ayuda para identificar organismos, que consiste en las respuestas a una serie de preguntas

diffusion the movement of particles from regions of higher concentration to regions of lower concentration (420)
difusión el movimiento de partículas de regiones de mayor concentración a regiones de menor concentración

digestive system the organs that break down food so that it can be used by the body (496)
aparato digestivo los órganos que descomponen la comida de modo que el cuerpo la pueda usar

domain in a taxonomic system, one of the three broad groups that all living things fall into (432)
dominio en un sistema taxonómico, uno de los tres amplios grupos al que pertenecen todos los seres vivos

dune a mound of wind-deposited sand that moves as a result of the action of wind (99, 117)
duna un montículo de arena depositada por el viento que se mueve como resultado de la acción de éste

E

Earth system all of the nonliving things, living things, and processes that make up the planet Earth, including the solid Earth, the hydrosphere, the atmosphere, and the biosphere (132)
sistema terrestre todos los seres vivos y no vivos y los procesos que componen el planeta Tierra, incluidas la Tierra sólida, la hidrosfera, la atmósfera y la biosfera

egg a sex cell produced by a female (523)
óvulo una célula sexual producida por una hembra

elevation the height of an object above sea level (280)
elevación la altura de un objeto sobre el nivel del mar

embryo in humans, a developing individual from first division after fertilization through the 10th week of pregnancy (525)
embrión en los seres humanos, un individuo en desarrollo desde la primera división después de la fecundación hasta el final de la décima semana de embarazo

empirical evidence (em•PIR•ih•kuhl EV•ih•duhns) the observations, measurements, and other types of data that people gather and test to support and evaluate scientific explanations (8)
evidencia empírica las observaciones, mediciones y demás tipos de datos que se recopilan y examinan para apoyar y evaluar explicaciones científicas

endocrine system a collection of glands and groups of cells that secrete hormones that regulate growth, development, and homeostasis; includes the pituitary, thyroid, parathyroid, and adrenal glands, the hypothalamus, the pineal body, and the gonads (514)
sistema endocrino un conjunto de glándulas y grupos de células que secretan hormonas las cuales regulan el crecimiento, desarrollo y homeostasis; incluye las glándulas pituitaria, tiroides, paratiroides y suprarrenal, el hipotálamo, el cuerpo pineal y las gónadas

endocytosis (en•doh•sye•TOH•sis) the process by which a cell membrane surrounds a particle and encloses the particle in a vesicle to bring the particle into the cell (422)
endocitosis el proceso por medio del cual la membrana celular rodea una partícula y la encierra en una vesícula para llevarla al interior de la célula

endoplasmic reticulum (ehn•doh•PLAHZ•mick rhett•ICK•yoo•luhm) a system of membranes that is found in a cell's cytoplasm and that assists in the production, processing, and transport of proteins and in the production of lipids (395)
retículo endoplásmico un sistema de membranas que se encuentra en el citoplasma de la célula y que tiene una función en la producción, procesamiento y transporte de proteínas y en la producción de lípidos

energy (EN•er•jee) the ability to do work or to cause a change (302)
energía la capacidad para trabajar o causar un cambio

enzyme (EN•zym) a type of protein that speeds up metabolic reactions in plants and animals without being permanently changed or destroyed (497)
enzima un tipo de proteína que acelera las reacciones metabólicas en las plantas y animales, sin ser modificada permanentemente ni ser destruida

erosion the process by which wind, water, ice, or gravity transports soil and sediment from one location to another (82)
erosión el proceso por medio del cual el viento, el agua, el hielo o la gravedad transporta tierra y sedimentos de un lugar a otro

esophagus (ih•SAWF•uh•gus) a long, straight tube that connects the pharynx to the stomach (498)
esófago un conducto largo y recto que conecta la faringe con el estómago

Eukarya in a modern taxonomic system, a domain made up of all eukaryotes; this domain aligns with the traditional kingdoms Protista, Fungi, Plantae, and Animalia (433)
Eukarya en un sistema taxonómico moderno, un dominio compuesto por todos los eucariotes; este dominio coincide con los reinos tradicionales Protista, Fungi, Plantae y Animalia

eukaryote (yoo•KAIR•ee•oht) an organism made up of cells that have a nucleus enclosed by a membrane; eukaryotes include protists, animals, plants, and fungi but not archaea or bacteria (377)
eucariote un organismo cuyas células tienen un núcleo contenido en una membrana; entre los eucariotes se encuentran protistas, animales, plantas y hongos, pero no arqueas ni bacterias

evaporation the change of state from a liquid to a gas (210)
evaporación el cambio de estado de líquido a gas

excretory system (EK•skrih•tohr•ee SIS•tuhm) the system that collects and excretes nitrogenous wastes and excess water from the body in the form of urine (501)
aparato excretor el sistema que recolecta y elimina del cuerpo los desperdicios nitrogenados y el exceso de agua en forma de orina

exocytosis (ek•soh•sye•TOH•sis) the process in which a cell releases a particle by enclosing the particle in a vesicle that then moves to the cell surface and fuses with the cell membrane (422)
exocitosis el proceso por medio del cual una célula libera una partícula encerrándola en una vesícula que luego se traslada a la superficie de la célula y se fusiona con la membrana celular

experiment (ik•SPEHR•uh•muhnt) an organized procedure to study something under controlled conditions (26)
experimento un procedimiento organizado que se lleva a cabo bajo condiciones controladas para estudiar algo

F

fetus a developing human from the end of the 10th week of pregnancy until birth (526)
feto un ser humano en desarrollo desde el final de la décima semana del embarazo hasta el nacimiento

floodplain an area along a river that forms from sediments deposited when the river overflows its banks (85)
llanura de inundación un área a lo largo de un río formada por sedimentos que se depositan cuando el río se desborda

force a push or a pull; something that changes the motion of an objec (336)
fuerza un empuje o un jalo'n; algo que cambia el movimiento de un objeto

free fall the motion of a body when only the force of gravity is acting on the body (356)
caída libre el movimiento de un cuerpo cuando la única fuerza que actúa sobre él es la fuerza de gravedad

front the boundary between air masses of different densities and usually different temperatures (232)
frente el límite entre masas de aire de diferentes densidades y, normalmente, diferentes temperaturas

function the special, normal, or proper activity of an organ or part (408)
función la actividad especial, normal o adecuada de un órgano o parte

Fungi a kingdom made up of nongreen, eukaryotic organisms that reproduce by using spores, and get food by breaking down substances in their surroundings and absorbing the nutrients (434)
Hongos reino compuesto por organismos eucarióticos sin clorofila que se reproducen por medio de esporas y que, para alimentarse, descomponen sustancias del ambiente y absorben sus nutrientes

genus (JEE•nuhs) the level of classification that comes after family and that contains similar species (430)
género el nivel de clasificación que viene después de la familia y que contiene especies similares

geosphere the mostly solid, rocky part of Earth; extends from the center of the core to the surface of the crust (133)
geosfera la capa de la Tierra que es principalmente sólida y rocosa; se extiende desde el centro del núcleo hasta la superficie de la corteza terrestre

glacial drift the rock material carried and deposited by glaciers (100)
deriva glacial el material rocoso que es transportado y depositado por los glaciares

glacier (GLAY•sher) a large mass of ice that exists year-round and moves over land (100, 113)
glaciar una masa grande de hielo que existe durante todo el año y se mueve sobre la tierra

gland (GLAND) a group of cells that make chemicals for use elsewhere in the body (514)
glándula un grupo de células que elaboran sustancias químicas para su utilización en otra parte del cuerpo

global wind (GLOH•buhl WIND) the movement of air over Earth's surface in patterms that are worldwide (172)
viento global el movimiento del aire sobre la superficie terrestre según patrones globales

Golgi complex (GOHL•ghee COHM•plehkz) a cell organelle that helps make and package materials to be transported out of the cell (395)
aparato de Golgi un organelo celular que ayuda a hacer y a empacar los materiales que serán transportados al exterior de la célula

gravity a force of attraction between objects that is due to their masses (352)
gravedad una fuerza de atracción entre dos objetos debido a sus masas

greenhouse effect the warming of the surface and lower atmosphere of Earth that occurs when water vapor, carbon dioxide, and other gases absorb and reradiate thermal energy (151)
efecto invernadero el calentamiento de la superficie y de la parte más baja de la atmósfera, el cual se produce cuando el vapor de agua, el dióxido de carbono y otros gases absorben y vuelven a irradiar la energía térmica

groundwater the water that is beneath Earth's surface (86)
agua subterránea el agua que está debajo de la superficie de la Tierra

heat the energy transferred between objects that are at different temperatures (158)
calor la transferencia de energía entre objetos que están a temperaturas diferentes

high-pressure system (HY PRESH•er SIS•tuhm) a usually calm and clear weather system that forms when air sinks down in a high-pressure center and spreads out near the ground toward areas of low pressure (234)
sistema de alta presión un sistema meteorológico comúnmente calmo y claro que se forma cuando el aire se hunde en un centro de alta presión y se dispersa cerca del suelo hacia áreas de baja presión

homeostasis (hoh•mee•oh•STAY•sis) the maintenance of a constant internal state in a changing environment (416, 458)
homeostasis la capacidad de mantener un estado interno constante en un ambiente en cambio

hormone a substance that is made in one cell or tissue and that causes a change in another cell or tissue in a different part of the body (514)
hormona una sustancia que es producida en una célula o tejido, la cual causa un cambio en otra célula o tejido ubicado en una parte diferente del cuerpo

humidity the amount of water vapor in the air (221)
humedad la cantidad de vapor de agua que hay en el aire

hurricane (HER•ih•kayn) a severe storm that develops over tropical oceans and whose strong winds of more than 119 km/h spiral in toward the intensely low-pressure storm center (248)
huracán una tormenta severa que se desarrolla sobre océanos tropicales, con vientos fuertes que soplan a más de 119 km/h y que se mueven en espiral hacia el centro de presión extremadamente baja de la tormenta

hydrosphere the portion of Earth that is water (134)
hidrosfera la porción de la Tierra que es agua

hypothesis (hy•PAHTH•eh•sys) a testable idea or explanation that leads to scientific investigation (28)
hipótesis una idea o explicación que conlleva a la investigación científica y que se puede probar

immune system the cells and tissues that recognize and attack foreign substances in the body (547)
sistema inmunológico las células y tejidos que reconocen y atacan sustancias extrañas en el cuerpo

immunity the ability to resist or recover from an infectious disease (550)
inmunidad la capacidad de resistir una enfermedad infecciosa o recuperarse de ella

inertia (ih•NER•shuh) the resistance of an object to change in the speed or direction of its motion (341)
inercia la resistencia de un objeto al cambio de la velocidad o de la direccio'n de su movimiento

infectious disease a disease that is caused by a pathogen and that can be spread from one individual to another (559)
enfermedad infecciosa una enfermedad que es causada por un patógeno y que puede transmitirse de un individuo a otro

jet stream a narrow band of strong winds that blow in the upper troposphere (174, 237)
corriente en chorro un cinturón delgado de vientos fuertes que soplan en la parte superior de la troposfera

joint a place where two or more bones meet (468)
articulación un lugar donde se unen dos o más huesos

kidney one of the organs that filter water and wastes from the blood, excrete products as urine, and regulate the concentration of certain substances in the blood (502)
riñón uno de los órganos que filtran el agua y los desechos de la sangre, excretan productos como orina y regulan la concentración de ciertas sustancias en la sangre

kinetic energy (kuh•NET•ik) the energy of an object that is due to the object's motion (303)
energía cinética la energía de un objeto debido al movimiento del objeto

lake (LAYK) a filled or partially filled basin of fresh or salt water surrounded by land (114)
lago una cuenca de agua dulce o salada total o parcialmente llena y rodeada de tierra

landslide the sudden movement of rock and soil down a slope (105)
derrumbamiento el movimiento súbito hacia abajo de rocas y suelo por una pendiente

large intestine the broader and shorter portion of the intestine, where water is removed from the mostly digested food to turn the waste into semisolid feces, or stool (499)
intestino grueso la porción más ancha y más corta del intestino, donde el agua se elimina de la mayoría de los alimentos digeridos para convertir los desechos en heces semisólidas o excremento

larynx (LAR•ingks) the part of the respiratory system between the pharynx and the trachea; has walls of cartilage and muscle and contains the vocal cords (488)
laringe la parte del aparato respiratorio que se encuentra entre la faringe y la tráquea; tiene paredes de cartílago y músculo y contiene las cuerdas vocales

latitude (LAHT•ih•tood) the angular distance north or south from the equator; expressed in degrees (278)
latitud la distancia angular hacia el norte o hacia el sur del ecuador; se expresa en grados

law a descriptive statement or equation that reliably predicts events under certain conditions (18)
ley una ecuación o afirmación descriptiva que predice sucesos de manera confiable en determinadas condiciones

law of conservation of energy the law that states that energy cannot be created or destroyed but can be changed from one form to another (307)
ley de la conservación de la energía la ley que establece que la energía ni se crea ni se destruye, sólo se transforma de una forma a otra

ligament a type of tissue that holds together the bones in a joint (466)
ligamento un tipo de tejido que mantiene unidos los huesos en una articulación

lightning an electric discharge that takes place between two oppositely charged surfaces, such as between a cloud and the ground, between two clouds, or between two parts of the same cloud (247)
relámpago una descarga eléctrica que ocurre entre dos superficies que tienen carga opuesta, como por ejemplo, entre una nube y el suelo, entre dos nubes o entres dos partes de la misma nube

lipid a fat molecule or a molecule that has similar properties; examples include oils, waxes, and steroids (384)
lípido una molécula de grasa o una molécula que tiene propiedades similares; algunos ejemplos son los aceites, las ceras y los esteroides

liver the largest organ in the body; it makes bile, stores and filters blood, and stores excess sugars as glycogen (500)
hígado el órgano más grande del cuerpo; produce bilis, almacena y filtra la sangre, y almacena el exceso de azúcares en forma de glucógeno

local wind (LOH•kuhl WIND) the movement of air over short distances; occurs in specific areas as a result of certain geographical features (176)
viento local el movimiento del aire a través de distancias cortas; se produce en áreas específicas como resultado de ciertas características geográficas

loess (LOH•uhs) fine-grained sediments of quartz, feldspar, hornblende, mica, and clay deposited by the wind (99)
loess sedimentos de grano fino de cuarzo, feldespato, horneblenda, mica y arcilla depositados por el viento

low-pressure system (LOH PRESH•er SIS•tuhm) a big and often stormy weather system that forms when air circles into a low-pressure center, then moves up to higher altitudes (234)
sistema de baja presión un sistema meteorológico grande y a menudo tormentoso que se forma cuando el aire circula alrededor de un centro de baja presión y luego sube a mayor altura

lymph (LIMF) the clear, watery fluid that leaks from blood vessels and contains white blood cells; circulates in lymphatic system; returned to bloodstream through lymph vessels (478)
linfa el fluido claro y acuoso que se filtra de los vasos sanguíneos y contiene glóbulos blancos; circula por el sistema linfático; regresa al torrente sanguíneo a través de los vasos linfáticos

lymph node (LIMF NOHD) small, bean-shaped masses of tissue that remove pathogens and dead cells from the lymph; concentrated in the armpits, neck, and groin; high concentration of white blood cells found in lymph nodes (480)
nodo linfático masas de tejido pequeñas y con forma de frijol que eliminan los patógenos y las células muertas de la linfa; están concentrados en las axilas, el cuello y la ingle; los nodos linfáticos presentan una alta concentración de glóbulos blancos

lymphatic system (lim•FAT•ik SIS•tuhm) a network of organs and tissues that collect the fluid that leaks from blood and returns it to blood vessels; includes lymph nodes, lymph vessels, and lymph; the place where certain white blood cells mature (478)
sistema linfático una red de órganos y tejidos que recolectan el fluido que se filtra de la sangre y lo regresan a los vasos sanguíneos; incluye los nodos linfáticos, los vasos linfáticos y la linfa; el lugar donde maduran ciertos glóbulos blancos

lysosome (LY•soh•zohmz) a cell organelle that contains digestive enzymes (398)
lisosoma un organelo celular que contiene enzimas digestivas

macrophage (MAK•ruh•faj) an immune system cell that engulfs pathogens and other materials (548)
macrófago una célula del sistema inmunológico que envuelve a los patógenos y otros materiales

mechanical energy (meh•KAN•ih•kuhl) the amount of work an object can do because of the object's kinetic and potential energies (306)
energía mecánica la cantidad de trabajo que un objeto realiza debido a las energías cinética y potencial del objeto

mesosphere (MEZ•uh•sfir) 1. the strong, lower part of the mantle between the asthenosphere and the outer core, 2. the layer of the atmosphere between the stratosphere and the thermosphere and in which temperature decreases as altitude increases (148)
mesosfera 1. la parte fuerte e inferior del manto que se encuentra entre la astenosfera y el núcleo externo, 2. la capa de la atmósfera que se encuentra entre la estratosfera y la termosfera, en la cual la temperatura disminuye al aumentar la altitud

mitochondrion (myt•uh•KAHN•dree•uhn) in eukaryotic cells, the organelle that is the site of cellular respiration, which releases energy for use by the cell (394)
mitocondria en las células eucarióticas, el organelo donde se lleva a cabo la respiración celular, la cual libera energía para que utilice la célula

mitosis (my•TOH•sis) in eukaryotic cells, a process of cell division that forms two new nuclei, each of which has the same number of chromosomes (419)
mitosis en las células eucarióticas, un proceso de división celular que forma dos núcleos nuevos, cada uno de los cuales posee el mismo número de cromosomas

model a pattern, plan, representation, or description designed to show the structure or workings of an object, system, or concept (17, 44)
modelo un diseño, plan, representación o descripción cuyo objetivo es mostrar la estructura o funcionamiento de un objeto, sistema o concepto

molecule (MAHL•ih•kyool) a group of atoms that are held together by chemical bonds; a molecule is the smallest unit of a substance that can exist by itself and retain all of the substance's chemical properties (383)
molécula un grupo de átomos unidos por enlaces químicos; una molécula es la unidad más pequeña de una sustancia que puede existir por sí misma y conservar todas las propiedades químicas de esa sustancia

motion (MOH•shuhn) a change in position over time (316)
movimiento un cambio de posición en el tiempo

mountain an area of significantly increased elevation on Earth's surface, usually rising to a summit (112)
montaña elevación considerable sobre la superficie terrestre que alcanza su punto más alto en la cima

muck fire a fire that burns organic material in the soil (268)
incendio de subsuelo incendio que quema el material orgánico del suelo

mudflow the flow of a mass of mud or rock and soil mixed with a large amount of water (105)
flujo de lodo el flujo de una masa de lodo o roca y suelo mezclados con una gran cantidad de agua

muscular system a collection of muscles whose primary function is movement and flexibility (470)
sistema muscular un conjunto de músculos cuya función principal es permitir el movimiento y la flexibilidad

nephron (NEF•rahnz) the unit in the kidney that filters blood (502)
nefrona la unidad del riñón que filtra la sangre

nervous system the structures that control the actions and reactions of the body in response to stimuli from the environment; it is formed by billions of specialized nerve cells, called neurons (508)
sistema nervioso las estructuras que controlan las acciones y reacciones del cuerpo en respuesta a los estímulos del ambiente; está formado por miles de millones de células nerviosas especializadas, llamadas neuronas

net force the combination of all of the forces acting on an object (338)
fuerza neta la combinación de todas las fuerzas que actúan sobre un objeto

neuron a nerve cell that is specialized to receive and conduct electrical impulses (510)
neurona una célula nerviosa que está especializada en recibir y transmitir impulsos eléctricos

noninfectious disease a disease that is caused by hereditary factors, environmental factors, or a combination of the two (558)
enfermedad no infecciosa una enfermedad que no se contagia de una persona a otra

nucleic acid a molecule made up of nucleotide subunits that carries information in cells (385)
ácido nucleico una molécula compuesta por subunidades de nucleótido que contiene la información de las células

nucleus 1. in a eukaryotic cell, a membrane-bound organelle that contains the cell's DNA and that has a role in processes such as growth, metabolism, and reproduction, 2. in physical science, an atom's central region, which is made up of protons and neutrons (376)
núcleo 1. en una célula eucariótica, un organelo cubierto por una membrana, el cual contiene el ADN de la célula y participa en procesos tales como el crecimiento, metabolismo y reproducción, 2. en ciencias físicas, la región central de un átomo, la cual está constituida por protones y neutrones

observation the process of obtaining information by using the senses; the information obtained by using the senses (27)
observación el proceso de obtener información por medio de los sentidos; la información que se obtiene al usar los sentidos

ocean current a movement of ocean water that follows a regular pattern (184)
corriente oceánica un movimiento del agua del océano que sigue un patrón regular

orbit the path that a body follows as it travels around another body in space (356)
órbita la trayectoria que sigue un cuerpo al desplazarse alrededor de otro cuerpo en el espacio

organ a collection of tissues that carry out a specialized function of the body (406)
órgano un conjunto de tejidos que desempeñan una función especializada en el cuerpo

organ system (AWR•guhn SIS•tuhm) a group of organs that work together to perform body functions (407)
aparato o sistema de órganos un grupo de órganos que trabajan en conjunto para desempeñar funciones corporales

organelle one of the small bodies in a cell's cytoplasm that are specialized to perform a specific function (376)
organelo uno de los cuerpos pequeños del citoplasma de una célula que están especializados para llevar a cabo una función específica

organism a living thing; anything that can carry out life processes independently (372, 404)
organismo un ser vivo; cualquier cosa que pueda llevar a cabo procesos vitales independientemente

osmosis the diffusion of water through a semipermeable membrane (420)
ósmosis la difusión del agua a través de una membrana semipermeable

ovary in the female reproductive system of animals, an organ that produces eggs (523)
ovario en el aparato reproductor femenino de los animales, un órgano que produce óvulos

oxidation (ahk•sih•DAY•shuhn) a chemical reaction in which a material combines with oxygen to form new material; in geology, oxidation is a form of chemical weathering (76)
oxidación una reacción química en la que un material se combina con oxígeno para formar un material nuevo; en geología, la oxidación es una forma de desgaste químico

ozone layer the layer of the atmosphere at an altitude of 15 to 40 km in which ozone absorbs ultraviolet solar radiation (150)
capa de ozono la capa de la atmósfera ubicada a una altitud de 15 a 40 km, en la cual el ozono absorbe la radiación solar

pancreas (PANG•kree•uhz) the organ that lies behind the stomach and that makes digestive enzymes and hormones that regulate sugar levels (500)
páncreas el órgano que se encuentra detrás del estómago y que produce las enzimas digestivas y las hormonas que regulan los niveles de azúcar

passive transport the movement of substances across a cell membrane without the use of energy by the cell (420)
transporte pasivo el movimiento de sustancias a través de una membrana celular sin que la célula tenga que usar energía

pathogen a microorganism, another organism, a virus, or a protein that causes disease (546)
patógeno un microorganismo, otro organismo, un virus o una proteína que causa enfermedades

penis the male organ that transfers sperm to a female and that carries urine out of the body (522)
pene el órgano masculino que transfiere espermatozoides a una hembra y que lleva la orina hacia el exterior del cuerpo

pharynx (FAIR•ingks) the part of the respiratory system that extends from the mouth to the larynx (488)
faringe la parte del aparato respiratorio que va de la boca a la laringe

phospholipid (FOSS•foh•LIH•pyd) a lipid that contains phosphorus and that is a structural component in cell membranes (386)
fosfolípido un lípido que contiene fósforo y que es un componente estructural de la membrana celular

photosynthesis (foh•toh•SYN•thuh•sys) the process by which plants, algae, and some bacteria use sunlight, carbon dioxide, and water to make food (418)
fotosíntesis el proceso por medio del cual las plantas, las algas y algunas bacterias utilizan la luz solar, el dióxido de carbono y el agua para producir alimento

physical weathering (FIZ•ih•kuhl WETH•er•ing) the mechanical breakdown of rocks into smaller pieces that is caused by natural processes and that does not change the chemical composition of the rock material (72)
desgaste físico el rompimiento mecánico de una roca en pedazos más pequeños que ocurre por procesos naturales y que no modifica la composición química del material rocoso

placenta the partly fetal and partly maternal organ by which materials are exchanged between a fetus and the mother (526)
placenta el órgano parcialmente fetal y parcialmente materno por medio del cual se intercambian materiales entre el feto y la madre

Plantae a kingdom made up of complex, multicellular organisms that are usually green, have cell walls made of cellulose, cannot move around, and use the sun's energy to make sugar by photosynthesis (434)
Plantae un reino formado por organismos pluricelulares complejos que normalmente son verdes, tienen una pared celular de celulosa, no tienen capacidad de movimiento y utilizan la energía del Sol para producir azúcar mediante la fotosíntesis

position (puh•ZISH•uhn) the location of an object (314)
posición la ubicación de un objeto

potential energy the energy that an object has because of the position, shape, or condition of the object (304)
energía potencial la energía que tiene un objeto debido a su posición, forma o condición

precipitation (pri•sip•i•TAY•shuhn) any form of water that falls to Earth's surface from the clouds; includes rain, snow, sleet, and hail (211, 222)
precipitación cualquier forma de agua que cae de las nubes a la superficie de la Tierra; incluye a la lluvia, nieve, aguanieve y granizo

prokaryote (proh•KAIR•ee•oht) a single-celled organism that does not have a nucleus or membrane-bound organelles; examples are archaea and bacteria (377)
procariote un organismo unicelular que no tiene núcleo ni organelos cubiertos por una membrana, por ejemplo, las arqueas y las bacterias

protein a molecule that is made up of amino acids and that is needed to build and repair body structures and to regulate processes in the body (384)
proteína una molécula formada por aminoácidos que es necesaria para construir y reparar estructuras corporales y para regular procesos del cuerpo

Protista a kingdom of mostly one-celled eukaryotic organisms that are different from plants, animals, and fungi (434)
Protista un reino compuesto principalmente por organismos eucarióticos unicelulares diferentes de las plantas, los animales y los hongos

radiation (ray•dee•AY•shuhn) the transfer of energy as electromagnetic waves (160)
radiación la transferencia de energía en forma de ondas electromagnéticas

reference point (REF•uhr•uhns POYNT) a location to which another location is compared (314)
punto de referencia una ubicación con la que se compara otra ubicación

relative humidity the ratio of the amount of water vapor in the air to the amount of water vapor needed to reach saturation at a given temperature (221)
humedad relativa la proporción de la cantidad de vapor de agua que hay en el aire respecto a la cantidad de vapor de agua que se necesita para alcanzar la saturación a una temperatura dada

respiratory system a collection of organs whose primary function is to take in oxygen and expel carbon dioxide; the organs of this system include the lungs, the throat, and the passageways that lead to the lungs (487)
aparato respiratorio un conjunto de órganos cuya función principal es tomar oxígeno y expulsar dióxido de carbono; los órganos de este aparato incluyen a los pulmones, la garganta y las vías que llevan a los pulmones

ribosome a cell organelle composed of RNA and protein; the site of protein synthesis (394)
ribosoma un organelo celular compuesto de ARN y proteína; el sitio donde ocurre la síntesis de proteínas

river (RIV•er) a large natural stream of water that flows across land surfaces within a channel (114)
río un gran curso de agua natural que fluye a través de superficies de terreno y dentro de un canal

rockfall the rapid mass movement of rock down a steep slope or cliff (105)
desprendimiento de rocas el movimiento rápido y masivo de rocas por una pendiente empinada o un precipicio

sandbar a low ridge of sand deposited along the shore of a lake or sea (90)
barra de arena un arrecife bajo de arena depositado a lo largo de la orilla de un lago o del mar

science the knowledge obtained by observing natural events and conditions in order to discover facts and formulate laws or principles that can be verified or tested (6)
ciencia el conocimiento que se obtiene por medio de la observación natural de acontecimientos y condiciones con el fin de descubrir hechos y formular leyes o principios que puedan ser verificados o probados

shoreline the boundary between land and a body of water (87)
orilla el límite entre la tierra y una masa de agua

sinkhole a circular depression that forms when rock dissolves, when overlying sediment fills an existing cavity, or when the roof of an underground cavern or mine collapses (267)
depresión una depresión circular que se forma cuando la roca se funde, cuando el sedimento suprayacente llena una cavidad existente, o al colapsarse el techo de una caverna o mina subterránea

skeletal system the organ system whose primary function is to support and protect the body and to allow the body to move (464)
sistema esquelético el sistema de órganos cuya función principal es sostener y proteger el cuerpo y permitir que se mueva

small intestine the organ between the stomach and the large intestine where most of the breakdown of food happens and most of the nutrients from food are absorbed (499)
intestino delgado el órgano que se encuentra entre el estómago y el intestino grueso en el cual se produce la mayor parte de la descomposición de los alimentos y se absorben la mayoría de los nutrientes

species (SPEE•seez) a group of organisms that are closely related and can mate to produce fertile offspring (430)
especie un grupo de organismos que tienen un parentesco cercano y que pueden aparearse para producir descendencia fértil

speed the distance traveled divided by the time interval during which the motion occurred (317)
rapidez la distancia que un objeto se desplaza dividida entre el intervalo de tiempo durante el cual ocurrió el movimiento

sperm the male sex cell (522)
espermatozoide la célula sexual masculina

spinal cord a column of nerve tissue running from the base of the brain through the vertebral column (508)
médula espinal una columna de tejido nervioso que se origina en la base del cerebro y corre a lo largo de la columna vertebral

stomach the saclike, digestive organ that is between the esophagus and the small intestine and that breaks down food by the action of muscles, enzymes, and acids (499)
estómago el órgano digestivo con forma de bolsa, ubicado entre el esófago y el intestino delgado, que descompone la comida por la acción de músculos, enzimas y ácidos

storm surge a local rise in sea level near the shore that is caused by strong winds from a storm, such as those from a hurricane (249, 263)
marea de tempestad un levantamiento local del nivel del mar cerca de la costa, el cual es resultado de los fuertes vientos de una tormenta, como por ejemplo, los vientos de un huracán

stratosphere the layer of the atmosphere that lies between the troposphere and the mesosphere and in which temperature increases as altitude increases; contains the ozone layer (148)
estratosfera la capa de la atmósfera que se encuentra entre la troposfera y la mesosfera y en la cual la temperatura aumenta al aumentar la altitud; contiene la capa de ozono

structure the arrangement of parts in an organism (408)
estructura el orden y distribución de las partes de un organismo

sublimation the process in which a solid changes directly into a gas (210)
sublimación el proceso por medio del cual un sólido se transforma directamente en un gas

surface current a horizontal movement of ocean water that is caused by wind and that occurs at or near the ocean's surface (184, 283)
corriente superficial un movimiento horizontal del agua del océano que es producido por el viento y que ocurre en la superficie del océano o cerca de ella

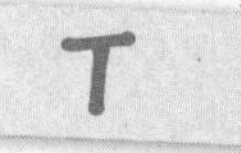

T

T cell an immune system cell that coordinates the immune system and attacks many infected cells (548)
célula T una célula del sistema inmunológico que coordina dicho sistema y ataca muchas células infectadas

temperature (TEM•per•uh•chur) a measure of how hot or cold something is; specifically, a measure of the average kinetic energy of the particles in an object (156)
temperatura una medida de qué tan caliente o frío está algo; específicamente, una medida de la energía cinética promedio de las partículas de un objeto

tendon a tough connective tissue that attaches a muscle to a bone or to another body part (471)
tendón un tejido conectivo duro que une un músculo con un hueso o con otra parte del cuerpo

testes the primary male reproductive organs, which produce sperm cells and testosterone; singular, testis (522)
testículos los principales órganos reproductores masculinos, los cuales producen espermatozoides y testosterona

theory the explanation for some phenomenon that is based on observation, experimentation, and reasoning; that is supported by a large quantity of evidence; and that does not conflict with any existing experimental results or observations (16)
teoría una explicación sobre algún fenómeno que está basada en la observación, experimentación y razonamiento; que está respaldada por una gran cantidad de pruebas; y que no contradice ningún resultado experimental ni observación existente

thermal energy the total kinetic energy of a substance's atoms (156)
energía térmica la energía cinética de los átomos de una sustancia

thermal expansion an increase in the size of a substance in response to an increase in the temperature of the substance (157)
expansión térmica un aumento en el tamaño de una sustancia en respuesta a un aumento en la temperatura de la sustancia

thermosphere the uppermost layer of the atmosphere, in which temperature increases as altitude increases (148)
termosfera la capa más alta de la atmósfera, en la cual la temperatura aumenta a medida que la altitud aumenta

thunder the sound caused by the rapid expansion of air along an electrical strike (247)
trueno el sonido producido por la expansión rápida del aire a lo largo de una descarga eléctrica

thunderstorm a usually brief, heavy storm that consists of rain, strong winds, lightning, and thunder (246)
tormenta eléctrica una tormenta fuerte y normalmente breve que consiste en lluvia, vientos fuertes, relámpagos y truenos

tissue a group of similar cells that perform a common function (405)
tejido un grupo de células similares que llevan a cabo una función común

topography (tuh•POG•ruh•fee) the size and shape of the land surface features of a region, including its relief (280)
topografía el tamaño y la forma de las características de una superficie de terreno, incluyendo su relieve

tornado a destructive, rotating column of air that has very high wind speeds and that may be visible as a funnel-shaped cloud (250)
tornado una columna destructiva de aire en rotación cuyos vientos se mueven a velocidades muy altas y que puede verse como una nube con forma de embudo

trachea (TRAY•kee•uh) thin-walled tube that extends from the larynx to the bronchi; carries air to the lungs; also called windpipe (488)
tráquea el conducto de paredes delgadas que va de la laringe a los bronquios; lleva el aire a los pulmones

transpiration the process by which plants release water vapor into the air through stomata; also the release of water vapor into the air by other organisms (210)
transpiración el proceso por medio del cual las plantas liberan vapor de agua al aire por medio de los estomas; también, la liberación de vapor de agua al aire por otros organismos

troposphere the lowest layer of the atmosphere, in which temperature drops at a constant rate as altitude increases; the part of the atmosphere where weather conditions exist (148)
troposfera la capa inferior de la atmósfera, en la que la temperatura disminuye a una tasa constante a medida que la altitud aumenta; la parte de la atmósfera donde se dan las condiciones del tiempo

umbilical cord the ropelike structure through which blood vessels pass and by which a developing mammal is connected to the placenta (526)
cordón umbilical la estructura con forma de cuerda a través de la cual pasan vasos sanguíneos y por medio de la cual un mamífero en desarrollo está unido a la placenta

upwelling the movement of deep, cold, and nutrient-rich water to the surface (190)
surgencia el movimiento de las aguas profundas, frías y ricas en nutrientes hacia la superficie

urine the liquid excreted by the kidneys, stored in the bladder, and passed through the urethra to the outside of the body (502)
orina el líquido que excretan los riñones, se almacena en la vejiga y pasa a través de la uretra hacia el exterior del cuerpo

uterus in female placental mammals, the hollow, muscular organ in which an embryo embeds itself and develops into a fetus (524)
útero en los mamíferos placentarios hembras, el órgano hueco y muscular en el que el embrión se incrusta y se desarrolla hasta convertirse en feto

vaccine a substance that is prepared from killed or weakened pathogens or from genetic material and that is introduced into a body to produce immunity (550)
vacuna una sustancia que se prepara a partir de organismos patógenos muertos o debilitados o de material genético y se introduce al cuerpo para producir inmunidad

vacuole (VAK•yoo•ohl) a fluid-filled vesicle found in the cytoplasm of plant cells or protozoans (396)
vacuola una vesícula llena de líquido que se encuentra en el citoplasma de las células vegetales o de los protozoarios

vagina the female reproductive organ that connects the outside of the body to the uterus (524)
vagina el órgano reproductivo femenino que conecta la parte exterior del cuerpo con el útero

variable (VAIR•ee•uh•buhl) any factor that can change in an experiment, observation, or model (29)
variable cualquier factor que puede modificarse en un experimento, observación o modelo

vector (VEK•ter) a quantity that has both size and direction (323)
vector una cantidad que tiene tanto magnitud como dirección

vein in biology, a vessel that carries blood to the heart (483)
vena en biología, un vaso que lleva sangre al corazón

velocity the speed of an object in a particular direction (323)
velocidad la rapidez de un objeto en una dirección dada

visibility The distance at which a given standard object can be seen and identified with the unaided eye (225)
visibilidad la distancia a la que un objeto dado es perceptible e identificable para el ojo humano

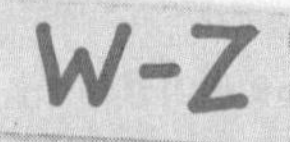

water cycle the continuous movement of water between the atmosphere, the land, the oceans, and living things (208)
ciclo del agua el movimiento continuo del agua entre la atmósfera, la tierra, los océanos y los seres vivos

weather the short-term state of the atmosphere, including temperature, humidity, precipitation, wind, and visibility (220, 276)
tiempo el estado de la atmósfera a corto plazo que incluye la temperatura, la humedad, la precipitación, el viento y la visibilidad

weathering the natural process by which atmospheric and environmental agents, such as wind, rain, and temperature changes, disintegrate and decompose rocks (72)
meteorización el proceso natural por medio del cual los agentes atmosféricos o ambientales, como el viento, la lluvia y los cambios de temperatura, desintegran y descomponen las rocas

wildfire (WYLD•fyr) an unplanned fire in land that is undeveloped except for roads and power lines and other such structures (268)
incendio forestal un incendio imprevisto en terrenos que no están urbanizados excepto por la presencia de carreteras, cables eléctricos y otras estructuras de ese tipo

wind the movement of air caused by differences in air pressure (170, 224)
viento el movimiento de aire producido por diferencias en la presión barométrica

Index

Page numbers for definitions are printed in **boldface** type.
Page numbers for illustrations, maps, and charts are printed in *italics*.

D

E

K

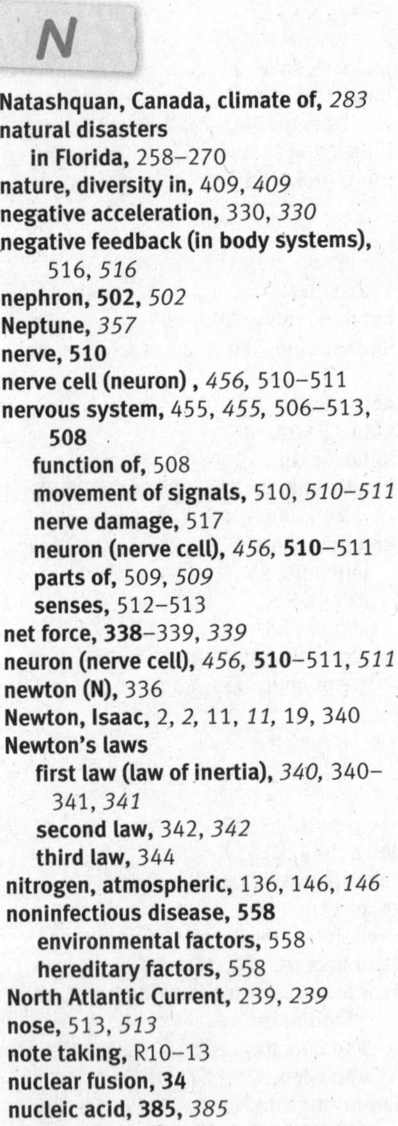

N

O

P–Q

T

U

V

X–Y

Z